ACCOUNTING THEORY

GRID SERIES IN ACCOUNTING

Consulting Editor
J. Leslie Livingstone

Jensen, Coffman, Burns, *Advanced Accounting and The Rule-Making Agencies*
Kollaritsch, *Cost Systems for Planning, Decisions, and Controls*
Most, *Accounting Theory,* Second Edition
Most and Lewis, *Cost Accounting*

ACCOUNTING THEORY

Second Edition

Kenneth S. Most
Professor of Accounting
Florida International University

Grid Publishing, Inc., Columbus, Ohio

2950 North High Street
Box 14466
Columbus, OH 43214

Printed in the United States

1 2 3 4 5 4 3 2

Library of Congress Cataloging in Publication Data

Most, Kenneth S.
Accounting theory.
(Grid series in accounting)
Includes bibliographical references and index.
1. Accounting. I. Title. II. Series.
HF5625.M65 1982 657'.01 81-13313
ISBN 0-88244-243-0 AACR2

TABLE OF CONTENTS

Cases

PREFACE

The encouraging response to the first edition of *Accounting Theory* confirmed the author's belief that there was a need for a rigorous and relatively concise survey of the current state of problem areas in financial reporting. The book has been used in both undergraduate and graduate programs at a large number of universities throughout the world. This revised edition has not merely been brought up-to-date with respect to the many important developments which have taken place since the first edition appeared in 1977, but also improved in the light of the suggestions and criticisms which have been received from users.

Those features which have been found valuable have been retained — the historical and international perspectives, the critical textual analyses, the additional readings and the socioeconomic viewpoint of the author. I have added cases to some of the chapters when the issues discussed have indicated that case study would be a useful method of seeking enlightenment. Questions have been appended to all chapters to assist readers in testing their understanding of the material and to provide instructors with suggestions for classroom discussion and examination material.

I have taken note of two serious criticisms of the first edition. Some readers found many of my statements somewhat elliptical; I have taken care to expand on them where this has been brought to my attention. Some readers have found fault with a tendency for personal opinions to intrude into objective discussion of questions which are still controversial; I have tried to separate these statements of opinion from the views of others. On the other hand, I have not sought to remove myself from the discourse, as some readers have welcomed a text in which the author takes clear positions.

It has been my belief from the beginning that a student using *Accounting Theory* will normally have had a heavy dose of financial and cost accounting courses beforehand, and that is why I have not devoted much space to an explanation of accounting methods. This underlies the "level of generality" referred to in the Preface to the first edition.

On the other hand, I believe that students will obtain the greatest value from this book if they use it in conjunction with the promulgated body of generally accepted accounting principles, preferably in the form of the current text rather than the original pronouncements.

This approach is confirmed by the following quotation which appeared in the *Journal of Accountancy* for January, 1980.

> The "why" vs. the "how"
>
> Accounting programs have become more technical with concentration on technical procedures — the "how" is taught at the expense of the "why." Of course, I recognize that this is a response to the explosion in rules and procedures that has hit the accounting profession in recent years. Twenty years ago, generally accepted accounting principles could be contained in a book about an inch-and-a-half thick. Now, that book is probably measured in feet. With the proliferation in rules, our textbooks are outdated before they're off the presses. However, the solution is not to publish more texts or add more courses but to make existing courses more significant. In a sense, we're coming back to the old theory vs. application problem. It's simply not enough to know accounting principles or auditing standards; students must also understand why a particular standard developed.
>
> From a keynote address by A. E. MacKay,
> Chairman, Main, Hurdman & Cranstoun, before a seminar
> sponsored by the business studies division of
> Catonsville Community College, Catonsville, Maryland
> May 18, 1979

I would like to encourage users to send me their comments and criticisms. I am particularly grateful to Dr. J. Leslie Livingstone of the University of Southern California and to Professors Philip W. Bell of Rice University, M. Eisa of Southern University, James Gozon of Ithaca College, Robert Morgan of the University of North Carolina, and Stanly C. W. Salvary of Canisuis College for their invaluable reviews and suggestions.

As in the first edition, I acknowledge with thanks permission of the Ronald Press Company to reproduce the extract from the *Accountant's Handbook*, of Prentice-Hall, Inc., for the extract from *A Dictionary for Accountants*, of Dr. Leon Herbert for Figure 1-1, and of the American Accounting Association for the excerpt from Sanders, Hatfield, and Moore in chapter 4. New acknowledgments are gratefully offered to Borg–Warner Corporation, The Southern Company, and The British Petroleum Company Ltd. for permission to reproduce extracts from their 1980 annual reports.

Mrs. Dorothy Kime has been a great support in the typing of the revised manuscript, and I thank her for her assistance in this regard.

Finally, I would again like to pay respect to two great thinkers who have influenced my life and work, and to whom I owe a deep debt of gratitude: Dr. Ralph H. Blodgett and the late Dr. Abram Mey. This book is offered in tribute to their great achievements, and in imitation of their scholarship.

Kenneth S. Most

Miami, Florida
1981

1

TOWARD A CONCEPTUAL FRAMEWORK FOR ACCOUNTING

A book entitled *Accounting Theory* should start with a disclaimer: There is no generally accepted theory of accounting. There are a number of accounting theories, and some theories of accounting, which will be examined from time to time in later chapters of this book. On the other hand, at the present time there is an unmistakable drive toward the formulation of an accounting theory, often referred to as a "conceptual framework". Perhaps this observation provides the best justification for this book.

DEFINITION OF ACCOUNTING

To start with, even the definition of the word *accounting* is in dispute. Until recently the most widely quoted definition was that in *Accounting Terminology Bulletin No. 1* of the American Institute of Certified Public Accountants (AICPA) (1941).

> Accounting is the art of recording, classifying, and summarizing in a significant manner and in terms of money, transactions and events which are, in part at least of a financial character, and interpreting the results thereof.

This appears to be a definition of accountancy, an *art*, rather than accounting, a *body of knowledge*. If the definition were clear, the objection would not count for much, as we could then define accounting as the product of accountancy. However, the AICPA definition has certain weaknesses, of which the most critical is the meaning of "financial." The word cannot mean "money" here or "capable of representation in money," because in both cases the previous phrase "in terms of money" would be redundant. "Financial" is therefore an unstructured concept calling for definition.

Secondly, the words "in part at least" introduce an uncertainty which must affect our ability to identify those "transactions and events" which are proper subjects of accounting. Thirdly, the phrase "transactions and events" limits the scope of accounting by excluding, for example, the accrual of interest receivable, the write-off of a bad debt or the recording of depreciation expense, unless we use the circular reasoning that everything the accountant records, etc. represents a transaction or an event.[1]

More recently, the Netherlands Institute of Registered Accountants defined accounting as:

> the systematic recording, processing and supplying of information for the management and operation of an entity and for the reports that have to be submitted thereon.

This definition is too wide because it would include the functions of newspapers, libraries, and centers of documentation as well as accounting itself. Indeed, one of the aims of the definition was to permit accounting to embrace nonmonetary items; unfortunately, which nonmonetary items cannot be determined. This same desire to extend the boundaries of accounting to include nonmonetary quantification is a feature of the American Accounting Association Committee Report, *A Statement of Basic Accounting Theory* (ASOBAT, 1966). This widely acclaimed publication defined accounting as "the process of identifying, measuring, and communicating economic information to permit informed judgments and decisions by users of the information."

The Accounting Principles Board, in its *Statement No. 4* (October, 1970) also attempted to define accounting with reference to the concept of information:

> Accounting is a service activity. Its function is to provide quantitative information, primarily financial in nature, about economic entities that is intended to be useful in making economic decisions, in making reasoned choices among alternative courses of action. Accounting includes several branches, for example, financial accounting, managerial accounting and government accounting.

This definition has been greeted as a significant step forward, but closer examination reveals that the improvement is more apparent than real. Reference to "economic decisions" does not help us to identify the quantitative information which is "intended to be useful," unless we adopt the quite untenable assumption that accountants produce data for input into the decision models used by economists. The obscurity of "in part at least, of a financial character" is carried forward intact in the phrase "primarily financial in nature." This problem has led to an attempt to distinguish between *financial statements* and *financial reporting*, which will be examined in chapter 7.

The first of the Financial Accounting Standards Board's (FASB) statements of financial accounting concepts leapfrogged the issue by concentrating on financial reporting. But it is not necessary to define accounting closely. Fields of knowledge are simply groups of problems studied together because the same methodology is used for their solution; this is the case with medicine or architecture or the law. Accounting is the solution of problems using accounts; the definition directs us to the types of problem amenable to this form of solution and to the methodology used by accountants. As a working definition we may accept the following creation of a Committee of the American Accounting Association. "The primary function of accounting is to accumulate and communicate information essential to an understanding of the activities of an enterprise." (*Accounting and Reporting Standards for Corporate Financial Statements–1957 Revision*.)

THE ROLE AND FUNCTIONS OF ACCOUNTANTS

The role of today's accountants has not been clearly spelled out, and their position in society is ambiguous. On the one hand, they are associated by tradition with the business world and are identified as servants of the capitalistic enterprise. This view directs attention to the accountant as keeper of the firm's records, preparer of financial statements used for inviting capital contributions to the enterprise, for verifying credit-worthiness, and as a basis for assessing income taxation. This is obviously an incomplete image of the accountant, who performs many of the same functions in a communistic economy as in a capitalistic one.

The accountant has another more public role in which he or she is identified as a person of trust, a professional to whom society can give a variety of tasks knowing they will be performed in the public interest. This view directs attention to the accountant as auditor, as tax counsel, and as government employee in many capacities, such as civil servant, consultant to regulators, and advisor to administrations.

A third role of accountants is that of the technician, skilled in the techniques of business management and knowledgeable about the organization and operations of particular industries. In this capacity they function as a part of management in both the private and public sectors, and as outside consultants on such matters as administrative systems and procedures, cybernetics, short and long range planning, mathematical modelling, and many other techniques, in addition to the design, installation, and operation of accounting systems.

The *Accountants' Handbook*[2] classifies accounting into the following fields:

1. *Financial reporting*—the preparation from raw data of financial statements, consisting of an income statement, a statement of financial position, and a statement of changes in financial position. These may be used within an organization, by its managers, or by outside parties, such as

stockholders, creditors, labor unions, income tax authorities, and regulatory agencies.

2. *Tax determination and planning*—the preparation of tax returns and reports in accordance with the laws and regulations governing such matters, for which purpose financial reports may serve as a point of departure. This field includes tax planning and representation of the taxpayer as counsel before the Internal Revenue Service and courts of law.
3. *Independent audits*—the examination of financial statements and other representations with the objective of expressing an opinion on their fairness.
4. *Data processing and information systems*—the design, installation and administration of systems for generating, processing, storing, and retrieving data required for a variety of purposes.
5. *Cost and management accounting*—objective analyses of costs and performances and the quantitative preparation of managerial decisions.
6. *Internal auditing*—an independent appraisal performed inside an organization, on a continuous basis, to ascertain the extent of compliance with sound business practices and established systems and procedures.
7. *Budgeting*—accounting for the future, and the related function of budgetary control by comparing financial statements with budgets and investigating variances.
8. *Fiduciary accounting*—the administration of trusts and the estates of deceased persons, bankrupts, minors, or the insane under the terms of a law, trust instrument, or court order.
9. *National income accounting*—the preparation of the financial statements of the nation or other macroeconomic aggregate. This role has been occupied by economic statisticians, with very little involvement by accountants; nevertheless, it belongs under our definition of accounting.
10. *Management consulting*—this residual field covers advising management on a variety of problem areas, to improve the profitability of business firms and the economy of not-for-profit organizations.

To this list we may add the field of government accounting, including government auditing, which is of considerable importance at the present time at international, federal, state, and local levels, and the field of accounting for nongovernmental not-for-profit institutions, which is certainly significant in the United States.

THE GROWTH OF ACCOUNTABILITY KNOWLEDGE

Figure 1-1 shows graphically the exponential rate of increase of the body of knowledge represented by accounting during the past two hundred years. Prior to 1750 there existed little literature on

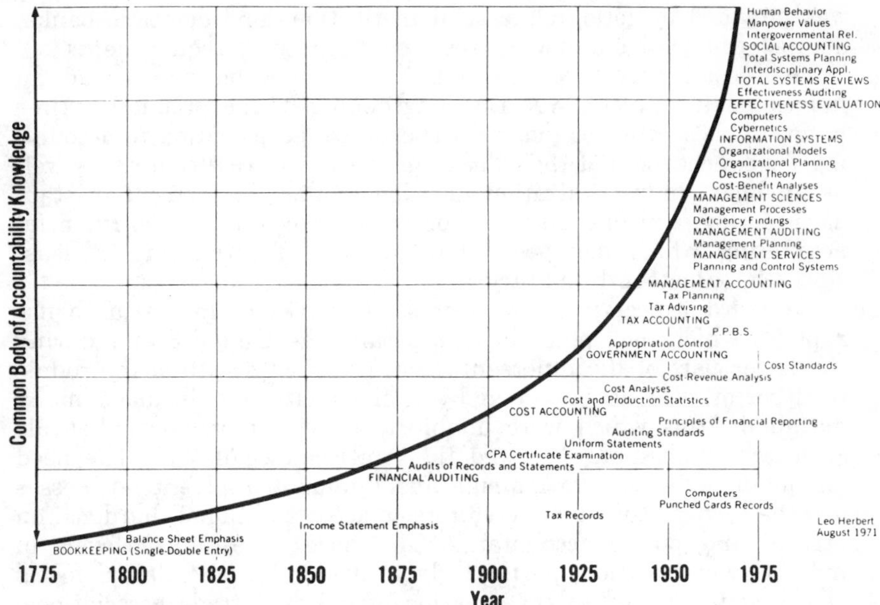

Source: Dr. Leo Herbert, U.S. General Accounting Office.[3]

FIGURE 1-1
Growth of Accountability Knowledge 1775-1975

the subject, consisting mainly of translations and adaptations of the relevant portions of Luca Pacioli's *Summa de Arithmetica, Geometria, Proportioni et Proportionalita* (1494), the first book to describe double-entry bookkeeping. Accountants were virtually all private accountants, working for a bank, merchant, chartered company, or as government employees, and their functions and responsibilities were restricted to the duties assigned by the employer. Public accounting, or the practice of offering accountancy services to the public against a fee, was unknown.

The principal factors listed in Figure 1-1 as responsible for the expansion of the accountant's functions, and thus, for the growth of this body of knowledge, were the following.

The Industrial Revolution One result of the transition from domestic production to factory production was the growth in the size of the firm and its capital requirements. To raise capital of the required magnitude, it was frequently necessary for the firm to incorporate; the number of registered corporations increased from a few hundreds to tens of thousands between 1800 and 1900. The need for meaningful accounts to be rendered by the promoters and managers to the stockholders greatly increased the responsibilities of accountants, and company legislation in Great Britain calling for these accounts to be audited created a need for public accountants. In the United States, where the greater part of industrial capital was provided by foreign financial institutions and domestic banks, audited financial statements resulted from their requirements.

A second aspect of the industrial revolution which had an impact on accounting was the lengthening of the production time period. This feature of industrialization called attention to accounting for overheads and the allocation of costs to cost centers as well as products. Industrialization also led to the development of standard costing, and to the separation of cost accounting from financial accounting which has been characteristic of accounting at least since the nineteenth century.

A third aspect was the successive waves of industrial bankruptcies which took place in Europe and the United States during the latter part of the nineteenth century. The growth of the industrial sector was accompanied by overcapacity and included many marginal firms which were unable to survive economic upheavals such as, for example, followed the American Civil War. The need for qualified persons to manage and liquidate insolvent businesses for the benefit of their creditors placed additional burdens on private and public accountants. The need to establish forms of industrial cooperation, particularly to avoid the more lethal forms of price-cutting, led to the creation of national trade associations, and many of these developed uniform accounting systems which were published for the benefit of members.

The Railroad Companies The biggest single users of corporate capital during the nineteenth century were the railroads. These companies were illustrative of additional problems presented by the industrial revolution because they were highly capital intensive, and their fixed assets had longer useful lives than customary. Many people in the industry believed that maintenance of the tracks and rolling stock would make railroad fixed assets virtually everlasting, and there was thus no need to charge depreciation in the income statement (then called the profit and loss account). Coupled with the overstatement of profits, many less excusable abuses occurred, such as paying dividends out of capital contributed for investment, and the creation of excess capacity leading to business failures, which caused investors and creditors substantial losses.

These problems directed attention to the critical necessity to distinguish capital from revenue, to the importance of the income statement, and to the need to calculate depreciation on a systematic basis. In many countries railroad finances became a matter of public concern, and legislation regulating their operations was enacted; in most countries the railroads have gradually been taken over by government and are now operated as state enterprises. In the United States certain states prescribed the form of railroad accounts; regulation was later taken over by the Federal Interstate Commerce Commission, which issued a uniform classification of accounts in 1894.

These developments were followed by regulation of other industries of public interest, such as public utilities, broadcasting, interstate gas pipelines, and aviation. In each case, regulation included the requirement to use a uniform accounting system for recording and reporting, and in each case the system was different. Thus, the case of the railroads provides an example not only of the growth of accountability knowledge but also of the emergence of acceptable alternatives in accounting, which is one of the reasons for a study of accounting theory.

The Rise Of The Accounting Profession The profession of public accountant gradually became organized in the English-speaking world during the nineteenth century. The Institute of Chartered Accountants in Scotland was the first such organization (founded 1854), followed by the Institute of Chartered Accountants in England and Wales (1880). The New York State Society of Certified Public Accountants was formed in 1896 and a national organization, the predecessor of the American Institute of Certified Public Accountants, in 1887.

These professional organizations laid down rules of conduct for their members and issued pronouncements on technical questions which added substantially to accountability knowledge from about 1900.

The Personal And Corporate Income Taxes After several abortive attempts, the U.S. Treasury finally succeeded in imposing an income tax in 1913. Although challenged as unconstitutional, this form of taxation was eventually validated by constitutional amendment. Other countries, notably Britain and Germany, imposed income taxation before the end of the nineteenth century.

The significance of this development lies both in the contribution it made to strengthening the accounting profession by opening to it a new field of accounting, and in the additions to knowledge made by a succession of revenue acts and related commentaries, case law, and textbooks. The necessity to determine income, as a preliminary to the determination of taxable income, provided a major impetus to the extension and improvement of accounting practice, and the essentially legal ideas and concepts of the tax laws influenced the development of accounting theory in subtle ways.

The First And Second World Wars In the first and second world wars the governments of the countries taking part utilized to the fullest extent the industrial sectors built up during the nineteenth and early twentieth centuries. In the United States large portions of the industrial sector were engaged in the production of weaponry, ships, ammunition, motor vehicles, military clothing and a wide variety of goods and equipment needed for the war effort.

Only a small part of this production was carried out by the government itself; the greater part was allocated to private industry through the medium of the defense contract. There was considerable fear—in many cases justified—that defense contractors would exploit the ignorance of civil servants by overcharging for their products, but the government was a powerful force in this situation and gradually succeeded in laying down regulations for costing defense contracts (Section XV of the Armed Service Procurement Regulation) and establishing audit agencies to ensure that costs were fairly reported.

The relations between government agencies and private firms created by defense contracting and its regulation led to further consideration of cost accounting problems, and the refinement of methods of standard costing and differential or incremental costing is attributable in large part to this situation.

Government Accounting Politicians do not favor disclosure. When in power they resist it, and the opposition does not fight too hard for fear it will inherit the obligation. It is no accident that in most countries government accounting is a byword for backwardness and obscurity.

The tremendous increase in government revenues which followed the introduction of income taxation, particularly at the level necessary to finance the first world war, vastly increased the problem of government accountability. In the English-speaking countries, government accounting has traditionally been accounting for receipts and payments, which paradoxically is less informative than the accrual system. It may be noted, however, that the Kingdom of Sweden in the seventeenth century, and the Austria of Maria Theresa in the eighteenth, developed sophisticated forms of government accounting comparable to contemporary business systems, and that the cash basis is no more essential to government accounting than to any other kind.

Beginning in the 1890s, attempts were made in the United States to reform the federal budgeting and financial reporting process, and similar movements were discernible elsewhere. The Taft Commission, which reported in 1912, resulted in the establishment of an executive budget only nine years later, and the Budget and Accounting Act of 1921 enacted some of the Taft recommendations. In 1949, the 81st Congress completed the task of legislating the Taft Commission's report by passing Public Law 784. Nevertheless, even now, the actual implementation of reforms proposed by the Taft Commission is a long way from completion.

In addition, state and local government accounting have developed their own techniques and literature as the revenues from sales and property taxes have increased through both legislation and inflation.

The Fruits Of Scientific Management By the end of the nineteenth century many of the problems of industrial organization and management had been identified, and a scientific approach to their solution was proposed by F.W. Taylor, the Gilbreths, and others between 1885 and 1920. Imitating the dictum of Lord Kelvin, this approach has been summed up in the phrase: "What cannot be measured, cannot be managed."

It was clear to the pioneers of scientific management that accounting had a large part to play in the measurement of cost and output and in the evaluation of managerial performance. The business schools established after the turn of the century placed emphasis on the study of accounting as a tool of management control, and a substantial literature has developed on this aspect of accounting. We may note as landmarks the early work of Garcke and Fells and Hamilton Church on standard costing[4] and the invention of breakeven charting by Henry Hess in 1904.[5] This literature, which grows more extensive daily, belongs to the area designated *management accounting*, which is also the title of the monthly publication of the National Association of Accountants in the United States.

The development of management accounting has been marked by two significant changes in emphasis, which cannot be ignored by any student of accounting theory. One is the attempt to apply to accounting data the mathematical methods which have proved powerful tools for investigating the world of natural phenomena. This field of *statistical method* has produced many experiments of varying success. The use of ratios and averages has a long history, but such techniques as discriminate analysis, multivariate analysis, and others, applied to accounting ratios in order to evaluate their usefulness as predictors, is a fairly recent development. Compound arithmetic as a tool of financial mathematics is likewise of some vintage, but present value techniques for accounting valuations are new.

The other change is the attempt to solve accounting problems within an interfunctional, and consequently interdisciplinary, framework of management. Before the industrial revolution it was common for merchants, bankers, and artisans to keep their own accounts. As specialization became necessary in the growth of manufacturing firms, accounting was one of the first functions which the manager transferred to someone else. The accountant became increasingly isolated from the decision-making centers of the firm, leading to the separation of accounting from operating management, and outside pressures created a tendency for accounting aimed at such external users as financiers, creditors, and the tax authority to acquire the major share of the resources available for the accounting function. The twentieth century has seen a reversal of this trend.

In the process, the accountant has both contributed to and taken from the other functions of management. To production planning and control he has given standard costing; from it the statistical techniques used in quality control have been taken over for variance analysis. To marketing he has given cost/volume/profit analysis, and from marketing he has taken one of the principles of valuation of joint products, the relative sales value method. Figure 1-1 suggests other flows of ideas of this type, as the accountant has interacted with specialists in finance, cybernetics, organization theory, systems analysis, decision theory, and human behavior.

It is this contributing factor to the growth of accountability knowledge which is mainly responsible for the sharp upturn in the graph since about 1950. A comparative study of the literature on management accounting prior to and since that date reveals the enormous impact which this cross-pollination has had on the development of accounting thought, an impact which has yet to work itself out in the body of knowledge we call accounting theory. However, we can perceive this impact in the form of the various approaches to accounting theory which will be identified in this book.

CRITICISMS OF ACCOUNTING

Such pervasive growth might suggest that accountants were doing something right. On the contrary, however, many serious criticisms of accounting have been voiced, both inside and outside the accounting profession. Accountants assert that their work is useful to stockholders, but financial statements do not show realized and liquidated profit available for dividends, or cumulative investment, profits, and dividends to date. They claim that their work is useful to creditors, but statements of financial position do not reveal current market values of assets and legal claims against them. They purport to assist in tax assessments, but financial statements must be reworked in accordance with fiscal legislation to calculate taxable income. Nor do financial statements report such important information as value added. Value added is the difference between a firm's sales and purchases, and it is therefore the amount which must cover wages, interest, rent, dividends, and capital recovery. For this reason, value added is an important factor in labor negotiations, since unions seek to maximize labor's share of this amount.

Until forty years ago there was little criticism of accounting by accountants.[6] A landmark was the publication in 1939 of Kenneth MacNeal's *Truth in Accounting*,[7] which attacked contemporary financial reporting standards with what the author himself called "ill temper and sweeping denunciation." A CPA with many years' experience, MacNeal dealt to some extent with generally recognized abuses, such as bypassing the income statement with profits and losses, and failing to recognize known investment losses. In the intervening forty years these abuses have ceased to be the main target and to a great extent accountants have been successful in eliminating them. Most of MacNeal's strictures, however, were leveled at the accountant's unwillingness to "value," that is, to depart from historical costs, with the result that the figures contained in financial statements had no relation to "the truth."

The truth, following Fisher and Canning,[8] lay in "the meaning of value in its economic aspect," which was well known and complete enough to serve most practical purposes. "A balance sheet and profit and loss statement purport to state values. In order to fulfil their purpose they must state values according to economic concepts. . . ." This is a very misleading proposition; economics is not a science of values but a theory of relative prices. It was precisely on this point that modern economic theory acquired its strength, namely, the recognition by the medieval Schoolmen that the domain of truths capable of being proved by reason was limited and that many doctrines must be accepted on the basis of faith alone. Thus, economists who followed Thomas Aquinas and Duns Scotus turned away from questions of value, a subjective concept, and occupied themselves with questions of price, an objective reality.

MacNeal predicted one of two outcomes: either accounting principles and practice would remain unchanged, with the accounting profession declining in reputation and remuneration, or accountants would supply the public with "the truth" and prosper accordingly. During the intervening forty years there has been very little basic change in accounting principles and practice, but the accounting profession has increased in numbers and prosperity as never before. This observation alone should ensure that MacNeal's criticisms are carefully examined and not simply taken at face value.

Since MacNeal wrote there have been innumerable restatements of his criticisms, but the rationale has changed subtly over the years.[9] Although many critics still proceed from the assumption that accounting can be referred to a framework of economic theory, it has become unfashionable to call this the truth. Instead, the critics direct attention to the need for information useful in making economic decisions. The desired values are not intrinsically good, but acquire their virtue from the decision models which call them forth.

> Thus accounting is being criticized for many reasons: that it is based on irrelevant historical costs instead of opportunity costs; that it provides only a description of the past, but no prediction of the future; that its models consist exclusively of identities but lack behavioral functions and do not lend themselves to optimization procedures; that it ignores psychological factors and uses 'arbitrary' allocation procedures... that the balance sheet is not comprehensive enough because its inclusion criterion of measurability is too superficial; that the additivity assumption on which it operates is illusionary [sic]; that its measures are not accompanied by error estimates, etc....[10]

It will be one of the aims of this book to examine these criticisms in some detail. The task is clearly a fascinating one; as Brief pointed out in a recent article, the revolt against accountants has been brewing for nearly 100 years and certain accounting problems appear to be perennial and impervious to regulation and legislation.[11] At this time, however, we are interested principally in their effect on the need for accounting theory.

It must be confessed, however, that the main thrust of the criticism of accountants, both within and without the profession, has been directed at practical problems. These include—

- The acceptability of multiple methods of reporting the same basic facts.

- Switches from more or less "conservative" accounting methods to the opposite.
- "Front-ending" income which should more appropriately be spread over several periods.
- Deferring costs in inventory and fixed asset accounts, followed by "big bath" write-offs.
- Overoptimistic estimates of recoverability of invested amounts
- Off-balance sheet financing to avoid financial statement disclosure and/or affect the computation of debt/equity ratios.
- Using assertions of immateriality to disguise failure to follow accounting practices recommended by GAAP.
- Allowing form to prevail over substance in accounting for transactions planned with their accounting treatment in mind.

THE POLITICIZATION OF ACCOUNTING

Whether the result of genuine dissatisfaction with the accounting profession—or simply a recognition on the part of society of the important role accounting plays, and can play, in the arrangement of human affairs—recent years have seen a variety of interventions of a political nature in the accounting process. These can be categorized as the politicization of the accounting standard-setting system together with overt governmental involvement with accounting practices.

Whereas the early attempts at establishing accounting principles were clearly guided by a sincere desire to assure users of reliable accounting information, in recent years a spirit of bargaining more resembling a political process has become increasingly evident.

Of the political influences on the accounting standard setters, the dominant force is the Securities and Exchange Commission (SEC). Since 1934 this Federal agency has had the power to set accounting standards, but it has rarely used it, preferring to allow the accounting profession, or organizations like the Financial Accounting Standards Board which depend on the accounting profession, to do the work. This is not to assert that the SEC has laid down no accounting rules; on the contrary, accountants concerned with SEC filings must be aware of a host of Accounting Series Releases (ASRs) and other pronouncements which affect their financial statements. The bulk of the body of knowledge called GAAP, however, emanates from other sources.

In recent years, the SEC has become increasingly visible as the hand behind the system, both as concerns specific forms of accounting (Reserve Recognition Accounting, for example) and detailed methods of handling individual transactions. A good example of the latter was provided by the origins of *FASB Statement No. 4*, "Reporting Gains and Losses from Extinguishment of Debt."

In 1974 the SEC became concerned with the number of firms which were realizing substantial gains from purchasing their own debt on the bond market, where rising interest rates had resulted in sharply lower prices. These gains were no longer being shown as extraordinary items in income statements because *APB Opinion No. 30* (1973) had virtually eliminated this class of item, and they were often lumped with other revenues or gains and not reported separately. The SEC intimated to the FASB that this situation demanded an immediate response and threatened to issue its own pronouncement if the FASB failed to act. The FASB announced its intention to issue a pronouncement and then produced an Exposure Draft within a few days; the customary public hearing was waived and the Standard itself was published in March, 1975, within the minimum time period allowed. The significant point is that by singling out gains and losses on extinguishment of debt for treatment as extraordinary items, the FASB clearly contradicted an important position of the Accounting Principles Board (APB) taken only two years previously, in the formation of which the chairman of the FASB at the time had been heavily involved.

Pressure from the SEC is the most tangible and irresistible, but far from being the only force with which accounting standard setters must contend. Affected corporations press for their own accounting methods, either because their accountants sincerely believe that these are the best, or simply to avoid the expense of making substantial changes. Often they can foresee economic consequences which the members of the FASB feel free to ignore, such as those which followed *FASB Statement No. 8*, dealing with accounting for foreign currency transactions and translation. Larger public accounting firms argue for the perceived interests of their clients, or against measures which they see as potentially increasing their legal liability. Small accounting firms lobby through the American Institute of Public Accountants (and sometimes individually) against rules which may increase their costs without necessarily permitting them to raise their fees. Financial analysts and other investment advisers oppose any attempt to force accountants to provide the kind of information which they, the analysts, regard as their specialty. Many commentators see managers of public corporations supporting self-serving positions, such as against rules which will make it more difficult for them to satisfy contractual obligations, or reduce the profit figure on which their bonuses are calculated, or increase the profit figure and thus arouse criticism from the press and public.

Besides these influences, the field of accounting is also the subject of direct governmental interest in almost all countries, and this phenomenon will be looked at in subsequent chapters. Specific U.S. legislative acts have laid down accounting rules; one of these states that no organization shall prescribe a particular method of accounting for the income tax investment credit. (Revenue Act of 1971). Senate Bill 1435, "Capital Cost Recovery Act of 1979," aimed to allocate annual depreciation charges based on designated recovery periods, rather than the productive life of the assets, indicative of a governmental interest in even the way accounting data are recognized. The most extensive attempt by the U.S. Congress to control accounting, however, started in 1974 and culminated in the Foreign Corrupt Practices Act of 1977, which will be examined in the next section of this chapter.

In 1974 and 1975 committees of the U.S. House of Representatives (the Moss Committee) and of the U.S. Senate (the Metcalf Committee) held extensive investigations of the public accounting profession and published reports severely critical of the SEC's oversight of the profession and of the FASB's failure to reduce the amount of substandard financial reporting. Although the Moss and Metcalf Committee reports were widely regarded as having been produced by overzealous staff members who were less than objective in their approach, they did have an effect on the practice of accounting. Since 1978 the SEC has been required to make an annual progress report on the "improvement" of the accounting profession, and since 1977 the ground rules for accounting liability have been radically changed by the Foreign Corrupt Practices Act.

THE FOREIGN CORRUPT PRACTICES ACT OF 1977 (FCPA)

The FCPA became law on December 19, 1977. Its ostensible purpose was to make illegal certain payments to foreign officials, politicians, and others. Because some of the bribery revealed by the investigations of the Securities and Exchange Commission was facilitated by the falsification of accounting records, however, the FCPA also contained an amendment to the Securities Exchange Act of 1934, adding two new sections, 13(b) 2 (A) and (B). The amendment reads:

> (2) Every issuer which has a class of securities registered pursuant to section 12 of this title and every issuer which is required to file reports pursuant to section 15 (d) of this title shall—
>
> (A) make and keep books, records and accounts, which, in reasonable detail, accurately and fairly reflect the transactions and dispositions of the assets of the issuer; and
>
> (B) devise and maintain a system of internal accounting controls sufficient to provide reasonable assurances that—
>
> (i) transactions are executed in accordance with management's general or specific authorization;
>
> (ii) transactions are recorded as necessary (I) to permit preparation of financial statements in conformity with generally accepted accounting principles or any other criteria applicable to such statements, and (II) to maintain accountability for assets;

An obvious question is why, in the light of the fact that good business practice mandates such actions and that the existing SEC rules and regulations permit the Commission to pursue contraveners both civilly and criminally, was it necessary for the U.S. Congress to enact this law?

Beginning in 1973, the work of the Special Prosecutor appointed to investigate what has become known as the Watergate scandal revealed widespread use of corporate funds for illegal domestic political contributions. The manner in which these contributions were made available to political fund-raisers frequently involved actions of significance to investors, nondisclosure of which entailed violations of federal securities laws. On May 12, 1976 the SEC submitted a detailed "Report on Questionable and Illegal Corporate Payments and Practices" to the Senate Committee on Banking, Housing, and Urban Affairs. One of the conclusions stated in this Report was that:

> The almost universal characteristic of the cases examined to date by the Commission has been the apparent frustration of our system of corporate accountability which has been designed to assure that there is proper accounting of the use of corporate funds and that documents filed with the Commission and circulated to shareholders do not omit or misrepresent material facts. Millions of dollars of funds have been inaccurately recorded in corporate books and records to facilitate the making of questionable payments. Such falsification of records has been known to corporate employees and often to top management, but often has been concealed from outside auditors and counsel and outside directors.

After the FCPA was passed the SEC adopted new rules 13b2-1 and 13b2-2 under the Securities Exchange Act of 1934, effective March 23, 1979. The former states that "no person shall directly or indirectly falsify or cause to be falsified any book, record or account subject to Section 13(b)(2)(A)." The latter prohibits materially false statements or material omissions by an officer or director of an issuer made to an accountant in connection with the examination of financial statements or filing of a document or report required to be filed with the Commission. These offences are not limited to material *falsifications*; anything incorrect, no matter how trivial, is indictable. The rules apply to oral as well as written statements to auditors and do not require *scienter*, a guilty mind. It appeared at the time to be the view of the Commission that the FCPA applied to corporate accountability generally, and not just to financial accounting.

Why were the FCPA and the Commission's new rules necessary? At least one Congressional participant in the hearings which preceded the Act believed that corporations were already covered by its provisions and that the SEC had all needed powers.[12] The fact is that prior to the FCPA the SEC had to rely exclusively on Section 13(a) of the 1934 Act, and the rules thereunder, in order to prosecute corporations and their officers. These rules covered misstatements or omissions deemed *material*, and *scienter* was a requirement. Thus, the key to understanding the accounting provisions of the FCPA is the lack of a materiality standard and the absence of *scienter*. Illegal payments which would previously have escaped the Commission's regulatory net are now caught.

Given the selective system of law enforcement by the SEC, it is too early to say what the practical consequences of the FCPA will be. The SEC's influence on disclosure and materiality generally will be discussed in chapter 7. From the viewpoint of an accounting theorist, however, the requirement that accounting records "accurately and fairly reflect transactions" provides a new challenge to determine the factors which characterize accounting standards. It is true that the FCPA requires financial statements to be prepared in conformity with generally accepted accounting principles, but the written statement of these principles is incomplete and changes from time to time.

THE NEED FOR A CONCEPTUAL FRAMEWORK

Possibly as a reaction to this politicization of the standard setting process the FASB has been, since its inception, attempting to establish a conceptual framework, a theory of accounting to which practical problems could be referred for solution in a relatively objective manner. The FASB, which was established in 1972, took over this project from the APB, which had made an unsuccessful first attempt in its *Statement No. 4*. The conceptual framework project, as it is called, has so far produced four Statements of Financial Accounting Concepts; an overview was published as *Scope and Implications of the Conceptual Framework Project* on December 2, 1976. Figure 1-2 shows the eight major components of the project.

FIGURE 1-2
Conceptual Framework for Financial Accounting and Reporting

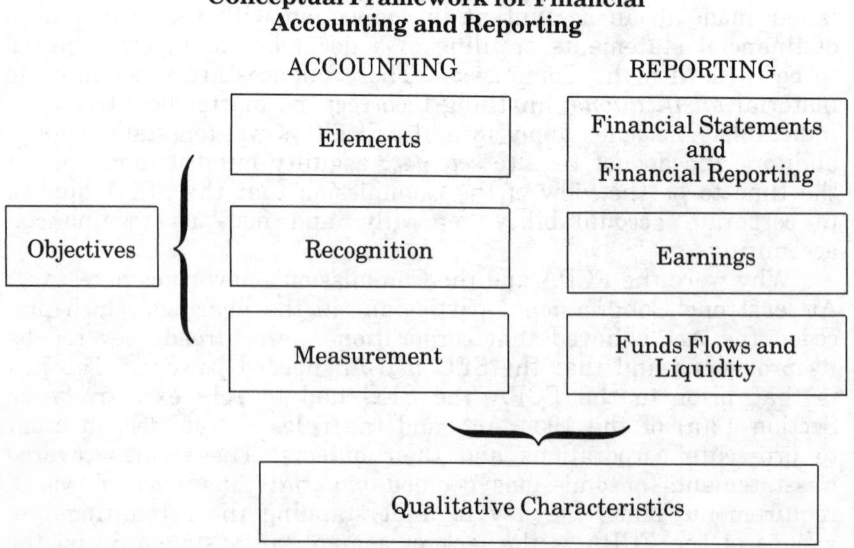

Adapted from Financial Accounting Standards Board publications.

The project was expected to lead to FASB pronouncements on—

- The objectives of financial statements (for what uses are they intended? to whom should they be aimed? what information should they contain? what are their limitations?)
- Qualitative characteristics of financial statement information (what qualities make the information useful? how to resolve questions concerning trade-offs between qualities?)
- Basic elements of accounting (what are assets, liabilities, revenues, expenses? how should earnings be defined? how should assets and liabilities be determined?)
- Basis of measurement (how should the basic elements be measured?)
- Measuring unit (should the monetary unit be adjusted for changes in general purchasing power over time?)

The FASB expressed a need for a *constitution*, "a coherent system of interrelated objectives and fundamentals that can lead to consistent standards and that prescribes the nature, function, and limits of financial accounting and financial statements." In particular, the conceptual framework was expected to—

1. Guide the body responsible for establishing accounting standards.
2. Provide a frame of reference for resolving accounting questions in the absence of promulgated standards.
3. Determine bounds for judgment in preparing financial statements.
4. Increase financial statement users' understanding of and confidence in financial statements.
5. Enhance comparability.

By the middle of 1981 the FASB had issued four Statements of Financial Accounting Concepts (SFAC) and a Discussion Memorandum on funds flows and liquidity.[13]

- SFAC No. 1, "Objectives of Financial Reporting by Business Enterprises," November 1978.
- SFAC No. 2, "Qualitative Characteristics of Accounting Information," May 1980.
- SFAC No. 3, "Elements of Financial Statements of Business Enterprises," December 1980.
- SFAC No. 4, "Objectives of Financial Reporting by Nonbusiness Organizations," December 1980.
- DM, "Funds Flows, Liquidity, and Financial Flexibility", December, 1980.

A Statement of Financial Accounting Concepts (SFAC), unlike a Statement of Financial Accounting Standards, does not establish Generally Accepted Accounting Principles. Its purpose is to set forth fundamentals on which GAAP will be based, and is primarily to be used by the FASB in promulgating new standards and in re-examining its own pronouncements and those of its predecessor standard-setting bodies.

OBJECTIVES OF FINANCIAL REPORTING

SFAC No. 1 establishes the objectives of general purpose external financial reporting by business enterprises.[14] It supersedes *APB Statement No. 4*, which was the Accounting Principles Board's attempt to establish an underlying accounting theory. *APB Statement No. 4* now describes the objectives which existed prior to the issue of SFAC No. 1. However, the same environmental postulates as those underlying the objectives stated in *APB Statement No. 4* were adopted.

- An exchange economy using cash as purchasing power.
- Consumption and saving on the basis of expectations.
- Production and marketing requiring saving for investments.
- Savings invested through financial intermediaries.
- Production carried on by investor-owned businesses.
- Divorce between ownership and management, with owners interested in returns (dividends plus appreciation).
- Management accountable to owner-investors.
- Investment of savings in the forms of debt and equity securities traded in markets.
- Market transactions set security prices.
- Investors balance expected risks and returns.
- Securities markets tend to allocate scarce resources to those enterprises which use them efficiently, and away from inefficient enterprises. Efficiency is defined as having expected profit sufficient to indicate returns to investors.
- Government intervenes in resource allocation, thus affecting the balance of market forces in an unspecified way.
- Government supplies economic statistics based to a considerable extent on financial report information.
- Resource allocation by individuals, enterprises, markets, and government is more effective if based on information that reflects the relative standing and performance of business enterprises.

From these assumptions follows the primary objective:

> Financial reporting is intended to provide information that is useful in making business and economic decisions—for making reasoned choices among alternative uses of scarce resources.

But information has a cost, and therefore methodological postulates are required to specify how it will be collected and displayed.

- Financial information, meaning "expressed in units of money."
- These numbers are usually exchange prices or amounts derived therefrom.
- It is constrained by the need to be verifiable, to enhance reliability and objectivity.
- It does not attempt to measure macroeconomic events, or the degree to which consumption satisfies consumer wants.
- It focuses on the creation and use of, and rights to, wealth and the sharing of associated risks.
- It involves estimates, classifications, summarizations, judgments and allocations, and is therefore approximate.
- It is primarily about the past and present, so that if users want to predict the future it must be supplemented by other information.
- Benefits are usually incalculable, and costs are often difficult to determine, therefore the cost/benefit ratio cannot be known.

Finally, SFAC No. 1 contains behavioral postulates concerning users and their needs. The objectives of general purpose financial reporting assume that it is designed for the informational needs of external users who lack power to obtain what they want, and who must use that which is provided for them by management.

From these assumptions flow the objectives themselves. Financial reporting should provide information that is useful to present and potential users in making rational decisions. The information should be comprehensible to those who have a reasonable understanding of business and economic activities and are willing to study the information with reasonable diligence. It should provide information to help present and potential users to assess the amounts, timing and uncertainty of prospective cash receipts from dividends and of interest and the proceeds from the sale, redemption or maturity of securities and loans. Information helping investors, creditors, and others to assess the amounts, timing, and uncertainty of prospective net cash inflows to the related enterprises will serve this purpose. However, information about cash receipts and disbursements is not the most useful information for this purpose.

More specifically, financial reporting should provide information about the economic resources of an enterprise, the claims to those resources, and the effects of transactions, events, and circumstances that change resources and claims thereto. It should provide information about an enterprise's financial performance during a period, and accrual accounting is a better measure of performance than accounting for receipts and payments. However, financial reporting should provide information about how an enterprise obtains and spends cash and about other factors that may affect an enterprise's liquidity or solvency. Financial reporting should provide information about how management has discharged its stewardship responsibility to owners and to managers and directors in making decisions in the interest of owners. It should include explanations and interpretations designed to assist users to understand the financial information provided.

In subsequent chapters we will examine the assumptions and stated objectives of SFAC No. 1 more closely, in order to identify the difficulties which they present and to evaluate the degree to which the statement will in fact serve the purposes for which it was prepared.

QUALITATIVE CHARACTERISTICS OF ACCOUNTING INFORMATION

SFAC No. 2 addressed the problem of what characteristics of accounting information make that information useful. It was assumed that choice between alternative accounting methods would be made more wisely if the ingredients that contribute to usefulness were better understood. By identifying and defining the qualities that make accounting information useful, SFAC No. 2 develops a number of generalizations or guidelines for making accounting choices and also provides a terminology which should promote consistency in standard setting. A special need was that for improved communication between the FASB and its constituents (the accounting and financial communities), which could be the principal benefit from this Statement.

The qualities which distinguish better (more useful) information from inferior (less useful) information are primarily relevance and reliability, subject only to considerations of cost and materiality.

If either of the qualities, relevance and reliability, is completely missing, the information will not be useful. *Relevant* includes timely; to be relevant, information must have predictive or feedback value, or both. *Reliable* includes representational faithfulness, verifiability, and neutrality. *Comparability*, which includes consistency, is also important, but of a secondary kind. To be useful, financial information should have each of these qualities to a minimum degree, but trade-offs will be necessary and will differ in different situations.

Relevance is defined as information's capacity "to make a difference" in a decision, either by helping to form predictions or to confirm or correct expectations. The fact that new information may add little to the knowledge of an informed decision maker may make the new information less useful, but it does not make it less relevant, only less valuable. Relevance can also be viewed as effectiveness.

Reliability combines the two concepts of *representational faithfulness* and *verifiability*. Representational faithfulness is the correspondence between a measure or description and the phenomenon it purports to represent. In other sciences this is often designated as "validity." "The financial statements of a business enterprise can be thought of as a representation of the resources and obligations of an enterprise and the financial flows into, out of, and within the enterprise—as a model of the enterprise."

Verifiability is a quality of representational faithfulness. It excludes the possibility of biased measurement. Conservatism implies bias if it connotes a deliberate, consistent understatement of net assets and profits. If conservatism is simply prudence, however—using the less optimistic of two equally likely estimates of amounts to be received or paid in the future—it is acceptable. Skepticism is warranted, bias is not.

Neutrality, another qualitative characteristic, means that either in formulating or implementing standards, the primary concern should be the relevance and reliability of the information that results, and not the effect that the new rule will have on a particular interest. Neutrality plus freedom from bias equals credibility.

With regard to comparability, investing and lending involve evaluation of alternatives. Different accounting methods make financial comparisons difficult. There cannot be one "right" method among available alternatives, and not all measurements must be standardized—only those characteristics necessary to comparison. Again, comparability and relevance/reliability may be incompatible; improving comparability may destroy or weaken relevance or reliability. Consistency is important over time, but it may inhibit accounting progress. Disclosure may permit inconsistency without eliminating comparability.

SFAC No. 2 also discussed cost and materiality. The benefits of information cannot be confined to those who pay for it, and its supply therefore cannot be left to the market. Costs are mostly passed on to users of the information and to consumers. *Materiality* is determined by the user; the importance of an item to the user determines the level at which it becomes material. The predominant view is that materiality judgments can be made only by those who have all the facts, and therefore the FASB will not formulate a materiality standard.

The concepts of relevance, verifiability, comparability, and materiality will be discussed in later chapters of this book, which adopts as a point of departure the representation view of financial statements underlying the concept of representational faithfulness.

ELEMENTS OF FINANCIAL STATEMENTS OF BUSINESS ENTERPRISES

The test of the usefulness of the first two Statements of Financial Accounting Concepts is difficult to devise. Most commentators will agree that accounting information should be useful, relevant, reliable, free from bias, and have more benefits than costs. The elements of financial statements are a different proposition, however; presumably we should be able to examine a set of financial statements and see whether its components correspond with the concepts adopted by the FASB.

SFAC No. 3 defines assets, liabilities, equity, investments by owners, distributions to owners, comprehensive income, revenues, expenses, gains, and losses. The FASB had previously indicated a preference for the word "earnings" for comprehensive income, but the Statement explained that the word earnings might be used to designate something else in the future. Since the definition and description of these ten concepts is a major portion of later chapters of this book, the FASB's definitions will not be listed at this time. Here we will deal generally with the accounting assumptions.

Elements are classes of items used to construct financial statements. They must be quantifiable in units of money. The financial statements in question are those of business enterprises, but several of the definitions have been worded so as to be applicable to nonbusiness financial statements. The type of statements in question are those prepared on the accrual basis, and the statement contains a lengthy discussion of accrual accounting, as accounting for events and circumstances as well as transactions.

An *event* is a happening of consequence to the entity. A *circumstance* is a condition or set of conditions that develop from an event or a series of events. A *transaction* is a particular kind of external event involving transfer of value between two or more entities. Value is defined as future economic benefit. A transaction may be an exchange or a nonreciprocal transfer.

Accrual is the accounting process of recognizing noncash events and circumstances as they occur. It is concerned with future cash receipts and payments, as contrasted with prepayment and deferral, which are concerned with past cash receipts and payments. Deferral is the accounting process of recognizing a liability for a current cash receipt or an asset for a current cash payment (or current incurrence of a liability) with an expected future impact on revenues or expenses. Thus, to defer is to postpone recognition of a revenue or expense.

Allocation is the accounting process of assigning or distributing an amount according to a plan or formula. It includes amortization and, therefore, depreciation and depletion. Amortization is the accounting process of systematically reducing an amount by periodic payments or write-downs.

Realization denotes the sale of assets for cash or claims to cash. *Recognition* is the process of formally recording or incorporating an item in the accounts and financial statements of an enterprise. Thus recognized means recorded.

The Statement describes the difference between accrual and cash accounting thus:

> A report showing cash receipts and cash outlays for an enterprise for a short period cannot indicate how much of the cash received is return *of* investment and how much is return *on* investment and thus cannot indicate whether or to what extent an enterprise is successful or unsuccessful.... Thus, recognition of revenues, expenses, gains and losses and the related increments or decrements in assets and liabilities ... is the essence of using accrual accounting to measure performance of business enterprises.

The Statement defines the elements as financial representations (depictions in words, numbers, and other symbols) of certain enterprise resources, claims to those resources and the effects of transactions and other events and circumstances that result in changes in those resources and claims. These representations stand for certain future economic benefits, sacrifices (of benefits) and events and circumstances. The same names are used for both the financial representations and the objects they represent. Performance measurement governs the definitions, and accrual accounting is necessary for performance measurement.

The other accounting assumption dealt with was *articulation*. The elements are divisible into two classes: Class 1—assets, liabilities, and equity; and Class 2—the remaining seven elements.

Elements of classes are changed by revenues, expenses, gains, and losses, and at any time are their cumulative result. Elements of class 1 are also changed by investment, borrowing, and repayment. When we say that financial statements are articulated, we mean that the change in class 1, other than that resulting from investment, borrowing, and repayment, is equal to the change in class 2, called comprehensive income.

Finally, the Statement points out that the definitions do not cover the recognition, measurement, or display of the elements, which will be dealt with in other concepts statements. The definitions are intended to screen out items that do not qualify as particular elements of financial statements because they lack one or more essential characteristics. Thereafter an item still must meet other criteria for recognition and measurement, and conform to the qualitative characteristics laid down by SFAC No. 2, before it can enter the financial statements as a part of one of the elements.

The first four Statements of Financial Accounting Concepts will be examined in more detail in chapters 6 and 12 through 14.

THE NEED FOR UNIFORMITY IN FINANCIAL REPORTING

Underlying the pronouncements of the Accounting Principles Board and the Financial Accounting Standards Board in the U.S.A., the International Accounting Standards Committee (IASC), and similar accounting regulators in other countries, is the belief that uniform accounting practices improve the reliability of financial reports as a source of information for investment decisions. It is also implied that disclosure is not a satisfactory substitute for uniformity, and that uniformity must be made mandatory through regulation.

The need for such regulation is ascribed to several factors.

1. The "free rider" aspect of public information, which is a way of saying that its benefits cannot be confined to those who

pay for it. Such information is a "public good," in the language of economics, and all public goods will tend to be undersupplied if not produced at public expense, or else the producers constrained to supply them. This argument is clearly contradicted by the facts, because public disclosure of information by the majority of public companies was both extensive and expanding prior to the establishment of the SEC in the United States.

2. The "inefficiency" of capital markets results when all traders do not have access to the same information. This "market failure" causes capital to flow to some firms, and away from others, in a pattern which is less than optimal, given the risk/reward preferences of investors.
3. The "cost/benefit" attitudes of managers, who seek to minimize the cost of capital by manipulating such relationships as the debt/equity ratio, or earnings before interest and taxes to interest expense.
4. The "agency theory" of the firm, which views the firm as a set of contractual relationships. These relationships include those between the firm and its financiers, and the firm and its managers. In the former, the contract may include an agreement to maintain a specified debt/equity ratio, a minimum dollar amount of stockholders' equity, and a minimum ratio of earnings to interest. In the latter, the contract may include bonus and other forms of manager remuneration dependent upon earnings. These accounting data are measured in accordance with generally accepted accounting principles, and if managers have alternatives they will tend to choose that method which is most favorable in the light of the contractual arrangement, rather than the one which best represents the actual situation of the firm.

On the other hand, it is fairly clear from many years of financial reporting that a purposeful effort to manipulate financial statements is not widespread. Indeed, given the complexity of human affairs, the consequences of manipulating financial data are often unpredictable, even from quarter to quarter. In addition, one may cite other factors which are believed to contradict the need for mandated uniformity.

1. The view that consistency of application of accounting methods is more important than uniformity between issuers of investment securities.[15]
2. The "situational" approach to accounting, which postulates that ostensibly similar transactions, events and circumstances may require different treatment. For example, the effect of an exchange rate change on the assets of a foreign subsidiary differs according as the subsidiary is financed with U.S. dollars or foreign currency.

3. The belief that the principal users of financial reports as a source of information for investment decisions are such "sophisticated" users as institutional investment managers and financial analysts, who are able to see through accounting practices which do not mirror economic events.

The need for disclosure regulations is not in question; they can readily be justified as belonging to the powers of government in its capacity of protector of the savings of the individual. The debate concerns the need for regulations imposing uniformity in accounting practices among different enterprises in the same jurisdiction.

CONCLUSION

We have traced the expansion of the field of accounting over the past two hundred years and identified some of the strains which this rapid growth has caused. Many commentators—and the FASB as the regulator of accounting and financial reporting—have pointed to the lack of an accounting theory as a principal factor responsible for these strains. The FASB has attempted to make good this deficiency through its conceptual framework project.

The project was reviewed at a conference held in the summer of 1980, at which a number of skeptics voiced the opinion that the end result of the exercise would be the ratification of the status quo. A review of the first outputs of the conceptual framework project support this observation. More important than the establishment of accounting theory, however, may be the fact that the project forces members of the FASB and its staff to think more carefully about their objectives and the methods they adopt to achieve these objectives. The FASB has acknowledged the importance of good communications with its constituency, which the definitions and express assumptions of the Statements of Financial Accounting Concepts may benefit.

Nor can it be said that the academic community has had more success until now in developing a widely usable theory of accounting. Indeed, a recent survey of work accomplished under this heading was extremely pessimistic about the lack of "theory closure" in this field.[16]

ENDNOTES

1. See also the expanded form of this definition in Grady, Paul, "Inventory of Generally Accepted Accounting Principles for Business Enterprises," *Accounting Research Study No. 7*, New York, AICPA, 1965.
2. Fifth edition, New York, The Ronald Press, 1970.
3. Reprinted by permission of the author. See also Herbert, Leo, "The Environment of Government Accounting in the Seventies," *The GAO Review*, Fall 1972, pp. 22-32.
4. Sowell, Ellis Mast, *The Evolution of the Theories and Techniques of Standard Costs*, Alabama, 1973.

5. Hess, Henry, "Manufacturing: Capital, Costs, Profits and Dividends," *The Engineering Magazine*, Vol. 26, December 1903, p. 367 *et seq*.
6. Accounting professors recognize as one of their functions to criticize accounting. An early example was Hatfield, Henry Rand, "What is the Matter with Accounting?" *Journal of Accountancy*, October 1927, pp. 267-9.
7. Philadelphia, University of Pennsylvania Press, 1939.
8. Canning, John B. His work will be discussed in chapter 8.
9. See Storey, Reed K., *The Search for Accounting Principles: Today's Problems in Perspective*, New York: AICPA, 1964.
10. Mattesich, Richard, *Accounting and Analytical Methods*, Homewood: Richard D. Irwin, Inc., 1964, p. 414.
11. Brief, Richard P., "The Accountant's Responsibility in Historical Perspective," *The Accounting Review*, April 1975, pp. 285-97.
12. 1977 House Hearings (remarks of Congressman Eckardt), *Foreign Corrupt Practices and Domestic and Foreign Investment Disclosure, Hearing Before the Committee on Banking, Housing and Urban Affairs*, United States Senate, 95th Congress of the United States, 1st Session, at 227 (March 16, 1977).
13. Other Discussion Memoranda were: "Criteria for Determining Materiality," March 21, 1975 and "Reporting Earnings," July 31, 1979. In addition, there were several Discussion Memoranda outstanding which depended in some way upon the outcome of the Conceptual Framework Project; one on accounting for business combinations and purchased intangibles was taken off the FASB's agenda in 1981.
14. It will be noted that the change in emphasis from financial statements to financial reporting appears to have taken place about the end of 1979 or the beginning of 1980.
15. Securities and Exchange Commission, *The SEC Major Issues Conference, Final Report*, January 13-15, 1977, Washington, D.C. p. 8.
16. Committee of the American Accounting Association, *Statement on Accounting Theory and Theory Acceptance*, Sarasota: American Accounting Association, 1977.

SELECTED ADDITIONAL READINGS

Brief, Richard P., "The Accountant's Responsibility in Historical Perspective," *The Accounting Review*, April 1975, pp. 285-97.

Chatfield, Michael, *A History of Accounting Thought*, Hinsdale, Illinois: The Dryden Press, 1974.

Committee of the American Accounting Association, *Statement on Accounting Theory and Theory Acceptance*, Sarasota: American Accounting Association, 1977.

Davies, Jonathan J., ed. *Accounting Research Convocation 1977*, University of Alabama, November 1977, especially Bedford, Norton M., pp. 1-26 and Koch, Albert A., pp. 27-40.

Financial Accounting Standards Board, FASB *Discussion Memorandum*, "An analysis of issues related to Conceptual Framework for Financial Accounting and Reporting: Elements of Financial Statements and Their Measurement," December 2, 1976.

Goldberg, Louis, *An Inquiry into the Nature of Accounting*, Monograph No. 4, Iowa City: American Accounting Association, 1965.

Hakansson, Nils H., "Where We Are in Accounting: A Review of *Statement on Accounting Theory and Theory Acceptance*," *The Accounting Review*, July 1978, pp. 717-25.

Mattessich, Richard, *Accounting and Analytical Methods*, Homewood, Illinois: Richard D. Irwin, Inc., 1964.

Merino, Barbara D. and Teddy L. Coe, "Uniformity in Accounting: A Historical Perspective," *Journal of Accountancy*, August 1978, pp. 62-69.

Metcalf Staff Reports: Subcommittee on Reports, Accounting and Management of the Committee on Government Operations of the United States Senate—A Staff Study, *The Accounting Establishment*, Washington, D.C.: U.S. Government Printing Office, 1976, and *Improving the Accountability of Publicly Owned Corporations and Their Auditors*, Washington D.C.: U.S. Government Printing Office, 1977.

Peasnell, K.V., "Statement of Accounting Theory and Theory Acceptance: A Review Article," *Accounting and Business Research*, Summer 1978, pp. 217-25.

Shenkir, William G., "Current Efforts to Develop a Conceptual Framework for Financial Accounting and Reporting," Working Paper No. 30 in *Working Paper Series Vol. 2*, The Academy of Accounting Historians, 1979.

Solomons, David, "The Politicization of Accounting," *Journal of Accountancy*, November 1978, pp. 68-72.

Case 1–1 International Harvester's McCardell

In 1977 Archie R. McCardell joined International Harvester Inc. as chairman and chief executive. Part of the package of benefits which attracted him to the position was a $1,796,250 loan to buy 60,000 shares of International Harvester stock. The terms of the loan included a provision that repayment would be forgiven if he managed to raise the corporation's profitability to the average ratio of six competitors within a seven-year period. At that time this average profitability (called parity) was 10.5 percent; Harvester's was 6.86 percent.

In fiscal 1978 it was proposed to change to the LIFO method of inventory valuation for that year's annual financial statements. It was anticipated that this change would reduce profits by about 5 percent compared with 1977, but provide an immediate cash saving, through deferring taxes on profits, of several million dollars. A similar depressing effect on profits, coupled with substantial tax savings, could be expected for subsequent years.

1. Discuss the factors which Archie McCardell would consider when preparing the decision whether to change to LIFO in 1978.
2. What do you think the decision was? (See *Fortune*, December 15, 1980, p. 90).

Case 1–2 Using the FASB's Conceptual Framework

At a public hearing on foreign currency translation in December, 1980, the Chairman of the FASB pointed out that this was the most controversial and complex issue the Board has faced. Its complexity arose out of the fact that it covered every aspect of the conceptual framework project: objectives of financial reporting, qualitative characteristics of accounting information, the unit of measure, accounting for changing prices, and the display of information about earnings and fund flows. It was controversial because responsible people disagreed on those conceptual issues.

1. Explain why the conceptual framework is perceived as useful to the FASB in arriving at an accounting standard for foreign currency translation.
2. Discuss the specific ways in which the FASB's concepts statements on objectives, qualitative characteristics, and elements can assist the FASB in arriving at a new statement of financial accounting standards on this subject.
3. Show how the FASB did in fact base its attempt to produce a successor to *FASB Statement No. 8* on the conceptual framework project.

END OF CHAPTER QUESTIONS

1. Define *accounting*. What is the purpose of such a definition?
2. What functions do accountants perform in a modern society, and what is the public perception of their social role? Do these correspond?
3. Explain what is meant by the "growth of accountability knowledge." What are its landmarks?
4. In recent years accountants have increasingly criticized the work which they perform and the basis of their methodology. Why?
5. What practical problems have plagued accountants during the period in question, and how are these related to the criticisms of accounting methodology?
6. Discuss the politicization of accounting, with particular reference to the role of the SEC in accounting standard setting.
7. State the main provisions of the Foreign Corrupt Practices Act of 1977 insofar as they affect accountants, and explain why this Act has aroused strong reactions from accountants since its passage.
8. All FASB Statements of Financial Accounting Concepts begin with the words: "Statements in the series are intended to set forth objectives and fundamentals that will be the basis for development of financial accounting and reporting standards." In other disciplines only general social objectives of an ethical nature are pronounced by the appropriate professional association, and the development of particular objectives and basic concepts is left to individuals and groups of scholars and practitioners. Why should accounting and financial reporting call for an authoritarian mode for the discharge of this function?
9. Describe the scope of the FASB's conceptual framework project

and state the extent to which the FASB has covered the subject at the present time.

10. What are *environmental postulates*? Why are they needed in a conceptual framework? What environmental postulates did the FASB adopt?
11. What assumptions concerning the use and limitations of accounting information were derived from the FASB's environmental postulates?
12. What primary objective did FASB SFAC No. 1 adopt for financial reporting?
13. List the qualitative characteristics of accounting information. Which ones are primary? What does *trade-off* mean in this context, and how would it be made?
14. What are *elements* and *items* of financial statements? Which elements did FASB SFAC No. 3 define? What, in addition to definitions, is required before we can identify the items of which financial statements consist?
15. Define: accrual, allocation, realization, recognition, articulation.
16. Discuss the need for uniformity in financial statements with particular reference to contemporary economic and management theories.
17. "Accounting is a service activity." Discuss this proposition in the contexts of (a) the historical development of accounting, (b) the financial reporting function, and (c) the managerial accounting function.
18. Generally accepted accounting principles require the use of accruals and deferrals in the determination of income.

    Required:

    a. How does accrual accounting affect the determination of income? Include in your discussion what constitutes an accrual and a deferral, and give appropriate examples of each.
    b. Contrast accrual accounting with cash accounting. (AICPA, November 1979)

2

THE DEVELOPMENT OF ACCOUNTING THOUGHT

It is sometimes interesting to trace the path which ideas have travelled. This chapter will attempt to point out the principal features of the development of accounting thought, some of which still influence the practice of accountancy to a marked degree.

While accounting appears to have been practiced at least since the beginning of recorded history, accounting theory is of comparatively recent origin. This may be due to the difficult, abstract nature of accounting thought, or perhaps to a gradual change in the scope and methods of accounting, which was thereby rendered more amenable to the formalized type of explanation which we call theory.

ORIGINS OF ACCOUNTING

According to evidence produced by recent archaeological research, both writing and arithmetic evolved from the need to account. That counting and accounting are intimately related has long been known, but the accounting origins of writing are of particular significance.

Scholars long believed that writing developed from pictographs which were graphic representations of objects—a sheep, a loaf of bread, and so on. Bone artifacts bearing incised markings have been found, which date from Palaeolithic times 30,000 to 12,000 years ago, and later clay tablets bearing similar representations show the use of pictographs in the Middle East. These pictographs resemble the earliest cuneiform writing of the Neo-Sumerian and Old Babylonian periods.

Archaeologists have also discovered large numbers of clay tokens of different shapes in ancient settlements. These clay tokens were an archaic recording system; the shape and the markings expressed the type and number of objects being represented. Thus, a token representing "sheep" was a disc with an incised cross. It is believed that these tokens could have been used in keeping track of the contents of silos and storage pits. They were also used in trade, and collections of tokens were transferred from one party to another as evidence of the transfer of ownership of the objects represented.

Another step was the invention of the *bulla,* a clay envelope containing clay tokens. The bulla became a kind of bill of lading, as its surface could bear the seal of a merchant who chose to authenticate the enclosed message. Because of its opacity, however, the recipient of the bulla could not know what it contained, and the practice arose of impressing on the surface of the bulla pictorial representations of the tokens it contained. A few hundred years later it dawned on the users that the tokens now were dispensable; all that was necessary was to incise their pictures on clay tablets. (The origin of the clay tablet is apparent from the fact that it had a convex surface.) The pictographs thus created, from which writing developed, were representations not of the objects, but of the clay tokens which were used to account for those objects.[1]

It appears that the scribes of those times were mainly occupied in recording business transactions and land sales. By about 3,000 B.C. they were also keeping accounts. Many of the early records which are recognizable as accounts, or the raw materials from which accounts may be constructed, lack those systematic attributes of form and content with which we associate accounting today. They consist mostly of inventories, lists of commodities used as payments, contracts of sale or loan, and, more rarely, simple journal entries. Nevertheless, ancient accounts were both used and useful. A modern archaeologist, studying the records which were kept by the Chaldean merchant Ea-Nasir nearly five thousand years ago, was able to assert that he was trading at a loss.[2]

The force which provided the necessary impetus for the development of modern accounting was the introduction of money as a means of exchange. As with so many other discoveries, it appears that the Chinese where the originators of this practice and that they used coined money some two thousand years before it appeared in Europe. Although Western knowledge of Chinese accounting in ancient times is very limited, we do know that sophisticated forms of government accounting, including both historical accounting and budgetary control, existed in China as early as 2000 B.C., accompanied by an audit function performed by a high and independent public official.

The coinage of money having a uniform value, therefore suitable for use as a medium of exchange, first took place in Europe in the seventh century B.C. Greek civilization, based on the secularization of an economy previously controlled by the priests, possessed a sophisticated system of public administration with accounting and auditing functions, of which details have survived. Banking and other commercial activities were conducted in ancient Greece, and accounting played an important role in them. Management accounting was used in business, as we know from the Zenon papyri. These rolls represent the records of the Egyptian estates of Appolonius, finance minister to the Greek ruler Ptolemy Philadelphus II, which were managed by one Zenon. It is clear from them that techniques of accounting control, which we associate with the modern corporate form of business enterprise, were known and understood more than two thousand years ago.

No accounting records have survived the fall of the Roman civilization, which extended from about 700 B.C. to 400 A.D. This has been attributed to the fact that the Romans kept their accounts on wax tablets, which turned out to be a most perishable material. No doubt the Goths and Visigoths did their part by destroying all remaining physical records. Tantalizing glimpses of Roman accounting occur in the legal codes of Gaius and Justinian, in the orations of Cicero, and in other literary sources. From these it has been surmised that the Romans used the bilateral account form and even that the double-entry system was known fifteen hundred years before Pacioli.

Evidence for the assertion that the Romans used the double-entry system comes mainly from surviving fragments of the Ciceronian oration *Pro Fonteio.* Fonteius was a Roman administator during a period when inflation was causing severe economic hardships throughout the Roman empire. There was even a shortage of money to pay the new high prices with. The Roman Treasury therefore undertook a currency reform, in which new units of currency were exchanged for old units in the ratio one to four. Fonteius was accused of having received taxes and debts owed to the treasury in the new currency, but of reporting the receipts as if they had been received in the old, keeping three-fourths of the amount for himself.

In Cicero's oration for the defense the advocate is reported to have said that Fonteius kept records "of the one-fourth and of the three-fourths." Why, it is asked, did he keep records of the three-fourths (the amount of the debt written off because of the conversion from old to new currency)? Some accounting historians have asserted that this would only be necessary in a double-entry system of accounting, in order to balance the accounts. It must be admitted that this tenuous supposition has not attracted much support.

We do know that large-scale commercial and industrial operations were a characteristic of the Greek and Roman civilizations, and that they operated complex organizations such as banking, shipping, and insurance. From the Zenon papyri and other records we know that basic principles of accounting, planning, and control such as budgeting, the journal entry, financial reporting, and auditing were used by the Greeks, and therefore probably by the Romans. We are on more certain grounds when we view the modern history of accounting.

THE RISE OF THE DOUBLE-ENTRY SYSTEM

The destruction of the Roman and Byzantine civilizations was followed by a period of European history known as the Dark Ages.

The feudal system of political organization rescued Europe from chaos and provided the stability necessary for the creation of economic surpluses. These surpluses represented the capital base on which the economic development of the Middle Ages was built. The conversion of a subsistence economy into a money economy was effected by the Norman adventurer-kings. The medieval period, therefore, saw the existence of conditions favorable for the development of accounting.

This development took place at several levels: government, business, and the medieval manor. Apart from banking, the conduct of business was largely a function of small traders and artisans who kept accounting records of a crude memorandum nature, sufficient for their restricted information needs. Large-scale business operations were carried on by the banks and the church, the latter through the manorial system, and we find the banks using financial accounting based on principles which eventually became double-entry bookkeeping, and the manors using management accounting, based on essentially statistical models.

We have mentioned the use of the bilateral account form long before this period. The integration of this form into a system of double-entry accounts appears to have evolved during the twelfth or thirteenth centuries A.D. It may or may not have been an invention of the Italians who at that time dominated banking, trade, and what little manufacturing there was. Largely as a result of the *Liber Abacci* of Leonardo of Pisa, the Italians adopted Arabic in place of Roman numerals, which was an additional factor favoring the expansion of the concept underlying accounting. Although it is believed that the idea of double-entry was originated by banks, the oldest surviving record which incorporates double-entry principles is the Giovanni Farolfi branch ledger (Salon, France) for the year 1299-1300. More familiar are the double-entry trading accounts of Donald Soranzo and Brothers, merchants of Venice, from the first quarter of the fifteenth century. The first professional organization of accountants was founded in Venice in 1581. The method of Venice then spread throughout the world, partly through translations and plagiarisms, partly through being transplanted to other countries by Venetian traders and clerks.

Giovanni Farolfi and Company were a firm of Florentine merchants, and it is noteworthy that the banking and manufacturing center of Florence experienced a parallel development of double-entry bookkeeping during the same period as Venice. In fact, Florentine accounting appears to have been more sophisticated than the method of Venice and more comparable with modern accounting systems. Datini (1335-1410) conducted a large-scale international business—what would today be called a multinational corporation—using a full double-entry system of accounts for the control of foreign as well as domestic operations. The Medicis not only kept complex accounts for their banking operations, but also integrated cost accounting records for textile manufacturing. In these latter records we find the first examples of accounting for depreciation, interest on capital, and cost of production.

THE FATHER OF MODERN ACCOUNTING

Luca Pacioli is considered the father of modern accounting because his *method of Venice* became the model for subsequent textbooks during a period of over two hundred years. In 1494 he published his *Summa,* which contained two chapters—*de Computis et Scripturis,* describing double-entry bookkeeping. Pacioli was a Franciscan monk and a collaborator of Leonardo da Vinci; Pope Leo X thought highly enough of his ability to appoint him in 1514 professor of mathematics in the Sapienza at Rome—the university of the highest standing in all Christendom. The fact that this noted mathematician was interested in bookkeeping is significant of the high esteem which this subject enjoyed in Venice.

Other European scholars who assisted in disseminating accounting ideas were the German *Grammateus* (Schreiber) (1518); the Dutchman Simon Stevin, who wrote an extended treatise on bookkeeping for his royal pupil, the Prince of Orange (1602), and Arthur Cayley, now known for his early studies of the principles of flight, who while professor of mathematics at Cambridge University in England wrote *The Principles of Double-Entry Bookkeeping.*

The Italian system of double-entry bookkeeping made slow headway in England, however, and was not generally accepted until towards the end of the nineteenth century when the growth of the corporation and the reintroduction of the income tax combined to make its virtues apparent.[3] On the European continent, these virtues were appreciated earlier; the famous Antwerp printer and publisher Christopher Plantin kept a set of books for his partnership covering the period 1563-67, consisting of a journal and double-entry ledger along the lines laid down by Luca Paciolo. The ledger accounts included equipment and paper inventory accounts, a manufacturing expense account, and a finished goods account for books in stock (inventory).

THE SOMBART PROPOSITIONS

Werner Sombart, a political economist of some note, was born in 1863 and died in Germany in 1941. He studied law, economics, history, and philosophy at the Universities of Berlin, Rome, and Pisa, eventually becoming a professor of economics in Berlin. His major work, *Der Moderne Kapitalismus,* is a book in praise of capitalism and in it he predicted that capitalism would reach its zenith in the twentieth century.[4]

Sombart's theme led him to examine the accounting records of the period during which capitalism developed in Europe, and he identified three causal factors which contributed to the growth of the capitalistic enterprise.

1. The law
2. Business management techniques
3. The market

The law provided a framework for the firm, the capitalistic enterprise as a legal entity, and the market provided a means for it to become a financial entity. Business management techniques relied primarily on accounting, and Sombart put forward four explanations for the role which accounting played in this connection.

(i) By representing the flow of capital through a business."... from the capital account to the transaction accounts through the profit and loss account and back into the capital account," accounting facilitated a concentration on the creation of wealth by means of profits.

(ii) By restricting the observations of the entrepreneur to that which could be captured in the accounts, accounting fostered the development of economic rationalism: *quod non est in libris, non est in mundo.* ("What's not in the book doesn't exist.")

(iii) Systematic organization of the affairs of the business was achieved through accounting.

(iv) Double-entry bookkeeping facilitated the separation of management from ownership by rendering the concept of capital objective and by permitting the separation of business accounts from household accounts.[5]

Winjum has examined these propositions in the light of accounting textbooks and records produced in England during the period 1500-1750 and has concluded that, while some evidence exists in support of all four, the primary advantage of double-entry bookkeeping was the creation of "order from chaos."[6] The main purpose of accounting revealed by the textbooks and the main use of accounting revealed by the records was the systematic organization of the affairs of the business.

ACCOUNTING IN ITS AGE OF STAGNATION

Largely as a consequence of the influence which Pacioli's work had upon the business world of its time, but also partly because that world changed very little between 1494 and 1775, the period which followed the invention of double-entry bookkeeping has become known as accounting's "age of stagnation."[7] The principal feature of this period is the extension of the method of Venice to other countries as they came to dominate world trade. Thus, we find double-entry accounting spreading to Germany, the Low Countries (now Belgium and Holland) England, Scotland, Portugal, and Spain during this period.

The emphasis of both literature and practice was on accounting as an aid to the management of a business, rather than as an information source for external users. The owner of a business was expected to keep accounts, and instruction in double-entry bookkeeping was a part of the education of the middle classes. Because the accounts were for one's own use, we do not find the preparation of financial statements and their audit occupying a central place in the expositions of textbook writers. Nor have we inherited any period income statements or balance sheets of the kind with which we are now familiar.

The prevailing practice was to continue the accounts through several years until some event occurred which called for a balance to be drawn up—the merchant's death, the filling of an account book, the disposal of the business. We know that the accountant-businessman sometimes prepared financial statements for specific periods, and the profit and loss account, precursor of the modern income statement, was, as its name implies, a listing of profits and losses on individual ventures or lines of business. Similarly, the balance sheet was a listing of balances left over after profits and losses had been closed out to the profit and loss account. Nevertheless, the concepts of capital as the difference between assets and liabilities, and of net profit as the change in capital between two dates (after adjusting for capital contributions and withdrawals) was well established during the age of stagnation.

THE ENGLISH COMPANIES ACTS

We will restrict ourselves here to a description of the way in which accounting and financial reporting developed in England from about 1775 (although a comparable sequence of events can be noted in other European countries), expanding on the reference to this in chapter 1.

The industrial revolution, which is conventionally regarded as beginning in the 1760s with the invention of production machinery, had several consequences of far-reaching importance to the history of accounting. One was the growth of the large-scale enterprise, beyond anything previously known, requiring quantities of capital greater than could be provided by one man or one family. Another was the introduction of the variable time period into production in the two senses of the time period required to amortize machinery and other equipment, and the time period required for production itself.

The demand for capital involved increasing numbers of savers in investment situations, either directly or through financial intermediaries such as banks and insurance companies. The corporation proved to be the most satisfactory form of business organization from this point of view. As more and more individuals and institutions were involved as stockholders, the financing function became separate from the management function, which has been designated the *managerial revolution*. In this situation the owners of the business were no longer able to inform themselves by keeping accounts for its operations, because they took no part in the management of the enterprise.

To afford these outside investors a measure of protection, the British government introduced a succession of Companies Acts. These laws placed certain obligations on the promoters and managers of corporations as part of the price they had to pay for the privilege of incorporation. The 1844 Act required the directors of a company to supply the stockholders with audited balance sheets annually, and the 1865 Act provided a model form of balance sheet for this purpose. This legislation has been progressively supplemented and refined to the present day. It is aimed at providing investors and other financiers with audited information in the form of accounts on which to base their investment and disinvestment decisions and from which to judge the manner in which the directors of the corporation have managed the business.

The lengthening of the time period of production had two principal effects. These were the development of business credit, as distinct from investment, and the gradual transfer of attention from the balance sheet to the profit and loss account. Business credit, by its nature short-term and revolving, required decisions for which short-term information about financial position and results was necessary. The need to prepare more frequent financial statements which would reveal profitability and liquidity gave considerable impetus to the development of accounting. In the preparation of financial statements, the analysis of changes in capital became necessary for a variety of operating decisions. This led to the establishment of rules for income statement preparation—in particular, for calculating depreciation, the valuation of inventories, revenue recognition, and provision for future expenditures arising out of past activities.

A by-product of the industrial revolution was the growth and refinement of management accounting. The use of accounting and other quantitative data for purposes of management planning and control has been noted in Ancient Greece, in the medieval manors, and by the traders of the age of stagnation. Some cost accounting was done,varying in sophistication from the *ad hoc* calculations of individuals to the integrated systems of the Medici factories and the French Royal Wallpaper Manufactory. The complex manufacturing processes and large-scale organizations which appeared during and after the industrial revolution required more detailed and systematic analyses of costs of production. Thus, the subject of cost accounting, encompassing the accounts necessary to plan, control, and analyze costs, acquired a separate existence during the second half of the nineteenth century. This separation of cost from financial accounting has persisted to the present, in spite of practical and theoretical efforts to integrate them.

ORIGINS OF EUROPEAN ACCOUNTING THEORY

Although the use of financial reports to assist owners of corporate stock to manage their investments can be said to have originated in nineteenth century England, accounting as a tool of management is of great antiquity. Long before American accounting theorists attempted to generalize about accounting, several European writers sought to do so.

Historically, there have been three basic approaches to the development of accounting theory. Attention was first directed to the account itself, and attempts were made to construct rules for the operation of accounts. This led to the *personification theories* in which the account was ascribed the qualities of a person who received and gave.[8] But an account is not a person, and recognition of this fact directed attention to the transactions and events which are in great part the subject matter of accounts. This led to attempts to formulate rules and standards designed to ensure that objective economic facts were recorded and reported. It then became clear that accounts contained values other than those represented by transactions and events, and that the very concept of value was subjective.

Early writers on accounting had great difficulty in explaining what it was that they were instructing students to do. Lacking an accounting theory, they resorted to precept and admonition, frequently bolstered by appeals to the deity. Personification was one device used to reduce the need to memorize rules and procedures. By viewing the account as a person, generalizations were made possible, such as "debit him that receives, credit him that gives." In fact, personification took three forms—

- The attribution of human qualities to inanimate objects or constructions such as accounts,
- The fiction that each account was an extension of the proprietor's personality ("John Smith his goods"),
- The view that each account represented a clerk who received and gave up value on behalf of the proprietor.

The second of these proved most fertile, as it suggested the classification of the accounts of the firm into *real* (impersonal) accounts, being accounts for objects owned by the proprietor, and *personal* accounts for persons other than the proprietor—suppliers, customers, and lenders. Personal accounts would correspond to accounts kept by others, and must therefore conform to general rules, whereas real accounts could be handled in different ways. As the practice of preparing a profit and loss account developed, some of the real accounts were seen to represent period phenomena; these were then named *nominal* accounts.

Note that this classification scheme presented its own problems. Suppose that the firm opened an account at a bank owned by another individual. Was this a real account (cash) or a personal account (X's Bank)? Nominal accounts created real strain for the writers; how does one personify the account for sales or cash discounts received? This, together with the growing realization that the device was artificial, led to the abandonment of personification in the nineteenth century.

THE PROBLEM OF CLASSIFICATION

The problem of classification is fundamental to any science, and early writers on accounting attempted to classify ledger accounts in a logical order. An example of the transition from personification to some other basis can be found in Abraham de Graef's *Instructie van het Italiaans Boekhouden* ("Instruction in Italian Bookkeeping") published in Amsterdam in 1693. He divided accounts into three groups.

1. Accounts of the merchant as a person: Capital, Profits and Losses, Insurances, Reserves, Housekeeping, Interest.
2. Accounts of other persons: Debtors, Creditors, Participations in Trade Ventures, etc.
3. Accounts for merchandise: Goods in store, Goods in Ships afloat, Cash available for purchases, etc. (the *real* accounts).

Edmond Degrange in his book *La Tenue des Livres Rendue Facile* ("Bookkeeping Made Easy"), published in Paris in 1795, divided these real accounts into five classes: Cash, Goods, Bills (Notes) Receivable, Bills (Notes) Payable, and Profits and Losses. It is noteworthy that what was a personal account to de Graef was a real account to Degrange. Followers of Degrange became known as the "Cinquecontistes" or five-account school.

In Belgium, H. Godefroid attempted to integrate cost and financial accounts for manufacturing concerns; requiring more classes, he borrowed from literary sources, and, in a textbook published in 1864, Godefroid suggested the use of titles, chapters, and sections for classifying accounts. In this scheme, one of the titles was used for departmental operating accounting, that is, for cost accounts. Because of its expanded content, Godefroid's scheme became popular in Europe, and some of his followers decimalized his classification. By the end of the nineteenth century the decimal chart of accounts, based primarily on a classification of balance sheet accounts but including a section for operations, was in widespread use for didactic purposes as well as in actual accounting systems.

THE FRENCH SCHOOL

Rene Delaporte was perhaps the outstanding French accounting theorist. A many-sided individual, he was a writer, colonial civil servant, professor of business, bank administrator, and the holder of six university degrees. He published several works on accounting, the most important in 1936, six years before he died.[10]

Delaporte denied the existence of real or personal accounts and drew attention to the arithmetical or statistical nature of the account. There were two classes, assets and liabilities; he included owners' equity under liabilities. Accounts represented values, which he interpreted as legal rights and was prepared to see include even obligations "not to do" something, such as to refrain from selling in a certain territory. Delaporte favored the use of the symbols + and − in place of the terms "debit" and "credit."

Another French contributor was J. F. Dumarchey, whose theoretical work was first published in 1914. Dumarchey attempted to establish a scientific foundation for accounting.[11] This scientific foundation lay in the economic and social sciences; Dumarchey was interested in the relationship between accounting and economics, because both dealt with questions of production, distribution, and consumption of wealth. To Dumarchey, value is economic value, and accounts may be *static* or *dynamic;* this dichotomy relates him to the German school discussed below.

Other contributions were made by Eugène de Fagès, a civil engineer; by J. Sigaut; and by Pierre Garnier, author of one of the best-selling modern French accounting texts.[12]

THE GERMAN SCHOOL AND A NOTABLE SWISS

In Germany, the major influence on the development of accounting theory was Eugen Schmalenbach. He founded the new discipline of business economics (*Betriebswirtschaftslehre*) and, in 1906, the journal *Der Zeitschrift für Handelswissenschaftliche Forschung,* the first business research periodical. Prior to Schmalenbach, a number of German writers had introduced legalistic theories of accounting, which Schmalenbach called *static.* Basing his theory on the study of the behavior of business corporations, he called it dynamic accounting, and his *Dynamische Bilanz* ("Dynamic Accounting"), originally published in Germany in 1916, was severely critical of the emphasis on the balance sheet.[13] He argued that the objectives which were generally ascribed to the balance sheet were incapable of realization. The balance sheet could not present the value of the business as a going concern, because that value was different (more or less) from the sum of the individual parts, of which only a selection appeared in the balance sheet. The balance sheet was not a statement of financial position for the same reason and also because the assets and liabilities were not shown at liquidation amounts. Instead of pursuing unattainable objectives with regard to the balance sheet, Schmalenbach argued, accountants should concentrate on improving the profit and loss account (income statement) with the objective of accurately measuring the results of operations. This would relegate the balance sheet to the role of a list of balances in suspense, or "a step between two income statements" as the contemporary phrase has it. An example of a modern chart of accounts derived from Schmalenbach's classification is reproduced as Table 2-1. It is noteworthy that more classes are allocated to income statement accounts than to balance sheet accounts, and for explicitly recognizing the necessity to incorporate revenue and expense accounts in the classification scheme.

TABLE 2-1
General Chart of Accounts for German Industry (a)

CLASS 0		**CLASS 1**	
Fixed Assets and Long-term Capital		**Current Assets and Current Liabilities**	
FIXED ASSETS	LONG-TERM CAPITAL	CURRENT ASSETS	CURRENT LIABILITIES
00 Land and buildings 000 Unbuilt land 001/2 Built-up land 003/7 Buildings 008 Buildings under construction 009 Depreciation on land and buildings	**06 Outside capital** 060/1 Loans, debentures 062/5 Mortgages 066/9 Other outside capital	**10 Cash** 100 Main cash 105 Petty cash	**16/17 Creditors** 160 Creditors for goods supplied 161/9 Analysis *(c)* 170 Other creditors 171 Advance payments received 172 Advances received from associated companies 173/4 Due to employees (savings schemes etc.) 175/8 Other creditors 179 Adjustments to creditors' accounts
01 Manufacturing plant and equipment 010/9 Machines and equipment	**07 Proprietors' capital** Companies 070/1 Subscribed capital 072 Legal reserve 073/6 Free reserves 077/8 Losses applicable to capital 079 Profit and loss account carry forward Sole traders and partnerships 070/3 Capital accounts Adjustments to balance sheet and profit and loss account	**11 Banks**	**18 Bills payable, due to banks** 180/1 Bills payable 182/9 Due to banks—over-drafts
02 Auxiliary plant and equipment 020/7 Machines and equipment 028 Machines under construction 029 Depreciation on plant and equipment	**08 Adjustments, reserves** 080/4 Credit adjustments 085/7 Reserves for losses 088/9 Liabilities for acceptances, guarantees, endorsements	**12 Cheques etc.** 120 Undeposited cheques 121/9 Bills receivable	**19 Transitory and confidential accounts** 190/1 Transitory account for invoices 192/3 Transitory account for receipts and payments 194 Amounts to be allocated 195/6 Other transitory accounts 197/9 Confidential accounts
03 Vehicles, tools, patterns, etc. 030/3 Vehicles 034/6 Tools, apparatus 037/8 Patterns etc. 039 Depreciation on vehicles, tools, patterns, etc.	**09 Suspense accounts** 090 Control account for apportionments 098 Control account for accrued expenses 099 Control account for accrued expenses	**13 Current (temporary) investments** 130/6 Quoted investments 178/8 Own and holding company's shares 139 Amounts written off current investments	
04 Control accounts for fixed asset movements 041/4 Additions: purchases 045 Additions: own manufacture 049 Eliminations		**14/15 Debtors** *(c)* 140 Due for goods delivered 141/9 Analysis 150 Other debtors 151 Advance payments 152 Advances to associated companies 153 Advances to directors, employees, etc. 154/8 Other advances 159 Adjustments to debtors' accounts (reserves etc.)	
05 Other fixed assets Valuable rights 050/2 Patents, trademarks, goodwill 053 Depreciation on patents, etc. **Financial fixed assets** 054 Investments in subsidiaries 055 Quoted investments 056 Advances on mortgages 057 Other long-term advances 058 Debits applicable to long-term capital *(b)* 059 Depreciation on financial fixed assets			

Author's Notes:

(a) The translation follows the original with some changes where accounts relate to local conditions only.

(b) e.g. formation expenses.

(c) Where applicable, nominal analysis only.

(d) Contra accounts to entries only affecting costing.

(e) May be confined to direct materials, indirect materials being included in Class 4.

TABLE 2-1 *(Continued)*

Issued by the Federation of German Industries–Business Economy Section

CLASS 2

Neutral Expenses and Income

20 Non-operating expenses and income
- 200/5 Extraordinary nonoperating expense and income
- 206/9 Recurring non-operating expense and income

21 Expense and income of land and buildings
- 210/9 Analysis

22 Free

23 Depreciation

24 Interest expense and income
- 240/1 Interest paid
- 242/4 Discounts given
- 245/6 Interest received
- 247/8 Discounts taken

25/26 Extraordinary operating expense and income

Applicable to the period
- 250/1 Sundry losses
- 252/9 Other expense and income accounts

26 Applicable to other periods
- 260 Fixed assets
- 261/5 Maintenance
- 266 Research
- 267 Taxes
- 268 Other expenses
- 269 Income

27/28 Contra accounts *(d)*

27 Expenses applicable to other periods included in cost accounts

28 Other calculations for cost accounts
- 280 Excess depreciation
- 281 Interest charged
- 282 Contingency reserves
- 283 Notional salary for proprietor
- 284 Other calculations

29 Expenses and income relating to operations as a whole (e.g. corporation taxes)

CLASS 3

Materials

30/37 Materials
- 300/79 Analysis *(e)*

38 Parts purchased and work given out

39 Manufactured goods purchased
- 390/6 Purchases *(f)*
- 397 Adjustments to inventories

CLASS 4

Expenses by Type

40/42 Materials *(h)*

40/1 Materials consumed
- 400 Control account—materials consumed
- 401/19 Analysis (direct, indirect; raw, finished etc.)

42 Fuel and power
- 420 Fuel
- 429 Power

43/44 Personnel expenses

43 Salaries and wages
- 431/8 Analysis

44 Social security expenses
- 440/6 Health, unemployment insurance, etc.
- 447 Voluntary contributions
- 448 Other welfare expenses

45 Maintenance
- 450 Land and buildings
- 451 Plant and machinery
- 452 Vehicles, tools
- 453 Equalization account
- 454 Other
- 455 Services
- 456 Laboratory and research

46 Taxes, licences, insurance premiums, etc.
- 460/3 Taxes on income and capital
- 464/7 Other taxes and licences
- 468/9 Insurance premiums etc.

47 Rent and administrative expenses
- 470/1 Rent and machine hire
- 472/3 Travel, transportation and carriage
- 474/5 Postage, telephone
- 476 Office expenses
- 477/8 Publicity and representation
- 479 Financial expenses

48 Notional expenses
- 480 Excess depreciation
- 481 Interest charged
- 482 Contingency reserve charges
- 483 Proprietors' salary charges
- 484 Other

49 Internal transactions

CLASS 5—CLASS 6

Cost Accounts

Reserved for departments other cost centres, products, processes, etc.

CLASS 7 *(g)*

Inventories of Finished Products and Work in Progress

70/77 Reserved for costs not allocated to cost centres, products, etc. (selling costs etc.)

78 Inventory of work in progress

79 Inventory of finished goods
- 799 Adjustments to book values of inventories

CLASS 8

Income

80/82 Reserved for selling cost accounts *(i)*

83/84 Income from products and services

85 Income from re-sale of goods purchased

86 Income from by-products and secondary activities

87 Income from services performed by the business for itself

88 Income adjustment accounts
- 880/2 Additions to income
- 883/9 Reductions of income

CLASS 9

Closing Accounts

90/96 Reserved for summarization and special needs *(i)*

97 Cost operating statements

98 Profit and loss accounts
- 980 Manufacturing accounts
- 981/4 Free
- 985/6 Inventory adjustments
- **987 Net result of** neutral expense and income
- 988 Expense and in- **income affecting** operations as a whole
- 989 Profit and loss accounts

99 Balance sheets
- 998 Opening balance sheet
- 999 Closing balance sheet

(f) Sub-accounts for purchases from other members of group.

(g) Accounts 78/9 can be combined with accounts 38/9 in Class 3.

(h) Accounting for materials may be restricted to this group of accounts, or it may be used only for materials included in overheads.

(i) Where Class 8 is required for selling and distribution cost accounts, accounts 83/8 can be incorporated in Class 9.

Switzerland was one of the earliest European countries to establish a business school (the Zurich *Handelshochschule*) and to found a chair in commercial science (*Handelsbetriebe*). J. F. Schär, the first occupant of that chair (in 1903) and Leon Gomberg of Geneva, founded a significant accounting school in Switzerland. Gomberg is now recognized to have made a substantial contribution to the history of accounting thought.

Gomberg opposed the German practice of including accounting in the study of business economics; himself a public accountant, Gomberg saw this as only one of its aspects. He criticized the concept "dynamic accounting" on the grounds that the balance sheet is necessarily static. Gomberg's version of fourteen basic account entries is interesting.[14]

<table>
<tr><td rowspan="4">Statistical results</td><td rowspan="2">Assets</td><td>Increase through transactions with property</td></tr>
<tr><td>Decrease through transactions with property</td></tr>
<tr><td rowspan="2">Liabilities</td><td>Decrease through transactions with property</td></tr>
<tr><td>Increase through transactions with property</td></tr>
<tr><td rowspan="4">Legalistic results</td><td rowspan="2">Receivables</td><td>Increase of a claim</td></tr>
<tr><td>Decrease of a claim</td></tr>
<tr><td rowspan="2">Payables</td><td>Decrease of a claim</td></tr>
<tr><td>Increase of a claim</td></tr>
<tr><td rowspan="6">Economic results</td><td rowspan="2">Losses</td><td>Increase of losses</td></tr>
<tr><td>Decrease of losses</td></tr>
<tr><td rowspan="2">Profits</td><td>Increase of profits</td></tr>
<tr><td>Decrease of profits</td></tr>
<tr><td rowspan="2">Capital</td><td>Increase of invested capital</td></tr>
<tr><td>Decrease of invested capital (disinvestment)</td></tr>
</table>

THE BASIC EQUATION

One idea to come out of this historical development was the basic equation, which can be found in both the European and American accounting literature of the nineteenth century. According to Fabio Besta, one of the Italian users of this equation, the central construct of a business is its capital, a pure abstraction without juridical meaning. It is found by deducting liabilities from assets. The American authors go a step further; they view capital as a representation of proprietorship. Thus, we call this early theory a proprietary theory of accounting.

The transactions of a business can now be referred to this equation to explain why we account for them as we do. If the transaction increases assets or decreases liabilities, it increases capital; Besta called this a *modifying* transaction. Transactions which alter assets or liabilities without modifying capital, he called *permutational* transactions. This permits the operation of accounts to be expressed in the following form:

Assets		=	Liabilities		+	Owners' Equity	
Debit for increases	Credit for decreases		Debit for decreases	Credit for increases		Debit for decreases	Credit for increases

Because this basic equation is a static representation of accounts it does not lend itself to an explanation of revenues, expenses, gains, and losses. It can be expanded for this purpose into the form:

Assets + Expenses = Liabilities + Revenues + Owners' Equity (Capital).

By cancellation of expenses against revenues, this becomes the basic equation again. The income statement represents the substitution of revenues for expenses, the result of which is net income or loss, an increase or decrease of capital.

One of the advantages of the basic equation is that it also explains the statement of changes in financial position, or funds statement. Cancellation of expenses against revenues in the expanded equation turns it into the following form:

$$\text{Assets} = \text{Liabilities} + \text{Owners' Equity} + \triangle\ \text{Owners' Equity}.$$

and the funds statement can then be expressed as:

$$\triangle\ \text{Assets} = \triangle\ \text{Liabilities} + \triangle\ \text{Owners' Equity}.$$

However, the basic equation still leaves the terms *asset, liability, owners' equity, revenue,* and *expense* undefined.

THE INTERNATIONAL CHART OF ACCOUNTS

The basic equation was expanded into a chart of accounts by Schmalenbach and others (see Table 2-1). An international accounting conference in Paris in 1951, *Les Journées Internationales de la Comptabilité*, put forward a proposal for a chart of accounts which would be truly international in scope. The chart would have to reflect the basic characteristics of the firm, independent of peculiarities of national legislation, accounting conventions, or professional standards. The conference committee adopted a classification published by Joseph Anthonioz in 1947, which was based on a paper "The Cycle of the Economy" prepared by Maurice Lucas for the International Accountants' Congress held at Barcelona in 1929.[15]

The classification is based on a proposition derived outside accounting: that a firm is an entity which takes savings from the economy, invests them in the forms of fixed and circulating capital, and by incurring costs produces goods and services for distribution to the economy. This proposition provides us with a model for the firm, depicted in Table 2-2. The model has two phases, a planning phase, which starts with the distributed product and proceeds backwards to determine the amount of savings required for investment, and an action phase, in which invested savings are transmuted into distributed products.

We then structure this model by including under each term the features which are empirically observable in the real world. Firms obtain savings in two forms, proprietorship and debt. Fixed capital takes many forms: land, plant, equipment, livestock, goodwill, and

TABLE 2-2
The Investment Cycle

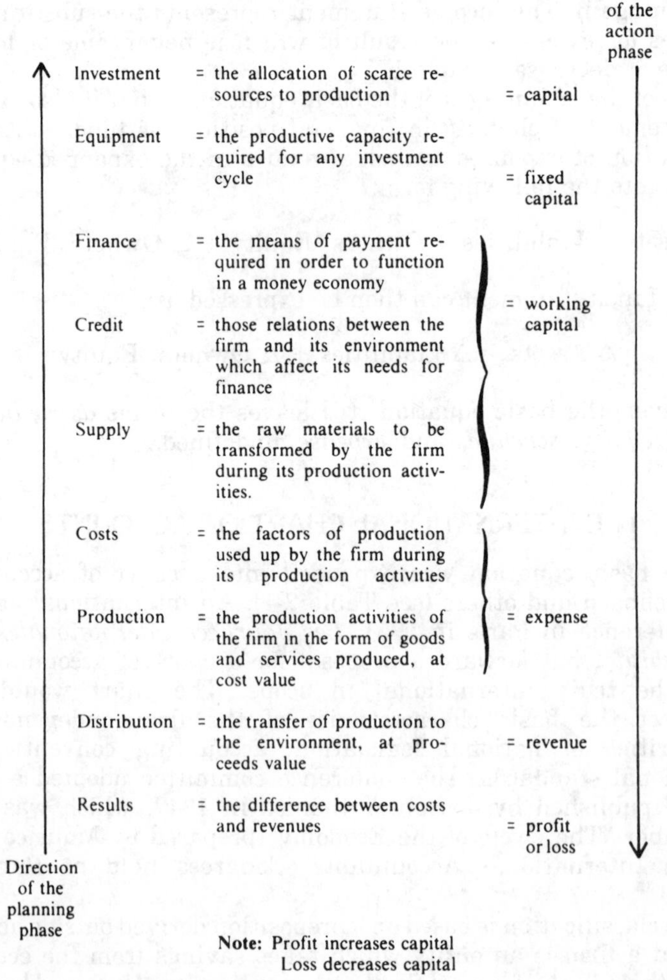

Investment	= the allocation of scarce resources to production	= capital
Equipment	= the productive capacity required for any investment cycle	= fixed capital
Finance	= the means of payment required in order to function in a money economy	= working capital
Credit	= those relations between the firm and its environment which affect its needs for finance	
Supply	= the raw materials to be transformed by the firm during its production activities.	
Costs	= the factors of production used up by the firm during its production activities	= expense
Production	= the production activities of the firm in the form of goods and services produced, at cost value	
Distribution	= the transfer of production to the environment, at proceeds value	= revenue
Results	= the difference between costs and revenues	= profit or loss

Note: Profit increases capital
Loss decreases capital

so forth. Circulating capital consists of the three elements: cash, credit, and inventories. Since credit is a two-way street, circulating capital (or working capital as it is called in business) is represented by the equation: working capital = current assets − current liabilities, where current assets is a summation of cash, inventories, and credit recognized *by* the firm, and current liabilities is a representation of the firm's credit.

Costs are observable in many forms and may be classified by type (*natural* classification), by object (*functional* classification), or by variability (*behavioral* classification). A classification by type is into wages and salaries, purchased supplies, depreciation, interest, and taxes. A functional classification is into production costs, selling costs, and administrative costs. A behavioral classification is into fixed and variable costs. Production is observable in the forms of work in process and distribution in the forms of individual products, or product groups, of goods or services.

It will be noted that profit or loss (*net income*) has not been mentioned. In this *theory of accounts* approach, profit is the difference between production and distribution measurements. It would be possible for the proceeds of distribution to be imputed back to the factors of production so that neither profit nor loss resulted. However, we observe that business firms operate under conditions of uncertainty, producing either a profit or a loss, which must be accommodated.

In the chart in Table 2-3, the model is depicted by representing the internal operations of the firm as a two-dimensional matrix, and the operations whereby the firm transacts with its environment (acquisitions and disposals) as a third dimension. The two dimensional matrix corresponds to the equation:

$$\text{Saving} = \text{Investment}$$

where

$$\text{Investment} = \text{Fixed capital} + \text{Working capital}$$[16]

This will be recognized as the basic equation used by finance theorists, in the form:

$$\text{Finance} = \text{Investment}$$

The model can also be represented by means of the expanded equation:

$$\text{Investment} + \text{Revenues} = \text{Fixed capital} + \text{Working capital} + \text{Costs}$$

leading by cancellation to:

$$\text{Investment} + \triangle\,\text{Investment} = \text{Fixed capital} + \text{Working capital}$$

TABLE 2-3
The Accounting Model of the Firm

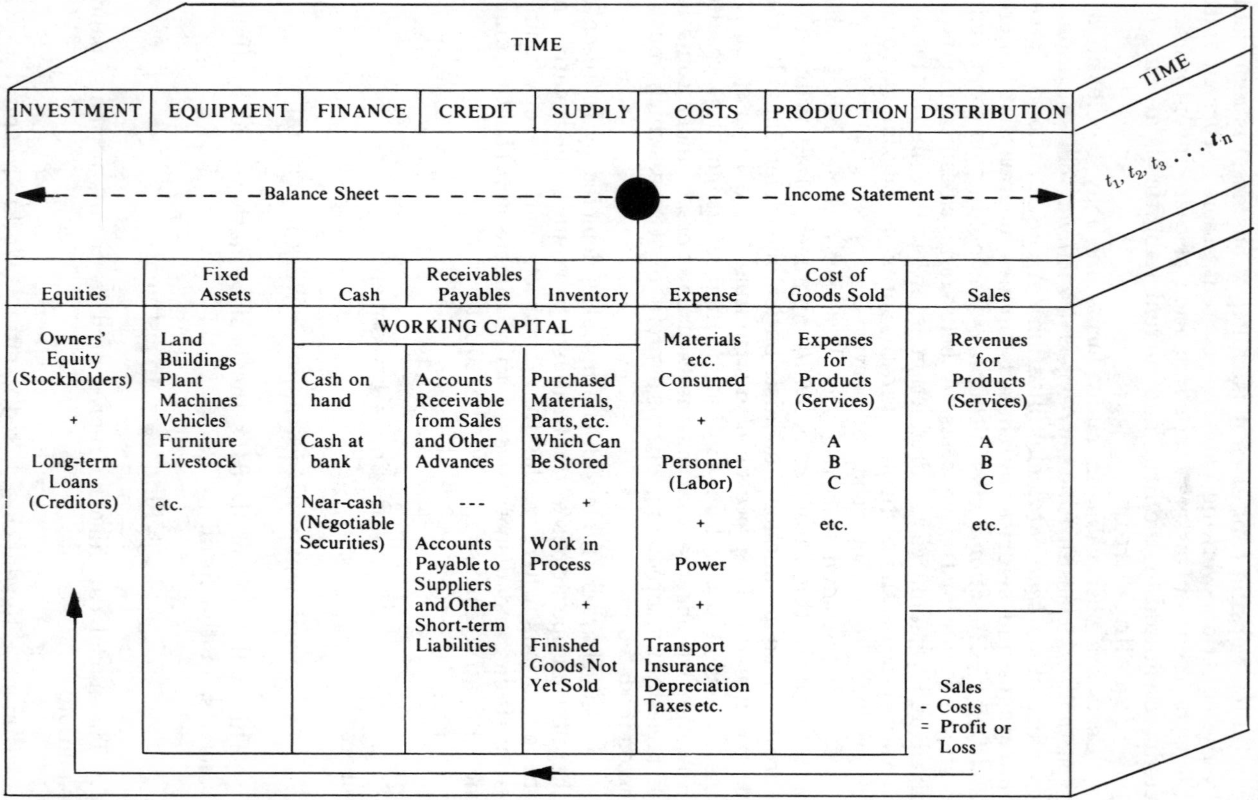

TIME

TIME $t_1, t_2, t_3 \ldots t_n$

INVESTMENT	EQUIPMENT	FINANCE	CREDIT	SUPPLY	COSTS	PRODUCTION	DISTRIBUTION
← Balance Sheet					● Income Statement →		
Equities	Fixed Assets	Cash	Receivables Payables	Inventory	Expense	Cost of Goods Sold	Sales
		WORKING CAPITAL					
Owners' Equity (Stockholders) + Long-term Loans (Creditors)	Land Buildings Plant Machines Vehicles Furniture Livestock etc.	Cash on hand Cash at bank Near-cash (Negotiable Securities)	Accounts Receivable from Sales and Other Advances --- Accounts Payable to Suppliers and Other Short-term Liabilities	Purchased Materials, Parts, etc. Which Can Be Stored + Work in Process + Finished Goods Not Yet Sold	Materials etc. Consumed + Personnel (Labor) + Power + Transport Insurance Depreciation Taxes etc.	Expenses for Products (Services) A B C etc.	Revenues for Products (Services) A B C etc. Sales - Costs = Profit or Loss

Equities = Fixed Assets + Working Capital rather than
Assets (Fixed + Current) = Liabilities (Equity + Current) + Residual (Owners') Equity

and the representation of the third dimension, which underlies the statement of changes in financial position, as:

$$\triangle \text{ Investment} = \triangle \text{ Fixed capital} + \triangle \text{ Working capital}$$

To demonstrate the universality of these concepts we may note that the Chinese have adopted as the basic accounting equation:

Total sources of funds = Total application of funds

From this proposition they classify economic events into the following four groups:

1. Increase of both source and application.
2. Decrease of both source and application.
3. Increase in one source, decrease in another.
4. Increase in one application, decrease in another.[17]

LIMITATIONS OF THE TRADITIONAL MODEL

One should be cautious in criticizing a model which has served so well, and so widely, for so many years. Nevertheless, the constraints imposed by this model are being felt and voiced more and more frequently. It is restrictive in its classification scheme when viewed from the information-providing perspective. Information is defined as purpose oriented data, that is, data which have been selected as inputs into a particular decision model. But selection of data presupposes a surplus of data, and the accountant is concerned first with data, and only produces information after the data have been collected. Should the accountant be concerned only with those data which fit neatly within the four corners of the classification?

The flexibility of the traditional model can be seen from the development of accounting, starting with accounting for transactions, then moving to transactions plus events, and now covering transactions, events, and circumstances. An event is the cost of goods sold; the transaction is the sale, which triggers another set of accounting entries leading to the cost of goods sold. A circumstance is the unstated interest on a receivable or payable not immediately due; accepting a note payable in one year's time in settlement of a receivable requires accounting for the interest foregone through not having received payment now. But events do not occur labelled "accounting event," and circumstances are even more difficult to identify. Indeed, one can observe a positive reluctance on the part of accounting standard-setting bodies to adopt a *situational* theory of accounting, which would make the applicable accounting principle dependent upon the attendant circumstances of the transaction.

Equally important, the traditional model does not deal explicitly with the problem of measurement. Valuation in accounting is defined as the representation of observations as amounts of money; a quantity (of goods, services, human relations, etc.) is multiplied by a price. The valuation problem concerns both quantities and prices; measurement involves pricing alone. Thus, given the fact that the traditional model enables us to identify what should be included, we are still not clear about how it shall be priced.

The model depicted in Table 2-3 shows that the pricing problem is really a succession of problems, as values move through the enterprise from original capital input to ultimate distributed output. For example, capital stock is originally priced according to the transaction by which it was issued. Once the firm's equipment has been acquired, however, the value of that stock may change, as investors perceive the profit-making opportunities which until then were apparent only to the promoter. By the time the firm's products start rolling off the production lines, the value of the company's shares may be different again.

The traditional model is associated with the cost principle, which has two elements (a) the unit of measure is the currency of the entity's country of domicile (in the United States, the U.S. dollar) and (b) observations should be recorded and reported at historical cost as long as the value in movement remains within the enterprise; only when it is realized can market value be used. The first proposition has been undermined by inflation, and experimental financial statements measured in *constant dollars*, or units of uniform purchasing power, are now being prepared and published. The second proposition has been rendered suspect by a number of practices sanctioned as generally accepted accounting principles; the lower of cost or market rule for inventories and marketable securities, use of market values for nonmonetary exchanges involving dissimilar assets, and accounting for restructured debt are obvious examples.

EXTENDING THE TRADITIONAL MODEL

For many years accounting writers sought to remedy these weaknesses by stating *behavioral theories of accounting*. Among them we find—

- The *proprietary* theory, which seeks to explain the content and measurement principles underlying financial statements by placing the owner of the enterprise in the center of the accounting universe. All observations are made from this viewpoint, the accountant sees only what the proprietor wishes to see, and values objects according to his or her interest. Assets are things owned; liabilities are debts owed; expenditures are expenses and receipts, revenues. Net income is the change in owners' equity during a given period.

- The *entity* theory, which seeks to explain from the assumption that the enterprise is an autonomous social entity, separate from its owners. The providers of capital become a kind of creditor interest, and assets, liabilities, expenses, and revenues are determined from the interest of management rather than that of stockholders.

Unfortunately these two theories proved of little help. The proprietary theory, for example, suggests that the proprietor's nonbusiness assets, such as the family home and furniture, be included, together with personal obligations, but except for isolated examples in the Middle Ages, this does not appear to have been done. Again, the proprietary viewpoint suggests the use of market values rather than cost, but historical cost was established as more useful than market value well before the growth of the corporation, with its essential separation of ownership from management, dictated that personal considerations be excluded from the accounts. Reference to contemporary textbooks reveals the disappearance of these theories from the intermediate accounting phase, and inconclusive remarks in the advanced phase, where treatment of consolidations makes the entity concept particularly important.

A similar fate has attended other such behavioral theories. The *residual equity* theory looks very much like the proprietary theory; it merely excludes the holders of preferred stock from the proprietor group. The *commander* theory assumes that decisions on content and measurement are made by a manager, or small managerial group; while this no doubt corresponds to the facts of the business world, it still leaves our problems unsolved. Behavioral theories derived from economics, communications theory, or psychology have proved equally frustrating.

Because of the clear similarity between the basic equations of accounting and finance, some accounting theorists have tried to build a crosswalk between the traditional model and the investment model used by finance theorists. The data used for investment models consist entirely of cash flows, and a modified traditional model expressed in cash flows has been put forward as a means for eliminating the obscurities and ambiguities of accrual accounting. This development is supported by the emphasis of the objectives statement of the FASB on assessing the amounts, timing, and uncertainty of prospective cash flows, yet the FASB has asserted that cash flow statements are not the best means of doing this.

CONCLUSION

The viewpoint adopted in this book, that the state of accounting theory development is still unsettled, received confirmation from a Committee of the American Accounting Association formed to study this problem.[18]

A study of accounting history reveals steady progress in explaining the development of accounting thought as evidenced by contemporary accounting practice. Modern critical scholarship, however, does not give much weight to the proposition that current accounting practice is sound because it is the consequence of a long evolutionary process. The role of deliberate, purposeful conduct in changing conditions is important in the study of human development, and the contemporary scene reveals a need for accountants to break out of the historical mold. But how?

ENDNOTES

1. The individual responsible for this discovery is Professor Denise Schmandt-Besserat, who has published her findings in, for example, "Reckoning Before Writing," *Archaeology,* Vol. 32, No. 3, 1979 pp. 23-31; "The Earliest Precursor of Writing," *Scientific American,* Vol. 238, No. 6, June 1978.
2. Bibby, Geoffrey, *Looking for Dilmun,* New York: Knoft, 1969.
3. Winjum, James Ole, *The Role of Accounting in the Economic Development of England: 1500-1750,* Illinois: Center for International Education and Research in Accounting, 1972.
4. A shorter work on the same theme, *Der Bourgeois,* was translated into English by M. Epstein as *The Quintessence of Modern Capitalism,* New York: L.P. Dutton & Co., 1915.
5. Sombart, Werner, *Der Moderne Kapitalismus,* 3rd edition, Munich and Leipzig: Duncker und Humblot, 1919, Vol. II, 1st half, Chapter X.
6. Winjum, *The Role of Accounting, p. 239.*
7. Winjum, James Ole, "Accounting in its Age of Stagnation," *The Accounting Review,* Vol. XLV, Oct. 1970, pp. 743-761.
8. Cerbone, Giuseppe, *Logismographie,* 1873.
9. For most of what follows I am indebted to Professor V.P. Filios of Greece, who has kindly allowed me to quote from his doctoral dissertation.
10. Delaporte, R., *Méthode Rationelle de la Tenue des Comptes,* Paris: Encyclopaedie Roret, 1936.
11. Dumarchey, J.F., *La Théorie Positive de la Comptabilité,* Lyon, 1914 and 1933. See also *Comptabilité Génèrale,* Paris, 1945.
12. Garnier, Pierre, *La Comptabilité (Algebre du droit et methode d'observation des sciences économiques*) Paris, 1947. Also *Comptabilité rationelle,* Paris, 1951.
13. Schmalenbach, E., *Dynamic Accounting,* transl. G.W. Murphy and K.S. Most, London: Gee & Co. (Publishers) Ltd., 1959.
14. Gomberg, Leon, *Eine geometrische Darstellung der Buchhaltungs methode in Annalen der Betriebswirtschaft,* Vol. 1, 1927, p. 102.
15. The history of the international chart of accounts is provided in *Le Plan Comptable International,* ed. Marcel Mommen, Brussels: Eds. Cambel, 1958.
16. The practice of deducting current liabilities from current assets is not unknown in the United States, although it is more common in the United Kingdom. Such statements conform to this equation.
17. Cheng, Philip C., "Political accounting in China: What the West should know," *Journal of Accountancy*, January 1980, p. 77.
18. Committee of the American Accounting Committee, *Statement on Accounting Theory and Theory Acceptance,* Sarasota: American Accounting Association, 1977.

SELECTED ADDITIONAL READINGS

The Academy of Accounting Historians, *Working Paper Series, Vol. I,* 1979 and *Vol. II,* 1979, ed. Edward N. Coffman, especially Working Papers Nos. 2, 3, 7, 11, 19, 21, 22, 25, 34, 35 and 39.

Accounting and Business Research, Vol. 10, No. 37A, Special Accounting History Issue, 1980.

The Accounting Review, Supplement to Vol. XLV, 1970, "Report of the Committee on Accounting History," pp. 53-64.

Chatfield, Michael, *A History of Accounting Thought,* Hinsdale, Illinois: Dryden Press, 1974, Chs. 1-7.

Costouros, George J., "Development of An Accounting System in Ancient Athens In Response to Socio-Economic Changes," *The Accounting Historians Journal,* Vol. 4, No. 1, pp. 37-54.

Frishkoff, Paul, "Capitalism and the Development of Bookkeeping: A Reconsideration," *The International Journal of Accounting,* Vol. 5, No. 2, pp. 29-38.

Edler, Florence, "Cost Accounting in the Sixteenth Century," *The Accounting Review,* Vol. XII, pp. 226-37.

Forrester, David A. R., *Schmalenbach and After, A Study of the Evolution of German Business Economics,* Glasgow: Strathclyde Convergencies, 1978.

Garner, S. Paul, *Evolution of Cost Accounting to 1925,* University of Alabama, 1954, Chs. 1 & 2.

Hatfield, Henry Rand, "A Historical Defense of Bookkeeping," *Journal of Accountancy,* April 1938, pp. 293-302.

Ijiri, Yuji, *The Foundations of Accounting Measurement,* Englewood Cliffs, N.J.: Prentice-Hall, Inc., 1967.

The Institute of Chartered Accountants, *Microfilmed Collection of Rare Books on Accounting and Related Subjects,* London: World Microfilms Publications, 2nd ed. 1975.

Käfer, Karl, *Theory of Accounts in Double-Entry Bookkeeping,* Illinois: Center for International Education and Research in Accounting, 1966.

Lee, Geoffrey Alan, "The Development of Italian Bookkeeping, 1211-1300," *Abacus,* December 1973, pp. 137-55.

———, "The Coming of Age of Double Entry: The Giovanni Farolfi Ledger of 1299-1300," *The Accounting Historians Journal,* Vol. 4, No. 2, pp. 79-96.

Littleton, A.C. *Accounting Evolution to 1900,* New York: American Institute Publishing Company, Inc., 1933.

——— and B.S. Yamey, ed., *Studies in the History of Accounting,* London: Sweet and Maxwell, Ltd., 1956.

Williams, John J. "A New Perspective on the Evolution of Double-Entry Bookkeeping," *The Accounting Historians Journal,* Vol. 5, No. 1, pp. 29-39.

END OF CHAPTER QUESTIONS

1. One obvious approach to the study of history is the division of events into time sequences.
   a. Prepare a time sequence ordering of events in the development of accounting thought.

b. What alternative approach to this aspect of history might be more instructive?

2. What significance do you perceive in the observation that the Romans used double-entry bookkeeping, if that were in fact the case?
3. Who is known as the "father of double-entry"? What evidence is there that this method of accounting was not new when first described in a book of 1494 A.D.?
4. Who was Sombart? What did he claim as the consequence of double-entry bookkeeping? How do you evaluate this claim?
5. What is meant by accounting's "age of stagnation"? What factors put an end to this stagnation?
6. Explain the role of personification in the development of accounting theory.
7. Important contributions to accounting theory were made by French, German, Italian, and Swiss writers in the nineteenth and early twentieth centuries. Name some of these authors and identify some of the contributions they made.
8. The basic equation has been described as a "static" or "legalistic" representation of accounting. What is meant by these terms? How can the basic equation be expanded into a "dynamic" representation of accounting?
9. What is a uniform (or general) chart of accounts? What is its utility from the viewpoint of accounting theory?
10. Discuss the limitations of the traditional accounting model in the light of contemporary accounting problems.
11. Write brief notes on each of the following accounting theories: proprietary, entity, residual equity, commander, situational.
12. Examine the implications of accounting for cash flows as a basis for financial reporting in the light of the historical development of accounting thought.

3

ACCOUNTING RESEARCH AND METHODOLOGY

THE NEED FOR ACCOUNTING THEORY

It is in the context of the tremendous growth in accountability knowledge and the accompanying fundamental criticisms of accounting and accountants that the need for accounting theory has manifested itself. In this chapter we shall examine the concept, and explain the relationship between theory formulation and research methodology.

A *theory* is a systematic statement of the rules or principles which underlie or govern a set of phenomena. A theory may be viewed as a framework permitting the organization of ideas, the explanation of phenomena, and the prediction of future behavior. *Accounting theory* is that branch of accounting which consists of the systematic statement of principles and methodology, as distinct from practice. Thus, the rule of conservatism belongs to the subject of accounting theory; the practice of providing for future losses from current doubtful receivables, being a question of practice, does not. It is clear, however, that theory cannot be divorced from practice, which it underlies, explains, and attempts to predict. There cannot be any basic contradiction between theory and facts, or between theory and practice.

A theory is above all an explanation. There is a widespread misconception that a theory must aid in prediction, but not all theories do. The theory of evolution, for example, has no predictive ability whatsoever; it is impossible to use it to forecast changes which will take place in living things. Similarly, a political theory may explain revolution in socioeconomic terms, but could not predict that Chile would become the first country to vote a communist government into power, or to liberate itself from one.

A theory is an explanation, but not every explanation is a theory in the scientific meaning of the word. *Epistemology* is the science of the method or grounds of knowledge, and a theory must conform to the rules of this science. In everyday language we use the word theory to denote a speculation, a conjecture, even a doctrine. In science, a theory is an explanation of phenomena which accounts for them to the satisfaction of knowledgeable persons, and this presupposes that the theory consists of propositions, each of which can be established by empirical research or is necessary for the explanation in question, and has not been demonstrated to be false. For example, an economic theory may utilize the empirically verifiable concept of a production function, and the unverified but undisproved motivational assumption of profit maximization, to explain the supply curve.

There are three main views of what a theory is—reductionism, instrumentalism, and realism.

Reductionism starts from the assumption that theories do not refer directly to observables (percepts) and do not make statements which are directly testable. They do, however, provide a disguised reference to observables, a kind of shorthand which can be translated back into the observables themselves. This view has been criticized on the grounds that all theories contain terms which cannot be translated in this way, including those which no reputable theorist wishes to abandon. Further, a theory which could be supported in all its terms by explicit definitions would be a static theory, incapable of growth and therefore useless for explaining or predicting new phenomena.

Instrumentalism views theory as an instrument, a tool bag or set of calculating devices, to be used on observation statements. This view emphasizes the abstract and systematic role of theories and their use for explanation or prediction, but makes no reference to content. In this framework, a theory cannot be true or false, only logical or illogical.

Realism is the term used for the view that theories are bundles of propositions, each of which may be a true or false statement referring to real world phenomena or objects. If each of the propositions is believed to be true, then we have a complete concordance of theory and fact. The approach to theory used in this book is best described as realistic.

Another distinction which is often encountered is between *positive* and *normative* theories. A positive theory explains *what is,* a normative theory, *what ought to be*. It is clear that, ideally, there should be no such distinction, and Gunnar Myrdal has drawn attention to the political assumptions underlying positive economic theories.[1] A good accounting theory is both positive and normative, as it will explain practice in terms of its usefulness.

As an illustration of the difference between a normative and a positive approach to accounting theory we may consider the definition of the word *value*. Definitions of terms used are an important part of any theory. In the Exposure Draft *Elements of Financial Statements of Business Enterprises,*[2] the Financial Accounting Standards Board defined value as "future economic benefit" (para. 69).

Examination of accounting textbooks and financial reports reveals that the word may denote—

- book value (a recorded account balance, or the algebraic sum of two or more account balances)
- carrying value (an amount reported in a financial statement)
- present value (the sum of a series of expected future net cash flows discounted over the period preceding their receipt or payment)
- net present value (present value minus the amount invested in producing the net cash flows)
- current value (= replacement cost)
- current value (= selling price)
- net realizable value (selling price less disposal costs)
- selling price less a normal markup
- a nominal amount used for memorandum purposes (an asset written down to $1, for example)

Not all of these can be embraced by the concept of "future economic benefit." Thus, to choose this definition is to state what value in accounting, *should be,* rather than *is*.

The uses of accounting are becoming more and more sophisticated and require explanations of what was in the past, perhaps, taken for granted. Many of those with whom accountants work are graduate scientists, engineers, and humanists well grounded in logic and other aspects of epistomology. It is no longer sufficient for these critics to reply to their questions by saying, "this is the way it has always been done," or "this is how it must be."

Further, the professional liability of accountants to clients and third parties having been established by the courts, an increasing number of accounting issues is being presented to judges for decision in cases where the accountant is the defendant. In these cases the judge will not accept as a defense the argument that a particular practice is acceptable to the accountant's professional association, or conforms with rules and principles arrived at outside the law, unless that practice or those rules and principles can be explained within the context of some body of knowledge recognizable as accounting theory.

Finally, accountants are being challenged by the existence of new problems, to which traditional explanations of accounting do not seem to apply. Areas of accountability opening up to accountants currently include social accounting,[3] human resource accounting,[4] and public sector accounting.[5] It is very significant that in 1975 the then chairman of the Securities and Exchange Commission, Ray Garrett, Jr.[6] and Commissioner A. A. Sommer, Jr.[7] called for "a recognition that traditional models, rules and modes for disclosure" may no longer be adequate. Specifically, the impact of inflation on financial reporting was the principal issue, and the commissioners drew attention to the need for "innovative presentations" where a "single-valued, articulated set of financial statements" did not tell the "economic story".

WHAT IS RESEARCH?

Explanation implies knowledge, and knowledge presupposes discovery. But just as every explanation is not a theory, so not every process of inquiry is research. The essence of research is the expansion of knowledge through problem-solving techniques which have been tried and tested in different fields. The following description provides a framework for understanding what we mean by research.[8]

The initial step in research is problem finding. Problem finding can be generated either formally or informally. Formal problem finding implies the use of punctilious and methodical procedures while the informal approach is subjective and nonroutinizable.

Observations of others in prior research is one of the most productive sources of formal problem finding, since new problems may arise which indicate that expanded research is needed. Other formal approaches to problem finding are as follows:

The Analog Method uses knowledge gained in one area to formulate a hypothesis in a related area.

Renovation is used to replace defective components with a view to restoring or improving the effectiveness of a theory.

The Dialectic Method consists of developing alternative methods for challenging, refining, or disposing of existing or proposed theories. It evaluates the advantages and disadvantages of different courses of action.

The Extrapolation Method extends current trends into the future and postulates questions relative to the predicted outcome.

The Method of Morpholopy analyzes all possible combinations of related problems.

The Decomposition Method breaks problems down into their component parts and analyzes each area.

The Aggregation Method takes research findings or theories from other areas and applies them to more complex problems. Informal methods are also utilized in problem finding.

Conjectures are hunches or intuitive feelings frequently used by decision makers.

Phenomenology is the description of the formal structure of phenomena abstracting from interpretation or evaluation.

Consensual activity is a group definition of a problem.

Experience is the observation of the problem itself.

THE RESEARCH PROBLEM

A research need arises when there is insufficient knowledge to solve an existing problem. The problem must first be defined or stated accurately. A quality of a well-defined problem is that it represents in all essential respects the environment from which it is drawn. Inadequate definitions can arise because of descriptive (what is) and normative (what should be) judgments or because of time-dimension deficiencies, such as taking a problem which has been critical in the past and assuming that it is also critical at the present.

Once the problem is identified and defined it should be put in a solvable form. This is referred to as hypothesis formulation. Frequently problems are posed in global or universal terms impossible to investigate.

A hypothesis is the building block from which a theory is constructed and can be most easily recognized as a proposition of an "if...then" variety. In this form it will suggest experiments whereby the proof or disproof of the proposition may be undertaken. It may be described to an accountant as the *journal entry* of research methodology, the means whereby a problem is translated into a convenient form for study; convenient because it is acceptable to the researchers seeking to replicate the experiments it suggests.

For example, the problem "What information should be provided to investors?" is incapable of solution in that form; it is too wide, too general, and suggestive of too many different solutions between which we are unable to choose. Research methodology requires that it be restructured as a set of hypotheses, such as—

Assumption Investors use information in arriving at their investment decisions.

Hypothesis If a corporation which is expected to report a profit reports a loss instead, some holders of the corporation's shares who would otherwise have continued to hold will sell.

This hypothesis suggests an experiment which could be conducted in order to prove or disprove it; such experiments will be discussed later in connection with the *efficient market hypothesis*.

RESEARCH METHODOLOGY

A prime factor in the concept of research methodology is something known as *scientific method*. While scholars argue interminably about what is meant by scientific method, they behave as though its meaning is generally understood. We shall therefore attempt an explanation, knowing that many will disagree.

Two primary methods of reasoning can be observed in the discoveries which lead to knowledge: induction and deduction. Induction can be defined as reasoning from the particular to the general; deduction from the general to the particular. Historically, Roger Bacon is identified with inductive reasoning; Descartes with deductive. Modern science, of which Galileo is the acknowledged father, combines induction and deduction interactively. Galileo observed that heavy objects fall with increasing speed, and from these particular observations he arrived inductively at a hypothesis—that the speed is directly proportional to the distance. Lacking the measuring equipment to test this hypothesis he used deductive reasoning to arrive at the conclusion that the hypothesis was incorrect, because it implied that objects falling unequal distances would require the same elapsed time, a proposition which could easily be disproved by observation. This led to a new hypothesis, that the speed is directly proportional to the time elapsed, suggesting the experiment of rolling balls down an inclined plane.

The research sequence can be viewed as a cycle of observation → hypothesis → experiment → conclusion → observation, in which the mode is sometimes inductive, sometimes deductive. Underlying the process is the indispensible element of inspiration, which feeds observation and the choice of the problem, the construction of the experiment, and the inference which supports the conclusion.

Research methodology can also be viewed narrowly as a set of strategies, domains, and techniques employed in hypothesis testing. Of these the central and most important is the selection or construction of a model. A model is a correct representation of something else, which nevertheless abstracts from some of the properties of the thing being modeled. A model automobile may have no motor; a model ship may be unable to float. These features have been assumed immaterial in view of the purpose which the models are to serve, the automobile as a toy, the ship for display. In the same way, a model in research is a construction which permits the observation of the effects of certain selected variables identified by the hypothesis, and may therefore abstract from aspects of the reality modeled which are unaffected by the variables selected, or effects in which the researcher is not interested.

In summary: a theory is a complex set of rules or principles based upon knowledge preferably derived from research. Research is characterized by a certain methodology, which is a reliable set of methods. A method is a family of models which have been found useful for hypothesis testing. A theory, therefore, is essentially a set of acceptable hypotheses.

Research in accounting is of relatively recent origin. It is clear, however, that abundant opportunities for research exist. Virtually every principle and rule of accounting is unsupported by knowledge scientifically obtained. This suggests that in spite of the need, little research has in fact been carried out.

The more important research strategies which have been used in accounting research appear to be (1) opinion, (2) empirical, (3) archival, and (4) analytical. Opinion research of an informal kind is widespread and underlies the pronouncements of professional institutions. Formal opinion research involves surveys using questionnaires and polls, with or without interviews. Empirical research, in which what is studied lies within the experience of the researcher, includes the descriptive work involved in writing case studies, as well as the observation of that which can be perceived either in the field or in a laboratory. Archival research is basically the examination of recorded facts, and since accounting by its very nature consists of recorded facts, much accounting research is archival. The library search is a characteristic method of archival research. Analytical research involves the adoption of analytical methods from other disciplines for the purpose of solving problems in accounting; the use of mathematical models is a frequent example.

The methodological limitations of accounting research, however, are not the central problem in the development of accounting theory. One critical problem is that an explanation of something in accounting must start with observations outside accounting. Just as a definition which contains the word being defined is useless—"cost accounting is accounting for costs"—so a hypothesis which relies on observations of what accountants do in order to explain why they do it is of little use in theory construction. The concepts "asset," "liability," "equity," "revenue," "expense," and "income" must be established without reference to their function in accounting before we can use them to explain accounting.

The other problem has been put succinctly in these words.

> But of all the phenomena science tries to deal with, it has been least successful with those involving human behavior. Few scientific findings in this sphere conflict to any great extent with the ordinary man's experience and common sense. And when they do, more likely than not it is science that turns out to have been wrong or incomplete.[9]

CLASSIFICATION AND ACCOUNTING THEORY

A taxonomy is a classification designed to aid the analysis and interpretation of a field of inquiry. A classification of accounting systems should be of value in many ways.

- By sharpening the focus of description and analysis
- By assembling a mass of data in a form suitable for explanation
- By permitting the isolation of critical factors which must be considered in setting accounting standards

By adaptation, a good taxonomy becomes a predictive tool, enabling the analyst to determine probable outcomes of decisions to change a system. More importantly, a taxonomy should lead to the development of models which permit inferences to be drawn from changes in causal and modifying factors to changes in accounting systems.

Classification in accounting has only recently begun to consider the theoretical implications of taxonomy. The most frequently encountered classification of accounting systems, into financial, tax, managerial, cost, government, and so on, lacks the qualities of an efficient classification in that the classes are not mutually exclusive.

For example, financial statements, which are the subject of financial accounting, are used for tax purposes, by managers as part of their information, and by governments which float loans from bankers and other financial institutions. Cost accounting is a necessary ingredient of financial statements of manufacturing enterprises, for ascertaining end of period inventories and for valuing machinery and other assets constructed by a firm for its own use.

The role of classification in financial accounting appeared to be well understood and generally agreed until recently. In the area of practice there was (and is) widespread use of charts of accounts which reflected the balance sheet and income statement categories underlying the well-known basic equation. In the area of theory, it was frequently pointed out that this was the fundamental process; Mattessich made it the point of departure in his quest for a measurement theory of accounting: "The most basic measurement is classification, a fundamental discriminatory process whereby the various categories can be identified and distinguished through numerals." The division into classes can be a scale of measurement, and he gives as his example a chart of accounts.[10] The same proposition is found in such widely different sources as a book on controllership, which identifies the five basic classifications as assets, liabilities, proprietorship, revenues, and expenses,[11] and a contribution to the normative theory of accounting, where the last three were given the names, residual equity, income, and cost.[12]

The area of managerial accounting, however, did not disclose any comparable uniformity of ideas, and the study of different classifications of costs not only threw up the possibility of alternative subclasses but also revealed a weakness in the basic classification used by financial accountants. This was the observation that a chart of accounts should not be based upon the balance sheet, because many accounts required by a business are eliminated in the preparation of the financial statements, in particular the so-called "clearing accounts."[13]

By 1969, when Sorter drew attention to the problem,[14] the idea that accounting events were not given in nature had been recognized widely, and attention was being devoted to "economic events" as the phenomena which accountants were attempting to interpret and represent. Unfortunately, this concept led to the identical classification scheme as did accounting events. Sorter postulated that accounts were needed to provide information to be used in decision models, that individual users would develop their own input values, and therefore a financial statement should include all items relevant to any decision model. The startling implications of this observation led Johnson to attempt to design a structure for a financial accounting system of this type.[15]

In one experiment comparing the decision-making effects of database (events) accounting and structured (aggregate, or value) accounting, it was found that the psychological type of the decision maker should have a bearing on information system design. Structured reports, while not necessarily leading to better profit decisions, were preferable because they were less costly.[16]

ACCOUNTING AND DECISIONS

A key element in understanding accounting is to understand the process whereby data is converted into information by the user. Two commonly used research models designed to investigate this process have been derived from information theory and information economics respectively. The former, introduced by Lev in 1968,[17] does not appear to have been productive and has been criticized by other researchers on both theoretical and practical grounds.[18] Information economics, an extension of decision theory which uses payoffs to value information, has seemed to some more promising. In this approach, the expected value of an information system is the difference between the expected values of two outcomes, one with and one without the system.[19]

In recent years accounting researchers have sought to use psychologists' models for this purpose. The "lens" model has been used extensively,[20] and cognitive style, a hypothetical construct which attempts to explain the process of mediation between stimuli and responses, appears to have wide applicability.[21] Protocol analysis is a form of psychological study which involves recording the thought processes of an individual, which may include filming eye movements and other external indicators of mental activity. Little in the way of definitive conclusions can be derived from such studies; they do appear to confirm the common sense observation that aggregation improves the usefulness of data up to a certain point and that the benefits of aggregation are thereafter decreased. The lower "tail" of this curvilinear function is referred to as *information overload*, and the upper "tail" as the absence of information content.

CONTEMPORARY APPROACHES TO ACCOUNTING THEORY

Accounting in a Macroeconomic Framework A social model of accounting would place the entity in the context of a national or international socioeconomic system. However, it should abstract from political assumptions about social welfare; it should be a nonexplicit model of economic behavior.

A different model could be constructed on the basis of postulates that government planning and direction are both feasible and desirable. It is here assumed that national economic goals are set, and that national policies guide entities toward actions which will lead to the implementation of these goals. In this situation, accounting could become an instrument of national economic policy.[22] Such a model may be used to explain accounting in the Soviet Union, for example, and certain aspects of accounting in a relatively free enterprise economy such as the United States—accounting for the investment tax credit, for example. This *macroeconomic* approach to accounting theory, it has been suggested, is useful for explaining tax accounting and accounting for regulated industries. We have pointed out earlier that accountants' actions in these areas can be explained in terms of the legal system, so that it is unnecessary for accounting theory to undertake this task.

A quite different normative model, however, might be based on the postulates that—

1. the firm is the essential unit in the economic fabric of the nation,
2. the firm accomplishes its goals best through close coordination of its activities with the national economic policies of its environment,
3. public interest is served best if enterprise accounting interrelates with national economic policies.[23]

Each of these postulates relies upon political assumptions which not all accountants will accept. Even though it were possible deductively to arrive at a set of logically consistent theorems which, together with hypotheses and other assumptions, constituted a theory of accounting, such a normative theory would be useless for explaining current practice or for evaluating it. Neither would this theory help with predicting change, unless it could be shown that accountants were willing to embrace the policies and beliefs implicit in it. The proposition that they could be *forced* to conform to such a behavioral model has of course no theoretical significance.

Accounting in an Ethical Framework Another approach to accounting theory can be identified which proceeds from assumptions, not about the nation or the economy, but about the individual who accounts. The characteristic features of this approach are pragmatism in the solution of accounting problems; a desire to reflect in financial statements the substance of a transaction or event, rather than be dominated by matters of form; and a belief in the need for financial statements to be in some sense "fair" to all parties who may rely on them.

The desire to be fair seems to underly the Anglo-Saxon audit function since the forms of the audit report used in the United States and the United Kingdom include the words "present fairly" and "give a true and fair view" respectively. The AICPA has recently attempted to define this concept in a *Statement on Auditing Standards*.[24]

Leonard Spacek, then managing partner of Arthur Andersen & Co., argued that the fairness of financial statements was a product of their compliance with predetermined principles.[25] Spacek pointed out that the reader of a financial report could not evaluate the accounting principles used simply on the basis of disclosure. Nor could the accountant or auditor discharge his or her duty to stockholders by resigning. He therefore proposed an accounting court to decide issues involving the appropriateness of accounting principles used in the preparation of financial statements.

Implicit in this approach is the belief that only one accounting treatment of a given phenomenon is fair to all parties, and the corollary, that such treatment would be identical for all corporations experiencing the same phenomenon. However, the analogy with the legal system is unfortunate; a court would lead to the substitution of forensic skills in place of accounting theory, and to the fossilization of rule making, which the APB and the FASB have so far managed to avoid. It is interesting to note that the SEC rule, which requires auditors to certify on a change in an accounting principle that the one adopted is preferable, has been vigorously opposed by CPAs who could find themselves in the position of certifying that changes in opposite directions by two clients at the same time were both preferable.

BEHAVIORAL APPROACHES TO ACCOUNTING THEORY

In recent years we have witnessed several attempts to adapt the ideas which management theorists have taken from the behavioral sciences in order to construct models for testing accounting theories. The main source of such ideas is the psychologist Alfred Adler (1870–1937), who was a frequent visitor to the United States after 1926 and who settled there in 1935. Adler saw man as goal-oriented, and this image proved attractive to management scientists such as Cyert and March.[26] Finance theorists have found some difficulty in identifying the goal or goals in question.[27]

Another source is the work of the behavioralists on motivation, principally derived from the study of animals. There are, of course, many other behavioral sciences, including sociology, cultural anthropology, social anthropology, and ethology, and even psychology is itself a field composed of different, often conflicting, views of man. Management scientists are starting to direct their attention to the ideas of Jung to explain qualitative aspects of management. This line of inquiry has led at least one accounting theorist to investigate accounting as a form of magical ritual.[28]

Some theorists have attempted to distinguish between accounting in large firms, controlled by managers, and in smaller firms, controlled by owners. It is argued that gradually improving profitability is the goal of manager firms, who will therefore tend to adopt accounting policies leading to income smoothing. Owner firms, controlled by those who know the true incidence of profits and losses on accounting periods, would be less likely to support deferral accounting which disguises that effect. Some empirical research appears to support this behavioral hypothesis.[29] However, there are difficulties in identifying "control" in large organizations and in measuring the effects of policy decisions on reported net income, and there are other reasons for the variability of reported earnings besides absence of smoothing policies. Further research in this area is necessary before the results can be used as behavioral hypotheses in accounting standard setting.

It may be observed that this preoccupation with behavioral assumptions arises out of the conflict inherent in economic theory, between the assumption of profit-maximization necessary to support the structure of price theory, and the different behavioral assumptions required for the investigation of other economic problems.[30] If the proposition that accounting does not require behavioral assumptions of a nonteleological kind is accepted much of the discussion summarized above would appear to be irrelevant.

A noteworthy feature of communication and decision-making approaches to the solution of accounting problems has been the stimulus which they have given to empirical research on the impact of accounting numbers on investor behavior, as observed in the stock market. In addition, Demski and others have attempted to construct models for observing the effects of alternative accounting policies,[31] and Mock has identified the uses of measurement theory in behavioral research in accounting.[32] Hofstedt investigated the decision maker as user of accounting information,[33] and there have been a number of statistical studies of uses of financial statements by individual investors, institutional investors, and financial analysts.[34]

In this connection, the last twenty-five years have seen a movement away from the determination of the *intrinsic value* of an investment to the determination of its *relative value*. The intrinsic value approach involved the analysis of the financial statements of a corporation in the light of expected general economic conditions and the position of the particular industry. A notional value per share was thus reached, and the decision to buy, hold, or sell resulted from comparison of this notional value with current market price.

Partly as a consequence of the gradual acceptance of the capital budgeting approach to investment decisions, and partly under the influence of the portfolio theories developed by Markowitz and others, there has been a noticeable tendency for accounting standards to move in the direction of assisting the determination of relative values. Capital budgeting theory emphasizes cash flows over revenue and expense flows; portfolio theory distinguishes between systematic risk, which is measured by the so-called *beta factor*, and unsystematic risk, which is measured by the difference between the specific price fluctuations of an individual security and the systematic risk. FASB pronouncements have tended to prohibit accruals and deferrals necessary for the measurement of revenue and expense, and to increase the variability of earnings of multinational corporations, insurance firms, businesses in high technology industries, and firms holding portfolios of marketable securities.

There is some evidence that the limitations of capital budgeting theory in this area are becoming more apparent. In particular, the use of earnings per share as a surrogate for net cash flow per share in valuation models of the relative kind has fallen into disrepute following the collapse of price/earnings ratios in 1974–1975. The relevance of portfolio theory to accounting standards is also an issue which calls for research at the present time.

The basic premise of this line of research can be simply stated: accounting numbers impound exogenous and endogenous phenomena in a form which permits them to be used for prediction. In this sense, financial statements are useful information for making decisions. Implicit in this premise is the notion of *causality*, the relationship of a cause to its effect, which underlies much scientific work. It can be expressed as the proposition that specific stimuli will produce standard results under controlled conditions. In modern times this proposition has been under continual attack, and a contemporary view of causality is more modest. The cause of any event is the preceding happening, without which the event in question would not have occurred. If *all* indispensable previous events could be identified, one would have the cause of the event in question.

Thus, if one attempts to explain accounting in terms of prediction, one must abandon the idea of a comprehensive explanation in favor of a partial explanation. In the ratio studies of Beaver and others, a situation precedent (the ratio) is compared with a situation subsequent (business failure, change in price of a stock) and, if a statistical relationship between a number of such cases can be identified, causality is assumed. It is clear that other factors can exist which either reinforce the effect of the situation precedent or cancel it, and therefore the observation has no normative significance. Nevertheless, researchers using this methodology rely on the Friedman hypothesis, that a theory permitting correct predictions more than 50 percent of the time is better than no theory at all.

Caspari has recently examined the philosophical basis for attempting to relate accounting numbers to decision models in this way, and has concluded that accounting data may provide the empirical statements necessary to explain nonaccounting decision models of the "invest/do not invest" type.[35] He did, however, point to areas of concern in this research such as the definition of terms, the confirmation of generalizations about the accounting numbers used, the confirmation of generalizations contained in the non-accounting theory, and the interface between the accounting and nonaccounting models.

Yet another form of behavioral research in accounting is concerned with the social choice aspect of accounting policy making. In this context, the selection of a particular accounting rule must be evaluated with reference to the objectives of the policy makers, not the users of financial statements. A priori research may be helpful in identifying the nature of the choices which policy makers face but cannot provide any assistance in making the choice. This reasoning leads to empirical research on the impact of accounting rule making and to the study of the relationship between organizational behavior and administrative decision making in such institutions as the APB, the FASB, and the CASB. In practical terms, the current debate on restricting the applicability of generally accepted accounting principles to small businesses can only be resolved on the basis of social choice.

THE EFFICIENT MARKET HYPOTHESIS

The assumption that financial reports are used as a source of information by investors, creditors, and others underlies the production and distribution of such reports by business and other entities, and the audit function is designed to assure the reliability of this information. A basic issue in accounting research is therefore whether accounting information is a factor in determining security prices, and thus in assuring efficient resource allocation through business investment. Efficient market research investigates this issue on the assumption that the behavior of the aggregation of users of this information differs from the behavior of any individual user.[36]

The proposition that security markets are "efficient" in the sense economists use the word is derived from the random walk hypothesis of finance theory. This hypothesis asserts that the best indicator of earnings is the previous period's earnings, perhaps adjusted upwards to recognize the consequence of the reinvestment of the earnings of the previous period. Economic studies have so far failed to contradict this proposition and have indeed drawn attention to the unpredictability of share prices, the movement of which has been likened to the path which a fly might take in its walk across a sheet of paper—hence the name "random walk." This hypothesis is in obvious contradiction to the proposition that a study of past earnings, in the form of a trend or moving average, can produce a prediction of future earnings, and eventually a growth rate to be used in stock valuation models of the form

$$P = \frac{d}{(i - g)^n}$$

where d = expected dividend for the current period, i = a time-value of money discount rate, and g = the expected rate of dividend growth.

The efficient market hypothesis proceeds to test this latter proposition, which is based upon the observed operations of a large number of financial analysts, using the following assumptions about the stock market.

1. There is a finite set of securities traded during a determinate period on a public stock exchange.
2. There are finite sets of buyers and sellers in this market, with a given income and marginal propensity to consume, and, thus, a determinate amount of saving for investment.
3. Buyers and sellers regard all securities traded in this market as substitutable at prices which adjust for different degrees of risk.
4. Risk is measured by variability of expected returns, the latter defined as dividend plus price change during a given period. Thus, return can be expressed as

$$R = \frac{d + (P_0 - P_1)}{P_0} \times 100$$

   where P_0 and P_1 are the security's price at the beginning and end of the period in question.
5. An optimal portfolio is a subset of no. 1 above which provides a return that cannot be increased at a given level of risk.
6. Investors hold optimal portfolios.
7. Risk and return are inversely related for all buyers and sellers (i.e. they are risk-averse).
8. Past returns are not predictive of future returns.
9. If the present price P_0 is the best indicator of the future price, P_1, then the security's beta can be used as a surrogate for the variability of expected returns. A security's beta represents the systematic risk of a security expressed in units of market risk and can be described graphically thus:

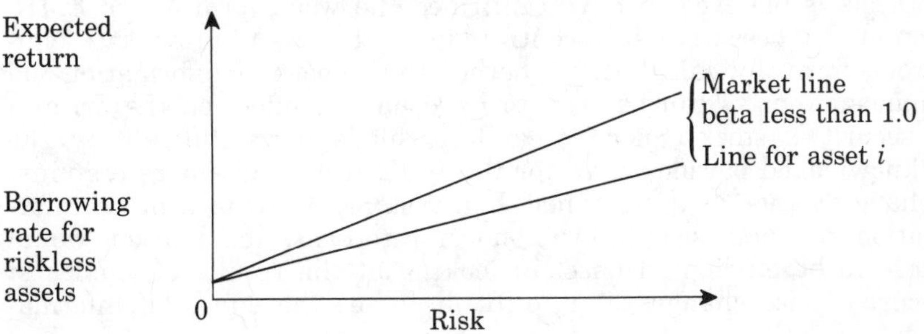

10. Supply and demand curves are "normal"; a security is not a Giffen good.
11. An efficient market permits buyers and sellers to acquire and maintain an optimal portfolio.

Note that the beta of a portfolio consisting of the entire securities market would have a beta of 1.0, and that beta can be more or less than 1.0 for any security.

The efficient market hypothesis (EMH) asserts that although unsophisticated individual investors may make incorrect decisions because of their inability to evaluate financial reports and other information, the market *as a whole* is efficient in the sense that—

1. prices of securities traded in that market act as though they fully reflect all available information, and
2. prices react instantaneously, or nearly so, in an unbiased fashion to new information.

The market may not be efficient at a particular time for a particular stock or stocks, and investors may still make incorrect decisions. However, the availability of information permits *arbitrargeurs* to buy stocks with prices lower than their risk/return characteristics justify, or to sell stocks with prices which are too high, and thus to correct these inefficiencies. It follows that, except in this last case, investors in securities traded on an efficient market cannot make abnormal returns, or profit from knowledge gained, for example, from financial reports and thus available to all.

The EMH can take one of three forms.

1. **Weak form** Current prices fully reflect the information implied by the historical sequence of prices. The information is said to be "impounded" in the price.
2. **Semi-strong form** Current prices fully reflect all publicly available information.
3. **Strong form** Current prices fully reflect all information, including that available only to insiders.

Research into security prices leading to the random walk hypothesis is believed to have confirmed the weak form of the EMH. Accounting research is concentrated on attempts to prove the semi-strong form, by calculating whether the release of information via financial reports can be seen to have had an effect on the price of a security's stock. Such research is made more difficult by the acknowledged paradox that, for the EMH to be true, investors must behave as though it were not. If investors ceased to acquire information in their search for abnormal returns, the market would cease to be efficient. Hence, in looking at the results of studies of security price changes, it is difficult to see the effects of information.

Consider, for example, research which found considerable market reaction prior to a stock split announcement, but no abnormal returns afterwards. Does this disprove the semi-strong form of the EMH or prove the strong form? Stock splits are only *believed* to have economic effects; some empirical research has failed to find that investors realize benefits from them. If the market did react to such an event, therefore, it could be said to be efficient (impounding information in the share price) or inefficient (fooled by false information).[37]

William Beaver, one of the pioneers of EMH research, has suggested that the EMH poses the following research problems:

1. Is the market "efficient" in the postulated sense? What is the role of inside information?
2. What is the cost to the investing public of abnormal returns earned by insiders?
3. What decision models do investors use? What information do these models call for?
4. Do financial reports aid in determination of risk, and if not, how could they?
5. Which financial statement items are most highly correlated with changes in stock market prices?

Answers to these questions can assist the FASB to minimize investor costs, specifically (a) costs resulting from abnormal returns accruing to insiders, and (b) costs of obtaining information from sources other than financial reports, which must be paid for.[38]

The effect of regulation on an otherwise competitive market is believed to be highly relevant to this kind of research. In an unregulated economy, it is argued, managers incur the costs of preparing and publishing financial statements in order to reduce other costs, such as debt service costs, or to justify increasing their own remuneration. In this situation, the need for accounting theory is purely pedagogic and explanations are dominated by legal considerations and managers' manipulative practices. In a regulated economy, such as the United States, financial statements aid the transfer of wealth and other constraining functions of government. Theories become advocacy proceedings to justify particular accounting practices.[39] In such a situation, interpretation of EMH research findings might not be unbiased.

ACCOUNTING THEORIES AND THEORIES OF ACCOUNTING

The EMH belongs to a group of accounting theories, or subtheories, of the same kind as GAAP in the United States, which are primarily quantitative in nature and attempt to answer the question: what kind of information should financial reports provide? Other examples of accounting theories are those of Chambers[40] and Sterling,[41] both primarily deductive in nature, and the situational responses of accounting practitioners, notably the firm of Ernst and Whinney, to problems posed by the FASB, which proceed from the assumption that accounting practices should respond to the facts of each situation. Table 3–1 attempts to classify these theories.

On a higher level of abstraction, however, are theories of accounting, which attempt to explain the role that accounting can and does play in the organization of society, in economic development, in the allocation of resources, and in resolving social conflicts. Theories of accounting are predominantly qualitative in nature, and lead inexorably to consideration of nonmonetary information in addition to, or perhaps instead of, monetary data. Such notable works as Paton's early *Accounting Theory*,[42] the Paton and Littleton monograph,[43] Gilman's *Accounting Concepts of Profit*,[44] and the Sanders, Hatfield, and Moore report[45] are early examples of attempts to derive accounting theory from theories of accounting. More recent attempts are those of Ijiri,[46] Gambling,[47] and Kosiol.[48] These theories may be normative or positive (descriptive); McDonald calls the former "theories *for* accounting."[49]

The traditional view of accounting as concerned solely with a historical description of financial activities is no longer acceptable. There is strong support for the expansion of accounting to embrace human resources, for example, and much of the argument to this end is sociopsychological.[50] Even more unsettling is the impact of the physical sciences, represented here by this quotation from Gambling.

> At present, the accountant always wants to talk of increments and decrements over a finite period of time, and of values at some point in time; this is fair enough as the description of the behavior of cash flow or any other physical flow, but it is very near meaningless when applied to a dynamic system.[51]

Among the possibilities of nonmonetary accounting we may note demographic accounting, attributed to the Frenchman, Pierre Garnier, and space accounting, a technique used by some architects to align building space available with space needed. More to the point, the topic of *corporate social accountability* has become an important item in corporate annual reports; according to the annual surveys of this type of reporting conducted by Ernst and Whinney, the form is predominantly nonmonetary.[52]

Professor V.P. Filios of Greece has conducted an extensive survey of theories of accounting in his as yet unpublished *A Retrospect of International Developments in Accounting Thought*. According to Filios, a pure theory of accounting can be attributed to Thomsen, who defines an event as a member of a sequential memory.[53] Each event in a sequential memory carries a unique description. The events are ordered by time of occurrence and classified into groups called event series. The entity concept defines the boundary of a sequential memory and establishes a set of relations between the participants in events. These constructs provide four categories of relations.

TABLE 3-1
Dominant Approaches to Accounting Theory

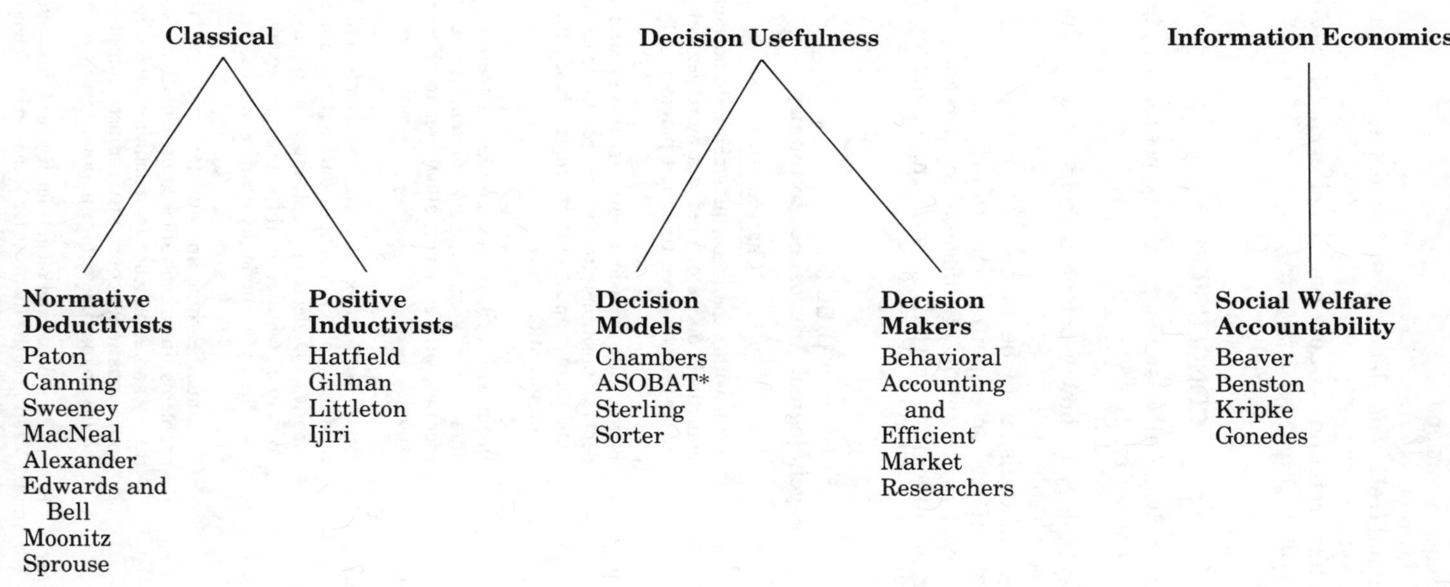

* *A Statement of Basic Accounting Theory,* American Accounting Association, 1966.

Schematic adaptation of *Statement on Accounting Theory and Theory Acceptance,* American Accounting Association, 1977.

1. Equivalence relations
2. Time relations
3. Definitional relations (leading to the determination of new quantities)
4. Cause/effect relations (where one set of events is stated as a function of another set).

CONCLUSION

In the last analysis, all systems of inquiry possess the following five structural characteristics:[54]

1. User psychology or how a person perceives and evaluates the world (see Table 3–2)
2. The type of decision to be made
3. The institutional or organizational context
4. The mode of presentation of information (personal or impersonal communication, verbal or written, public or private)

TABLE 3-2
Psychological Approaches to Inquiry

System	Characteristics
1. Lockean	Begin with experience, judgments, basic facts, and inductively derive or predict a more general theory. Heavy weight given to expert judgment.
2. Leibnitzian	Begin with a basic theory or axioms and deduce general positional truths; collect evidence to validate theory and develop single "best" model for communication to users.
3. Kantian	Begin with at least two *alternative* theories; collect data to verify each theory; present several explicit theories, with evidence; allow user to choose "best" model.
4. Hegelian	Begin with at least two *completely antithetical* theories; collect a single data set to evaluate all theories. Dialectical confrontation of models in conscious conflict enables user to formulate his own theory or model by creative synthesis.
5. Singerian	Continual learning and adaptation; define "wicked" problems in a solvable approximation; combine theory and experience to redefine problem in closer approximation; constantly adjust complexity of inquiry to maximize information.

Weathersby, George B., "Design Paradigms and Models for Higher Education," a paper presented at the 48th Annual Meeting of the Institute for Management Sciences and the Operations Research Society of America, November 17, 1975.

5. A philosophy of evidence congruent with number 1.

Important in this process is the distinction between *percepts* and *concepts*. Percepts are the objects of perception; concepts are the ideas we form concerning the objects perceived. The confusion of the two is a major logical error, responsible for many of the difficulties which accompany the exposition of accounting theory.

The FASB has accepted the proposition that the economy of the United States is based upon private ownership of the means of production and free competition in markets for the output of productive units. Under this view, resource allocation decisions are made in capital markets by individuals who seek to maximize profits. In order to function, these investors and lenders need information, one source of which is provided by financial accounting and reporting. The principal role of financial reporting is therefore to furnish investors and lenders with information useful in assessing prospective risks and returns associated with a specific enterprise.

ENDNOTES

1. Myrdal, Gunnar, *The Political Element in the Development of Economic Theory*, Harvard, 1955.
2. (Revised), Financial Accounting Standards Board, Stamford, Conn.: December 28, 1979.
3. Seidler, Lee J. and Lynn L., *Social Accounting: Theory Issues and Cases*, Los Angeles: Melville Publishing Co., 1975.
4. Hermanson, Roger, *Accounting for Human Assets*, Michigan State University: Bureau of Business and Economic Research, 1964.
5. *Sound Financial Reporting in the Public Sector, A Prerequisite to Fiscal Responsibility*, Chicago: Arthur Andersen & Co., 1975.
6. In an address before the National Conference of the AICPA in January, 1975.
7. In an address before the NAA, March 18, 1975.
8. With acknowledgment to chapters 1 and 2 of Buckley, John W., Marlene H. Buckley and Hung-Fu Chiang, *Research Methodology and Business Decisions*, National Association of Accountants, 1975.
9. Alexander, Tom in *Fortune*, April 1975, p. 150.
10. Mattesich, Richard, *Accounting and Analytical Methods*, Homewood, Ill.: Richard D. Irwin, Inc., 1964, p. 58.
11. Anderson, David R., Leo A. Schmidt and Andrew M. McCosh, *Practical Controllership*, Homewood, Ill.: Richard D. Irwin, Inc. 1961, pp. 129-52,
12. Chambers, Raymond J., *Accounting, Evaluation and Economic Behavior*, Englewood Cliffs, N.J.: Prentice-Hall, Inc., 1966.
13. Most, Kenneth S., *Uniform Cost Accounting and the Classification of Accounts*, London, Gee & Co. (Publishers) Ltd., 1961.
14. Sorter, George H., "An Events Approach to Basic Accounting Theory," *The Accounting Review*, January 1969, pp. 12-19.
15. Johnson, Orace, "Towards an 'Events' Theory of Accounting," *The Accounting Review*, October 1970, pp. 641-53, and "On Taxonomy and Accounting Research," *The Accounting Review*, January 1972, pp. 64-74.
16. Benbasat, Izak and Albert S. Dexter, "Value and Events Approaches to Accounting: An Experimental Evaluation," *The Accounting Review*, October 1979, pp. 735-49.
17. Lev, B., "The Aggregation Problem in Financial Statements: an informational approach," *Journal of Accounting Research*, Autumn 1968, pp. 247-61.

18. Abdel-Khalik, A.R., "The Entropy Law, Accounting Data and Relevance to Decision-making," *The Accounting Review*, April 1974, pp. 271-83.
19. Mock, T.J., "Measurement and Accounting Information Criteria," *Studies in Accounting Research #13*, Sarasota, AAA, 1976.
20. Hofstedt, T.R. "Some Behavioral Parameters of Financial Analysis," *The Accounting Review*, October 1972, pp. 679-92.
21. Driver, M.J. and T.J. Mock, "Human Information Processing, Decision Style and Accounting Information Systems," *The Accounting Review*, July 1975, pp. 490-508.
22. Mueller, Gerhard G., *International Accounting*, New York: The Macmillan Company, 1967, Ch.1.
23. Ibid, p. 12.
24. *SAS No. 5*, "The Meaning of "Present Fairly in Conformity With Generally Accepted Accounting Principles" in the Independent Auditor's Report," New York: AICPA, 1975.
25. Spacek, Leonard, "The Need for an Accounting Court," *The Accounting Review*, July 1958, pp. 368-379; *A Search for Fairness in Financial Reporting to the Public*, Selected addresses by Leonard Spacek, Chicago: Arthur Andersen & Co., 1969. See also Spacek's comments on Sprouse, Robert T. and Maurice Moonitz, "A Tentative Set of Broad Accounting Principles for Business Enterprises," *Accounting Research Study No. 3*, New York: AICPA 1962, p. 78.
26. Cyert, R. and J. March, *A Behavioral Theory of the Firm*, Englewood Cliffs, N.J.: Prentice-Hall, Inc. 1963.
27. Findlay, M. Chapman III and G.A. Whitmore, "Beyond Shareholder Wealth Maximization," *Financial Management*, Winter 1974, pp. 25-35.
28. Gambling, Trevor, of the University of Birmingham, England.
29. Smith, E. Daniel, "The Effect of the Separation of Ownership from Control on Accounting Policy Decisions," *The Accounting Review*, October 1976, pp. 707-723.
30. Machlup, Fritz, "Theories of the Firm: Marginalist, Behavioral, Managerial," *American Economic Review*, March 1967, pp. 1-33.
31. Demski, Joel S., "Choice Among Financial Reporting Alternatives," *The Accounting Review*, April 1974, pp. 221-232.
32. Mock, T.J., "Measurement and Accounting Information Criteria," *Studies in Accounting Research #13*, Sarasota, Fla.: American Accounting Association, 1976.
33. Hofstedt, Thomas J., "The Processing of Accounting Information: Perceptual Biases," *Behavioral Experiments in Accounting*, ed. Thomas J. Burns, Columbus, Ohio: College of Administrative Science, Ohio State University, 1972, pp. 285-315.
34. Chang, Lucia S. and Kenneth S. Most, *Financial Statements and Investment Decisions,* Miami: Florida International University, 1979.
35. Caspari, John A., "Wherefore Accounting Data—Explanation, Prediction and Decisions," *The Accounting Review*, October 1976, pp. 739-746.
36. Dyckman, Thomas R., David H. Downes and Robert P. Magee, *Efficient Capital Markets and Accounting*, Englewood Cliffs, N.J.: Prentice-Hall, Inc., 1975. See also Eskew, R.K., "The Forecasting Ability of Accounting Risk Measures: Some Additional Evidence," *The Accounting Review*, January 1979, pp. 107-18. The statistical method used has been criticized; see Elgers, Pieter T., "Accounting-Based Risk Predictions: A Re-examination," *The Accounting Review*, July 1980, pp. 389-408.
37. Several researchers, notably O'Donnell (1965 and 1968), Mlynarczyk (1969), Gonedes (1969), Comiskey (1971), Archibald (1972), Ball (1972), and Sunder (1975), have studied the effects of changes in accounting principles and methods which did not necessarily represent economic effects. See Dyckman *et al*, (n. 36) pp. 28-30.
38. Beaver, William H., "What should be the FASB's objectives," *Journal of Accountancy*, August 1973, pp. 49-56.
39. Watts, Ross L. and Jerold L. Zimmerman, "The Demand for and Supply of Accounting Theories: The Market for Excuses," *The Accounting Review*, April 1979, pp. 273-305.

40. Chambers, *op. cit.*
41. Sterling, Robert R., *Theory of the Measurement of Enterprise Income*, Kansas, 1970.
42. Paton, William Andrew, *Accounting Theory*, New York: The Ronald Press, 1922.
43. Paton, W.A. and A.C. Littleton, *An Introduction to Corporate Accounting Standards*, American Accounting Association, Monograph No. 3, 1940.
44. Gilman, Stephen, *Accounting Concepts of Profit*, New York: The Ronald Press, 1939.
45. Sanders, T.H., H.R. Hatfield and U. Moore, *A Statement of Accounting Principles*, American Accounting Association, 1938.
46. Ijiri, Yuji, *The Foundations of Accounting Measurement*, Englewood Cliffs, N.J.: Prentice-Hall, Inc. 1967.
47. Gambling, Trevor E., *Societal Accounting*, London: Allen and Unwin, Ltd., 1974.
48. Kosiol, Erich, *Pagatoric Theory of Financial Income Determination*, Urbana, Ill.: Center for Accounting Education and Research, 1978.
49. McDonald, Daniel I., *Comparative Accounting Theory*, Reading, Mass.: Addison-Wesley Publishing Co., 1972, p. 92.
50. Lev, Baruch and Aba Schwartz, "On the Use of the Economic Concept of Human Capital in Financial Statements," *The Accounting Review*, January 1971, pp. 103-18; also Flamholtz, Eric G., "Toward a Theory of Human Resource Value in Formal Organizations," *The Accounting Review*, October 1972, pp. 666-78. See also chapter 17.
51. Gambling, Trevor E., "A Systems Dynamics Approach to Human Resource Accounting," *The Accounting Review*, July 1974, p. 541.
52. Ernst & Ernst, *Social Responsibility Disclosure, 1978*, Cleveland, Ohio: Ernst & Ernst, 1978.
53. Thomsen, Torben Carl, *An Event Relation Approach to a Metatheory of Accounting*, Ph.D. dissertation, Michigan State University, 1973.
54. Churchman, C. West, *The Design of Inquiring Systems: Basic Concepts of Systems and Organization*, New York: Basic Books, 1971, as adapted by Weathersby, George B. in "Design Paradigms and Models for Higher Education," paper presented at the 48th National Meeting of the Institute for Management Sciences and the Operations Research Society of America, November 17, 1975.

SELECTED ADDITIONAL READINGS

Accounting Research 1960-1970: A Critical Evaluation, ed. Dopuch, Nicholas and Lawrence Revsine, Illinois: Center for International Education and Research in Accounting, 1973, pp. 3-34 and 137-94.

American Accounting Association, Committee on Accounting Theory Construction and Verification, Report in *The Accounting Review*, Supplement to Vol. XLVI, 1971, pp. 51-79.

———, Committee on Internal Measurement and Reporting, Report in *The Accounting Review*, Supplement to Vol. XLVIII, 1973, pp. 209-41.

Beaver, William H., "The Behavior of Security Prices and its Implications for Accounting Research Methods," in the Report of the [American Accounting Association] Committee on Research Methodology in Accounting, *The Accounting Review*, Supplement to Vol. XLVII, 1972, pp. 407-37.

———, *Financial Reporting: An Accounting Revolution*, Englewood Cliffs, N.J.: Prentice-Hall, Inc. 1981.

Benston, George J., *Corporate Financial Disclosure in the UK and the USA*, Lexington: Lexington Books, Inc., 1976.

Buckley, John W., Paul Kircher and Russell L. Mathews, "Methodology in Accounting Theory," *The Accounting Review*, April 1968, pp. 274-83.

———, Marlene H. Buckley and Hung-Fu Chiang, *Research Methodology and Business Decisions*, National Association of Accountants, 1975.

Carlson, Marvin L. and James W. Lamb, "Constructing a Theory of Accounting—An Axiomatic Approach," *The Accounting Review*, July 1981, pp. 554-73.

Chambers, R.J., "Towards a General Theory of Accounting," *The Australian Society of Accountants Annual Lecture, 1961*. The University of Adelaide, Australia, 1961.

———, "Blueprint for a Theory of Accounting," *Accounting Research*, January, 1955. (Reprinted in Davidson, Sidney, David Green Jr., Charles T. Horngren, and George H. Sorter, *An Income Approach to Accounting Theory: Readings and Questions*, Englewood Cliffs, N.J.: Prentice-Hall, Inc., 1964, pp. 57-65.

Devine, Carl Thomas, *Essays in Accounting Theory*, Vols. I-III, Tallahassee, Fla., Private printing, 1962-71.

———, "Research Methodology and Accounting Theory Formation," *The Accounting Review*, July, 1960, pp. 387-99.

Goldberg, Louis, *An Inquiry into the Nature of Accounting*, American Accounting Association Monograph No. 4, Iowa City: American Accounting Association, 1965.

Mattessich, Richard, *Accounting and Analytical Methods*, Homewood, Ill.: Richard D. Irwin, Inc., 1964, Chs. 1 and 2.

May, Robert G. and Gary L. Sundem, "Research for Accounting Policy: An Overview," *The Accounting Review*, October 1976, pp. 747-63.

Mayer-Sommer, Alan P., "Understanding and Acceptance of the Efficient Markets Hypothesis and its Accounting Implications," *The Accounting Review*, January 1979, pp. 88-106.

Sterling, Robert R., "An Explication and Analysis of the Structure of Accounting, Part One," *Abacus*, December, 1971, pp. 137-52 and "Explication, Part Two," *Abacus*, December 1972, pp. 145-62.

———, *Theory of the Measurement of Enterprise Income*, Kansas, 1970.

Tilley, Ian, "Accounting as a Scientific Endeavour—Some Questions the American Theorists Tend to Leave Unanswered," *Accounting and Business Research*, Autumn 1972, pp. 287-97.

Watts, Ross L. and Jerold L. Zimmerman, "The Demand for and Supply of Accounting Theories: The Market for Excuses," *The Accounting Review*, April 1979, pp. 273-305.

Wells, M.C., "A Revolution in Accounting Thought," *The Accounting Review*, July 1976, pp. 471-82.

Yu, S.C., *The Structure of Accounting Theory*, Florida: 1976.

Other Works on Research and the Scientific Method

Look up "theory" in reputable dictionaries, encyclopedias and other reference works.

Churchman, C. West, *The Design of Inquiring Systems: Basic Concepts of Systems and Organization*, New York: Basic Books, 1971.

Cohen, Morris R. and Ernest Nagel, *An Introduction to Logic and Scientific Method*, London: Routledge & Kegan Paul, Ltd. 1934.

Dewey, John, *Logic, The Theory of Inquiry*, New York: Holt, Rinehart and Winston, 1938.

Friedman, Milton, *The Methodology of Positive Economics*, Chicago: 1953.

Hicks, J.R., *Capital and Growth*, New York and Oxford, 1965, Ch. 1.

Kuhn, Thomas S., *The Structure of Scientific Revolution*, Chicago, 1962.

Myrdal, Gunnar, *The Political Element in the Development of Economic Theory*, Harvard, 1955.

Popper, Karl R., *The Logic of Scientific Discovery*, London: Hutchinson & Co., 1959.

Schumpeter, J.A., *The Theory of Economic Development*, New York: Oxford University Press, 1961, Ch. 1.

Case 3-1 Who are "the Accountants"?

The diagram below indicates the scope of what might loosely be called "the accounting profession" in the U.S.

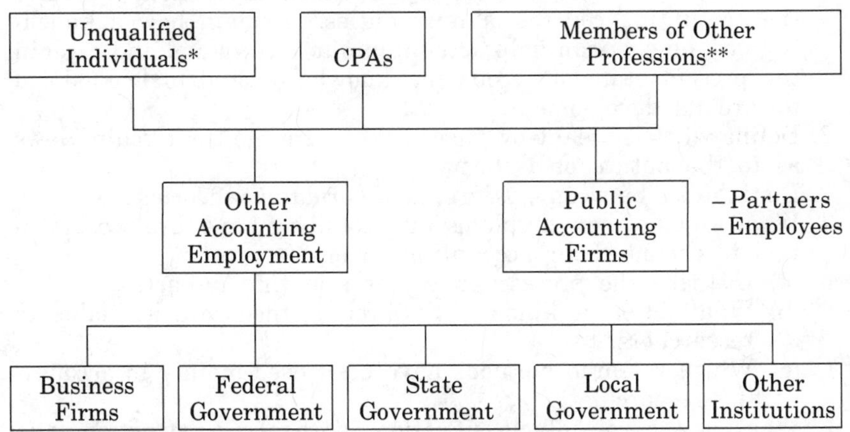

* May be qualified, by experience or education, to undertake accounting tasks
** Engineers, personnel consultants, computer systems analysts, etc.

1. How would you define the word *accountant* to embrace so many different occupational categories?
2. What are the implications of this problem for accounting research?

Case 3-2 The Bank Fraud

In 1981 a bank fraud came to light which involved cash in transit. A bank officer took advantage of the fact that the bank's computers were programmed to allow five days for a remittance from one office to turn up as a receipt at another, before signalling that the funds had gone astray. The officer would create a transfer and suppress the notification to the receiving office; within the five-day period he would then create another transfer to the office in question for a larger amount, and refund the embezzled funds out of this. (*Time*, March 9, 1981, p. 64)

1. Is this an accounting problem?
2. Since it does not involve the definitions of the basic elements of accounting, or the structure of accounting's basic equation, in what way is it a proper subject of accounting theory?
3. What accounting (not auditing) solution is there to this problem, and how does accounting theory assist in arriving at it?

END OF CHAPTER QUESTIONS

1. "Exposure to accounting history is seldom a significant part of the accounting courses of universities." Explain how a knowledge of the past can help accountants to understand and explain the present state of accounting knowledge, and to look ahead toward its development.
2. Define what is meant by *theory*. What are the three main views as to the nature of a theory?
3. Distinguish between *positive* and *normative* theories.
4. What kinds of new problems in accounting have directed attention to the need for accounting theory?
5. (a) Describe the process known as scientific research.
   (b) What different kinds of research methods are available to researchers?
   (c) Which research methods have been used mainly in accounting research?
6. What is the role of classification in theory construction, and in what form does this role present itself to accounting researchers?
7. Human information processing (HIP) is the name given to the field in psychology which deals with the way in which the mind receives and processes information in order to produce a decision. What is the relevance of this field to accounting, and in what ways have accounting researchers attempted to use its methodology?
8. Explain the following approaches to accounting theory:
   (a) Macroeconomic
   (b) Ethical
   (c) Behavioral

9. What types of research has the behavioral approach to accounting theory inspired, and which of these assumed particular importance in the 1970s?
10. What is the efficient market hypothesis? What forms does it take, and for which of these forms have accountants directed their research efforts?
11. Which questions of accounting policy formulation is it suggested that efficient market research can help to solve?
12. Discuss the relationship between accounting theory and policy and security market regulation.
13. What is the distinction made between accounting theories and theories of accounting? Does the distinction between pure and applied research, which characterizes other scientific fields, hold also for accounting research?
14. Discuss the validity of the proposition that the economy of the United States is one of free enterprise, a term which embraces the characteristics of free competition and private enterprise. How would rejection of this proposition affect the relevance of the FASB's conceptual framework project?
15. "The FASB's function is important because decisions regarding allocation of capital (investment) are based on financial information, much of which is the product of the financial accounting/reporting process." (*Facts about FASB*, February 1981.)
    (a) What do you think *capital (investment)* means in the above quotation?
    (b) Is the statement one of fact or a belief?
    (c) How can this statement be converted into a hypothetical proposition suitable for testing so as to become a part of an accounting theory?

4

THE SEARCH FOR GENERALLY ACCEPTED ACCOUNTING PRINCIPLES

FOUR PERIODS

Storey, writing in 1963, identified three periods during which accountants were preoccupied with the need for accounting principles.[1] The first, starting about 1930 and ending at the outset of World War II, saw the enactment of the 1933 and 1934 securities legislation and was marked by cooperation between the (then) American Institute of Accountants and the New York Stock Exchange. The American Accounting Association published two statements of accounting principles, in 1936 and 1941,[2] and Paton and Littleton *An Introduction to Corporate Accounting Standards.*[3] Sanders, Hatfield, and Moore summarized the state of the art in *A Statement of Accounting Principles* (1938),[4] and the American Institute's Committee on Accounting Procedure published the first Accounting Research Bulletins.

The second started shortly after World War II and was characterized by a temporary abandonment of the task of developing a comprehensive statement of accounting principles. Rather, attention was directed toward particular reporting problems, including accounting for the effects of price-level changes. Accounting Research Bulletins on a variety of topics were revised and restated; *ARB No. 43* (1953), although it was followed by eight more ARBs, marked a high point of institutional action.

The third period, which was stimulated by increased discontent with the scope of these institutional actions, saw the formation of the Accounting Principles Board in 1957 and the establishment of a research arm to support its pronouncements. To these three periods we may add a fourth, which saw the demise of the APB and the creation of the Financial Accounting Standards Board in 1972.

In this chapter we shall describe, in summary form, the salient features of these four periods, concentrating on the pronouncement process. We shall also see that at least two earlier attempts to establish uniform financial accounting and reporting proved abortive, providing a contrast with the developments in continental

Europe referred to in chapter 2. In chapter 5 we will review the substantive contributions of these periods to accounting theory formulation.

The first period was characterized by a number of influential publications which effectively set the stage for the practice of accountancy and auditing during the next fifty years. These documents (a) laid down what were, and were not, acceptable accounting practices, (b) established doctrines, such as the view of accounting as a process of cost allocation, which were to dominate generations of accounting thought, and (c) defined accounting principles narrowly, by reference to *Webster's New International Dictionary,* which led inexorably to the axiomatic, or *a priori,* approach to accounting theory formulation of the 1960s.

THE PROTAGONISTS

The principal participants in this were the accountancy profession, the New York Stock Exchange (NYSE), and the Securities and Exchange Commission (SEC). Playing significant roles were the American Accounting Association (AAA) and the National Association of Accountants (NAA).

The first American professional association of accountants, the American Association of Public Accountants, was formed in 1887. When it was succeeded by the Institute of Public Accountants in 1916, membership was only 1,150; the name was changed to American Institute of Accountants (AIA) the following year. In 1921 the American Society of Certified Public Accountants, a federation of state societies, came into existence; it merged with the AIA in 1936 when the latter agreed to restrict its membership to CPAs. After 1936 there was continuous pressure on the AIA to include the letters CPA in the Institute's title, which did not succeed until the National Society of Public Accountants was organized. Members feared that the existence of the two organizations might confuse the public about which one represented professional, accredited public accountants. A by-law changing the name of the AIA to the American Institute of Certified Public Accountants was adopted in 1957. The AIA established a Board of Examiners in 1917 to create a uniform CPA examination, now administered by the National Association of State Boards of Accountancy.

The New York Stock Exchange was organized as such in 1794 to facilitate the transfer of government and corporate securities. As early as 1866 it attempted to obtain financial statements from corporations listed on the exchange, but the NYSE had little success until 1900, when it required all corporations applying for listing to agree to publish annual financial statements. In 1926 the NYSE required listed companies to provide stockholders with financial statements prior to the company's annual general meeting, which was already a provision of the company laws in other countries.

The Securities and Exchange Commission was established by an act of Congress in 1934 to protect the public from loss through ignorance. The Securities Act of 1933 required companies to register new offerings of securities, and the Securities Exchange Act of 1934 stipulated for the registration of any securities listed for sale to the public. The SEC was set up to administer these two acts and given broad powers to prescribe the form and content of disclosure documents filed, including financial statements.

The American Accounting Association began life as the American Association of University Instructors in Accounting in 1916; its name was changed in 1935. The AAA in 1935 expanded its scope to include research and the development of accounting principles and standards.

The National Association of Accountants (formerly the National Association of Cost Accountants) was established in 1919. From its inception the NACA, later the NAA, published research studies and monographs on managerial accounting, including both financial and cost accounting. Emphasis was on problems of practice, and many managerial accounting techniques were first presented to the public through the medium of the monthly *NACA Bulletin* (now *Management Accounting*).

Other organizations which have concerned themselves with the development of accounting principles in the United States include the Financial Executives Institute, the Financial Analysts Federation, and research groups centered on universities.

BEGINNINGS OF UNIFORM ACCOUNTING

The search for uniform cost accounting in the United Kingdom and the United States began in the late nineteenth century as a response to lethal cutthroat competition. The adoption of uniform cost accounting schemes by a number of trades and industries did not of itself lead to any degree of standardization of accounting generally.[5]

Most of the capital needed in the United States for economic development in the nineteenth century came from Europe, and the financiers sent their accountants to check on the use of their money. These accountants, mainly Scottish and English, brought with them standards for the form and content of financial statements which were those laid down in the United Kingdom Companies Acts. As the American economy developed, the banking system became the principal source of capital, and bankers tended to set standards for financial accounting. Not surprisingly, they tried to make business financial statements as much like bank accounts as possible.

As early as 1894 the American Association of Public Accountants adopted a resolution recommending that the order of presentation of balance sheet items should correspond with the order of their liquidation. In 1910 a committee was formed to establish uniform definitions of technical accounting terms, and the income tax regulations which followed the enactment of the corporate income tax spurred pressures for uniformity in accounting.

In response to this pressure, the Federal Reserve Board and the Federal Trade Commission in 1917 requested the AIA to put forward proposals for standardized financial statements. The resulting memorandum received the endorsement of the Federal Reserve Board and, after being submitted to the banking community nationally for their reactions, it was published in the April 1917 issue of the *Federal Reserve Bulletin.* This memorandum became the publication *Uniform Accounting*[6] and was republished in 1918 as *Approved Methods for the Preparation of Balance Sheet Statements.* The Federal Reserve Board published a revised edition, *Verification of Financial Statements,* in 1929.[7]

Uniform Accounting placed emphasis on the balance sheet. As might be expected in the context of its publication, assets were to be presented in order of decreasing liquidity, liabilities in the order in which they were to be met. Inventories must be stated at the lower of cost or market value. Fixed asset changes must identify value changes recorded separately from movements. As for the profit and loss statement (note the terminology), depreciation was to be shown as a "deduction from income" together with interest and taxes. Net income became profit or loss by the addition or deduction of special credits or charges.

A 1936 revision of this publication was published by the AIA; entitled *Examination of Financial Statements by Independent Public Accountants,* it proclaimed its object to be financial statements for creditors and also annual reports to stockholders.[8] The 1936 revision adopted the going concern convention and the cost basis of valuation and provided new emphasis on the income statement.

The transition from net income to profit or loss, noted above, was dealt with in many countries (and still is in some) by a two-part profit and loss account. The first part, sometimes called a *trading account,* offsets the beginning inventory and operating costs against the revenues of the period and the ending inventory, to arrive at a trading profit, or profit from operations. This figure is then carried down to the second part, called the profit and loss account, where extraordinary gains and losses and prior period adjustments are added or deducted to arrive at the net profit (or loss) for the period.

In spite of the emphasis on the income statement, and on what George O. May called "earning power," this solution was not adopted, and the uniform financial reporting schemes listed above led to a unitary form of income statement embracing all revenues, gains, expenses, and losses *in* the period, including those *for* prior periods. The inclusion of nonoperating gains and losses as other income or expense, which the 1936 revision required, has created special income statement problems, such as the treatment of prior period adjustments, which will be discussed in chapter 14.

THE GREAT DEPRESSION

In the 1920s the general public, flush with cash from World War I and the subsequent boom, began buying corporate securities heavily. The United States went through a period of speculation similar to the English "South Sea Bubble" of the early 1700s or the Dutch "tulipomania" of the preceding century. Lacking any company laws worth mentioning, these investors were unprotected from fraud or the consequences of their own ignorance. In particular, they could not rely on audited financial statements for their information.

As we have seen, the American audit began as a means of verifying transactions for absentee owners. It developed as a means of providing banks with information about solvency and liquidity; hence the peculiarly American concept of a *balance sheet audit.* Audit techniques used by English auditors to verify transactions and report on the profit and loss account were largely neglected. Thus, financial statements presented to investors were either over-conservative, showing assets at their liquidation values, or over-optimistic, showing assets at written-up values and manipulated income figures.

In a speech at the 1930 convention of the AIA, J. M. B. Hoxsey voiced several criticisms of contemporary accounting, which were particularly painful coming from the executive assistant of the Committee on Stock List of the NYSE. He drew attention to the diversity of approaches to depreciation accounting and the lack of information about depreciation policy, diversity of approaches to consolidation, absence of sales volume figures and a clear separation of nonoperating income, failure to identify earned surplus in the balance sheet, recording stock dividends received at higher amounts than those shown by the companies declaring the dividends, and practices designed to understate profits. These criticisms echoed the earlier findings of William Z. Ripley, a Harvard University professor of economics, made public in a 1926 article. The results of this public pressure have been documented by May, one of the leaders of the accountancy profession at that time, in his book *25 Years of Accounting Responsibility.*[9] This book contains much of the correspondence which passed between representatives of the protagonists at that time.

The AIA's special committee on cooperation with stock exchanges was established to deal with the problem that listed companies were using a variety of different accounting methods to report ostensibly similar transactions and situations. The committee, headed by George O. May, considered the possibility of having a competent authority select a detailed set of binding rules, but rejected this in favor of another approach

> ...to leave every corporation free to choose its own methods of accounting within... broad limits... but require disclosure of the methods employed and consistency in their application from year to year.

The idea was for each listed company to prepare a statement of the methods of accounting and reporting used in the preparation of its financial statements. This statement would be adopted by the directors of the company, filed with the Stock Exchange, and available to any shareholder on request. Corporations would provide the Exchange with an assurance that these methods would be applied consistently from year to year, and that the Exchange would be informed when changes took place. The audit certificate would be changed to require auditors to state whether these methods had been used, whether they were in accordance with generally accepted accounting standards, and whether they had been applied consistently.

It is widely believed that May's professional development (he started his career as a Chartered Accountant in England) led him to put forward this proposal as a modification of the company reporting rules contained in the English Companies Acts.* These Acts prescribed the form of disclosure, but did not lay down rules for the accounting methods and procedures to be followed in preparing financial statements for publication. They did, however, require the financial statements to be audited, and for the auditor to report whether they presented a "true and fair view." These were the basic elements of the committee's proposal.

The May committee did however specify the following five "principles":

1. That income accounts should not include unrealized profit, realization being the consequence of an act of sale.
2. That capital surplus (reserves) should not be used for revenue items of charge.
3. That earned surplus (revenue reserves) of a subsidiary created prior to acquisition was not part of the consolidated earned surplus of the parent.
4. That dividends paid by a corporation to itself in respect of holdings of its own stock should not be credited to income.
5. That amounts receivable from officers, employees, and affiliated companies should be shown separately.

This modest list of principles was quoted with approval in a statement issued the following year by the president of the New York Stock Exchange (NYSE) when it was announced that after July 1, 1933, all applicants for listing must henceforth agree to have their financial statements audited, and submit them on application (with the exception of certain railroads). The correspondence concluded with a draft form of audit report, and *The Accountant* (London) of May 19, 1934 commented favorably on the manner in which this result was reached, by cooperation between the AIA and the stock exchange authorities, and not by legislative sanction.

*But May himself denied this, in his *Financial Accounting*, New York, The Macmillan Company, 1961.

ORIGINS OF THE SHORT-FORM AUDIT REPORT

The correspondence mentioned included a letter from the NYSE Committee on Stock List to the Governing Committee of the NYSE dated October 24, 1933. This letter said:

> It would... be advantageous if audit reports were so framed as to constitute specific answers to the last three questions embodied in the (NYSE) President's letter to listed companies of January 31, 1933, namely:
>
> 4. Whether in their opinion the form of the balance sheet and of the income or profit-and-loss account is such as fairly to present the financial position and the results of operation.
> 5. Whether the accounts are in their opinion fairly determined on the basis of consistent application of the system of accounting regularly employed by the company.
> 6. Whether such system in their opinion conforms to accepted accounting practices, and particularly whether it is in any respect inconsistent with any of the principles set forth in the statement attached hereto. [i.e., the May Committee's five principles].

The *Revised Suggestions of a Form of Accountants' Report* produced by the May Committee reads as follows:

> To the XYZ Company:
>
> We have made an examination of the balance sheet of the XYZ Company as of December 31, 1933 and of the statement of income and surplus for the year 1933. In connection therewith, we examined or tested accounting records of the Company and other supporting evidence and obtained information and explanations from officers and employees of the Company; we also made a general review of the accounting methods and of the operating and income accounts for the year, but we did not make a detailed audit of the transactions.
>
> In our opinion, based upon such examination, the accompanying balance sheet and related statement of income and surplus fairly present, in accordance with accepted principles of accounting consistently maintained by the Company during the year under review, its position at December 31, 1933 and the results of its operations for the year.

The short-form audit report subsequently adopted by the AIA for use by its members was as follows:

> Addressee   Date
>
> We have examined the balance sheet of X Company as of December 31, 19–, and the related statement(s) of income and surplus for the year then ended. Our examination was made in accordance with generally accepted auditing standards, and accordingly included

> such tests of the accounting records and such other auditing procedures as we considered necessary in the circumstances.
>
> In our opinion the accompanying balance sheet and statement(s) of income and surplus present fairly the financial position of X Company at December 31, 19–, and the results of its operations for the year then ended, in conformity with generally accepted accounting principles applied on a basis consistent with that of the preceding year.

It appears, therefore, that the short-form audit report in use in the United States is in essence the product of suggestions made by a former president of the NYSE.

THE SEARCH FOR PRINCIPLES

The implications of an audit report resting on generally accepted accounting principles were immediately apparent to the profession, which cast about for something more substantial than the five principles produced by the May Committee. A prize was offered for the best paper on the subject, and the winner, Gilbert R. Byrne, presented his list at the Fiftieth Anniversary celebration of the AIA in 1937.[10] Byrne quoted with approval the Webster definition of a principle as "a fundamental truth; a comprehensive law or doctrine, from which others are derived, or on which others are founded; an elementary proposition or fundamental assumption; a maxim; an axiom; a postulate."

Byrne accepted the assumption that accounting principles "like the axioms of geometry . . . are few in number. . . ." It was Byrne likewise who stated the postulate that "accounting is essentially the allocation of historical costs and revenues to the current and succeeding fiscal periods." He also postulated that "while it is not in many cases of great importance which of several alternative accounting rules is applied in a given situation, it is essential that, once having adopted a certain procedure, it be consistently adhered to in preparing accounts over a period of time." Finally, Byrne postulated that "income shall include only realized profits" and "profit is deemed to be realized when a sale in the ordinary course of business is effected." From these four unnecessary assumptions the theory and practice of accounting are only now, forty years later, painfully liberating themselves.

The five rules which Byrne laid down as principles of accounting (having "a coercive or compelling quality" based on business laws which must be obeyed if an enterprise is to survive) are—

- Depreciation on plant must be charged against operations,
- All expenses incurred in producing net income must be provided for,
- Probable losses should also be provided for,

- Proprietors' contributions of capital consist of capital stock and capital surplus, and
- Earned surplus should represent accumulated earnings less distributions to stockholders.

Byrne's ideas can still be found in writings on accounting, and even his precise phrasing, as in *APB Opinion No. 10* (December 1966). "Profit is deemed to be realized when a sale in the ordinary course of business is effected unless the circumstances are such that the collection of the sale price is not reasonably assured" (para. 12).

In 1935, the Haskins and Sells Foundation decided to assist in the identification of accounting principles by requesting a committee of academics to study the subject and prepare an impartial report. The committee consisted of two accounting professors, Thomas Henry Sanders of Harvard University Graduate School of Business Administration and Henry Rand Hatfield of the University of California, and a legal scholar, Underhill Moore of Yale University. Their report, *A Statement of Accounting Principles,* was published by the American Institute of Accountants in 1938.

The trustees of the foundation, in their letter of invitation to Dr. Sanders, specified the reasons why the need for accounting principles had become apparent. They were—

- Inconsistency between corporation and other statutes, some of which permitted indefensible accounting practices.
- Contradiction between federal agencies issuing regulations involving accounting, and between federal and state regulatory bodies.
- Questions raised by the stock exchanges and the SEC in their efforts to ensure adequate disclosure. In particular

> Notwithstanding the difficulties involved, accountants who certify to financial statements filed with the Securities and Exchange Commission have been required by the regulations of that commission to express an opinion concerning such financial statements and the practices of the registrant in the light of accepted principles of accounting.[11]

In the letter of transmittal, the committee reported that they had "made inquiry in four directions." These were as follows:

- Personal interviews, supplemented by correspondence, with competent persons.
- Review of accounting literature.
- Study of statutes and court decisions.
- Examination of current corporate reports.

The report stated as the objective of accounting, "Making effective and effectively maintaining... the distinction between capital and income of a particular enterprise ...."[12] Hence, its findings could only be expected to apply to business accounting. The report recognized as conventional the balance sheet/income statement complex and the going concern assumption, and the effect of legal considerations on liabilities; also the importance of the notes to financial statements.

The Common Law nature of accounting principles, that they exist in unwritten form, was one of the findings of the committee, based on their observation that controversy within the profession was restricted to a relatively small number of situations out of the much greater number which might lead to disagreement. However, instead of proceeding empirically to list those objects of agreement, the committee based its statement of accounting principles on economic definitions of capital and income in an attempt to force the principles into a framework of deductive reasoning. Hence the proposition—"Income normally arises from the sale of goods or services for amounts greater than their cost".[13]

The bulk of the report consisted of an enumeration of the items which were found in financial statements together with justification for contemporary practices. From this descriptive material generalizations were made in part VI of the report, "Summary of Accounting Principles." Part VI is reproduced below as it represents a milestone, dated 1938, in the development of accounting principles.

PART VI
SUMMARY OF ACCOUNTING PRINCIPLES

The following enumeration of accounting principles is to be read as a very general summary of the report. Each proposition is to be construed in the light of the relevant discussion in the body of the report.

I. GENERAL PRINCIPLES

A. Accounting should make available all material information of a financial nature relating to (a) the financial condition or status of the business, (b) its progress in earning income.

B. Transactions which add to or subtract from capital must be distinguished from those which add to or subtract from revenue, and, where both kinds of change occur in one transaction, the extent of each must be shown.

C. A reliable historical record must be made of all transactions of the business; but this record must also be analytical, or susceptible to subsequent analysis, to preserve the necessary distinction between capital and income.

D. The use of long-term assets involves the apportionment of capital and income over the several accounting periods; the accuracy of the accounts depends in large measure upon the exercise of competent judgment in making these apportionments.

E. The basis of the treatment applied to the several items should be adhered to consistently from period to period; when any change of treatment becomes necessary, due attention should be drawn to the change.

F. The possible extent of unforeseen contingencies of adverse character calls for a generally conservative treatment of items to which judgment must be applied.

II. INCOME STATEMENT PRINCIPLES

A. The income statement should show, for the period it covers, (a) income from all sources, (b) costs and expenses of all kinds, and (c) net income.

B. Only income realized by the sale of goods or rendering of service is to be shown in the income statement. Unrealized income should not be recorded, nor utilized to absorb proper charges against earnings.

C. Income from sources other than the main operations of the business should be stated separately.

D. Costs and expenses must include:
(a) all current operating costs,
(b) inventory losses of the period,
(c) provision for losses on other current assets, which have become imminent in the period,
(d) proper allocations for the depreciation, depletion, or amortization of all capital assets subject to those processes.

E. Nonrecurring items should be reported in terms which indicate their nature.

F. As far as possible net income should be so determined that it will need no subsequent correction. When, however, such correction becomes necessary, it may be made through current income only if it is not so large as to distort the statement of that income; otherwise it should be made through earned surplus.

III. BALANCE-SHEET PRINCIPLES

A. A balance-sheet should show (a) the nature and amounts of the assets, (b) the nature and amounts of the liabilities, (c) the nature and amounts of the invested capital, (d) the amounts of earned and of capital surplus.

B. With reference to fixed or capital assets in the balance sheet:
1. The amounts should be based upon the amounts invested in such assets.

2. Reserves for depreciation, depletion, and amortization should show the cumulative progress of prorating their cost over their useful lives.
3. Proper distinction should be made between (1) tangible assets, (2) intangibles, and (3) investments.

C. The proper showing of current assets requires:
1. That inclusion or exclusion of particular items be determined on the same time basis as is applied to current liabilities;
2. That the values in general be the lowest of cost, replacement market, or realization, as may be applicable for the several items;
3. That reserves be plainly associated with the current assets to which they apply;
4. That separate mention be made of items not in the ordinary course of business.

D. Particular care must be given in reporting deferred charges:
1. To the distinction between charges inuring to the benefit of future periods and losses actually sustained;
2. To the basis of amortization, which in general should be the periods to be benefited by the deferred charges.

E. Contingent liabilities should be noted in the balance-sheet or in a footnote, if they are material, imminent, and of reasonably determinable amount.

F. Reacquired stock should be shown as a deduction from capital stock, unless exceptional circumstances justify showing it as an asset, when the reason should be given.

G. The restatement of capital assets at higher values results in capital surplus. Restatement at lower values may result in a subtraction from capital, capital surplus, or earned surplus, depending on circumstances.

H. Capital surplus should not be utilized to relieve either earnings or earned surplus of charges which should be made against them.

IV. CONSOLIDATED STATEMENTS

A. Consolidated statements should include only units which are effectively controlled by the parent company.

B. The amount at which the stock of a subsidiary is carried in the parent company books constitutes in effect a revaluation of the subsidiary properties, either tangible or intangible, and is reflected as such in the consolidated balance-sheet.

C. Surplus of subsidiaries existing at the time when control of them was acquired by a parent company should not be shown in the consolidated balance-sheet.
D. Minority interests in subsidiaries may be shown in the consolidated balance-sheet at their net value in the subsidiary books.

V. COMMENTS AND FOOTNOTES
A. Comments, footnotes of reasonable length, and supplementary schedules may be used to elucidate items in the statements calling for explanation, or to supplement the statements.

A Statement of Accounting Principles was criticized at the time because it appeared to sanction accounting practices which were even then suspect, such as carrying forward a loss as an asset in the balance sheet.

THE SEC AND GAAP

Section 13 (b) of the 1934 Securities Exchange Act provides that:

> The Commission may prescribe, in regard to reports made persuant (*sic*) to this title, the form or forms in which the required information shall be set forth, the items or details to be shown in the balance sheet and the earnings statement, and the methods to be followed in the preparation of reports, in the appraisal or valuation of assets and liabilities, in the determination of depreciation and depletion, in the differentiation of reoccurring and nonreoccurring income...

It was this power which permitted the SEC to require that the information contained in financial statements and supporting schedules be certified by an independent accountant, and that the independent accountant follow the rules and procedures laid down by the SEC. The SEC was later called upon to administer other federal investment laws: the Public Utility Holding Company Act of 1935; the Trust Indenture Act of 1939; the Investment Company Act of 1940; the Investment Advisers Act of 1940; the National Bankruptcy Act (as amended); and the Investors Protection Act of 1970. All of these gave a role to independent accountants as auditors.

The SEC issued its principal accounting rules, Regulation S-X, in 1940. This Regulation stated that "no public accountant should attempt an examination of financial statements intended for filing under any of these acts without having an up-to-date copy of Regulation S-X at hand." Thus, although initially the SEC allowed considerable flexibility providing the registrant disclosed the methods used, gradually this flexibility was severely reduced. As a result, some friction developed between the SEC and the accountancy profession. This friction came into the open after the SEC published *ASR No. 177* which required that companies changing from one acceptable method to another file a letter from their auditors indicating whether the change was to an alternative principle which, in their judgment, was "preferable under the circumstances." Appalled by the possibility that it might find itself supporting one client's change in one direction, and the opposite change for another client, the firm of Arthur Andersen & Co. filed a petition in May 1976 objecting to both *ASR No. 150** and *ASR No. 177*. Their point was that the distinction between the SEC's role in setting *disclosure standards* and the accountancy profession's responsibility to set *measurement standards* had been eroded. Subsequent events were to show that this erosion had become permanent. The Arthur Andersen petition was set aside by the court on the grounds that it did not have jurisdiction in the matter, so that the dispute as to the SEC's precise duties remains unresolved.

The role of the SEC as an influence on accounting practice in the United States cannot be overstated. The SEC's requirement that corporations file data on sales, other operating revenue, cost of goods sold, operating expenses, and other details, undoubtedly led to the expansion of financial reporting generally to the same ends. Again, the SEC's stand in opposition to recording appreciation has been a major factor in restricting the growth of current value accounting in the U.S. The influence of the SEC was exercised largely behind the scenes, but it seems obvious that, possessing the authority of the legislature, the SEC must prevail on any issue joined with an essentially voluntary body such as the Accounting Principles Board or the Financial Accounting Standards Board.

In the fiscal year ended June 30, 1936, two years after the passage of the Securities Exchange Act of 1934, there were 2,303 issuers required to file annual financial reports with the SEC, and 781 registration statements were filed for $4.8 billion under the 1933 Act. Twenty-five years later, in 1961, 4,789 issuers were required to file annual reports, and 1,830 registration statements were filed for $20.7 billion. It is clear that the task of ensuring that this flow of information was reliable rested on the public accounting profession, as the SEC, which has never had more than a few hundred professional employees, could only look at a fraction of the total volume of filings.

From the beginning the SEC relied upon the accounting profession to set standards, although it reserved the right to prescribe for financial statements generally and to advise on specific matters

**ASR No. 150* stated that accounting principles, standards and practices theretofore or thereafter promulgated by Statements and Interpretations of the FASB, the Opinions of the APB and the Accounting Research Bulletins of the Committee on Accounting Procedure of the AICPA that are still in effect will be considered by the Commission as having substantial authoritative support, and that financial statements containing accounting practices for which substantial authoritative support was lacking were presumed to be misleading.

through its *Accounting Series Releases*. The first chief accountant of the SEC, Carman G. Blough, stated before the commission that:

> ...the policy of the Securities and Exchange Commission was to encourage the accountants to develop uniformity of procedure themselves, in which case we would follow...only as a last resort would the Commission feel the necessity to step in....If the time comes when the Commission is convinced that a procedure which is not generally accepted in the profession is a procedure that should nevertheless be followed, the matter will be handled not through the release of an opinion by the chief accountant, but *through a rule or regulation of the Commission requiring that such procedure be followed.* (Emphasis supplied.)[14]

From the viewpoint of the SEC, generally accepted accounting principles are those having "substantial authoritative support." This phrase was first used in the SEC's *Accounting Series Release (ASR) No. 4* (1938) which stated that the Commission would accept for filing only financial statements prepared using accounting principles having such support or in accordance with rules, regulations, or other official pronouncements of the Commission or its chief accountant. *ASR No. 4* says in part:

> Financial statements...prepared in accordance with accounting principles for which there is no authoritative support...will be presumed to be misleading or inaccurate...providing the matters are material.

Although this was the SEC's first explicit recognition of the existence of generally accepted accounting principles established by another body, there appears to be no precise definition of "substantial authoritative support" in the Commission's rules or elsewhere. The term was repeated in *ASR No. 150* and was used in the Special Bulletin adopted by Council of the AICPA in October 1964 (see Appendix A to *APB Opinion No. 6*). This called for AICPA members in their capacity as independent auditors to see that departures from AICPA pronouncements were adequately disclosed. The Special Bulletin made several recommendations, including the following:

> 1. 'Generally accepted accounting principles' are those principles which have substantial authoritative support.

The APB again referred to this term in Chapter 6 of *APB Statement No. 4:*

> Inasmuch as generally accepted accounting principles embody a consensus they depend on notions such as *general acceptance* and *substantial authoritative support,* which are not precisely defined. (Footnote to para. 137).

In an article in the *Journal of Accountancy,* Marshall S. Armstrong presented his views on how the problem of finding generally accepted accounting principles is resolved.[15] The steps to be followed were—

1. Define the problem.
2. Survey the relevant literature.
3. Survey present practice.
4. Evaluate the information so gathered.
5. Reach a conclusion.

There was, however, one exception to this pragmatic approach. If the principle in question were one on which the SEC had previously taken an informal position contrary to the present consensus, discussions would take place with the staff of the SEC, particularly if the company were subject to SEC regulation.

To conclude this historical review, on March 1, 1973 the AICPA adopted a revised Code of Ethics which included Rule 203. This rule includes the words:

> A member shall not express an opinion that financial statements are presented in conformity with generally accepted accounting principles if such statements contain any departure from an accounting principle promulgated by the body designated by Council to establish such principles....

ORIGINS OF THE APB

Two major influences on the pronouncements of the AICPA were (1) the "Student Department" of the *Journal of Accountancy,* dating back to 1914, and (2) a series of Special Bulletins published by the AIA in the 1920s. The former was "a gold mine of information on the accounting principles of the time and the reasons for their existence."[16]

THE COMMITTEE ON ACCOUNTING PROCEDURE

Prior to 1938 various committees of the AIA worked on specific projects aimed at clarifying points of practice. In 1936 the AIA publication *Examination of Financial Statements* ... referred to the phrase "generally accepted accounting principles." During the period 1936-1938 a Committee on Accounting Procedure (CAP) existed, consisting of the seven chairmen of various AIA committees, which responded to specific questions from members of the AIA and thus built up a collection of precedents. In 1938 the membership of the CAP was increased to twenty-one, and appointed for one-year terms, which may have accounted for a certain lack of continuity; after that date what continuity there was came from the CAP's research staff, a small and diminishing number.

In spite of the need for generally accepted accounting principles, the CAP devoted itself to decisions of an *ad hoc* nature; few of its pronouncements were based on research studies. They were called *Accounting Research Bulletins* (ARBs), and forty-two ARBs were published during the first fifteen years. Most of these were consolidated into *ARB 43,* and between 1953 and 1959 a further eight were published, bringing the total to 51. The consolidated *ARB 43* included eight reports of a Committee on Terminology, published separately in 1953 as *Accounting Terminology Bulletin No. 1,* "Review and Resume." This publication has been of great significance in that, to the extent that definitions and practices have not been revised subsequently, it represents the prime source of "generally accepted accounting principles" in the United States. *ARB's 1-51,* together with the *APB Opinions* available at the time, provided the basis for *Accounting Research Study No. 7.*[17]

The shortcomings of the CAP were revealed in the period following World War II, when new financing techniques, such as conglomerate acquisitions, equipment leasing, convertible securities, and leaseback arrangements, created accounting problems which could not be solved from precedents. In addition, the decline in the purchasing power of money raised the prospect of the abandonment of historical costs, and changes in technology threw up intangibles of great value which were inadequately expressed at a memorandum figure of one dollar. G.O. May wrote at this time that there was a need for the following:

1. Continuous research on a high level; a service that a rapidly changing Committee on Accounting Procedure cannot render.
2. Consideration of questions in a longer historical perspective.
3. Consideration of problems, not in isolation, but in their relationship one to another.
4. More penetrating discrimination between phenomena that have in the past been considered as indistinguishable for the purposes in hand,...
5. A receptiveness to change...
6. More rigorous logic and presentations in which there shall be no begging of the question by making assumptions which leave the conclusions apparently inevitable.[18]

THE ESTABLISHMENT OF AN ACCOUNTING PRINCIPLES BOARD

As if in response to these proposals, the then president of the AICPA, Alvin R. Jennings, addressed himself to the question "how successful we have been in narrowing areas of difference and inconsistency in the preparation and presentation of financial information."[19] He proposed that a new approach be taken and that the development of accounting principles should be regarded as "in the nature of pure research." A proper research organization should be set up, staffed with academically qualified persons, and financed by the profession and industry jointly. The function of the research organization should be to carry on continuous examination and reexamination of basic accounting assumptions and to develop authoritative statements for the guidance of both industry and the profession. Such statements would be submitted for approval or rejection to the Council of the AICPA.

Jennings set up a Special Committee on Research Program in 1957, and in 1958 the Special Committee recommended the dissolution of the CAP and its research department.[20] They were to be replaced by an Accounting Principles Board (APB) and an appointed director of accounting research, with a permanent research staff. The Council of the AICPA accepted these recommendations in 1959, and the APB was duly established and given the mission "to advance the written expression of what constitutes generally accepted accounting principles."

The Special Committee's report stated that the problem required attention at four levels: the basic postulates, the principles themselves, rules or guides for the application of the principles, and research. It was again asserted that "postulates are few in number"; environmental postulates were indicated. A broad set of coordinated principles should be formulated on the basis of the postulates. Rules and other guides should be developed in relation to the postulates and principles. Adequate accounting research was necessary in all of these contexts.

The report suggested that although primary attention be given to published financial statements, in the long-run this work should be extended to institutions other than corporations regulated by the SEC.

The APB consisted of between eighteen and twenty-one members, mainly representatives of public accounting firms but also including representatives of industry and government and academics. The Accounting Research Division consisted of a director and a research staff.

ACCOUNTING RESEARCH STUDIES

The Special Committee's report specified that "immediate projects of the accounting research staff should be a study of the basic postulates underlying accounting principles, and a study of the broad principles of accounting."[21] The first director of research was Dr. Maurice Moonitz, an academic of the California school, strongly influenced by Fisher and Canning. He started work on the postulates study, and appointed Dr. Robert T. Sprouse to work on the principles study. The products, *Accounting Research Studies Nos. 1* and *3,* were published in 1961 and 1962 respectively.[22]

The Accounting Research Division was intended to produce rigorously argued studies heavily dependent on deductive reasoning, and these two publications disappointed the AICPA and the accounting profession. Instead of a carefully argued position, Moonitz and Sprouse produced two polemical papers attempting to move the profession toward basing financial statements on exit values, valuing assets at market prices. Deinzer has shown that the postulates presented in *ARS No. 1* could have equally supported diametrically opposed principles.[23]

The principles laid down by Sprouse and Moonitz included the assertion that "profit is attributable to the whole process of business activity," which contradicted the realization principle. The restatement of capital for general price-level changes, and the recognition of specific price changes as gains or losses, whether due to accretion or market events, were asserted as principles. Valuation principles involved three steps: determine if future services exist; quantify the estimate; multiply the quantity by a past, present, or future price. Monetary assets and liabilities should be recorded at present values.

Of these, the two propositions which proved most unacceptable to the AICPA were probably the necessity to account for general and specific price-level changes and the need to record inventories which are readily salable at known prices at net realizable value. The two studies were rejected by the AICPA and published with a leaflet insert stating that the postulates and principles were not acceptable at the present time. A statement by the APB to the same effect which appeared in the May 1962 issue of the *Journal of Accountancy* contained these words.

> The Board believes, however, that while these studies are a valuable contribution to accounting thinking, they are too radically different from present generally accepted accounting principles for acceptance at this time.
>
> After a period of exposure and consideration, some of the specific recommendations in these studies may prove acceptable to the Board while others may not.

The rejection of ARS No. 1 and No. 3 resulted in the commissioning of Paul Grady's ARS No. 7 which merely inventorized accounting methods sanctioned by ARBs, APB Opinions, or other precedent. Other products of the Accounting Research Division proved more fruitful. They were as follows:

ARS No. 2, "Cash Flow Analysis and the Funds Statement," by Perry Mason, AICPA 1961.

ARS No. 4, "Reporting of Leases in Financial Statements," by John H. Myers, AICPA 1962.

ARS No. 5, "A Critical Study of Accounting for Business Combinations," by Arthur R. Wyatt, AICPA 1963.

ARS No. 6, "Reporting the Financial Effects of Price-level Changes," by the staff of the Research Division, AICPA 1963.

ARS No. 8, "Accounting for the Cost of Pension Plans," by Ernest L. Hicks, AICPA 1965.

ARS No. 9, "Interperiod Allocation of Corporate Income Taxes," by Homer A. Black, AICPA 1966.

ARS No. 10, "Accounting for Goodwill," by George R. Catlett and Norman O. Olson, AICPA 1968.

ARS No. 11, "Financial Reporting in the Extractive Industries," by Robert R. Field, AICPA 1970.

ARS No. 12, "Reporting Foreign Operations of U.S. Companies in U.S. Dollars," by Leonard Lorensen, AICPA 1972.

ARS No. 13, "The Accounting Basis of Inventories," by Horace G. Barden, AICPA 1973.

ARS No. 14, "Accounting for R & D Expenditures," by Oscar S. Gellein, and Maurice S. Newman, AICPA 1973.

ARS No. 15, "Stockholders' Equity," by Beatrice Melcher, AICPA 1973.

APB OPINIONS AND STATEMENTS

The APB added to the body of generally accepted accounting principles by issuing Opinions. Between 1959 and 1973 the APB produced thirty-one Opinions. In 1964 the council of the AICPA resolved that after 1965 all departures from APB Opinions and surviving Accounting Research Bulletins must be disclosed in footnotes to financial statements or in audit reports signed by members. The Code of Ethics of the AICPA lays down the procedure to be followed if a member believes that an alternative accounting method should be used in place of one prescribed as part of GAAP. The Standards issued by the FASB are now included in the body of generally accepted accounting principles.

In addition to the Opinions, the APB also published four Statements, of which the response to the publication of *ARS No. 1* and *3* was the first. The Statements, which can be viewed as tentative opinions designed to inform the public on specific issues, included:

APB Statement No. 2, "Disclosure of Supplemental Financial Information by Diversified Companies," APB, September 1967.

APB Statement No. 3, "Financial Statements Restated for General Price-Level Changes," APB, June 1969.

APB Statement No. 4, "Basic Concepts and Accounting Principles Underlying Financial Statements of Business Enterprises," APB, October 1970.

Within a decade, considerable dissatisfaction with the operation of the APB had arisen. The same faults identified in relation to the CAP were discerned in the APB—a "fire-fighting" approach to accounting problems, disregarding its own research in favor of decisions reflecting the pre-conceived ideas of board members, lack of a theoretical framework resulting in inconsistencies, failure to deal with new questions resulting from change. A new fault was also attributed to the APB: failure to resist pressure from outside interest.

While these outside pressures included public accounting firms and their clients and industry associations, the most significant source was the SEC. The APB's position on accounting for the investment tax credit, which presented quite new accounting issues, was expressed in *APB Opinion No. 2* and came into conflict with the SEC's position as expressed in *ASR No. 97.* As a consequence, the APB abandoned its requirement of a uniform treatment and, in *Opinion No. 4,* permitted alternatives. Returning to the task in *Opinion No. 11* on "Accounting for Income Taxes," the APB was again forced to abandon its position, this time by the opposition of the Internal Revenue Service.

Prior to this controversy the SEC had objected to *ARB No. 32* on "Income and Earned Surplus" because it disagreed on allowing direct charges and credits to surplus (retained earnings). At that time the Commission authorized its chief accountant to take exception to financial statements which "appear to be misleading" even though they reflected the application of *ARB No. 32.* The SEC then forced the accounting profession to serve its needs through item 17 of Regulation S-X, reporting special items of income or loss not included in arriving at net income. By changing *Opnion No. 2,* the APB prevented similar embarrassment.

In a thoughtful article, Professor Horngren looked back over four years as a member of the APB and attempted to diagnose its weakness.[24] In his view a great mistake had been made in believing that the power to set principles rested in the private sector. "The increasing role of the federal government in our society", wrote Horngren, "is an unstoppable phenomenon." The APB had formulated principles subject to the constraints set by the SEC, to which organization Congress had delegated its powers in this area. The APB had been used by the SEC as a buffer, insulating the SEC from pressures and criticisms and doing an enormous amount of unpaid work for the government. Horngren cited as evidence the sequence of events accompanying *APB Opinions 2* and *4* on accounting for the investment tax credit; the establishment by Congress in 1972 of a *Cost Accounting Standards Board* has served to underline this point. As if to emphasize the political nature of this accounting decision, the Congress of the United States provided a clause in the Revenue Act of 1971 prohibiting any restriction on the method of accounting for the investment tax credit.

By 1970 it was apparent that the days of the APB were numbered. The reasons for this were as follows:

1. It was weakened by major controversies such as the one concerning the investment tax credit. There were also less visible subjects of discord, such as the petroleum industry struggle to select either the successful efforts or the full cost method of accounting for preproduction costs.
2. It lacked an explicit framework both for its own decisions

and to help practitioners in responding to new accounting problems.

3. Some viewed it as being dominated by the "Big Eight" accounting firms, others as a servant of the SEC.
4. It lacked any representation of users of financial statements.
5. It ignored the findings of its own Research Division, as previously the Institute had passed up its own Research Department's findings on inventories.
6. Its ad hoc approach—"piecemeal principles" and the "fire-fighting" image.
7. It was not even achieving its own objective of reducing available accounting alternatives, which remained a major problem.

Dale Gerboth asserted that such criticisms arise out of "the comprehensive approach to policy-making" and pointed out that it postulates an ideal world which is useless as a standard.[25] In his opinion, the APB had adopted the "incremental approach" as a standard, which consists of rational behavior as a substitute for perfection. The allegations that the APB acted *ad hoc,* repeatedly confronted the same problems, and adopted short-run solutions at the expense of long-run objectives, were misguided and arose from a false conception of policy making. The subsequent history of the successor organization, the Financial Accounting Standards Board, lends some credence to Gerboth's position.

Finally, it has been suggested that the increasing volume of litigation against public accountants in the United States was a factor in the demise of the APB. Most APB members were partners in CPA firms, and there was a real possibility that the defense of compliance with generally accepted accounting principles might be rejected in court on the grounds that these principles had been laid down by those who sought to hide behind them.

BIRTH OF THE FINANCIAL ACCOUNTING STANDARDS BOARD

Following the 1968 stock market crash the usual drive to blame the accountancy profession began. It was alleged that "creative accounting" was responsible for fostering imaginary earnings growth, and the SEC publicly charged some accounting firms with failure to safeguard investors. Many investors had recourse to the courts for compensation; such lawsuits as Westec, Mill Factors, Four Seasons Nursing Homes, Continental Vending, Revenue Properties, Black Watch Farms, Orvis Brothers, and Penn-Central threatened to undermine the auditing profession's reputation for reliability and independence.

The thrust of this criticism was that accountants had been "managing" the income statement by selecting from different generally accepted accounting principles those methods which would result in the highest reported earnings per share. In a report to Congress on the Penn-Central bankruptcy, dated August 3, 1972, the SEC stated that:

> The whole pattern of income management which emerges here is made up of some practices which, standing alone, could perhaps be justified as supported by generally accepted accounting principles, and other practices which could be so supported with great difficulty, if at all. But certainly the aggregate of these practices produced highly misleading results.

The chairman of the SEC blamed the APB for writing detailed opinions, pointing out that some circumstances were bound to occur which would make the literal application of these rules produce misleading disclosure.

In response to this kind of criticism the AICPA announced in April 1971 the formation of two study groups. One, entitled "The Study Group on the Objectives of Financial Statements" was chaired by Robert M. Trueblood, a prominent CPA, and will be analyzed in chapter 6. The other, entitled "The Study Group on Establishment of Accounting Principles," was chaired by Francis M. Wheat, a former SEC commissioner and long-time critic of the profession. The Wheat Committee reported on March 9, 1972[26] and proposed a new structure for establishing accounting rules and standards, based on a Financial Accounting Standards Board. The organization of this new structure is shown in Exhibit 4-1.

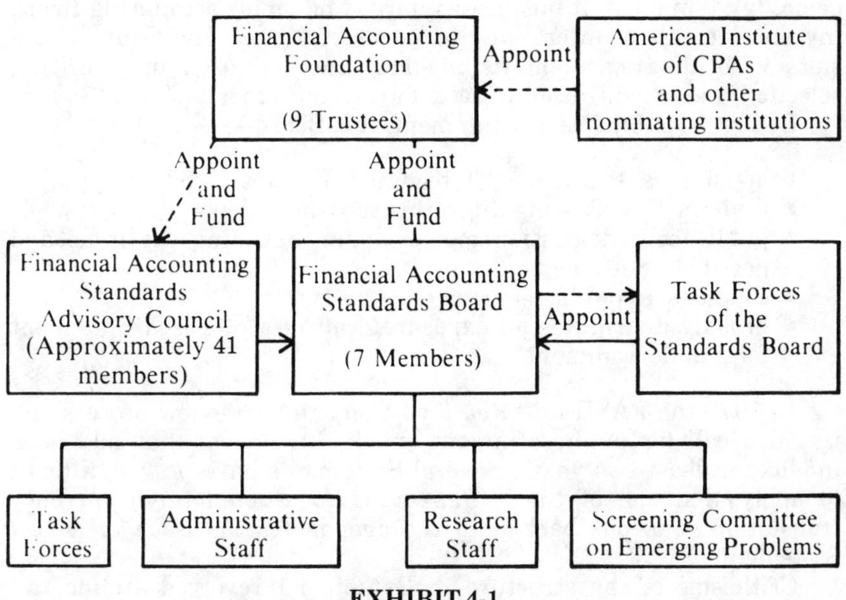

EXHIBIT 4-1

Financial Accounting Foundation Organization Structure

ORGANIZATION OF THE FASB

The FASB is the operating part of a tripartite structure independent of other professional and business organizations. Its 1980 budget of more than $8 million was obtained from contributions and sales of publications. Contributions are made to the Financial Accounting Foundation, approximately one-half from business firms and one-half from public accounting firms. No single contribution exceeding $50,000 may be accepted. The Foundation selects the members of the Board* and of its Advisory Council and is responsible for general oversight, which excludes technical accounting matters. Its Board of Trustees is made up of nominees of the six sponsoring organizations, which are the—

- American Accounting Association
- American Institute of Certified Public Accountants
- Financial Analysts Federation
- Financial Executives Institute
- National Association of Accountants
- Securities Industry Association

There is also a trustee-at-large representing the banking industry.

The other part of the structure is the Financial Accounting Advisory Council which now consists of 41 members broadly representative of the Board's constituencies in government, law, academe, large and small businesses, large and small accounting firms, investors, credit grantors, and other user groups. The Council consults with the Board on its agenda, the allocation of priorities, selection and organization of task forces, and other technical issues.

Before it publishes a Statement the Board—

- appoints a task force of technical experts
- reviews the existing literature on the subject
- publishes a discussion memorandum outlining the issue and possible solutions
- conducts a public hearing
- broadly distributes an exposure draft of a proposed Statement for public comment

In 1978 the FASB initiated a post-enactment review process and issued a call for public comment on all Statements that had been in effect at least two years. Several Statements have proved difficult to apply, and one of them, *Statement No. 8* on foreign currency translation, was put back onto the agenda for the issue of a new Statement.

Criticisms of the structure in Exhibit 4-1 revolved around the FASB and its funding. It was feared that the seven members would

*Members must possess "knowledge of accounting, finance, and business, and a concern for the public interest in matters of financial accounting and reporting."

operate in an ivory tower environment far removed from actual practice, a fear reinforced when the FASB moved into an elegant new building in Stamford, Connecticut. It was also feared that a substantial commitment called for from the accounting profession would result in the Big Eight firms, some of which offered to pay as much as one million dollars each over a five-year period, forming a powerful pressure group. Organizationally it was pointed out that, by being separated from the AICPA, the FASB would have no true constituency and that the system had no appeals mechanism.

In spite of these criticisms, the Wheat Report met with a remarkable display of enthusiasm, and the FASB was endorsed by the AICPA at its 85th annual meeting in 1972 and was in operation by the following year. On May 7, 1973 an AICPA Council resolution gave the FASB authority to establish accounting principles, and on July 1 of that year it succeeded the APB in this. Problems immediately emerged; the Advisory Council had no real role; the APB had cleared nearly every move with the SEC but the FASB did not even show the SEC draft documents. In spite of the latter, the SEC adopted the FASB as a source of GAAP in *ASR No. 150* dated December 20, 1973.

The initial agenda included some topics inherited from the APB: the conceptual framework project, foreign currency translation, leases, price-level adjustment. Others originated with the SEC; contingencies, certain practices of insurance companies, prior period adjustments. Even Congress got into the act, with oil and gas accounting. The Accounting Standards Executive Committee (AcSEC) of the AICPA, through which the Institute had retained a residual standard-setting function, put forward classification of short-term obligations expected to be refinanced; marketable equity securities; accounting for restructured debt. Only the users of financial statements failed to make their wishes known.[27]

The business community was apprehensive about the possible intervention of the United States government in the accounting standard-setting process; Reginald Jones, then chairman of General Electric, warned his counterparts not to react when their "ox was gored." Thus, FASB *Statement No. 2* on accounting for research and development costs and *No. 5* on accounting for loss contingencies aroused no opposition even though a number of corporations were unfavorably affected. Even FASB *Statement No. 8* on accounting for foreign currency translation was received fairly docilely at first; opposition to this Statement began to build only after its economic impact became clearly apparent.

Criticism of the FASB mounted until, in 1976, the trustees of the Financial Accounting Foundation decided that a comprehensive review of the workings of the Board was necessary. They appointed a "structure committee" to review the first three years of operations and make recommendations for changes. The structure committee reported in April, 1977.[28]

One important factor underlying the timing of the review was the publication of two government reports critical of the accounting

Accounting Principles Board	Financial Accounting Standards Board
Composed of eighteen members	Composed of seven members
Members part-time, not remunerated	Members full-time, well paid
A senior committee of the AICPA	Semiautonomous; subject to Financial Accounting Foundation
Viewed as not independent because of continued source of remuneration	Viewed as independent because members sever ties with former employers
Members required to be CPAs	Only four members required to be CPAs, therefore a broader public represented
Relatively small budget	Large budget, averaging five million dollars yearly
Views stated through issue of *Opinions* and *Statements,* preceded by exposure drafts.	Views of others solicited by issue of *Discussion Memorandum*, usually followed by public hearings; own views through *Exposure Drafts,* finally through *Statements* and *Interpretations*.
Discussed conceptual issues in *Statements* which did not lay down GAAP.	Undertaking a formal conceptual framework project, leading to issue of *Statements* which are said to underlie GAAP.
Issued Interpretations to apply Opinions to specific cases	Issues Technical Bulletins for guidance on specific application problems.

EXHIBIT 4-2

Comparison Between the APB and FASB

profession, which raised the specter of a government takeover of the accounting standard-setting process. The structure committee's report reaffirmed the FASB's role as the private sector's standard-setting body and confirmed the existence of public support for the FASB in this role.[29]

The FASB adopted several organizational changes as a direct result of the structure committee's recommendations. One of the most significant was the appointment of the trustees of the FAF by a board of six electors, each representing one of the sponsoring organizations, instead of by the Board of Directors of the AICPA. Others were designed to make the FASB more responsive to user needs, and included—

- that the majority of the members of the Board are no longer required to have had the greater part of their professional experience in public accounting,
- that pronouncements of the FASB are now adopted by a simple majority, instead of five out of seven,
- that meetings of the Board, the Advisory Council, and the Foundation are now open to the public,
- that there be a major reorganization of staff duties, giving the research and technical staff more responsibility for preparing and drafting pronouncements,
- that outside capacity be used in research projects,
- that there be broadened financial support to eliminate the criticism that large donors might have undue influence,
- that special consideration be given to the needs of small businesses, in the form of differential disclosure requirements.

Another significant element of the structure committee's report was the statement that "accounting standards are not immutable truths, but are instead conventions that are accepted and used by all who are involved because they are understood to be in the best interests of all."

The changes of form initiated by the structure committee have been more marked than the recommended changes of substance. Statements and interpretations are not noticeably better than before; an early move to fund outside research was not productive; differential disclosure has been restricted to the areas of segment reporting, earnings per share and accounting for price-level changes; and the emphasis on the conventional nature of accounting standards has not resulted in any change to the audit report, which still certifies conformity with generally accepted accounting *principles*.

THE AMERICAN ACCOUNTING ASSOCIATION (AAA)

Although the AAA started life as an association of university instructors in accounting, it has long since broadened its membership to include practicing accountants in the profession, business, and government. Only one-third of its current membership consists of accounting professors. In the reorganization which started this transformation in 1935, the Executive Committee of the AAA was assigned the responsibility for creating broad, fundamental accounting principles and standards which could provide a framework for corporate financial statements. The first attempt to discharge this duty—*A Tentative Statement of Accounting Principles Underlying Corporate Financial Statements*—was, like the Sanders, Hatfield and Moore report, a mixture of standards and rules. It did, however, contain some propositions aimed at improving contemporary accounting practices.

In 1940 the AAA published Paton and Littleton's *An Introduction to Corporate Accounting Standards* which was destined to become the most influential AAA effort in this field. Paton and Littleton had been members of the original AAA Executive Committee which had prepared the 1936 Tentative Statement. The 1936 statement was revised in 1941 and again in 1948, under the title "Accounting Concepts and Standards Underlying Corporate Financial Statements." Eight supplementary statements were prepared between 1950 and 1954, clarifying or expanding on the 1948 statement.

In 1957 a fourth revision appeared, entitled "Accounting and Reporting Standards for Corporate Financial Statements—1957 Revision." Five supplementary statements to this revision were published between 1957 and 1964.

During this period, 1940-1965, the AAA also published a number of research studies, notably Louis Goldberg's *An Inquiry into the Nature of Accounting* (Monograph No. 7, 1964) and R.C. Jones' *Price-Level Changes and Financial Statements: Case Studies of Four Companies* (1955).

A new departure was taken in 1964 with the appointment of a Committee to Develop a Statement of Basic Accounting Theory. The resulting report is known as ASOBAT.[30] ASOBAT placed particular emphasis on qualitative standards and laid down basic standards of relevance, quantifiability, verifiability, and freedom from bias. These ideas were taken up by the authors of *APB Statement No. 4* and have found their way, in an expanded form, into the FASB's Statement of Financial Accounting Concepts No. 2, *Qualitative Characteristics of Accounting Information,* May 1980.

The AAA's involvement in identifying accounting standards reveals a shift from the inductive to the deductive mode of reasoning, the 1957 Revision being the transition point. The first statement placed emphasis on correcting improper current practices and while assuming the need for "a single coordinated body of accounting theory" nevertheless adopted the profession's view of accounting as a process of allocation. This Statement took the position that accounting was not a process of valuation; by 1941 the concept of value was being discussed, but in the 1940 Monograph Paton and Littleton set their faces sternly against such an idea.

The 1957 Revision proceeded from the principles of economics in general, and particularly the theory of corporation finance which had been developed from Fisherian economics. Revenue was defined as the monetary expression of the aggregate of products or services transferred to customers during a period. Assets were "aggregates of service-potentials," which become expenses (or losses) as they "expire," and stockholders equity "the residual claims to corporate assets." This framework was conspicuous in two subsequent supplementary statements, which recommended current cost for long-lived assets and replacement cost for inventories.[31]

The significance of this move from a positive to a normative theoretical framework is that it provided the profession with a rationale for the abandonment of historical cost. By identifying an attribute to be measured in money (quantities of units of future services) the way is opened up to multiplying those quantities by prices other than the ones which relate to their acquisition. The immediate response to the 1957 Revision, however, was critical, although in time much of its terminology became familiar to U.S. accountants through classroom contact during their educational experiences.

ASOBAT was a "new and different kind of effort"; its authors' ambitions went beyond anything previously attempted. They sought to occupy the field of information generally, not merely that part which can be expressed in terms of money. They arrived at propositions which would be applicable to all accounting—financial and managerial; individual, corporate, and governmental; not-for-profit enterprises, and so on. They did not restrict themselves to concepts of income and wealth, but spilled over into "the concepts arising from the growing body of knowledge about management."

This approach appears today as something of a swan song; the AAA has now confined its standard-setting activities to establishing committees for the purpose of responding to FASB Discussion Memoranda and Exposure Drafts. Empirical research in accounting has left the academic branch of the profession much less certain that it knows the answers to the very difficult questions posed in accounting theory, and the FASB disposes of so much greater resources in its conceptual framework project that competition with that project appears to some to be a futile undertaking.

OTHER CONTRIBUTIONS

The National Association of Accountants has investigated many of the same problems as the AICPA but from the viewpoint of the business executive—controller or financial vice-president. For reasons which are unclear, the NAA has failed to make an impact, in spite of several initiatives designed to improve the quality of its contributions, except perhaps in respect of foreign currency translation. Even a professed intention to place great importance on research to identify "the entire range of socioeconomic information needed by those who manage a business and by those who provide its capital" has failed to produce a tangible result.

The various associations of financial executives and analysts from time to time publish studies of accounting problems, some of which draw attention to areas avoided by the professional bodies, such as accounting for multinational corporations. It is noteworthy that the international field was neglected by the AICPA and the APB.

In other English-speaking countries there has been a comparable surge of interest in reducing the number of alternative treatments available for apparently similar transactions. The extent to which associations of accountants outside the United States have been influential in developing accounting principles, as distinct from improving the general level of accounting practice in those countries, is debatable. The Institute of Chartered Accountants in England and Wales has since 1942 issued "Recommendations on Accounting Principles" to its members. In recent years the Accounting Standards Steering Committee (ASSC), a body jointly managed by five of the principal British and Irish accounting associations, has issued exposure drafts and standards on many of the same topics as the APB and the FASB, often with contrary opinions. The Canadian Institute of Chartered Accountants has a research committee which has tended to propose more adventurous solutions than those favored by the AICPA but with little to show for its trouble. In Australia, the Institute of Chartered Accountants in Australia and the Australian Society of Accountants have both engaged in accounting research and publications, often of a high standard. Several Australian scholars enjoy considerable reputations in the United States.

Although accounting bodies outside the United States have tended to follow the APB and the FASB in selecting accounting topics for discussion, in one particular area they have taken the lead. This is the area of *current value* or *current cost* accounting which will be discussed in chapters 10 and 11. The idea of a gearing adjustment to avoid some of the unacceptable implications of accounting for inflation originated in the United Kingdom.

TOWARD INTERNATIONAL ACCOUNTING STANDARDS

A feature of accounting which has gone almost unnoticed until recent years is its international aspect.

Prior to World War II accountants from different countries met infrequently at International Congresses, starting in St. Louis in 1904. The purpose of these meetings was largely social and fraternal, although technical sessions were an important part. The largest British and American firms of public accountants already had worldwide practices. The growth of international trade, particularly international money markets, following World War II accelerated the internationalization of public accounting but did not lead to the establishment of any supra-national organization to regulate the profession.

The development of an international structure for the profession has proceeded since World War II on three levels:

1. Regular International Congresses of Accountants and regular meetings such as the Inter-American Accounting Conferences

and the Asian and Pacific Accounting Conventions. A permanent organization, the *Union Européenne des Experts Comptables Economiques et Financiers* (U. E. C.) was established in Europe. In addition to biennial congresses, it has standing committees which work toward the goal of harmonizing the public accounting, auditing, and taxation systems of the European countries, particularly those belonging to the European Common Market.

At the International Congress of 1972 a committee was entrusted with the task of coordinating public accounting worldwide. This International Coordination Committee for the Accounting Profession (ICCAP) reported in March 1976 and recommended the formation of an International Federation of Accountants (IFAC) which was established in 1978 and has its offices in New York City. IFAC is primarily concerned with modalities of professional practice throughout the world, and its first activities have been directed to laying down worldwide auditing standards.

2. The formation in 1973 of the International Accounting Standards Committee (IASC). Its nine original members had each been hosts to one of the International Congresses. With the admission of Kenyan and Egyptian professional associations in mid-1980 the number of member societies has risen to 75, from 57 countries. The IASC is headquartered in London and has pushed ahead with the process of establishing international standards for published financial statements. The IASC has published international accounting standards, and in many cases these have paralleled similar standards of the APB and the FASB. In some cases they have differed, as with accounting for research and development costs. It appears as though the accounting professional institutions have started to enforce conformity with these international accounting standards, although regrettably this is not possible in the United States, where the IASC member, the AICPA, is no longer capable of ensuring that domestic (FASB) accounting standards conform with those accepted internationally.
3. The Accountants International Study Group was organized in 1966 by the three British Institutes of Chartered Accountants, the Canadian Institute of Chartered Accountants, and the AICPA. It has published fifteen comparative studies of practices in the principal countries of the English-speaking world.[32]

The Study Group was disbanded in 1979. A Working Party established in 1978 recently proposed a formal relationship between the IASC and IFAC; this proposal will be put forward for ratification at the 1982 International Congress in Mexico.

PROSPECTS FOR THE INTERNATIONAL HARMONIZATION OF ACCOUNTING STANDARDS

As accounting standards and laws proliferate, the problem of harmonization becomes more urgent. Accounting is an international profession; financial reports prepared in one jurisdiction are used as information for investment decisions in a different one. At the present time this problem is being given serious study only in the countries of the European Economic Community, but accountants practicing internationally are well aware that it affects the world scene.

The European Economic Community (the European Common Market) has adopted a Fourth Directive on company law which contains detailed accounting and financial reporting rules, and the member states have until 1982 to bring their domestic laws and regulations into line. The French *Projet de Plan Comptable National* of 1979 was made explicitly subject to legislation which would have to be forthcoming in France to achieve this harmonization. The Fourth Directive was ten years in the making; the proposed Seventh Directive dealing with groups of companies and consolidated financial statements may take longer. However, there is no EEC mechanism for setting accounting standards outside the legal system, and the IASC cannot perform this task because many of the member bodies do not possess the requisite authority. The Organization for Economic Cooperation and Development (OECD) established an *ad hoc* working group on accounting standards, and its September 1979 report indicated that this body saw itself as a suitable institutional mechanism for European accounting harmonization.

The United Nations Commission on Transnational Corporations (more generally known as multinational corporations) set up a group of experts in 1975 to consider international standards of accounting and reporting for this type of corporation. A public report was issued in 1977 which provided lists of minimum items of financial and nonfinancial information to be included in such reports. Following this, a meeting took place in New York in February 1980 of the UN's *ad hoc* intergovernmental group of experts on international standards of accounting and reporting. About 30 governments took part, together with representatives of the EEC, OECD, IASC, IFAC, and the International Chamber of Commerce. The finance minister of the Philippines was elected chairman and the vice-chairmen were from the Netherlands and Egypt. The rapporteur was from Argentina. The group approved a restatement of paragraph 43 of the draft UN Code of Conduct for transnational corporations which resembles the OECD guidelines; the UN paper of 1977 was not discussed but may be the subject of a subsequent meeting. These developments can be followed in publications of the United Nations Economic and Social Council, notably the periodical reports of the Secretary-General on the Centre on Transnational Corporations. They show accountants being inexorably sucked into a vortex of political issues, such as those surrounding the Union of South Africa, by including corporate financial information in the various devices used to pressure certain nations into changing their governments.

CONCLUSION

Criticism of accountants prior to 1930 was largely due to a belief that there were ways in which they could improve their practices; since 1930 it has been suffused with the view that accountants have been involved in widespread management misinformation of investors. For example, theories that investor losses arising out of the Great Depression and out of the substantial recession of 1975 were directly attributable to deceptive financial reporting were principal reasons for the Securities Acts and for the Foreign Corrupt Practices Act.

The factual basis for these beliefs were examined by Dillon in a 1979 article.[33] Early SEC filings for 110 corporations listed on the New York Stock Exchange were examined for the purpose of finding the extent of asset revaluation during the period 1925-34. It was found that the conventional wisdom could not be supported; more firms revalued assets downwards during this period than revalued them upwards, and, significantly, no firm in the sample increased reported earnings by this means.

Critics are unlikely to be silenced by these factual revelations. The accountant is the modern bringer of bad news, and as in primitive times, the response of the ruler is to demand his head.

ENDNOTES

1. Storey, Reed K., *The Search for Accounting Principles—Today's Problems in Perspective,* New York: American Institute of Certified Public Accountants, 1964.
2. *A Tentative Statement of Accounting Principles Underlying Corporate Financial Statements,* revised in 1941 with the words "A Tentative Statement" omitted.
3. American Accounting Association *Monograph No. 3,* 1940.
4. Reprinted by the American Accounting Association, 1959, 1963, 1968.
5. Most, Kenneth S., *Uniform Cost Accounting and the Classification and Coding of Accounts,* London: Gee & Co. (Publishers) Ltd., 1961.
6. See the *Journal of Accountancy,* June 1919, pp. 401-33.
7. Washington, D.C.: U.S. Government Printing Office, 1929.
8. New York, January 1936.
9. May, George O., *25 Years of Accounting Responsibility,* New York: American Institute Publishing Co. Inc., 1936.
10. Byrne, Gilbert R., "To What Extent Can the Practice of Accounting be Reduced to Rules and Standards," *Journal of Accountancy,* November 1937, pp. 364-79.
11. Sanders, Hatfield, and Moore, p. xii
12. *Ibid,* p. 1
13. *Ibid,* p. 12
14. Barr, Andrew, "Accountants and the Securities Exchange Commission," *Journal of Accountancy,* April 1962, p. 33.
15. Armstrong, Marshall S., "The FASB and Emerging Practice Problems," *Journal of Accountancy,* July 1975, pp. 63-65.

16. Moonitz, Maurice, "Three Contributions to the Development of Accounting Principles Prior to 1930," *Journal of Accounting Research,* Spring 1970, p. 148.
17. Grady, Paul, "Inventory of Generally Accepted Accounting Principles for Business Enterprises," *Accounting Research Study No. 7,* New York: AICPA 1965. 1965.
18. May, George O., "Generally Accepted Principles of Accounting", *Journal of Accountancy,* January 1958, p. 26.
19. Jennings, Alvin R., "Present-Day Challenges in Financial Reporting," *Journal of Accountancy,* January 1958, pp. 29-34.
20. "Report to Council of the Special Committee on Research Program," *Journal of Accountancy,* December 1958, pp. 62-68.
21. *Ibid,* p. 64
22. Moonitz, Maurice, *The Basic Postulates of Accounting,* New York: AICPA 1961, and Sprouse, Robert T. and Maurice Moonitz, *A Tentative Set of Broad Accounting Principles for Business Enterprises,* New York: AICPA 1962.
23. Deinzer, Harvey T., *Development of Accounting Thought,* New York: Holt, Rinehart and Winston, Inc., 1965, Ch. 9.
24. Horngren, Charles T., "Accounting Principles: Private or Public Sector?" *Journal of Accountancy,* May 1972, pp. 37-41.
25. Gerboth, Dale L., "Muddling Through' with the APB," *Journal of Accountancy*, May 1972, pp. 42-49.
26. *Establishing Financial Accounting Standards,* New York: AICPA 1972.
27. Schuetze, Walter P., "The early days of the FASB," *World,* New York, Peat, Marwick, Mitchell & Co., Summer 1979, pp. 34-39.
28. *The Structure of Establishing Financial Accounting Standards,* report of the Structure Committee of the Financial Accounting Foundation, April 1977.
29. Metcalf Staff Report: Subcommittee on Reports, Accountancy and Management of the Senate Committee on Government Affairs; and Moss Subcommittee Report: Subcommittee on Oversight and Investigations of the House Committee on Interstate and Foreign Commerce.
30. American Accounting Association Committee to Prepare a Statement of Basic Accounting Theory, *A Statement of Basic Accounting Theory,* American Accounting Association, 1966.
31. Committee on Concepts and Standards—Long-Lived Assets, Supplementary Statement No. 1, "Accounting for Land, Buildings and Equipment"; Committee on Concepts and Standards—Inventory Measurement, Supplementary Statement No. 2, "A Discussion of Various Approaches to Inventory Measurement," *Accounting Review,* July 1964, pp. 693-99 and 700-14.
32. Mueller, Gerhard G. and Lauren M. Walker, "The Coming of Age of Financial Transnational Reporting," *Journal of Accountancy,* July 1976, pp. 67-74.
33. Dillon, Gadis J., "Corporate Asset Revaluations: 1925-1934," *The Accounting Historians Journal,* Spring 1979, pp. 1-15.

SELECTED ADDITIONAL READINGS

American Accounting Association Committee to Prepare a Statement of Basic Accounting Theory, *A Statement of Basic Accounting Theory,* American Accounting Association, 1966.

Arpan, Jeffrey S. and Lee H. Radebaugh, *International Accounting and Multinational Enterprises,* Boston: Warren, Gorham & Lamont, 1981, Ch. 3.

Beaver, William H., "What Should be the FASB's Objectives?" *Journal of Accountancy,* August 1973, pp. 49-56.

Bevis, Donald J., "How It Feels to be a Gored Ox," *TEMPO* (House Journal of Touche Ross & Co.) Vol. 21, No. 1, 1975, pp. 45-49.

Blough, Carman, "Development of Accounting Principles in the United States," *Berkeley Symposium on the Foundations of Financial Accounting,* Berkeley: School of Business Administration, University of California, 1967, pp. 1-14.

Burton, John C., "Some General and Specific Thoughts on the Accounting Environment," *Journal of Accountancy,* October 1973, pp. 40-46.

Byrne, Gilbert R., "To What Extent Can the Practice of Accounting be Reduced to Rules and Standards?" *Journal of Accountancy,* November 1937, pp. 364-79.

Chambers, R. J., "The Anguish of Accountants," *Journal of Accountancy,* March 1972, pp. 68-74.

Chatov, Robert, *Corporate Financial Reporting,* New York: The Free Press, 1975.

Deinzer, Harvey T., *Development of Accounting Thought,* New York: Holt, Rinehart & Winston, Inc., 1965, chs. 2, 8 and 9.

Enthoven, Adolf J. H., *Accountancy and Economic Development Policy,* New York: American Elsevier Publishing Co. Inc., 1973.

Grady, Paul, "Inventory of Generally Accepted Accounting Principles in the United States of America," *The Accounting Review,* January 1965, pp. 21-30.

Hicks, Ernest L., "APB: The First 3600 Days," *Journal of Accountancy*, September 1969, pp. 56-60.

Higgins, Thomas S., and Herman Bevis, "Generally Accepted Accounting Principles—Their Definition and Authority," *The New York Certified Public Accountant,* February 1964, pp. 93-94.

Horngren, Charles T., "Accounting Principles: Private or Public Sector?" *Journal of Accountancy*, May 1972, pp. 37-41.

May, George O., *25 Years of Accounting Responsibility,* New York: American Institute Publishing Co. Inc., 1936.

Moonitz, Maurice, "Three Contributions to the Development of Accounting Principles Prior to 1930," *Journal of Accounting Research,* Spring 1970, pp. 145-55.

Mueller, Gerhard G., and Lauren M. Walker, "The Coming of Age of Financial Transnational Reporting," *Journal of Accountancy*, July 1976, pp. 67-74.

Paton, W. A., "Earmarks of a Profession—And the APB," *Journal of Accountancy,* January 1972, pp. 37-45.

Rappaport, Louis H., *SEC Accounting Practice and Procedure,* New York: The Ronald Press Co., 2nd ed., 1963.

Report, Conclusions and Recommendations, The Committee on Auditors' Responsibilities, New York: AICPA, 1978.

"Report to Council of the Special Committee on Research Program," *Journal of Accountancy,* December 1958, pp. 62-68.

Sanders, T. H., H. R. Hatfield and U. Moore, *A Statement of Accounting Principles,* American Accounting Association, 1938.

Skousen, Fred K., *An Introduction to the SEC,* Cincinnati: South-Western Publishing Co., 1976.

Storey, Reed K., *The Search for Accounting Principles—Today's Problems in Perspective,* New York: American Institute of Certified Public Accountants, 1964.

Study on Establishment of Accounting Principles, *Establishing Financial Accounting Standards* (The Wheat Report), New York: American Institute of Certified Public Accountants, March 1972.

Zeff, Stephen A., *Forging Accounting Principles in Five Countries: A History and An Analysis of Trends,* Champaign, Ill.: Stipes Publishing Company, 1971.

United Nations Economic and Social Council, Report of the Secretary-General on the Centre on Transnational Corporations, New York: U.N., E/C 10/45, 30 April 1979.

END OF CHAPTER QUESTIONS

1. The history of the establishment of generally accepted accounting principles has been said to be one of "twists and turns." Explain why.
2. What do you understand to be the key difference between accounting *principles* and accounting *standards*?
3. Which publications were of major importance in guiding the accounting profession to the pronouncement of generally accepted accounting principles? Give a brief summary of the significant contribution of each.
4. Which institutions were the protagonists in the process of developing generally accepted accounting principles?
5. What is meant by "uniform accounting"? Why do you think that this concept did not prevail in the United States, either on an industry basis or generally, through the development of a uniform chart of accounts?
6. Discuss what is meant by "the transition from net income to profit or loss" and its significance for financial reporting.
7. What were the sources of criticism of accountants prior to the Depression, and what kinds of deficiency did they point out?
8. Discuss the contribution made by George O. May to the establishment of generally accepted accounting principles.
9. Explain how the short form of audit report used in the United States came into existence. What criticisms have been leveled against this report, and what happened to the attempt to improve it?
10. How did the search for generally accepted accounting principles begin? What was the contribution of Gilbert Byrne?
11. Analyze the accounting principles laid down by Sanders, Hatfield, and Moore, and discuss the ideas which they reveal in the light of contemporary problems of accounting theory and practice.
12. What is the Securities and Exchange Commission (SEC)? Why and how was it created? What are its powers and duties?
13. Describe the methods used by the SEC to discharge its legislated duties.

14. Explain the difference between disclosure standards and measurement standards in accounting. What is the position of the accounting profession on the responsibility for each of these two types of standard?
15. Explain why "the role of the SEC as an influence on accounting practice in the United States cannot be overstated."
16. What is meant by "substantial authoritative support"? What is the importance of this phrase to accountants?
17. Explain why the SEC's accounting rules are important to accountants who are not concerned with SEC filings.
18. What was the Committee on Accounting Procedure (CAP), and how did it contribute to GAAP?
19. Why was the CAP replaced by the APB, and how?
20. Describe the APB's contributions to (a) GAAP and (b) the development of accounting thought.
21. Why was the APB replaced by the FASB, and how?
22. How is the FASB organized, and how does the process of accounting standard-setting function?
23. How does the FASB differ from the APB, and to what extent does it suffer from the same shortcomings and encounter the same difficulties?
24. Discuss the contribution of the American Accounting Association (AAA) to the development of generally accepted accounting principles. Does this organization continue to be a contributing factor at the present time?
25. Explain the need for international accounting standards. What do you understand by the phrase "conflict of standards"? Give examples.
26. What international accounting organizations have contributed to the move toward international accounting standards? Explain the contribution of each.
27. Why did the United Nations become involved in the problems of accounting standard setting? What is the present status of UN initiatives in this regard?

5

ACCOUNTING THEORY IN THE USA BEFORE 1970

The involvement of government with accounting has had a long history. It goes back to the Code of Hammurabi, the oldest surviving legal code, dating from Babylonia of the eighteenth century B.C., which contained a clause requiring bailees to keep accounts. Its extreme form is that laid down by V.I. Lenin in his 1917 work, *The State and the Revolution*, which made accounting the primary control system for the Communist state. Between those two poles lie a variety of social uses of accounting; the United States provides us with only one example of many.

In this chapter we will examine some of the main sources of modern accounting theory, with particular reference to the influence of government through corporation laws, income taxation, and other regulatory systems. We will also look at the type of accounting theory which these brought forth.

ORIGINS OF PROBLEMS OF ACCOUNTING THEORY

Until the twentieth century the English-speaking world's approach to accounting was entirely pragmatic. Little attention was paid to theoretical or historical aspects of the subject, and even today the phrase "accounting theory" is often used to denote the accounting methods sanctioned under United States generally accepted accounting principles. Few theoretical controversies enlivened discourse among accountants prior to the 1930s, and the most celebrated of these, resulting from Jones of Bristol's claim to have invented a method of accounting which was superior to double-entry, concerned the form of records to be kept.[1] Littleton's *Accounting Evolution to 1900* is largely a description of European developments.[2]

The twentieth century has seen a radical reversal of roles. During this period a number of English-speaking countries (the United States, the United Kingdom, Australia, Canada, and New Zealand in particular) have become the leaders in developing new ideas about accounting: what it is and what it should be. In this chapter we shall attempt to trace the course of this transformation with the spotlight on accounting in the United States.[3]

Accounting was essentially a private activity when carried on by merchants, bankers, and rulers for their own benefit, or for a small group of partners. It began to affect a wider public when used for city and state government finances, beginning in Italy in the fourteenth century, and for large-scale businesses involving many investors, in nineteenth century Europe.

The need for a method of accounting to outsiders became apparent before the nineteenth century. Beginning with the sixteenth century a number of large-scale projects, such as canals and ports, were undertaken by groups of investors, often through the medium of a corporation specially chartered by the government for that purpose. Early attempts at financial reporting to these investors were given extra impetus by the Industrial Revolution.

Accounting problems requiring accounting theory for their solution began to present themselves. In order to see why, we must explain how the lengthening of the time period of production, which was the consequence of the Industrial Revolution, created a need to account for the use of factors of production separately from their acquisition.

The processes of mass production may be contrasted with those of an artisanal economy. In the latter, manufacture was accompanied by payments at every stage—for materials when the work was put in hand and for labor as the work was executed, either in the workshop or in the worker's home. The difference between the money payments and the eventual money receipt when the work was completed was called profit and had to cover the craftsman's expenses, which were virtually all domestic in nature. This concept of profit is still used by economists, even though it is a pre-industrial one. It underlies the analysis of investment situations in terms of cash flows.

In factory production, however, the nexus between acquisition and use and between production and market was broken. The manufacturer produced for an unknown customer, in advance of demand, and, therefore, could not associate the eventual selling price with specific production. He acquired raw materials, machinery, and often labor in advance of production and therefore could not identify the cost of production without making assumptions about *cost flows*. The conceptual nature of allocation has been demonstrated by Thomas, who points out the artificiality—he calls it arbitrariness—of all accounting allocations.[4]

We must also be aware of a semantic problem which exists in the United States because of the use of the word "allocation" to refer to three distinct accounting processes. The first of these is *assignment*, the identification of payments with objects. The second is *allocation*, tracing the use of objects in a production process. The third is *absorption*, tracing the use of a production process in the production of a product or service. In this section we are contrasting the simplicity of assignment with the complexity of allocation and absorption.

The immediate problems raised by the necessity to allocate and absorb costs concerned the calculation of depreciation and depreciation accounting, the valuation of inventories of work in process and finished goods and accounting for cost of goods sold, and accruals and deferrals generally, in relation to uses which preceded or followed acquisitions. In course of time the same necessity has led to a vast area of accounting problems, covering virtually the entire field of accounting, and created what one writer has referred to as "explanation strains."[5]

These strains were rendered more acute by the traditional separation of financial and cost accounting. Because of the critical importance of these allocation decisions for pricing policy, they were often retained by the proprietor of the business long after he had delegated accounting for acquisitions to a clerk.

Cost accounting went through three stages in the nineteenth century. In the first, it was performed by nonaccounting calculations illustrated by the papers of Josiah Wedgwood and Charles Babbage. In the second, the need to create order out of chaos led to the introduction of accounting method and the growth of systems of cost accounts separate from the financial accounts. These separate accounts might be reconciled with the financial accounts, or made to interlock with them through the medium of control accounts: a cost ledger control account in the financial books and a general ledger control account in the cost books. Finally, the integration of financial and cost accounts in one accounting system was achieved.[6]

THE GROWTH OF THE CORPORATION

Corporations are nothing new; the Romans used them, together with elevators, central heating, and divorce. An extensive world trade was conducted from the sixteenth century on by the chartered corporations formed by rulers and entrepreneurs in the mercantilist period. During the nineteenth century, however, and particularly in the United Kingdom and the United States, the number of commercial corporations grew at an accelerating pace, from several hundreds to tens of thousands. Laws were passed to facilitate their formation and administration and to render them accountable to the governments which gave them life.

The characteristic features of the corporation are its relatively long life (perpetual succession) and the transferability of its capital. Both of these are the consequence of it being an artificial person, but a legal person nonetheless. Because the corporation does not die, or become sick or insane, it is a convenient device for executing contracts, including contracts to supply capital for industrial undertakings. Because of the transferability of its capital, it is also an attractive device to businessmen and other investors concerned about their future liquidity needs. Add to these the bonus feature of limited liability, and the corporation becomes the irresistible instrument of business growth.

Use of the corporation as a device for channelling savings into business investment effected a separation between capital and its management, formal in the case of the "one man corporation," but very real in the case of those corporations which raised capital from a number of investors. In order to provide these "anonymous partners," as the French law called them, with some means of ascertaining what was happening to their investment, a succession of Companies Acts was legislated in the United Kingdom which required corporations to keep records and to render account to their stockholders. Most of the English-speaking world has enacted comparable legislation; only in the United States has it proved impossible to make the states, in whom the power resides, exercise social control over corporate officials. The situation is now changing slightly, as the states see the corporations as taxpayers and require accounts to be kept for the purpose of demonstrating taxable capacity.

Typically, a Companies Act would contain sections requiring accounts to be kept and financial reports to be rendered to stockholders. More important, to protect stockholders from the deception of being paid dividends to keep them quiet while the managers were losing the company's money, the law would stipulate that dividends may be paid only out of profits. This led of necessity to the preparation of period accounts, or annual financial statements, and to problems of allocation similar to those which were raised by the factory system.

As the manufacturer required information about depreciation, work in process and finished goods, and cost of sales in relation to specific products or services, so the corporation required this type of information in relation to specific periods. The major problems in financial reporting arise from segmenting the life of the firm into artificial lengths only remotely related to the time period of production. As a consequence, we find accountants adopting the *going concern* assumption, that raw materials acquired will be put into production, that work in process will be completed in the form of salable finished goods, and that finished goods will be sold at prices higher than their production costs. The going concern assumption also involves a belief that the business will continue to operate in more or less the same way until it has recovered its investments in fixed assets from its customers as part of the selling prices of its products.

The going concern assumption is one of the earliest explanatory devices found in the accounting literature in the United States. It is also known as the continuity assumption, and it is necessary to justify many accounting practices which we tend to take for granted. For example, imagine a trading concern which has purchased a large quantity of a commodity of which one-quarter remains unsold at the date when financial statements are to be prepared. Without the going concern assumption, the cost of these goods must be written off to the income statement as a loss. The assumption that the firm will be able to sell them in the future at a profit underlies the practice of valuing them at cost for inclusion among the assets in the statement of financial position.

Other assumptions which can be identified with the growth of corporate accounting are—

- The *entity* assumption, that an economic organization such as a corporation can be separated from its owners and accounted for as if it were independent from them.
- The *cost* assumption, that a resource can be represented using the price paid for it at the time it was acquired, regardless of intervening change in value.
- The *lower of cost or market* assumption (or rule), which causes us to abandon the cost assumption if the resource in question is a current asset and its market value is below cost. The lower of cost or market rule, originally restricted to inventories, has recently been extended to marketable securities by *FASB Statement No. 12*.
- The *stable monetary unit* assumption, that changes in the purchasing power of the monetary unit from one date to another, or during a period of time, are to be disregarded.

An important contribution of the corporation laws was the specification of the capital of the corporation in legal terms. The Companies Acts provided for the registration of corporations to include a description of their capital stock and for the reduction of this capital stock only by legal proceedings, under the mistaken belief that persons dealing with the corporation would be protected in some way by the maintenance of this legal fiction. A variety of ancillary problems were gradually incorporated in the statutes: how to account for amounts subscribed in excess of par; how to account for treasury stock; how contributed capital in excess of par and retained earnings could be converted into issued capital. The legal problem of *capital maintenance* was extended to emphasize the separation of income from capital through the legal rule prohibiting a corporation from paying a dividend in an amount exceeding undistributed net income to date. But this legal concept came in conflict with the concept of economic capital maintenance.

Consider the situation of the board of directors of a mill which has not paid its stockholders a dividend for several years and has virtually no retained earnings brought forward at the beginning of the current year. During this year it is necessary to make major repairs to the mill's machinery to keep its productive capacity intact. Without these repairs, the income statement will show a net income sufficient to justify a dividend; if the repairs are put in hand, it will not. The legal concept of capital maintenance, which requires a net income to cover the dividend, is in conflict with the economic concept of capital maintenance, which requires an expenditure on repairs.

In spite of legal provisions for the protection of stockholders and creditors, unscrupulous managers nevertheless found ways to make capital look like profits, to pay dividends to one set of shareholders out of capital paid in by another set, and to defraud creditors by liquidating while keeping legal capital intact. To a certain extent, they always will. One of the objectives of accounting theory is to develop rules of conduct which will make this behavior more difficult. This explains the normative nature of many propositions in accounting; they are attempts to dissuade people from behaving dishonestly.

A fascinating byway of the growth of corporations in the United States is the antitrust law. By the end of the nineteenth century a number of corporations had grown, by retention of profits or by acquisitions, to a size which represented a visible concentration of wealth and a real source of social and economic power. The name for a corporation which grows by acquiring control over other corporations is a *holding company*. In 1890 the U.S. Congress passed the Sherman Antitrust Act, to prevent corporations which did not possess powers to own stock in other corporations from acquiring control over such stock by means of a trust instrument. This forced corporations to obtain powers to own stock in other corporations directly, and a number of state corporation laws were amended to permit this. In 1914 the Clayton Act was passed, which made illegal the acquisition of stock of another corporation if this tended to reduce competition. In spite of these and other measures, mergers and acquisitions thrived and the vertical and horizontal integration of industries has been succeeded by the conglomerate, a holding company owning controlling interests in corporations operating in different industries.

The consequence of the combination of corporations was a demand for financial reports which would reveal the combined assets of the combined entity. This led to the development of consolidated financial statements as early as 1886, although the first annual report of the United States Steel Corporation in 1902 is usually acknowledged as the prototype of consolidations.

THE RAILROADS AND GOVERNMENT REGULATION

The importance of the railroads in the process of identifying accounting problems cannot be exaggerated. They were the first really large-scale enterprises spawned by the Industrial Revolution. The first capital-intensive enterprises, they presented in unmistakable terms the separation of capital and management, and they provided the first scenario for government regulation of business, including its financial statements. This resulted in large part from the misdeeds of a host of promoters who sold railroad stock and acquired control over railroad assets with no intention other than to enrich themselves.

The New York Stock Exchange dates from before the American Revolution, but only in 1866 did it prescribe that listed corporations should file their financial statements. Not until 1900 did this influence become effective. One of the principal reasons for the involvement of the New York Stock Exchange was the tremendous fluctuation in the prices of railroad stocks, a consequence of the ignorance of investors as well as the manipulations of the railroad barons.

The railroads were the center of a historic struggle which resulted in the recognition that use should be accounted for, and not merely acquisition. The railroad managers argued that regular maintenance and replacement of worn equipment would cause the permanent way and the rolling stock to last indefinitely. Depreciation was therefore not a relevant concept, and replacements should be charged to expense as incurred. This solution had obvious attractiveness, since it made the expense a discretionary item—in good years more and in lean years less or possibly none.

In 1876 the Railway Commissioners of Massachusetts required railroads to keep accounts, and by 1879 a uniform system of accounting had been adopted nationally on the initiative of the Interstate Commerce Commission (ICC). The Hepburn Act of 1906 authorized the ICC to prescribe railroad accounting, which it did in part by publishing "Classification of Operating Expenses" in 1907 and finally a complete "Accounting Classification for Steam Railroads" in 1914.

The 1907 scheme provided for depreciation to be charged to operating expenses on a monthly basis, but gave individual railroads the option not to do so (or to include accrued expenses) if, for example, they were losing money. In 1923 the ICC proposed to make depreciation accounting mandatory; the railroads opposed, using arguments which are still heard today when additional disclosure is sought—that it was unnecessary, deceptive, and impossible to calculate with accuracy. The railroads' opposition delayed the imposition of mandatory depreciation until 1932, when it was immediately suspended because of the depression. It finally came into force in 1943. The omission of depreciation was undoubtedly one of the factors which permitted railroads to operate and attract capital long after obsolescence and inefficiency had made them a burden on the economy.

The outcome of the struggle just described was irrelevant because of the development of generally accepted accounting principles in the United States, which required railroads to charge depreciation in their published financial statements. The struggle itself is important because it documents the transition from a pre-industrial to an industrial accounting system. Government regulation in the United States has had some of the effects of the Companies Acts in the United Kingdom and elsewhere, in that a number of commissions besides the ICC (the Federal Power Commission, the Federal

Communications Commission, the Federal Aviation Authority, etc.) have prescribed accounting systems for the enterprises they regulate. Although some accounting problems have been identified and solutions found through this process, the consensus is that government regulation has had an unfavorable effect on the accounting of regulated enterprises, through discouraging experimentation and innovation. Further, the accounting systems have ceased to be oriented toward disclosure, as in the unregulated sector, and have increasingly become instruments of politics. This is because the commissions have become rate makers, thus taking the pricing function out of the market. One of the principal means for a government to effect a political purpose is by fixing prices.

Thus, although a number of accounting issues have been raised by the regulation of public utilities, they can be readily explained in the context of the political problems of rate setting and do not form part of the set of issues which accounting theory seeks to explain.[7]

THE CORPORATE INCOME TAX

Perhaps the single most pervasive influence on the growth of accounting has been the corporate income tax, since it affects all business firms, large or small, incorporated or unincorporated, regulated or unregulated. Here we are concerned with the influence of the corporate income tax on the development of modern accounting theory.

The critical point is that the corporate income tax is a legal structure, and therefore the solutions to tax problems are legal solutions. To the extent that the tax laws recognize accounting solutions, accounting becomes part of the law. There is, for example, no definition of income to be found in the tax code, and the logical tendency of the taxing authority is to tax movements of cash. The first attempts at a corporate income tax in the United States, the 1909 Excise Act and the 1913 Revenue Act, measured net income as cash receipts less cash disbursements, and a battle had to be fought to establish the acceptability of accrual accounting as *the basis* for income taxation.

A striking illustration of the difference between accounting and taxation is found in the United Kingdom, where the objective is also to tax receipts, and the business accounts are accepted as a point of departure. The tax laws were laid down before the need to charge depreciation was clearly identified, and to this day, depreciation is not deductible in the U.K. However, businessmen were eventually successful in persuading the tax authority that fixed assets may be losing value through time, and the tax laws were amended to introduce *capital allowances*. These are a quite separate legal system for calculating depreciation for tax purposes, having no connection with accounting depreciation and applicable only to specified classes of depreciable fixed assets; store fixtures and office buildings are excluded. In preparing a business tax return therefore, the U.K. accountant adds back depreciation to net income and deducts a different amount, calculated according to the law.

The distinction between accounting net income and taxable income has given rise to a set of accounting problems, under the general title of *tax allocation*, to handle timing differences as distinct from permanent differences. The two income concepts are essentially distinct. It appears that the original intention of Congress in the United States was to establish a concept of taxable income which corresponded with business net income, but the harmonization of the two has become impossible. In the first place, tax avoidance through technical accounting methods created loopholes which led to legislation forbidding certain tax accounting practices; the valuation of inventories at prime cost, for example, is not permissible, however logical this might be in a specific context. In the second place, use of the income tax laws to effect a redistribution of wealth and to promote political objectives has led to the enactment of a multitude of provisions concerning what is or is not to be included in taxable income, and what may or may not be deducted therefrom.

We should not look, therefore, to the corporate income tax as a source of modern accounting theory. Its importance lies in—

1. Extending the need for accounting to many businesses which would not otherwise have prepared financial statements.
2. Influencing many businesses to adopt tax rules or guidelines for the recognition of items of revenue or expense, because of the complications involved in operating two accounting systems.[8]
3. Stimulating debate on such questions as depreciation and inventory accounting, accrual and deferral, and asset and liability valuation, by revealing alternatives to conventional practices.
4. Introducing a new subset of accounting problems, accounting for taxation, which have strained the ability of accountants to explain the application to them of accounting principles developed in a different context.
5. Distorting accounting to conform with taxation where the tax laws provide that a particular deferral or deduction may be claimed only if the requisite tax treatment becomes also the financial statement treatment. This is the situation in the United States with regard to the use of the LIFO method of determining cost of goods sold. In some countries (France, Germany) many of the items in the financial statements are there because of the requirements of the tax laws.
6. Providing a false trail for accounting theorists, such as the rule in *Eisner v. Macomber* (see chapter 7), who have been tempted to adopt legal explanations for practices found outside the legal framework.

7. Providing a source for generally accepted accounting principles applicable to inventory valuation, nonmonetary exchanges, accounting for loss contingencies, and other financial statement items.

THE ECONOMISTS

Until the nineteenth century economics was political economy; most economists were occupied in studying the production and distribution of wealth as a source of political power. By the middle of the nineteenth century some leading economists had begun to appreciate the role which industry played in creating and distributing wealth, and that some large corporations were more powerful than some political entities. Alfred Marshall in England, J.B. Clark in the United States, and Eugen von Böhm-Bawerk in Austria did empirical work on business enterprises and attempted explanations of such accounting concepts as income, capital, cost, and depreciation. The victory of the marginalist school gradually drove economic and accounting definitions of these concepts further apart.

Nevertheless, the apparent similarity of the subject matter of economic studies led some early accounting theorists to assume that the disciplines of accounting and economics were essentially one, so that accounting problems could be solved within the framework of economic theory. This assumption pervades much of the contemporary literature on accounting theory, and its origins can be traced to books written in the early years of the twentieth century.

The interests of economists lie primarily in macroeconomics, the study of the national income and its generation, and their work in microeconomics, the study of economic behavior at the level of the firm, is designed to support the major field of interest. For this reason, economists have never made the transition from the pre-industrial model of the firm, where acquisitions and uses, and capital and assets, cannot be distinguished, where financial institutions as sources of money can be disregarded, and where time can be reduced to an average or omitted entirely as a significant variable. As we have noted, this transition was accomplished by accountants in the nineteenth century and resulted in the valuation method we call allocation.

An example of the incompatibility of the marginalist school of economics with the needs of accounting theory is the problem of fixed costs. By definition, a fixed cost (such as a period rent) is paid out before any production is undertaken; its amount is constant regardless of the level of production. It can therefore never enter into the calculation of marginal cost (change in total cost) of anything produced with the facility or equipment rented. In accounting, the relationship between a fixed cost and a level of production is of the greatest interest; investment decisions are taken on the basis of an assumption about this level and one of the accountant's tasks is to provide information to validate this assumption. Without allocating fixed costs to products this cannot be done. In economics, marginal cost is *the* cost; in accounting it is only one of a number of possible costs.

One notable exception to the failure of economists to adapt to the industrial (and indeed, the post-industrial) realities was J.M. Clark.[9] Clark recognized the existence of situations in which economic valuation could not be effected by imputing marginal amounts to production inputs or outputs; he dealt specifically with the nonimputable overhead costs of manufacturing firms. Another American economist who attempted to adapt microeconomics to the industrial scene was Thorstein Veblen. Unfortunately the pioneering work of these theorists proved abortive, as their colleagues were unwilling or unable to abandon the Ricardian images on which their science was based.

The struggle to liberate economics from its restrictive assumptions is still going on. In a recent lecture given at Harvard University, no less an economist than Nicholas Kaldor, referring to the Cambridge "monists," stated that

> they believe that there is a single basic logical objection to the theory of marginal productivity that is alone sufficient to pull the rug out from under the neoclassical value theory. I am referring to the difficulty of isolating or measuring the change in the quantity of capital when the inventory of capital goods changes—which...makes it impossible to attribute to capital a marginal productivity of its own.[10]

Kaldor himself found other things in general equilibrium theory to object to besides the application of marginal productivity theory to the division between wages, interest, and profits. On the other hand, many equally distinguished economists would doubtless argue that these objections do not undermine the usefulness of economic theory for the purposes for which it was designed. Our point is that accountants who seek to base accounting theory on a foundation of economic theory must be aware of the intrinsic difficulties of doing so.

THE AMERICAN SCHOOL OF ACCOUNTING THEORY

Much the same sequence of events can be identified in other countries. The situation in the United Kingdom, where the Industrial Revolution and the income tax originated, can be contrasted with that in the United States, where government regulation played a unique role. The Anglo-American jurisdictions can be contrasted with those jurisdictions which forced financial accounting to conform to tax accounting. Nevertheless, it is noteworthy that the responses of accountants in different parts of the world to similar situations was highly comparable. By the beginning of the twentieth century the form and content of financial statements did not differ to any considerable extent throughout the Western world.

From 1930 on, however, special factors have caused the U.S. to act as a trail-blazer in the development of accounting theory. There is a distinct "American School of Accounting Theory." The characteristics of this school are (1) the involvement of a relatively large number of academics and practitioners in defining, researching, and debating accounting issues; (2) the existence of institutions which publicize and focus attention on the views of accounting theorists, for example the AICPA and the AAA; (3) the general acceptance of the neoclassical economic theory of investment, as adapted by scholars in corporation finance; and (4) an experimental approach to accounting aimed at producing a framework which will justify and explain a more significant social role for the accountant than he has appeared to play in the past.

One striking absence from this list of characteristics is research into accounting practices. Apart from the annual AICPA publication *Accounting Trends and Techniques*, annual selections of extracts from financial reports prepared by some public accounting firms, and an occasional research study undertaken by an individual, there has been very little attempt to find out what practices are used by U.S. accountants, and why. What inquiry is undertaken, apart from scholarly dissertations, sometimes lacks scientific method.

The first American author to identify himself clearly as an accounting theorist was Paton, whose seminal work was originally published as a doctoral dissertation in 1916.[11] It was Paton who emphasized the entity theory, which earlier American writers had used and Littleton has identified in nineteenth century European publications.[12] Paton pointed out in the preface to his book that "the conception of the business enterprise as in all cases a distinct entity or personality—an extension of the fiction of the corporate entity—is adopted, although not without important qualifications. . . ."

A.C. Littleton was another accounting scholar of this period whose works took an explicitly theoretical form and whose ideas contributed significantly to modern accounting thought. Both Paton and Littleton made a number of important contributions to the literature between 1925 and the latter's death in 1974; Dr. Paton is still at work in this field. The two combined forces to produce an influential monograph widely regarded as an accounting classic.[13]

Littleton's view of theory was as an explanation of practice; it was positive and not normative. Contemporary scholarship is concerned with leading practice rather than knowing it, and for this reason Littleton's contribution today appears insufficient to many. Nevertheless, it has been summarized as—

1. The inductive approach to the development of accounting knowledge,
2. The historical method of relating accounting practice to its social and economic development,
3. The development of the idea of general purpose financial statements which permitted the initial development of an organized structure of accounting thought,

4. The view of accounting theory construction as explanations of varying levels of validity of relations among concepts,
5. The comprehensive view of accounting as one common interrelated body of knowledge to be studied and examined as a single discipline.[14]

To which may be added his 1938 proposal to substitute the word "standards" for "principles," adopted by the FASB in 1973.

Littleton is now viewed as a figure of the past; current accounting scholarship adopts contrary assumptions on virtually every point. Nevertheless, his definitions and interpretations have not yet been demonstrated false and for that reason are still part of accounting theory.

During this period a number of other accounting writers occupied themselves with a variety of accounting questions. Some, such as G.O. May, Maurice E. Peloubet, Wilmer L. Green, Thomas Henry Sanders, and Perry Mason, concentrated on explaining current financial accounting practices and their origins. S. Paul Garner performed a similar service for cost accounting. DR Scott attempted to reconcile accounting with statistical method, and John B. Canning, with the economic theories of Irving Fisher. Henry W. Sweeney investigated the problems of accounting in a time of changing price-levels. Robert H. Montgomery attempted to develop a theory of auditing, and Stephen Gilman, to produce agreed definitions of accounting terms and a common concept of income.

Since 1950 the number and quality of contributions to accounting theory have increased rapidly as the subject of accounting has been firmly placed in the mainstream of academic life in American universities. In part this has been a function of an increase in the number of Ph.D.s in accounting, since the Ph.D. is generally regarded as a research degree and carries the moral obligation to continue to explore and publish after the completion of the doctoral dissertation. But many practitioners and accounting teachers who did not acquire this degree have also contributed richly to the expanding body of accountancy knowledge. It is impossible to provide a complete list in a book of this kind, but reference will be made to the work of many individuals at appropriate places. In any case, it is clear that the world has never seen a comparable concentration of talents on the problems of accounting as that in the United States during the past seventy years.

Much of this work was made possible by institutional arrangements which were ahead of the rest of the world by many decades. Public accountants established foundations which awarded funds for research and publication: Sanders, Hatfield, and Moore, for example, were commissioned by the Haskins and Sells Foundation to produce *A Statement of Accounting Principles* in 1938. The American Institute of Accountants, and its successor body, the American Institute of Certified Public Accountants, sponsored research often ignored by their committees responsible for promulgating accounting principles, and provided a forum for ideas in an official publication, the *Journal of Accountancy*. The American Accounting Association's quarterly publication *The Accounting Review*, launched in 1926, quickly became the leading vehicle for exposing new ideas and discussing theoretical problems. The AAA created a committee structure for scholars with similar research interests, who were encouraged to work together and publish jointly-authored papers. The AAA also established its monograph series, permitting outstanding scholars to publish works of high quality which would be unlikely to attract the support of a commercial publishing house. Similar support to that provided by the AICPA and the AAA was available to scholars interested in cost and management accounting from the National Association of Cost Accountants (now the National Association of Accountants) and through its journal the *NACA Bulletin*, (now called *Management Accounting*). In recent years these institutional arrangements have increased, and many other sources of support are now offered to accounting theorists in the United States.

METHODOLOGY OF ACCOUNTING THEORY FORMULATION

The view that accounting theory should consist of principles "relatively few in number" goes back a long way. It was adopted by the AIA's Joint Committee with the New York Stock Exchange, which provided the link between the pre- and post-SEC periods, and by Gilbert Byrne in his celebrated paper of 1936.[15] It is possible that economics provided the inspiration for this viewpoint; in economics the law of demand is deduced from the postulate of utility maximization, and the law of supply from the twin postulates of the production function and profit maximization.

This view contrasts sharply with the inductive approach favored by Littleton. Littleton saw the derivation of accounting principles from the observation of good accounting practices; good business practices were accompanied by good accounting practices. Although the formal structure of postulates, principles, and rules did not appear explicitly in this process, the Littleton-Chambers debate suggests that a set of normative postulates underlie Littleton's reasoning; to him, accounting was what accountants *should* do.[16]

Paton, on the other hand, summarized the postulates on which his theory was based.

1. The separate existence of the business entity from its owners or managers
2. The going concern assumption of continuity as the normal case
3. The balance sheet equation, Assets = Equities
4. The exhaustive nature of financial condition, in which every significant fact is expressed in dollars
5. The stability of the measuring unit (dollars)
6. The equivalence of cost and value on original entry
7. The transitivity of cost, which "passes over and attaches"

8. The accrual of costs, their expiry over time and attachability to production[17]

A more formal approach is that taken by Mattessich, who starts with the following definition:

> Accounting is [a discipline concerned with] the quantitative description and projection of [the] income [circulation] and [of] wealth [aggregates] by [means of] a method based on the following set of assumptions. . . .[18]
>
> There are eighteen assumptions, specifically:

1. Monetary valuation
2. Time
3. Structure (accounting as a closed system)
4. Duality (double-entry)
5. Aggregation (algebraic operations)
6. Economic objects (scarce resources)
7. Inequity of monetary claims (stability of the measuring unit)
8. Economic agents (human actors)
9. Entities (social institutions)
10. Economic transactions (movements of values)
11. Valuation (operational rules for measuring movements of values)
12. Realization (operational rules for measuring income)
13. Classification (operational rules for analyzing movements of values)
14. Data input (operating rules for bookkeeping)
15. Duration (operating rules for relating entities to time)
16. Extension (operating rules for consolidating entity accounts)
17. Materiality (operating rules for identifying data)
18. Allocation (operating rules for imputing values to parts of entities)

In spite of the elements of overlap, this is the most precise statement of assumptions which has been presented as such by an accounting theorist and from which explanations of accounting practices have been derived. However, we are moving further away from the proposition that accounting principles are few in number.

Another approach to methodology is that taken by Sterling.[19] In his book, Sterling adopts expressly and by reference economic theories of income (chapter II), price theory (chapter III), information and communication theory (chapter IV), and measurement theory (chapters V and VI). Because of the contradictions inherent in any theoretical framework it would have been preferable for Sterling to specify more closely which definitions, assumptions, and models were used in the construction of his theory, particularly because Sterling's theory is normative in nature.

APB Statement No. 4, "Basic Concepts and Accounting Principles Underlying Financial Statements of Business Enterprises" lies somewhere between these two extremes, including as it does both specific postulates and the adoption of general frames of reference as integral parts of the exposition. *APB Statement No. 4* is still an important component of accounting theory and is recognized as such by the FASB Statements of Accounting Concepts, which identify *Statement No. 4* as evidence of the state of accounting theory at the time it was published. In the context of this chapter it may be said to have attempted to integrate the sources of accounting theory enumerated here: corporate accounting; the federal income tax; neoclassical economic theory; and the writings of outstanding scholars prior to the 1970s.

APB STATEMENT NO. 4

The need for a formal structure of accounting theory was apparent to academics from the 1920s on, but the accounting profession in the United States did not appear to recognize this need until 1958. In that year the president of the AICPA called upon the Institute to establish an adequate research organization continuously to reexamine basic accounting assumptions and to develop authoritative statements.[20] A Director of Accounting Research was appointed and the publication of a series of accounting research studies commenced. Unfortunately, the AICPA did not live up to these high expectations and the first attempts to formulate an accounting theory, *Accounting Research Study No. 1* and *No. 3*, were rejected by the Accounting Principles Board which sponsored them.[21] There was a return to the piecemeal approach to formulating accounting pronouncements without reference to a general framework, but the search for such a framework was not abandoned. It resulted in the publication, in 1970, of APB *Statement No. 4*.

The questions which were addressed by *Statement No. 4* were—

- what is accounting?
- what environmental factors influence it?
- how can it provide useful information?
- what are the objectives of accounting?
- what are "generally accepted accounting principles"?

The approach taken by the authors was based primarily on observation of accounting practice, precisely because generally accepted accounting principles had not yet been formally derived. The aims of the Statement were both educational and developmental; the latter intended to provide a basis for guiding the future development of financial accounting. But the two aims were essentially distinct. The educational part contained a description of what were then generally accepted accounting practices; the developmental part contained general propositions about the environment, the objectives, and the basic features of financial accounting. The contradiction between these two aims was not resolved.

What was perhaps new was the decision to define accounting in terms of information. The first paragraph of the Statement asserts that "accounting is a service activity. Its function is to provide quantitative information, primarily financial in nature, about economic entities that is intended to be useful in making economic decisions." Financial statements are the means by which the information is periodically communicated to users. There are two basic types of information, on financial position and on changes in financial position. Financial position was defined in terms of the proprietary equation, owners' equity being a difference between assets and liabilities. Changes in financial position included the income statement, which contained the most important information. Statements of retained earnings and of other changes in owners' equity were required to complete the description of the total change in owners' equity. A statement of changes in financial position showed the major sources of increase in an enterprise's assets for a period.

The Statement subsequently laid down disclosure principles which defined basic financial statements as consisting of the above five items (the first called a balance sheet) plus descriptions of accounting policies and related notes. The audit certificate was not referred to as part of the financial statements, although most accountants would regard it as such.

Generally accepted accounting principles determine the information, how it is organized, measured, combined and adjusted, and finally, how it is presented. This information refers to economic activity; the balance sheet is concerned with economic resources and obligations together with a residual interest, and the other components of financial statements describe the effects of the economic activities which change them. However, assets, liabilities, owners' equity, revenue, expenses, and net income are related to economic elements but not identical thereto.

The following environmental postulates were introduced:

1. Financial accounting information is used by a variety of users for diverse purposes. (The Statement expressly refrains from distinguishing information from data.)
2. There is a presumption that a significant number of users need similar information.
3. All societies engage in production, income distribution, exchange, consumption, saving, and investment.
4. In the United States most productive activity is by investor-owned business enterprises of a complex kind. This complexity is a function of
   a. Continuity of economic activity (underlying the need for allocation)
   b. Jointness of products (underlying the need for arbitrary assumptions)

c. Uncertainty

5. Modern economies function within a stabilizing framework of law, custom, and tradition affecting corporate existence and contractual rights and obligations.

The Statement provides the following definitions:

1. *Economic resources*—Scarce means, consisting of productive resources (owned and leased), products, money, claims to money, and ownership interests in other enterprises.
2. *Economic obligations*—Present responsibilities to transfer economic resources to other entities in the future.
3. *Residual interests*—Economic resources minus economic obligations.
4. *Economic events*—Acquisition and disposal of resources, incurrence and discharge of obligations, and changes in the utility or prices of resources held. These are classified into external and internal events; the former include exchanges and nonreciprocal transfers, and the latter, production and casualties. Although the classification is intended to be complete and to avoid overlapping, it will be observed that there is no place for waste (economic theory likewise abstracts from waste), and casualty losses could as readily be classified as external events.
5. *Cost*—Economic cost is the sacrifice incurred in economic activities.

At least one distinguished economist has argued that accounting and economics are so unrelated that the methodology of the former should not be made dependent upon the definitions and concepts of the latter.[22]

Do the general-purpose financial statements which accountants produce fulfill the objectives of providing information which is useful for economic decisions? The Statement provided an answer.

> The objectives of financial accounting and financial statements are at least partially achieved at present, although improvement is probably possible in connection with each of them.

The Statement listed the basic features and basic elements of financial accounting, which are shown in Table 5-1. The similarity between the basic features and the assumptions of Paton and Mattessich is apparent. It is not indicated how these assumptions are to be combined with the objectives in order to arrive at the economic elements recognized and measured in the form of the basic elements.

There are three types of generally accepted accounting principles.

- *Pervasive*, which embrace measurement principles and modifying conventions

TABLE 5-1

APB Statement No. 4

Basic Features of Financial Accounting	Basic Elements of Financial Accounting
1. The accounting entity	Assets
2. The going concern	Liabilities
3. Measurement of economic resources and obligations	Owners' equity
4. Time periods	Other Balance Sheet elements (commitments, contingencies and other financial matters)
5. Money measurement	Revenue
6. Accrual	Expenses
7. Exchange price as the "basis" for financial accounting measurements	Net income (net loss)
8. Approximation (allocation)	
9. Judgment required	
10. General-purpose financial information	
11. Fundamentally related financial statements (double entry system)	
12. Substance over form	
13. Materiality	
+	
Objectives	
=	
Economic elements recognized and measured in the form of the Basic Elements	

- *Broad operating*, which are principles of selection, measurement, and presentation generally
- *Detailed*, the rules and procedures laid down for the application of broad operating principles

All three types of principles are conventional and emphasize verifiable measures, and are based on assumptions that certain causal relationships exist and can be traced. They are illustrated below. The Statement emphasized that "no attempt is made... to indicate specific relationships between principles" nor indeed, between postulates, objectives, basic features, and elements, as these terms are used in the Statement. The pervasive principles "establish the basis for implementing accrual accounting" and determine (1) the types of events to be recognized, (2) the bases on which to measure the events, (3) the time periods with which to identify the events, and (4) the common denomination of measurement. The pervasive principles are six in number.

Pervasive principles Since these are relatively few in number, we shall list them all.

P-1. Initial recording of assets and liabilities "generally...on the basis of *events* in which the enterprise acquires resources...or incurs obligations...the assets and liabilities are measured by the *exchange* prices at which the *transfers* take place." (emphasis supplied) The events do not include own construction of assets.

P-2. Revenue recognition requires (1) that the earning process be complete and (2) that an exchange has taken place. [Note: this was a new realization assumption and did not correspond with current generally accepted accounting principles.]

P-3. *Some* costs are recognized as expenses on the basis of a presumed direct association with specific revenue. (The *matching* principle)

P-4. In the absence of a direct cause and effect measurement *some* costs are allocated to periods using a systematic and rational relationship to benefits.

P-5. *Some* costs are expenses because no future benefits are likely, or allocation between periods seems pointless.

P-6. The U.S. dollar is the unit of measure in the United States. Changes in its general purchasing power are not recorded in the basic financial statements. [This is an example of a principle which is clearly incompatible with the economic theories of the developmental section, and the Statement refers to the use of LIFO and accelerated depreciation in the U.S. as attempts to minimize the effects of not recording changes in purchasing power.]

Modifying conventions have evolved to mitigate the unwanted effects of rigidly applying these pervasive measurement principles. They are: *conservatism* (understatement of net assets and net income preferred to overstatement); *emphasis on income* (the income statement takes precedence over the balance sheet); *judgment of the accounting profession* may modify the principles, by approving measurements which are in direct conflict with the fundamental, pervasive, accounting principles of measurement.

Broad operating principles are much more numerous, and we will therefore illustrate these by listing those relating to balance sheet items. In so doing we will follow the Statement by placing measurement principles together with selection principles. (p. 141).

This sample of broad operating principles of selection and measurement reveals the difficulty of rationalizing and explaining what were, in 1970 (and still are, to a great extent), generally accepted accounting practices.

The third category of broad operating principles are those of presentation, that is, those necessary to meet qualitative standards of "fair presentation in accordance with generally accepted accounting principles." There are twelve of these principles; we have already mentioned the first, which laid down the meaning of "basic financial

Broad Operating Principles

1. *of selection*	2. *of measurement*
S-1 Exchanges are recorded	M-1 at exchange prices
S-1A Resources acquired in exchanges are recorded as assets	M-1A at exchange prices

(but money and claims to money are recorded at their face amount or sometimes at their discounted amount).

1. *of selection*	2. *of measurement*
	M-1A at fair value if no money changes hands, or in the case of a "bundle" purchase, or if goodwill acquired.
S-1B Disposal of assets in exchanges recorded as decreases in assets	M-1B at recorded amounts
S-1C Obligations incurred in exchanges are recorded as liabilities	M-1C at amounts established in the exchanges
S-1D Decreases in liabilities are recorded when they are paid or replaced by other liabilities or otherwise.	M-1D at recorded amounts
S-1E Commitments are not recorded until one party at least partially fulfills its commitment, except for some leases and losses on firm commitments.	No measurement principle stated

statements." Others were aimed at ensuring completeness. The basic time period was defined as one year, and consolidated financial statements were said to be "usually" necessary if one of a group of enterprises owns more than 50% of the outstanding voting stock of the others. Equity accounting and foreign currency translation were mentioned. Of particular interest at the present time, because of attacks on the concept of working capital, is the following principle.

> R-9A *Working capital*. Disclosure of components of working capital (current assets less current liabilities) is presumed to be useful in manufacturing, trading, and some service enterprises.

As an aside, this principle contained a note (3) which illustrates nicely the difficulty of making progress in defining accounting concepts. The note states that the difference between current assets and liabilities is sometimes described as *net working capital* because the term *working capital* is sometimes used to describe current assets alone. It is obviously incorrect to use one term, which refers to a precise construct, to describe another precise construct which has its own unique name.

The section of principles of presentation went on to state the rules for offsetting assets and liabilities, for showing gains and losses separately from revenue and expenses, and for other financial statement disclosures.

The Statement concluded by pointing to ways in which generally accepted accounting principles might change, even the pervasive and broad operating principles, in response to changes in economic and social conditions, technology, and user demands. Orderly change depended upon the consistency of proposed principles with the general tenor of the Statement.

Suggestions for change included (1) eliminating differences in accounting practices not justified by differences in circumstances, (2) making accounting principles more consistent internally, (3) improving their effectiveness, and (4) reflecting more adequately the economic activities represented. Specific proposals related to including commitments, contracts, and leases in financial statements as assets and liabilities; developing unique methods for charging costs, including depreciation, against revenue; recording revenue under the accretion method; substituting output values for input values; recognizing price-level changes; and including budgets as part of the basic financial statements.

Other proposals concerned new financial statements; use of ratios in place of money amounts; more effective visual communication by graphs and charts. The Statement also pointed toward the development of international accounting standards, the world equivalent of generally accepted accounting principles.

CONCLUSION

We have examined APB *Statement No. 4* at length because it represented, as late as 1970, the current state of accounting theory.[23] As we shall see in chapter 6 and in subsequent chapters on the financial statements and their basic elements, the conceptual framework proposed by the FASB is not too far removed from *Statement No. 4*. The Statement is noteworthy because it adopted explicitly user needs as the objective of accounting, and introduced the concept of an attribute to be measured, which has become a central issue in the movement toward accounting for price-level changes.

The Statement also revealed the need to rationalize existing practices, which is strongly indicative of resistance to change. Many of the ideas it contains are phrased in ambiguous or unclear terms, indicative of a desire not to confront conceptual issues which might prove controversial. The term "economic reality" is attractive, but it means different things to different users. Some see the outlines of events perceived dimly through the "veil of money." Others interpret it to mean replacement cost, net realizable value, present value, future cash flows, physical goods and services, or "real values"; this last term is usually undefined. The attempt to root accounting concepts in economic theory was misguided; economists and accountants study the same phenomena, but for different purposes.

This point was acknowledged by the chairman of the FASB, Donald J. Kirk, at an FASB public hearing on the subject of accounting for foreign currency translation which was held in December 1980. People disagree on what constitutes information useful for investment and credit decisions; they disagree on what accounting information is consistent with economic reality. "Economic reality may be as elusive as is a popular answer to this controversial subject.... We all must recognize the limits of accounting information to portray economic reality."

ENDNOTES

1. Jones, Edward Thomas, *English System of Bookkeeping by Single or Double Entry*, 1796; available from World Microfilms Publications, London.
2. Littleton, A.C., *Accounting Evolution to 1900*, New York: American Institute Publishing Co. Inc., 1933. See also Littleton, A.C., *Structure of Accounting Theory*, American Accounting Association, 1953.
3. Chatfield, Michael, *A History of Accounting Thought*, Hinsdale, Ill.: The Dryden Press, 1974, chs. 8-11.
4. Thomas, Arthur L., *The Allocation Problem: Part Two*, Studies in Accounting Research No. 9, American Accounting Association, 1974.
5. Deinzer, Harvey T., "Explanation Strains in Financial Accounting," *The Accounting Review*, January 1966, pp. 21-31.
6. Sowell, Ellis Mast, *The Evolution of Theories and Techniques of Standard Costs*, Alabama, 1973.
7. The financial and accounting problems of the railroads were brilliantly exposed by A.S. Dewing in *Financial Policy of Corporations*, New York: The Ronald Press Co., 5th ed., 1953.
8. A list of the items in the financial statements of 44 corporations reporting in 1954/55 which were seen as providing examples of the influence of income taxation on accounting was provided by Peter A. Firmin in his doctoral dissertation, *Some Manifestations of the Influence of the Provisions of the Federal Income Tax on Generally Accepted Accounting Practices*, Michigan, 1957.
9. Clark, J.M., *Studies in the Economics of Overhead Cost*, Chicago, 1923.
10. Kaldor, Nicholas, "What is Wrong with Economic Theory?" *The Quarterly Journal of Economics*, August 1975, pp. 347-57.
11. Paton, William Andrew, *Accounting Theory*, New York: The Ronald Press, 1922.
12. *Ibid*.
13. Paton, W.A. and A.C. Littleton, *An Introduction to Corporate Accounting Standards*, Monograph No. 3, American Accounting Association, 1940.
14. Bedford, Norton M. and Richard E. Zeigler, "The Contribution of A.C. Littleton to Accounting Thought and Practice," *The Accounting Review*, July, 1975, p. 443.
15. Byrne, Gilbert R., "To What Extent Can the Practice of Accounting be Reduced to Rules and Standards?" *Journal of Accountancy*, November 1937, pp. 364-79.

16. Chambers, R.J., "Blueprint for a Theory of Accounting," *Accounting Research*, Vol. 6, 1955, pp. 17-25; A.C. Littleton, "Choice Among Alternatives," *The Accounting Review*, July 1956, pp. 363-70; Chambers, R.J., "Detail for a Blueprint," *The Accounting Review*, April 1957, pp. 206-15.
17. Paton, op. cit.
18. Mattessich, Richard, *Accounting and Analytical Methods*, Homewood, Ill.: Richard D. Irwin, Inc., 1964. The parentheses identify redundancies.
19. Sterling, Robert R., *Theory of the Measurement of Enterprise Income*, Kansas, 1970.
20. Jennings, Alvin R., "Present-Day Challenges in Financial Reporting," *Journal of Accountancy*, January 1958, pp. 28-34.
21. Accounting Research Study No. 1, *The Basic Postulates of Accounting*, by Maurice Moonitz and No. 3, *A Tentative Set of Broad Accounting Principles for Business Enterprises*, by Robert T. Sprouse and Maurice Moonitz were rejected by the APB in *APB Statement No. 1*.
22. Boulding, Kenneth E., "Economics and Accounting: The Uncongenial Twins," in *Studies in Accounting Theory*, ed. W.T. Baxter and Sidney Davidson, Homewood, Ill.: Richard D. Irwin, Inc., 1962, pp. 44-55.
23. The FASB Statements of Financial Accounting Concepts contain the following note: "Pronouncements such as APB Statement No. 4, *Basic Concepts and Accounting Principles Underlying Financial Statements of Business Enterprises*, and the Accounting Terminology Bulletins will continue to serve their intended purpose—they describe objectives and concepts underlying standards and practices existing at the time of their issuance."

SELECTED ADDITIONAL READINGS

Accounting Principles Board, *Statement No. 4*, New York: AICPA, 1970.

Arnett, Harold E., "Taxable Income vs. Financial Income: How Much Uniformity Can We Stand?" *The Accounting Review*, July 1969, pp. 482-94.

Arnold, Jerry L. and Earl C. Keller, "The Influence of Accounting Rules on Tax Policy Objectives: An Empirical Investigation," *The Journal of the American Taxation Association*, Winter 1980, pp. 10-15.

American Accounting Association Committee on Concepts and Standards, "Accounting Principles and Taxable Income," *The Accounting Review*, October 1952, pp. 427-30.

Canning, John B., *The Economics of Accountancy*, New York: The Ronald Press, 1929.

Carey, John L., *The Rise of the Accounting Profession*, New York: American Institute of Certified Public Accountants, Vol. 1, 1969 and Vol. 2, 1970.

Chambers, Raymond J., *Accounting, Evaluation and Economic Behavior*, Englewood Cliffs, N.J.: Prentice-Hall, Inc., 1966.

Chatfield, Michael, *A History of Accounting Thought*, Hinsdale, Ill.: Dryden Press, 1974.

————, ed., *Contemporary Studies in the Evolution of Accounting Thought*, Belmont, California: Dickenson Publishing Co., 1968.

Deinzer, Harvey T., *Development of Accounting Thought*, New York: Holt, Rinehart and Winston, Inc., 1965.

Deinzer, Harvey T., *The American Accounting Association-Sponsored Statements of Standards for Corporate Financial Reports*, College of Business Administration, University of Florida, 1964.

Gilman, Stephen, *Accounting Concepts of Profit*, New York: The Ronald Press, 1939.

Hackney, William P., "Accounting Principles in Corporation Law," *Law and Contemporary Problems*, Autumn 1965, pp. 791-823.

Ijiri, Yuji, *Theory of Accounting Measurement*, American Accounting Association, 1975.

———, "Critique of the APB Fundamentals Statement," *Journal of Accountancy*, November 1971, pp. 43-50.

Lambert, Samuel Joseph III, "Basic Assumptions in Accounting Theory Construction," *Journal of Accountancy*, February 1974, pp. 41-48.

Littleton, A.C., *Structure of Accounting Theory*, Monograph No. 5, American Accounting Association, 1953.

———, and V.K. Zimmerman, *Accounting Theory: Continuity and Change*, Englewood Cliffs, N.J.: Prentice-Hall, Inc., 1962, pp. 1-102.

Paton, William Andrew, *Accounting Theory*, 1922, repr. Lawrence, Kansas: Scholars Book Co. 1973.

———, and A.C. Littleton, *An Introduction to Corporate Accounting Standards*, Monograph No. 3, American Accounting Association, 1940.

Previts, Gary John and Barbara D. Merino, *A History of Accounting in America: An Historical Interpretation of the Cultural Significance of Accounting*. New York: The Ronald Press, 1979.

Stabler, Henry Francis, *George O. May: A Study of Selected Contributions to Accounting Thought*, Atlanta: Georgia State University, 1977.

Staubus, George J., "An Analysis of APB Statement No. 4," *Journal of Accountancy*, February 1972, pp. 36-43.

Solomons, David, "Economic and Accounting Concepts of Income," *The Accounting Review*, July 1961, pp. 374-83.

———, "Economic and Accounting Concepts of Cost and Value," *Modern Accounting Theory*, ed. Morton Backer, Englewood Cliffs, N.J.: Prentice-Hall, Inc., 1966, pp. 117-40.

END OF CHAPTER QUESTIONS

1. How did the need for accounting allocations arise?
2. Explain two different reasons for allocation, one based on the need to calculate costs, and the other based on the need to determine period income.
3. Explain the "going concern assumption" fully, with particular reference to asset valuation.

4. List and describe other assumptions which were made (and continue to be made) by accountants in order to prepare financial reports for corporations.
5. What are the legal and economic concepts of capital maintenance? How can they be in conflict?
6. The corporate income tax influences accounting practice in subtle ways. Discuss this proposition with particular reference to (a) inventories, (b) nonmonetary exchanges, (c) depreciation, (d) imputing interest on receivables and payables, and (e) income tax allocation.
7. "Economic theory properly underlies all accounting theory and practice." Do you agree?
8. What are the principal contributions made by the income tax laws to the development of accounting thought?
9. It is usual for developments in the sciences to be the result of a synthesis between observation of what is and speculation about what might be. On the other hand, T.S. Eliot defined poetry as "the assimilation of tradition and the exercise of the individual talent." Does the development of accounting thought indicate whether accounting is an art, like poetry, or a science?
11. Compare and contrast the inductive method of arriving at accounting standards with the axiomatic method, the latter defined as the attempt to derive general propositions from a few basic principles (= assumptions).
12. Compare and contrast the assumptions of Paton, Mattessich, and the authors of *APB Statement No. 4*.
13. What are the "basic financial statements"? Is there any difference between your answer and that given by *APB Statement No. 4?*
14. Explain the relationship between the three kinds of principles postulated by *APB Statement No. 4,* viz: pervasive, broad operating, and detailed. Give examples of each.
15. What is the current status of *APB Statement No. 4* in relation to the FASB's conceptual framework project?

6

THE OBJECTIVES OF ACCOUNTING AND FINANCIAL REPORTING

The belief that financial reporting standards can only be useful and effective if they are seen to be based upon agreed objectives appears to have found widespread acceptance during the past decade. This can be seen in the work of both the APB and the FASB, starting with *APB Statement No. 4* and culminating in the publication of the FASB's *Statement of Financial Accounting Concepts No. 1*.

Prior to this development, attention had been directed to the financial statements themselves as the objectives of the accounting and financial reporting process. Acceptance of the wider view, that the preparation of financial reports must proceed from a perception of user needs, leads to consideration of two subsidiary alternatives—

- Providing information for unknown users having multiple decision objectives, or
- Providing information for specific user groups having a known decision objective.

The former implies *general purpose financial reporting* which contains data rather than information as such; this data is transformed into information by the user. General purpose financial reporting is the objective adopted by *FASB Statement of Financial Accounting Concepts No. 1*. The latter implies special purpose financial statements addressed to specified users; because their needs and decision processes are assumed to be known, these statements would contain information relevant to their particular decision models, or "different figures for different purposes." So far this approach has not proved capable of being made operational.

An interesting example of the difference between these two viewpoints is found in the field of transnational financial reporting. This involves the publication in a particular country of financial statements originating in, and prepared in accordance with the financial accounting principles of, another country. The alternatives are—

- The single domicile approach, under which essentially the same financial statements are issued in the foreign country, differing from the domestic financial statements only by being translated into another language, and sometimes by expressing money amounts in the foreign country's currency, and
- The primary and secondary statements approach, with different financial statements being issued in the two countries, prepared according to the accounting principles of each, with or without translation of currency amounts.

Both practices are in general use, and so far no attempt has been made to establish international accounting standards in this regard.

THE WHEAT AND TRUEBLOOD COMMITTEES

APB Statement No. 4 contained a section on objectives which will be discussed later in this chapter. The immediate reason for *FASB Statement of Financial Accounting Concepts No. 1*, however, can be appreciated only in relation to the birth of the FASB.

In response to criticisms of corporate financial reporting and the lack of a framework for developing accounting principles, in April 1971 the president of the AICPA announced the formation of two study groups. One was called "The Study Group on the Objectives of Financial Statements," the other "The Study Group on the Establishment of Accounting Principles." The objectives study group was headed by Robert M. Trueblood, a practicing public accountant, and became known as "The Trueblood Committee." The principles study group was headed by Francis M. Wheat, a former Securities and Exchange commissioner and critic of the accountancy profession, and became known as "The Wheat Committee."

These actions followed a conference of thirty-five prominent CPAs, representing twenty-one major accounting firms, held in Washington, D.C. in January 1971. The crucial issues raised by this conference included the desirability of undertaking a broad review of how accounting principles should be established. It was intended that the Wheat and Trueblood Committees should report at approximately the same time, and that the Trueblood Committee's statement of objectives should support the Wheat Committee's recommendations. The Wheat Committee reported in March 1972, but the report of the Trueblood Committee did not appear until October 1973. The Wheat Committee report and its consequences were discussed in chapter 4.

In its charge to the Trueblood Committee the Board of Directors of the AICPA laid down four questions to be considered by the study group.

1. Who needs financial statements?
2. What information do they need?
3. How much of the needed information can be provided by accountants?
4. What framework is required to provide the needed information?

To answer these questions the Trueblood Committee assembled a staff of academicians, practitioners, and consultants, solicited the views of more than 5,000 corporations and other organizations, conducted more than 50 interviews and held 35 meetings with institutional and professional groups and a three-day public hearing in New York.[1]

THE TRUEBLOOD COMMITTEE OBJECTIVES

The Trueblood Report contained twelve objectives which were stated within a context of assumptions and argument purporting to support the objectives and underline their logical derivation. As Anton has demonstrated, they can be viewed as a hierarchy,[2] the principal objective being stated in these terms: "The basic objective of financial statements is to provide information useful for making economic decisions."

As a general proposition this objective acquires its meaning from the further objectives stated in the report which Anton refers to as: identifying users and uses, specifying information needed, and implementing. The report also contains nine "imperative recommendations" and two "nonhierarchical" objectives, the latter relating to governmental and not-for-profit organizations and to social reporting. The further objectives are as follows:

TRUEBLOOD COMMITTEE OBJECTIVES

Identifying Users And Uses

An objective of financial statements is to serve primarily those users who have limited authority, ability, or resources to obtain information and who rely on financial statements as their principal source of information about an enterprise's economic activity.

An objective of financial statements is to provide information useful to investors and creditors for predicting, comparing, and evaluating potential cash flows to them in terms of amount, timing, and related uncertainty.

Specifying Information Needed

An objective of financial statements is to provide users with information for predicting, comparing, and evaluating enterprise earning power.

An objective of financial statements is to supply information useful in judging management's ability to utilize enterprise resources effectively in achieving the primary enterprise goal.

Implementing

An objective of financial statements is to provide factual and interpretive information about transactions and other events which is useful for predicting, comparing, and evaluating enterprise earning power. Basic underlying assumptions with respect to matters subject to interpretation, evaluation, prediction, or estimation should be disclosed.

An objective is to provide a statement of financial position useful for predicting, comparing, and evaluating enterprise earning power. This statement should provide information concerning enterprise transactions and other events that are part of incomplete earnings cycles. Current values should also be reported when they differ significantly from historical cost. Assets and liabilities should be grouped or segregated by the relative uncertainty of the amount and timing of prospective realization or liquidation.

An objective is to provide a statement of periodic earnings useful for predicting, comparing, and evaluating enterprise earning power. The net result of completed earnings cycles and enterprise activities resulting in recognizable progress toward completion of incomplete cycles should be reported. Changes in the values reflected in successive statements of financial position should also be reported, but separately, since they differ in terms of their certainty of realization.

An objective is to provide a statement of financial activities useful for predicting, comparing, and evaluating enterprise earning power. This statement should report mainly on factual aspects of enterprise transactions having or expected to have significant cash consequences. This statement should report data that require minimal judgment and interpretation by the preparer.

An objective of financial statements is to provide information useful for the predictive process. Financial forecasts should be provided when they will enhance the reliability of users' predictions.

The nine imperative recommendations are a mixture of disclosure standards, valuation methods, postulates concerning the production process, and behavioral assumptions. The two nonhierarchial objectives are as follows:

- An objective of financial statements for governmental and not-for-profit organizations is to provide information useful for evaluating the effectiveness of the management of resources in achieving the organization's goals. Performance measures should be quantified in terms of identified goals.
- An objective of financial statements is to report on those activities of the enterprise affecting society which can be determined and described or measured and which are important to the role of the enterprise in its social environment.

The Trueblood Report also presented, in a separate chapter, seven qualitative characteristics which financial statement information should possess in order to satisfy user needs.

1. Relevance and Materiality
2. Substance rather than Form
3. Reliability
4. Freedom from Bias
5. Comparability
6. Consistency
7. Understandability

Of these last items, the FASB has separated two of them (qualitative characteristics and objectives of financial reporting by nonbusiness organizations) to become the subject matter of *Statements of Financial Accounting Concepts Nos. 2* and *4*, respectively. Social accountability remains a controversial issue, which will be discussed in chapter 17.

PREDECESSORS OF THE TRUEBLOOD COMMITTEE OBJECTIVES

The thrust of the basic objective can be traced to Staubus' pioneering work *A Theory of Accounting to Investors*.[3] However, the Trueblood Report was directly influenced to a very considerable extent by chapter 4 of *APB Statement No. 4* on the objectives of financial statements. This chapter divided objectives into particular, general, and qualitative, and placed them under a set of constraints. The following paragraphs summarize the chapter.

PARTICULAR OBJECTIVE

To present fairly in conformity with generally accepted accounting principles, financial position, results of operations, and other changes in financial position.

GENERAL OBJECTIVES

1. To provide reliable information about economic resources and obligations of a business

   a. To evaluate its strengths and weaknesses
   b. To reveal its financing and investment
   c. To evaluate its solvency
   d. To demonstrate its resource base for expansion
2. To provide reliable information about changes in net resources* resulting from its profit-directed activities
   a. To indicate to investors expected dividend return.
   b. Successful operations indicate to creditors that they will be paid, employees that they will receive employment, government that it will collect taxes.
   c. To provide management with planning and evaluation information.
   d. To help users make predictions about earning potential.
3. To provide other information about changes in economic resources
4. To provide other information relevant to financial statement users' needs

* in context, resources minus obligations, or residual equity.

QUALITATIVE OBJECTIVES

1. Relevance to common needs of users is primary.
2. Understandability (but users must have "some understanding").
3. Verifiability, which involves specifying attributes to be measured and measurement methods.
4. Neutrality—absence of bias toward particular user needs.
5. Timeliness—for economic decisions.
6. Comparability—differences should not be the result of financial accounting treatment.
7. Completeness—"reasonable" in order to fulfill the other qualitative objectives.

The comparability objective covers form, content, accounting principles, and disclosure of changes in principles or circumstances. Consistency is an important factor in attaining comparability, which also requires identifying circumstances necessitating a particular accounting principle or method and eliminating alternatives under these circumstances.

Constraints on achieving the objectives consist of conflicts of objectives (relevance being primary); environmental influences (user needs v. cost of satisfying them); and incomplete understanding of the objectives, that is, human error. The Statement concluded that, notwithstanding these constraints, "the objectives of financial accounting and financial statements are at least partially achieved at present." The basic purpose was to provide quantitative financial information about a business enterprise that is useful to statement users, particularly owners and creditors, in making economic decisions.

Decision-usefulness is presumably a characteristic which can be tested, and it is interesting to observe that the period which preceded the publication of *APB Statement No. 4* also saw the first publications of results of testing the efficient market hypothesis. The accounting implications of the efficient market hypothesis were discussed in chapter 3. Briefly, supporters of this hypothesis regard securities markets as efficient in the sense that prices fully reflect publicly available information about the securities traded, and react virtually instantaneously to new information. Thus no individual buyer or seller can profit from information (earn excess returns), and, therefore, financial reports are not useful for investment decisions designed to permit the decision maker to earn more than a normal return on investment. An abnormal return cannot be obtained by studying annual reports.

It is not certain, however, that securities markets are efficient, for which information availability is a necessary but not a sufficient condition. Some traders do make abnormal returns, some consistently. There are conceptual and methodological problems associated with efficient market research which affect the interpretation of research findings. Evidence relating to some markets (the American Stock Exchange; Over-the-counter) is less than unequivocal. "In general, those who are disposed to accept the hypothesis find all of the support they need in existing evidence, while those who reject it also find support for their beliefs."[4]

THE FASB STATEMENT ON OBJECTIVES

FASB Statement of Financial Accounting Concepts No. 1, entitled "Objectives of Financial Reporting by Business Enterprises," was issued in November 1978. It laid down the following objectives:

1. To provide information which is useful to investors, creditors, and others in making rational decisions.
2. To assist investors and creditors in assessing future net cash flows to the enterprise in respect of amount, timing, and uncertainty.
3. To identify entity resources (assets) and claims against resources, both creditor claims (liabilities) and owner claims (owners' equity).
4. To provide information about enterprise performance and earnings potential.
5. To show how an enterprise obtains resources and what it uses them for.

In this list, the second has been most widely quoted as *the* objective laid down by the FASB and, therefore, deserves fuller quotation.

> Financial reporting should provide information to help present and potential investors and creditors and other users in assessing the amounts, timing and uncertainty of prospective cash receipts from dividends or interest and the proceeds from the sale, redemption or maturity of securities or loans. The prospects for those cash receipts are affected by an enterprise's ability to generate enough cash to meet its obligations when due and its other cash operating needs, to reinvest in operations, and to pay cash dividends and may also be affected by perceptions of investors and creditors generally about that ability, which may affect market prices of the enterprise's securities. Thus, financial reporting should provide information to help investors, creditors, and others assess the amounts, timing, and uncertainty of prospective net cash inflows to the related enterprise. (para. 37)

As suggested earlier, and subsequently confirmed by the FASB, the Trueblood Report was intended as guidance when accounting standards were being formulated. The idea was then for the FASB's standards to contribute to the achievement of the objectives of financial reporting. That seven years went by between the establishment of the FASB and the publication of a statement of the objectives of financial reporting, years which saw the publication of over thirty Standards and a similar number of Interpretations, might be viewed as a handicap. In one respect, at least, it proved a blessing.

One of the Trueblood objectives was "to provide information useful to investors and creditors for predicting, comparing and evaluating potential cash flows to them in terms of amount, timing and related uncertainty." Another spoke to the need to distinguish between "completed earnings cycles" and "uncompleted earnings cycles." Some commentators interpreted this to mean that the authors of the Trueblood Report were advocating a return to cash accounting in order to evade the uncertainties and allocations necessitated by accrual accounting, an impression which some members of the Trueblood Committee reinforced with their public utterances. *FASB Statement of Financial Accounting Concepts No. 1* corrected this by firmly adopting accrual accounting as the necessary basis for financial reporting.

The Statement asserts that "accrual accounting attempts to record the financial effects on an enterprise of transactions and other events and circumstances that have cash consequences for the enterprise in the periods in which those transactions, events and circumstances occur rather than only in the periods in which cash is received or paid by the enterprise." The reason for accrual accounting is clearly stated, even though the need to tie it to cash consequences is redundant. The Statement goes on to say, "Thus, accrual accounting is based not only on cash transactions but also on credit transactions, barter exchanges, changes in prices, changes in form of assets or liabilities and other transactions, events and circumstances that have cash consequences for an enterprise but involve no concurrent cash movement." Note that an exchange of one similar asset for another has no cash consequences, unless we define cash consequences so as to include the absence of a cash receipt or payment.

In one connection the Statement came too late, however. The SEC in 1978 required oil and gas producing companies to base supplementary financial statements on economic accounting principles, a form known as Reserve Recognition Accounting (see chapter 8). In the publication announcing this decision, the SEC stated that

> Because historical costs do not furnish meaningful information concerning economic resources of oil and gas producing companies, the data presented in the balance sheet and income statement do not adequately assist investors in assessing prospective cash flows.[5]

This ASR quoted extensively from the FASB Exposure Draft "Objectives of Financial Reporting and Elements of Financial Statements of Business Enterprises," December 1977, in support of its position.

It may be observed that RRA, as the system has come to be known, relies just as much on uncertainties and allocations, and is just as far removed from cash accounting, as is accrual accounting. It can be stated categorically that prediction (or assessment, as it is now called) of future cash flows is far more difficult from RRA than from conventional financial reporting, particularly if the latter can be assumed to demonstrate a net income figure from which can be derived the long-run average annual cash flow in or out of the firm. RRA's combination of assumed constant prices and a ten percent discount factor, together with the undisclosed assumptions about rates of production and length of production period, and the known unreliability of the proven reserves to which these assumptions are applied, render the valuations of proven reserves and the changes in these valuations which RRA attempts to disclose, particularly opaque.

The argument supporting the cash prediction objective states that investors primarily want to know prospective net cash flows to them (amount, timing, and relative uncertainty), and want to know net cash flows to the enterprise in order to predict net cash flows to themselves. Govindarajan studied the *Wall Street Journal* for a one-year period and analyzed professional reports prepared by security analysts.[6] The results are summarized in Table 6-1.

TABLE 6-1

Results of Content Analysis of 976 Analyst Reports

	%
No mention of earnings	0.5
Earnings analysis less important than cash flow analysis	2.5

Earnings analysis and cash flow analysis equally important	10.5
Earnings analysis more important than cash flow analysis	43.5
Earnings analysis only, except for mention of dividends	22.5
No mention of cash flow	20.5
Total	100.0

Source: Vijayaraghan Govindarajan. "Objectives of Financial Reporting by Business Enterprises: Some Evidence of User Preference," (see n. 6) p. 341.

Govindarajan pointed out that the nature of the industry covered in the analyst's report did influence the use of cash flow analysis, which featured in respect of real estate companies, for example. His overall conclusion was that security analysts used earnings more often than cash flows in preparing their professional reports. It is interesting to speculate whether the emphasis on predicting cash flows which characterized the Trueblood Report, and which has been carried forward in a modified form into *Statement of Financial Accounting Concepts No. 1*, originated with accountants whose main area of expertise lay in accounting for real estate companies.

Several public accounting firms issue end-of-year advice to corporate managements concerning financial questions which may be asked at shareholders' meetings. These rarely contain references to questions aimed at assessing future cash flows. Ernst & Whinney's publication *1981 Shareholders Meetings*, for example, included a section entitled "Future Expectations," listing questions which shareholders might be expected to ask about the company's forecasts. Not one of these questions asked about, or suggested an interest in, future cash flows to the enterprise.

In the process of arriving at a concepts statement on objectives the FASB published a number of exploratory documents.

- Discussion Memorandum, *Conceptual Framework for Accounting and Reporting: Consideration of the Report of the Study Group on the Objectives of Financial Statements*, June 6, 1974.
- Three documents dated December 2, 1976, entitled—
  Tentative Conclusions on Objectives of Financial Statements of Business Enterprises.
  Conceptual Framework for Financial Accounting and Reporting: Elements of Financial Statements and their Measurement.
  Scope and Implications of the Conceptual Framework Project.
- Exposure Draft, *Objectives of Financial Reporting and Elements of Financial Statements of Business Enterprises*, December 29, 1977.

The Discussion Memorandum included the diagram shown in Figure 6-1, which represented the thinking of the FASB at that

FIGURE 6-1

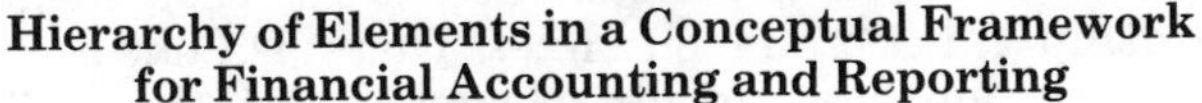

Hierarchy of Elements in a Conceptual Framework for Financial Accounting and Reporting

BASIC OBJECTIVE(S)

SUBSIDIARY OBJECTIVE(S)

QUALITATIVE CHARACTERISTICS

INFORMATION NEEDED

FUNDAMENTALS OF ACCOUNTING AND REPORTING

ACCOUNTING AND REPORTING STANDARDS

INTERPRETATIONS OF STANDARDS

ACCOUNTING PRACTICES
APPLICATIONS TO SPECIFIC SITUATIONS BY MANAGEMENT AND AUDITORS

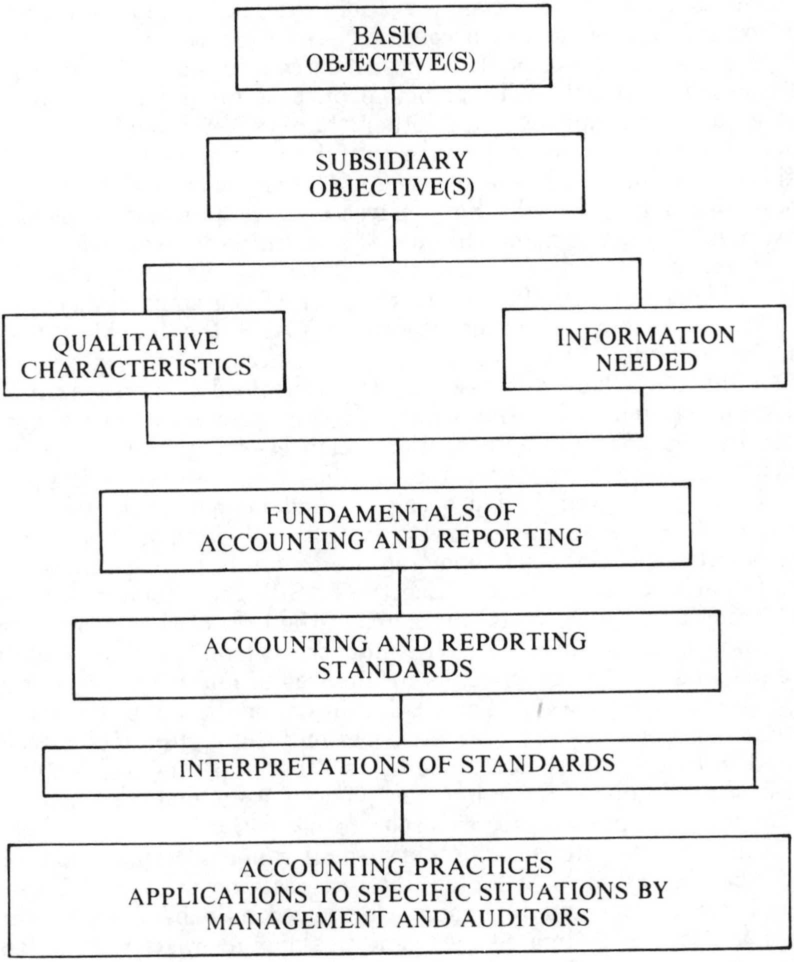

time about the structure of the conceptual framework project and the important role played by objectives in this framework.

A CRITICAL LOOK AT THE NEED FOR THE OBJECTIVES STATEMENT

The objectives adopted by the FASB can be viewed in the light of a historical emphasis on the *stewardship function* of accounting. This view originated in former perceptions of a narrow role for the accountant, that of providing evidence of the honest custodianship of resources. Because modern accounting emphasizes the measurement and evaluation of performance, it has been suggested that the stewardship function is obsolete. There is, however, no real conflict between the stewardship objective and that of providing information useful for decision making; the latter simply recognizes an expanded view of the accountant's role in society.

The reconciliation of these positions can be found in the words of Edwards and Bell: "The principal purpose to be achieved by the collection of accounting data (other than prevention of fraud and theft and the like) is to provide useful information for the evaluation of past business decisions and of the methods used in reaching those decisions." A subsidiary purpose is to provide a basis for taxation.[7] By emphasizing the role of accounting in evaluations both by management and of management, Edwards and Bell included in their objectives virtually the entire range of contemporary accounting functions inexplicably omitted by the APB, the Trueblood Committee, and the FASB. The management, taxation, regulatory, and other functions were dismissed by the Trueblood Committee on the specious grounds that financial reporting primarily serves users with limited power to obtain information elsewhere. *The representation view* of the purpose of financial reporting embraces everything in the Edwards and Bell proposition, and budgeting as well.

Nor does it seem necessary to state the obvious in this respect; the objectives of financial reporting are certainly known throughout the financial community in which the FASB's constituency lies. The SEC report on the financial problems of the City of New York dated February 5, 1979 stated that "the most critical deficiency in existing municipal securities practices is in the area of municipal accounting and financial reporting." The SEC pointed out that the market for municipal securities provides investors only limited protection compared with corporate, government, or other types of issuers. It is clear that financial reporting was viewed as a major element in protecting the purchasers of corporate securities.

Further, the failure to provide useful financial reports imposes penalties in the form of higher interest costs on municipal issuers whose accounting and reporting are viewed as substandard. Standard & Poor has estimated that penalties may average 0.125 to 0.25 percentage points; on a typical $100 million bond issue with a 10-year average life this adds up to $1,250,000 to $2,500,000 in additional costs.

If this is so widely known, why has it been necessary to state it again at great length?

The belief that the provision of information to investors and others having limited ability to obtain it elsewhere should be a primary objective of financial statements can be traced directly to the work of the noted economist J.K. Galbraith. Galbraith has publicized the concept of the "technostructure," meaning that a business is run by those who have information.[8] This management elite—managers, scientists, lawyers, accountants, and so on—wield power because information is the real source of power. The owners of the business, the investors, lack power and the way to give it to them is by providing them with information via the financial statements.

The fallacy of this argument (quite apart from the problem that the technostructure would always have the information before the investors) is the assumption that information is required in order to exercise power. The study of political science reveals that all that is required to exercise power is power; hence the concept of absolutism. Even if we look at the democratic form of organization which supposedly characterizes the modern corporation, all that is required to exercise power is a simple majority. The reason why stockholders have lost control of the modern corporation is not because they have been denied access to information, but because they have not formed a majority. The resulting power vacuum has been occupied by the technocrats, but this is an accident outside their control; the government will take power away from them even though they memorize the contents of their computer storage nightly.

Some other propositions which may be worthy of consideration in this regard follow.

- That all problems of user needs can be resolved within an accounting framework. The need to decide questions of taxation in a legal framework, and questions of regulation generally in a political framework, was not recognized, but it should be clear that the scientific determination of the question "what are the objectives of the financial reports required by the IRS, or the SEC?" is a quite distinct process from the scientific determination of the question "what are the objectives of the financial reports required by investors?"
- That the objectives of financial reporting can ignore the operating needs of managers, who are responsible for the preparation and publication of financial statements and pay for them to be audited.
- That agreement on objectives will lead to agreement on standard rules and practices. The field of capital budgeting provides direct evidence to the contrary. In the theory of finance the objective is the one thing all agree on: to prepare and evaluate investment decisions. From that point, finance theorists can agree on nothing—not on the form of their algorithms, the meaning of their terms, or even the name for what they are doing. A vast contradictory literature has arisen since the early 1950s in which writers draw attention to the superiority of their methods over those of others.

Perhaps the most significant fallacy, however, is the assumption that it is necessary generally to specify objectives for financial reporting to establish standards or rules governing the form and content of financial statements. This view may originate in the current preoccupation with Management by Objectives (MBO) which would support the proposition that an accountant should specify his objectives before producing a set of financial statements. There can, however, be a number of objectives for the preparation of financial statements.

1. To satisfy a legal obligation, such as the one imposed by the SEC, or the Companies Acts in the United Kingdom
2. To inform stockholders about what has happened to their investments, and what is expected to happen
3. To provide the basis for a tax assessment
4. To attract new equity or loan financing
5. To assist in the negotiation of a labor contract
6. To satisfy a contractual agreement with a customer, including to conform to the standards laid down by the Cost Accounting Standards Board
7. To arrive at a price for a business, or a share in a business, on sale or merger
8. To determine the amount available for dividends or for reinvestment
9. To support a request for government assistance, as for example in the form of a subsidy
10. To decide whether to liquidate a going concern
11. To participate in an interfirm comparison scheme

It is no more necessary to specify objectives to develop rules and standards for financial reporting than to specify user needs to discuss the rules for drawing or analyzing a critical path network.

In the first edition of this book, the above point was made by redesigning the "hierarchy of elements" shown in Figure 6-1 to abstract from the need for objectives. Figure 6-2 has been redrawn to show how it supports the remaining elements of the FASB's conceptual framework project.

THE PROBLEM OF INFORMATION

Overriding all other difficulties is the problem presented by the use of the word "information." It is unlikely in this context that the word means any communication of knowledge, because its users refer to information "useful for making economic decisions." It is clear that the expectation is for financial statements to contain inputs into a specific decision model.

We may recall the components of a decision. They are: the available actions that can be taken, the states of nature which could occur, the consequences of each combination of action and state of nature, an experiment or other device for obtaining information about the states of nature, the available strategies, the action probabilities, and a choice criterion. The decision model requires information, which is defined as *purpose oriented data*, and only when the purpose is known can the device for obtaining information be constructed or used.

Further, if we accept this definition of information as *evaluated data*, we must accept the possibility of a surplus of data in all but the limiting case. If the accountant is concerned with data col-

FIGURE 6-2

Hierarchy of Elements in a Conceptual Framework and their Relationship to the FASB's Conceptual Framework Project

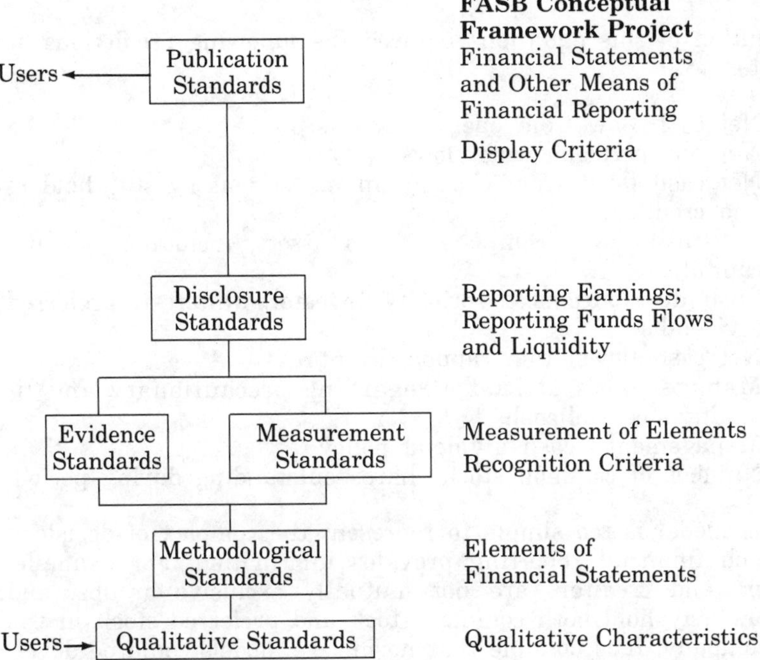

Source: Discussion Memorandum, "Conceptual Framework for Accounting and Reporting: Consideration of the Report of the Study Group on the Objectives of Financial Statements," Financial Accounting Standards Board, June 9, 1974, p. 15.

lection, aggregation, and presentation, he is leaving to the user the task of selecting the data which satisfy his needs.

Thus, on the one hand "information" forces us to distinguish accounting information from other kinds, and on the other hand, it places us upon the horns of a dilemma: data are not information, yet the accountant must work with an unknown user need. One way out is to specify the decision model, and thus the user need.

The Trueblood Committee's preoccupation with predicting cash flows appears to have grown out of acceptance of a particular investor decision model. A committee of the American Accounting Association described such a model in a 1969 report, pointing out that the model was normative in nature; it showed how investors and creditors *should* make decisions, not how they actually do so. The model assumed that the principal variable to be predicted (or estimated) was dividends per share, represented as D_{ik}. The formula for expected dividends per share involved expectations about cash dividends to common stock holders and number of shares at issue. Thus:

$$D_{ik} = \frac{CDS_{ik}}{N_{ik}} \quad \begin{matrix}\text{(total cash dividend to stockholders)} \\ \text{(number of shares outstanding)}\end{matrix}$$

Solution of this equation required the following predictions or estimates:

- Net cash flow from operations
- Net nonoperating cash flows
- Net cash flows from changes in investment by stockholders and creditors
- Net cash flows from changes in assets, including working capital
- Cash distributions to priority investors (interest, preferred dividends)
- Net cash flows from random events
- Management's attitudes regarding precautionary and liquidity stocks of cash
- Management's cash dividend policy
- Number of common stock shares outstanding during period

This model is too simple to represent the complex of decisions for which financial reporting provides information. For example, investors and creditors are not mutually exclusive groups, and investors may hold both common stock and preferred stock in the same company. It is possible that normative models could be developed for these three main subgroups of financial report users.

Investors: those responsible for resource allocation decisions (subgroups: owners, lenders, managers/financial investors, and real investors).

Regulators: those responsible for establishing the rules of the investment game, and for policing the players (subgroups: the stock exchanges, financial analysts, and the SEC/financial institutions generally).

Stabilizers: those responsible for making adjustments to the economic environment in which investment decisions are made (subgroups: the Federal Reserve Board, the U.S. Treasury, and the IRS; many other federal, state, and local government agencies).

However, recent research has established that *investors* are not a homogeneous group, rather they consist of sizable subgroups of (a) sophisticated and unsophisticated investors, and (b) long-term and short-term investors (speculators).[9] It is likely that the decision models of these subgroups and their combinations and permutations will differ materially.

A NEW LOOK AT OBJECTIVES

Perhaps the principal objection to the present state of the objectives controversy is the emphasis on investors and creditors and the assumption that satisfaction of their information needs will automatically satisfy the needs of other users. The opposing viewpoint is that of *The Corporate Report* published in England in 1975.[10] Instead of placing themselves in the corner of one type of user of financial statements, the authors of *The Corporate Report* concerned themselves with the accountability of economic entities of all kinds, although the emphasis was on the business enterprise. This accountability lies with equity investors, loan creditors, and suppliers, but also with employees, financial analysts and investment advisers, business connections of different types, the government, and the public in general. Accountability arises from the social role of the entity and not solely from legal requirements. "Such organizations, which exist with the general consent of the community, are afforded special legal and operational privileges, they compete for resources of manpower, materials, and energy, and they make use of community owned assets such as roads and harbors."

From this proposition *The Corporate Report* derived its criticism of current financial statements, that they are primarily concerned with supplying measurements and information of use to shareholders and creditors. The report also listed the following defects of current financial reports:

1. Emphasis on period earnings encourages users to believe, erroneously, that the maximization of short-term profits is the goal of the enterprise.
2. The audit certificate combines with the financial statements to give the figures a false impression of certainty.
3. The form of the financial statements encourages users to evaluate the enterprise on the basis of short-term results and may thus influence management to take a short-run view.
4. The financial statements implicitly direct attention to proprietors as the dominant interest group, which they may not be.

The Corporate Report rejects the assumption that general-purpose financial statements can satisfy the information needs of all user groups. It suggests that employees may require special reports at the plant or site level, and proposes the following six additional statements:

(i) A statement of value added to show the wealth produced by the firm and how it has been distributed.
(ii) An employment report, dealing with efficiency, productivity, personnel policies, industrial relations, and other matters of interest to workers.

(iii) A statement of money exchanges with government, to show the firm's role in financing the public sector not only through taxes on its own profits, but also through collections and payments of withholding taxes and social security contributions, sales taxes, and other imposts. The statement would also show receipts from government, such as grants and subsidies.

(iv) A statement of transactions in foreign currency, distinguishing between current and capital transactions and showing overseas borrowings and repayments and dividends received and paid.

(v) A statement of future prospects, attempting to forecast profits, employment, and investments.

(vi) A statement of corporate objectives.

The report draws attention to the concept of "social accounting," and attempts to move in that direction. Naturally, those countries where the government sets standards of accounting and financial reporting are more likely to adopt social accounting than are those where standards are set by the private sector.

The additional statements suggested by the report appear to be of primary interest to economists, particularly those employed by the government, and it is difficult to see how businesses can be made to pay for providing such information unless required to do so by legislation containing effective sanctions for noncompliance. This may well be the consequence of *The Corporate Report* and, if so, will result in an increase in the role and remuneration of the accounting profession. In this respect it contrasts markedly with the Trueblood Report, which attempted to hitch the profession to the declining star of the individual investor.

In the author's view, the objective of financial reporting is to represent formally, using the methodology of accounting and in conformity with contemporary standards of evidence, measurement, disclosure, and publication, the actual or planned activities of an organization for a given period of time and its capacity to continue at a given moment in time.

OBJECTIVES OF FINANCIAL REPORTING BY NONBUSINESS ORGANIZATIONS

Financial difficulties experienced by a number of nonbusiness organizations during the 1970s, notably the incipient bankruptcy of the City of New York, brought to light serious deficiencies in the accounting and financial reporting methods of such entities. In August 1977 the FASB initiated a project designed to enable it to assume the same role in setting accounting standards for nonbusiness organizations as it plays for business firms. A research study aimed at identifying the objectives of financial reporting for nonbusiness organizations resulted in a 1978 research report,[11] closely followed by a Discussion Memorandum and public hearings. An Exposure Draft was issued in March, 1980 and *Statement of Financial Accounting Concepts No. 4*, "Objectives of Financial Reporting by Nonbusiness Organizations," in December 1980.

The project covered initially three types of nonbusiness organization.

- State and local governments
- Private nonprofit and philanthropic organizations, which includes colleges and universities, hospitals, churches, and foundations
- Other social institutions such as trade and professional associations, called "membership organizations" because they exist to benefit their members

The scope of the project would exclude investor-owned hospitals and colleges, clubs with transferable equity interests, and mutual insurance companies and other mutuals and cooperatives.

Prior to the initiation of this project, guidelines for accounting for nonbusiness organizations were provided from several sources. The AICPA had published industry audit guides for hospitals, colleges and universities, and voluntary health and welfare organizations; also *Statement of Position No. 78-10* "Accounting and Reporting for Certain Nonprofit Organizations." As a consequence of *FASB Statement No. 32*, which specified that specialized accounting and reporting principles laid down in certain AICPA Statements of position and accounting and auditing Guides are preferable accounting principles, these Statements of Position can be used to justify a change in accounting principle accounted for according to the method prescribed by *APB Opinion No. 20*. The National Council on Governmental Organizations (NCGA) and other groups representing particular types of nonbusiness organization had also laid down guidelines for accounting and financial reporting, and by including state and local governments in the scope of its project, the FASB aroused considerable controversy, and even opposition. In December 1979 the NCGA recommended that the FASB either defer publication of its Exposure Draft or else exclude governmental units from its scope. (*FASB Statement No. 32* explicitly restricted its scope to nonbusiness organizations other than government.) An interorganizational study group consisting of representatives of the AICPA, NCGA, Municipal Finance Officers Association, National Association of State Auditors, Comptrollers and Treasurers, the U.S. General Accounting Office, and the Financial Accounting Foundation was formed to examine the issue and recommend who should set accounting standards for government. As a result, *Statement of Financial Accounting Concepts No. 4* specifically excluded state and local governments from its scope. The Statement emphasized that the FASB believed that the objectives of financial reporting by governmental agencies engaged in activities that are not peculiar to government, such as hospitals, universities, and utilities, should be similar to those of business or nongovernmental nonbusiness enterprises engaged in the same type of activities.

The Statement defines nonbusiness organizations as possessing three characteristics.

1. A significant portion of their receipts comes from persons who expect neither repayment nor corresponding benefits
2. Absence of a profit motive
3. Absence of transferable ownership interests

It points out that although some economic factors are absent, nevertheless nonbusiness organizations operate in the same economic environment as do business enterprises, and although their objectives, and those of resource providers, may be largely noneconomic, they are nevertheless involved in money transactions and other activities involving economic resources and obligations. Many people base economic decisions on their relationship to and knowledge about nonbusiness organizations and are thus interested in their financial reports. These users include members, taxpayers, contributors, grantors, lenders, suppliers, creditors, managers, service beneficiaries, financial analysts, brokers, underwriters, civil servants, and many more categories. Notably absent, of course, are investors.

Thus, the general objective of financial reporting for nonbusiness organizations differs somewhat from the primary objective of financial reporting by business enterprises:

> Financial reporting by nonbusiness organizations should provide information that is useful to present and potential resource providers and other users in making rational decisions about the allocation of resources to those organizations.

Statement of Financial Accounting Concepts No. 1, it will be recalled, specified "business and economic decisions" as the area for making reasoned choices among alternative uses of scarce resources.

The following specific objectives were enumerated for nonbusiness organizations' financial reporting:

1. To provide information to help users to assess the services the organization provides and its ability to continue to provide those services.
2. To provide information that is useful in assessing how managers have discharged their stewardship responsibilities and other aspects of their performance.
3. To provide information about the economic resources, obligations and net resources [presumably the algebraic difference between these two] of an organization and the effects of transactions, events, and circumstances that change resources and interests in those resources.

4. To provide information about the performance of an organization during a period through the information covered by numbers 1 through 3 above.
5. To provide information about the amounts and kinds of inflows and outflows of resources during a period.
6. To provide information about how an organization obtains and spends cash and other liquid resources.

It seems clear from these objectives that the FASB regards the provision of basic financial statements together with notes and an audit certificate as the kind of information which meets them. Paragraph 1. of the Statement says that "the Board has concluded that it is not necessary to develop an independent conceptual framework for any particular category of entities (e.g. nonbusiness organizations or business enterprises)." Thus, the contents of the basic financial statements and notes may be assumed not to require different accounting treatment if the entity is a nonbusiness organization.

Nowhere does the FASB face up to the two basic problems in accounting for nonbusiness organizations which have made the financial reporting function for such entities so difficult. These are the lack of an agreed output measurement, which affects attempts to provide a period statement indicative of services provided and performance results, and the lack of an agreed valuation perspective, which affects the measurement of assets and liabilities in the balance sheets of nonbusiness organizations.* Until these important and fundamental issues are addressed the objectives of the Statement cannot be achieved, and the application of generally accepted accounting principles to nonbusiness organizations remains a judgmental question.

CONCLUSION

The debate on objectives demonstrated a struggle between the conventional view of financial statements as a report by management on its stewardship of the wealth entrusted to it, and the more recent view that they should be useful to investors and others for prediction, evaluation, and comparison designed to support resource allocation decisions. The debate took place against a background of research which purported to show that financial reporting does not contain information which is useful for investment decisions.

The results of the debate have been to provide a rationale for the definition of financial reporting to include statements of financial position, results of operations, and other changes in financial position. Yet basic financial statements do not currently reveal information permitting the assessment of future cash flows, and we cannot deduce from the objectives what form and content of financial reporting would permit the objectives to be achieved. In

*The FASB recently published a research study entitled "Reporting of Service Efforts and Accomplishments Information."

the circumstances, it cannot be a matter of much surprise to find accounting and financial reporting largely unaffected as yet by the attempt to define their objectives.

The author has before him as he writes the annual report for 1978 of a profitable oil company which started paying cash dividends in that year, after fourteen years of stock dividends. Could the preceding thirteen years' financial reports have been designed to lead the user to conclude that 1978 would be the beginning of net cash flows to investors?

The proposition that the objectives of financial reporting for nonbusiness organizations are essentially the same as those for businesses implies that all accounting standards should be set by one agency, such as the FASB. Establishment of a new GASB suggests five problems.

1. Proliferation of agencies may lead to a lessening of the credibility of the FASB, and to a demand for creation of yet more specialized agencies.
2. Conflict of standards is already a fact of life internationally, on common problems such as pension accounting.
3. Qualified and experienced professionals are not available to perform the same tasks at two agencies.
4. Providing resources for the GASB would reduce those available to the FASB.
5. It would be difficult, if not impossible, to assure the independence of an agency so directly concerned with regulating the actions of government and other political institutions.

In February 1981 the Organizing Committee for a governmental accounting standards board (GASBOC) reported its proposals. They involve establishing a structure similar to that of the FASB, namely—

- a five-member full-time board located in Washington, D.C.
- a governmental standards advisory council to advise the GASB
- a governmental accounting foundation to appoint the Board and Advisory Council, raise money, approve budgets, and "exercise oversight." The foundation would be sponsored by key organizations having an interest in governmental accounting.

The Trustees of the Financial Accounting Foundation (FAF) did not support these proposals, but did approve a revised draft issued by GASBOC in July 1981. The new factor was that oversight responsibility for a separate GASB would be given to the FAF, and that the FAF would be responsible for fund-raising.

ENDNOTES

1. *Objectives of Financial Statements*, Report of the Study Group on the Objectives of Financial Statements, New York: AICPA, October 1973 (usually referred to as the Trueblood Report).
2. Anton, Hector R. "Objectives of Financial Accounting: Review and Analysis," *Journal of Accountancy*, January 1976, pp. 40-51.
3. Staubus, George J., *A Theory of Accounting to Investors*, Berkeley: University of California Press, 1961.
4. FASB's *Tentative Conclusions on Objectives of Financial Statements of Business Enterprises*, Financial Accounting Standards Board, December 2, 1976, p. 40.
5. *Accounting Series Release No. 253*, Securities and Exchange Commission, August 31, 1978, SEC Docket/939.
6. Govindarajan, Vijayaraghavan, "Objectives of Financial Reporting by Business Enterprises: Some Evidence of User Preference," *Journal of Accounting, Auditing & Finance*, Summer 1979, pp. 339-43.
7. Edwards, Edgar O. and Philip W. Bell, *The Theory and Measurement of Business Income,* Berkeley: University of California Press, 1961, p. 271.
8. Galbraith, John Kenneth, *Economics and the Public Purpose*, Boston: Houghton, Mifflin Company, 1973, p. 82.
9. Chang, Lucia S. and Kenneth S. Most, *Financial Statements and Investment Decisions*, Miami: Florida International University, 1979.
10. *The Corporate Report*, London, Accounting Standards Steering Committee, 1975. See also "Aims and Scope of Company Reports," Department of Trade, May 1976, and "Company Accounting and Disclosure—A Consultative Document," Cmnd. 7654, 1979 (both U.K. government documents).
11. Anthony, Robert N. *Financial Reporting in Nonbusiness Organizations*, Financial Accounting Standards Board, May 1978.

SELECTED ADDITIONAL READINGS

American Accounting Association Committee to Prepare a Statement of Basic Accounting Theory, *A Statement of Basic Accounting Theory*, Evanston, Ill: AAA 1966.

American Institute of Certified Public Accountants *Statement No. 4 of the Accounting Principles Board*, "Basic Concepts and Accounting Principles Underlying Financial Statements of Business Enterprises," New York: AICPA, 1970.

Anthony, Robert N., *Financial Accounting in Nonbusiness Organizations*, Stamford, Conn.: FASB, May 1978.

Anton, Hector R., "Objectives of Financial Accounting: Review and Analysis," *Journal of Accountancy*, January 1976, pp. 40-51.

Beaver, William H. and Joel S. Demski, "The Nature of Financial Objectives: A Summary and Synthesis," *Studies in Financial Accounting Objectives*, 1974, Supplement to Vol. 12, *Journal of Accounting Research*, pp. 170-187.

Chastain, Clark E., "Accounting Objectives and User Needs: A Behavioral View," *National Public Accountant*, May 1974, pp. 24-27, and Part II, *National Public Accountant*, June 1974, pp. 26-31.

Chen, Rosita S., "Social and Financial Stewardship," *The Accounting Review*, July 1975, pp. 533-543.

Climo, Tom, "What's Happening in Britain?" *Journal of Accountancy*, February 1976, pp. 55-59.

The Corporate Report, Accounting Standards Steering Committee discussion paper, London, August 1975.

Cyert, Richard M. and Yuji Ijiri, "Problems of Implementing the Trueblood Objectives Report," in *Studies on Financial Accounting Objectives: 1974*, Supplement to Vol. 12, *Journal of Accounting Research*, pp. 29-42.

Dopuch, Nicholas and Shyam Sunder, "FASB's Statements on Objectives and Elements of Financial Accounting: A Review," *The Accounting Review*, January 1980, pp. 1-21.

FASB *Statements of Financial Accounting Concepts*, No. 1, November 1978 and No. 4, December 1980.

Hinton, Raymond P., "Objectives of Financial Statements," *Journal of Accountancy*, November 1972, pp. 56-58, 60.

Kenley, W.J. and G.J. Staubus, *Objectives and concepts of financial statements*, Melbourne, Australia: Accountancy Research Foundation, 1972.

Mautz, R.K., "Accounting Objectives—The Conservative View," *CPA Journal*, September 1973, pp. 771, 774-777.

Objectives of Financial Statements, Report of the Study Group on the Objectives of Financial Statements, New York: AICPA, October 1973.

Objectives of Financial Statements, Volume 2/Selected Papers, ed. Joe J. Cramer, Jr., and George H. Sorter, New York: AICPA, 1974.

Pannell, Richard L., "Stewardship in financial accounting," *Journal of Accountancy*, October 1979, pp. 90-93.

Ramanathan, Kavasseri, "Toward a Theory of Corporate Social Accounting," *The Accounting Review*, July 1976, pp. 516-28.

Schattke, R.W., "Accounting Principles Board Statement No. 4—Promise for the Future," *CPA Journal*, July 1972, pp. 552-556.

Staubus, George J., *A Theory of Accounting to Investors*, Berkeley: University of California Press, 1961.

Sorter, George H. and Martin S. Gans, "Opportunities and Implications of the Report on Objectives of Financial Statements," in *Studies on Financial Accounting Objectives*, 1974, Supplement to Vol. 12, *Journal of Accounting Research*, pp. 1-12.

Thomas, Arthur L., "Evaluating the Effectiveness of Social Programs," *Journal of Accountancy*, June 1976, pp. 65-71.

Robert M. Trueblood Memorial Conference Studies on Financial Accounting Objectives, 1974, Chicago: The Institute of Professional Accounting, Graduate School of Business, University of Chicago, 1974.

Williams, Robert Jan, "Differing Opinions on Accounting Objectives," *CPA Journal*, August 1973, pp. 651-656.

Case 6-1 Florida East Coast Railway

Florida East Coast Railway (FEC) is a small, little-known railroad which some believe to be the most efficient in the United States. It was made profitable by a financier named Ed Ball, who acquired control in 1959 through buying its bonds cheaply and then taking it out of insolvency. In order to make the railroad profitable, Ball fought a long war against "featherbedding," the common practice of requiring a train to be overmanned. A nine-year strike against the FEC finally ended in the early 1970s with victory for FEC; as a result a Jacksonville–Miami train has only two crew members compared with the more customary 12 to 15 mandated by the union. FEC's transportation operating costs were only 29 percent of revenues in 1980, compared with an industry norm of 40 percent.

One of FEC's principal assets consists of over 30,000 acres of prime Florida real estate, some of it bought when an acre cost under one dollar at the turn of the century. In 1978 part of FEC's Miami holdings were condemned for city use; Ball finally negotiated $28 million for land which had a book value of $2.5 million. Another parcel of condemned Miami land was sold for $23.3 million in 1981; its book value was $4 million. The former property consisted of a 10.2 mile right of way; the latter, of only 32 acres. Negotiations for these sales took several years.

Earnings per share in 1980 was $8.29 without any land sale profits; these inflated 1979 earnings to nearly double this amount and 1981 was expected to resemble 1979. For many years Ball refused to pay a dividend on the FEC common, but by 1980 he had relented to the extent of 40 cents per share, a mere 0.5% of the market price of $82. It was reliably estimated that the shares had an asset value of $150 at that time. Although stockholders were dividend poor they could get rich; a stockholder who paid $16 in 1975 saw the stock quintuple by 1980.

1. What is the relevance of the FASB's objectives of financial reporting to the preparation of FEC's annual report?
2. What should be the objectives of financial reporting by a corporation such as FEC?

Case 6-2 Other Comprehensive Basis of Accounting

A CPA can properly give a "clean" report on statements prepared on an "other comprehensive basis of accounting"—OCBOA for short. *Statement of Auditing Standards No. 14* of the AICPA identifies several OCBOAs, illustrates the appropriate audit reports, and suggests appropriate statement titles. None of the related publications provides guidance on content and form, on what the line-item and subtotal captions should be, how items are to be defined, or what specific information should be disclosed. A review of the literature shows that this subject has been largely avoided by academic and professional writers on accounting and auditing. However, in 1981 the Technical Information Division of the AICPA began to publish examples of OCBOA reporting to assist practitioners; these examples, however, do not establish standards.

1. Give examples of "other comprehensive bases of accounting."
2. What is the purpose of a professional rule which permits accountants to publish, and auditors to provide "clean" audit reports on, financial statements which are not in accordance with GAAP, providing that this is made clear to the reader?
3. What are the implications of this situation for the FASB's conceptual framework project?

Case 6-3 Financial Reporting by Hospitals

There are several different ways by which hospitals in the United States can be organized and financed. Some are run by the federal government, such as those administered by the Veterans Administration. Many are the creations of local governments, particularly of cities. Many are funded by charitable trusts, or financed by the fund-raising efforts of fraternal and religious organizations. Finally, there are many hospitals operated as business ventures, including some hospital chains which are quoted public companies.

Regardless of ownership, virtually all hospitals depend upon the public sector to finance part of their operations. The federal Medicare (for the elderly) and Medicaid (for the needy) programs pay all or part of the bills for these two groups, regardless of which type of hospital provides the service. Hospitals which receive Medicare and Medicaid refunds must report their costs to these federal agencies in accordance with particular accounting rules in order to be eligible for reimbursement. Disallowed costs can be substantial.

1. Explain the concept of "conflict of accounting principles" in relation to hospitals.
2. Discuss different methods of reporting costs disallowed by Medicare and Medicaid which might be made mandatory for business hospitals by the FASB and for nonbusiness hospitals by the GASB.

END OF CHAPTER QUESTIONS

1. What are the alternative views of the usefulness of financial reporting? Which has been adopted by the APB and the FASB?
2. What was the Trueblood Committee Report, and what was its connection with the birth of the FASB?

3. Which of the Trueblood Committee's objectives were not adopted by the FASB, and what part of the Commitee's report led to a separate Statement of Financial Concepts being issued by the FASB?
4. Compare and contrast the objectives of the Trueblood Committee Report with those identified by *APB Statement No. 4* three years previously. What is the most significant single difference between these lists of objectives?
5. Discuss the objectives of financial reporting for business enterprises laid down by the FASB, with particular reference to the following quotation from an FASB Exposure Draft dated June 30, 1981: "Financial statements are intended to present in financial terms the performance, financial position, and cash flows of an enterprise."
6. Explain the relationship between accrual accounting and cash flow accounting as perceived by the FASB. What is the "cash prediction" objective, and to what extent is it supported by empirical evidence?
7. What is the stewardship function of accounting, and in what respects does it embrace the function of providing information useful to investors?
8. What is the role of accounting in Galbraith's technostructure? To what extent does this view fit into a theory of accounting as an instrument of social control? What is the extreme form of this view of accounting?
9. List twelve possible uses of financial reporting by a business in a modern society.
10. Define *information* in a decision theory framework. What dilemma does this place accountants in?
11. Which type of decision model requires prediction of cash flows to investors, and what type of financial reporting can best provide the information on which such predictions can be based?
12. Who are the users of financial accounting information? How do we distinguish direct from indirect users? Why is it important to study user needs and user characteristics? What view of human behavior tends to make the study of user needs unimportant?
13. Explain the reasoning which underlay *The Corporate Report*, and list the components of financial reporting to which this reasoning led the authors of that Report.
14. How do the objectives of nonbusiness reporting differ from those of business reporting? What kind of financial reporting and accounting standards do nonbusiness entities need?
15. What is the GASB, and what is its relationship to the FASB?
16. What do you understand by the phrase "conflict of principles" of financial reporting? Explain how this conflict could arise through the existence of separate accounting standards boards for business and nonbusiness entities.

7

THE SEC: DISCLOSURE AND MATERIALITY

DISCLOSURE

In April, 1932 the U. S. Senate Banking and Currency Committee began public hearings on stock exchange practices. The investigation concluded that complete disclosure of financial information would prevent misrepresentation and cited the British Companies Acts as a model. President Roosevelt took up this suggestion and made it a plank in his 1932 presidential platform. Thus were born the Securities Act of 1933 and the Securities Exchange Act of 1934.

The Securities and Exchange Commission (SEC) was created in 1934 by the Securities Exchange Act to administer the federal laws enacted in 1933 and 1934. The 1933 law aimed at protecting investors by requiring the issuer of a security to be sold to the public to make a full disclosure of material facts affecting the security and its issuance. A material fact is defined as a fact the average prudent investor would be expected to rely on. Disclosure is made by filing a registration statement and prospectus for review by the staff of the SEC. In its review the SEC determines whether there has been compliance with the Securities Act of 1933 and with the rules, regulations, and instructions issued by the SEC. If not, the SEC can refuse to accept the registration, and the issuer of the securities can become criminally liable for causing the public to subscribe for them.

The 1934 Act required ongoing disclosure by corporations whose securities were publicly traded, by means of annual, quarterly, and irregular filings, the main component of which was and is the financial statements of the corporation. The SEC expresses its views on this subject in the following five ways:

1. Regulation S-X which governs the form and content of financial statements filed with the SEC.
2. Accounting Series Releases (ASRs), which are major opinions of and rules laid down by the SEC.

3. SEC decisions and reports, including periodical Staff Accounting Bulletins.
4. Speeches and articles by members of the Commission, particularly important being those of the Chairman.
5. The SEC's annual reports.

Among the principal ongoing reports which an affected corporation must file with the SEC are the 10-Q quarterly report, the 8-K irregular report of unscheduled events or corporate changes of importance to shareholders, or to the SEC, and the 12-K report for certain regulated companies. Of major importance is the 10-K or annual filing by corporations which have issued securities that are publicly traded. Accounting Series Releases Nos. 279, 280, and 281 of 1980 drastically revised the SEC's system of corporate disclosure.

ORIGIN OF REGULATION S-X AND REASON FOR CHANGE

Regulation S-X was introduced by *ASR No. 12*, "Adoption of Regulation S-X," on February 21, 1940. At that time there was little in the way of authoritative accounting literature, and the SEC found it necessary to codify its own requirements for financial statement disclosure. Since that time, however, the task of publishing generally accepted accounting principles has been pursued vigorously by the accounting profession and the FASB. In its 1978 and 1979 "Report to Congress on the Accounting Profession and the Commission's Oversight Role," the SEC expressed its continued faith in the system of establishing accounting standards through a private sector institution subject to SEC supervision. However, this supervision involves the SEC taking position from time to time on some of accounting's more important unresolved problems.

Early in 1976 the SEC established an Advisory Committee on Corporate Disclosure, which reported in November 1977.[1] The Committee concluded that "the disclosure system established by the Congress in the Securities Act of 1933 and the Securities Exchange Act of 1934, as implemented and developed by the Securities and Exchange Commission since its creation in 1934, is sound and does not need radical reform or renovation." In order to establish a basis for changes to be made when needed the Committee recommended that the SEC adopt the following statement of objectives:

> The Commission's function in the corporate disclosure system is to assure the public availability in an efficient and reasonable manner and on a timely basis of reliable, firm-oriented information material to informed investment and corporate suffrage decision-making. The Commission should not adopt disclosure requirements which have as their principal objective the regulation of corporate conduct.

This Committee also recommended the revision of Form 10-K in order to eliminate rules of general applicability which cause differences between financial statements prepared according to GAAP and those prepared according to Regulation S-X. These differences can be illustrated by the following examples.

1. *ASR No. 236*, "Industry Segment Reporting" was necessitated by the publication of *FASB Statement No. 14*, "Financial Reporting for Segments of a Business Enterprise."
2. *ASR No. 242*, "Notification of Enactment of Foreign Corrupt Practices Act of 1977" outlined the provisions of the FCPA, which can lead to criminal action under the securities acts.
3. *ASR No. 253*, "Adoption of Requirements for Financial Accounting and Reporting Practices for Oil and Gas Producing Activities" which effectively revoked *FASB Statement No. 19*, "Financial Accounting and Reporting by Oil and Gas Producing Companies."
4. *ASR No. 272*, "Recision of Moratorium on Capitalization of Interest Cost" which amended the SEC's rules following the publication of *FASB Statement No. 34*, "Capitalization of Interest Cost."

The information contained in Regulation S-X disclosures can be classified into—

- Disclosures which are important to all financial report users,
- Disclosures which are important to a more restricted group of sophisticated users,
- Disclosures which duplicate GAAP or have ceased to be important to users.

Thus, a reform which distinguished clearly between the first and second type of disclosure and which eliminated the third type was undertaken.

The 1980 reforms created an integrated system of corporate disclosure containing a *basic information package* as shown in Figure 7-1.

The practical effect of the three Accounting Series Releases is to require the information in the basic information package to be the same for both corporate annual reports and SEC filings. Thus, a registrant's financial statements in its annual report to shareholders will be subject to the provisions of Regulation S-X. To understand the significance of this one must realize that prior to 1980 the form and content of financial statements in corporate annual reports were governed by GAAP, and the auditor certified that the financial statements were in accordance with GAAP. There were substantial differences between SEC rules and GAAP in respect of detailed items to be disclosed, which are far more numerous under Regulation S-X, and in respect of the ideas underlying disclosure. GAAP tends to be more general and permit variations for different circumstances; the SEC tends to be more specific as befits an organization dominated by lawyers.

FIGURE 7-1

SEC's New Form 10-K Requirements

General instructions
Part I
1. Description of the business
2. List of properties
3. Report of any significant legal proceedings
4. Ownership of securities—special features

Part II

5. Market for the registrant's stock 6. Selected financial data 7. Management's discussion and analysis of financial condition and results of operations 8. Financial statements and supplemental (e.g. quarterly) data	basic information package

Part III
9. Directors and executive officers
10. Management remuneration and transactions

Part IV
11. Exhibits, financial statement schedules, and Form 8-K reports

Signatures
Supplemental information

It is feared that, as a result of these changes, the importance of GAAP as a foundation for financial reporting and of the private sector's responsibility for setting accounting standards are both due to decline sharply.

Significant additional non-GAAP disclosures which will now be required in annual reports include the following:

1. Balance sheets for the two most recent years, income statements and statements of changes in financial position for the most recent three. (GAAP does not require the publication of comparative statements, but the SEC's previous requirement of two years has been universally followed.) The financial statements also must analyze changes in shareholders' equity for three years.
2. Management's discussion and analysis must cover three years of financial statements instead of two.
3. Pretax income must be segregated between domestic and foreign to identify the source of taxable income.
4. Segregate both current and deferred income taxes as domestic or foreign.
5. Disclose any timing difference which exceeds 5 percent of the product of pretax income and the tax rate.
6. Reconcile income tax expense and the product of pretax income and the tax rate.

7. Redeemable preferred stock must be classified separately from shareholders' equity and certain additional information disclosed.
8. Reserve recognition accounting for oil and gas producing companies.
9. Different materiality tests. Certain SEC S-X rules require disclosure not called for by GAAP, for example:
   - Notes receivable representing more than 10 percent of aggregate receivables must be shown separately.
   - If LIFO is used, the excess of replacement over LIFO cost.
   - In retained earnings, the undistributed earnings of unconsolidated subsidiaries and affiliates accounted for under the equity method.
   - Net sales of tangible products and, separately, revenue from rentals, services, and other sources if any of these exceeds 10 percent of total revenue.
   - Cost of tangible goods sold and cost of sales of other revenues, separately.

Regulation S-X requires disclosure of cost of sales, selling, general and administrative expenses, and interest and amortization of debt discount and expenses, regardless of the form of income statement used by the registrant.

Regulation S-K specifies the contents of the items required by Form 10-K, and it is interesting to study these requirements in detail as indicative of one view of full disclosure.

Item

1. Description of business;
   (a) General development of business,
   (b) Financial information about industry segments for three most recent years,
   (c) Narrative description of business,
   (d) Financial information about foreign and domestic operations and export sales.
2. Description and location of principal plants, mines, and other properties, and how held.
3. Significant legal proceedings (pending or in progress) in which the corporation is involved. Separate forms are to be filed for such agreements as to underwrite securities and for legal opinions rendered.
4. Security ownership of certain beneficial owners and management, particularly holders of more than 10 percent of any class of securities.
5. Market price of the registrant's common stock and related security holder matters. Involves specifying the market where the securities are traded, highs and lows for the two prior years, approximate number of shareholders, frequency and amount of dividends paid.

6. Selected financial data for each of the last five fiscal years or the life of the registrant and its predecessors, if less. Includes net sales or operating revenues; income (loss) from continuing operations (also on a per share basis); total assets; long-term obligations; capital leases; redeemable preferred stock; and cash dividends declared per common share.
7. Management's discussion and analysis (MDA) of financial condition and results of operations. It is in this part of the corporate filing that changes in S-K requirements are most significant. The stated objective of the new section is to require (1) a complete commentary on the changes in financial position as reflected in all the financial statements presented and (2) a specific discussion of liquidity and capital resources. The latter requires an evaluation of the amounts and certainty of cash flows from operations and from external sources. The SEC has emphasized the importance of this item by stating, "Management is in the best position to know what it is about its company that is important to the users of its reports, and management need not await the development of specific disclosure requirements by the Commission."

   The MDA section covers the three years of information provided in the financial statements. It must discuss three financial aspects of the registrant's business: liquidity, capital resources, and results of operations. Forward-looking information is encouraged, but not required.
8. Financial statements and supplementary data. Two years' balance sheets and three years' income statements and statements of changes in financial statements are to be filed on a consolidated basis. Financial statements and notes thereto shall be presented in Roman type at least as large and legible as 10-point modern type. The form and content of the financial statements are specified in Regulation S-X.
9. Names and addresses of directors and executive officers together with certain other information.
10. Indemnities of officers and directors and other transactions with them.

Regulation S-X also calls for a considerable number of exhibits and schedules listing various items summarized in the financial statements, and for notes describing accounting policies, methods, and changes. Provision has been made for smaller companies to file an abbreviated Form 10-K, thus giving effect to the concept of *differential disclosure*.

Somewhat contradicting the view that the SEC has provided more information for sophisticated users is the new role which management's financial discussion and analysis has been given. The change is from a discussion of percentage changes on a line-by-line basis to a discussion of selected items which places more emphasis on trends and on the balance sheet. In particular, it must include an analysis of the company's liquidity, which sophisticated users can provide for themselves from the financial statements.

Noteworthy, however, is the absence of any inflation accounting requirement. The Chairman of the SEC was an active proponent of inflation accounting throughout the years prior to 1980, and in speeches and articles he expressed the SEC's intention to do something about accounting for price-level changes if the FASB failed to act. In 1979 the FASB issued *Statement No. 33* requiring the largest U. S. corporations to publish supplementary information on both a constant dollar and a current cost basis, and the SEC thereupon withdrew its own replacement cost disclosure requirements, laid down in *ASR No. 190*. Presumably, the SEC has been convinced that users of financial statements would find price-level adjusted financial statements difficult to evaluate, and require a period of experimentation before such statements are incorporated into Regulation S-X.

However, early in 1981 the SEC amended Regulation S-K, Item 12, to require that companies subject to *FASB Statement No. 33* disclosure requirements on the effects of changing prices, include such information in most SEC filings. It would automatically be included in Form 10-K via the annual report; the new requirement extends disclosure to various registration statements, proxy statements and the like. In addition, discussion concerning the effects of inflation and changing prices is required for all companies, in the management discussion and analysis section.

There is a considerable area of overlap between the GAAP promulgated by the APB/FASB and the accounting standards of the SEC. The SEC's disclosures are those required by one who holds, or contemplates holding, the securities issued by a corporation; the APB/FASB disclosures are aimed at preventing such disclosures from being incomplete or misleading. Most importantly, however, the SEC places the financial statements in the context of the business which they purport to represent and the stock markets on which its securities are traded; this broader perspective seems to have escaped both the APB and the FASB.

THE GENERAL PROBLEM OF CORPORATE DISCLOSURE

The United States is probably unique in that corporate disclosure in the states is not governed by corporation laws. In the United Kingdom, for example, the Companies Acts specify what must be reported by the directors and other officers of a company, and legal liability attaches to noncompliance. In Germany the precise form of the financial statements is laid down in the corporation laws (*Aktiengesetz*), and departure from this form can have serious legal consequences.

Nevertheless, even in those jurisdictions where the law dictates the form and contents of corporate reports there is a problem of disclosure. We observe that many companies include more data and additional information in their annual reports than called for by the law and are therefore obliged to ask the same question.

The question is: what should be disclosed in financial statements and in the reports of which financial statements form the central part? It is one which has become a subject of wide ranging debate in the accounting literature. The main objective of the SEC is disclosure through registration statements, prospectuses, and other filings, and insofar as the SEC has permitted the accountancy profession to establish its own principles and standards, disclosure has acquired special significance for the accountant.

In spite of this, no meaningful concept of disclosure can be identified either in SEC or AICPA sources. It is generally agreed that accounting reports should disclose that which is necessary to make them not misleading[2]—but this appears to be an open-ended construct, and attempts to make it more specific lead only to confusion. At first sight the potential area of disclosure is commensurate with the information available to management, and thus a workable construct of disclosure could be derived from analysis of management decisions. An attempt will be made later in this chapter to examine this approach. Recent developments have indicated that such a construct is inadequate, since some interested parties look to financial statements and the reports in which they are presented to disclose matters not normally part of a management information system. Such matters could include data believed useful for macroeconomic models and data having assumed relevance to the solution of social problems, such as employment of the disadvantaged and environmental quality control. It is easily perceived that these data could include observations not required by managers to perform their functions efficiently. It therefore appears that the concept of disclosure extends beyond the search for fairness and that problems of disclosure cannot be solved by reference to the legal rules against *suppressio veri* or *suggestio falsi*.

A major problem can arise when different governmental regulatory agencies prescribe for different disclosures of the same, or similar, information, often defining the object of disclosure in different terms. Line of business (LOB) sales, costs, and assets; direct and portfolio investments by foreigners in the United States and by U. S. corporations overseas; expenditures on pollution control and environmental protection are examples of this situation. Even within the area of accounting rule making there is an acute problem; can one reconcile the disclosure requirements of the SEC, APB, FASB, and IRS on a change to the LIFO basis of inventory valuation?

The question of materiality also has to be answered in this new context. The conventional view of materiality as a function of size arises from the definition of materiality as that which is capable of affecting judgment. But if disclosure must be related to the purposes of unspecified users, no size determinants can be identified. In the United Kingdom, for example, companies are required by law to report charitable donations, a very insignificant corporate expenditure. The current debate on materiality will also be examined in this chapter.

Among the references to disclosure we meet the modifiers "adequate," "fair," and "full," which appear to some to designate a progression. As Hendriksen has pointed out, there is no real difference between the three concepts; adequate disclosure must be full and fair, and so on.[3]

THE TRADITIONAL VIEW OF DISCLOSURE

We have observed that the boundaries of disclosure extend beyond the financial statements themselves and even beyond the reports in which these statements appear. However, we shall first examine the traditional view—that disclosure is theoretically commensurate with financial reporting.

This view proceeds from the assumption that the principal or sole objective of financial reporting is to assist in buy/hold/sell decisions of investors, particularly those investors lacking the powers to obtain information at will.[4] Extension of this assumption to a definition of investment resource allocation directs attention to the needs of others besides present and potential future stockholders. These have been classified as *direct users* and *indirect users*, and the two classes are listed in Table 7-1.

TABLE 7-1
Users of Financial Statements

Direct Users		**Indirect Users**
Owners	Present	Financial Analysts and Advisers
Creditors and Suppliers	and Potential	Stock Exchanges
Managers		Lawyers
Taxing Authorities		Regulatory or Registration Authorities
Employees		
Customers		Financial Press and Reporting Agencies
		Trade Associations
		Labor Unions

It should be emphasized that these groups are not mutually exclusive; the same individuals, corporations, and financial institutions which supply goods on credit or loan money also hold equity or ownership interests. The indirect users can exist only as providers of services to direct users. Further, the lists are not definitive; since *APB Statement No. 4* was written, social action groups have become influential users of financial statements. Although this fact has not been formally acknowledged by the FASB, *Statement of Financial Accounting Concepts No. 4* included in the user group for nonbusiness financial reporting "legislators, the financial press and reporting agencies, labor unions, trade associations, researchers, teachers, and students."

At this point we encounter the difficulty exposed in chapter 6 on the objectives of financial statements. The concept of information disclosure can be structured only by reference to the perceived or assumed needs of a specified user or user group, because different users have different information needs. For example, even where investors are narrowly defined as present and potential future stockholders, a distinction may be made between the standard user, who is assumed to understand accounting, and the unskilled user, who cannot interpret financial statements. This observation leads to the idea of *differential disclosure* which SEC spokesmen have exposed since 1974, and to the current state of "smørgasbord" financial reporting, in which different figures for different purposes are laid out, in the manner of hors d'oeuvres, for the user to select.[6] These ideas contrast sharply with the current AICPA official position that financial reports should be general-purpose sources of financial information designed to serve the common needs of those interested in them.

Recent research aimed at identifying the user group has discovered that the "investor" category is not homogeneous.[7] Institutional investors are one user group, the members of which are highly comparable in terms of personal characteristics, such as education and training, experience, and other qualifications. Financial analysts, who mainly assist institutional investors, also resemble the latter in these respects. Individual investors, however, of whom there are approximately 30 million in the United States, are not homogeneous in any respect. There is a sizeable subgroup which resembles the institutional investors and financial analysts in respect of the personal characteristics mentioned. However, perhaps the majority of individual investors would have to be classified as unskilled users or nonusers.

This same research has elicited the information that the most important investment objective of both institutional and individual investors is long-term capital gain (or a combination of dividend income and long-term gain). It has also been discovered that the majority of those surveyed acknowledge multiple objectives, that is, they also place some importance on short-term gains. Thus, investment (resource allocation) decisions are being taken by those unskilled in financial report analysis, and also by those sometimes referred to as sophisticated users in situations where it may be surmised that they act on information other than that contained in financial reports.

Assuming that the difficulty of identifying the user can be overcome, the traditional view of financial reporting states that the problem of disclosure can be referred to the two qualitative characteristics of relevance and reliability.[8] But information which is relevant for one purpose is not necessarily relevant for another, and *Statement of Financial Accounting Concepts No. 2* reminds us that some relevant information may have little value. Decision theory postulates a set of parameters which must be known before the criterion of relevance can be met.[9]

Suppose that we can apply the criterion of relevance; the next question is how much to disclose? The traditional view specifies the following elements of the disclosure model:

1. Income statement,
2. Statement of financial position (including statement of retained earnings and statement of stockholders' equity),
3. Statement of changes in financial position,
4. Notes to financial statements,
5. Audit report.

These elements, as we have seen, do not automatically dictate the quantitative aspects of disclosure. The perception, classification, accumulation, and aggregation of data are subject to what *APB Statement No. 4* referred to as constraints, such as—

- Conflicts of objectives, or the trade-off between verifiability and relevance.
- Environmental influences, of which the most important is the economic question of value of information compared to cost of providing it.
- Incomplete understanding of the purpose of the information.

Statement of Financial Accounting Concepts No. 2 does not assist us in finding the proper balance between characteristics, such as relevance and reliability, or in distinguishing between conservatism as bias and conservatism as prudence. Enumeration of the elements of financial statements does not answer such disclosure questions as detail of analysis or method of aggregation. Acceptance of the accrual system does not necessarily lead to articulation between the income statement and balance sheet. There are many problems of financial reporting which are dependent for their solution on the investigation of the concept of disclosure.

DISCLOSURE OF FORECAST AND OTHER INFORMATION

A new twist to the disclosure problem has been given by the debate on whether or not to include forecast information in financial reports. For some years the SEC vacillated on this issue, before coming out guardedly in favor of some forecast information. Dr. John C. Burton, when chief accountant of the SEC, directed attention to the continuous aspect of business operations, suggesting that while quarterly, annual, or other periodic reports may be useful, continuous timely reporting may be preferable to reporting the results of a single time period. As an example of this approach, Dr. Burton suggested the use of exception reporting; historical reporting would occur only at times when a change in expectations arose.

The Trueblood Report regarded forecast information as important to meet the objectives of financial statements, a position which met with almost unanimous opposition from corporate executives, public accountants, lawyers, and even financial analysts, who prefer to make their own projections. Table 7-2 summarizes the arguments for and against the publication of forecasts.

TABLE 7-2
Arguments Concerning Forecast Information

For publication	Against publication
• The sophisticated investor will understand the uncertainty inherent in forecasting and be able to use the information.	• There will be "undue credibility" and an inevitable tendency to mislead.
• The effect on an unsophisticated investor should not dominate disclosure decisions.	• Failure to achieve projected results would undermine investor confidence in management and capital markets.
• Continuous forecasting would direct attention away from short-run results and lead to greater attention to long-term trends.	• Forecasts would lead to an undue preoccupation with management's ability to achieve results in the short-run.
• Investors need forecasts.	• There is no evidence of such a need; both management and investors seem to want to make their own projections separately.
• Projections are routinely obtained by financial analysts who make the public pay for "stale" information.	• Projections which have been "filtered" through the mind of a skilled analyst are more useful to the public.
• No more liability would attach to an inaccurate forecast than now attaches to an erroneous going concern assumption.	• The risk of legal liability for erroneous forecasts would result in their being misleadingly conservative.
• Publication of forecasts would help investors by putting pressure on management to achieve forecast results.	• Shareholder pressure to achieve forecasts would lead to short-run decision making.
• Since management is best able to command information about the business, it is best able to make projections.	• Management may benefit from, and be in a position to effect, the manipulation of stock prices through the publication of unrealistic projections.

At various times during the 1970s the SEC also promoted ideas to require corporations to disclose social information, that is, information that might be useful to the public in making political decisions, and for management to report on internal control. The Advisory Committee on Corporate Disclosure recommended against the former, but a report on the state of internal control appeared to be appropriate following the passage of the Foreign Corrupt Practices Act and the issuance of *ASR No. 242*. The proposal met with strong opposition, not only because it might lead to self-incrimination but because of its implications for the accounting profession generally. These are as follows:

- The implications of the FCPA being as yet unclear, and its provisions the subject of debate, accountants could not be expected to know what the report should address.
- Internal control is but one of the responsibilities of management to which the accountant directs attention and which an auditor may be called upon to examine. A comprehensive management audit would be more appropriate than a selective statement on internal control.
- By requiring auditors to test all components of the internal control system every year, the SEC would be, in effect, setting audit standards, which remain the prerogative of the accounting profession.

The SEC's proposals on internal control reporting were withdrawn during 1980. Among the factors leading to this is the view that government-mandated disclosure tends to chill both creativity and competition in commercial "speech." It therefore contravenes the First Amendment, and it has been remarked that the U.S. Supreme Court will only uphold "time, place and manner" restrictions on free speech. Even publication of forecasts could probably not be prevented if the case went to the Supreme Court.

In its *Guide for a Review of Financial Forecasts* (1980) the AICPA permitted independent accountants to report on forecasts. The report should merely state that the accountant has reviewed management's forecast information, that it conforms with the AICPA *Statement of Position (SOP) 75-4*, "Presentation and Disclosure of Financial Forecasts," and that no claim is made that the forecast results will be attained.

ACCOUNTING AS A COMMUNICATION PROCESS

The disclosure problem belongs within the general area of communication.

> Accounting is the process of identifying, measuring, and communicating economic information to permit informed judgments and decisions by users of the information.[10]

Sterling has presented a graphic model to handle accounting as a measurement-communications system.[11]

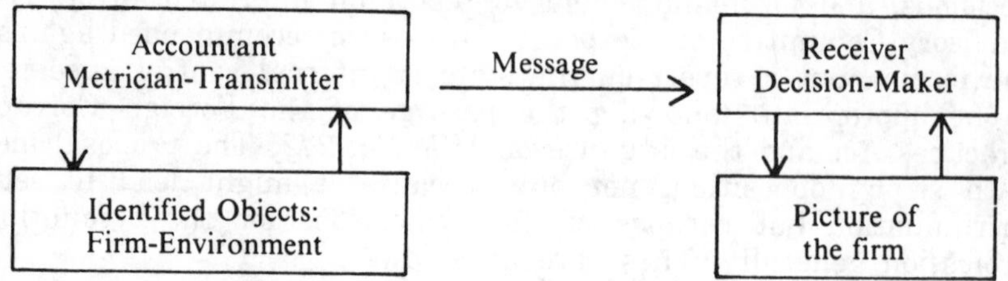

In this model, the accountant measures observed attributes of the firm in relation to its environment and transmits these measurements in message form (the financial statements) to the investor-user. The investor-user has an image of the firm in which he is interested, permitting him to interpret that message.

There are a number of conceptual problems to be solved before this model can be validated.

1. Does the accountant measure? Measurement is itself a science called metrology, with its own methodology in which accountants are not trained.
2. If the accountant does not measure, then he receives messages containing measurements and transmits them. The simpler Shannon and Weaver model seems more relevant to this situation.[12]

   Source→Transmitter→Channel→Receiver

3. There can be a considerable variance between the reality as perceived by the transmitter and as perceived by receiver; indeed, the problem of separating the identified object from the person observing it is a fundamental philosophical difficulty. Chambers has abstracted from it by postulating as an ideal the neutrality of the accountant; Chambers' actor must be able to perceive what the accountant has observed as if he, the actor, had observed it himself.[13]
4. If accounting is only a part of the information system serving the user, it is necessary to identify the position of financial statements in a vector of messages or to assume that the user utilizes financial statements exclusively.

In spite of these criticisms, the communication approach to disclosure has considerable promise.[14] It forces us to analyze disclosure into parts: the *elements*, as in the Shannon and Weaver model; the *dimensions*, as in questions of materiality and other constraints; and the *process*, which is the accountant's role. It also permits us to examine the message without reference to user needs. In a sense, the accountant becomes a mapmaker, and financial statements can be viewed as maps of the territory they represent.

The critical feature of the message is that it is independent of transmitter and receiver. Thus, there is no concordance between message and meaning; meaning lies in the minds of the transmitter and the receiver. Further, the communication process can be disturbed, a phenomenon known as "noise." Noise consists of those factors which interfere with the message, such as overloading the channel (too much data) or using a linguistic code for inputs which differs from the one used for outputs. This occurs when the user of financial statements cannot understand (decode) them. Terminology is still the fundamental accounting problem.

METHODS OF DISCLOSURE

Disclosure in accounting takes a number of forms, principally—

1. The basic financial statements, consisting of an income statement, a statement of financial position, and a statement of changes in financial position, together with, where necessary, a statement of retained earnings and a statement of changes in stockholders' equity.
2. The auditor's certificate. This is more properly defined as a report by the auditor disclosing the reliability of the financial statements. Thus, the auditor's certificate would be the appropriate place to disclose departures from generally accepted accounting principles and their effects, changes from one generally accepted accounting principle to another and their effects, and differences of opinion between auditor and client on these and other questions.
3. Footnotes, which are conventionally viewed as forming part of the financial statements. Analysis of the contents of footnotes reveals that they are likely to be of three kinds:
   - A. Schedules and exhibits more properly viewed as part of the financial statements themselves, as for example, analysis of the item, "Property, plant and equipment—net." Before the obligation to present a separate funds statement, sources and application of funds were frequently shown in a footnote, as is still the case in some European countries.
   - B. Explanations of items appearing in the financial statements, such as methods of valuation of inventories, depreciation policy, effects on future years of lease and pension obligations.

C. Information additional to the contents of the financial statements and auditor's certificate. This information may either throw light on the financial statements as a whole (e.g. consolidation policy; effects of translating foreign currencies), or refer to specific matters not included in the financial statements, such as contingent liabilities and subsequent events.[15]

4. Statistical data derived from the financial statements, of which earnings per share is the prime example. Such data are sometimes presented in a separate, supplementary report.

5. Supplementary financial statements, such as those required under *FASB Statement No. 33* on the effects of price-level changes. Segment reporting under *FASB Statement No. 14* may be viewed as belonging here, and also the SEC-mandated Reserve Recognition Accounting for oil and gas producing companies.

Unfortunately, the footnotes have tended to become substitutes for financial statement items; the possibility of avoiding an accounting decision by mentioning the item in a note has acted as a severe brake on the modernization of financial statements. For example, where unquoted investments have substantially altered their value since acquisition, companies which disclosed the fact tended to do so by way of footnote, rather than by amending the asset valuation directly.

In practice, the number and size of footnotes should be severely scrutinized, as they are often obscure and may even contradict the financial statements themselves. Information which does not fall under categories (1) to (3) above should be disclosed in a non-accounting part of the report, such as the president's letter or directors' review. Information which purports to specify accounting policies and methods used is critical,[16] but the complexities of practice cannot be explained in a short note, and a long one would remain unread.

Adoption of the phrase "objectives of financial reporting" in *FASB Statement of Financial Accounting Concepts No. 1* drew attention to the need to specify more clearly the difference between financial reports and financial statements as vehicles for disclosure. The FASB exposed this problem in an *Invitation to Comment* (a rarely used type of document embracing characteristics of both a Discussion Memorandum and an Exposure Draft), entitled "Financial Statements and Other Means of Financial Reporting" on May 12, 1980.

The publication made use of the "information spectrum" concept. For the purpose of this concept the FASB separated the notes from the "body" of the statements, even though financial statements invariably state that the notes form part of them. The FASB's objective was to attempt to identify *what*, *who*, and *where* questions: what information should be disclosed, by whom, and where. The following possibilities were suggested:

	All Enterprises	Designated Enterprises
Required information in financial statements		
Required information in notes to financial statements		
Required supplementary information		
Information required to be made available on request		
Voluntary information		

The *Invitation to Comment* discussed these possibilities within the framework of the qualitative characteristics adopted by the FASB in *Statement of Financial Accounting Concepts No. 2*, and came to no conclusions. The problem places the FASB on the horns of a dilemma. If "financial reporting" is defined as communicating information derived from an accounting system, it is difficult to see what should *not* be included in the financial statements (notes being part thereof). If financial reporting extends to information not found within the accounting system it becomes an open-ended construct without clear meaning.

The road to disclosure of nonaccounting information is a difficult one, as earnings per share illustrates. This statistic is used by financial analysts as a variable in their share valuation models; prior to *APB Opinion No. 15* it was being computed in a variety of different ways. The APB attempted, in its longest opinion, to standardize this nonaccounting measure; its attempt was not successful, and an even longer Interpretation had to be issued (*Computing Earnings per Share*). Even this failed to provide financial analysts with the information they seek; more to the point, earnings per share has diverted attention from the opportunity to provide a much more useful accounting ratio, return on invested capital.

The "who" part of the *Invitation to Comment* raised the issue of differential disclosure which is dealt with next.

DIFFERENTIAL DISCLOSURE—"LITTLE GAAP"

Since the APB began its proliferation of rules in the early 1960s, accountants have criticized their application to small businesses, virtually all of which are privately owned. Many owners of such businesses have complained to Congress, to the AICPA, and to the standard-setting agencies about the cost and inconvenience of applying rules which were designed for large public corporations.

In 1976 a committee of the AICPA recommended the establishment of less stringent reporting requirements for small businesses.[17]

Disclosure requirements for nonpublic corporations were first made different from those for public corporations by *FASB Statement No. 21*, "Suspension of the Reporting of Earnings per Share and Segment Information by Non-public Enterprises" (1978). A nonpublic enterprise is a firm other than one whose debt or equity securities are traded in a public market, or is required to file financial statements with the SEC. Such a firm is not required to report earnings per share or segment information in financial statements which purport to have been prepared according to GAAP. Thus was born what has come to be referred to as "Little GAAP."

Slightly different is the fact that *FASB Statement No. 33*, "Financial Reporting and Changing Prices" (1979) was made applicable only to corporations with net assets of $1 billion or more, or gross property, plant, and equipment of $125 million or more. In the first place, the Statement requires the publication of *supplementary* financial statements to show the effect of price-level changes, and secondly, it was an avowed experiment designed to pave the way for a subsequent Standard which presumably would have a wider applicability. It could, therefore, eventually become applicable to small businesses.

Different again is the argument that not only are disclosure rules, but also measurement rules, oppressive to small businesses. Although accrual accounting is widely used by small businesses, such features of GAAP as lease capitalization under *FASB Statement No. 13* and tax allocation under *APB Opinion No. 11* are viewed as complicating and adding cost to the preparation of financial statements for small businesses without adding to their informational content.

MATERIALITY

Many financial reporting decisions hinge on the question of materiality; all FASB statements and interpretations explicitly state that they apply only to material items. Yet materiality is a quality or state, and to seek to answer the question "what is materiality?" is a philosophical exercise. There is no materiality, but there are material things. How can we recognize them?

Accounting Research Study No. 7 of the AICPA defined materiality by saying that "a statement, fact or item is material, if giving full consideration to the surrounding circumstances, as they exist at the time, it is of such a nature that its disclosure, or the method of treating it, would be likely to influence or to 'make a difference' in the judgment and conduct of a reasonable person." The SEC's definition for the purposes of Regulation S-X, Rule 1.02(m) is basically the same. But this definition requires explanations of such phrases as "surrounding circumstances," "likely to influence," and "a reasonable person."

Some attempts to identify quantitative measures of materiality have been made; they differ. In one case the SEC specified 1 percent of a given amount; in another, the effects of timing differences necessitating tax allocation need be disclosed only when the amount exceeds 5 percent of the product of income before tax and the "applicable statutory Federal Income Tax rate." In *APB Opinion No. 15* a 3 percent reduction in earnings per share through dilutive securities can be disregarded. The SEC's *ASR No. 159* provides alternatives: 10 percent of the corresponding amount in the previous period or more than 2 percent of the average net income or loss from the three preceding years.

On the other hand, accountants acknowledge that materiality is a qualitative concept. This is clear from *APB Opinion No. 30*, para. 24, which states under this heading:

> The effect of an extraordinary event or transaction should be classified separately in the income statement... if it is material in relation to income before extraordinary items or to the trend of annual earnings before extraordinary items, or is material by other appropriate criteria. Items should be considered individually and not in the aggregate in determining whether an extraordinary event or transaction is material.

Pattillo and Siebel provided four classes of factors which influence materiality:[18]

1. Financially related quantitative factors,
2. Financially related qualitative factors,
3. Nonfinancial quantitative factors, and
4. Nonfinancial qualitative factors.

The FASB's Discussion Memorandum on the subject reduced these to three: quantitative, nonquantitative, and a combination of the two.[19] As an example of the last, the Discussion Memorandum gave this statement.

> a. If the amount of its current or potential effect equals or exceeds 10 percent of a pertinent financial statement amount, the matter should be presumed to be material.
> b. If its amount or current or potential effect is between 5 and 10 percent of a pertinent financial statement amount, the materiality of the matter depends on the surrounding circumstances.

Appendices C and D of the Discussion Memorandum contained a list and, in one case, a reproduction of empirical studies designed to investigate how materiality decisions are made. After reviewing these studies the Discussion Memorandum concluded that "although the literature suggests the desirability of authoritative criteria for the determination of materiality, a sufficient basis for the development of operational criteria that would be responsive to the needs of users has not been developed."

Appendix D of the Discussion Memorandum contained a similar statement from a different viewpoint:

> The question remains however, whether that objective of providing the 'average prudent investor' with information necessary to make an informed investment decision is attainable without knowledge of the characteristics of the average investor or the decision model that he uses.[20]

The authors proposed additional research to test the association between security price changes and the magnitude of unexpected changes in accounting variables, on the assumption that the securities market is "efficient" in the sense that prices fully reflect all presently available information. The research which has been conducted reveals the researchers divided on the issues.[21] Benston and Gonedes found either no significant impact or an impact which suggested that the quantitative criteria generally proposed are far too low. Ball and Brown found that reported earnings correlated with price movements and consequently would constitute an appropriate base for judging materiality, but other studies have shown a clearer correlation between share prices and earnings reported subsequently.

Statement of Financial Accounting Concepts No. 2 relegated materiality to a place of lesser importance, behind the primary qualitative characteristics of relevance and reliability (see Figure 7-2). It emphasized the circumstantial aspect of materiality judgments and the significance of the degree of precision with which a particular item can be measured. The FASB accepted the proposition advanced by many respondents to the Discussion Memorandum, that materiality judgments can be made only by those who have all the facts.

> The Board's present position is that no general standards of materiality could be formulated to take into account all the considerations that enter into an experienced human judgment....The essence of the materiality concept is clear. The omission or misstatement of an item in a financial report is material if, in the light of surrounding circumstances, the magnitude of the item is such that it is probable that the judgment of a reasonable person relying upon the report would have been changed or influenced by the inclusion or correction of the item.

An illustration of the difficulty of the materiality problem was provided by the publication of *FASB Statement No. 34*, "Capitalization of Interest Costs" at the end of 1979, just a few months before the publication of *Statement of Financial Accounting Concepts No. 2* in May, 1980. *Statement No. 34* stated that "notwithstanding the requirements of this Statement, if the effect of interest capitalization and its subsequent amortization or other disposition is not material, compared with the effect of charging interest to expense as incurred, capitalization is not required." Some readers interpreted this as meaning that capitalizing interest, otherwise required under the Statement, could be avoided under certain circumstances, thus creating a new materiality test. *FASB Statement No. 42*, "Determining Materiality for Capitalization of Interest Cost—an amendment of *FASB Statement No. 34*," deleted that language and made clear that the usual tests of materiality apply for implementing *Statement No. 34*. Given that Concepts Statement No. 2 acknowledged that the usual tests are incapable of precise formulation, it is difficult to see what *FASB Statement No. 42* means.

FIGURE 7-2
A Hierarchy of Accounting Qualities

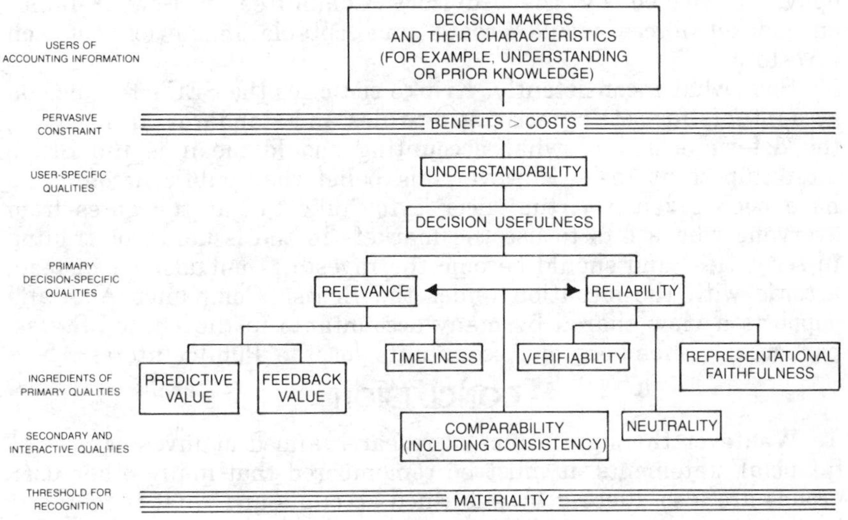

Source: FASB Statement of Financial Accounting Concepts No. 2, 1980.

DOES THE SEC PROTECT INVESTORS?

One of the most informed critics of the SEC's disclosure system is Homer Kripke, who served on the SEC's staff for five years, and was the lone member refusing to sign the final report of the SEC's Advisory Committee on Corporate Disclosure. His dissent has been republished in a book which criticizes the SEC's procedures.[22]

Kripke's basic point is that the SEC has consistently tried to ensure that corporate disclosures include only objective facts, and has, therefore, ensured that projections and hopes for the future are kept in the dark. The SEC apparently believes that investors do not have the knowledge or experience to handle "soft" information in a critical fashion. Prospectuses, which should be of the greatest importance to investors, are therefore valueless, and publication of useful information is often delayed by the SEC staff until it has become stale. Nor has the SEC been successful in attempting to reduce corporate fraud; the growth of the Enforcement Division and the accelerating rate of enforcement actions may even be construed to mean that increasingly restrictive regulation breeds violation. Again, even though the Commission sees itself as the stockholder's protector, it has done little or nothing to protect against predatory, and sometimes fraudulent, brokers and investment advisers.

Kripke's view is that everything we know about stock markets points to the importance of predictions, rather than historical facts, and the effects of macroeconomic factors, rather than firm-specific developments. Efficient market research indicates that even if left alone firms will provide adequate information about their activities, because market forces oblige them to do so. The SEC's basic philosophy, reaffirmed by the Advisory Committee, is that reliance on market forces would create unacceptable inequities between investors.

Somewhat inconsistently, Kripke criticizes the SEC's reliance on accountants for setting accounting rules and standards. In his view, the determination of what accounting should mean is the SEC's most important task. However, his belief that public accountants have been given a virtual license to "take toll at the gates from everyone who wants to use the markets in the issuance or trading in securities" and should become the investors' ombudsmen instead, accords with the situation under the British Companies Acts and supports a view shared by many accountants in the United States, particularly members of Accountants for the Public Interest.

CONCLUSION

Whatever the significance of research aimed at investor uses of financial statements, it must be remembered that many other user groups are also affected by published accounts and what is material to them may be quite different. In a recent Supreme Court case (*TSC Industries*, *Inc. v. Northway*, *Inc.*) the opinion of Justice Thurgood Marshall contained this statement:

> The question of materiality, it is universally agreed, is an objective one, involving the significance of an omitted or misrepresented fact to a reasonable investor. Variations in the formulation of a general test of materiality occur in the articulation of just how significant a fact must be or, put another way, how certain it must be that the fact would affect a reasonable investor's judgment.[23]

In this case, the Court concluded that omission of a fact in a proxy statement was material if there was a substantial likelihood that a reasonable shareholder would consider it important in deciding how to vote. Expanding this proposition to cover other user groups suggests that the search for a specific materiality criterion must prove abortive.

The Foreign Corrupt Practices Act of 1977 confirmed that the concept of "significance" was more important in the law than that of materiality. "Significant" includes "material" but is more comprehensive; the SEC, which is entrusted with the enforcement of the FCPA contends that compliance with section 13(b)(2) of the Act should be tested against a threshold of importance lower than the level of materiality ordinarily applied by auditors when reporting on financial statements.

Coupled with the SEC's new disclosure provisions, which make the annual report the principal vehicle for corporate financial disclosure and therefore permit the SEC to dictate the form and content of financial reporting generally, the substitution of significance for materiality effectively transfers responsibility for determining disclosure questions to the legal system.

The prospect of government as a setter of accounting standards does not inspire confidence, for several reasons. First, the level of corporate disclosure in those countries where accounting standards are set by legislation is noticeably lower than that in countries where the accounting profession is responsible for the task. Secondly, the government is basically a modifier of behavior and does not seek to initiate. If this "rule of conduct" approach tries to restrain behavior viewed as unfair, disclosure standards must change frequently in response to public perceptions of fairness. If the government seeks to modify behavior by offering incentives for actions believed to contribute to the government's economic goals (such as, for example, stimulating investment), then it must be realized that there is no general agreement among economists about how such goals are attained.

In the last analysis, however, government is not concerned with individuals but with abstractions: "the people" or "the public." Government standards must be uniform, leaving no discretion in the hands of those who apply them to individual circumstances. In its extreme form, that of accounting standard setting in the Soviet Union, government standards abandon all pretence at impartiality or objectivity; the financial statements must show what should be, not what is.[24]

ENDNOTES

1. *Report of the Advisory Committee on Corporate Disclosure to the Securities and Exchange Commission*, Vols. 1 and 2, Washington, D.C.: U.S. Government Printing Office, November 3, 1977.
2. Maurice Moonitz, "The Basic Postulates of Accounting," *Accounting Research Study No. 1*, New York: AICPA, 1961, p. 50. See also AICPA, *By-Laws*, *Code of Professional Ethics*, Art.2.02 and Rule 3.06, and Regulation S-X, Securities and Exchange Commission.
3. Hendriksen, Eldon S., *Accounting Theory*, Homewood, Ill.: Richard D. Irwin, Inc., 1977, p. 546.
4. *Objectives of Financial Statements*, New York: AICPA, 1973.
5. Accounting Principles Board, *Statement No. 4*, New York: AICPA, 1973.
6. Devine, Carl T., "Some Conceptual Problems in Accounting Measurement," in *Research in Accounting Measurement*, ed. Jaedicke, Ijiri, and Nielson, American Accounting Association, 1966, pp. 13-27.
7. Chang, Lucia S. and Kenneth S. Most, *Financial Statements and Investment Decisions*, Miami: Florida International University, 1979.
8. *Statement of Financial Accounting Concepts No. 2*, "Qualitative Characteristics of Accounting Information," Financial Accounting Standards Board, May 1980,

para. 15. The proposition derives from *A Statement of Basic Accounting Theory* (ASOBAT), American Accounting Association, 1966, p. 7.
9. Halter, Albert N. and Gerald W. Dean, *Decisions under Uncertainty*, Cincinnati: South-Western Publishing Co., 1971, p. 9
10. ASOBAT, op. cit. p. 1.
11. Sterling, Robert R., "A Statement of Basic Accounting Theory: A Review Article," *Journal of Accounting Research*, Spring 1967, pp. 95-112.
12. Shannon, Claude and Warren Weaver, *The Mathematical Theory of Communication*, Urbana: University of Illinois, 1949, p. 5.
13. Chambers, R.J., *Accounting, Evaluation and Economic Behavior*, Englewood Cliffs, N.J.: Prentice-Hall, Inc. 1966.
14. Bedford, Norton M. and Vahe Baladouni, "A Communication Theory Approach to Accountancy," *The Accounting Review*, October 1962, pp. 650-59.
15. It has been suggested that footnotes should be classified by importance into primary and secondary classes. This dual classification scheme was proposed by Coyner, Randolph S. and Lawrence J. Stern in "A Classification Scheme for Financial Footnotes," *Management Accounting*, May, 1981, pp. 43-46 and 55.
16. APB Opinion No. 22, *Disclosure of Accounting Policies*, 1971.
17. *Report of the Committee on Generally Accepted Principles for Smaller and/or Closely Held Businesses*, New York: AICPA, August 1976.
18. Pattillo, J.W. and J.D. Siebel, "Factors Affecting the Materiality Judgment," *CPA Journal*, July 1974, pp. 39-44. See also position papers by Arthur Young & Company (1976), Ernst & Ernst (1975), and other public accounting firms.
19. FASB Discussion Memorandum, *An Analysis of Issues Related to Criteria for Determining Materiality*, Financial Accounting Standards Board, March 21, 1975.
20. O'Connor, Melvin and Daniel W. Collins, "Toward Establishing User-oriented Materiality Standards," *Journal of Accountancy*, December 1974, pp. 171-74.
21. Benston, George J., "Published Corporate Accounting Data and Stock Prices," *Empirical Research in Accounting: Selected Studies 1967*, supplement to *Journal of Accounting Research*, pp. 1-54; Gonedes, Nicholas J. "Some Evidence on Investor Actions and Accounting Messages—Parts I and II," *The Accounting Review*, April 1971, pp. 320-28 and July 1971, pp. 135-51; Ball, Ray and Philip Brown, "An Empirical Evaluation of Accounting Income Numbers," *Journal of Accounting Research*, Autumn 1968, pp. 159–77. See also ch. 3, pp. 68–71.
22. Kripke, Homer, *The SEC and Corporate Disclosure: Regulation in Search of a Purpose*, New York: Law & Business, Inc., Harcourt Brace Jovanovich, 1979.
23. 426 U.S. 438 (1976).
24. In 1981 the Federal Home Loan Bank Board, faced with the fact of substantial losses by savings and loan associations, adopted a rule designed to improve the appearance of their financial statements. A loss incurred when a mortgage is sold to a government agency for a price below book value may be deferred and written off over the remaining life of the mortgage loan. A more obvious example of the approach of a governmental agency to accounting standards could hardly be found.

SELECTED ADDITIONAL READINGS

American Accounting Association Committee on Non-Financial Measures of Effectiveness, "Report of the [AAA] Committee on Non-Financial Measures of Effectiveness," *The Accounting Review*, January 1971, pp. 47-49.

Asebrook, Richard and D.R. Carmichael, "Reporting on Forecasts: A Survey of Attitudes," *Journal of Accountancy*, August 1973, pp. 38-48.

Barlev, Benzion, "On the Measurement of Materiality," *Accounting and Business Research*, Summer 1972, pp. 194-197.

Bedford, Norton M., *Extensions in Accounting Disclosure*, Englewood Cliffs, N.J.: Prentice-Hall Inc., 1973.

Benston, George J., "Evaluation of the Securities Exchange Act of 1934," *Financial Executive*, May 1974, pp. 28-36; 40-42.

———, "Public (U.S) Compared to Private (U.K.) Regulation of Corporate Financial Disclosure," *The Accounting Review*, July 1976, pp. 483-98.

———, "The Baffling New Numbers Game at the FTC," *Fortune*, October 1975, pp. 174-179.

Bernstein, Leopold, "The Concept of Materiality," *The Accounting Review*, January 1967, pp. 86-95.

Birnberg, Jacob G. and Nicholas Dopuch, "A Conceptual Approach to the Framework for Disclosure," *Journal of Accountancy*, February 1963, pp. 56-63.

Blumberg, Phillip I., "Public's 'right to know': disclosure in the major American corporation," *Business Lawyer*, July 1973, pp. 46-50, 52-54.

Buzby, Stephen L., "The Boundaries of Adequate Disclosure," *The Singapore Accountant*, Vol. 10, 1975, pp. 83-91.

Carmichael, D.R., "Reporting on Forecasts: A U.K. Perspective," *Journal of Accountancy*, January 1973, pp. 36-47.

Chambers, R.J., "Usefulness—The Vanishing Premise in Accounting Standard Setting," *Abacus*, December 1979, pp. 71-92.

Financial Accounting Standards Board, *Analysis of Issues Related to Criteria for Determining Materiality*, Stamford, Conn.: FASB, March 21, 1975.

———, *Statement of Financial Accounting Concepts No. 2*, "Qualitative Characteristics of Accounting Information," Appendix C. Stamford, Conn.: FASB, May 1980.

Foster, George, "Accounting Policy Decisions and Capital Market Research," *Journal of Accounting and Economics*, Vol. 2, 1980, pp. 29-62.

———, *Financial Statement Analysis*, Englewood Cliffs, N.J.: Prentice-Hall, Inc., 1978.

Frishkoff, Paul, "An Empirical Investigation of the Concept of Materiality in Accounting," and Rose, J., W. Beaver, S. Becker, and G. Sorter, "Toward an Empirical Measure of Materiality," *Empirical Research in Accounting: Selected Studies*, 1970, *Journal of Accounting Research*, pp. 116-129 and 138-153.

Gonedes, Nicholas J., Nicholas Dopuch, and Stephen H. Penman, "Disclosure Rules, Information Production, and Capital Market Equilibrium: The Case of Forecast Disclosure Rules," *Journal of Accounting Research*, Spring 1976, pp. 89-106.

Holmes, William, "Materiality—Through the Looking Glass," *The Journal of Accountancy*, February 1972, pp. 44-49.

Longstreth, Bevis, and H. David Rosenbloom, *Corporate Social Responsibility and the Institutional Investor*, New York: Prager Publishers, 1973.

Nelson, Carl L., "Case for Accounting Disclosure," *CA Magazine*, March 1975, pp. 35-38.

Rappaport, Alfred and Eugene Lerner, *A Framework for Financial Reporting by Diversified Companies*, New York: National Association of Accountants, 1969.

Report on the Advisory Committee on Corporate Disclosure to the Securities and Exchange Commission, Vols. 1 and 2, Washington, D.C.: U.S. Government Printing Office, 1977.

Sterling, Robert R., "A Statement of Basic Accounting Theory: A Review Article," *Journal of Accounting Research*, Spring 1967, pp. 95-112.

Sunder, Shyam, "Why Is The FASB Making Too Many Accounting Rules," *The Wall Street Journal*, Manager's Journal, April 27, 1981.

Woolsey, Sam, "Approach to Solving the Materiality Problem," *Journal of Accountancy*, March 1973, pp. 47-50.

———, "Materiality Survey," *Journal of Accountancy*, September 1973, pp. 91-92.

Case 7-1 Dunes Hotels and Casinos, Inc.

Dunes Hotels and Casinos Inc. (formerly Continental Connector Corporation) operates the Dunes Hotel and Casino in Las Vegas. One of the management problems of operating a casino is how to collect gambling debts, which can be substantial and are not usually recoverable by legal action.

According to the 1979 annual report of this corporation, a former Dunes director named Sydney Wyman authorized advances of $607,500 to various gaming customers. Management was subsequently unable to determine the identity of the individuals receiving the advances, which were fully reserved and, following Mr. Wyman's death in 1978, written off as irrecoverable. The Executor of Mr. Wyman's estate denied any obligation in this matter. Indeed, Mr. Morris A. Shenker, chairman of the Dunes board and virtual owner of the corporation,* felt personally obligated to protect Mr. Wyman from liability for these advances prior to his death because of their long personal friendship and successful business association.

Note 3 to the 1979 financial statements recounted that a Mr. David Reese, manager of the Dunes' poker room, perceived that the Dunes reputation, and its poker business, were being damaged by the gaming community's knowledge of attempted collection from the Wyman estate. He concluded that if he were to personally repay the advances by purchasing the receivables from the Dunes his personal reputation would be greatly enhanced and poker business at the casino increase substantially.

According to affidavits prepared at the request of the Dunes Audit Committee, Mr. Reese brought this plan to Mr. Shenker, with the information that he was unable to arrange his own financing. Mr. Shenker thereupon borrowed $650,000 from a bank which also lends money to the Company, and loaned $600,000 to Mr. Reese. Mr. Reese then paid the Company $607,500 in settlement of the Dunes claim against Mr. Wyman's estate, which was accounted for as a recovery of a bad debt. The terms of the Shenker-Reese note were the same as those of the bank-Shenker note, and the Company did not endorse or accept liability for either.

*Mr. Shenker owned, directly or indirectly, 46 percent of the common stock of the Company. A further 36 percent was owned by I.J.K. (Nevada) Inc., wholly owned by Mr. Shenker and family.

This transaction took place on June 7, 1979. In March, 1980 the Company renewed Mr. Reese's employment contract for a period of one year, at a salary of $5,000 monthly plus 50 percent of the poker room's operating profit in excess of $45,000 monthly.

The Dunes reported a net income of over $2 million for each of the years 1978 and 1979, after deducting substantial losses on discontinued operations, principally retailing and trucking. The Company's auditors provided a clean audit certificate for both years.

1. Why did the notes to financial statements disclose the details of these events and circumstances?
2. Does this situation shed light on the difference between financial statements and financial reporting?
3. How can accounting standards ensure that financial affairs, which may be as bizarre as those recounted in this case, are disclosed in financial reports, and aid auditors to satisfy themselves that the financial statements "present fairly" what they purport to represent?

Case 7-2 The Topper Toy Corporation

In 1970, The Topper Toy Corporation was the second largest U.S. toy manufacturer. Sales for 1970 were about $64 million, made on the terms which were customary in the industry at that time. Customers had from five to eight months to pay for the goods or return them, but the sale was recorded when the goods were shipped.

In December 1971, shareholders received a letter announcing that the Corporation expected to report a loss of between $10 and $15 million in 1971. A nine-month report previously received had showed net income of about $15 million, which was about five times the 1970 net income. The main cause of the turnaround was that $14 million of 1970 sales had been returned by customers. By early 1972, Topper's inventory had ballooned and its receivables had to be written down to net realizable value. By February, 1973, the Corporation had filed for bankruptcy under Chapter II and ceased operations.

It was not until January 1973 that the Corporation's auditors, one of the Big Eight, finally withdrew its report on Topper's 1970 financial statements, which had been unqualified.

1. Did Topper's 1970 accounting practice reflect an acceptable definition of revenue?
2. Which would be more informative:
   a. to not report sales until the customer paid, or
   b. to report sales on invoiced delivery and make full provision in cost of sales for estimated returns, or
   c. to report sales as invoiced deliveries minus the estimated provision for returns?
3. What standard did the FASB subsequently lay down to cover this type of problem?

END OF CHAPTER QUESTIONS

1. Why was the SEC created, and how? By what means does it make its views known? What force does an Accounting Series Release possess?
2. Explain the need for Regulation S-X.
3. Why were the 1980 disclosure reforms necessary? What was the principal long-term effect of the new system?
4. Give examples of non-GAAP disclosures required by the SEC.
5. What is the required content of the Management's Discussion and Analysis section of the Annual Report?
6. What is the basic issue in corporate disclosure? How is this issue faced in the United States and in other countries?
7. Explain what is meant by the "traditional view of disclosure."
8. Who are the users of financial statements? Are investors a single user group? How do we know that financial reports are used for investment decisions?
9. What are the "elements of the disclosure model"? What are the issues which recognition of these elements leaves unresolved?
10. Discuss the reasons for disclosure of forecast information, and the probable reasons why there has been so much resistance to such disclosure. What are the current positions of the AICPA and the SEC on forecast disclosures?
11. Explain the relationship between the communication model of financial reporting and the problem of disclosure.
12. What problem has emerged from the use of footnotes to explain and expand upon financial statement items?
13. Why was the FASB constrained to publish an invitation to comment on "Financial Statements and Other Means of Financial Reporting"? What dilemma did this reveal?
14. What is meant by "differential disclosure"? Describe the efforts which have been made so far to implement this concept.
15. Define *materiality*, and discuss whether it is a quantitative or a qualitative construct.
16. Why do you think that it is so difficult to lay down uniform materiality standards?
17. Explain why Professor Kripke and others maintain that the SEC does not protect investors. What is the relevance of this argument to the theory of corporate disclosure?
18. Distinguish between the accountant's concept of materiality and the lawyer's concept of significance.
19. Discuss the reasons for and against placing the responsibility for accounting standard setting in the public sector.

8

INCOME AND CAPITAL

The distinction between income and capital has become a topic of debate because the price-level changes resulting from inflation have drawn the accountant's attention to the problem of recognizing the maintenance of capital. We have become aware that *capital maintenance* can be measured in units of money, in units of constant purchasing power, and in monetary representations of physical means of production.

The concept of income has great importance to accountants; many believe that income measurement is the central accountancy function. The shift in the emphasis of financial reporting from the balance sheet to the income statement was recognized by writers on accounting during the 1930s. It is tempting to attribute interest in the measurement of business income to this cause, but there is evidence of deeper roots. As Brown has pointed out,[1] the phenomenon we have remarked is merely an *external* shift; the income statement was increasingly important *internally* by the second half of the nineteenth century at the latest because of—

1. The separation of management from ownership in the corporate form of business enterprise, which substituted profitability for technical efficiency as the criterion of success;
2. The need for management information to plan and control operations to this end;
3. The growth of short term credit repayable from operations and the need to track changes in liquidity resulting from changes in profitability.

The introduction of income taxation in 1916 provided the trend with additional impetus as the income tax laws do not define the word "income."

THE SEMANTIC PROBLEM

The problems associated with the measurement of income and capital have been compounded by a semantic one. The businessman's "profit" is subtly different from the economist's "income," and the word "earnings" which some accountants have sought to use in this context is different again. Comprehensive income, a term used by the FASB in *Statement of Financial Accounting Concepts No. 3*, is defined as the change in equity (net assets) of an entity during a period from transactions and other events and circumstances from nonowner sources, but this does not correspond with current accounting usage. A donation of land to a business by a local authority, for example, would be included in the FASB's definition, but not recognized as an element of income in preparing an income statement.

These semantic differences have practical implications. The economist's view of profit as income derived from taking risks does not correspond with the lawyer's view of profit as a source of dividend income, which is encountered in corporate charters as early as the year 1600. The legal view, originating in the agreement of prudent businessmen that it is unsound to pay dividends out of capital except when liquidating a firm, is known as the *capital impairment rule* or the *profits test*. The concept of comprehensive income appears to be neutral with regard to where the money came from or how it is to be used; it is a static concept, not a dynamic one.

Another semantic problem is the belief that taxable income and business income are different views of the same economic phenomenon. The definition of "taxable gross income" in the Internal Revenue Code is a pure legal construct, arrived at without reference to accounting principles. The deductions allowed by the income tax code have functions quite different from those of expenses in income statement preparation, even though the amounts may be identical in many cases.

A more fundamental question, however, remains. Why did American corporations choose to report income rather than profit or loss? Examination of early published financial reports which included an income statement reveals a longstanding disinclination to report profits. The corporations concerned were using the term *net income* as early as 1903 (U.S. Rubber Company) and by the 1920s it was in general use. In 1928, an editorial in the *Journal of Accountancy* commented on the importance of Irving Fisher's definition of income to accounting[2] which Canning attempted to demonstrate the following year.[3]

The significance of this can be seen from the observation that until the present time businesses outside the United States have reported profit or loss and used a *profit and loss account* for the purpose. Even in Germany, where economists' views have been influential in that the Companies Acts require a value-added form of income statement, it is called a profit and loss account and ends with a figure for profit (or loss), not net income. Net income is an economic concept meaning something quite different, specifically the net return (from production) which must be spent to keep the process going[4] and, more generally, net monetary receipts.

Generally accepted accounting principles are not very helpful in responding to this question. In 1941, *ARB No. 9* rejected the word "profit" in favor of "income" largely because of the *Eisner v. Macomber* legal definition, which no longer represents legal thinking on this subject. In *ARB No. 43* it was pointed out that "the word income is used to describe a general concept, not a specific and precise thing." And *Accounting Terminology Bulletin No. 2* (1955) defined net income as synonymous with earnings, which FASB *Statement of Financial Concepts No. 3* categorically denies.

There have been a number of attacks on the *entity income* concept in recent years. Vatter pointed out that "the measurement of income is not the sole, or even the most important, aim of accounting" and that "it is impossible to present a single income figure that will begin to meet all the demands which will be made upon it.... It may well be that accountants should avoid the complications, confusions and disappointments which arise from overemphasis on 'net income.'"[5]

Dissatisfaction with the income statement results from—

1. The lack of an agreed concept of net income in accounting theory.
2. The many ways in which business net income can be derived in accounting practice, the consequence of multiple generally accepted accounting principles for arriving at revenue and expenses.
3. Inability to agree on the effects of inflationary price-level changes and how to report them in the income statement.
4. Its uselessness for short-run decisions.
5. The absence of physical or behavioral data which would make it more useful for analysis.

In this chapter we shall review the legal, economic, and accounting concepts of income and examine the related concept of capital, to better understand the modern income statement and its relationship to the balance sheet and statement of changes in financial position. This discussion is predicated on the general observation that prices of goods and services change; the problem of inflationary price-level changes is left for chapters 10 and 11.

THE USES OF NET INCOME

The most pervasive use of a net income figure is probably as the numerator of a ratio, the denominator of which is some number of shares, a ratio called *earnings per share*. This ratio is believed to be an important factor in investment decisions, because a share price can be found by multiplying earnings per share by a price-earnings multiplier, or P/E ratio. In fact, the required magnitudes are *predicted* earnings per share and a *future* P/E ratio; in the absence of these, financial analysts use surrogates, of which earnings per share is one.

The income statement *as a whole* has a wider function or set of uses. Management uses it as a *planning model*, and a target net income figure may be a key variable in operating such a model. Because of its use as a planning model, management also uses the income statement for *control*, comparison of actual results against planned to determine variances from the plan. In this sense, income can be said to provide a measure of efficiency. The income statement also provides a point of departure for determining taxable income, since many of the elements of business and taxable income are common.

The net income figure is also used as a predictor of future net income, particularly when valuing a business on sale of all or part of the ownership interest. It is required for calculating distributable amounts (dividends) where corporation law or the company's charter restrict the amount of dividends in this way. Financiers look at the net income of a business as "cover" for interest payments on money lent to the business. Regulatory agencies and politicians regard net income as an indicator of exploitation of monopoly powers and issue regulations or enact laws designed to restrict it. Unions frequently look to net income as a fund for wage increases.

The conflict of objectives represented by this variety of uses is depicted in Table 8-1.

TABLE 8-1

Uses of Net Income	Net Income Concept
1. Earnings per share	Future net income and number of shares outstanding
2. Investors	Net income
3. Managerial planning and control	Revenue minus expenses (operating income)
4. Taxable income	Excess receipts
5. Business valuation	Maintainable profit
6. Dividend cover	Distributable profit
7. Interest cover	Income before interest and income taxes
8. Political and regulatory	Pure profits
9. Labor unions	Value added

This conflict of objectives reflects itself in a conflict of measurements. Managers require an all-inclusive, long-run concept of income, the ultimate return on investment; this includes holding gains and losses, as well as the result of revenue and expenses on operations, and necessitates accruals and deferrals which many accountants regard as subjective. Investors look to business net income as an indicator of future managerial performance; they would rather exclude irregular and extraordinary items. The concepts of pure profits and value added imply charging to expense interest on capital employed, a practice clearly at odds with the needs of financiers who would like to see as an expense, interest actually paid out. Prediction necessitates excluding extraordinary items and prior period adjustments, which must be included in determining distributable income.

For this reason the search for a single income concept has been abandoned by some theorists in favor of measuring and reporting several concepts of net income. Although associated initially with Devine,[6] this view was popularized by ASOBAT[7] which looked forward to an expansion of the scope of accounting. "The committee believes that initially this expansion will be reflected in accounting reports with multiple valuations."

Acceptance of this proposition by the FASB can be seen from *Statement of Financial Accounting Standards No. 33*, "Financial Reporting and Changing Prices," which calls for the presentation of several different measurements of income from operations.

INCOME AND CAPITAL

Income is a flow of wealth; capital is a stock of wealth. The wealth represented as a flow is capital at any point in time. There can thus be no fundamental difference between income and capital. Yet examination of the literature on accounting and economics reveals the extent of misunderstanding on this point.

For the difficulties which economists have experienced it suffices to refer to Irving Fisher's great work.[8] Some of their different viewpoints will be presented later in this chapter. As examples of accountants' problems, extracts from Kohler's *A Dictionary for Accountants* and the *Accountants' Handbook* are provided.

CAPITAL

1. Goods produced and intended for further production.
2. The amount invested in an enterprise – proprietorship, partnership, or corporation – by its owners; paid-in capital.
3. Legal capital: that portion of stockholder's contributions allocated to capital-stock account by the board of directors, bylaws, articles of incorporation, or agreement with stockholders; stated capital.
4. The amount so invested plus retained income (or earned surplus); net worth; net assets; stockholders' equity.
5. Net worth plus long-term liabilities; also, the equity of security-holders.
6. (economics) (a) One of the factors of production: goods produced by man and used in further production; wealth (of an individual) devoted to

obtaining money income; any wealth employed with productive intent; e.g., consumers' capital; producers' capital. See capital asset. (b) Hence, net worth plus all liabilities; the total of assets. See assets (2).

Because of these varied meanings, all of which have wide currency, a better understanding results where the intended meaning is made clear.

Source: Eric L. Kohler, *A Dictionary for Accountants*, Englewood Cliffs, N.J.: Prentice-Hall, Inc., 5th Ed., 1975, p. 80.

PAID-IN CAPITAL

Corporate Capital and the Accounting View of Corporations

DEFINITION—THE ACCOUNTING CONCEPT The capital of a business enterprise has been defined in various ways. In the business sense, it is considered to be the wealth or investment in the total assets. The accountant thinks of capital as the total assets of the business enterprise less the total liabilities. For the corporate form of business it is synonymous with "shareholders' equity." "Paid-in capital" is considered by the accountant as that part of shareholders' equity contributed by shareholders.

Although paid-in capital (contributed capital) may be defined in still narrower terms, some difficulties have been encountered in arriving at a precise definition. Consider the following:

> The total amount of cash, property, and services contributed to a corporation by its stockholders.... It may be reflected in a single account, now generally preferred, or divided between capital stock and paid-in surplus accounts. (Kohler, A Dictionary for Accountants)
>
> The full amount invested by stockholders is recognized as paid-in capital or invested capital. [It may be increased by transfers from retained earnings.] (Simons and Karrenbrock, Intermediate Accounting)
>
> Invested capital refers to the portion of stockholders' equity which arose from the commitment of assets to the enterprise, including transfers from retained earnings.... (Sprouse and Moonitz, Accounting Research Study No. 3)
>
> Paid-in capital is measured by the cash, or fair market value of other assets or services, contributed by stockholders or persons acting in a capacity other than that of stockholders or creditors, or by the amount of liabilities discharged upon the transfer of an equity from a creditor to a stockholder status. (American Accounting Association, Accounting and Reporting Standards for Corporate Financial Statements)

Source: Accountants' Handbook, New York: The Ronald Press Company, 5th ed., 1970, 21-1.

And the AICPA (Accounting Terminology Bulletin No. 1) recommends that the contributed portion of proprietary capital include amounts paid in by shareholders and capital received other than for shares, whether from shareholders or from others.

The shareholders' equity section of currently published financial statements usually presents the paid-in or contributed capital as consisting of two portions: (1) the par or stated value of shares of stock issued and (2) the excess of the paid-in or contributed capital over and above the stated or par value of the shares issued. In general, the accounting usage of the term paid-in capital includes contributions of assets by shareholders and nonshareholders, as well as retained earnings capitalized by stock dividends. Paid-in capital is simply the amount put into (invested in) the business enterprise by shareholders. Some accountants would also include as part of paid-in capital, assets arising from changes in the purchasing power of money even though technically they do not represent a source of capital.

Typifying the confusion of thought referred to above, Kohler included both assets and liabilities in his definition, whereas the authors of the *Accountants' Handbook* preferred assets *minus* liabilities.

In economic theory, capital is *always* a stock concept, in part because economic theory abstracts from time. For the same reason, the economist need not distinguish between capital and assets, between the source of the wealth and its use at any point in time. The primary meaning of capital in accounting is the relationship between an entity and the source of its wealth. In the case of the sole proprietorship or the partnership, the source can be clearly seen to be the proprietor or partners, hence their *capital accounts*. In the case of the corporation, the position is not so clear because of legal concepts of capital, and we distinguish between contributed capital and retained earnings, both of which are, directly or indirectly, provided by the stockholders. Inability to name the source of the wealth causes accountants to avoid the term capital in accounting for government entities and not-for-profit organizations generally.

Other meanings of the word are derived from this one. We speak of *loan capital* to indicate that the source of the wealth it represents was a loan. The total capital employed by an entity, or total assets, is the wealth it employs at any point in time, but its total capital is also the wealth of those who have transacted with the entity to put this wealth at its disposal. We are not dealing with a simple identity: loan capital endures after the related assets have disappeared.

The economist's concept of capital is consistent with this interpretation, although few economists have been able to put it into words which indicate this fact. One who did was Bernard Shaw.

> Take the case of a workman with an allotment [smallholding]. He discovers that he can get nothing out of it until he digs it; and he cannot dig it without a spade. Therefore he must save enough out of his wages to buy a spade... and with it the workman makes

> his allotment produce vegetables enough for his table and perhaps a few over which he can sell. The vegetables are the income which he derives from his capital, as we call the sum he saved to buy the spade... although the digger possesses the spade he does not still possess the money the spade cost. That has been eaten up by its makers and the ironmonger, and is gone for ever.... And whether the capital contributed... be six shillings for a spade or six millions for a colossal industrial plant or a fleet of transatlantic liners, once the plant and ships are constructed and the six millions spent on the subsistence of the workers whose labor has constructed them, those millions are consumed irrevocably, and their appearance as figures in the balance sheets is only a memorandum having no substance in fact.[9]

The concept of capital maintenance implies that in measuring flows of wealth through time, the sources must be clearly separated. The flow of wealth from customers (retained earnings) must be accounted for separately from the flow of wealth from investors, or financiers, or the government in the form of subsidies. It does not mean what economists mean, maintaining physical assets intact, or their value equivalent, which construct is used *for the measurement of social income*.[10] Only if this is understood can the meaning of Goudeket's much-quoted proposition be grasped:

> At Philips we hold to the view that there can be no recognition of income for a period unless the capital employed in the business at the beginning of the period has been maintained, that is to say, after it has been established that the purchasing power of that capital at the end of the period is equal to that at the beginning of the period.[11]

Clearly, this refers to capital and not to assets; one cannot speak of the purchasing power of raw materials, work in process, finished goods, land, buildings, or plant and equipment.

LEGAL CONCEPTS OF INCOME

The distinction between capital and income, between "the tree and the fruit," was known to Roman law, if not before. This legal concept had great importance in the development of the concept of taxable income.

Another distinction, originating in the common law, was probably equally influential on business accounting. The trust was a common law creation designed to break the feudal system of land tenure. In a trust we distinguish the *corpus*, or capital, from the trust income. The capital of a trust is the property which the trust acquired from the trustor, as modified by acts allowed under the trust instrument. It will be seen that this concept resembles closely the accounting concept of capital, and it appears from accounting decisions of the English courts during the nineteenth century that judges saw company directors as trustees for the shareholders.

The significance of this observation for income determination lies in the concept of waste. The common law recognized three types of waste: permissive, voluntary, and equitable. Permissive waste—allowing the stately home to fall into disrepair—did not have to be made good (charged against income), and the trustee was not liable for voluntary waste, some act of the trustee which caused damage to the property. Only acts which were clearly inequitable, that is, which were a purposeful reduction of the value of the trust estate, would be restrained by the courts. Early English court decisions seem to have approached income determination by looking at sales revenue as gross trust income and requiring the deduction of ordinary expenses incurred, which did not include depreciation or depletion.

The absence of a federal corporation law and the inadequacy of state laws have denied us a comparable case history in the United States. The legal concept of income has been debated primarily in income tax cases, of which *Eisner v. Macomber* is the best known.[12] The issue there was whether Congress could tax a corporate stock dividend as income, and a lengthy opinion of the U.S. Supreme Court held that stock dividends did not constitute income within the meaning of that term in the Sixteenth Amendment. This is called the *narrow holding of Eisner v. Macomber*, which supports the broad view that profits exist only when an increment in wealth is realized.

> Income may be defined as the gain derived from capital, from labor or from both combined, provided it be understood to include profit gained through sale or conversion of capital assets... enrichment through increase in any value of capital investment is not income in any proper meaning of the term.

This broad view excludes holding gains and losses from the definition of taxable income. Justices Holmes and Brandeis dissented; the majority view was severely criticized by lawyers as well as economists. In *Helvering v. Bruun*[13] the Supreme Court considered whether the value of a lessee's structure which reverted on expiry of the lease constituted income to the lessor. The Court held that the realization rule in *Eisner v. Macomber* was only intended in the narrow context of stock dividends. The Court stated that:

> While it is true that economic gain is not always taxable as income, it is settled that the realization of gain need not be in cash derived from the sale of an asset.... It is not necessary to recognition of taxable gain that he should be able to sever the improvement begetting the gain from his original capital.

By the 1960s the remains of *Eisner v. Macomber* were ready for interment. The Supreme Court equated realization with "realizability"[14] and held that a nonreciprocal transfer of assets from husband to wife in a divorce settlement could create income in the difference between the fair market value of the property transferred and its cost.[15]

Professor Lowndes has commented on the disappearance of realization as an element in the constitutional definition of income.[16] It would appear that the legal concept of taxable income in the United States is no longer dominated by Roman and medieval English law, but it is not clear what concept of income will result. Professor Lowndes has suggested that the authority for this lies with Congress.

ECONOMIC CONCEPTS OF INCOME

Like many other terms in economics, income has no one clear meaning. Among the concepts which economists have used at various times we find income being—

1. A fund for consumption
2. A series of periodic receipts
3. The product of a particular productive activity
4. The increase in value of a particular asset or group of assets
5. Specified classes of receipts
6. Any receipts

Net income, of course, is one of these less some other variable.

Until the latter part of the nineteenth century, it was clear to economists that all were cash concepts. A fund for consumption was equated with expenditure; the increase in the value of assets was an increase in money capital; naming classes of receipts involved excluding from consideration those benefits not received in cash.

Toward the end of the nineteenth century we find a growing realization that income was not adequately described in terms of cash, culminating in the capital and income theories of Böhm-Bawerk and Wicksell. Briefly, the preindustrial model of the firm used by the economic theorists of the early nineteenth century was that of the farm. Since there could be only one crop a year (in Western Europe), time could be ignored as an economic variable; all time periods were the same size. The only way in which time could enter the picture was to equate cash flows at the beginning of the year (for seed and other investment expenditures) with receipts from sale of the crop one year later. This equation was effected by discounting the future receipt to its present value at the earlier date. Böhm-Bawerk and Wicksell attempted to adapt this model to industrial reality by means of the assumption of an average time period of production, comparable with the one year agricultural production cycle. Their discounting procedure was taken up by Fisher in order to determine capital and income.

The attempt to develop a *real* (= nonmonetary) analysis of income came to grief in the monetary mainstream of economic theory from Quesnay to Keynes, which produced a cash-based macro or aggregative analysis of *social income*. The great achievement of Irving Fisher was to adapt the ideas of the Austrian and Swedish Schools to the mold of classical economic theory by translating them back into a cash form.[17] It is remarkable that Schumpeter should have referred to this book as "the first economic theory of accounting," as the accrual basis of accounting is wholly incompatible with Fisher's approach.

It appears that Fisher made a major break with previous economic usage of the income concept. He did state explicitly that "a corporation as such can have no net income.... Its stockholders may get income from it but the corporation itself, considered as a separate person apart from these stockholders, receives none."[18] Nevertheless, since Fisher defined capital as income capitalized, it has become commonplace to speak of the income of an investment, a machine, or a corporation. This is fundamentally different from Cantillon's system, where income from agriculture must be spent to keep the production process going, or Keynesianism, where income is the sum of consumption plus saving.

As we shall see, Fisher's concept of income resembles that of a series of periodic receipts. Keynes' concept resembles a fund for consumption, often referred to in the Hicksian version.[19]

> ...it would seem that we ought to define a man's income as the maximum value which he can consume during a week, and still *expect to be* as well off at the end of the week as he was at the beginning. (emphasis supplied)

A number of serious problems are associated with this definition. Hicks had previously pointed out that no difficulty arose in using an income concept in statics, where "a person's income can be taken without qualification as equal to his receipts (earnings of labor, or rent from property)." This is our concept number 3. In representing a dynamic system, however, Hicks did not believe that income (or depreciation, or investment) were suitable tools for analysis because "there is too much equivocation in their meaning, equivocation which cannot be removed by the most painstaking effort." This equivocation arises out of the words, *expect to be*, and the remainder of his chapter six is devoted to a meticulous examination of the nature of the equivocation involved. In this examination, Hicks refers to the idea of making everything depend on the capitalized money value of the individual's prospective receipts as a first approximation, suitable for personal income from property, but unsuitable for more complex situations.

Indeed, the German economist F.B.W. Hermann had already written in 1874 that "income is that portion of an individual's receipts which that individual may consume without injury to his capital stock." The unsatisfactory nature of this concept arose out of the fact that it did not establish definite limits.[20]

FISHER'S THEORY OF INCOME

In summarizing Fisher's theory of income one is conscious of the effort made by Canning to clarify the relationship between the theory and accounting.[21] It may be observed, however, that while Fisher claimed to present an all-embracing theory of income, he narrowed the concept in some respects but left it ambiguous in others. This arose, no doubt, from his "instinctive feeling that there exists a definite income concept" which need not be complete. The approach has been called the *income is* postulate.

Fisher distinguished between three dimensions of income.

1. "Psychic," receipt of satisfactions
2. "Real," receipt of services producing satisfactions
3. "Money," receipt of cash

The *definite income concept* was a flow through time of services yielded by property. This restriction raised the question whether a propertyless laborer could have an income; Fisher concluded that he could. Nevertheless, it is doubtful whether a firm could have an income in this sense, representing as it does "satisfactions." Thus, "business income" must be interpreted as "income of the stockholders," whether distributed to them in the period earned or retained and reinvested.

Fisher assumed that his *money income* dimension was that of the businessman and defined it as *receipts less payments*; hence, no doubt, Schumpeter's interpretation of the theory as an economic theory of accounting. His first example, that of the rent of a house less "actual expenses" (undefined) illustrates both the nexus with human satisfactions and the overriding cash flow concept, rationalized by the statement that services and payments for services are the same thing. One of the most significant accounting innovations has been the development of techniques to measure use separately from acquisition where they occur at different times.

Fisher also achieved a superficial resemblance to accounting by relating income closely to property, resulting in his view of income as an increase of capital. The need to attach income to a particular object, and to define it as services rendered by that object, was a necessary feature of the valuation model which he proposed. This model is essentially the valuation of capital (= asset, for we are discussing an economic theory) as the sum of a series of discounted expected future net receipts, and income as the difference between present value at two points in time. Under conditions of certainty that difference would be interest accruing because of the passage of time (the SEC has called this "accretion of discount"). With uncertainty, changes in present value could also result from other factors, such as revising the estimate of expected future receipts. It may be noted that this valuation model has been used for hundreds of years to value monetary assets and liabilities, Fisher's contribution being to adapt it to serve as a general valuation model.

It is from this that Canning derived his concept of *total lifetime income*:

> Ultimate total income is the final fruition in money both of the enterprise assets and of those other services not listed as assets that... have the economic attributes of assets.[22]

It is difficult to make this transition from expected periodic net receipts to an amount of capital, or assets, at a point in time. We shall attempt to show how Alexander, Solomons, *et al*. have combined the Hicksian and Fisherian concepts of income to produce a more generalized concept which permits *economic income* (sometimes called *business income*) to be closely related to *accounting income*.

Fisher's *ideal* or *standard* income is the algebraic sum of expected net receipts from a specific property, and Canning extended this to cover value changes during the life of the property, realized on liquidation. The net proceeds of liquidation of a firm, minus the capital introduced by its proprietors, and plus any sums withdrawn by them during its lifetime, thus constitute *ultimate total income*. Hicks' view of income as a relationship between expected net receipts and expected consumption resembles this construct except that it abstracts from the time dimension.

THE FISHERIAN APPROACH TO "ECONOMIC INCOME"

Assume that X buys 10,000 shares of common stock in AB Inc. for $11,479 at t_0 in expectation of dividend income. He receives dividends of $1,000 at t_1, $2,500 at t_2, and $3,700 at t_3. He sells the shares at t_4 for $7,000. The period between the *t*'s is one year.

Note that one economic concept of income would calculate the amount as $14,200 (the sum of the dividends and the proceeds of sale) being the cash receipts which could be consumed or saved.

The Fisher-Hicks model can be explained as follows. Let Y_e be income, C be net cash flow from the investment, and K be capital. Then $Y_e = C + (K_n - K_{n-1})$. The present value of the capital at t_1 (K_n); using the 7% discount rate implicit in this problem is $11,282.

Period	C	K_n	K_{n-1}	Y_e	Implicit depreciation
$t_0 - t_1$	$1,000	$11,282	$11,479	$ 803	$ 197
$t_1 - t_2$	2,500	9,572	11,282	790	1,710
$t_2 - t_3$	3,700	6,542	9,572	670	3,030
$t_3 - t_4$	7,000	0	6,542	458	6,542
Total income				$2,721	
Total depreciation (saving)					$11,479

Note that total income is the difference between the expected cash flows of $14,200 and the initial net cash outflow of $11,479 or $2,721. Now add the possibility of reinvesting the income, and we have an infinite return of $803, which is economic income on the constant capital K.

Periods	Y_e	Interest on saving	Total return	Interest computation
$t_0 - t_1$	$803	$ 0	$803	
$t_1 - t_2$	790	13	803	(7%×$197)
$t_2 - t_3$	670	133	803	(7%×$1,907)
$t_3 - t_4$	458	345	803	(7%×$4,937)
$t_4 - t_5$	803	0	803	(7%×$11,479)

Now we introduce uncertainty, in the shape of a change in expectations: at t_2 the proceeds of sale at t_4 change from $7,000 to $8,000. The difference is known as a *windfall* or *holding* gain. Income changes as follows.

Periods	C	K_n	K_{n-1}	Y_e	Adjustment to Ye
$t_2 - t_3$	$3,700	$7,477(1)	$10,445(2)	$732	$873(3)
$t_3 - t_4$	8,000	0	7,477	523	65

(1) $8,000/1.07=$7,477
(2) $3,700/1.07+$8,000/1.07²
(3) Y_e is now $732+$873=$1,605.

Note that the present value at t_2 of $9,572 is *rolled forward* to the new present value of $10,445, and the present value of $6,542 at t_3 is *rolled forward* to $7,477. We shall meet this concept again in chapter 10. The new total income is ($803 + 790 + 1,605 + 523 =) $3,721, exactly $1,000 higher than before.

ECONOMIC INCOME AND ACCOUNTING INCOME

According to Alexander, as revised by Solomons, problems result solely from periodizing income (because ultimate total income is a fact). Since economists discuss *ex ante* income under conditions which imply certainty, it is necessary to coin a new term for a concept of income under conditions of uncertainty. This they called *variable income*; that is, the amount which a person can consume in a year and feel as well off at the year's end as at the beginning may vary from year to year, capital remaining constant.

In a paper which is roughly contemporary with his revision of Alexander, Solomons attempted to specify the distinction between this new concept of economic income and accounting income, as follows:

Accounting income
\+ Unrealized tangible asset changes
− Realized tangible asset changes which occurred in prior periods
\+ Changes in the value of intangible assets
= Economic Income.[23]

The question whether tangible asset changes should be recognized when there is evidence that they have occurred, or only when this evidence is a sale at the new value (realization) is a relatively minor point and would hardly necessitate a borrowing from economic theory to explain accounting income. The key difference is "changes in the value of intangible assets." This does not refer to those intangible assets which appear in business balance sheets but to something called *subjective goodwill* which is implicit in the application of the Fisherian valuation model to the business situation and in the concept of variable income.

Subjective good will is the net present value of expected income-receipts. In the previous example, it will be observed that the amount of the investment ($11,479) included the present value of the dividends, and that net present value was 0.

Although economic accounting is based on a conceptual framework which is quite different from that recognized by the FASB, it has recently produced one financial reporting application.

On August 31, 1978 the SEC published a requirement for oil and gas producing companies to publish supplementary financial statements based on an economic accounting concept of income, by a method called Reserve Recognition Accounting (RRA). This system necessitates finding the present value of proved reserves of oil and gas at a particular date, using then current selling prices and an annual discount factor of 10 percent. Thereafter, a Statement of Results of Oil and Gas Producing Activities must be prepared for each year.[24]

The positive determinants of results are: accretion of discount; effects of revision of present value due to increases in selling prices, changes in reserve estimates, and shortening the production time period; and discoveries and other additions to reserves. The negative determinants of results are: exploration, development and production costs; changes in reserve estimates; purchases of reserves; and eventually, changes in present value due to decreases in selling prices. The difference between these positive and negative elements is reduced by a hypothetical income tax expense to arrive at a figure which the SEC called "RRA results." Oil companies have preferred to call this figure "net income (loss) on the basis of RRA," and it has become customary to refer to it as "RRA earnings." The SEC's original intention was to make economic accounting obligatory for oil and gas producers in regard to their production operations, after a period of experimentation with supplementary statements. (The then Chairman of the SEC, Harold Williams, was an economist.) By early 1981, however, it had become apparent that the usefulness of these statements was a matter of serious question, and the SEC announced that RRA would not be required for the primary financial statements, although supplementary RRA statements would continue to be obligatory. This must be regarded as a serious blow to the *critical function theory* that profit (income) is earned at the time of making the most critical decision, or of performing the most difficult part of the operating cycle.

The following concepts of accounting income are believed to be consistent with the FASB's conceptual framework.

1. *Money income* The excess of assets over liabilities (both found using generally accepted accounting principles) at one date minus the excess at a prior date, after deducting contributions of proprietor capital and adding back dividend payments.
2. *Constant dollar income* Money income indexed to changes in the purchasing power of the money unit by adjusting the elements of financial statements for the effects of changes in the price-level.
3. *Current cost income* Money income indexed to changes in the specific prices of assets and liabilities by adjusting the elements of financial statements for changes in specific prices.
4. *Current cost/constant dollar income* A combination of 2. and 3.

To these accounting concepts of income we must add *replacement cost income*, which involves an attempt to measure in money the physical capacity aspects of assets, and which appears to lie outside the FASB's framework. We must also add *realizable income*, a construct publicized by Chambers and Sterling, and based on accounting at selling market prices.[25] The formula for this is

$$Y_r = D + (R_n - R_{n-1})$$

where Y_r denotes realizable (or current value) income
R_n is similar to K_n above, but is valued at selling price at t_n, and
D is the dividend or distribution for any period.

This system differs from economic accounting in that expected future receipts are not valued at their discounted amounts, but assets are valued at their selling prices. Thus, in place of the accretion of discount and implicit depreciation of the economic income calculation, we have depreciation calculated from the decline in selling price of an asset between two points in time.

In their influential book, *The Theory and Measurement of Business Income*, Edwards and Bell attempted a reconciliation between economic and accounting income.[26] They first examined the Fisher-

Hicks model and rejected it as too simplistic; they were also influenced, it may be surmised, by the desire not to break with traditional accounting method. They then proposed an income concept similar to current cost income, which they called "business income," together with a method of adjustment for the effects of general price-level changes.

The Edwards and Bell model postulates that management decision making requires that the results of operating decisions be evaluated separately from the results of holding decisions. In order to accommodate the results of holding assets while their prices change, they abandon the principle of realization and the unitary concept of income as a change in net assets. The result is structurally different from accounting income. Using Y_a to refer to the latter, and Y_b to refer to business income

$\mathbf{Y_a}$	$\mathbf{Y_b}$
Sales	1. Sales
−Historical cost of goods sold	2. − Current cost of goods sold
±Realized holding gains/losses	3. ± Realized holding gains and losses arising during the period
	4. ± Unrealized holding gains and losses

Using the term *current operating profit* (COP) for 1. minus 2., *realized holding gains* (RHG) for 3. and *unrealized holding gains* (UHG) for 4., then Y_b=COP+RHG+UHG of past periods realized in the current one. As an example, suppose that goods bought for $1,000 at t_0 have a replacement cost of $1,500 at t_1 and are sold for $2,000 at t_2, then $Y_a t_2$=$1,000, $Y_b t_1$=$500 and $Y_b t_2$=$500. If replacement cost rose to $1,800 in t_2 before sale, then COP=$200, RHG=$300, and UHG=$0 for t_2.

The FASB attempted to bring the income measurement and capital maintenance issues together in these terms.

Income Statement approach	**Asset/Liability approach**
historical cost	financial capital measured in units of money
constant dollar	financial capital measured in units of the same purchasing power
current cost	physical capital measured in units of money
current cost/constant dollar	physical capital measured in units of the same purchasing power

The issue of choice between these concepts remains unresolved.

INCOME AS RETURN ON INVESTMENT

The Fisherian concept of income assists us in distinguishing between a return *of* capital and a return *on* capital, which Fisher expressed as a *rate of return on cost*. This construct, which has also been called the marginal efficiency of capital (Keynes), the internal rate of return (Boulding), the discounted cash flow (DCF), rate of return (Dean), and by many other names, is that rate of discount which makes the present value of an expected stream of net receipts equal to the investment in the property producing the receipts. At that rate of discount, net present value (subjective goodwill) is zero.

The reason for the contemporary interest in the measurement of economic income is because of its importance for the neoclassical theory of investment. According to that theory—

- The objective of the firm is to maximize its present value in order to maximize the value of investor capital,
- Present value is a function of future income,
- Future income is a function of present investment, and
- In the absence of other evidence, the best indicator of future income is present income.

An analogous concept in accounting is *return on investment* (ROI) or the profitability ratio, calculated as

$$\frac{\text{Net Income} \times 100}{\text{Total Assets}}$$

In this form it is a measure of the profitability of assets. The purpose of this ratio is to compare profitability (1) between periods (vertical comparisons), (2) between firms (horizontal comparisons), (3) against targets, and (4) between projects (investment choices).

The calculation of ROI takes several forms. In financial analysis, it is usual to exclude interest and taxes from the numerator in evaluating profitability from the lender's viewpoint, and to deduct loan capital from the denominator in evaluating it from the proprietor's viewpoint. The formula illustrated is presented as an overall measure in which the value of resources allocated to production (assets) is compared with the part of the value added by production which is not subject to social claims, such as those of lenders, workers, and government.

The discounted cash flow rate of return used by Dean and the capital budgeting school is a target return, in the sense that *ex ante* calculations resulting in a given DCF rate are the basis for investment decisions. Similarly, the ROI calculation is used in business as a standard, in that achievement of an acceptable ROI is regarded as a measure of efficiency. It has been clear for some time that the coexistence of these two frameworks has serious implications for accountants since reliance by businessmen on a capital budgeting approach to decision making would require a control system based on capturing net cash flows by periods. This problem underlies the preoccupation of the Trueblood Committee with "cash flows to investors."

Given the survival and development of the accrual basis of accounting and financial reporting and its acceptance by the FASB, it would be logical to assume that it is better suited to the needs of users than is the cash flow basis. We may note here some of the more obvious disadvantages to basing income determination on cash flow accounting.

1. It is more difficult to predict cash flows than revenues and expenses, since the latter require one less uncontrollable variable.
2. The DCF concept of income restricts the depreciation plan to the implicit amortization table.
3. It is difficult, if not impossible, to interpret a DCF rate without specifying a named individual or small group to whom it will be meaningful. The acceptance of the idea of a target rate raises the question: for whom?
4. The use of a DCF model restricts attention to cash flows, time, and the discount factor. While the investment decisions of savers may be so simply represented, it is possible that the model is too crude to serve for producers.
5. If net cash flows are only in part a function of revenues and expenses they should be analyzed separately, for example, in the statement of changes in financial position.

A more fundamental criticism, however, is that cash flows are not necessary for accrual accounting and financial reporting, and, therefore, income determination cannot be made dependent on them, as the following situation demonstrates.

> A corporation is established by an oil company and a chemical company, to produce a petrochemical. The oil company transfers to the new corporation valuable patents, and receives 50 percent of the share capital in exchange. The chemical company constructs the process plant, and receives 50 percent of the share capital in exchange. The oil company supplies the corporation with agreed quantities of petroleum feedstock, delivered to the corporation's plant in the oil company's trucks. This raw material is invoiced to the corporation at current prices. The chemical company supplies all managerial and operative personnel, who are paid by the chemical company. The relatively minor other expenses are paid by the chemical company, which invoices them and the payroll to the corporation monthly. The production of the corporation is taken on a 50/50 basis by the joint owners, who collect it in their own trucks; it is invoiced to them at current market prices. No dividend is paid, but profit is simply credited to retained earnings, which are capitalized from time to time by issuing fully paid up shares to the joint owners in proportion to the balances on their current accounts.

Obviously, the financial reporting of such a corporation would be no different from the financial reporting of any other corporation, but it would have no cash flows to report. It can be seen that the viewpoint that accrual accounting is an attempt to normalize the irregularities of cash flows is simply a rationalization.

PROFIT, INCOME, AND EARNINGS

The FASB has adopted the name comprehensive income for the change in owners' equity during a period from nonowner sources, consisting of items B.1.a. and b. in Figure 8-1. The name earnings has been reserved for some intermediate measure of period activity, which has not yet been decided upon. The name profit, still used in virtually every other country but the United States, for the same construct, and still widely used by accountants and others in the U.S. in everyday communication, is frowned upon.

Yet the concept of profit, or net profit, is well understood. In economics it is a difference arising from transactions in two markets, one buying (the *input* market) and one selling (the *output* market). Knight pointed out that this difference arises from uncertainty and is therefore a function of forecasting errors in the two markets.[27] The more complex process of substituting revenues for expenses which produces a figure for accounting profit is no different in nature.

The process was described by Littleton thus:

> ...the point of view of the businessman is that *output* is the result of definitely planned work—the consequence of a prior *service-input* made with intent to create output; *money-income* is the earning flowing from the planned work—the consequence of a prior *money-outlay* made with intent to generate income...we may say then that the costs thus incurred express quantitatively the *causes* which actuate the inflow of services or that the chosen input of services causes the *outflow* of cost-expenditures...net income is the result of a favorable or unfavorable *relation* between revenue and cost.[28]

And, later in the same article:

> Profit (net income) is the result of providing an outflow of economic services (thereby causing an inflow of gross revenue) which services are valued by the purchaser at an amount higher than the input of economic factors (brought about by an outflow of expense) required to produce the services put out.

CONCLUSION

We have noted the increased interest in the income statement during the twentieth century, and the frustration encountered by some analysts when faced with the complexities of accrual accounting. The essential features of accrual accounting are the separate allocation of payment, acquisition, use, and output to periods of time, and many critics would feel easier with a system which focused on cash flows. Nevertheless, the paradox remains that it is easier to

FIGURE 8-1

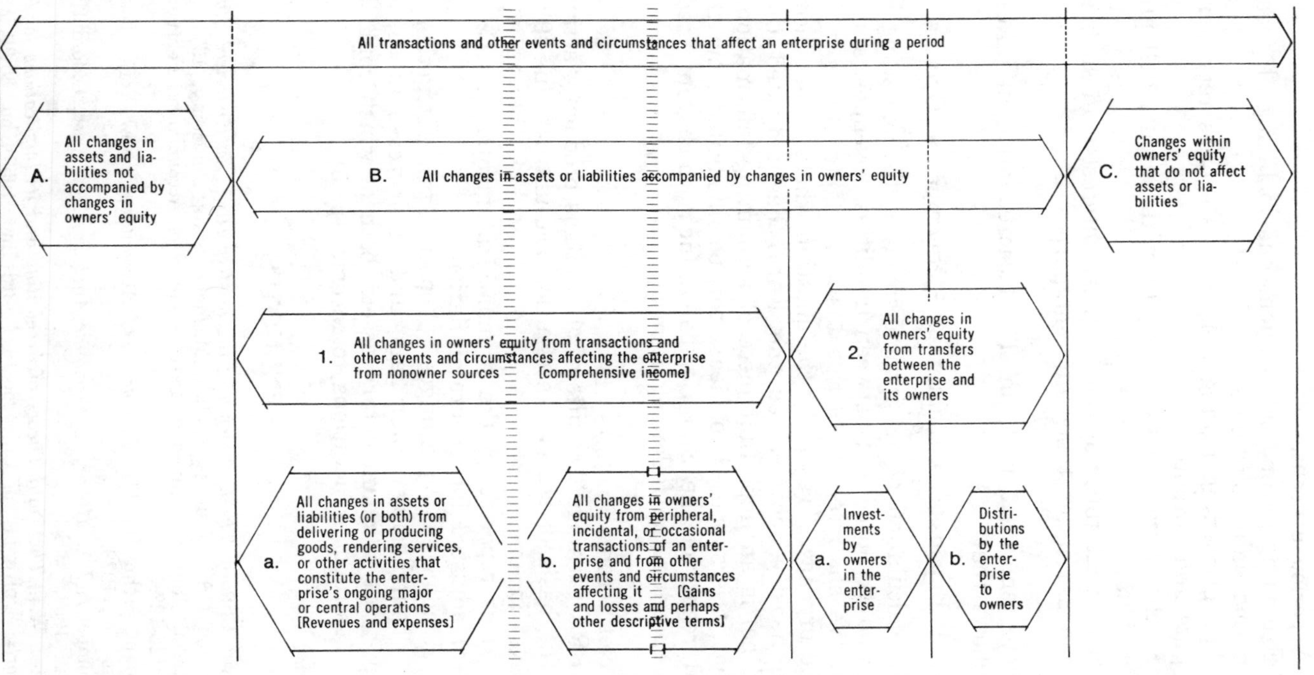

Source: Financial Accounting Standards Board, *Statement of Financial Accounting Concepts No. 3*, December, 1980, p. 23.

predict cash flows from accrual accounting than from cash flow accounting.

The accounting concept of net income is as follows:

1. A period concept,
2. Extending beyond transactions and including all measurable period value phenomena,
3. And permitting aggregation into categories representing inputs and outputs,
4. So that a comparison of inputs with outputs will produce a residual,
5. Such that the majority of those interested in such a figure can use it for their different purposes.

There remains a problem. The basic equation in its expanded form shows that

Assets + Expenses = Liabilities + Revenues + Owners' Equity

and the calculation of net income involves distinguishing between assets and expenses and between liabilities, revenues, and owners' equity. We shall return to this task in chapter 14.

The urgency of resolving the question whether "net income" (or "comprehensive income," as the FASB has indicated the name should be) is an important piece of accounting information, and if so, what it is supposed to mean, can be illustrated from the 1980 annual report of the Sun Company, Inc., which contained statements showing the following items:

- Net income (p. 26);
- RRA earnings ("results of oil and gas producing activities on the basis of reserve recognition accounting") (p. 49);
- Net income:
  - (a) as reported in the primary statements,
  - (b) adjusted for general inflation,
  - (c) adjusted for changes in specific prices together with a purchasing power gain, and an increase in the current cost of nonmonetary assets, both of which could be construed as additions to income. (p. 58).

ENDNOTES

1. Brown, Clifford, *The Emergence of Income Reporting: An Historical Study*, East Lansing: MSU Business Studies, Michigan State University, 1971.
2. Editorial, "Income Defined at Last," *Journal of Accountancy*, February, 1928, pp. 125-127.
3. Canning, John B., *The Economics of Accountancy*, New York: The Ronald Press Co., 1929.
4. Schumpeter, J.A., *History of Economic Analysis*, New York: Oxford University Press, 1954.
5. Vatter, W.J., *The Fund Theory of Accounting and its Implications for Financial Reports*, University of Chicago, 1947 (3rd Imp. 1959), pp. 35-36.

6. Devine, Carl T., "Some Conceptual Problems in Accounting Measurements," in *Research in Accounting Measurement*, ed. Jaedicke, R.K., Y. Ijiri and O. Nielsen, American Accounting Association, 1966, pp. 13-27.
7. *A Statement of Basic Accounting Theory*, American Accounting Association, 1966.
8. Fisher, Irving, *The Nature of Capital and Income*, New York: The Macmillan Co., 1912, Ch. 1.
9. Shaw, Bernard, *Everybody's Political What's What?* London: Constable and Company Limited, 1944, pp. 93-5.
10. Hicks, J.R., "Maintaining Capital Intact: A Further Suggestion." Reprinted from *Economica* in *Readings in the Concept and Measurement of Income*, ed. Parker, R.H. and G.C. Harcourt, Cambridge, England: The University Press, 1969, p. 133.
11. Goudeket, A., "An Application of Replacement Value Theory," *Journal of Accountancy*, July, 1960, p. 38.
12. 252 U.S. 189, 40 S. Ct. 189 (1920).
13. 309 U.S. 461, 60 S. Ct. 631 (1940).
14. *James v. U.S.*, 366 U.S. 213, 81 S. Ct. 1052 (1961).
15. *U.S. v. David*, 370 U.S. 68, 82 S. Ct. 1190 (1962).
16. Lowndes, Charles L.B., "Current Conception of Taxable Income," 25 *Ohio State L. Rev.*, 152 at 158 (1964).
17. Fisher, Irving, op. cit.
18. Fisher, Irving, "Income and Capital," in *Readings in the Concept and Measurement of Income*, p. 46.
19. Hicks, J.R., *Value and Capital*, Oxford: Clarendon Press, 2nd ed. 1946, p. 172.
20. See Mueller, Paul H., "Concepts of Taxable Income: The German Contribution," reprinted from *Political Science Quarterly* in *Readings in the Concept and Measurement of Income*, p. 146.
21. It is, perhaps, too late to point out that Canning demonstrated some confusion. See, e.g. op. cit. pp. 91, 95, 99, 143, 160.
22. Op. cit. p. 95.
23. Alexander, Sidney S., "Income Measurement in a Dynamic Economy," revised by David Solomons in *Studies in Accounting Theory*, ed. Baxter, W.T. and Sidney Davidson, Homewood, Ill.: Richard D. Irwin, Inc., 1962, pp. 126-217; and Solomons, David, "Economic and Accounting Concepts of Income," *The Accounting Review*, July 1961, pp. 374-83.
24. *Accounting Series Release No. 269*, Securities and Exchange Commission. See also SEC Rel. 33-6126 and 6128 and Staff Accounting Bulletin No. 35.
25. Chambers, R.J., *Accounting, Evaluation and Economic Behavior*, Englewood Cliffs, N.J.: Prentice-Hall, Inc. 1966; Sterling, Robert R., *Theory of the Measurement of Enterprise Income*, Lawrence: University Press of Kansas, 1970.
26. Edwards, E.O. and Philip W. Bell, *The Theory and Measurement of Business Income*, The University of California Press, 1961.
27. Knight, Frank H., *Risk, Uncertainty and Profit*, New York: Harper Torchbooks, 1955.
28. Littleton, A.C., "Concepts of Income Underlying Accounting," *The Accounting Review*, March 1937, pp. 17-18.

SELECTED ADDITIONAL READINGS

Adkerson, Richard C., "Can Reserve Recognition Accounting Work?" *Journal of Accountancy*, September 1979, pp. 72-81.

Alexander, Sidney S., "Income Measurement in A Dynamic Economy," in *Five Monographs on Business Income*, New York: AICPA, 1950; rev. Solomons, David in *Studies in Accounting Theory*, ed. W.T. Baxter and Sidney Davidson, Homewood, Ill.: Richard D. Irwin, Inc., 1962, pp. 126-217.

Bartin, A.D., "Expectations and Achievements in Income Theory," *The Accounting Review*, October 1974, pp. 664-81.

Beams, Floyd A., "Income Reporting: Continuity with Change," *Management Accounting*, August 1972, pp. 23-7.

Bedford, Norton M., "Income Concept Complex: Expansion or Decline," in Robert R. Sterling, *Asset Valuation and Income Determination*, Lawrence, Kansas: Scholars Book Co., 1971, pp. 135-44.

———, , *Income Determination Theory: An Accounting Framework*, Reading, Mass: Addison-Wesley, 1965.

Bodenhorn, Diran, "Entity Approach to the Measurement of Wealth, Income and Product," *Abacus*, December 1972, pp. 127-144.

Böhm-Bawerk, Eugen von, *Capital and Interest*, Vol. II, "Positive Theory of Capital," South Holland, Ill.: Libertarian Press, 1959, pp. 16-66.

Brief, Richard P., "The Accountant's Responsibility in Historical Perspective," *The Accounting Review*, April 1975, pp. 285-97.

Brown, Clifford, *The Emergence of Income Reporting: An Historical Study*, East Lansing: MSU Business Studies, Michigan State University, 1971.

Canning, John B., *The Economics of Accountancy*, New York: The Ronald Press Co., 1929.

Chambers, R.J., "Income and Capital: Fisher's Legacy," *Journal of Accounting Research*, Spring, 1971, pp. 137-149.

FASB Discussion Memorandum, "An Analysis of Issues Related to Conceptual Framework for Financial Accounting and Reporting: Elements of Financial Statements and Their Measurement", Stamford, Conn.: Financial Accounting Standards Board, December 2, 1976, Part I.

FASB Discussion Memorandum, "An Analysis of Issues Related to Reporting Earnings," Stamford, Conn.: Financial Accounting Standards Board, July 31, 1979, Ch. 2.

Hansen, Palle, *Accounting Concept of Profit: An Analysis and Evaluation in the Light of the Economic Theory of Income and Capital*, Amsterdam: North-Holland Publishing Co., 1962.

Lawson, G.H., "The Measurement of Corporate Profitability on a Cash Flow Basis," *International Journal of Accounting, Education, and Research*, Fall 1980, pp. 11-46.

Lee, T.A., "Note on the Nature and Determination of Income," *Journal of Business Finance and Accounting* Vol. 1, Spring 1974, p. 145-147.

———, *Income and Value Measurement: Theory and Practice*, Baltimore: University Park Press, 1975.

Louderback, Joseph G., III, "Projectability as a Criterion for Income Determination Methods," *The Accounting Review*, April 1971, pp. 298-305.

Morris, R.C., and G.H. Breakwell, "Manipulation of Earnings Figures in the United Kingdom," *Accounting and Business Research*, Summer 1975, pp. 177-84.

Parker, R.H. and G.C. Harcourt, *Readings in the Concept and Measurement of Income*, Cambridge: University Press, 1969, pp. 123-138.

Peters, Robert A., *Return on Investment: Practical Theory and Innovative Applications*, New York: AMACOM (American Management Association), 1974.

Revsine, Lawrence, "Predictive Ability, Market Prices, and Operating Flows," *Accounting Review*, July 1971, pp. 480-489.

Schumpeter, Joseph A., *The Theory of Economic Development*, Cambridge, Mass.: Harvard University Press, 1934, pp. 115-123.

Schwayder, Keith, "A Critique of Economic Income as an Accounting Concept," *Abacus*, August 1967, pp. 23-25.

Simmons, John K. and Jack Gray, "An Investigation of the Effect of Differing Accounting Frameworks on the Prediction of Net Income," *The Accounting Review*, October 1969, pp. 757-76.

Solomons, David, "Economic and Accounting Concepts of Income," *The Accounting Review*, July 1961, pp. 374-83.

Sterling, Robert R., *Theory of the Measurement of Enterprise Income*, Lawrence, Kansas: University Press of Kansas, 1970, pp. 7-19.

Thomas, Arthur L., "The FASB and the Allocation Fallacy," *Journal of Accountancy*, November 1975, pp. 65-68.

Weber, Charles, "Income Determination Theory: Some Mathematical and Graphical Approaches," *The International Journal of Accounting Education and Research*, Fall 1966, pp. 35-47.

CASE 8-1 Simon Blumenfeld, Inc.

Simon Blumenfeld incorporated his business in 1978 with a capital of $60,000. Having many family and cultural contacts in Eastern Europe, he felt that he could obtain orders for American firms from Communist countries in that part of the world. In 1978 he travelled to the Soviet Union and brought back orders worth $50,000 for delivery in 1979 on which his commission was 20 percent. Office and travel expenses during 1978 amounted to $15,000. Data regarding similar trips for the years 1978-80 are given below.

	1978	1979	1980
Orders received	$50,000	$200,000	$500,000
Commissions earned through invoiced deliveries	0	10,000	40,000
Travel expenses	5,000	5,000	5,000
Office expenses	10,000	10,000	10,000
Withdrawn as salary	20,000	25,000	30,000

In 1979, Simon Blumenfeld Inc. obtained a bank loan of $10,000 on Blumenfeld's personal guarantee. In 1980 the company applied for a further loan, and the bank requested income statements for 1978 and 1979 and a projected income statement for 1980. Simon

Blumenfeld showed the above figures to a CPA, who appeared perplexed by them and gave his opinion that there was no point in preparing such income statements as the bank would not find them acceptable as evidence of the suitability of such a loan.

1. Prepare accrual-basis income statements for 1978, 1979, and 1980.
2. What additional information might help to obtain the bank loan?

CASE 8-2 High Technology Electronics Inc. (Hi-Tech)

Hi-Tech was established in 1965 with the objective of using advanced electronics technology to execute defense contracts for the United States government. The initial capital was $1 million. Hi-Tech obtained a series of contracts of increasing amount, the largest being one for $50 million in 1979. All of these contracts had a significant research component although they were primarily for the manufacture of aircraft equipment. The company's income statements showed net losses every year from 1965 through 1980, the cumulative total of which at December 31, 1980 amounted to over $1 million. Cash inflows and outflows were approximately equal for each of these years. At the end of 1980, a large aircraft manufacturer acquired all the voting equity of Hi-Tech for $20 million.

Discuss the problem of *disclosure* with particular reference to the facts of this case.

END OF CHAPTER QUESTIONS

1. "The problem of defining and measuring income is a current and practical matter of concern to the accounting profession." Explain the nature of this problem.
2. Discuss the semantic problems associated with the word *income*. Is there a distinction between the concepts of *business income* and *taxable income*? In what way are they related?
3. What is *profit* in accounting? In economic theory? Is the accounting meaning of earnings synonymous with that of profit?
4. *Income to whom?*

   Income measurement can be divided into different income concepts classified by income recipients. The following income concepts are tailored to the listed categories of income recipients.

Income Concepts	Income Recipients
1. Net income to residual equity holders	Common stockholders
2. Net income to investors	Stockholders and long-term debt holders
3. Value-added income	All employees, stockholders, governments, and some creditors

For each of the concepts listed above, explain in separately numbered paragraphs what major categories of revenue, expense, and other items would be included in the determination of income. (AICPA, November 1974).

5. Distinguish between income as a flow concept and capital as a stock concept.
6. List the different definitions of capital encountered in the accounting literature. Do they share any common feature? Can the economist's concept of capital be reconciled with the accountant's?
7. Explain what is meant by *capital maintenance* in accounting.
8. What was the rule in *Eisner v. Macomber*? How has it been interpreted? Does it represent a contemporary legal view of income?
9. List economists' concepts of income. What difficulty prevents economists from agreeing on one concept?
10. What is the Hicks concept of income? Why is it not useful?
11. Explain Fisher's theory of income. What method of calculating income does it underlie? What is *accretion of discount*?
12. Explain the concept of *ultimate* or *total lifetime* business income.
13. How does a rolling forward adjustment arise in calculating economic income?
14. Compare and contrast the structure of economic income calculation with that of traditional accounting net income.
15. What is *subjective goodwill*? How is it calculated?
16. Investigate the reasons why the SEC abandoned its attempt to make economic income accounting obligatory for oil and gas producers.
17. What four income concepts are believed to be consistent with the FASB's conceptual framework?
18. Explain Edwards and Bell's reconciliation of economic and accounting income.
19. How did the FASB attempt to join income concepts and capital maintenance concepts?
20. What is meant by *income as return on investment*? What are the accounting implications of this construct?
21. Can income determination be made dependent upon a cash flow model of the business entity? If not, why not?

9

ASSET VALUATION AND ACCOUNTING MEASUREMENTS

Because of the articulation of accrual accounting income statements and balance sheets, asset and liability valuation inevitably affects income measurement. In its most primitive form, the comparison of balance sheets approach, income measurement is primarily dependent upon asset valuation. Under this method, which is still the basic approach to calculating taxable income in France, for example, net income is found as the difference between the owner's equity at two dates, deducting capital contributed during the period, and adding back dividends distributed during the period.

Accountants have developed a different approach, which has been called *operational* because it attempts to ascertain net income as the result of operations. This requires monitoring the flow of resources and obligations through the accounting entity during the period selected. Various parts of this flow are given the names revenue, gain, expense, and loss, and net income is calculated by deducting expenses and losses from the sum of revenues and gains. The operational approach has also been called a *transactions* approach because so many nontransaction-based value changes, such as the effects of price-level changes, are ignored. The FASB's repeated use of the phrase "transactions, events and other circumstances" may be interpreted as an attempt to encourage accountants to move nearer to the operational approach.

It might be thought that the existence of different income constructs would lead to the production of "different figures for different purposes," a situation in which the net income figure did not necessarily balance the balance sheet. The possibility of such a nonarticulated accounting structure has been widely debated, but it is based on a different concept. The double-entry system of bookkeeping, on which accounting and financial reporting are based, is a closed system in which every observation recorded is related functionally to the image of the entity being observed. The arithmetical equivalence of debits and credits, which produces a balance, is a forced equivalence and does not necessarily reflect any value equivalence in the real world, although it may do so in a restricted class of simple cases. Herein lies the source of certain questions which appear in the contemporary literature on accounting theory: Is the administrative convenience of double-entry bookkeeping in promoting the creation of order out of the apparent chaos of business operations an overriding consideration? Should the analytical and predictive uses of income determination be given priority, if necessary, at the expense of the closed system? Can we represent the entity as an open system, in which some features are of necessity left unmeasured, and at the same time maintain control over the data base from which the accountant derives his measurements?

In other words, nonarticulated financial statements will be the products of an open system of bookkeeping, such as the database management systems which computer scientists are trying to create. The accounting problem is complicated by the fact that the system within which net income is determined must also furnish management with control information. Control information consists of measurements made during operations, or management accounting. One of the features of control is comparison of the measurement with some predetermined value in order to establish variances for analysis. Control measurements must correspond structurally with these predetermined values, so that any variances resulting from the comparison represent differences between plans and achievements and not simply differences between methods of measurement. Managerial planning and control in practice, therefore, constitute a constraint on valuation in accounting.

WHAT IS VALUE?

The word *value* is derived from the French word *valoir* meaning "to be worth."[1] This construct has two dimensions, an ethical and a material. The ethical meaning involves considerations of respect and esteem, so that valuation consists of appreciating the intrinsic merit of a thing: what it is worth for its own sake. This meaning is difficult to quantify, even though its significance to civilized existence cannot be overestimated. The material meaning of *value* is often confused with price, a ratio between some thing and a monetary scale, representing an amount which has been paid for that thing, or for which it could be bought or sold. Clearly, this is a special case of the general meaning of value, and prices are material values observable in transactions. Generally, however, the mathematical definition of a value is the number or quantity represented by a figure or symbol, and, in accounting, valuation is the representation of anything in terms of money. Another way of putting this proposition is to define valuation in accounting as any operation which results in the representation of an object as an amount of money.

Valuations of this kind pervade many aspects of business life. In taxation, for example, valuations are frequently necessary for income, gift, and estate tax computations, and vary greatly from one situation to another. Examples of such valuations occur in the cases of charitable contributions in kind and casualty loss deductions, which are arrived at by valuing the property contributed or destroyed.

For tax purposes *value* is deemed to be fair market value of the property at the time of transmittal or loss or, in the case of estate taxes, death of the owner. IRS regulations define fair market value as the price at which a property would change hands between a willing, knowledgeable and unrelated buyer and seller. In many cases a price can only be imagined, because the item in question is unique, or because the last such sale took place many years ago, and the IRS, the courts, and taxpayers use experts to appraise such property. Courts have frequently found themselves better able to value, however, and have set aside expert valuations in favor of their own, going so far as to establish criteria for the selection of experts, and factors which must be considered when determining the fair market value of a rare or unusual object.[2]

Perhaps influenced by IRS practice, accountants have often used the word *value* to denote fair market value, or selling price. Some of the opposition to "value accounting" has arisen because of the implied assumption that this would require all assets and liabilities to be reported at selling or liquidating values, with a corresponding effect on net income as these values moved up or down. Such is not the case: market value is relevant only for assets which are on the market, and many business assets are intentionally withheld from the market on which they are normally traded, often for many years. For such assets, another value concept known as *value in use* is more appropriate. The FASB, in *Statement No. 3*, has defined value in use as the present value of expected future net cash flows from an asset, which assimilates this value concept to the fair market value concept.[3] Many accountants would prefer Bonbright's *value to the owner*, now called *deprival value.*[4] Deprival value defines value in use as a quantitative representation in money of the loss which the owner of an item would suffer by being deprived of it; in some cases this would be the amount for which it could be sold, but in many others it would be the cost at which the item could be acquired and brought to its place and state of use.

Again, preoccupation with fair market value leads to neglect of the problems involved in the use of transfer prices. The integration of production processes arising out of mechanization and automation causes products to be moved from one process to another over a considerable period of time; in batch production this time period may include movements into and out of storage. Vertical and horizontal integration involve the combination of firms responsible for successive manufacturing processes (vertical) or the same process (horizontal) into one entity. Movements of goods and services between processes within one entity are called *internal events* to distinguish them from *external* involving markets and hence prices. Artificial prices used to record internal exchange events are called transfer prices.

There are three basic types of transfer price, depending on whether the price is found by reference to selling markets, buying markets, or otherwise. They are known respectively as the market, cost, and negotiated bases. Thus, two out of the three basic types of transfer price are not fair market value, and it is important to bear in mind this accounting problem when considering how assets should be valued for financial reporting purposes.

THE AGGREGATION PROBLEM

One of the objections to the retention of the present *historical cost* basis of accounting, under which assets and liabilities may be reported at acquisition prices, selling prices, present values, and even figures which have no existential significance outside accounting method (book values, such as "Fixed assets, net of depreciation") is that these different values are not aggregative. By this is meant that the money amounts have different *attributes.* The word is explained in n. 2 to the FASB's *Statement of Financial Accounting Concepts No. 1:*

> 'Attributes to be measured' refers to the traits or aspects of an element to be quantified or measured, such as historical cost/historical proceeds, current cost/current proceeds, etc. Attribute is a narrower concept than measurement, which includes not only identifying the attribute to be measured but also selecting a scale of measurement (for example, units of money or units of constant purchasing power). 'Property' is commonly used in the sciences to describe the trait or aspect of an object being measured, such as the length of a table or the weight of a stone. But 'property' may be confused with land and buildings in financial reporting contexts, and 'attribute' has become common in accounting literature and is used in this Statement.

This quotation shows that the aggregation problem concerns the monetary scale to be used, as well as the basis whereby value is derived. A 1981 dollar is worth roughly one-third of a 1967 dollar; a German mark is worth roughly one-half of a U.S. dollar. No one would think of adding together amounts expressed in different currencies, yet acquisitions made in U.S. dollars at different dates are routinely added together, even though the relative difference may be greater.

The problem is more acute than it appears at first sight. Consider fair market value in the light of what economists call the *fallacy of composition.* This is the belief that what is true for one member of a group is true for all; that if one person gets a better view by standing up at a football game, all present will improve their views of the game by doing likewise. A manufacturer of pianos may realize quite different amounts of money by selling pianos one at a time as compared with selling the entire inventory to a department store. The problem presents itself also in relation to replacement cost.

For example, suppose that a firm employs three machines as a group, each of which is different. At one point in time their replacement costs are: $300, $150, and $180. If any of the machines wears out, it will be replaced if the present value of the net cash flows from the group is greater than the replacement cost of the machine. But the whole group will not be replaced if the present value of the net cash flows is less than the sum of the costs of all the individual machines ($630). What is the deprival value of these machines?

MEASUREMENT AND VALUATION

Measurement is a method of representing an object or other perception. Kohler, in his *A Dictionary for Accountants*, defined measurement as

> The assignment of a system of *ordinal* or *cardinal* numbers to the results of a scheme of inquiry or apparatus of observation in accord with logical or mathematical rules.

The economist who is responsible for modern systems of national income accounting, J. R. N. Stone, described the objective of measurement as being to "define the degree of difference between distinguishable objects, and bring them into a certain relation with a scale of numbers."

The subject of measurement acquired importance to accountants at the time when they transferred their attentions from the balance sheet to the income statement. We speak of the *valuation* of assets and liabilities but the *measurement* of income. Valuation in accounting is the representation of anything in terms of money of account, but is it a form of measurement? We could equally well speak of asset and liability *measurement*, or the *valuation* of income. The purpose of this section is to examine the concept of measurement and its relation to valuation and to analyze the different valuation concepts used by accountants. By this means, it is hoped, subsequent discussion of the elements of financial statements will be more readily understood.

It should be pointed out that there is considerable doubt whether the word *measurement* has any meaning in this context. In the following summary of the approach to measurement in accounting which can be found in the contemporary literature, it is assumed that money constitutes a unit of measure and that a monetary system constitutes a ratio scale. Neither of these propositions appears to be empirically verifiable.[5]

The saying of Lord Kelvin, the celebrated physicist, that without being able to measure an object we cannot know much about it, is frequently quoted with approval.

> I often say that when you can measure what you are speaking about and express it in numbers, you know something about it, but when you cannot measure it, your knowledge is of a meager and unsatisfactory kind.

This saying implies that measurement invests the object measured with some quality which adds to the informational content of observations using that measurement. The question is: how?

Some authors have suggested that measurements improve observations by making them more precise, although precision lies in language as well as in numbers. Measurement, in this view, is a system for distinguishing objects, for ordering, and comparing them. A scale of measurement is a correspondence between objects and numbers; the system of weights and measures which we use is a set of scales. By representing properties of objects in scalar units, we establish a one-to-one correspondence of the property with the unit, known as an *isomorphic* relationship. The process of relating the property with the scale is known as mapping. Clearly, if we can represent a property of an object in units of a scale, we invest it with a kind of precision.

Precision in representation, however, is not the end of the story. By quantifying the observation we are able to utilize the logical processes of mathematics in order to understand it. The powerful operations which mathematicians have devised throughout the ages can be applied to many quantities for purposes of explanation, prediction, planning, and control. If we cannot measure we can still describe, reproduce, and alter the property; if we can measure we can also add it, subtract it, multiply it, and divide it. If we can count, we can also account.

The essential ingredients of measurement are therefore (1) a property to be quantified and (2) a scale, or set of units of measure, prepared for the purpose of quantifying that property.

Use of the word "attribute" in place of "property," helpful though it may be to those who have difficulty in reading financial statements, only serves to confuse the significance of this concept in accounting measurement. Historical cost, for example, is a property of a transaction, but not a property of the object being exchanged. The question of how to measure or value an asset is quite separate from the question of how to measure the transaction by which it was acquired.

Examine the proposition:

X weighs 20 lbs.

In this proposition we have four terms, each of which can be independently verified. Both X and weight can be perceived directly; X can be both seen and lifted. No scale is required for these purposes. The number 20 can be found from a system of numbers, and isomorphism with the avoirdupois scale can be verified. The avoirdupois scale can be verified by experimentation with other objects having the property of weight. Thus, the weight of X can be experimentally demonstrated to be 20 pounds.

Now examine the apparently identical proposition:

X costs \$20

Again, the terms X and 20 can be verified by experiment, as also can the existence of a currency designated in units called dollars, isomorphic with the system of numbers, of which 20 is a part. But how can we verify cost? If I give the owner of X \$20 and he gives me X, then cost equals price. If the owner of X sees it destroyed in a fire, and claims \$20 from an insurance company, cost equals sacrifice. If I own X, and will give it to you in exchange for \$20, it may be argued that for me \$20 equals value. Under no conditions can cost equal current purchasing power since current purchasing power, expressed in money of account, is a scale and measures a property only of money as a medium of exchange.[6]

One view, then, is that valuation is a form of measurement different in kind from that used in the physical sciences; one to which the concepts of error measurement and range of estimates do not apply. To hold this view would be to misunderstand the nature of measurement in the physical sciences, which is not "exact" in the way a layman tends to believe. Another view holds that accounting, in the words of Churchill and Stedry, is "the assignment of numerical values to events that are observed as impinging on an enterprise in order that these events can be recorded in a fashion suitable for aggregation in combination with other events to which numerical values have been assigned."[7]

Number is a property which is represented by a numeral.[8] In economics there is a well-known assumption that money can be used as a scale for measuring economic events. The objective is to measure physical phenomena incident to the operations of exchange; that is why prices are relevant measurements. But prices are supplemented by what Fisher called "appraisements" and are in fact imputations. For example, the proceeds of sale of a product (the price) are assumed to be divided among the providers of the factors of production by a procedure which involves the calculation of marginal cost. In this procedure, money is called the *numéraire*; borrowing from economics, Chambers calls the property being represented by a numeral, *numerosity.* The need to establish a broader concept of measurement has been felt by several social scientists, and a bold attempt was finally made by a psychologist, S. S. Stevens. In a short article which appeared in the journal *Science* (Vol.

103, Jan-June 1946), entitled "On the Theory of Scales of Measurement," Stevens took a great step toward satisfying this need. Subsequent work has refined and extended the field.

Stevens defined measurement simply as "the assignment of numerals to objects or events according to rules." It is significant that he used the word numeral, the symbol, and not number, the quantity. The definition means what it says: any rules. Only random numeral assignment is excluded.

It follows that the most basic measurement in this broad sense is classification; traditional "narrow" measurement scientists such as C. West Churchman join issue at this point.[9] Stevens postulates a hierarchy of four classes of scales—the nominal, ordinal, interval, and ratio. These classes are found by reference to the transformation processes which leave the scale form invariant, and therefore correspond to well-known mathematical groups.

The nominal scale simply uses the numeral as a label. These scales belong to the permutation group $x' = f(x)$ where $f(x)$ means any one-to-one substitution. The numbering of accounts provides many illustrations. In ordinal scales, properties being measured are subject to order rank in accordance with the number system, thus permitting discrimination of the type "greater than," "equal to," or "less than." The ordinal scales belong to the isotonic group $x' = f(x)$ where $f(x)$ denotes any increasing monotonic function. Numbering accounts in a bound ledger or ranking responses to a questionnaire are examples of ordinal scales. Some measurement theorists would argue that this is the most basic measurement, since it is at this point that a scale is created. (Latin: *scala* means steps).

An interval scale enforces regularity in the ordering of the steps of a scale, without having an absolute or natural zero or point of departure. The mathematical group is linear, where $x' = zx + b$ and $z > 0$; examples are the Fahrenheit and Celsius temperature scales and the calendar dimension of time. A ratio scale is the highest form in the hierarchy because it is constrained by the same qualities which ordinal and interval scales must possess plus one more, a zero point which is given experimentally and not simply by convention. A ratio scale belongs to the mathematical group $x' = cx$, where $c < 0$; money of account is said to be a typical ratio scale (as are also avoirdupois and linear and square measures).

A frequently cited illustration of Stevens' classification of measurement is the temperature of water. In place of "hot" and "cold" we could use the numerals 1 for hot and 2 for cold; a nominal scale with no quantitative significance. Should we require a third type of warm water we might use 1 for hot, 2 for warm, and 3 for cold, to indicate that warm lies between hot and cold: an ordinal scale. The inequality of the intervals limits the use of this scale to the very general discrimination between hot, warm, and cold; cold goes from −273°C to perhaps 20°C, warm goes from perhaps 20°C to perhaps 90°C and hot from, say, 90°C to as high as 1200°C! Three of the widely used temperature scales are interval scales, having class intervals of constant size: Fahrenheit, Réamur, and Celsius. The fourth, the Kelvin scale, is a ratio scale because its zero point is set nonarbitrarily at −273°C, and its intervals are of equal size.

The utility of Stevens' classification for measurement theorists has been generally acknowledged, but the admission of nominal scales, and classification itself, as a form of measurement has not been accepted. It will be appreciated that Stevens, as a psychologist, was concerned with adding to the informational content of observations which are not expressed in quantitative terms—the degree of schizophrenia or the force of a suicidal tendency. For him, any use of numerals offered promise. In accounting, however, where most observations are expressed in quantitative terms, the problem was viewed differently. Accepting the fact that money of account is a ratio scale, the question posed is: what property or properties can we measure?

ERROR MEASUREMENT

The significance of this question lies in the observation that if we can identify the property to be measured by accountants we can indicate the degree of accuracy of a particular accounting figure. In science, the best method of measuring is the one which produces the lowest error measurement, sometimes expressed as a standard deviation. The application of this approach to accounting was described by Morgenstern.[10]

A balance sheet can be viewed as a cell, like this.

This cell has a hard core, or kernel, of accurate figures to which customary concepts of error measurement apply. Surrounding layers are progressively different from this core because of the manner in which the figures are arrived at; even though in outward appearance they are identical. Morgenstern concludes:

> ...we see that the adoption of a correct statistical view on the nature of information produced by financial statements has profound *operational significance.* It must now be realized that combinations of financial statements yield far more information than is assumed by the nature and extent of the numerical operations carried out with these figures.... Business gives itself the illusion of dealing with "accuracy" where there is none in an

> ordinary sense; nor does there exist a subtitute notion....This has deep significance in judging the possibilities and effects of policy, or prediction and is, of course, of paramount importance for economic theory.

In the second (1963) edition of this work, Morgenstern explained further this view of the balance sheet. The different assets have different probabilities of being realized (converted into cash). The probability of cash is, of course, 1, and error measurement attaching to different methods of counting cash can be made explicit. Marketable securities have somewhat lower probabilities, with government securities approaching 1; accounts receivable and inventories can be similarly viewed. Equipment will have a lower probability than inventories, and any figure for intangibles could have a very low probability indeed.

This formulation, which resembles closely the Chambers' construct of current cash equivalents, assumes explicitly that the property to be measured is liquidity (which Chambers calls numerosity) and can be seen as an attempt to produce a balance sheet in terms of probable cash inflows:

Probabilistic Structure of Assets

	Stated	**Marginal Probability**	**Mathematically Expected Value**	**Standard Errors**
Cash	1,000,000	1.00	1,000,000	0
Securities	2,000,000	.95	2,075,000	50,000
Inventory	5,000,000	.80	5,400,000	600,000

Oskar Morgenstern, *On The Accuracy of Economic Observations*, 2nd ed., 1963, pp. 76-79.

Liabilities can be similarly expressed in terms of probable cash outflows.

If the property being measured by accountants is liquidity, then the idea of measuring everything in terms of the probability that it will become a receipt or a payment has obvious merit. But we have seen that the emphasis in modern accounting is on the measurement of profitability and not liquidity; hence the primacy of the income statement which has stimulated the search for a measurement theory of accounting. Cash is general purchasing power, and the assumption that liquidated assets will produce cash is a dubious proposition; the firm is likely to spend the proceeds of sale of goods on other goods and services, not to hold it in spendable form. But the most important argument against the Chambers/Morgenstern approach is that it renders the income statement less able to measure profit, or business income. Overhead allocation and absorption, depreciation, depletion and amortization—these are valuation processes of great complexity, designed to produce a *better* measurement of profit or loss than would result from a mere chronicle of liquidity changes.

ENTROPY AND THE ECONOMIC PROCESS

This probabilistic approach to asset and liability measurement produces figures in a range, rather than the point values of deterministic approaches. A different probabilistic approach is suggested by analogy with thermodynamics.

In thermodynamic terms, disorder is represented by a situation in which the outward appearance of an object is consistent with a large number of different possible arrangements. Order is increased if the overall appearance will permit fewer arrangements of the constituent parts. Heaps of lumber can have the same exterior form, yet the boards may be arranged internally in thousands of different ways. To represent a heap of lumber as a barn, however, requires reducing the number of possible internal arrangements to a few. In physical systems, order is a concept of the degree to which certain overall properties dictate the internal and external arrangements of the parts. Entropy is the name given to a spontaneous, one-way, irreversible process which erodes such order.[11] Time is evidence of the process of entropy.

If an ordered, and therefore unique, arrangement becomes disordered spontaneously through time, an improbable situation will tend to become more probable. The Second Law of Thermodynamics states: "Every system which is left to itself will *on the average*, change toward a condition of maximum probability." But what is "on the average"? The probability of any given event may be minuscule, and a probable state contains less information than the one which preceded it.

The principal contribution of this type of thinking to the development of accounting theory has been to draw attention to the relativity of accounting measurements. It probably underlies the distinction between the SEC's role in setting disclosure standards and the accounting profession's role in setting measurement standards. The distinction between a measurement and an attribute to be measured is perhaps another result.

The thermodynamic idea of distinguishing between the preparation of a state and the measurement of a state has been applied to the economic process by Georgescu-Roegen.[12] In this formulation, analysis requires—

1. Setting a boundary (frontier) between the *process* (the part of reality being studied) and the *environment* (the part not being studied).
2. Defining a purpose for which the boundary is set.
3. Specifying a finite duration for the boundary observation.
4. Observing a "happening," or a boundary crossing.

The economic process can therefore be defined broadly as a change in the universe or, narrowly, as a change in a state. Clearly, this type of analysis has been a commonplace of accounting throughout the ages, and underlies the distinctions between capital and revenue and between stocks and flows. The fundamental difference between economics and accounting is the use by the former of Euclidean space to accommodate its point values, and by the latter of abstract space. Many of the weaknesses of economic theory could be eliminated by a transition to a more abstract concept of space, but this would require the economist to become an accountant.

VALUATION IN ACCOUNTING

Valuation in accounting is the assignment of numerals to objects according to rules, where the numerals are found within a monetary system. We shall call this system the *money of account*. Money of account is one of the uses of money in a modern economy. These uses are generally said to be four in number:

1. As a medium of exchange.
2. As a store of value.
3. As a measure of value.
4. As a unit of account.

Money as a measure of value and a unit of account predates money as a medium of exchange. Loans have been recorded since the beginning of history; old Sumerian documents, circa 3,000 B.C., reveal a systematic use of credit based on loans of grain by volume and loans of metal by weight. Often these loans carried interest. This type of loan, repayable in kind, required standards of quality and measurement, which appear to have led to monetary standards of a measurement kind. Originally a commodity, such as grain, the unit of measure eventually became independent of such commodities. Part of this process can be seen in the survival of the words *capital* and *pecuniary*, both derived from the use of cattle or other beasts as a measure of value.

Metals such as gold and silver were also loaned out at interest, and before coined money, were exchanged by weight. Coined money probably first appeared in Asia Minor in the seventh century B.C., but uncoined metal was used for money long before that time. It is noteworthy that the Code of Hammurabi, circa 1,800 B.C., called for accounts to be kept, and recognized negotiable bills of exchange. This was before the introduction of money as a means of exchange.

It is important analytically to distinguish between separate and separable phenomena. Money may exist as a store of value independently from being a medium of exchange, as any numismatist knows. Another term for this use is *asset money*, and monetary theorists recognize the distinction between money used for exchanges and money held for precautionary and other purposes. The use of money as a measure of value can be observed in any catalog or department store. The use of money as a unit of account is quite different from any of these; a debit of $100 to the account "provision for doubtful receivables" resulting from the write-off of a bad debt is explicable only in terms of money of account.

The problem here is to explain the rules used by accountants for assigning money values to their observations. These rules fall into two classes—direct and indirect. By direct valuation, we mean a measurement which specifies the property to be measured; indirect valuation, on the other hand, cannot be verified in this way.

DIRECT VALUATION

To put the subject of direct valuation into proper perspective, the following quotation should be of some interest to accountants.

> Without the threat of a thumbscrew, and indeed with no urging at all, an economist may often be found to declare that his idea of a measure for a stock of capital is to equate it to the present discounted value of the future stream of earnings that the stock of capital will generate. This is so inherently unmeasurable that it will amuse a statistician until he perceives that the suggestion is offered somewhat more than half-seriously.[13]

The distinction between direct and indirect valuation was first made by Canning, based on the economic theories of Irving Fisher.[14] Fisher had defined value as *present value*, which is the sum of a series of expected cash flows, discounted by the time value of money. If the property to be measured is the future net cash receipts to be produced by the object to be valued, then present value is the direct valuation of future net cash receipts, which, together with the positive discount rate associated with the waiting period, can be expressed by means of a mathematical formula.

This formula requires three known factors, from which the unknown, the value, can be inferred. The three factors are the future net cash receipts, the periods of time with which they are associated, and the discount rate. Using V for value, R for the receipts, d for the discount rate, and n for the number of time periods, the formula is—

$$V = \frac{R_1}{1 + d} + \frac{R_2}{(1 + d)^2} + \ldots, \ldots \frac{R_n}{(1 + d)^n}$$

It will be observed that this formula embraces only the variables specified, although some analysts have expanded it to include other factors, such as risk and price-level changes, where they can be estimated and quantified. A purist might object that the concept of present value is based on outcomes known with certainty, and therefore the introduction of a risk factor is anomalous. The formula takes a linear view of time, and this feature, which simplifies the mathematics, is fundamental. The formula is used in accounting to value some accounts receivable and, by analogy, some accounts payable and long-term obligations, pension liabilities, and certain lease agreements.

A critical element in the use of the present value formula is the determination of the discount factor. In the macroeconomic models with which Fisher was concerned, the discount factor is the interest rate, being the marginal rate at which society will substitute future satisfactions for present satisfactions. It was long believed that the equivalent concept as far as the entity was concerned was the firm's cost of capital, being the weighted average of the payments required to attract capital in its various forms to the firm, expressed as a rate. This concept had theoretical and practical weaknesses, and the currently prevailing view is that the appropriate discount rate is a risk-adjusted rate of interest.

This is not a problem in attributing the model to individual investors, who can be assumed to know their own discount rates. That is the justification for the normative asset valuation model discussed in chapter 6 in relation to the information needs of investors. Difficulty in finding the discount factor is invariably present when using this model for asset and liability valuation. What discount rate should be used in finding the present value of noninterest-bearing receivables and payables under *APB Opinion No. 21*? How should one determine whether a nominal interest rate differs from a real interest rate? What is the "lessee's incremental borrowing rate" under *FASB Statement No. 13*, which must be used if it is lower than the lessor's implicit interest rate? The SEC's requirement that expected future cash receipts from the sale of oil and gas should be discounted at 10 percent for RRA (reserve recognition accounting) purposes aroused widespread criticism on the grounds that (a) the rate was too low and (b) one rate should not be applied to all situations.

An associated problem is what to do when interest rates change. The accounting implications of changes in present value arising from this cause are so complex that none of the standard-setting bodies has mentioned the possibility. Even accounting textbooks are silent on this question.

The direct or present value method of valuation is used in accounting where future net cash receipts can be predicted with certainty. When we consider applying the algorithm to future net cash receipts which, while not expected with certainty, can nevertheless be converted to certainty equivalents if probabilities are known, we are faced not only with the problem of agreeing on a probability distribution, but also with the problem of how precisely to adjust the valuation model. We can modify the term R or d, the number of time periods n or the value V, and each of these in a variety of different ways. The price-level change adjustment is also capable of a variety of treatments.

Further, direct valuation is not appropriate for individual assets where net cash receipts are a function of their joint operations.

Although conceivably a method of imputation could be used to allocate expected future net cash receipts to all objects deemed to contribute to them, this solution is cumbersome and must be discarded as impractical. The use of marginal net receipts is subject to the difficulty that their sum is unlikely to equal total net cash receipts predicted. For all of these reasons the use of direct valuations is restricted to those objects whose properties can be confidently defined in terms of future net cash receipts, which may be negative.

A second type of direct valuation is where the property to be measured is selling price, and there exists a relevant market for the object in question. It goes without saying that the object must be ready to be placed on the market; the use of selling price in this context can only be justified if there is no impediment of form, time, or space preventing the sale of the object in question. In virtually every case it would have to be argued that the object was being kept off the market for speculative reasons, in the hope of a higher price, and that there was no chance of a price decline.

RRA provides an interesting example of this situation. Changes in present value are admitted as increases in results (RRA earnings) if selling prices of oil and gas reserves increase. Realization of oil and gas reserves at the prices used at the date of the last RRA statement produces no increase in RRA earnings, since the inventory is already carried at selling prices. In a time of rapidly rising prices, therefore, it is apparently more profitable to leave the oil and gas in the ground than to produce and sell it, because the end of year price will always be higher than the average price for the year. Obviously, this type of statement does not reflect the decision processes of the industry's firms, which are busy trying to sell as much oil and gas as they can.

Where relevant, valuation at selling price is reduced by any costs necessary to bring the object into the hands of the buyer, such as commission, transportation, taxes, finishing, and installation. This construct is known as *net realizable value* and has only limited acceptance in accounting, principally for certain natural resources in the extractive industries. It is also used as a *highest value* alternative for inventories.

Some analysts have suggested that valuation at selling price, or net realizable value, should be effected by using the present value algorithm, whereby the current selling price would be reduced by the application of a discount factor for the waiting period prior to sale. This is illogical; selling price is not an expected future net receipt in this case, and if the expected future net cash receipt were known with certainty or certainty equivalence, it would be higher than current selling price, or else the object in question would have been sold.

Interestingly, cash, which would appear to be an obvious candidate for direct valuation, is valued by count and not discounted if held in noninterest-bearing checking accounts. The present value of cash is only equal to the amount reported as cash in the balance sheet if it is earning a realistic rate of interest.

INDIRECT VALUATION

Where the property to be measured cannot be clearly identified, it may be assumed. In many cases, no property can be identified or assumed, and value is equated with price paid. This class of valuation method is known generally as *input measures of value*. There are three types of input measures of value used in accounting, known as *historical cost*, *current cost*, and *imputed cost*. The problem is compounded by the fact that each of these may be the point of departure for other types of valuation, all known as *fiat* values because of the apparently arbitrary manner in which they are arrived at.

The expression *historical cost* is often used as a code word for "those methods of valuation acceptable to accountants," in which use it embraces a variety of different valuation constructs. In a more precise sense, however, historical cost means acquisition price. This terminological problem underlies *APB Statement No. 4*, "Basic Concepts and Accounting Principles Underlying Financial Statements of Business Enterprises." The statement attempts to distinguish external from internal events as causal factors in valuation, and within the first category, between transfers of resources and other events. External transfers are then divided into exchanges and nonreciprocal transfers.

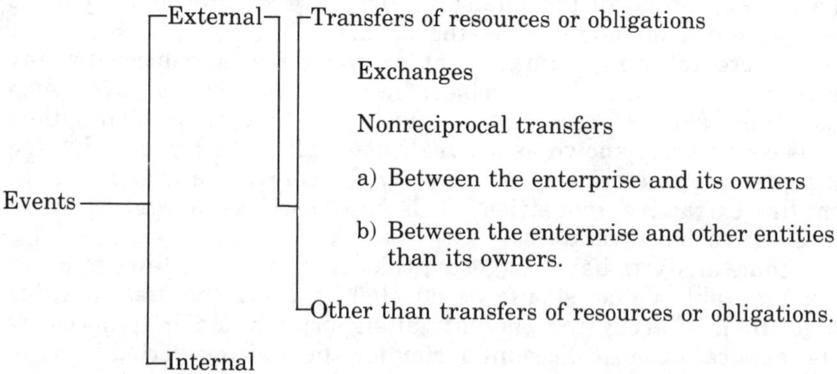

It is evident from this classification that prices are relevant only to external events involving exchanges, and, therefore, that historical cost is an imprecise term for the valuation of other events in the classification.

APB Statement No. 4 defined external events as "events that affect the enterprise in which other entities participate," and internal events as "events in which only the enterprise participates." The Statement classified such events as earthquakes and floods as internal events. *FASB Statement of Financial Accounting Concepts No. 3* defined an internal event as one "that occurs within an entity," such as using materials in production. An earthquake or a flood are therefore external events in this classification.

With regard to cost, *APB Statement No. 4* asserted that "resources are measured in terms of money through money prices," and several types of money prices were listed—price in past purchase exchanges, price in a current purchase exchange, price in a current sale exchange, price "based on" future exchanges. The Statement went on to say that "each of these concepts has at least some current application in financial accounting." Thus, by illicitly stating that every monetary measurement is a price, the Statement purported to homogenize what are, in fact, very different valuation models. However, the Statement clearly specified under "Price in past purchase exchanges of the enterprise" that "this price is usually identified as *historical cost* or *acquisition cost* because the amount ascribed to the resource is its cost, measured by the money or other resources exchanged by the enterprise to obtain it."

Statement of Financial Accounting Concepts No. 3 has taken a large step toward recognizing the heterogeneity of accounting valuation by defining cost more generally.

> Cost is the sacrifice incurred in economic activities—that which is given up or foregone to consume, to save, to exchange, to produce, etc. For example, the value of cash or other resources given up (or the present value of an obligation incurred) in exchange for a resource measures the cost of the resource acquired. Similarly, the expiration of future benefits caused by using a resource in production is the cost of using it.

This cost concept is in widespread use for accounting valuations of inventories and other kinds of assets, tangible and intangible. It does not, however, apply to the valuation of accounts receivable and there are many cases in which accountants depart from the cost concept even in respect of other assets.

In other words, historical cost is an acquisition price in some cases, but not all, and even then it is not necessarily a measurement in money in exchange. It is a measurement in money of account.

In the simple case, where the exchange is money for goods (or services) we can equate the price paid with the utility of the object acquired. In this case, historical cost has obvious advantages over other indirect valuations; it lies to hand, in the form of an invoice or check; it is objective and verifiable, being free from subjective appreciations; and it may be assumed to represent "value to the acquirer at the time of acquisition," if one can equate value with utility. Naturally, these advantages exist only at the moment of acquisition; price and utility change over time and other evidence than the invoice or check may become more objective and verifiable—the object may break or be destroyed through use.

In the more complex case of a nonmonetary exchange the initial valuation at cost is less easily explained. *APB Opinion No. 29* distinguishes two kinds of such barter transactions; those which are, and those which are not, the culmination of an earning process. In the latter case the asset acquired is recorded and reported at the book value of the asset given up. In the former case, the asset acquired is either recorded and reported at the fair market value of the asset given up (corresponding to the FASB definition of cost) or at the fair market value of the asset acquired, if this is more clearly apparent.

Finally, recall that some assets are measured by allocating costs and other recorded amounts in accordance with methods which may vary from firm to firm and from situation to situation. This is the case of a manufacturer's inventories or equipment constructed by a firm for its own use. The phrase "historical cost" is particularly difficult to interpret in this context.

OTHER METHODS OF VALUATION

Other methods of valuation used or proposed can be divided into the two categories of input and output measures of value, depending on whether the source of the measure is based on assumed acquisition of factors of production or assumed disposal of the item to be valued. The Sandilands report attempted to bring these different methods into a decision framework.[15] Using RC for replacement cost, RV for realizable value, and PV for present value of expected net cash flows, we have the following six alternative situations, in which value to the firm is marked with an asterisk.

1	**2**	**3**	**4**	**5**	**6**
PV	RC	RC	PV	RV	RV
>	>	>	>	>	>
RC*	PV*	RV*	RV	PV	RC*
>	>	>	>	>	>
RV	RV	PV	RC*	RC*	PV

Bonbright's value to the firm (deprival value) would lead to the use of replacement cost as the measure of cost, in a decision involving the use of an asset, in all but two cases, in one of which presumably the asset would have been sold.

There are a number of objections to this approach. In the first place, it does not address the additivity issue; we will still be aggregating different kinds of measurement. Secondly, it assumes that we can apply each of these measurements to any asset (or liability). Such is not the case: the work in process of an electronics manufacturer, consisting largely of coated copper wire cut to different lengths, cannot be said to have a realizable value, and there are many items of plant and equipment which are unique and for which a replacement cost may not be calculable. Value to the firm is only capable of being made operational if we find, for each asset or liability, that value which represents its significance to the entity.

Thirdly, there is a problem of finding the measure once we have decided upon the applicable concept. We have referred to problems in calculating present values; similar difficulties are associated with replacement cost and realizable value.

Replacement cost is defined generally as the current cost of obtaining the same or equivalent services. Do we mean the same or equivalent? Consider the airline which owns a forty-year-old DC3 airplane. We could contemplate how much it would cost to construct the identical aircraft; this estimate, reduced by assumed depreciation for the loss of service life experienced by the existing asset, is called *reproduction cost*. Or do we mean the estimated cost of acquiring the same service potential, that is, the ability to deliver the same number of passenger miles, which is usually referred to as replacement cost? Or do we mean how much we could buy a used DC3 for today, which will fluctuate according to the state of the market and vary with the condition of the aircraft in question? The SEC, in *ASR 190*, and the FASB, in *Statement No. 33*, gave different answers to this question.

SEC Replacement Cost	**FASB Replacement Cost**
The lowest amount that would have to be paid in the normal course of business to obtain a new asset of equivalent operating or productive capacity. Found by indexation, direct pricing, unit pricing, or functional pricing.	Property, plant, and equipment— (1) current cost of a used asset of the same age and conditions, or (2) current cost of a new asset with the same service potential, less a deduction for depreciation, (3) current cost of a new asset with a different service potential, less a depreciation deduction and adjusted for the cost of the difference in service potential Inventory—the current cost of purchasing or producing the goods concerned. Found by direct pricing, functional or unit pricing, or indexation.

Neither of these sets of definitions envisioned that replacement cost might be affected by technological changes. For example, an electric utility contemplating replacing a large generator will take advantage of scientific and technological discoveries to permit the generation of electricity at the lowest unit cost. The difference between the existing and the future unit costs could be capitalized at some relevant interest rate, and this amount would represent a factor in the calculation of the replacement cost of the generator.

The Dutch system of *replacement value accounting* discussed in chapter 11 accommodates this kind of calculation.

Another criticism of replacement cost is that it confuses problems of acquisition with those of use. Objects are purchased by an entity in relation to their availability, the availability of finance, the economics of ordering, expectations of future prices, and other factors independent of the act of use or sale on a particular day. The relevant concept for the calculation of current cost is the sacrifice incurred on the day of use or sale, not the price which will be paid at some future date when the asset is replaced.

Replacement cost is used in financial accounting mainly as an upper limit for inventory valuation under the *lower of cost or market* rule. It is more widely used in management accounting, and the concept of replacement value underlies *standard cost* as a management accounting valuation method. Standard costs are neither historical nor replacement costs, but target or "should" costs similar to replacement values.

The standard cost eliminates from the representation of the object being valued all inefficiencies arising out of waste, whether of factors of production or of productive capacity. This is clearly desirable, bearing in mind the meaning of value with which we started; otherwise we accept the Marxist fallacy, that an object made by a slow and inefficient worker is worth more than the same object made by a quick and efficient one. Standard costing is in widespread use in many firms and industries, and some of these base their inventory valuations on standard costs, which are admitted under generally accepted principles of accounting if not too far removed from "actual" costs, whatever these may be. It should be remembered that standard costs are *imputed costs* or estimates, no matter how scientifically arrived at, and do not represent prices paid, whether historical, current, or future.[16]

Opportunity cost is a useful concept in arriving at usable valuations. The opportunity cost of any asset is the value it would have in its best alternative use. The opportunity cost of any liability is the obligation which would have to be incurred if it did not exist. The problem lies in determining what is a real alternative use, or source of funds.

"Current cash equivalent" and "continuously contemporary accounting" are names which have been given to a proposed uniform valuation system devised by an Australian theorist, R. J. Chambers.[17] Chambers argues that the firm is an entity which operates in markets, and therefore the only data which are relevant to its decisions, and to those of its owners, are exit prices or selling prices assuming normal realization. The sum of the realization values of resources minus obligations would indicate the entity's financial position, defined as its ability to operate in markets. The property to be measured is called *numerosity* and represents simply the number of units of the currency of account which can be produced by sale of the object being valued. It resembles the economist's concept of the *numéraire*, or money as a measurement scale as opposed to money as a commodity.

Chambers' use of numerosity seems to differ from the dictionary meaning of "the quality of being numerous." It would appear that Sterling uses numerosity to mean the quality of being stated in terms of a measurement unit, in this case, money of account.[18]

Marginal value is a concept derived from economics. In price theory, the *marginal cost* of a product is the differential cost of one incremental unit of that product and, because every unit is identical, it is therefore the cost of any unit produced at that level of activity. This marginal cost tends to equal the price of the product, since the tendency of the market is to eliminate profit. In the slightly different form of *direct cost* (variable cost), we find the marginal cost concept used for many purposes in the considerable literature on management accounting. Direct cost is not a valuation method used in financial accounting, except under quite special and relatively rare conditions.

Net realizable value is a term encountered frequently in accounting. It means the proceeds of sale of an asset minus any necessary costs associated with making it salable; costs to complete and costs to sell. Net realizable value is used in arriving at the lower of cost or market for inventories and in accounting for other assets which are destined for immediate sale.

Current value (sometimes, current cost) is a term which is applied to several different valuation methods, including replacement cost, net realizable value, present value, current cash equivalent, and proceeds of a liquidation of assets.

MEASUREMENT AND THE QUALITATIVE CHARACTERISTICS OF ACCOUNTING INFORMATION

Although the FASB has not yet published its views on the problems of valuation and measurement, an indication of its thinking can be found in *Statement of Financial Accounting Concepts No. 2*.

Relevance and reliability are the two primary qualities which make accounting information useful for decision making. They are subject to the constraints of cost and materiality. To be relevant, information must be timely and it must have predictive or feedback utility, or both. To be reliable, information must have representational faithfulness and it must be verifiable and neutral. In all cases, information which is not material need not be disclosed, nor should we expect disclosure in cases where cost exceeds benefit.

Relevance and reliability are not fixed, but variable points along a spectrum, and cost/benefit considerations are subjective. Consider the valuation of a painting. The most reliable information about a particular painting could be the date on which it was painted; the most relevant, how much an art collector would pay for it. How can there be a trade-off between these two types of information? The owner of the painting will not pay an expert to value it unless there is an expectation that the price at which the painting can be sold exceeds the cost of valuing. But the act of obtaining an expert's valuation may make the painting marketable.

Even the much-maligned historical cost basis of accounting proved relevant when some overseas subsidiaries of United States companies were nationalized and the governments concerned agreed to compensation based on historical cost.

Representational faithfulness is a quality which can apply to any valuation. In order for this quality to exist, it must be clear what claim is being made for an accounting number. This means that the basis of valuation of assets and liabilities should be stated in all types of financial reports, and an auditor attest to the truth of the assertion.

Conservatism is another aspect of valuation which pervades accounting practice. Conservatism was described in Concepts Statement No. 2 as follows:

> Conservatism is a prudent reaction to uncertainty to try to ensure that uncertainties and risks inherent in business situations are adequately considered. Thus, if two estimates of amounts to be received or paid in the future are about equally likely, conservatism dictates using the less optimistic estimate; however, if two estimates are not equally likely, conservatism does not necessarily dictate using the more pessimistic amount rather than the more likely one.

CONCLUSION

Financial statements are assembled from a wide variety of valuations, each of which impacts on the measurement of income as well as the statement of financial position. Among them we find the following:

1. Inventories reported at acquisition cost, replacement cost, or net realizable value.
2. Probable liabilities where the amount is uncertain, but can be expressed as a range of probable amounts, reported at the lowest value of the range. Acquisition price is an interesting conceptual problem in such cases.
3. If a resource is acquired in exchange for some other resource, the fair market value of the resource given up is reported as the cost of the resource acquired, even though fair market value may be a subject for legitimate debate.
4. Some resources, such as commodities, are reported at exit market values before their exteriorization by sale to customers, even though market values are higher than cost.
5. Many estimates recorded in accounts are based on relatively subjective considerations, such as depreciation expense, credit losses (or bad debts expense), and income tax expense.

6. Anticipated profits are often added to cost in recording long-term contracts in process (and anticipated losses should be deducted).
7. Natural resources are often revalued—for example, land in which mineral deposits are discovered, on the basis of expert opinion concerning the quantity of the minerals found and their current exit market price.
8. Many acquisition prices are not used to record resources, examples being expenditure on advertising to build up goodwill, cost of recruiting and training personnel, research and development expenditure.
9. Where a corporation has a substantial investment in another corporation under such conditions that the accounts of the two corporations are not combinable into *consolidated accounts*, the investment may be recorded at cost of acquisition *plus* the investor's share of the investee's profits earned during the investment period (and minus the share of losses for that period) using the equity method.

The implication of these observations is that some other explanation of valuation in accounting is needed. An attempt to use modern measurement theory for this purpose appears to have been unsuccessful. Indeed, Vickrey argues that money does not constitute a unit of measure and that the assumption that money constitutes a ratio scale cannot be empirically verified.[19] The approach of Georgescu-Roegen involves defining a purpose for which the "happening" is to be measured, and "disclosure," or "SEC filing" are not purposes. We seem to be left with accounting valuation as the use of measurements made for other purposes, in the preparation of financial statements.[20]

ENDNOTES

1. The English poet Shelley, in his book *In Defense of Poetry*, wrote that reason is the enumeration of things already known, whereas imagination involves their valuation, either singly or in combination.
2. *Maurice Jarre*, 64 TC No. 15.
3. *Statement of Financial Accounting Standards No. 33*, "Financial Reporting and Changing Prices," Financial Accounting Standards Board, September 1979.
4. Bonbright, J.C., *Valuation of Property*, New York: McGraw-Hill, 1937; repr. Charlottesville, Va.: Michie Company, 1965. Bonbright defined *value to the owner* as the lower of replacement cost and (a) sales value and (b) value in use.
5. Vickrey, Don W. "General Price-Level-Adjusted Historical Cost Statements and the Ratio-Scale View," *The Accounting Review*, January 1976, pp. 31-40, especially the bibliography, pp. 39-40.
6. The error in logic was first exposed by Gustav Adolf Gross in *Die Wirtschaftstheoretischen Grundiagen des "Modernen Kapitalismus" Von Sombart*, Jena: Verlag Von Gustav Fischer, 1931, p. 142. It is also the subject of Don W. Vickrey, "Is Accounting a Measurement Discipline?" *The Accounting Review*, October 1970, pp. 731-42.
7. Churchill, Neil C. and Andrew C. Stedry, "Some Developments in Management Science and Information Systems with Respect to Measurement in Accounting," in *Research in Accounting Measurement*, ed. Jaedicke, Ijiri, and Nielson, American Accounting Association, 1966, p. 28, n.l.

8. For an introduction to modern measurement theory see Sterling, Robert R. *Theory of the Measurement of Enterprise Income*, University of Kansas, 1970, pp. 65-115, and the two Vickrey articles cited above.
9. Churchman, C. West, *Prediction and Optimal Decision: Philosophical Issues of a Science of Values*, Englewood Cliffs, N.J.: Prentice-Hall, Inc., 1961, ch. 1.
10. Morgenstern, Oskar, *On the Accuracy of Economic Observations*, Princeton University Press, 1st ed. 1950, pp. 30-32.
11. Information theorists also use the word *entropy* to designate the amount of information expected from a message (the sum of the probability of each possible event times the amount of information associated with its occurrence).
12. Georgescu-Roegen, Nicholas, *The Entropy Law and the Economic Process*, Cambridge, Mass.: Harvard University Press, 1971.
13. Evans, W. Duane, "Some Comments on Measures of Changes in Capital Stock Aggregates", *Proceedings of the 37th Session*, International Statistical Institute, London 1969, Vol. XLIII, Book 1, pp. 265-275.
14. Canning, John B., *The Economics of Accountancy*, New York: The Ronald Press, 1929, pp. 182-4.
15. Sandilands, F.E.P., *Inflation Accounting—Report of the Inflation Accounting Committee*, London: Her Majesty's Stationery Office, Cmnd. 6225, 1975.
16. Many accountants overlook the prevalence of imputed, or "as if" costs, in GAAP. Examples are: accounting for employee stock option plans under APBO No. 25, and interest on long-term receivables and payables under APBO No. 21.
17. Chambers, R.J., *Accounting, Evaluation and Economic Behavior*, Englewood Cliffs, N.J.: Prentice-Hall, Inc., 1966.
18. Sterling, op. cit. pp. 77-8.
19. According to Vickrey, the most extensive "attribute" of the money unit is purchasing power, and if we do not measure in purchasing power units, we are not measuring at all.
20. The issues addressed in this chapter have been recently reviewed by Yuji Ijiri in *Historical Cost Accounting and its Rationality*, Research Monograph No. 1, Vancouver B.C.: Canadian Certified General Accountants Research Foundation, 1981.

SELECTED ADDITIONAL READINGS

Benke, Jr., Ralph L. and James Don Edwards, *Transfer Pricing: Techniques and Uses*, National Association of Accountants, 1980.

Chambers, Raymond J., *Accounting Evaluation and Economic Behavior*, Englewood Cliffs, N.J.: Prentice-Hall, Inc., 1966, pp. 42-49 and 84-96.

Chatfield, Michael, *A History of Accounting Thought*, Hinsdale, Ill.: The Dryden Press, 1974, pp. 231-249 and 254-266.

Dewhirst, John F., "Dealing with Uncertainty," *Canadian Chartered Accountant*, August 1971, pp. 139-146.

Financial Analysts Federation, Statement of the Financial Accounting Policy Committee, "Part II: Measurement of the Elements of Financial Statements," *Financial Analysts Journal*, March/April, 1978, pp. 22-30, 54, 72, 73.

Financial Accounting Standards Board, *Discussion Memorandum*, "an analysis of issues related to Conceptual Framework for Financial Accounting and Reporting: Elements of Financial Statements and Their Measurement," Stamford, Conn.: Financial Accounting Standards Board, December 2, 1976, Parts II and III.

Ijiri, Yuji, *The Foundations of Accounting Measurement: A Mathematical, Economic and Behavioral Inquiry*, Englewood Cliffs, N.J.: Prentice-Hall, Inc., 1967.

Mattessich, Richard, *Accounting and Analytical Methods, Measurement and Projection of Income and Wealth in the Micro- and Macro-Economy*, Homewood, Ill: Richard D. Irwin, Inc., 1964.

———, "On the Perennial Misunderstanding of Asset Measurement by Means of Present Values," *Cost and Management*, March-April 1970, pp. 29-31.

McDonald, Daniel L., "Feasibility Criteria for Accounting Measures," *The Accounting Review*, October 1967, pp. 662-679.

McKeown, James C., "Comparative Application of Market and Cost Based Accounting Models," *Journal of Accounting Research*, Spring 1973, pp. 62-99.

Mock, Theodore Jaye, "Measurement and Accounting Information Criteria," *Studies in Accounting Research #13*, Sarasota, Fla.: American Accounting Association, 1976.

Revsine, Lawrence, *Replacement Cost Accounting*, Englewood Cliffs, N.J.: Prentice-Hall, Inc., 1973.

———, "Technological Changes and Replacement Costs: A Beginning," *The Accounting Review*, April 1979, pp. 306-22.

Sterling, Robert R., "Conservatism: The Fundamental Principle of Valuation in Traditional Accounting," *Abacus*, Vol. 3, December 1967, pp. 109-132.

———, "Elements of Pure Accounting Theory," *The Accounting Review*, January 1967, pp. 62-73.

———, *Theory of the Measurement of Enterprise Income*, Lawrence, Kansas: The University Press of Kansas, 1970, pp. 65-115 and 117-132.

———, (ed.) *Asset Valuation and Income Determination*, Lawrence, Kansas: Scholars Book Co., 1971.

Vickrey, Don W., "Is Accounting a Measurement Discipline?" *The Accounting Review*, October 1970, pp. 731-742.

———, "General Price-Level Adjusted Historical-Cost Statements and the Ratio-Scale View," *The Accounting Review*, January 1976, pp. 31-40, especially bibliography, pp. 39-40.

Wright, T.K., "A Theory of Inventory Measurement," *Abacus*, December 1965, pp. 150-155.

———, "Relationship between Present Value and Value to the Owner," *Journal of Business Finance*, Summer 1973, pp. 19-25.

Yu, S.C., *The Structure of Accounting Theory*, Florida University Press, 1976.

Case 9-1 Problem in Inventory Valuation

A fully automated plant is set up to manufacture a unique product from one raw material. The material is the waste product of another industry, and delivered cost is nil since the other industry pays the cost of transporting the material from its premises to the place of use.

The cycle time of the plant is 32 days from receipt of material to finished product. It can produce 1,000 units of product at the end of each 32 day period. Fixed costs, including depreciation, total $365,000 a year and accrue evenly from day to day. There are no variable costs.

1. If the plant is put into operation on January 1 at full capacity to supply the February market, what is the value of inventory at January 31?
2. If the plant is put into operation on January 1 at 50 percent of capacity to supply the February market with 500 units of product, what is the value of inventory at January 31?
3. Suppose that the finished product must be held in store for 365 days in order to mature, and that the plant operates at full capacity during January. What is the value of January production included in inventory at December 31?

A selling price of $400 per unit during January can be assumed.

END OF CHAPTER QUESTIONS

1. Valuation of assets is an important topic in accounting theory. Suggested valuation methods include the following:

   Historical cost (past purchase prices)
   Historical cost adjusted to reflect general price-level changes (constant dollars)
   Discounted cash flow (future exchange prices)
   Market price (current selling prices)
   Replacement cost (current purchase prices)

   Required:

   a. Why is the valuation of assets a significant issue?
   b. Explain the basic theory underlying each of the valuation methods cited above. (AICPA November 1976).
2. What is meant by *articulation* in accounting, and what influence does this concept have on the valuation of assets?
3. What is meant by *value* in accounting? Why is the word often assumed to mean selling market value?
4. Explain the concept of *value in use.* Distinguish between the use of this phrase in FASB Statement No. 33 and Bonbright's meaning, now referred to as *deprival value*.
5. What is a transfer price? Why is it important to include transfer prices in a discussion of valuation in accounting?
6. Explain what is meant by the word *attribute* in accounting theory.
7. What is the *fallacy of composition* and what is its significance for valuation in accounting?
8. Define *measurement*, and explain what is meant by a measurement scale.

9. "Measurements of physical phenomena differ from measurements of value in accounting in respect of the greater precision of the former." Discuss.
10. Some theorists reject the proposition that accounting valuations are measurements. Why?
11. Discuss the problem of error measurement. What techniques are used to determine this value? Could they be applied to financial accounting data?
12. Define *entropy*. What is its relevance to understanding accounting information?
13. Explain what is meant by direct valuation. Give examples of its use in financial accounting.
14. Explain what is meant by indirect valuation. Give examples of its use in accounting.
15. What definition has been adopted by the FASB for the word *cost*. Is it consistent with the proposition that assets are valued for financial reporting purposes at historical costs?
16. Distinguish between the different uses of money in a modern society. What relevance does this distinction have for accounting?
17. What is the valuation decision framework presented by the Sandilands Report? Does it explain accounting practice in relation to balance sheet valuation?
18. Discuss the alternative approaches to the measurement of replacement cost of an asset.
19. Conservatism is usually cited as a basic accounting convention. What does it mean, and how is it applied?
20. List the different valuation methods which might be encountered in the financial statements of a large manufacturing corporation. In what way are they described by the phrase "historical cost"?

10

ACCOUNTING FOR CHANGING PRICES

THE UNITED STATES OF AMERICA

Because of supply and demand factors the prices of assets and liabilities may change while they are held by an entity even in the absence of inflationary price-level changes. Until now we have restricted our view of price changes affecting financial accounting to market price changes and noted that such changes may be recorded when they occur or when they are realized. These "holding gains or losses" may be recognized during the period in which the price of an asset changes, or during the period in which the product is sold, given away, or destroyed in a casualty loss.

In this and the next two chapters, we shall examine further the implications of accounting for changing prices, with special reference to inflationary price-level changes. These have been a common feature of all economies since World War II and have tended to become more pronounced through time. Thus, the context of this discussion is an inflationary period, and the thrust of efforts by accountants to account for inflationary price-level changes has been toward supplementary financial statements which adjust the basic statements for the effects of inflation. This is known in the United States as *accounting in constant dollars* since the FASB made this terminology official in its *Statement No. 33*.[1] It has also been called general price-level (GPL) accounting, current purchasing power (CPP) accounting, and purchasing power units (PuPU) accounting.

We can also account for general price-level changes together with accounting for changes in specific prices. This observation points to four possible categories of financial statement.

Category	Concept of Capital
historical cost	"financial" capital
historical cost-constant dollar	"real" capital in the economist's sense
current value	"real" capital in the businessman's sense (an aggregate of physical goods combined for production)
current value/constant dollar	Edwards and Bell's "real business capital" (see chapter 11).

The consequence of *FASB Statement No. 33*, and other accounting standards which are being set in countries outside the United States, is the gradual acceptance of the smørgasbord approach to financial reporting, in which the user can choose from an array of figures those which appear most relevant to the decision at hand.

The smørgasbord approach implies that no one method of determining income is acceptable for all users at the present time. The same statement can be made for profit, as those countries in which profit or loss is the last figure of the income statement are experiencing a similar difficulty in deciding what to put in and what to leave out of the profit and loss account. In the preparation of financial statements which permit a number of different income, or profit, figures, therefore, accountants appear to be responding to user needs.

In chapter 10 we examine accounting for changing price-levels, or constant dollar accounting. In chapter 11 we extend the analysis to changes in specific prices, under the heading "Current value accounting." *FASB Statement No. 33* covers both constant dollar and current cost accounting, and it is convenient to discuss its requirements in one place. For this reason, the explanations which follow will refer to both methods of accounting for changing prices.

INFLATION AND ITS MEASUREMENT

It is difficult to define what we mean by inflation more precisely than to call it a considerable and prolonged rise in most prices caused by too much money chasing after too few goods and services. This definition draws attention to the complex of factors responsible for inflation: an expansion of the money supply, increases in both demand and costs (demand-pull and cost-push), and restrictions on production through unionism and government regulation or because of inefficiencies, notably in the public sector. It also reveals the difficulties inherent in measuring "too much" and "too few." Some prices fall during inflation, and supply and demand change even when the purchasing power of money remains otherwise constant. Deflation is the opposite of inflation, and although this chapter is predicated on the existence of an inflationary condition at the time of writing, its contents are equally relevant to a deflationary condition.

The prices of all individual goods and services do not change at the same rate; some rise faster than others, and some may fall. The general price-level is a measure of relative price change for all goods and services. There are several such measures used by statisticians in the United States for observations concerning the social income. The Bureau of Labor Statistics of the Department of Labor publishes a Consumer Price Index, using a "basket" of weighted consumer goods and services to represent the universe of consumer goods and services. To construct the index, the prices of all the items in the basket are summed at one point in time, designated t_o. At any subsequent point in time (t_n) the items in the basket can be priced and the prices summed. The ratio of the sum of prices at t_n to the sum of prices at t_o gives the index, or relative price change between the two dates. A similar index for goods and services, having a somewhat bigger basket and using wholesale prices rather than retail prices, called the Producer Price Index is published by the Bureau of Labor Statistics. This was formerly called the Wholesale Price Index published by the Department of Commerce.

The most representative price index is the gross national product implicit price deflator (GNP Deflator) published quarterly by the Office of Business Economics of the Department of Commerce. National income statisticians collect data on all market transactions throughout the economy and to facilitate comparisons of one period with another, they keep track of price changes in each market. These price changes are then combined into one index to relate GNP data at different points in time in constant dollars—dollars having ostensibly the identical purchasing power. The GNP Deflator is regarded as the most comprehensive index of price-level changes in the United States but for technical reasons the FASB required an index which is published monthly and not revised repeatedly, and only the Consumer Price Index for all urban consumers satisfied that criterion. For this reason the CPI-U, as it is called, is the index to be used in applying *FASB Statement No. 33*. With a base year of 1967 = 100, the CPI-U had risen to more than 200 by the year 1981. Such an index measures the purchasing power of money, which moves inversely to the movements of the index. During this same period, therefore, the purchasing power of the U.S. dollar was more than halved. Another way to say this is that a 1981 dollar could buy about one-half of the consumer goods and services that a 1967 dollar could buy.

ACCOUNTING FOR CHANGING PRICES

We have identified two kinds of price change.

1. For a given good

   If market price at t_o = \$2.00
   And market price at t_n = 3.00
   The price change is + 1.00 and $\frac{1.00}{2.00} = 50\%$

This is called the specific change and the rate of specific price change is 50 percent. An index of these two prices would show their ratio, and look like this:

$$t_o = 100 \qquad t_n = 150$$

2. For all goods

   If market prices at t_o = \$200.00
   And market prices at t_n = 240.00
   The price change is + 40.00 and $\frac{40}{200} = 20\%$

This is called the general price change and the rate of general price change is 20 percent. An index of these two sets of prices would show:

$$t_o = 100 \qquad t_n = 120$$

We can combine these two pieces of information for the specific good described in 1. above.

$$\$2.00 \times \frac{120}{100} = \$2.40 - \$2.00 = \$0.40 \text{ (the inflation effect)}$$

$$\$2.40 \times \frac{150}{120} = \$3.00 - \$2.40 = \$0.60 \text{ (the market effect)}$$

The FASB calls the inflation effect the "effect of general price-level change," and the market effect the "increase in current cost net of inflation."

It is possible to justify general price-level accounting on the grounds that it improves the additivity of accounting measurements by expressing them in a homogeneous measurement scale. Other arguments have been put forward both for and against, and are summarized below.

Price-Level Adjustment

Advantages	**Disadvantages**
Reveals the effects of inflation on the particular entity.	Inflation means different things to different firms.
Improves interperiod and interfirm comparisons.	General price-level adjustments are not meaningful to business firms.
Assists the user to "assess future cash flows" better.	Adjusted figures do not reflect cash flows.
Refines ratios calculated from financial statement figures.	Ratios are crude indicators in any case.

As previously mentioned, the capital maintenance concept is often cited as the reason for general price-level accounting; the preparation of an income statement on this basis assures the maintenance of the purchasing power of invested capital before distribution of any profit as income to the stockholder. A typical argument of this kind uses the example of a baker who sells a loaf of bread. If the loaf cost the baker 50 cents and is sold for 80 cents, historical cost accounting shows a profit of 30 cents. The baker would be tempted to use this to buy a couple of rolls for himself. If, however, flour and other ingredients have increased in price, and a loaf of bread now costs the baker 65 cents, his consumable (distributable) profit is only 15 cents. Capital maintenance involves keeping intact sufficient purchasing power to buy a loaf of bread before distributing anything for consumption purposes.

Such examples are confusing because bread is a consumption good. It is clear, however, that this example concerns specific prices and not the general price-level; it might support current value accounting but not constant dollar accounting. The main problem with it, however, is that it oversimplifies the business accounting problem. Capital maintenance in historical cost terms is a most imprecise and subjective concept; how it is to be made more precise by changing the unit of measure is unclear. And in any case, the capital to be maintained is that of the shareholders in the corporate enterprise, which is a function of factors of many kinds (share market prices, portfolio selection, arbitrage, marginal propensity to save, etc.), only one of which is the calculation of retained earnings.

When the problem is presented in terms of economic capital and income, however, these complications can be avoided. Using the example of two end-of-year receipts of $1,000, the present value of which at 10 percent is $1,735, an amortization table looks like this:

Period	**PV_o**	**Income at 10%**	**PV + Income**	**Receipts**	**PV_n**
1	$1,735	$174	$1,909	$1,000	$909
2	909	91	1,000	1,000	0

Any other figure than $826 ($1,735 − $909) for depreciation will fail to produce the correct figure for income ($174) in year 1. In other words, there is a unique value for income, defined as $Y_1 = K_1 - K_0$ and that value is dependent upon the measurement of capital (K). If the purchasing power of money changes, it is obvious that K may be repriced in order to find that amount which could be spent during year 1 without diminishing the purchasing power of K_1 as seen at t_0. The question is, what does this proposition mean?

The other aspect of general price-level accounting which is mentioned frequently is that it purports to match current costs with current revenues. In other words, revenues are transactions measured in terms of current purchasing power, but cost of sales, depreciation, and perhaps other income statement expenses are measured in historical costs, purchasing power at the time the factors were acquired. If the costs are remeasured in constant dollars, this problem is solved. In this view, the primary purpose of constant dollar financial statements is the measurement of income as the result of operations. *FASB Statement No. 33* highlights the effect of inflation on income from operations.

The following advantages are claimed for constant dollar accounting:

1. It is more meaningful. The user of financial statements approaches them with a schema of current prices. Assuming that each value contained in a set of financial statements is a real quantity Q multiplied by a price P, then substituting P_n for P_0 permits the user to fit the magnitude P_nQ into his schema, where the magnitude P_0Q does not belong.
2. It eliminates misleading information. The realization of assets during periods when the price-level is rising conventionally

results in a credit to income for both the inflation effect and the market effect. If income is defined as profit, then the market effect alone should enter into its determination. If income is defined in terms of the Fisher-Hicks model, the real capital of the firm must be maintained before income can be said to have arisen, and this involves eliminating the inflation effect by restating capital at t_0 in terms of the purchasing power index at t_n. The balance sheet will then show assets and liabilities in terms of the purchasing power at t_n; if the income statement is presented in the same terms, ratio calculations are improved, particularly the profitability (return on investment) ratio.

3. It separates the accidental effects of inflation from the results of business operations. By separating those windfall gains and losses which occur in times of inflation from the market gains and losses which are the consequences of business decisions, the financial statements become more useful for judgments on profitability and the efficiency of management.
4. It reveals more clearly the taxable capacity of the entity. If the inflation effect is removed from the income statement, so-called paper profits are eliminated, and the price-level adjusted net income represents the base on which the effective tax rate should be calculated. It may be surmised that the hope that this type of presentation will be a strong argument for some kind of tax reduction underlies the support for constant dollar accounting in the accounting profession.

From the viewpoint that accounting should provide information useful for making economic decisions, a committee of the American Accounting Association arrived at six uses for price-level adjusted statements. These included appraisal of management's effectiveness in maintaining capital, analysis of earning power in the light of current economic conditions, and judgment of managerial policies concerning the matters dealt with in the accounts.[2]

Some writers go further and claim that constant dollar accounting helps maintain capital and prevents capital from being distributed to stockholders in the form of dividends. It is also suggested that, by reducing the amount of reported profit in an inflationary period and increasing it during deflation, constant dollar accounting has counter-cyclical implications for the economy as a whole, acting as a brake on overinvestment during the upswing, and *vice versa*.

It is perhaps regrettable that the FASB has forced the use of the term "constant dollar accounting" for two different methods of price-level adjustment. In order to express the effects of inflation one must select a particular unit of purchasing power as the unit of measure. Prior to *FASB Statement No. 33*, there were two common approaches to this problem, the use of *base period* dollars (called constant dollars) and the use of *current period* dollars (called current dollars). The end-of-year index was invariably used in order to express in current dollars, for the reason given in number 1 above.

There are two main advantages to using base period dollars, which involves translating all values into the base year index. First, the "rolling forward adjustment" necessitated by changing the index used each year is avoided. Once stated in base period dollars, the amounts reported never change until the asset or liability is disposed of. Secondly, any graphs or charts prepared can be maintained and extended; current dollar accounting involves the preparation of new graphs and charts every year. A secondary advantage is the fact that the effects of inflation are reflected in smaller numbers.

The main advantage of current dollars is that they are better understood. No one remembers what objects they were spending their money on in 1967, or how much they cost. Expenditure patterns and prices at the end of last year, on the other hand, are still fairly fresh in ones mind. Thus, to say that something now costs twice as much tells the listener more than to say that fifteen years ago it was one-half the price.

In the event, the FASB opted for current dollars, but for technical reasons chose *average of the current year* dollars, which minimizes the amount of restatement necessary. On the other hand, average of the current year dollars have the disadvantage of restating end-of-year values at lower amounts than their money dollar values, which must be disconcerting to some who expect inflation effects always to go in the same direction.

HISTORY OF CONSTANT DOLLAR ACCOUNTING IN THE UNITED STATES

Attention was drawn to the problems of accounting in times of changing prices by Henry Sweeney's writings during the 1920s and 1930s.[3] Sweeney reviewed the literature on inflation accounting which originated in Germany in the 1920s, notably the work of Fritz Schmidt, and examined various possibilities, of which constant dollar accounting was one. The subject of accounting for inflation was considered by the Committee on Accounting Procedure and mentioned in chapter 9A of *ARB 43*, where it was suggested that supplementary schedules, explanations, or footnotes would be appropriate, but no change was recommended in the historical cost basis of financial statements. Several research studies were conducted in the 1950s; we may mention Hendriksen's case study of two public utility firms,[4] and Jones' influential case study of four steel companies.[5]

In 1963 the AICPA authorized publication of *Accounting Research Study No. 6*, "Reporting the Financial Effects of Price-Level Changes," by the Staff of the Institute's Accounting Research Division. *APB Statement No. 3*, "Financial Statements Restated for

General Price-Level Changes," was published in 1969; in it the Accounting Principles Board presented recommendations on how to prepare and report information restated for general price-level changes. The board retained the ideas put forward in *ARS 6* and, as the FASB has also endorsed these ideas, the manner in which they were arrived at deserves some attention here.

ARS 6 "REPORTING THE FINANCIAL EFFECT OF PRICE-LEVEL CHANGES"

On April 28, 1961, the APB minutes recorded agreement that to ignore fluctuations in the value of the dollar was unrealistic. The minutes instructed the Director of Accounting Research to make recommendations for disclosing the effect of price-level changes on financial statements, preferably using supplementary statements for this purpose.

The result of this initiative was a research study (*ARS No. 6*) concentrating on one concept, the general price-level or purchasing power concept, and explicitly rejecting any other approach to the problem. In particular, changes in the prices of individual goods and services arising from supply and demand—that is, from nonmonetary factors— were assumed to reflect the normal functioning of a market economy and to account for them before realization would contravene the conventional principles of accounting.

To make comparisons between accounting figures at two dates meaningful, it was recommended that differences resulting from the inflationary or deflationary price-level changes of nonmonetary assets be eliminated by the use of a measure of the general level of prices. The reciprocal of the GNP Deflator was proposed for this purpose; $10,000 invested at a time when this index stood at 125 becomes $14,000 when the same index rises to 175, or $8,000 when the index falls to 100. No profit or loss accompanies the valuation change, because it does not represent a market price change; there is simply a restatement of capital.

In the case of monetary assets and liabilities, however, a gain or loss occurs as purchasing power falls or rises, namely, a gain or loss in purchasing power. By restating monetary assets and liabilities using the general price-level index, a realized gain or loss emerges. The study recommended that this gain or loss be reported either as the last element in the calculation of net income or immediately following net income, before showing changes in retained earnings.

The study has dominated professional thinking on the subject, and closely parallels the current purchasing power method recommended by the UK Institutes of Chartered Accountants. The official reason given is that it is the unit of measure that is being changed and not the accounting principles involved. In particular, the relationships between the elements of the financial statements, it has been alleged, are undisturbed by this type of price-level adjustment, a proposition which is patently false.[6] Restating, or rolling forward, prior years' nonmonetary assets and liabilities without producing reported gains and losses, is an important feature of *ARS No. 6* which has been retained in *FASB Statement No. 33*.

It might have been thought that, by providing official support for the disclosure of the effects of price-level changes in supplementary financial statements and by demonstrating that similar statements had been produced and published in other countries without apparent unfavorable effects, the AICPA would have encouraged U.S. corporations to experiment with them. The APB, after receiving the study and comments from interested parties, prepared a research draft of a proposed pronouncement but decided to conduct a field test of the method before committing itself on the proposal.

Eighteen companies were asked to restate their financial statements in the manner proposed by the study. The companies were of varied size and from a variety of industries; most of them were listed on stock exchanges. Each company restated the financial statements of two years; in general, the statements covered 1966 and 1967, years of low inflation rates of 2.7 percent and 3.0 percent, respectively. As might be expected, adjusting for general price-level changes showed companies reporting higher or lower net income, price-level gains or losses, higher or lower effective tax rates, and so on. The results of the study were reported in *The Journal of Accountancy*, with the conclusion that "the participants in general agreed that with proper preparation practical problems should not present a significant barrier to preparation of general price-level financial statements."[7] However, none of these companies found it useful voluntarily to publish price-level adjusted financial statements. In 1978 General Motors did publish adjusted figures for net income and dividends in its annual report; these were indexed financial statement amounts and not the result of constant dollar accounting. GM's initiative was welcomed by some public accountants and financial journalists, but criticized by Zeff on the grounds that restatement was not comprehensive and that the method used was not the one recommended by the FASB.[8] GM's recognition of user needs in this case came too late to influence the course of events.

APB STATEMENT NO. 3

In its *Statement No. 3*,[9] the APB recommended that price-level adjusted financial statements should be presented in addition to the basic historical cost statements, but not as the basic statements. It did not believe that price-level adjusted information was required at that time (1969) for fair presentation of financial position and results of operations in conformity with generally accepted accounting principles in the United States.[10] Such statements were "an extension of and not a departure from" historical cost accounting.

Statements should be presented in terms of the general purchasing power of the dollar at latest balance sheet date, and monetary items distinguished from nonmonetary items because general purchasing power gains and losses occur only in relation to the former. These general price-level gains and losses should be reported as a separate item in price-level adjusted income statements and included in current net income. Financial statements of earlier periods should be updated to year-end dollars of a subsequent period when presented as comparative information. The publication of price-level adjusted financial statements should be accompanied by explanations sufficient to prevent the reader from confusing the figures they contain with those in other financial statements; in particular, the effects of the roll-forward procedures on retained earnings should be explained. This requirement has not been carried forward into *FASB Statement No. 33*, which also does not call for the inclusion of gains and losses on monetary items in price-level adjusted net income.

The reconciliation would have taken this form.

Retained earnings at the beginning of the year:

Restated to general purchasing power at the beginning of the year	XXXX
Amount required to update to general purchasing power at the end of the year	XXXX
Restated to general purchasing power at the end of the year	XXXX

The Statement included an Appendix B which distinguished monetary from nonmonetary assets and liabilities. In paragraph 18, the Statement defined monetary assets and liabilities for purposes of general price-level accounting: "Their amounts are fixed by contract or otherwise in terms of numbers of dollars regardless of changes in specific prices or in the general price-level." There was some discussion of gray areas such as foreign currency receivables and payables, which some Board members regarded as similar to domestic monetary items, and a few assets and liabilities which might be either monetary or nonmonetary, such as marketable debentures held as an investment and convertible debt owed. Prepaid expenses other than interest, deferred charges and credits from income tax, and advances received and paid on sales and purchase contracts were items classified as nonmonetary which could equally have been classified as monetary. Indeed, the difficulty of classifying assets and liabilities other than money as monetary is one of the signs that we may be dealing with a normative rather than a positive theory of accounting, one which deals with what should be rather than what is.

This definition of monetary items, and the related definition of these items as "claims to a fixed quantity of the monetary unit," would restrict the category to domestic currency cash and bank deposits, accounts receivable and accounts, notes and bonds payable, and unmarketable loans held as investments. Mandatorily redeemable preferred stock would also qualify. *FASB Statement No. 33*, however, recognizing the complications involved in treating them as nonmonetary items, arbitrarily classified foreign currency cash, receivables and payables and deferred taxation balances as monetary items. This last concession to practicality no doubt resulted from the FASB's exposure draft, "Financial Reporting in Units of General Purchasing Power," which contained an example of accounting for the deferred taxation account on the assumption that it was a nonmonetary item.

The accelerated rate of inflation through 1973 led the Financial Accounting Standards Advisory Council to urge the FASB to consider the subject of accounting for price-level changes, which was placed on the FASB's agenda in January, 1974. A discussion memorandum was published by the FASB on February 15, 1974, which simply reaffirmed *APB Statement No. 3*. At this time the Trueblood Report took the position that the objectives of financial statements could not be best served by the exclusive use of a single valuation basis and recommended the use in the basic statements of historical costs, exit values, current replacement costs, and present values.

In spite of this diversion, the FASB issued an Exposure Draft in December 1974, "Financial Reporting in Units of General Purchasing Power," which fully endorsed *ARS 6* and *APB Statement No. 3*. This publication included an extensive worked example and proposed to require, for fiscal years beginning on or after January 1976, price-level adjusted financial statements together with the basic (historical cost) financial statements.

REPLACEMENT COST DISCLOSURE

After exposing the idea in August, 1975, the Securities and Exchange Commission (SEC) issued *Accounting Series Release No. 190* in March, 1976, requiring disclosure of certain replacement cost data by corporations over a specified size. The effect of *ASR 190* was to force about one thousand United States corporations to footnote the following in their annual financial statements, for years ending on or after December 25, 1976:

Assets—The estimated current replacement cost of inventories and productive capacity at each fiscal year-end for which a balance sheet is required to be filed. This means the estimated current cost of replacing (new) the productive capacity on hand, together with the depreciated cost of such capacity. Assets held under financing leases are to be included in productive capacity.

Cost and Expenses—Approximate amount of cost of sales for the two most recent fiscal years, computed using replacement cost of goods and services at the time sales were made. The approximate amount of depreciation, depletion, and amortization for the two most recent years based on the average current replacement cost of productive capacity.

Other— A description of the methods used in determining the above amounts, together with any consideration given to the related effects on direct labor costs, repairs and maintenance, utility and other indirect costs as a result of the assumed replacement of productive capacity.

Replacement cost was defined as "the lowest amount that would have to be paid in the normal course of business to obtain a new asset of equivalent operating or productive capacity."

The SEC gave as its reason the commission's belief that these data were important and useful to investors and not otherwise obtainable. Whatever the justification for this proposition, it cannot be denied that these data are important and useful to managers, particularly of the marketing function. It is therefore a matter of astonishment to note the difficulties which this simple request presented to the firms in question. Their auditors and many of the corporations which commented on the requirement asserted that the method of calculating replacement cost was virtually unknown, that they had no experience in this area, that there were no conventional methods or standards available, and that insoluble practical problems stood in the way of disclosing meaningful amounts.

Critics noted the absence of a definition of replacement cost, which the SEC purported to provide in *Staff Accounting Bulletin (SAB) No. 7*.

> Replacement cost is the lowest amount that would have to be paid in the normal course of business to obtain a new asset of equivalent operating or productive capability. In the case of depreciable, depletable or amortizable assets, replacement cost (new) and depreciated replacement cost should be distinguished....
>
> Productive capacity...would be measured by the number of units [a manufacturer] can presently produce and distribute within a particular time frame....

SAB 7 excluded intangible assets from this definition, an illustration of the irrational response to intangible assets later remarked upon in this book. *SAB 9* and *10* discussed the year of grace which *ASR 190* gave for mineral resources and foreign assets and explained the inclusion of one kind of intangible asset, capital leases, as productive assets. *SAB 10* and *11* pointed out that replacement cost was not required to be disclosed for nonreplacement assets; the total amount included in historical cost for such assets was to be reported. *SAB 10* listed the following four types of replacement cost measure:

1. Indexing—i.e. applying a specific index to an acquisition cost.
2. Direct pricing—i.e. using current factor prices to build up the cost of the asset.
3. Unit pricing—i.e. identifying the appropriate unit of measure of the asset in question (such as square feet of a building) and multiplying by their current prices.

4. Functional pricing—i.e. identifying the output of a process and developing a current cost to create capacity to produce that output.

In the summer of 1976 the FASB announced a decision to defer further consideration of constant dollar accounting, and many commentators saw this as an indication that the exposure draft proposing supplementary constant dollar statements would be withdrawn. The Board announced that it had not reached a conclusion about the merits of this type of financial statement, which was not sufficiently well understood by preparers and users. This suggested that the need had not been so well demonstrated as to justify imposing the cost of implementation on all preparers of financial reports.

Pressure from the SEC and other sources continued to be exerted upon the FASB to oblige it to bring out a standard on this subject, and the SEC's restricted approach to replacement cost disclosure pointed to the solution to the problem. In early 1979, the FASB published an exposure draft of a proposed standard which would have required supplementary price-level adjusted financial statements to be published by the largest public companies in the United States, numbering about 1,300. The proposed statement would have permitted these companies to choose whether to use constant dollar or current cost supplementary statements; the prospect of companies making this choice on the basis of which system made them look better, and possibly switching from one system to the other from year to year for this reason, was not acceptable to the FASB's technical staff. When the statement finally appeared in September, 1979, it required the affected companies to publish both constant dollar and current cost supplementary information for a five-year experimental period, starting with years ended on or after December 25, 1979. Unlike *ASR No. 190* which called only for Form 10-K disclosure, this information must accompany any annual financial statements which purport to be in conformity with GAAP if the accounting entity is a public enterprise with either (1) inventories and property, plant and equipment (gross) amounting to more than $125 million or (2) total assets (net of depreciation) amounting to more than $2 billion.

Following the pronouncement of *FASB Statement No. 33* the SEC waived the requirements of *ASR No. 190* for registrants providing current cost data for 1979, and repealed *ASR No. 190* in 1980.

FASB STATEMENT NO. 33

Prior to the issuance of *FASB Statement No. 33*, many of those who favored disclosing the effect of inflation, but who opposed the complexity of restating financial statements as a whole, recommended some form of partial adjustment. They suggested that the greatest effect of inflation (other than the purchasing power loss or gain on the net monetary position) impacted the entity through the valuation of inventories and fixed assets. It was alleged that the effect of inventory price changes on cost of goods sold could be accommodated by using the LIFO method of valuation, and some even suggested a LIFO-like adjustment to depreciation as well.

Many firms adopted LIFO as a tax-saving device and were required to report cost of goods sold and inventories on a LIFO basis because of the conformity rule. In times of rising prices, LIFO resembles current value accounting insofar as it charges the income statement with the current cost of goods sold. However, it differs from current value accounting in that the balance sheet valuation is far removed from current cost, and the holding gain or loss is nowhere disclosed.

Note that the conventional effect of LIFO is an average result; in some cases LIFO has the opposite effect on cost of goods sold, either through involuntary or voluntary liquidation of preceding year layers, or because of purchases at unusual prices shortly before the end of the fiscal year. To the extent that LIFO is acceptable for tax accounting, however, it serves to shield some of the inflation effect on business profits from taxation during a period of inflation, and the methods of accelerated depreciation allowed by the IRS have had a similar effect in respect of fixed assets. These measures may have dampened the desire of corporate executives to experiment with accounting for inflation in order to achieve tax reductions.

FASB Statement No. 33 is a method of partial adjustment, which requires the restatement only of the following figures:

- Cost of goods sold
- Inventories
- Depreciation expense
- Property, plant, and equipment, and accumulated depreciation

together with the disclosure of—

in constant dollar statements—purchasing power gain or loss on net monetary items (monetary assets minus monetary liabilities)

in current cost statements—increase or decrease in current cost amounts of inventories and property, plant and equipment, net of inflation

Restatement of cost of goods sold and inventories is required in order to arrive at income (loss) from continuing operations in either constant dollars or current cost/constant dollars.* This is an after-tax amount, before adjustment for extraordinary items, losses and gains on discontinued operations, and effects of changes in accounting principles, the last three on an after-tax basis.

*Recall that constant dollars are average of the year dollars. Most income statement items other than cost of goods sold and depreciation are expressed in average of the year dollars; hence, in the general case, current cost statements will include historical cost amounts which are also constant dollar amounts.

The FASB's decision to restrict adjustments to two income statement items appears to be a substantial saving of clerical and computational effort. The Statement also requires five-year summaries of net sales and other operating revenues and income (loss) from continuing operations in both constant dollars and current costs. The five-year summary in constant dollars may be measured in base-year purchasing power.

The Statement called for a period of experimentation by firms required to present this supplementary information on a constant dollar and current cost basis. This experimentation was not for the preparation of constant dollar and current cost financial statements, which had been demonstrated to be feasible by a variety of trials including the APB study mentioned above and a similar FASB study of 101 enterprises which restated their figures for the years 1972-74.[11] Rather, the experimentation referred to concerns the usefulness of this kind of information. In its para. 7 the Statement supported the continued dominant focus on historical cost statements because of their lack of subjectivity, verifiability, relation to cash flows, and because "users are accustomed to the present financial statements." The implication of the experimentation view was that the burden of proof lay on these new sets of figures to establish themselves as necessary information for financial statement users.

In 1980, the first samples of 1979 published annual reports containing data required by *Statement No. 33* revealed little that was unexpected. Corporate income from continuing operations on a constant dollar basis declined in every instance from the historical cost amount; in some cases, profits became losses. The reduction in reported profit averaged 40 percent. Those corporations reporting current cost data (not required until 1980 reports) also reported current cost operating income some 40 percent less than historical cost amounts. However, a few corporations (notably high technology and computer firms) reported higher current cost income from continuing operations, reflecting lower depreciation and other operating costs resulting from improved technology and increased productivity.

Most of the corporations reporting lower constant dollar income also reported substantial purchasing power gains and losses, which in some cases exceeded the diminution in operating income on a constant dollar basis. Current cost data showed large holding gains for many of the corporations reporting this figure. Several analyses of these 1979 results were published in 1980, including one by the FASB itself, which confirmed these observations.[12] They also highlighted the fact that constant dollar results showed effective income tax rates averaging 65 percent of constant dollar operating income, without attempting to distinguish the effects of income tax allocation, which results in many cases in the expense reported being considerably higher than the tax liability for the year.

An example of *Statement No. 33* supplementary financial reporting is reproduced on pages 274–60.

Notes to financial statements

Impact of changing prices (unaudited)

Management analysis of the impact of changing prices on the company is discussed on pages 16-18. The following supplemental information completes the disclosures required by the Financial Accounting Standards Board (FASB) Statement No. 33, "Financial Reporting and Changing Prices."

Reflected in the information is the effect of inflation on the reported results of the company using two different approaches as to adjusting property, plant and equipment for inflation. First, the effect of general inflation as determined by the Consumer Price Index (CPI) has been reflected as it relates to the depreciation of property, plant and equipment. Second, the effect of specific price changes on property, plant and equipment since initial purchase has been estimated and reflected in an adjusted depreciation amount based upon the "current cost" of the depreciable assets. The adjusted net earnings are not the result of a comprehensive restatement of earnings but more simply reflect earnings as adjusted for the impact of changing prices on property, plant and equipment. No specific adjustment is normally required for inventory as substantially all inventories are valued using the dollar value LIFO method which eliminates the impact of changing prices on inventory value from earnings. However, effect is given to the liquidation of LIFO inventories at current cost, which in 1980 amounted to $14.8 million.

Net earnings adjusted for changing prices

(millions of dollars)	Constant dollar earnings (adjusted for general inflation)	Current cost earnings (adjusted for specific price changes)
Net earnings—as reported	$126.1	$126.1
Excess of constant dollar depreciation over historical cost depreciation	34.2	
Excess of current cost depreciation over historical cost depreciation		35.4
Effect of liquidation of LIFO inventories	18.1	14.3
Net earnings as adjusted	$ 73.8	$ 76.4

Unrealized gain (loss) from decline in purchasing power of net monetary amounts owed or receivable

(millions of dollars)	Consolidated operations	Unconsolidated services operations	Net
	$28.7	$(13.8)	$14.9

Effect of the increase in current cost on December 31, 1980 ending balances

(millions of dollars)	Beginning of year current cost	Increase due to general inflation	Incremental amount due to change in specific prices	End of year current cost
Inventories	$515.5	$ 68.3	$(39.5)	$544.3
Fixed assets	$873.3	$102.2	$(73.9)	$901.6

Comparison of selected data adjusted for effect of changing prices

(millions of dollars except share data)	As reported **Adjusted (1980 dollars)** 1980	1979	1978	1977	1976	1975	Average annual rate of change
Sales	$2,673.3	$2,717.4	$2,326.0	$2,031.9	$1,862.4	$1,639.0	10.3%
	2,673.3	**3,084.9**	**2,937.8**	**2,762.9**	**2,695.8**	**2,509.3**	**1.3**
Net earnings	126.1	155.6	133.8	104.0	81.7	44.5	23.2
	126.1	**176.6**	**169.0**	**141.1**	**118.3**	**68.1**	**13.1**
Earnings per share	5.85	7.25	6.24	4.93	4.21	2.31	20.4
	5.85	**8.23**	**7.88**	**6.70**	**6.09**	**3.53**	**10.6**
Common stock dividend	2.35	2.08	1.85	1.65	1.41	1.35	11.7
	2.35	**2.36**	**2.34**	**2.24**	**2.04**	**2.07**	**2.6**
Book value per common share	54.51	50.99	45.64	41.10	38.36	35.51	9.0
	54.51	**57.89**	**57.65**	**55.89**	**55.53**	**54.36**	**.1**
Market value per share	42.75	35.88	28.38	27.88	30.50	20.00	16.4
	42.75	**40.73**	**35.85**	**37.91**	**44.15**	**30.62**	**6.9**
Capital expenditures	134.2	130.7	115.3	77.0	36.0	55.9	19.1
	134.2	**148.4**	**145.6**	**104.7**	**52.1**	**85.6**	**9.4**
Depreciation	64.4	59.6	55.2	50.9	43.4	42.8	8.5
	98.6	**100.6**	**97.6**	**92.8**	**88.0**	**94.9**	**.8**
Effective tax rate	46.1%	34.7%	43.2%	43.9%	48.5%	36.6%	4.7
	69.4	**42.9**	**50.5**	**50.9**	**55.9**	**64.2**	**1.6**
Net earnings adjusted for constant dollar depreciation	**91.9**	**143.7**	**141.0**	**117.7**	**93.1**	**38.7**	**18.9**
Consumer price index urban yearly average (base year: 1967)	**246.8**	**217.4**	**195.4**	**181.5**	**170.5**	**161.2**	**8.9**

Net assets at year-end

(millions of dollars)	**1980**	1979	1978	1977	1976	1975
As reported	**$1,153.7**	$1,076.9	$ 966.1	$ 872.2	$ 742.3	$ 689.1
Constant dollar	**1,581.8**	1,597.2	1,441.6	1,345.8	1,182.2	N/A*
Current cost	**1,619.6**	1,644.9	1,485.3	1,397.3	1,244.9	N/A*

*Not available

Impact of changing prices on operating margins

	Operating margin (LIFO)		Operating margin current cost*	
	1980	1979	**1980**	1979
Air Conditioning	**4.9%**	4.3%	**4.2%**	3.6%
Chemicals & Plastics	**9.3**	9.6	**7.8**	8.2
Industrial Products	**12.2**	13.0	**10.9**	11.9
Transportation Equipment	**3.5**	8.4	**1.9**	7.0
Total	**6.9%**	8.6%	**5.6%**	7.5%

*Operating margin on a LIFO basis, as adjusted for current cost depreciation. No effect is given to the 1980 liquidation of LIFO inventories at current cost, which amounted to $14.3 million.

Reproduced with permission from the Annual Report of Borg-Warner Corporation for 1980.

FINANCIAL ANALYSIS AND FASB STATEMENT NO. 33

Many corporate controllers have remarked on the fact that financial analysts rarely, if ever, ask them to provide constant dollar or current cost data for their companies. Researchers have found little interest in such data on the part of users of financial statements. This may be explained by the fact that some analysts are able to make any necessary adjustments to historical cost financial statements themselves.

One example of this is the Chicago firm of Duff and Phelps, Inc. which has its own Inflation Accounting Model, results of which are expressed in what the analysts call "real" or purchasing power terms.[13]

This model made the following adjustments to a corporation's historical cost financial statements:

1. Cost of goods sold was adjusted to reflect higher replacement cost of materials used in production.
2. Depreciation was recalculated using current replacement cost of plant and equipment instead of historical cost.
3. Inventories and net fixed assets were adjusted to replacement cost values.
4. Holding gains were excluded from "sustainable income" (which resembles the concept of distributable income because it can be paid out as dividends or reinvested without impairing the existing level of operations) but included in "economic income" whether realized or unrealized.

A purchasing power gain or loss on monetary items was not calculated, but a monetary working capital adjustment was made in order to show the additional funds required for working capital resulting from inflation. Finally, the adjustments permitted the analysts to prepare a funds statement on the capital maintenance basis of replacement cost accounting, which was believed to be the first attempt to prepare such a statement using inflation accounting.

It is difficult to believe that the partial and compromise constant dollar and current cost data required by *FASB Statement No. 33* will provide this type of financial analyst with information superior to that which it was capable of generating for itself. On the other hand, the FASB undoubtedly believed that many analysts and other users were not adjusting reported figures for the effects of price-level changes, either because they were unaware that it is a necessary feature of financial analysis, or because they lacked the technical skills. The Statement may be viewed as an attempt to reach this kind of user, and if its applicability is extended to firms outside the restricted number now covered, it will undoubtedly do so.

One member of the Board dissented on the grounds that it confuses the analyst with too many different income concepts. At the beginning of this chapter we pointed to four of them, based on the four different concepts of capital maintenance. However, the separate statement of purchasing power gains and losses on monetary items, and holding gains and losses on nonmonetary items, permits a number of additional combinations and permutations, so that the hypothetical "standard user" may yet cry in perplexity, "Will the real income number please stand up?" This Board member would have preferred a categorical move to current cost accounting, a position which will be discussed in more detail in chapter 11. Another dissenting Board member, however, was willing to live with constant dollar accounting but believed that "the weight of evidence suggests that the Board is promulgating a current cost model that is not ready, for a constituency that is not ready for it."

FASB Statement No. 33 has also been criticized because it did not require affected firms to disclose either constant dollar or current cost amounts for investments in nonconsolidated subsidiaries, marketable and other portfolio investments, and intangible assets generally. *FASB Statements Nos. 39, 40,* and *41* apply some or all of the provisions of *Statement No. 33* to mining and oil and gas, timberlands and growing timber, and income-producing real estate, respectively, but in an inconsistent manner. Moreover, with the exception of monetary liabilities, the effects of changing price levels on the equities side of the balance sheet have been ignored, and even in that instance there is no requirement to account for changing prices of notes, bonds, and other obligations; only the purchasing power aspect must be calculated and disclosed.

FASB Statement No. 33 prescribes minimum disclosure; a corporation which submits complete price-level adjusted financial statements is given wide latitude, particularly in respect of using end-of-period (current) constant dollars in place of average-of-the-year.

ACCOUNTING FOR CHANGING PRICES IN OTHER COUNTRIES

It was pointed out earlier that studies of price-level accounting in the United States relied heavily in their early days on the work of German accountants. The catastrophic German inflation of the 1920s stimulated accountants to attempt to account for its effects, and also to produce financial statements useful to managers and others in spite of the fluctuating purchasing power of the monetary unit. This pioneering work was continued and extended in other European countries, particularly France and Holland. Following World War II, inflation characterized the economies of most countries of the free world, directing the attention of accountants to this problem in the United Kingdom, Australia, New Zealand, and Canada. South America was the area of the world most sorely troubled by monetary disorders in recent times, and several South American countries have adopted a unique solution to the problems of accounting for inflation, called indexing, which is similar to constant dollar accounting. We shall examine several of these situations here.[14]

GERMANY

Germany suffered extreme forms of inflation after both World Wars and contemplated the problems of price-level adjustment as early as the 1920s. An accounting law, the *Goldmarkbilanzgesetz* of 1924, attempted to improve the reliability of financial statements in this way, but the creation of a stable currency made such accounting changes unnecessary. However, because of the problems presented by the temporary worthlessness of the paper mark, the subject of revaluation in accounting was explored by a number of German accountants.

After World War II there was another complete collapse of the German currency, the Reichsmark (RM), following military defeat and its economic consequences. The German Companies Act required financial statements based on historical costs, which were now meaningless. In any case, a large part of the total volume of transactions was effected by barter, so that market prices were not available for valuation purposes. Again the situation was corrected by monetary reform, the introduction of the Deutsche Mark (DM) on June 20, 1948. The conversion ratio of RM for DM was 10:1, but it could not be applied to historical costs, which bore no relation to money values at that time. A new law, the *DM Eröffnungsbilanzgesetz* dated August 21, 1949, required all balances to be restated for financial reporting, including income tax accounting. Revaluation was to take place as of June 21, 1948, the day after the new currency was introduced and from which new price indices were to be calculated. All items appearing in the historical cost financial statements were to appear in the revalued statements.[15]

S.5 of the law made the upper limit to valuation "current value" at the date of the balance sheet, but understatement was not prohibited. Rules were laid down for the valuation of fixed assets and for depreciation to be calculated on the new value. Firms were given the right to use replacement costs at either August 31, 1948, or August 31, 1949, by which latter date the market prices of goods could be expected to have some relative significance. After 1948 the Companies Acts and the Commercial Code returned to historical costs, and German laws do not permit revaluations. Thus, the benefit to German firms from the 1949 law was restricted to restatement of depreciation on fixed assets acquired before June 20, 1948.

The distinguished German accounting theorist Schmalenbach commented on stabilized accounting in the 12th edition of *Dynamische Bilanz*.[16] During inflation, he stated, managers at first attempted to minimize cash balances, to borrow as much as possible, to force debtors to pay promptly, and to use any excess working capital for the purchase of goods, equipment, foreign currency, or other hedges. However, by 1920 they had discovered that a currency suffering from inflation tended to show occasional improvement, which could cause losses for those short of marks. This led to the adoption of "measures of internal equalization," whereby payments would be made to prevent becoming a net monetary debtor, and purchasing power losses were compensated by purchasing power gains. Working capital and its changes were now the central components of financial statements, but to be comprehensive these statements had to include the effects of transactions in currencies other than the sick one, as well as of outstanding sales and purchase orders. Eventually, the practice of contracting at variable prices based on indices became common, and the accounting systems of firms involved in these tactics became most complicated.

In spite of this, wrote Schmalenbach, thoroughly usable and reliable accounts can be prepared during inflationary periods if meaningful price indices are available. To be meaningful, such indices must reflect the supply and demand factors existing within the economy. However, if government intervenes by fixing prices for certain items, the result is controlled-price inflation, and indices prepared using such government-controlled prices do not reflect relative utilities. As a consequence, during controlled-price inflation accountants are unable to prepare reliable financial statements. The passage concluded: "Since controlled-price inflation has now won the day, and it may be assumed that if Germany should ever experience another inflation it will also be accompanied by price controls, there is no further point in writing about accounting methods appropriate to a time of unstable currency values." And indeed, the admittedly gradual inflation which Germany has experienced since 1948 has not been accompanied by any preoccupation with price-level adjusted accounting.

Since Schmalenbach wrote, governments have found new ways to control prices by intervening in the foreign currency markets on which their money is traded, and the significance of domestic price indices has been even more seriously undermined.

It must be understood that under German and French tax laws, an expense is only tax-deductible to the extent that it is shown as such in the business financial statements of the firm. Thus, the issue of accounting for changing prices affects not only the computation of net income for financial reports, but also the computation of taxable income in tax returns. It is, therefore, a much more sensitive issue in countries such as Germany and France than it is in the United States and the United Kingdom, where the two types of accounting lead separate lives.

FRANCE

Between 1930, when Poincaré "stabilized" the value of the franc, and 1960, French currency changed its official value eighteen times. During this period the French government gradually allowed businesses to reflect these devaluations in their accounts. The first initiative came from the taxation authorities. A circular letter dated January 25, 1930 was addressed by the *Direction des Impots* (Internal Revenue Service) to firms, permitting them to revalue certain fixed assets to compute depreciation upon them on the basis of the relation between the franc and the gold dollar (as it then was). The exceptions were freehold land and intangible assets, on which no allowances were given. The depreciation calculations of past years were to be similarly revalued, and the revaluation surplus (*plus-value de re-évaluation*) would be tax free until distributed or capitalized, or until the assets from which it arose were realized by sale. This measure was designed to exempt from tax that part of profit which was inflated by the under-charge of depreciation on the basis of historical cost.

However, it aroused such a storm of opposition, principally from legal quarters, where it was felt to contravene the whole tradition of fiscal legislation, that attempts to apply it were rarely successful, and the Supreme Court (*Conseil d'Etat*) finally repudiated the letter in a decision dated November 14, 1938. But it is interesting to note the spectacle of a fiscal authority proceeding from an economically sound, and even sociological, concept of maintaining a healthy and productive private sector, which would then be all the better able to contribute financially toward the needs of the government. It was to return to this idea after the war.

Failure to withdraw from circulation the French francs issued during the occupation of that country by the Germans from 1940-45 resulted in accelerating inflation after the end of World War II. The latter part of the period 1930-1960, therefore, saw the successful introduction of revaluation accounting on a wide basis, enabling it to be generally applied. By a law dated August 15, 1945, firms were authorized to revalue certain assets, and the scope of this was progressively widened until the measure enacted on December 28, 1959.

Besides limiting the scope of the revaluation, the 1945 law also laid down rules for the method to be adopted. It prescribed use of the index of industrial prices (*l' indice des prix de gros industriels*) and applied only to those tangible assets which were not the subject of special tax regulations permitting the creation of tax-free replacement reserves. Of these, the index presented the greatest problems.

The problems arose out of the fact that price-level changes during the period for which operations are being revalued do not follow a regular and constant pattern. In the first place, during a time of monetary disorder, the state intervenes frequently to regulate either the general level of prices or else individual prices of particular commodities. Such intervention was quite common in France. In the second place, the indices represented annual averages, whereas price movements within the years were invariably upwards. Thirdly, prices of individual items within the range of the industrial price index did not move consistently; there were time-lags and other causes of variation. Finally, the French government was at times constrained to block price measurements and their official publication for political reasons.

In spite of its errors of omission and commission, the new law was greeted as a sincere attempt to clarify a confused situation, and it was acknowledged as providing firms with the possibility of avoiding the worst effects of inflation upon their survival and prosperity. Many business managers, however, were suspicious of the possible consequences of disclosing their hidden reserves, and in many cases only a partial revaluation resulted. In this way, it was thought, there would be a limitation of benefits, but also of potential inconvenience. This was influenced by the law's imposition of a special nondeductible tax of 5 percent on that part of revaluation surplus which originated from investment undertaken with loans contracted prior to 1944; this could, of course, be imposed only on firms which revalued their assets.

A permanent authorization to revalue was given on May 13, 1948, and was followed by a decree dated June 19, 1948, requiring all businesses which adopted the revaluation facility to submit their accounts on a uniform basis in accordance with certain rules. The *Plan Comptable Général* (National Chart of Accounts) which had originally been obligatory only for certain state and nationalized industries and firms receiving government subventions was thus extended to a number of independent private firms.

A law of December 28, 1959, put a dateline on revaluation which, in view of the stabilization of the franc effected during 1959, was believed to be unnecessary after June 30, 1959. Firms were given until December 31, 1962 to accomplish their revaluations, which were obligatory for all businesses, whether public or private, having an average annual turnover during the previous three years of more than 500 millions of old francs. It is estimated that this affected about 5,000 firms. Revaluation must be complete, although the law contained certain rules designed to mitigate some effects of applying the procedure. Obviously, the use of a general index of prices could produce values in certain cases which were well in excess of market values, or those which would be found by the application of a more rational procedure.

The revaluation coefficients to be used for the last revaluation were published in a decree dated March 19, 1960. Two sets of indices were to be used, one for fixed assets and depreciation, the other for equity securities and obligations; they were substantially different. Accounts had to be submitted in the uniform presentation and include, besides the balance sheet and a full profit and loss account with statement of retained earnings, schedules summarizing the movements on revaluation surplus account, fixed asset and depreciation and other provision accounts, and a tax computation.

The French system had several major defects: the index problem, not being mandatory for all firms, and the use of a quite separate system for inventory valuation. Because it was not mandatory, the door was opened to the manipulation of accounts and elimination of comparability with preceding financial statements. Because FIFO was required for the valuation of inventories, the calculation of the inventory valuation adjustment became unnecessarily clumsy whenever the level of inventory changed.[17]

Since 1959 inflation has continued in France, although at a lesser rate than in the preceding years. Whether to require firms to provide financial statements adjusted for general price-level changes remains a subject of intense debate throughout the area of the European Common Market, in which Germany, France, and the United Kingdom are all members.

THE UNITED KINGDOM (BRITAIN)

There have never been any strong feelings about upward revaluation of assets in Britain, and the Companies Act of 1948 expressly instructed companies to revalue fixed assets where their current values were substantially different from their historical costs. This arose from a belief that conservatism conflicted with fairness and that the understatement of asset values was as great a problem as their overstatement. Most companies did undertake such a revaluation, many of them at frequent intervals after 1948, and the resulting differences were credited to reserves (stockholders' equity). Depreciation was thereafter calculated on the revalued amount.

The clear separation between business profit and taxable income in Britain permitted the income tax authority (the Inland Revenue) to provide businesses with tax deductions which mitigated the effects of inflation to some extent, leading to virtual freedom to write off the entire cost of fixed assets acquired against the income of the period.

As far as inventories are concerned, although LIFO has never been an acceptable method of inventory valuation either for financial reporting or for tax accounting, direct costing has been widely used for both. Otherwise, until 1975 there was no specific provision for inventory accounting as a partial solution to the price-level problem. In 1975 a complicated form of stock (inventory) valuation adjustment was introduced as a tax accounting device to shield inventory profits from income taxation.

Prior to 1974 the position of the Institute of Chartered Accountants in England and Wales, and of the other official accountancy bodies, was similar to that of the AICPA, as evidenced by this quotation:

> The Council also recommends to members... that they should draw attention to the desirability of:... (c) experimenting with methods of measuring the effects of changes in the purchasing power of money on profits and on financial requirements....[18]

The position of accountants was also similar; very few involved themselves in the preparation of price-level adjusted statements and none was published. A rapid and severe increase in the rate of inflation during the 1960s, however, rendered financial statements prepared on a historical cost basis increasingly suspect, and the fact that many companies stopped charging depreciation on real property, arguing that the yearly appreciation exceeded any possible depreciation, drew more attention to the problem.

In 1971 the Institute of Chartered Accountants in England and Wales recommended that, in addition to the basic historical cost accounts, companies should convert balance sheet and income statement items to a current price-level basis, and in January, 1973, the Institute issued an exposure draft of a statement of standard practice on inflation accounting (ED 8). In May, 1974, the Institute issued *Statement of Standard Accounting Practice* (SSAP) 7, "Accounting for changes in the purchasing power of money," strongly recommending that the accounts of quoted companies published for a year commencing on or after June 30, 1974 contain inflation-adjusted supplementary financial statements. The supplementary statements should provide figures for the year-end financial position and for the results for the year, with comparative current purchasing power (CPP) figures for the preceding year and a reconciliation with the profit on a historical cost basis.

As a result of wider preoccupations with the effects of inflation on company financial statements and the relationship between such statements and taxation, the British government in 1974 established a committee to study and report on the need to amend the Companies Acts in this respect. The committee was headed by a prominent businessman, Francis Sandilands and became known as the "Sandilands Committee." Apprehensive of the outcome of this move, the Institute of Chartered Accountants immediately made *SSAP 7* a provisional statement; hence, it is referred to as *PSSAP 7*. Of the 300 quoted companies included in the 1974 *Survey of Published Accounts* in Britain, only 9 presented CPP financial statements, which increased to 48 of the 300 companies included in the 1975 *Survey*, although a further 9 companies referred to CPP accounts and published selected figures. An analysis of the first 42 published CPP financial statements appeared in *The Accountant* in April, 1975.[19]

The Sandilands Committee started work in 1974, when the rate of inflation was 11 percent per annum. Its report, twenty-one months later, came out firmly against CPP accounting and for current cost accounting (CCA).[20] The basic objection of the Sandilands Committee was to using a different unit of measurement (the unit of current purchasing power) because it was believed that this would confuse the user. In addition, the consumer price index was believed to be irrelevant. Sandilands recommended that all company accounts should be prepared under CCA, and that certain historical cost information should be produced as a supplement. The Sandilands Report was approved by the Confederation of British Industry, the London Stock Exchange, and eventually the accounting profession. The last-named, however, held out for a means of reflecting the impact of inflation on monetary items.

A steering committee representative of various interest groups was established as a subcommittee of the Accounting Standards Committee. By the time this Committee met in 1976, inflation was up to 19 percent. This was important in securing the acceptance of CCA not only for financial reporting but as a tool for management accounting. The Steering Committee (known as the Morpeth Committee) was financed by government and industry, as well as the accounting profession. Within one year the Accounting Standards Committee had accepted the Morpeth Committee's work and issued Exposure Draft (ED) 18 on inflation accounting. The detailed provisions of ED 18 met with much opposition within the profession. The potential abolition of the historical cost system; auditor involvement with what appeared to be subjective judgments of directors; the absence of a clear concept of capital maintenance; the complications presented by accounting for leases and deferred taxation; and finally, the fact that the vast majority of companies would report substantially lower profits using CCA (some, indeed, would report losses) all combined to arouse opposition.

This opposition was focused by two small practitioners who proposed a special resolution to members of the Institute of Chartered Accountants in England and Wales, that CCA not be made mandatory. In July 1977 the resolution was passed by a majority of about 2,500 votes in a poll responded to by approximately one-half of the Institute's 65,000 members. With this information, and about 700 responses to the Exposure Draft, the process began again. In the meantime, the Accounting Standards Committee issued the "Hyde Guidelines"[21] calling for listed (public) companies to produce, on a voluntary basis, supplementary profit and loss accounts containing three adjustments to the historical cost profit figure.

1. Additional depreciation based on current values.

2. A cost of sales adjustment based on current cost.
3. A gearing (leverage) adjustment to show the extent to which firms had benefited from borrowed money during inflation.

The next Exposure Draft—ED 24 (April 1979)—was limited to large companies. It called for a CCA statement in addition to, and not in place of, historical cost accounts.

On March 31, 1980 the Accounting Standards Committee (ASC) issued Statement of Standard Accounting Practice (SSAP) No. 16, entitled *Current Cost Accounting*. For accounting periods beginning on or after January 1, 1980 most listed companies and larger unlisted ones must report—

- Primary current cost statements with supplementary historical cost statements, or,
- Current cost statements accompanied by certain historical cost disclosures, or,
- Primary historical cost statements with supplementary current cost statements "prominently displayed," plus,
- A "gearing adjustment," and a "net monetary working capital" adjustment.

To come under this SSAP a nonpublic company must possess two of the following three characteristics: sales exceeding £5 million; assets exceeding £2.5 million; more than 250 employees.

Gearing Adjustment This idea was first advanced by economists Wynne Godley and Francis Cripps in *The Times* dated October 1, 1975.[22] They suggested that the so-called CCA holding gain be split into two components, one financed by shareholders and the other by creditors. They argued that only the latter represents a gain to shareholders, the former simply restating invested capital. The gearing adjustment under SSAP 16 allows companies to reduce the higher charges for current cost of sales and current cost depreciation (plus, where applicable, the monetary working capital adjustment) by an amount found from the following formula:

$$\text{total current cost adjustments} \times \frac{\text{loan capital}}{\text{total capital employed}}$$

Gearing is the British word for leverage, which is measured by the ratio on the right of this equation.

The following illustration is taken from an article in the *Journal of Accountancy* for July, 1980 at page 84.

Assume a steady-state company with these figures:

	December 31, 19X0	December 31, 19X1
Assets	$ 500	$ 600
Stockholders' equity	300	400
Loans	200	200
Total capital employed	$ 500	$ 600

The increase in assets of $100 is due to an increase in the current cost of inventory, fixed assets, and monetary working capital requirements.

In order to maintain their capital, the stockholders would have had an equity of 60 percent of the assets (= total capital employed) at the end of 19X1, or $360. The holders of the loan capital had claims on 40 percent of the assets at the beginning of the year, which would have amounted to $240 at year-end prices. The liability being fixed at $200 (money dollars), there has been a transfer of $40 (at year-end prices) to stockholders. This benefit offsets the increased current costs charged to the current cost income statement.

The gearing adjustment does not represent an amount available for distribution; by definition, it is a part of the increase in the current cost of capital employed (= assets). The debit to stockholders' equity is compensated by a credit to retained earnings via the current cost income statement. Because it is argued that lenders allow for the equity gain through higher interest rates, some accountants favor offsetting the gearing adjustment against interest expense, and this treatment can be seen in many of the current cost accounting statements published for 1980.[23]

The *net monetary working capital adjustment* is the purchasing power gain or loss on monetary working capital. This would normally be a loss because cash plus receivables would exceed current liabilities. However, in a period of high interest rates many companies operate with liquid ratios less than 1; in such cases, the adjustment will be a gain. Under *SSAP 16* the net monetary working capital adjustment is charged or credited before restated operating income, whereas the purchasing power gain on long-term debt is treated as an addition to operating income.

AUSTRALIA

Several notable academic contributions to the theory of accounting for changing prices were made by Australians during the period 1950-1970, notably by Chambers, Gynther, and Mathews. Chambers recommended adjustment to exit values; Mathews favored replacement cost accounting.[24] Gynther, who more than anyone else, has identified assumptions and analyzed alternatives, recommended a replacement cost approach using specific indices.[25] Until 1974, however, the two professional bodies, the Institute of Chartered Accountants in Australia and the Australian Society of Accountants, had associated themselves with the same wait and see attitude identified in the United States and the United Kingdom.

In December, 1974, a joint committee of the two bodies, the Australian Accounting Standards Committee (AASC), issued an exposure draft entitled, "A Method of Accounting for Changes in the Purchasing Power of Money." The content was substantially the same as that of *PSSAP 7*. In June, 1975, the AASC issued another exposure draft, "Current Value Accounting," which recommended the adoption of current value for the balance sheet, based on the concept of maintenance of the operating capability of the enterprise. This second exposure draft bore clear evidence of Gynther's analytical work; starting with a statement of the deficiencies of historical cost accounts, it stated the three alternatives: GPP accounting, replacement cost accounting, and the combination of the two which UK accountants were attempting to salvage from the wreck of *PSSAP 7*. This second (provisional) exposure draft defined profit as the excess of monetary and physical resources ("operating capability") at the end of an accounting period over operating capability at the beginning.

As in the United States and the United Kingdom, the Australian government became involved in the controversy. In November 1974, it appointed a committee to examine the effects of inflation on both the personal and corporate income taxes. The committee was chaired by Mathews and its report has become known as the Mathews Report.[26] It is interesting to note that the Mathews and Sandilands Reports both supported a current value (or current cost) approach to income measurement, rejected the arguments for GPP accounting, and failed to see a gain arising from long-term borrowing during a period of inflation.

The duality resolved in the United States by requiring two sets of price-level adjustment was resolved in Australia, as in the United Kingdom, in favor of current cost accounting. In October, 1976 the Australian accounting professional associations issued a Statement of Provisional Standards (DPS 1.1) entitled, *Current Cost Accounting*, and an exploratory Statement (DPS 1.2) entitled, *The Basis of Current Cost Accounting*. Application was recommended for financial reports published on or after July 1, 1977, a date which was subsequently put back to July 1, 1979 in view of implementation difficulties. A "CCA Working Guide" was published by the Australian Society of Accountants and the Institute of Chartered Accountants of Australia in July 1978. It called for adjustments to fixed assets and inventories, with corresponding adjustments to depreciation charges and cost of goods sold. Again, the data were to supplement the basic financial statements.

New Zealand has gone the way of the United Kingdom and Australia, but Canada has been strongly influenced by the United States. In December, 1974 the Accounting Research Committee of the Canadian Institute of Chartered Accountants issued an Accounting Guideline, "Accounting for the Effects of Changes in the Purchasing Power of Money." In July 1975 the Committee issued an Exposure Draft with the same title, proposing comprehensive restatement in constant (end of year) dollars and the inclusion of the purchasing power loss or gain on monetary items in income. However, by 1979 the situation had changed, and a new Exposure Draft abandoned constant dollar disclosures in favor of current costs. Two current cost income figures were proposed: income of the enterprise and income attributable to stockholders. The purchasing power loss or gain which would be included in enterprise income was restricted to monetary working capital items, whereas the income attributable to stockholders would include the purchasing power gain on long-term borrowing.[27]

SOUTH AMERICAN EXPERIMENTS WITH INDEXING

Galloping inflation destroys the capital of bond and mortgage holders. There are ways in which a society can protect these savers, one of which involves legislating transfers to them from other members of society. A specific method of making these transfers, which has been adopted in such high-inflation countries as Brazil, Argentina, Chile, and Uruguay, is known as *indexing*. Brazil presents a good illustration of this method in practice.[28]

Brazil has experienced extremely high rates of inflation for many years, which rendered traditional accounting irrelevant and called for a new approach to the entire problem of financing business. A new government in 1964 introduced inflation accounting into the tax laws and adopted a system of monetary correction, which has become known as *indexing*, as the basis of financial reporting.

Indexing affects all monetary operations in Brazil from personal savings to government debt. The nominal amounts are changed by the use of a purchasing power index, so that the saver's deposit or the government loan actually increases in monetary amount, and interest is paid on the higher amount; the monetary correction is tax free. In the same way, monetary assets and liabilities of a business change as the index changes. In addition, the system calls for annual restatement of fixed assets, with depreciation calculated on the restated amounts; the net increase in asset amount is credited to capital. There is a provision for a "maintenance of stockholders' investment" charge to the income statement, which is tax deductible, on all assets and liabilities other than fixed assets, and which includes the monetary correction adjustment. Thus, the cost of indexing loans is a tax-deductible charge, even when the loans are used to purchase fixed assets.

It will be appreciated that there are major differences between the Brazilian situation and those described in the preceding sections of this chapter. Because the Brazilian lender is protected, no question of a gain through being a net monetary debtor arises. In addition, it should be noted that inventories are dealt with as a monetary asset because firms "correct" the amount in accordance with purchasing power changes.

EVIDENCE AGAINST CONSTANT DOLLAR ACCOUNTING

As in several other places, we must here draw attention to a paradox. The move toward presenting price-level adjusted financial statements together with the conventional historical cost basic statements is the result of accountants' assertions that the former will provide information useful for economic decisions, information which is not available from conventional statements. Yet the Trueblood Report did not contain this assertion, and the users of financial statements (the SEC, financial analysts, economists) almost invariably call for something else, namely the abandonment of historical cost statements in favor of current cost statements.

Further, several research studies aimed at identifying user needs do not support unequivocally the view that supplementary price-level adjusted statements provide useful information. Estes requested financial analysts, bankers, and financial executives to rate such statements. He reported that 32 percent of those sampled felt they were "very useful," 39 percent indicated they were "somewhat useful," and 30 percent considered them "not useful."[29] In another study, Dyckman asked financial analysts to respond to a statement that price-level adjusted statements should be prepared and reported. The results indicated that 23 percent either mildly or strongly agreed; 20 percent were neutral; and 57 percent either mildly or strongly disagreed.[30] He also presented financial statements for two firms to three independent groups of financial analysts, consisting of (1) conventional statements, (2) conventional statements with price-level adjusted statements as supplements, and (3) price-level adjusted statements alone. Firm 1 was made to appear a better investment in the conventional statements, Firm 2 in the adjusted statements. It was hypothesized that the analysts would express an increasing preference for Firm 2 as they observed the contents of the adjusted statements. Dyckman found the correlation between choice of firm and method of reporting to be .34; he would have been satisfied with a correlation of .7 and concluded that the correlation was not a strong one.

The contradiction may be explained by reference to the fact that users have not, in the past, received price-level adjusted financial statements and therefore do not yet know what information can be derived from them. In this case it is surprising that the accountancy profession has made so little attempt to educate users on this subject. On the other hand, the argument that users find the information they require from conventional financial statements must confront the mounting tide of criticisms of such statements, even though other studies support the proposition that unadjusted financial statements perform as well (or as badly) as adjusted statements as predictors of future results.

CONCLUSION

We have seen how inflation, if severe enough, forces people and their governments to recognize the difference between "real" and "nominal" values. The consequence of severe inflation is either monetary reform or a kind of indexing. During relatively mild forms of inflation the immediate response of accountants is invariably some form of constant dollar accounting. This solution is rejected by users of financial statements, for both theoretical and practical reasons.

The basic theoretical argument arises from the observation that accounting uses money of account, not money. Keynes explained the difference between money of account, the description or title, and money, the thing that answers to that description:

> The difference is like that between the King of England (whoever that may be) and King George. A contract to pay 10 years hence a weight of gold equal to the weight of the King of England is not the same thing as a contract to pay a weight of gold equal to the weight of the individual who is now King George. It is for the state to declare, when the time comes, who the King of England is.[31]

There is, therefore, no valid distinction between a 1965 dollar or a 1975 dollar; the apparent change in the dollar is really a change in the value of commodities other than money. In Keynes' words, "there can be no real breach in the continuity of descent in the pedigree of the money-of-account." If valid, this proposition negates the rationality of constant dollar accounting, based as that method is on the assumption that a 1965 dollar and a 1975 dollar are different currency.

The practical reasons are—

1. The index number problem, which is discussed in the Appendix to this chapter. Critics argue that the use of an index of general purchasing power, however accurate, is inappropriate for a business which spends its money on a narrow range of objects.
2. The credibility problem. Constant dollar statements can never be more than supplements to financial statements prepared on another basis, whereas current cost statements can be the primary financial statements, thus avoiding the necessity to report several "income" figures.
3. The arbitrariness of the monetary/nonmonetary classification, on which the purchasing power gain or loss depends.
4. The disappearance of the effects of price-level changes on nonmonetary assets in the procedure known as *rolling forward*.
5. Specific unresolved issues such as: translating foreign company current cost or constant dollar statements into U.S. dollars; long-term contracts in process; intangible assets generally; and liabilities which are affected both by interest-rate changes and the firm's relative solvency.

In addition, there are two behavioral problems which require investigating in connection with the introduction of constant dollar financial reporting. First, if the difference between a monetary liability at one date and the same liability at a different date is a gain (which arises when the amount is adjusted for a change in purchasing power during a period of inflation), the pursuit of profit would require businessmen to borrow at least to the point where the cost of the debt (less the gain) equalled the return on investment which could be financed by the borrowing. If the rate of inflation exceeded the cost of the debt, this would lead firms to invest in uneconomic ventures, or ventures which are only economic at the expense of creditors. A more certain recipe for business failure can hardly be imagined.

Secondly, the definition of a monetary liability as an obligation fixed in monetary amount turns all other obligations into nonmonetary liabilities.[32] The latter would be adjusted for price-level changes using the ratio of the price index at t_1 to the price index at t_0, even in those cases where management had prudently estimated the liability to include the inflation factor when making its provision at t_0. This would of necessity lead to counting the same inflation twice, once as a loss and once as a gain, in two different accounting periods. It has occurred to some critics that the same argument applies to assets. If in times of inflation, firms bid up the prices of fixed assets, inventories, and other investments, it is possible that recently acquired nonmonetary assets are already "adjusted for inflation." To adjust them again in subsequent years is to double-count inflation.

APPENDIX: A NOTE ON THE INDEX NUMBER PROBLEM

A price index is a series of measurements, expressed as percentages, of the prices of goods and services at a succession of dates, with the base date set equal to 100 percent. In this form a price index does not measure purchasing power, but the reciprocal of a price index may be said to do this: if the index is 150, the dollar can purchase only two-thirds of what the dollar could have bought at the base date.

An index is usually weighted, to give consideration to the relative importance of each good or service to the subject of the index—the consumer, or the economy as a whole. The best known indices in the United States—the consumer price index, the producer price index, the composite construction cost index, and the GNP deflator—each represents a different basket of goods and services, weighted differently. For this reason, although they tend to move together, they may show variations from time to time, and occasionally move in opposite directions.

Any index is general unless it is specific; the consumer price index is specific to consumers. However, it is customary to distinguish between three general indices—the CPI, the PPI, the GNP deflator—and indices based on a narrower selection of items, such as the construction cost index. It is, of course, important that an index be used for the commodities it represents and not for other commodities.

In terms of financial statements, we may state value in the form pq. Capital maintenance implies that—

$$\Sigma p_2 q_2 = \Sigma p_2 q_1$$

or "the money value of the real resources at the end of period 2 is equal to the money value of the real resources at the end of period 1, valued at end of period 2 prices."

This proposition assumes the following:

1. The same distribution of q's—if a new q is introduced, the apparent symmetry disappears.
2. The same individuals are valuing—if there is a new group at t_2, the quantities at t_1 are not relevant to their uses.
3. Usable, if not perfect, index numbers, meaning that the pattern of consumption of the entity to which the index is being applied must be approximately the same as the structure of the index implies.

As Mathews has written: "Such general measures are fictional representations of wealth, and have little relevance to the individual firm that has used its purchasing power to buy specific assets."[33]

ENDNOTES

1. *Statement of Financial Accounting Standards No. 33*, "Financial Accounting and Changing Prices," Stamford, Conn.: Financial Accounting Standards Board, September 1979.
2. American Accounting Association Committee on Concepts and Standards Underlying Corporate Financial Statements, Supplementary Statement No. 2, *Price-Level Changes and Financial Statements*, American Accounting Association, 1951.
3. Sweeney, Henry W. *Stabilized Accounting*, New York: Harper and Bros., 1936. But articles on the subject appeared as early as 1918. See *Asset Appreciation, Business Income and Price-Level Accounting: 1918-35*, ed. Stephen A. Zeff, New York: Arno Press, 1975.
4. Hendriksen, Eldon S., *Price-Level Adjustments of Financial Statements—An Evaluation and Case Study of Two Public Utility Firms*, Pullman: Washington State University Press, 1961.
5. Jones, Ralph Coughenor, *Price Level Changes and Financial Statements, Case Studies of Four Companies*, American Accounting Association, 1955.
6. Consider the following exceptions to the rule that only the unit of measure is being changed.
   (a) Inventories, property, plant, and equipment are to be valued no higher than "recoverable amount," which is sometimes net realizable value, sometimes present value of expected future net cash flows.
   (b) The *rolling forward* adjustment effectively causes part of the realized gain or loss on disposal of a nonmonetary asset to bypass the income statement altogether.
   (c) Stockholders' equity is found as a residual and not by restatement of its component parts.
   (d) Some assets, and all liabilities, are omitted from the restatement process.
   An interesting illustration of (a) is found in the supplementary statements of electric and other utility companies, which are prevented by regulatory agencies from recovering more than the historical cost of their fixed assets in prices charged to consumers.

7. Rosenfield, Paul, "Accounting for Inflation—A Field Test," *Journal of Accountancy*, June 1969, pp. 45-50.
8. Zeff, Stephen A., "Professional Notes," *Journal of Accountancy*, October 1979, p. 96.
9. *Statement No. 3*, "Financial Statements Restated for General Price-Level Changes," New York: AICPA, 1969.
10. The problem of adjusting the financial statements of foreign operations for the effects of price-level changes has not been satisfactorily resolved.
11. FASB Research Report, "Field Tests of Financial Reporting in Units of General Purchasing Power," Stamford, Conn.: Financial Accounting Standards Board, 1977.
12. *Examples of the Use of FASB Statement No. 33, Financial Reporting and Changing Prices*, Stamford, Conn.: FASB, November 1980.
13. Similar studies in the United Kingdom have been published for the London stockbroking firm, Phillips & Drew, by one of its partners, Mr. Martin Gibbs, who is himself a Chartered Accountant.
14. Lack of agreement on the method to be used for adjusting financial statements to show the effects of price-level changes led the International Accounting Standards Committee, in its IAS 6, *Accounting Responses to Changing Prices*, June 1977, to admit virtually any approach to this problem.
15. Holzer, Peter H. and Hanns-Martin Schonfeld, "German Solution of the Post-War Price-Level Problem," *The Accounting Review*, April 1963, pp. 377-81.
16. Schmalenbach, E., *Dynamic Accounting* (transl. G.W. Murphy and K.S. Most, London: Gee & Co. (Publishers) Ltd., 1959, pp. 219-20 and 295-6.
17. Holzer, Peter H. and Hanns-Martin Schonfeld, "French Approach to the Post-War Price-Level Problem," *The Accounting Review*, April 1963, pp. 382-8.
18. *Recommendation on Accounting Principles N. 15*, Institute of Chartered Accountants in England & Wales, 1952.
19. Westwick, C.A. and N.J. Ballanger, "How Companies Account for Inflation," *The Accountant*, April 10, 1975, pp. 455-61 and April 17, 1975, pp. 496-500.
20. Sandilands, F.E.P., *Report of the Inflation Accounting Committee*, London: Her Majesty's Stationery Office, 1975.
21. Inflation Accounting Steering Group of Accounting Standards Committee, *Interim Recommendations*, London, November 1977.
22. Godley, Wynne and Francis Cripps, "Profits, stock appreciation, and the Sandilands Report," *The Times*, 1 October 1975.
23. For further discussion of the Sandilands report see Gibbs, Martin, Keith Percy and Richard Saville, "Sandilands and the effect on dividends," *Accountancy*, August 1976.
24. Mathews, R.L. and J.M.B. Grant, *Inflation and Company Finance*, Sydney: The Law Book Company of Australia, 1958.
25. Gynther, R.S., *Accounting for Price-Level Changes: Theory and Procedures*, Oxford: Pergamon Press, 1966.
26. *Inflation and Taxation*, Canberra: Australian Government Publishing Service, May 1975.
27. Exposure Draft, "Current Cost Accounting," Accounting Research Committee, Canadian Institute of Chartered Accountants, Toronto, December 1979.
28. Robinson, Christopher H., "Living with Inflation—Brazilian Style," *Tempo*, New York: Touche Ross & Co., Vol. 21, No. 1, 1975, pp. 18-20. See also *Client Inflation Clinic: The Brazilian Method of Indexing and Accounting for Inflation*, Chicago: Arthur Andersen & Co., May 1975.
29. Estes, Ralph W., "An Assessment of the Usefulness of Current Cost and Price Level Information by Financial Statement Users," *Journal of Accounting Research*, Autumn 1968, pp. 207.
30. Dyckman, Thomas R., "Investment Analysis and General Price Level Adjustments," *Studies in Accounting Research No. 1*, Evanston, Ill.: American Accounting Association, 1969. For a contrasting view see Russell, T. Alan, "An Application of Price-Level Accounting," *Financial Executive*, February 1975, p. 21.
31. Keynes, J.M., *A Treatise on Money*, London: MacMillan, 1923, p. 3.
32. See *FASB Technical Bulletin No. 81-4*, "Classification as Monetary or Non-

monetary Items," February 6, 1981, for an acute illustration of the problem.

33. Mathews, R. L., "The Price-Level Controversy: A Reply," *Journal of Accounting Research*, Spring 1967, p. 114.

SELECTED ADDITIONAL READINGS

United States of America

Accounting Principles Board, Statement No. 3, "Financial Statements Restated for General Price-Level Changes," New York: AICPA, June 1969.

Bradford, William D., "Price-Level Restated Accounting and the Measurement of Inflation Gains and Losses," *The Accounting Review*, April 1974, pp. 296-305.

Burton, John C., "Financial Reporting in an Age of Inflation," *Journal of Accountancy*, February 1975, pp. 68-75.

Chambers, R. J., *Accounting Evaluation and Economic Behavior*, Englewood Cliffs, N.J.: Prentice-Hall, Inc., 1965, pp. 223-227.

———, "NOD, COG and PuPU: See How Inflation Teases," *Journal of Accountancy*, September 1975, pp. 56-62 and *Errata, J. of A.* February 1976, p. 41.

Croll, John R., "General Price-Level Indexing: A Delusion, a Mockery and a Snare," *CA Magazine*, March 1975, pp. 29-34.

Davidson, Sidney and Roman L. Weil, "Inflation Accounting: What Will General Price-Level Adjusted Income Statements Show," *Financial Analysts Journal*, January/February 1975, pp. 27-31, 70-84.

Dyckman, T. R., "Investment Analysis and General Price-Level Adjustments—A Behavioral Study," *Studies in Accounting Research No. 1*, American Accounting Association, 1969.

Financial Reporting in Units of General Purchasing Power, Proposed Statement of Financial Accounting Standards, Stamford, Conn.: Financial Accounting Standards Board, December 31, 1974.

Financial Accounting Standards Board, *Statement No. 33*, "Financial Reporting and Changing Prices," Stamford, Conn.: FASB, September 1979.

Handbook of Accounting and Auditing, ed. Burton, John C., Russell E. Palmer and Robert S. Kay, Boston; Warren, Gorham & Lamont, Inc., 1981, ch. 8.

Heath, Loyd C., "Distinguishing Between Monetary and Nonmonetary Assets and Liabilities in General Price-Level Accounting," *The Accounting Review*, July 1972, pp. 458-468.

Ijiri, Yuji, "The Price-Level Restatement and its Dual Interpretation," *The Accounting Review*, April 1976, pp. 227-243.

Largay, James A. III and John Leslie Livingstone, *Accounting for Changing Prices*, New York: John Wiley and Sons, 1976.

Moonitz, Maurice, *ICRA Occasional Paper No. 3*, "Changing Prices and Financial Reporting," International Center for Research in Accounting, Lancaster: University of Lancaster, 1973.

———, "Restating the Price-Level Problem," *CA Magazine*, July 1974, pp. 26-31.

Peterson, Russell J., "A Portfolio Analysis of General Price-Level Restatement," *The Accounting Review*, July 1975, pp. 525-532.

Rosenfield, Paul, "The Confusion Between General Price-Level Restatement and Current Value Accounting," *Journal of Accountancy*, October 1972, pp. 63-68.

———, "GPP Accounting-Relevance and Interpretability," *Journal of Accountancy*, August 1975, pp. 52-59.

Sterling, Robert R., "Relevant Financial Reporting in an Age of Price Changes," *Journal of Accountancy*, February 1975, pp. 42-51.

Stickney, Clyde P., and David O. Green, "No Price-Level Adjusted Statements, Please (Pleas)," *CPA Journal*, January 1974, pp. 25-31.

Zeff, Stephen A., ed., *Asset Appreciation, Business Income and Price-Level Accounting: 1918-1935*, New York: Arno Press, 1976, espec. Henry W. Sweeney articles reprinted.

Other Countries

Arthur Andersen & Co., Client Inflation Clinic: *The Brazilian Method of Indexing and Accounting for Inflation*, Chicago: Arthur Andersen & Co., May 1975.

Australian Accounting Research Foundation, *Exposure Draft*, "The Recognition of Gains and Losses on Holding Monetary Resources in the Context of Current Cost Accounting," Insert to *The Australian Accountant*, July 1978.

CICA Accounting Research Committee, Proposed Accounting Recommendations, *Current Cost Accounting*, Toronto: Accounting Research Committee of the Canadian Institute of Chartered Accountants, December 1979.

Gynther, R.S., *Accounting for Price-Level Changes: Theory and Procedures*, Oxford: Pergamon Press, Ltd., 1966.

———, "Why Use General Purchasing Power," *Accounting and Business Research*, Spring 1974, pp. 141-157.

———, "Accounting Concepts and Behavioral Hypotheses," *The Accounting Review*, April 1967, pp. 274-290.

Hanna, John R., "An Application and Evaluation of Selected Alternative Accounting Income Models," *The International Journal of Accounting Education and Research*, Fall 1972, pp. 135-167.

Holzer, Peter H. and Hanns-Martin Schonfeld, "German Solution of the Post-War Price Level Problem," *The Accounting Review*, April 1963, pp. 377-381.

———, "French Approach to the Post-War Price Level Problem," *The Accounting Review*, April 1963, pp. 382-388.

Inflation and Taxation, Canberra: Australia Government Publishing Service, May, 1975.

International Accounting Standards Committee, "Treatment of Changing Prices in Financial Statements: A Summary of Proposals," New York: AICPA, 1977.

Katano, Ichiro, "Structure of Accounting for Changing Money Values," *The International Journal of Accounting Education and Research*, Spring 1967, pp. 21-36.

Kosiol, Erich E., "Price Changes, Money Value and Profit Distribution Within the Framework of Financial Accounting," *The International Journal of Accounting Education and Research*, Fall 1966, pp. 1-24.

Popoff, Boris, "The Price Level Adjustment and Accounting Realism: A Case Study of a New Zealand Company," *The International Journal of Accounting Education and Research*, Spring 1971, pp. 15-35.

Robinson, Christopher H., "Living with Inflation—Brazilian Style," *TEMPO* (Touche Ross & Co.) Vol. 21, No. 1, 1975, pp. 18-20.

Sandilands, F. E. P., *Inflation Accounting—Report of the Inflation Accounting Committee*, London: Her Majesty's Stationery Office, Cmnd. 6225, 1975.

Scapens, R. W., "Treatment of Inflation in Published Accounts of Companies in Overseas Countries," *Research Committee Occasional Paper No. 1*, London: The Institute of Chartered Accountants in England & Wales, August, 1973.

Standish, Peter, "Inflation Accounting Down Under," *Accountancy*, March 1976, pp. 48-52.

Staubus, George J., "Price-level Accounting: Some Unfinished Business," *Accounting and Business Research*, Winter 1975, pp. 42-47.

Tritschler, Charles A., "A Sociological Perspective on Accounting Innovation," *The International Journal of Accounting Education and Research*, Spring 1970, pp. 39-67.

Westwick, C. A. and N. J. Ballanger, "How Companies Account for Inflation," *The Accountant*, April 10, 1975, pp. 455-61 and April 17, 1975, pp. 496-500.

Zeff, Stephen A., ed., *Asset Appreciation, Business Income and Price-Level Accounting: 1918-35*, New York: Arno Press, 1976, especially articles by Fritz Schmidt and Max J. Wasserman, and Henry W. Sweeney, "Effects of Inflation on German Accounting" and "German Inflation Accounting."

Case 10-1 Rowntree Mackintosh Ltd.

Rowntree Mackintosh Ltd. is a multinational corporation registered in the United Kingdom. Its principal product lines are confectionary items (sweets and candies) and food items, all of which utilize chocolate, which is made from cocoa beans. The principal source of cocoa beans is an African country, and the price of cocoa fluctuates according to the size of the crop there. It is a common practice for such companies to buy futures contracts in order to protect themselves against sudden rises in the price of cocoa.

As a result of misjudging market trends, the company lost £32 million (before tax allocation) in 1973 when it had to close out unfavorable trading positions. The company was forced to borrow heavily to meet the cash outflow, which amounted to £21 million on an after-tax basis. This caused Rowntree Mackintosh to report interest expense of £3 million on the loan for the year 1974. The rate of inflation that year was 20 percent, and the company's annual report included constant dollar supplementary statements which showed that there had been a purchasing power gain of over £4 million during 1974 as a consequence of owing £21 million throughout the year. Because interest expense accrued evenly during the year, the restated amount was only £3.3 million. Thus, the constant dollar financial statements showed a higher profit than they would have done had the loss never occurred and the loan never been obtained.

1. Is it true to say that the company made a profit in 1974 as a direct result of losing money in 1973? How else can you explain the constant dollar results described in the case?
2. What would be the response of a chief executive when presented with financial statements showing that a company can make more money in times of inflation through borrowing than through trading? in words? in deeds?

Case 10-2 The Confounded Price Index

Under this heading *The Wall Street Journal* published an editorial critical of the Consumer Price Index (CPI) on May 13, 1981. This was followed by another editorial, *CPI: Confusing Price Index*, on September 30, 1981.

In the May editorial, the *Journal* identified the following criticisms of the CPI which were relevant to concern over federal spending and runaway budgets, over half of which were indexed.

1. The CPI relates current prices to a base year, currently 1972-1973. But changes in prices since then have also changed buying habits, so that the weights of items in the consumer "basket" are no longer the same.
2. The index purports to measure the prices of things consumed, yet includes the prices of durables such as television sets and wedding rings, which are not consumed during the year. Most troublesome is the inclusion of housing, which constitutes 40 percent of the market basket; prices and mortgage payments are added in as though they occurred during one year.
3. Quite apart from the impact of including these multiyear expenditures as if they occurred during one year, the CPI fails to reflect the fact that many people are still paying for mortgages at lower rates.
4. Part of the payment for a house mortgage, including insurance and property taxes, reflects increase in capital values, which do not affect the CPI.
5. Some of the payments included gross in the CPI are in fact tax deductible, and therefore cost the consumer less.

These last two points were the subject of the September editorial, which concluded:

> We wonder, then, just what kind of portents or auguries can be read into movements in the CPI. Even more troubling, we wonder why the government insists on leveraging the perceptions of the success of its policies and the indexing of its entitlement programs to the CPI. If there are reasons to keep an index called the Consumer Price Index, then let's at least make it a more accurate barometer. If there aren't, then let's use something else, or create something else...

1. Do these criticisms include all the known defects of the CPI as a measure of inflation?

2. What are the implications of these criticisms for the use of the CPI to measure the effects of inflation on corporate financial statements?

END OF CHAPTER QUESTIONS

1. A prominent businessman once said, "I have often bought a company on the basis of its balance sheet, but never sold one that way." Discuss.
2. What are the four principal types of financial statement, and what concept of capital underlies each of them?
3. What is the *smørgasbord* approach to financial reporting? What problem does it present the user?
4. The gross margin is an important business construct, and many decisions (including accounting decisions) depend upon this figure. Assume that an item of inventory cost \$100 at t_0 and that its replacement cost had risen to \$125 at t_1. It sold at t_1 for \$150. The rate of inflation between t_0 and t_1 was 10 percent. What is the gross margin percentage?
5. Explain the relevance of the capital maintenance concept to accounting for changing prices. What concept of capital maintenance was explicitly adopted by FASB *Statement No. 33*?
6. What technical problem was solved by requiring constant dollar measurements using average-of-the-year dollars? Explain how the restated operating income of one year will be restated in the five-year summary of the following one.
7. Discuss constant dollar accounting as a contribution to the better matching of costs with revenues.
8. List the advantages which are claimed for constant dollar financial statements.
9. What is meant by *rolling forward* in the context of constant dollar accounting?
10. As early as 1961 the accounting profession acknowledged the problem of accounting in historical costs when inflation was causing prices to increase. Investigate the extent to which the profession was successful in persuading corporations to publish price-level adjusted financial statements in the fifteen-year period ending with the promulgation of FASB *Statement No. 33*.
11. What feature of the rolling forward adjustment proposed by *APB Statement No. 3* was not incorporated in FASB *Statement No. 33*? Why is this feature important to the financial statement user?
12. What are "monetary assets and liabilities" in the context of constant dollar accounting? What complications are associated with treating foreign currency monetary items and deferred taxation as nonmonetary? How did FASB *Statement No. 33* decide they should be classified?
13. What is replacement cost? How does it differ from reproduction cost? Which of these was required for disclosures by (a) the SEC and (b) the FASB? Why do you think that the FASB adopted a different concept than that of the SEC?

14. How did the SEC permit replacement cost to be measured? Did the FASB adopt the same, or different, measurement rules for current cost?
15. Explain what is meant by the proposition that FASB *Statement No. 33* lays down a method of partial adjustment. How does a company's decision to publish constant dollar financial statements on a comprehensive basis affect its obligation under that Statement?
16. In a period of rising prices, what effect on operating income would you expect restatement of depreciation and cost of goods sold to have? (Purchasing power gain or loss does not enter into the determination of operating income.) What kind of businesses would experience the opposite effect, and why?
17. What is a net monetary debtor? A net monetary creditor? Which of these gains purchasing power during inflation, and which loses?
18. Have other countries faced the problems of accounting for changing prices? How did the United States learn from their experiences?
19. Discuss the proposition that constant dollar accounting depends on the existence of meaningful price indices, in the light of government regulation of prices over a substantial segment of the economy.
20. Prior to FASB *Statement No. 33* many corporate annual reports explained the absence of constant dollar supplementary statements on the grounds that such statements were not acceptable for income tax reporting. Is this a valid explanation in the United States? Would it be in countries like France and Germany?
21. What was the basic difference between revaluation accounting in France and constant dollar accounting in the United States?
22. Most countries with financial reporting environments similar to that of the United States have opted for current cost accounting; only the United States has placed primary emphasis on constant dollar accounting. Why do you think this difference exists?
23. Describe the parallels between the process whereby the United States accounting profession adopted FASB *Statement No. 33* and the United Kingdom accounting profession adopted *SSAP 16*.
24. What is gearing adjustment? How is it calculated? What is a net monetary capital adjustment? How is it calculated?
25. Discuss the reasons why many critics within the accounting profession, as well as many users of financial statements, do not accept that constant dollar financial reporting solves any of the problems of accounting for changing prices.

11

CURRENT VALUE ACCOUNTING

The need for current value accounting extends beyond the periodical preparation of the financial report, and can be seen in the internal, or management, reports of a business. This aspect of the subject has received little exposure, and we shall continue to direct our attention to periodical financial reporting. In this context, accounting for the effects of changing prices is perceived as a set of end-of-period adjustments, rather than a continuous process.

There are at least six valuation measures which could be used in current value accounting.

1. Replacement cost
2. Current market price (net realizable value)
3. Present value of future net cash receipts
4. Replacement value
5. Potential proceeds of sale (Chambers' current cash equivalents)
6. Distress sale (liquidation) proceeds

It is generally agreed by current value accountants that 6. is unnecessarily conservative, at least for a going concern. Although some would restrict current value accounting to one valuation method, the more common approach is to admit several; for example, use replacement cost for raw materials and work in process inventories and net realizable value for finished goods. Such a mixture of values has been criticized for being nonadditive because the money amounts do not measure the same attributes (properties). As we have pointed out in chapter 9, all valuation is subjective (a proposition which has recently received unexpected support from Beaver[1]) and does not involve the correspondence of units of money with perceived units of some other quantity. That is why we can add $100 in counted cash to $1,000 in equipment and call the result $1,100 of assets, in the same way that the zookeeper can add together one lion, two tigers, and three bears and call the total six animals.

If we accept the proposition that financial statements are part of the information on which investment decisions are based, it is easy to see that constant dollar financial statements add to the informational content of financial reports.[2] On the other hand, to report the inflation effect and not the market effect may compound the misleading aspects of historical cost statements. Current value accounting generally starts from the view that market effects should be disclosed, whether realized or not. Current cost/current dollar accounting, in the FASB's terminology, attempts to report both the inflation effect and the market effect of changing prices on an enterprise.

In this chapter we will trace the development of current value accounting theory in the United States, examine more closely the current cost provisions of *FASB Statement No. 33*, and look at the Dutch system of *replacement value accounting*, which has been in use in the Netherlands for many years.

THE POSTULATES AND PRINCIPLES OF MOONITZ AND SPROUSE

Accounting Research Study No. 1 began with the statement that "pressures have been building up in recent years for more use of future, and hence estimated, events and prices in order to make accounting reports 'more useful'."[3] The context revealed an attempt to justify the use of a variety of valuation models, of which replacement cost may be one. This motive also underlies the normative postulate C2:

> **Objectivity.** Changes in assets and liabilities and the related effects (if any) on revenues, expenses, retained earnings, and the like, should not be given formal recognition in the accounts earlier than the point of time at which they can be measured in objective terms.

Postulate C4, however ("Accounting reports should be based on a stable measuring unit"), suggests a taste for constant dollar accounting.

A subsequent publication by Sprouse and Moonitz moved closer to providing a theoretical basis for replacement cost.[4] This was the significance of the new postulate that "profit is attributable to the whole process of business activity, not just the moment of sale." The underlying concept of profit as an increase in net assets identifies it as income in the Fisher-Hicks tradition. Sprouse and Moonitz argued as follows:

1. All changes in asset and liability values are components of profit.
2. Movements in the market prices of specific goods and services, and movements in the general level of prices, are changes in asset and liability values. Market prices can be either replacement costs or selling prices.

3. The use of replacement cost is already sanctioned as objective in LIFO accounting, and a number of authorities have rejected realization as a basis for revenue recognition.
4. "We propose to use a classification [of asset changes?] that distinguishes...*(a)* the amount attributable to changes in the dollar (price-level changes), *(b)* the amount attributable to the acquisition of goods and services prior to their utilization, and *(c)* the amount attributable to sales in a current market." (p. 17)

The key assumptions are that replacement cost is a change in asset value, and that all changes in asset values are gains or losses. These assumptions were illustrated in an example:

> Assume that an item of merchandise is acquired for $3,000 in Year I and is sold for $5,400 in Year II. Both at the end of Year I and at its date of sale, its replacement cost is $3,600. Two kinds of questions need to be considered: (1) Is the increment (gain, profit) of $2,400 attributable entirely to Year II, to Year I, or to both? (2) Is the increment a gain, or is it partly or wholly something else?

These questions do not exhaust the possibilities, because on page 27 Sprouse and Moonitz asserted that "inventories which are readily salable at known prices with negligible cost of disposal, or with known or readily predictable costs of disposal should be measured at net realizable value." It cannot be said, therefore, that Sprouse and Moonitz established a theoretical foundation for the use of replacement cost as the value of nonmonetary assets; they simply admitted it as one of several alternatives aimed at disclosing holding gains and losses, defined as changes in assets and liabilities unaccompanied by realization. The problem, however, is to explain the terms assets and liabilities; without this explanation, the concept of change is meaningless, and we remain in the realm of unsupported assertion.

Another of the problems presented by *ARS No. 1* was the unreconciled acceptance of both present value and replacement cost as the meaning of value. The view that expenditure creates assets which either expire unused or survive as unrecovered costs and thus find their way into the balance sheet can be traced to the revised versions of the American Accounting Association *Tentative Statement*.[5] The interpretation of these costs as representing units of service potential came in the 1957 revision, where assets were defined as economic resources: "They are aggregates of service-potential available for or beneficial to expected operations."[6] By this means an attempt was made to link the balance sheet with Fisherian capital theory: the value of an asset at any point of time is simply the sum of its discounted future services and salvage, if any. The valuation problem becomes this—to (1) identify the expected services in each future period, (2) price each service and sum for each future period, (3) determine a discount rate, and (4) apply the present value algorithm. This model was explicitly adopted by Sprouse and Moonitz (p. 20), and it suffices here to point out its incompatibility with a concept of asset value as equal to replacement cost found by reference to input markets.

This same unresolved problem emerged again in connection with the definitions of asset and revenue adopted by the FASB in its third concepts statement, which will be discussed in chapters 13 and 14.

THE EDWARDS AND BELL CONTRIBUTION

In their seminal work,[7] Edwards and Bell explicitly relaxed three assumptions which they viewed as constraints on accounting.

1. Money as a stable measuring scale which does not change its value
2. Realization as the condition for recognizing revenue, or increase in net assets resulting from operations
3. The "unitary income statement," which does not separate operating from holding gains and losses

They first presented the concept of economic income, but discarded it as *ex ante* and "essentially short-run in nature." They then introduced a new term, *business profit*, as a comparable long-run *ex post* concept. Business profit is contrasted with something called *accounting profit*, which corresponds with net income found using historical costs.

Current value of outputs	Revenues
− Current value of inputs	− Expenses
= Current operating profit	= Accounting operating profit
+ Realizable capital gains	+ Realized capital gains
= Business profit	= Accounting profit

The authors reconciled business profit with economic income. *Subjective goodwill* is the term used by some economists for net present value; it is the excess of the present value of expected future net cash flows from an investment over the amount of the investment, the former discounted at the cost of capital. Economic income amortizes this subjective goodwill over the life of the investment; the SEC called the procedure "accretion of discount." Economic income would also include realizable capital gains, which are the result of changes in expectations.

Realized capital gains, of course, are the selling prices of surplus assets minus their book values.

Side by side with the business profit construct Edwards and Bell presented two additional constructs, real business profit and real realized profit. The composition of each of these is shown in Figure 11-1, the use of average of 19XX dollars underlying the addition of the word *real*. Edwards and Bell note that the same result could be reached using end-of-period adjustments to translate the figures into end-of-period dollars.

FIGURE 11-1
Supplementary Statement 1
Real Profit and Loss—XYZ Corporation for the year 19XX
in thousands of average-of-19XX dollars

Sales		4,000
Less: Cost of sales (including depreciation & interest)		3,813
Current operating profit (COP)		187

COP	187	COP	187
Real realized cost savings	87	Real realizable cost savings	205
Real realized capital gains	5		
Real realized profit	279	Real business profit	392

Disposition of real business profit

Federal income taxes	170
Dividends	74
Real realized surplus[1]	35
Real realized profit	279
Real unrealized surplus	113
Real business profit	392

[1]Change in retained earnings

Source: Edwards and Bell, op. cit., p. 246.

The definitions of these profit constructs are—

Current operating profit (COP) = Profit on operations
Business profit = COP + Realizable cost savings
Realized profit = COP + Realized cost savings
Real business profit = Business profit + price-level adjustment for net monetary assets.

In these constructs, a cost saving is an increase in the current cost of assets held. Realized cost savings are the excess of current cost over historical cost of inputs used in producing output sold. Holding gains and losses are thus a combination of realized cost savings and windfall gains and losses on inventories and equipment.

A reconciliation of current operating profit with historical cost net income is shown in Figure 11-2.

The concept of current cost was not explained by Edwards and Bell, but in view of their assumption that a primary use of financial statements is to evaluate the past, and that there must therefore be a clear delineation between holding gains and operating gains, we are justified in concluding that replacement cost was meant. Failure to structure the concept of current cost was one of the weaknesses of Edwards and Bell's imaginative and comprehensive proposal, which remains the most carefully thought out scheme of incorporating price changes in financial statements.

This system was presented as a set of end-of-period adjustments, rather than as a continuous process. It did, however, point to the separate disclosure of the inflation effect and the market effect, and it was based on the assumption that the components of the financial statements represented something more than just purchasing power.

To make the transition from the inflation effect to the specific price change, by incorporating the market effect, involves eliminating the practice of rolling forward. Asset values are restated at current entry prices when price changes can be objectively deter-

FIGURE 11-2

Reconciliation of Edwards and Bell's Current Operating Profit (COP) with Historical Cost Net Income

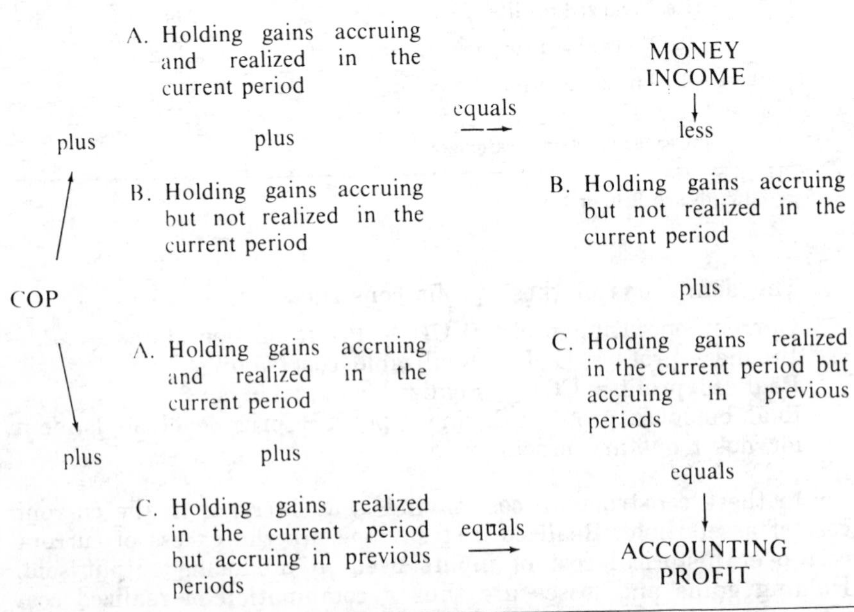

Source: *Readings in the Concept and Measurement of Income*, ed. R. H. Parker and G. C. Harcourt, Cambridge University Press, 1969, p. 6.

mined, which involves not only their identification but also a judgment as to their significance. In the case of assets which are removed from the market, and for which actual entry or exit market prices are therefore irrelevant (equipment, inventories), technological factors should also be recognized as causing value changes.

While Edwards and Bell's proposals received wide acclaim from academic accountants, they have had little effect on accounting practice in the U.S., unless the FASB's current cost requirements can be attributed to this source. The aspect which has aroused the widest criticism is the proposal to include the effects of specific price changes (the so-called holding gains and losses) in the determination of income.

Edwards and Bell argued that the distinction between operating margins and holding gains and losses should be of interest to managers and investors, whether due to holding inventories or fixed assets. This position has received widespread support, but has also been attacked on the grounds that it contradicts the realization principle ("fails to distinguish between sacrifice values and benefit values") and that holding and operating gains and losses are in fact inseparable.[8] Another view holds that it is incorrect to refer to these differences as gains and losses, as they are simply restatement effects from expressing capital in terms of current prices. As an illustration, suppose that a company owns an office building which cost $100,000 and is revalued in current cost at $300,000. There has been no change in net assets (the building), and there can, therefore, be no income resulting from the revaluation. In this framework, a difference of this kind is a constituent part of equity.

REVSINE'S REPLACEMENT COST THEORY

A major contribution to replacement cost theory has come from Revsine, who attempted to justify Edwards and Bell's unexplained transition from economic income to business income.[9] Revsine adopted the decision model approach criticized in chapter 6. Having selected long-term equity investors as the user group, he assumed a decision model derived from finance theory and approved by a committee of the American Accounting Association[10]:

$$V_0 = \left(\sum_{i=1}^{n} \frac{D_i \alpha_i}{(1+\beta)^i} + \frac{I_n \alpha_n}{(1+\beta)^n} \right) - I_O$$

where:

V_0 = subjective net present value of one equity share purchased at time O at price I_0.

D_i = dividend per share expected during period i.

α_i = a factor to adjust for uncertainty; if the investor is risk averse, $0<\alpha_i<1$.

β = opportunity rate of discount for a risk free investment.

I_n = expected value of this equity share at the end of the planning period, time n.

Two functions of accounting information were assumed: to serve as a lead indicator, because the data impounds exogenous factors, and to serve as a basis for extrapolation, because the data incorporates endogenous factors. The lead indicator argument for replacement cost income (current sales minus the current replacement cost of sales) is that it approximates economic income. Revsine presents the argument that replacement cost income equals economic income in a perfectly competitive economy. Economic income can be separated into two components, (1) expected income (subjective goodwill) and (2) unexpected income, arising out of changes in expectations. Revsine equates expected income to Edwards and Bell's COP and unexpected income to those authors' "realizable cost savings." Because the capital maintenance assumption of the economic model postulates the distributability of expected income, the use of replacement cost permits the estimate of the *D* term in the valuation model.

This is not the place to list the many assumptions which are necessary to deduce the implications of a perfectly competitive economy and, while the invalidity of any one of them might not be critical, the fact that they are virtually all irrelevant to the conditions under which accounting is performed renders untenable inferences such as those drawn by Revsine. There is no justification for his conclusion that "current operating profit" is merely an approximation for expected income in an imperfectly competitive economy. The argument presented in this book is that there is no relationship between any income construct of economic theory and the concept of business net income as found by accounting methods.

The extrapolation argument is that actual current operating profit (COP) is the best estimate of future COP, and future COP is a surrogate for future distributable cash flow. If assessment of future cash flows into and out of the enterprise is an important objective of users of the income statement, this argument would be critical to the adoption of replacement costs. If, however, assessing future cash flows is not a major use of financial statements, or alternately, if users can find the data required for such projections from statements of changes in financial position, this argument is less convincing. Another problem not dealt with is the role of holding gains and losses; they are included in future net cash flows but not in COP.

Revsine's advocacy of replacement cost may have influenced the SEC to require replacement cost disclosures in *ASR 190*.[11] These disclosures did not involve calculating current operating profit, since they only required publication of replacement cost of goods sold and depreciation, together with the replacement cost of inventories and property, plant and equipment. However, current operating profit and holding gains and losses could be calculated from the historical cost financial statements if they were adjusted using the replacement cost disclosures.

THE CONCEPT OF REPLACEMENT COST

Replacement cost, sometimes called *current input cost* is technically the price which will have to be paid to replace an object used or given up on an exchange. This concept relies upon the need to replace the object to be valued, so that it is not applicable to non-replacement situations. In order to value at replacement cost it is necessary, because of the closed system feature of accounting, to record the difference between historical cost and replacement cost. This difference arises out of changes in input market price between the date of acquisition and the date of valuation and is often referred to as a *holding gain* or *holding loss*.

Two criticisms of this concept of replacement cost are: that it confuses problems of acquisition and use, and that it abstracts from technological change. As to the former, objects are purchased by an entity in relation to their availability, the availability of finance, the economics of ordering, and other factors independent of the act of use or exchange. The relevant price for the decision to use or give up is not a future acquisition price but the price on the date of use or exchange. As to the latter, technological changes cause the replacement object to differ somewhat from the object being replaced. Both of these criticisms have been levelled against the SEC's replacement cost disclosure requirements and the more recent current cost disclosure requirements of *FASB Statement No. 33*.

Replacement cost can be viewed in the form of a valuation model in which value is the sum of discounted future costs saved, or payments which will not have to be made if the asset is acquired. The expression for value would be

$$V_c = \frac{C_1}{1+i} + \frac{C_2}{(1+i)^2} \dots\dots\dots\dots + \frac{C_n}{(1+i)^n}$$

where C denotes the sum of each period's cash payments and i the rate of discount (a borrowing rate).

This formulation permits the effects of technological change to be incorporated as reductions in C; even a learning curve can be incorporated in this way.

In March, 1976 the SEC amended Regulation S-X to require the disclosure of replacement cost information by certain very large corporations subject to its filing requirements. This requirement was cancelled following the pronouncement of *FASB Statement No. 33*. SEC staff interpretations of *ASR 190* outlined several different methods of determining replacement cost, and *ASR 190* itself announced that "alternative approaches will be acceptable." Attempts to formulate a replacement cost theory have not helped in the solution of this problem.

Among the interesting and difficult technical questions which must be answered in constructing a system of accounting using replacement costs are—

- The treatment of intangibles;
- The treatment of liabilities;
- The relationship between replacement cost and constant dollar accounting;
- The treatment of the so-called holding gains and losses;
- How to account for backlog (or "catchup") depreciation.

Subsequent paragraphs will deal with these issues either in connection with *FASB Statement No. 33* or with the Dutch system of replacement value accounting. At this point we shall summarize some of the arguments for and against replacement cost as the valuation basis for nonmonetary assets.

For replacement cost (RC)	Against replacement cost
1. Corresponds with *deprival value*.	1. When RC is greater than both present value and net realizable value, it does not measure *deprival value*.
2. Provides a physical productive capacity concept of capital maintenance. (This was implicit in the SEC's position.)	2. Money values cannot measure physical capacity; operating capability is a more appropriate concept.
3. Matches current costs with current revenues, leading to a profit figure which measures current operating results.	3. Involves charging backlog depreciation and crediting holding gains, which have no relationship to current operating performance.

The proposition that replacement cost income statements are more useful for evaluation, comparison, and prediction, which Edwards and Bell assumed to be true, can be seen to rest in large part on the treatment of backlog depreciation and holding gains and losses. There is, however, an additional complication.

The ability of an enterprise to maintain its operating capability, which is the capital maintenance concept from which replacement cost results-measurement starts, depends on the enterprise being able to command certain quantities of assets, classified in accounting into fixed assets and working capital. Replacement cost represents those quantities in money only if they are inventories or equipment. Many firms, however, must also have monetary working capital (excess of cash plus receivables over current liabilities) with which to operate. The effect of specific price changes on this amount needs to be taken into account in determining how much of the current inflow of assets from operations must be retained to maintain operating capability. This "net monetary working capital adjustment" was explained in chapter 10.

Finally, the gearing adjustment also described in chapter 10 is clearly relevant to this point, since maintenance of operating capability can be assured by borrowing, as well as by retaining shareholders funds.

BACKLOG DEPRECIATION

Depreciation presents an aspect of replacement cost accounting which is revealing of current value accounting problems. Consider a machine which cost $500 at the start of 19X0 and has a five-year useful life and no salvage value. Historical cost depreciation on the straight-line basis will be $100 each year through 19X4. Suppose that the replacement cost of the machine increases at the rate of 10 percent each year on the basis of its specific price. Current cost depreciation should, therefore, increase at the rate of 10 percent each year. In this case, however, accumulated depreciation will total only $610 at the end of the machine's life, whereas replacement value will be $731. This can be demonstrated graphically.

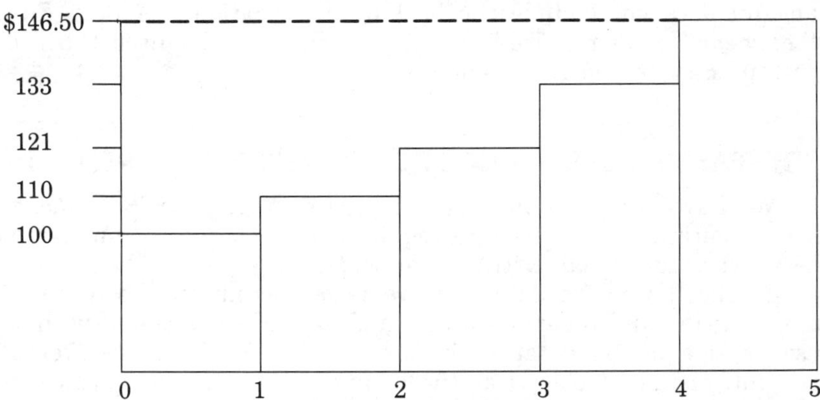

The area above the solid line and below the dotted line represents the difference of $121 and is called *backlog depreciation*. In order to increase accumulated depreciation to the required amount, it is necessary to charge this backlog depreciation to expense each year, in addition to the year's replacement value depreciation; or else debit the amount required year by year to stockholders' equity, as a prior period adjustment. In the former case expense will be as follows:

	19X0	19X1	19X2	19X3	19X4	Total
Regular	$100	$110	$121	$133	$146	$610
Backlog	0	10	21	36	54	121
Total depreciation	$100	$120	$142	169	$200	$731

Backlog depreciation expense is never disclosed by the constant dollar method required by *FASB Statement No. 33*, as a prior period adjustment is concealed in the rolling forward adjustment to retained earnings. It is automatically excluded under the FASB's current cost method as long as the data are prepared using end-of-period adjustments. These are illustrated below, for end 19X3 and end 19X4 only.

	End 19X3	End 19X4
Adjusted historical cost	$665.00	$732.50
Accumulated depreciation	532.00	732.50
Net amount	$133.00	$ 0

The carrying amount of $133 at the end of 19X3 is increased by the restatement of the asset ($67.50) and decreased by the restatement of the depreciation ($54.00) to $146.50, which is then charged to expense as the current cost depreciation for 19X4. This amount does not include the backlog depreciation, nor does *FASB Statement No. 33* require backlog depreciation to be disclosed in the current cost financial statements.

THE FASB'S CURRENT COST DISCLOSURE REQUIREMENTS

We have remarked on several aspects of the *FASB Statement No. 33* current cost disclosure requirements. These are summarized here, with additional critical comments.

1. The Statement defines current cost accounting as a method of measuring and reporting assets and expenses associated with the use or sale of assets at their current cost (or lower recoverable amount, discussed below) at the balance sheet date or at the date of use or sale. Because the disclosure is presented as a set of end-of-period adjustments, however, cost of goods sold or depreciation expense may be stated at current cost at end-of-period, not at date of use or sale.

2. The Statement requires partial restatement only, namely, of inventory; tangible property, plant and equipment; cost of goods sold; and depreciation, depletion, and amortization (of tangible property only). Any other income statement item which must be used in arriving at income from continuing operations is unchanged from the same item in the historical cost income statement. Since most revenue and expense items can be assumed to accrue evenly throughout the year, these items will already be expressed in average-of-the-year dollars, or constant dollars as defined by the Statement. However, any amortization of intangibles or other expenses, or gains and losses on the sale of such items, derived from historical cost figures originating in prior years will be included at their historical cost amounts. Income from continuing operations, therefore, is an amalgam of current cost, prior period adjustments, constant dollars, and historical costs.

3. The Statement includes a "lower of cost or market" rule which requires assets, the restated current cost of which exceeds the "recoverable amount," to be written down to the latter figure. Lower recoverable amount is defined as net realizable value for inventories

and other items held for sale (proceeds value in the replacement value terminology) and value in use for property, plant, and equipment not destined for sale. Value in use is defined as present value of expected future net cash inflows, found by using a discount rate which reflects the risk involved in the investment.

The principal type of company affected by this rule is the regulated utility which is prevented from recovering an amount in excess of historical cost in the rates charged to users. Such companies will show a reduction of current cost to lower recoverable amount in their current cost disclosures, but the reduction does not enter into the calculation of income from continuing operations. An enterprise which owns obsolete equipment will not be in this position, but will charge current cost depreciation based on the lower recoverable amount.

4. Current cost is defined as reproduction cost (current price of a similar used or equivalent asset) and not replacement cost (as required by the SEC) or replacement value. It can be found in several different ways: specific pricing, indexing using a specific price-level index, standard costs for inventories, unit pricing, and any other usable approach. The Standard specifies the method whereby current cost is to be found, but not in sufficient detail to enable answers to be found to many critical questions.

For example, assume that a company owns a building which cost $100,000 in 19X0, and the current reproduction cost of the identical building is $200,000 ten years later. The building has been depreciated to a net book value of $40,000. Construction costs of such a building have doubled, but the company could redesign the building so that it could be built for $170,000. A similar building is on the market for $150,000 in the next street; it is five years old. Problem: how many current cost amounts can be calculated?

5. The Statement failed to resolve the question whether the "holding gain or loss" is a restatement of capital or a component of income. Instead, companies were required to report this item under the heading "increase or decrease in the current cost of inventory, property, plant and equipment," after the presentation of income from continuing operations and not added to or deducted from that figure. This item is to be shown before and after inflation, thus permitting the market effect to be shown separately from the inflation effect.[12]

There is no requirement to disclose the effect of leverage on this holding gain or loss, as is the case with the United Kingdom gearing adjustment. Nor is there any need to calculate interest on capital employed during the holding period, thus ensuring that the market effect is overstated by at least this factor.

6. There is no requirement to disclose the effect of inflation on the amount of monetary working capital required to support operations. True, the purchasing power loss or gain on net monetary assets or liabilities is required to be shown in the constant dollar disclosures. This figure, however, includes long-term receivables and payables which will not be realized until long after the balance

sheet date, and in respect of which the concept of a purchasing power loss or gain is difficult to interpret.

7. The Statement points out that it "emphasizes measurement of the assets owned by the enterprise," that is, it takes a static view of the effects of changing prices rather than a dynamic one. Thus, the inflation effect is separated from the market effect only in connection with the so-called holding gain or loss. This is a major difference between current cost accounting and replacement value accounting.

REPLACEMENT VALUE THEORY

The Dutch system of accounting known as replacement value accounting differs from the replacement cost approaches previously mentioned in a number of important respects. Above all, it is based on a theory of value; hence the name "replacement value" and not "replacement cost."

Replacement value theory was developed by Theo Limperg, both a professor at the University of Amsterdam and a practicing public accountant, during the period 1912-1918. We have drawn attention to the limitations of the marginal approach to value and its inapplicability to the individual firm, a problem which was to engage the attention of economists in the United States and the United Kingdom in the 1920s. Quite apart from the obvious assumptions of the microeconomic theory of perfect competition, the significance of the marginal concept in behavioral models of the firm depends upon money being a physical quantity, costs being payments to factors of production, and sales being receipts from product sales. If cash is not a physical quantity, the meaning of a product demand curve as a supply schedule for money and a product supply curve as a demand schedule for money becomes unclear. If costs are not factor payments, it is not obvious that more product will be supplied at a higher price and if sales are not receipts, the whole question of imputation to the marginal quantity of a factor input fails.

Limperg perceived the need for a theory of value to the firm, as distinct from value to the consumer, where the concept of diminishing marginal utility is clearly an appropriate point of departure. The flow model of the economy used by economic theorists looks like this:

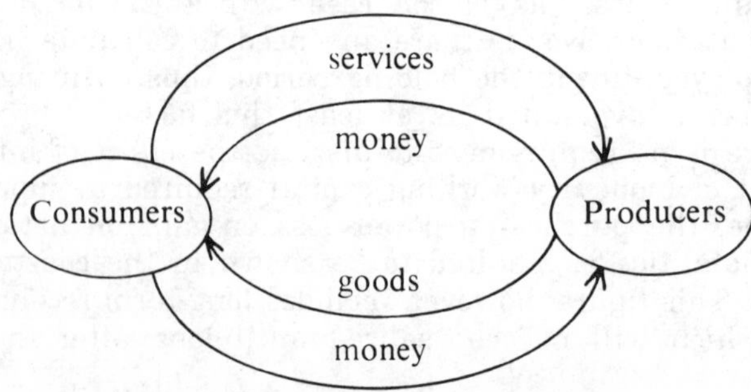

Having established this model, the economist then places himself firmly at the consumer pole; producers behave as a special kind of consumer, profit maximization substituting for utility maximization. From the economist's viewpoint there is nothing wrong with this emphasis as he is studying the production and distribution of the social income, and in this process the consumer plays a central role. From the accountant's viewpoint the emphasis is misplaced, as his work puts the firm, production entity, in the central position.

By the 1920s it had become clear to some economists that the marginal approach to value theory, invaluable for the construction of a theory of relative prices, was incapable of supporting a more complex production theory. One alternative, the monetary theory of value associated with Fisher's work on interest and capital, was not yet familiar to European economists. Another alternative, the social labor theory of value which Marx had constructed on the labor theories of Adam Smith and Ricardo, had already been demonstrated logically untenable.

The significance of replacement value theory for accounting arises from the Limpergian view of the economic function of management, to take economic decisions relating to production quantities and prices. Financial accounting is then viewed as a subset of management accounting in that financial decisions are the consequences of production decisions. To make rational decisions, the manager must at all times know the value of what he must use to produce or what he must give up to replace that which he sells. This involves the continuous updating of historical values to current input values and also the calculation of the effects of changing prices on working capital requirements.

The first generation of Limperg's students achieved management responsibility in the 1930s, during the Great Depression, a period of deflation. The logic of replacement value at that time called for writing down the historical costs of equipment and inventories to their lower current values, and in retrospect it can be seen that this was the correct approach to management decisions at the time. Several large Dutch concerns, notably the multinational electrical and electronics giant Philips Gloeilampenfabrieken N. V., adopted replacement value accounting and flourished; we are not told about those which may have done so and declined. Nevertheless, it is not correct to assert that Dutch accountants have all adopted replacement value accounting, and in 1971 only 28 of the 129 companies with securities quoted on the Amsterdam Stock Exchange prepared financial statements based on replacement value accounting.

In recent years there has been considerable criticism of replacement value accounting in Holland, on the grounds that it has been a restrictive influence on the development of accounting in that country. Dutch accountants are usually familiar with intellectual developments in the United States and the United Kingdom, and the more progressive among them have moved toward the concepts of current cost accounting.

Limpergian value theory is not a macroeconomic theory. One analogy which has been used compares the macroeconomist to the tourist who stands at the top of the Empire State Building and marvels, as he looks down, at the order of the traffic flows below. The microeconomist, however, in whose ranks the accountant must be numbered, is like the driver of one of the vehicles, whose preoccupations are to get from one point to another without falling foul of the traffic laws. Thus, although some have attempted to draw macroeconomic conclusions from Limpergian value theory, these tend to be contradictory. For example, it is argued that the use of historical costs leads to disinvestment during the upswing of the business cycle, because firms distribute capital in the form of income, and also that it leads to overinvestment during such periods, because firms appear more profitable than they really are.

REPLACEMENT VALUE ACCOUNTING

Abstracting from the macroeconomic issues which lie at the center of replacement cost theory, Limperg presented the following basic assumptions.

1. An object can have only one value to a specified entity in the same place at the same time. This effectively rules out historical cost under conditions of changing prices.

2. For any object which can be replaced, value cannot exceed the sacrifice which replacement involves. This is replacement value.

3. Replacement value can be calculated by finding the *technically necessary and economically unavoidable* cost of the object to be valued.

4. Cost is a measure for which "payment" and "expense" are not surrogates. Expense is a measure of consumption of resources during a period of time. We may have expenses without costs, as in the shut-down situation. Payment is a measure of financial sacrifice involved in acquisition, whereas cost is a measurement of use, not acquisition. Some factors of production used are not paid for, or are used for purposes other than those contemplated at the moment of acquisition. We have drawn attention to this allocation problem.

5. An accounting system is an organic whole which integrates the information requirements of all levels of management, insofar as they can be satisfied by accounting methods. Thus, cost as a value datum is relevant to all levels of management within the firm and, by implication, to those outside the firm who are interested in management's effectiveness. "In other words, the application of the replacement value theory is not merely a technique used in preparing the annual statements of the concern. It is integrated in the accounting system of all sections of the concern at every stage... thus the replacement value automatically enters into all management considerations and decisions."[13]

6. Cost is a representation of the standard quantities of factor inputs required for production, in terms of their money price at the moment of use. This can be presented algebraically as:

Unit cost

$$\sum_{i=1}^{i=n} iP_{ri} = \sum_{i=1}^{i=n} i\bar{a}_i \times \bar{V}_i' + \sum_{i=1}^{i=n} i\bar{b}_i \times \bar{V}_i'' + \sum_{i=1}^{i=n} i\bar{c}_i \times \bar{V}_c'''$$

Total cost and Cost of sales

$$N\sum_{i=1}^{i=n} iP_{ri} \qquad Q\sum_{i=1}^{i=n} iP_{ri}$$

where

P_r is the *integral* (we would say "full") cost of the unit of production.
$\bar{a}$ is the required quantity of direct materials, varying according to successive stages of production as $\bar{a}_1$, $\bar{a}_2$, etc.
$\bar{b}$ is the required quantity of direct labor, varied as $\bar{b}_1$, $\bar{b}_2$, etc.
$\bar{c}$ is the quantity of machine hours or other measure of capacity utilization, varied as $\bar{c}_1$, $\bar{c}_2$, etc.
$\bar{V}$ is the price or rate for each of these three quantities, varied as $\bar{V}_1$, $\bar{V}_2$, etc.
N is the volume of production in a particular period.
Q is the volume of production sold during a period.

The difference between total expense for a period and $N\sum_{i=1}^{i=n} iP_{ri}$ is a loss or gain in this model and does not enter into any of the uses for which cost figures are required, such as calculating operating profit or valuing inventory.

The relationship between replacement value accounting and standard costing is clear from the above observation. The differences referred to are those which in standard costing are called variances. Standard costing is also a system in which the technically necessary and economically unavoidable sacrifices involved in production and sale are offset against the proceeds of sale in order to determine profit. Standard quantities are found by reference to technical coefficients, and standard prices by reference to current market prices. Where these two systems part company is in the treatment of depreciation and other cost elements which are based on the price level of a prior period. In replacement value accounting, through continuous updating of costs for all factors of production, overheads are stated at current costs for all components. In both systems the losses and gains arising out of price-level changes and operating levels are reported "below the line," that is, after the computation of income from operations.

7. For any object which cannot be replaced, or which will not be replaced because net realizable value is less than replacement cost, value cannot exceed net realizable value (called *proceeds value*).

8. Value to the firm for any decision is the relevant cost; replacement value for replaceable items, proceeds (net realizable) value for nonreplaceable items, and zero for sunk costs.

In the Dutch system of replacement value accounting, holding gains are first recognized by charging assets, such as inventories and property, plant, and equipment, with interest for the *necessary* holding period (not the actual period held). This interest is credited against interest expense or taken to the credit of the income statement. The holding gain is then reduced by a transfer to deferred taxes in respect of the income tax with which it will be imposed when realized, and the balance credited to a revaluation account, part of stockholders' equity.[14] In Ijiri's terminology, it is a sacrifice value differential, and not a benefit value differential, and therefore cannot be part of profit added by sale.[15] Losses of this nature are debited against the revaluation account, but when it has been exhausted, any losses are debited to the income statement for the period.

This duality of treatment has led some to criticize the Dutch system for being biased against the shareholder, who bears some holding losses but is never credited with holding gains, even when realized. If these gains are illusory, however, then the shareholder's interest in the firm is protected to the extent that crediting such gains to capital prevents the distribution of capital in the form of income.

The replacement value theory of accounting leads to the revaluation of nonmonetary assets for balance sheet purposes and, because it is used for cost accounting, to the calculation of cost of sales for the income statement. It is important to note that the difference between total expenses and total costs previously referred to must appear in the income statement as a loss or gain.

We see here another reason why accounting and economics do not meet. The economist's models assume that all factors of production are fully employed at their optimal efficiency; only if this is the case can the theorems of perfect competition be deduced. For an accountant to make such an assumption, however, would be to abstract from the central issues in accounting: the analysis of return on investment and the evaluation of management's effectiveness.

The effect of changing price levels on monetary assets is not covered by replacement value theory. However, the purchasing power of these assets declines in times of inflation and increases in times of deflation. This "inflation effect" is dealt with in Goudeket's article; the explanation is couched in terms of capital maintenance.

> Since part of the stockholders' equity is invested in other (monetary) assets, the purchasing power of that part will diminish in case of a decrease in value of currency of the country. For this reason we calculate, on the basis of the cost-of-living index, how many currency units represent the same purchasing power as the

part of the capital which at the beginning of the period was invested in monetary assets.... This balance, multiplied by the inflation-factor based on the cost-of-living index, leads to the entry:

Dr.	Cost of inflation	(income account)
Cr.	Reserve for diminishing purchasing power of capital invested in monetary assets	(capital account)

Thus the income statement shows a result after the purchasing power of stockholders' equity has been maintained.[16]

This is an interesting example of a false assumption leading to an incorrect accounting procedure. It is assumed that the business enterprise has the responsibility of maintaining the purchasing power of the stockholders' investment. This is surely the responsibility of the individual stockholder, who uses the stock market for this purpose. It is concluded that the inflation effect on the enterprise should be calculated by means of an index of general purchasing power. Since the monetary assets of the firm are not used for consumption expenditures, the consumer price index must be irrelevant. An index of the factors on which the enterprise spends money should be used. Finally, the reference to monetary assets should probably read "monetary working capital," or liquid assets less current liabilities, since purchasing power losses (or gains) must be calculated with reference to the net monetary position. The United Kingdom gearing adjustment referred to in chapter 10 is used, in part, to reduce the cost of inflation in respect of that part of net monetary assets financed by creditors.

INTEREST ON CAPITAL EMPLOYED

The Dutch system of replacement value accounting is applied differently by different firms, but all applications reflect the above basic principles. It is important to note that these principles are predicated on a managerial approach to financial reporting and assume that the external user is best served by the information which is used by management for its decisions. A budgetary control system is a prerequisite to financial reporting under this viewpoint.[17]

One aspect of the managerial approach to financial reporting which differs from prevailing practice in the United States is the treatment of interest on capital employed. It is assumed that interest must be included as an element of cost in all accounting information about objects which contain a time element. The FASB, in *Statement No. 34*, "Capitalization of Interest Cost," restricted the inclusion of interest as an element of cost to interest actually paid, and to certain qualifying assets. Again, the prevailing practice in the United States is to regard interest expense as a "financial expense" and not an operating cost, although the relationship between financing and operations is quite clear. The Dutch system of replacement value accounting involves capitalizing in the cost of fixed assets and inventories the interest cost of bringing them to their state and place of use. Thus, even inventories routinely produced in large quantities on a repetitive basis would be charged with interest if the current rate of interest and the period of time involved in their production are sufficiently important to warrant inclusion of interest as an element of cost.

This capitalization of interest does not involve the necessity to pay interest; we are dealing with interest as a cost (a measure of a sacrifice incurred by production) and not as a payment. This is a good illustration of the use of money as a unit of account which is quite distinct from money as a medium of exchange, and results in the cost of capital being charged to the customer, and not to the provider of that capital. It is an imputation, not a transaction.

Interest on capital employed affects mainly two factors of production, materials and overheads (cost of capacity). The debit to inventory of materials, for example, includes the price payable to the supplier, credited to accounts payable, and the changes (increases) in the specific price level, credited to a Revaluation (capital) account. Materials handling and storage costs will also be debited to the inventory account, the credit being to the Materials overhead account. Storage costs will include calculated (imputed) interest on average capital invested in inventory for the normal holding period; the credit for this component will be to an Interest account, comparable with the account, "allowance for interest on equity funds employed in construction," found in the income statements of public utility companies. The total credit for the period is brought to credit of the income statement, after the determination of current operating profit, or credited against a larger amount of interest expense for the period. The current borrowing rate is used, whether or not any borrowings actually occur. In this way, interest on capital employed is accounted for as a part of the cost of production or sale of a manufacturing or merchandise inventory; and the interest expense charged to the investors in the company is the excess of interest expense incurred over the time value of money used for production.

The two-part income statement would look like this:

Operating Statement

Sales for the period		XXX
Less: Cost of sales (current cost at date of sale)		XXX
Operating profit		XXX
Add: Calculated interest	XX	
Favorable variances	XX	
Less: Unfavorable variances	(XX)	
Excess of interest expense over calculated interest	(XX)	XX
Net income		XXX

REPLACEMENT COST AND REPLACEMENT PRICE

The concept of cost in economic theory is most elusive—sometimes opportunity cost, sometimes replacement cost, sometimes cash payment, sometimes implicit cost, which can represent anything the economist chooses. It is important to bear in mind, however, that economic models are decision models, aimed at choosing between alternatives, and therefore always prospective. Every economic cost is a future cost. Accounting, on the other hand, is a planning and control model, aimed at producing information. Accounting cost, therefore, must be more closely defined as it serves both a prospective and a retrospective function. Accountants also are responsible for ambiguities in this connection; they use the word cost to mean variously, payment, acquisition, consumption through time (expense), or sacrifice through use in production or sale. Even where an effort is made to reconcile these uses, it is rarely successful, as the following quotation indicates.

> Cost is an exchange price, a foregoing, a sacrifice made to secure benefit. In financial accounting, the foregoing or sacrifice at date of acquisition is represented by a current or future diminution in cash or other assets.[18]

It seems relatively easy to convince accountants that, if a trailer manufacturer's workers procure materials to fix up their homes by charging the issue to one or more job orders, the materials so issued are not part of the cost of production of trailers. It is not so easy to convince them that a price may be excessive and require adjustment. One case which does seem to have achieved acceptance is that of fixed asset obsolescence, even though the generally accepted accounting principle—charge it to the current and future years' expenses—is obviously less than informative. Note that in this case no change has taken place in the physical state of the equipment, or in its capacity to produce at the rate established by the decision to purchase. Only the prices of these future services have changed.

The lack of correspondence between price at time of acquisition and at time of use is illustrated by the accounting rule for valuing materials and equipment. The rule states that cost includes all expenditure necessary to bring the asset to its state and place of use. In the case of inventories, freight, insurance, customs and other taxes, handling costs, and storage should be added to the invoice price; this is usually done on a flat percentage basis. In the case of equipment, legal and design fees and installation will be included in cost. Thus, it is recognized that value to the purchaser is higher than value to the vendor by the amount of these *location specific* costs, and, therefore, price and cost part company.

Similarly, if the production process requires time, interest on the capital invested is an element of cost. In the case of assets covered by *FASB Statement No. 34*, this is explicitly recognized by charging to cost interest during the construction period.

Thus, the significance of *value in exchange* is limited to the act of exchange, in which it represents a kind of average of the possible prices which might have been paid by all those interested in the object in question, and an average of all the possible uses to which it might have been put. On acquisition, however, the use is specified, and factors other than purchase price influence value. The suggestion by many authors that replacement cost can be found by reference to suppliers' price lists is clearly wrong.

Further, replacement value means the technically necessary and economically unavoidable quantity multiplied by the price at the time of use. This is not the price that will be paid to replace the quantity used, which is a problem of acquisitions and belongs to the conceptual framework of financing the business, not that of measuring and analyzing profit.

A complication exists in the case of businesses which execute forward contracts to avoid price fluctuations by assuring a regular flow of materials at predetermined prices. In such cases the long-run supply price, supplemented by the various costs necessary to bring the materials to their state and place of use, is the replacement value and not the price on the day of use.

With reference to the difference between replacement cost and the replacement price; if it were possible to finance the reacquisition of quantities used on a day-to-day basis, the two concepts would be the same. The fact that reacquisition is dependent upon non-production factors renders necessary further study of the problem. One must start from the proposition that identical objects cannot have different values in the same place at the same time. The acquisition of replacement materials at prices different from those used to evaluate inventories necessitates an accounting entry to recognize the fact. This, which Edwards and Bell and their followers call a "holding gain or loss," the Dutch school treat as a deferral; undoubtedly the correct treatment where prices fluctuate around some measure of central tendency. In a time of inflation, the assumption is not generally valid, since price movements are all in the same direction, but for specific prices this need not be the case. If specific price movements are continually upwards, it would be possible to avoid allowing these "paper profits" to enter into the calculation of business net income, by deferring them and charging against them purchasing power losses through holding monetary assets, the purpose of which is to finance the acquisition of materials in accordance with the conditions governing such acquisitions. This appears to be the logic underlying the monetary working capital adjustment.

CURRENT VALUES AS EXIT PRICES

The use of current exit (net realizable, or selling) prices to account for and report all asset and liability values has two clear benefits.

1. In terms of capital maintenance, profit can be determined at any point by calculating the difference between opening and closing net assets, adjusted for contributions and distributions.
2. In terms of management decisions, the continuous updating of prices provides management with the information required for making decisions to sell or to hold assets, or to repay or extinguish by repurchase, liabilities.

Note that in a complete accounting system of this kind, stockholders' equity would also be restated at selling market prices, so that goodwill would be a constantly changing asset in the balance sheet.

Some small investor associations have in fact adopted accounting and reporting systems of this kind, in order to provide investors with a valuation for their interests, should they desire to sell, in the absence of a market for those interests.

The problem with using exit prices is that the goal desired, namely, the continuous representation of the cash which could be raised by liquidating assets and liabilities in an orderly manner, is unobtainable. Work in process and specialized assets which are not readily marketable are obvious examples of the valuation problem; few accountants would support the proposition that such items should be omitted from the category "assets" simply because the exit price at the balance sheet date is not known, and to find their value by imputing the proceeds of sale of the firm's products is both impractical and rife with allocation inconsistencies.

Moreover, by selecting exit prices to value assets and liabilities, the accounting system necessarily renders itself less able to discharge its functions of accountability and control. Assume that a manager purchases an item for $10 which regularly sells for $15, and is recorded in inventory at $15, with a credit to income of the period of purchase for the assumed profit of $5. Why should he bother to sell it? How much should it be insured for, given that the replacement cost is still $10? Is it reasonable to borrow $5 in order to distribute the profit as a dividend? These are among the questions which an accounting system must provide information for, if it is to serve its social function. The experience with Reserve Recognition Accounting does not really address these questions, as the method was based on present values of future exit prices.

Edwards has stated the reasons for preferring entry values to exit values as a normal method of valuation (that is, for inputs).

1. The use of exit values necessitates anomalous revaluations on acquisition because the value of an object to its possessor is greater than its value to another by at least the amount of transport costs, installation and removal charges, and location specific benefits.

2. The use of exit values is of necessity a short-run approach to valuation. A positive excess of net realizable value over cost at a balance sheet date indicates nothing about the eventual result of disposing of the asset in question, or some other asset for the manufacture of which it will be used.
3. The use of exit values anticipates profit (or loss) and assumes that which the income statements should demonstrate, a difference between inputs and outputs. Abandoning entry values renders more difficult—perhaps impossible—the work of tracing how a set of acquisitions of factors of production have resulted in value added to the recipients of factor income.[19]

Edwards points out the importance of distinguishing between markets in which the firm is normally a buyer and markets in which the firm is normally a seller; exit prices are clearly irrelevant to the former, except in the unusual case of asset liquidation coupled with nonreplacement. In this case, the highest value of an asset to its possessor is its net realizable value, by definition.

CONCLUSION

It is clear that current value accounting is a set of techniques in process of development. The author's point of view is that attempting to deal with the problem of accounting for specific price changes by end-of-period adjustments avoids many of the technical issues which accountants should be facing in order to arrive at a comprehensive solution to the problem. Management accountants have not involved themselves actively in the process, and such a solution awaits their participation. General price-level adjustment to current cost financial statements is an unnecessary refinement, and the effect of inflation on the monetary position can be shown in the current cost financial statements themselves.

An example of the application of the United Kingdom SSAP 16 on current cost accounting appears on the following pages. It will be seen that the acceptance of these supplementary statements as the basic financial statements is only a matter of time. We will then be able to say that the problem of accounting for changing prices has been solved.

It may be pointed out that neither constant dollar nor current value (or cost) accounting makes any contribution to the assessment of future cash flows to the enterprise. In the case of constant dollar accounting, all figures adjusted are expressed in units of a particular purchasing power, which is not cash but money of account. In the case of current value accounting, all figures adjusted are expressed in units of money at the date of use or sale, or, in the case of balance sheet items, at the end of an accounting period. Although the last could be interpreted to mean the amount which would have to be paid out in order to replace the assets in question at that date, there is no implication that this amount *will* have to be spent at some future date when they are replaced, or when equivalent operating capability is acquired.

GENERAL NOTES ON CURRENT COST ACCOUNTS

Current cost accounting (CCA) is a system of accounting which makes allowance for the estimated effects of specific price changes on the net operating assets of a business. The main difference between historical cost accounting and CCA is that under historical cost accounting assets are accounted for in terms of their original cost whereas under CCA assets are generally accounted for in terms of the cost of replacing them.

The group current cost accounts are prepared in accordance with Statement of Standard Accounting Practice No. 16 and are supplementary to the historical cost accounts. The accounting policies set out on page 22 are followed in preparing the current cost accounts except where they are inconsistent with CCA principles. Current cost amounts in respect of associated companies and trade investments are included for the first time in 1980. Corresponding figures for 1979 have not been adjusted.

Current cost income

The following adjustments are made to the historical cost net income in computing the current cost net income:

(a) Cost of sales adjustment – the difference between cost calculated on the first-in first-out method under the historical cost convention and the estimated cost as if, using normal sources and methods of supply, the products sold had been acquired at the time of sale.

(b) Monetary working capital adjustment – the change as a result of inflation in the amount of monetary working capital (trade debtors and liquid resources less trading liabilities) needed to support the day-to-day operations of the group.

(c) Depreciation adjustment – the difference between depreciation calculated by applying the group's depreciation policies to the current cost of existing properties and operating assets and the depreciation charge in the historical cost income statement.

(d) Associated companies' income adjustment – the estimated difference between the group's share of income of associated companies calculated on current and historical cost bases.

(e) Gearing adjustment – this reflects the fact that part of the finance needed to provide the increased value of assets which is required to maintain the same level of business during periods of inflation comes from the lenders of borrowed funds and other creditors. It is calculated by applying to the above adjustments the ratio of average net borrowings to the sum of such borrowings and average shareholders' funds on a current cost basis. Net borrowings comprise all liabilities other than trading balances included in monetary working capital, less excess liquid resources.

Current cost balance sheet

Items are restated in the current cost balance sheet as follows:

(a) Properties and operating assets are stated at their current cost which is mainly established by the application of indices, appropriate to their function and location, to their original cost. In the remaining cases valuations have been obtained.

(b) Investments in associated companies are stated at the group's share of their estimated net assets calculated on a current cost basis or directors' valuation where lower.

(c) Trade investments are stated at market value for listed companies or directors' valuation for unlisted companies.

(d) Stocks and stores are stated at the lower of estimated replacement cost, from normal sources of supply, and net realisable value.

The difference between the amounts at which assets are stated in the historical and current cost balance sheets, together with the adjustments charged in the current cost income statement, are transferred to the current cost reserve after adjusting for minority shareholders' interest. This reserve should not be regarded as available for distribution to shareholders.

REPORT OF THE AUDITORS

To the members of The British Petroleum Company Limited

We have examined the accounts of The British Petroleum Company Limited prepared under the historical cost convention and the supplementary current cost accounts set out on pages 22 to 34 and pages 39 and 40. Our audit has been carried out in accordance with approved auditing standards.

In our opinion the historical cost accounts give, under that accounting convention, a true and fair view of the state of affairs of the Company and of the group at 31 December 1980 and of the net income, changes in reserves and source and application of funds of the group for the year then ended, and comply with the Companies Acts 1948 to 1980.

In our opinion the supplementary current cost accounts of the group have been properly prepared to give the information required by Statement of Standard Accounting Practice No. 16.

Ernst & Whinney
Chartered Accountants
London, 12 March 1981

SUPPLEMENTARY GROUP INCOME STATEMENT ON CURRENT COST BASIS

For the year ended 31 December 1980

Figures in £ million

	Note	1980	1979
Sales and operating revenue		**25,347**	22,705
Customs duties and sales taxes		**4,691**	4,462
Net sales and operating revenue	1	**20,656**	18,243
Other income		**298**	274
Revenues		**20,954**	18,517
Operating costs	2	**17,250**	15,564
Current cost operating result before deducting petroleum revenue tax and production taxes of £2,000m (£1,506m)		**3,704**	2,953
Interest	3	**264**	351
Income before taxation		**3,440**	2,602
Taxation	4	**2,959**	2,266
Income after taxation		**481**	336
Gearing adjustment		**383**	596
		864	932
Minority shareholders' interest		**287**	330
Current cost net income		**577**	602
Distribution to shareholders	5	**322**	274
Retained income for year		**255**	328
Current cost earnings per ordinary share	16	**36·9p**	38·9p

GROUP RESERVES ON CURRENT COST BASIS

	Note	1980	1979
At 1 January		**3,152**	2,934
Retained income for year		**255**	328
Special dividend	5	**—**	(30)
Premium on acquisition	8	**(31)**	43
Exchange fluctuations		**(297)**	(123)
At 31 December	17	**3,079**	3,152

SUPPLEMENTARY BALANCE SHEET ON CURRENT COST BASIS

At 31 December 1980

Assets employed	Note	Group 1980	Group 1979
Properties and operating assets	6–7	**12,890**	10,836
Investments			
Associated companies	10	**859**	478
Trade investments	11	**140**	8
Long-term receivables		**333**	273
Current assets less current liabilities	12	**4,489**	3,561
Total assets less current liabilities		**18,711**	15,156
Deferred liabilities	13	**944**	724
Deferred taxation	4	**173**	221
Pension and insurance provisions	14	**271**	274
		1,388	1,219
		17,323	13,937

Financed by			
Share capital	15	**409**	399
Share premium	15	**335**	199
Current cost reserve	18	**7,234**	4,782
Group reserves	17	**3,079**	3,152
Shareholders' interest		**11,057**	8,532
Minority shareholders' interest		**2,196**	1,722
Finance debts	19	**4,070**	3,683
		17,323	13,937

ENDNOTES

1. Beaver, William H., *Financial Reporting: An Accounting Revolution*, Englewood Cliffs, N.J.: Prentice-Hall, Inc., 1981, ch. 2.
2. Peterson, Russell J., "A Portfolio Analysis of General Price Level Restatement," *The Accounting Review*, July 1975, pp. 525-32.
3. Moonitz, Maurice, "The Basic Postulates of Accounting," *Accounting Research Study No. 1*, New York: AICPA 1961, p. 29.
4. Sprouse, Robert T. and Maurice Moonitz, "A Tentative Set of Broad Accounting Principles for Business Enterprises," *Accounting Research Study No. 3*, New York: AICPA 1962,
5. First revision, "Accounting Principles Underlying Corporate Financial Statements," *The Accounting Review*, June 1941, pp. 133-39 and second revision, "The Accounting Concepts and Standards Underlying Corporate Financial Statements, 1948 Revision," *The Accounting Review*, October 1948, pp. 339-44.
6. Committee on Concepts and Standards of the American Accounting Association, "Accounting and Reporting Standards for Corporate Financial Statements—1957 Revision," *The Accounting Review*, October 1957, p. 538.
7. Edwards, Edgar O. and Philip W. Bell, *The Theory and Measurement of Business Income*, University of California Press, 1961.
8. Samuelson, Richard A., "Should Replacement Cost Changes be Included in Income?" *The Accounting Review*, April 1980, pp. 254-68.
9. Revsine, Lawrence, *Replacement Cost Accounting*, Englewood Cliffs, N.J.: Prentice-Hall, Inc., 1973.
10. Committee on External Reporting, "An Evaluation of External Reporting Practices: A Report of the 1966-68 Committee on External Reporting," Supplement to *The Accounting Review*, Vol. XLIV, 1969, pp. 82-83.
11. See also Revsine, Lawrence, "Replacement Cost Accounting: A Theoretical Foundation," in *Objectives of Financial Statements, Volume 2/Selected Papers*, ed. Joe J. Cramer, Jr. and George H. Sorter, New York: AICPA, 1974.
12. *FASB Statement No. 33* only requires disclosure of the increase/decrease of current cost amounts over historical cost amounts net of inflation, but virtually all companies affected have construed this to mean both before and after, i.e., the market effect and the inflation effect.
13. Goudeket, A., "An Application of Replacement Value Theory," *Journal of Accountancy*, July 1960, pp. 37-47.
14. Report of the American Accounting Association Committee on International Accounting, 1974-75, *The Accounting Review*, Supplement to Vol. XLXI, 1976, pp. 107-33.
15. Ijiri, Y., *The Foundations of Accounting Measurement*, Englewood Cliffs, N.J.: Prentice-Hall, Inc., 1967.
16. Goudeket, op. cit., p. 41.
17. Mey, Abram, "On the Application of Business Economics and Replacement Value Accounting in the Netherlands," *International Business Series No. 8*, Seattle, Washington: University of Washington, 1970.
18. Sprouse and Moonitz, op. cit., p. 25.
19. Edwards, Edgar O., "The State of Current Value Accounting," *The Accounting Review*, April 1975, pp. 235-45.

SELECTED ADDITIONAL READINGS

Accounting Series Release No. 190 (March 23, 1976) and *Staff Accounting Bulletins Nos. 7, 9, 10, 11* (1976), Washington, D.C.: Securities and Exchange Commission.

Accounting Standards Steering Committee, Statement of Standard Accounting Practice No. 16, *Current Cost Accounting*, London, 1979.

Alexander, Michael O. and J. Douglas Barrington, "A Feasible Method of Current Value Accounting," *CA Magazine*, September 1975, pp. 33-39.

Backer, Morton, *Current Value Accounting*, New York: Financial Executives Research Foundation, 1973.

Burgert, R., "Reservations about 'Replacement Value' Accounting in the Netherlands," *Abacus*, December 1972, pp. 111-26.

CICA Accounting Research Committee, "Proposed Accounting Recommendations," *Current Cost Accounting*, Toronto: Canadian Institute of Chartered Accountants, December 1979.

Committee on International Accounting, "Report of the AAA Committee on International Accounting, 1974-75," *The Accounting Review*, Supplement to Vol. XLXI, 1976, pp. 107-33.

Current-Value Accounting: Economic Reality in Financial Statements: A Program for Experimentation, New York: Touche Ross & Co. 1975.

Davidson, Sidney and Roman L. Weil, "Inflation Accounting: The SEC Proposal for Replacement Cost Disclosure," *Financial Analysts Journal*, March/April 1976, pp. 57-66, included in *Replacement Cost Accounting: Readings on Concepts, Uses and Methods*, ed. Vancil, Richard F. and Roman L. Weil, Glen Ridge, N.J.: Thomas Horton and Daughters, 1976.

Depreciation and Replacement Policy, ed. J.L. Meij, Chicago: Quadrangle Books, 1961.

Edwards, Edgar O., "The State of Current Value Accounting," *The Accounting Review*, April 1975, pp. 235-245.

Edwards, Edgar O. and Philip W. Bell, *The Theory and Measurement of Business Income*, Berkeley, Calif.: The University of California Press, 1961.

Elvik, Kenneth O., "Acquisition Cost Versus Revaluation: A Historical Perspective," *The International Journal of Accounting Education and Research*, Spring 1974, pp. 155-79.

Enthoven, Adolf J.H., "Replacement Value Accounting: Wave of the Future," *Harvard Business Review*, Jan/Feb. 1976, pp. 6-8.

Goudeket, A., "An Application of Replacement Value Theory," *Journal of Accountancy*, July 1960, pp. 37-47, included in *Replacement Cost Accounting: Readings on Concepts, Uses and Methods*.

Institute of Chartered Accountants in Australia and Australian Society of Accountants, Statement of Provisional Accounting Standards, *Current Cost Accounting*, October 1976 (amended August 1978).

King, Alfred M., "Current Value Accounting Comes of Age," *Financial Executive*, January 1976, pp. 18-24.

Mey, Abram, "On the Application of Business Economics and Replacement Value Accounting in the Netherlands," *International Business Series No. 8*, Seattle, Washington: University of Washington, 1970.

New Zealand Society of Accountants, CCA Guidelines, *Supplementary Financial Statements in Terms of Current Costs and Values*, December 1978.

Revsine, Lawrence, *Replacement Cost Accounting*, Englewood Cliffs, N.J.: Prentice-Hall, Inc., 1973.

———, "On the Correspondence Between Replacement Cost Income and Economic Income," *The Accounting Review*, July 1970, pp. 513-23.

———, and Jerry J. Weygandt, "Accounting for Inflation: The Controversy," *Journal of Accountancy*, October 1974, pp. 72-78.

Rosenfield, Paul, "Current Replacement Value Accounting—A Dead End," *Journal of Accountancy*, September 1975, pp. 63-73.

Rosen, L. S., "Replacement Value Accounting," *The Accounting Review*, January 1967, pp. 106-113.

Ross, Howard, *Financial Statements—A Crusade for Current Values*, New York: Pitman Publishing Company, 1969.

Sandilands, F. E. P., *Inflation Accounting*, London: Her Majesty's Stationary Office, Cmnd. 6225, 1975, especially chs. 4, 10.

Van Seventer, A. "The Continuity Postulate in the Dutch Theory of Business Income," *The International Journal of Accounting Education and Research*, Spring 1969, pp. 1-19.

Case 11-1 The Southern Company and Inflation Accounting

The Southern Company is the parent of a group of electric utility companies operating in the south of the United States. Its 1980 annual report included note 14. to the financial statements, reproduced on the following page. Also included was the five-year summary required under *FASB Statement No. 33*, not reproduced in this Case.

The Statement of Income Adjusted for Changing Prices reported the same constant dollar and current cost amount of "Income Applicable to Common Stockholders, as Adjusted" of $56 million.

1. Did the Southern Company prepare this supplementary information in accordance with the rules laid down in *FASB Statement No. 33*? If not, state the precise differences from the requirements of that Statement.

   (Note: The financial statements affirm that the notes form part of the financial statements, and the auditor's report was unqualified, making no reference to this supplementary information.)

FINANCIAL REVIEW

14. Supplementary Information Concerning the Effects of Changing Prices (Unaudited):

The following supplementary information concerning the effects of changing prices is presented in accordance with the general concepts set forth in Financial Accounting Standards Board Statement No. 33, as modified to reflect the economic effects imposed on the Southern electric system by regulatory authorities. It should be viewed as an estimate of the approximate effects of inflation, rather than a precise measure.

Constant dollar amounts represent historical cost stated in terms of dollars of equal purchasing power, as measured by the Consumer Price Index for All Urban Consumers. Current cost amounts reflect the changes in specific prices of plant from the date the plant was acquired to the pesent. They differ from constant dollar amounts to the extent that specific prices have increased more or less rapidly than the general rate of inflation. The current cost of plant was determined by indexing each major class of plant using the Hardy-Whitman index of Public Utility Construction Costs. Current cost does not necessarily represent the replacement cost of existing productive capacity because the utility plant is not expected to be replaced precisely in kind.

The accumulated provision for depreciation for current cost was developed by applying, for each major class of plant, the same percentage relationship that existed between gross plant and accumulated provision for depreciation on a historical basis to the adjusted prescribed. Depreciation expense for both methods was determined by applying the current depreciation rates to the respective indexed plant amounts reduced by the amortization of investment tax credits which were first adjusted to average 1980 constant dollar amounts by year of addition.

Increases in the cost of electric generating fuel are recoverable in revenues through operation of fuel cost recovery mechanisms. Such increases effectively are receivables from customers. Therefore, such increases are not included in income but instead are treated as monetary assets. Income tax expense was not adjusted because only historical costs are duductible for income tax purposes.

Holding assets such as receivables, prepayments, and inventory results in a loss of purchasing power during periods of inflation because the amount of cash received in the future for these items will purchase less. Conversely, holding monetary liabilities, primarily long-term debt, results in a gain because the payment in the future will be made with nominal dollars having less purchasing power. The Southern electric system has a net gain due to the significant amounts of long-term debt outstanding.

Under the ratemaking prescribed by the regulatory commissions to which the subsidiaries of The Southern Company are subject, only the historical cost of plant is recoverable in revenues as depreciation and plant in rate base is limited to original cost. Therefore, the cost of plant stated in terms of constant dollars or current cost that varies from the historical cost of plant is not presently recoverable in rates as depreciation. The amount of this variance that accrued as a result of inflation in the current year is reflected as an adjustment to net recoverable cost. While the use of debt financing reduced the effect of this loss on common stockholders, earnings were not adequate to offset the erosion in the purchasing power of their investment.

Statement of Income Adjusted for Changing Prices
For the Year Ended December 31, 1980 *(in thousands of average 1980 dollars)*

	Constant Dollar	Current Cost
Income Applicable to Common Stockholders, as Reported	$ 344,395	$ 344,395
Erosion of Common Stockholders' Equity Because of Changing Prices:		
Cost in excess of the original cost of productive facilities not recoverable in rates as depreciation—		
Reportable as an additional provision for depreciation	310,021	383,542
Reported as a reduction to net recoverable cost	693,571	303,557
	1,003,592	687,099
Excess of the general level of prices ($2,009,519) in the current year over increase in specific price changes ($1,693,026)*		316,493
Offsetting effect of debt financing	(715,242)	(715,242)
Net erosion of common stockholders' equity	288,350	288,350
Income (Loss) Applicable to Common Stockholders, as Adjusted** (including the effect of debt financing)	$ 56,045	$ 56,045

*At December 31, 1980, current cost of property, plant and equipment, net of accumulated depreciation, was 10 billion, and historical cost or net cost recoverable through depreciation was $10 billion.

**Adjusted income (loss) applicable to common stockholders would be $34 million on a constant dollar basis and ($39 million) on a current cost basis if only the amount reportable as an additional provision for depreciation were deducted from the reported amount of such income.

2. Can you explain from the note why the income applicable to common stockholders was the same in current cost as in constant dollars?
3. What do you think was the purpose of the footnote marked with a double asterisk, at the bottom of the page?

Case 11-2 The Gearing Adjustment

The first official description of a gearing adjustment was contained in an Interim Recommendation by the United Kingdom Accounting Standards Steering Committee, issued December 1977. It stated that:

> It is recognised that there are different views on the question of how monetary items should be dealt with in inflation adjusted statements and that such differences are unlikely to be resolved quickly or without experiment. Nevertheless, it is considered that it would not be acceptable for the statement recommended to be limited to adjustments for depreciation and cost of sales....There are two different situations to be met, each of which calls for a different treatment:
>
> (a) if the total liabilities of the business, including for this purpose preference share capital, exceed its total monetary assets, so that part of its operating capability is effectively financed by the net monetary liabilities, an adjustment should be made to reflect the extent to which the depreciation and cost of sales adjustments do not need to be provided in full from the current revenues of the business in showing the profit attributable to the shareholders.
>
> (b) if the total monetary assets of the business exceed its total liabilities, an adjustment should be made to reflect the increase in the net monetary assets needed to maintain its scale of operation.

Appendix 2, Illustration of the Gearing Adjustment, is reproduced on the next page. (Note that "stocks" are inventories, and "reserves" include retained earnings and all other components of stockholders' equity other than the par value of outstanding common and preferred stocks.)

1. Why did the United Kingdom accountants consider it necessary to include a gearing adjustment in current cost financial statements?
2. What would be an "appropriate index" for calculating the gearing adjustment in a case where there are net monetary assets?
3. Would a gearing adjustment be a useful element of general price-level adjusted (constant dollar) financial statements?

ILLUSTRATION OF THE GEARING ADJUSTMENT

Example 1

TOTAL LIABILITIES OF THE BUSINESS EXCEED ITS TOTAL MONETARY ASSETS

SUMMARISED BALANCE SHEET, AFTER ADJUSTMENT FOR THE DIFFERENCE BETWEEN THE CURRENT VALUES AND HISTORICAL COST AMOUNTS FOR FIXED ASSETS AND, IF MATERIAL, FOR STOCKS:

	£'000
Equity share capital and reserves	684
Long-term liabilities	350
Current liabilities	406
	1,440
Fixed asset	600
Stocks	540
Monetary assets	300
	1,440

(1)	CALCULATE NET BALANCE OF MONETARY LIABILITIES		£'000
	Long-term liabilities		350
	Current liabilities		406
	Total liabilities		756
	Deduct: Monetary assets		300
	Net balance of monetary liabilities		456
(2)	CALCULATE NET BALANCE OF MONETARY LIABILITIES PLUS THE EQUITY SHARE CAPITAL AND RESERVES		£'000
	Net balance of monetary liabilities		456
	Add: Equity share capital and reserves		684
			1,140
(3)	CALCULATE GEARING PROPORTION	£'000	
	Net balance of monetary liabilities	456	
	divided by: Net balance of monetary liabilities plus equity share capital and reserves	1,140	= 40%
(4)	CALCULATE GEARING ADJUSTMENT		£'000
	Depreciation adjustment		70
	Cost of sales adjustment		80
			150
	Multiply by gearing proportion		40%
	Gearing adjustment		60

Example 2

TOTAL MONETARY ASSETS OF THE BUSINESS EXCEED ITS TOTAL LIABILITIES

In this case, the net balance of monetary assets should be calculated as shown in (1) above. The adjustment should be calculated by multiplying the net balance of monetary assets by the percentage change in an appropriate index during the accounting year.

END OF CHAPTER QUESTIONS

1. What different valuation methods could be used in a current value accounting system? Would the use of several of these methods in a set of current value financial statements make them basically different from financial statements prepared under the historical cost method?
2. Which valuation methods were stated to be acceptable in Accounting Research Studies Nos. 1 and 3?
3. Explain the Edwards and Bell contribution to the development of current value accounting. Which features of their system were not adopted by *FASB Statement No. 33*?
4. Discuss the significance of realization in the treatment of holding gains and losses arising from changing prices?
5. Distinguish between: current operating profit, business profit, realized profit, and real business profit.
6. How can the concept of current operating profit be reconciled with net income under historical cost accounting?
7. What is the argument which opposes the inclusion in net income of gains and losses arising out of changing prices?
8. Explain how Revsine justified the use of replacement cost as an accounting valuation method.
9. Define *replacement cost*. Discuss the various methods whereby it can be calculated. Are they capable of producing different results?
10. List the arguments for and against the use of replacement cost for nonmonetary assets.
11. What concept of capital maintenance underlies replacement cost accounting? How do the net monetary working capital position and the firm's leverage affect capital maintenance?
12. Explain the concept of backlog depreciation. How should it be handled in a current value accounting system? Does *FASB Statement No. 33* provide for its disclosure?
13. Analyze critically the current cost provisions of *FASB Statement No. 33* from the viewpoint of a proponent of current value accounting. Answer the question whether following the Statement does in fact measure the current cost of producing revenues for a period at the date of the sale or use of the resources consumed for that purpose?
14. What is the case for including interest as an element of the cost of assets employed, and incorporating it in cost of goods sold as the assets in question become expenses? How would this treatment affect the computation of the increase in an asset due to the effects of changing prices?
15. In what way does replacement value theory differ from current cost accounting as proposed in the English-speaking countries?
16. What are the macroeconomic implications of replacement value accounting? Do the same implications hold for current cost accounting?

17. List the assumptions of replacement value accounting. In what ways do these assumptions resemble those underlying standard costing?
18. How are the so-called holding gains and losses handled in replacement value accounting? What are the implications of this accounting for shareholders?
19. Explain the relationship between replacement cost and replacement price. Why is there confusion among accountants on the meaning of replacement cost? Under what conditions would replacement cost and replacement price be identical?
20. Discuss the reasons for and against accounting in exit prices.
21. Contemporary views on accounting for changing prices present a choice of measurement bases between: historical cost; historical cost/constant dollars; current value; current value/constant dollars. These measurement bases can be presented as a matrix, thus:

	Money dollars	**Constant dollars**
Historical cost	1	2
Current value	3	4

Block 1 of the matrix represents the traditional historical cost basis of measurement.

A. Explain the reasons for using 2, 3, and 4 as measurement bases.

B. Explain the implications of each of these bases for the determination of business income in a period of changing prices. Discuss specifically the problems of the purchasing power gain or loss on monetary assets and liabilities, and the increase (decrease) in the current value of nonmonetary assets, before and after elimination of the inflation effect.

12

THE BALANCE SHEET, OR STATEMENT OF FINANCIAL POSITION

In spite of the primacy of the income statement in modern accounting, we start our examination of the basic financial statements with an investigation of the balance sheet. The balance sheet is the account for the entity as a whole. The values of the resources with which it operates are registered as they enter, and claims against the entity as they are determined to arise. Thereafter, the resources may be consumed, lost, or liquidated, and the claims satisfied or set aside, but accounting begins and ends with the balance sheet. Sprague, in *The Philosophy of Accounts,* referred to it as "the origin and terminus for every account." It must be explicable within the framework of an accounting theory, and it must itself provide a framework for every other account.

The idea that the balance sheet juxtaposes economic resources and economic obligations was examined by Paton more than fifty years ago. Having identified two classes, properties and equities, Paton asked whether assets conformed to the economic concept of properties and found that they did not: economic resources were assets, but not all assets were economic resources.[1] One of the principal examples of assets which are not economic resources is the category of intangibles; Fisher and other economists are quite clear that resources are material objects, which is necessary if the proposition that we can measure changes in them of a marginal nature is to have any validity. The economist's distaste for intangibles is also a response to the fact that their value originates in monopolistic advantages, and this may be a strong influence on accounting for intangibles.

Paton defined equities in legal terms, but this is equally untenable since it explains only legal obligations. The identification of properties and equities as legal concepts has this overriding disadvantage; it requires the accountant to be a lawyer, since questions of title and obligation are among the more complex of life's daily problems. *APB Statement No. 4* defined assets as "economic resources... that are recognized and measured in conformity with generally accepted accounting principles. Assets also include certain deferred charges that are not resources...," and liabilities as "economic obligations...that are recognized and measured in conformity with generally accepted accounting principles...include certain deferred credits that are not obligations." Thus, while appearing to improve on the former *Accounting Terminology Bulletin* definitions of assets and liabilities (debit and credit balances respectively, carried forward upon closing the books as representing property values or rights), *Statement No. 4* left the question in the same obscure state as did Paton.

Statement No. 4 also raised the question which pervades this chapter, by stating that:

> The *financial position* of an enterprise at a particular time comprises its assets, liabilities and owners' equity...plus those contingencies, commitments, and other financial matters...required to be disclosed under generally accepted accounting principles. The financial position of an enterprise is presented in the *balance sheet* and in notes to the financial statements.

BALANCE SHEET OR STATEMENT OF FINANCIAL POSITION?

"I am confident that no group of responsible independent public accountants would delibarately [*sic*] encourage the impression that one of its objectives was to achieve an accurate portrayal of financial position." So wrote Alvin R. Jennings, then president of the AICPA in "Present-Day Challenges in Financial Reporting" (*Journal of Accountancy,* January 1958, p. 33).

"An objective is to provide a statement of financial position useful for predicting, comparing and evaluating enterprise earning power." This was the view of the Accounting Objectives Study Group, (*Objectives of Financial Statements,* New York: AICPA, October 1973).

We shall refer to the financial statement in question as the balance sheet, although the title "Statement of Financial Position" is favored by most textbook writers.[2] The AICPA in its proposed revised form of audit certificate used "balance sheet" and the term appears with increasing frequency in publications of the FASB.

Historically, the balance sheet originated in an attempt to list the resources and obligations of the proprietor of a business. It conformed to the equation

What I own = what I owe + my capital

The double entry equation abstracted from the ownership of capital; the ownership or *proprietary* theory of accounts placed the person of the owner in the definitive position. It was therefore likely that the owner of the business, after closing the nominal accounts to the profit and loss account, would estimate the worth *to him* of the values reflected in the remaining accounts. Differences between book value and worth to him, if recorded, would result in debits and credits to the profit and loss account, the balance of which would be credited to the capital account to close the system.

The *entity* theory, on the other hand, regarded the owner as one of a number of claimants on the resources of the business, and supported the balance sheet equation

$$\text{Assets} = \text{Equities}$$

where equities are any claims capable of being settled in money. In the English common law, such claims had to be pursued in a court of equity, hence the name.

By abstracting completely from the person who owned the business, the entity theory balance sheet was particularly appropriate to the business corporation, whose stockholders were, and still are, often anonymous. Since worth could not be decided upon in the absence of a named individual or small group, the values reflected in the accounts remaining open after the closing of the nominal accounts could not be adjusted. However, the doctrine of *conservatism* developed during the period when the entity theory emerged, to protect shareholders from the effects of failing to retain funds to meet uncertain future losses. Conservatism can be stated in the form: accrue all possible future losses, but only highly probable future gains. Thus, the entity approach to the balance sheet involved recording one class of differences between book value and net realizable value and debiting them to the profit and loss account.

The surprising feature of modern accounting is the survival of the proprietary theory long after it would appear to have outlived its usefulness, except perhaps to sole proprietorships and partnerships. Paton, in the 1922 edition of *Accounting Theory,* wrote:

> As commonly presented in current textbooks and other writings, the theory of accounting is saturated with the "proprietorship" concept.

Paton attempted to base his theory of accounting on the image of a business enterprise in all cases distinct and separate from the personalities of its owners. Thus, in a comparatively recent textbook coauthored with Dixon he wrote:

> The assets are the economic *resources* of the enterprise and the equities represent the *sources* of the funds—and the legal rights—reflected in the total assets.[3]

The view of the balance sheet as a list of valuations was fairly common in corporate financial reports until the 1930s. A few corporations wrote assets up as well as down, and in the boom period of the 1920s used increased net asset totals as a basis for financing. The practice was alleged to have resulted in deceptions, particularly after the boom collapsed; the name of Samuel Insull is associated with its aftermath. Following the stock exchange crash of 1929, many corporations wrote down their assets substantially, and writing-up has never regained respectability in the United States, though it is common enough in other countries.[4]

Fifty years later the proprietary theory reemerged in *APB Statement No. 4.*

> The relationship among assets, liabilities, and owner's equity . . . is:
> Assets − Liabilities = Owners' Equity

In this context it is important to note that Paton used the words "financial condition" to describe what the balance sheet represents, thus emphasizing the static nature of the balance sheet as an image at a point in time, a photograph of the entity at a fictitious full stop. The change to financial position implies a more dynamic view of the balance sheet which has been stated clearly by Chambers.[5] Starting from the economist's concept of the entity as entrepreneur, designated "the actor," Chambers defined his role as that of taking decisions in markets, and the purpose of accounting to provide him with information to assist him to take those decisions. From this it follows, bearing in mind the fact that credit and inventory situations have no place in the economic model of the firm (which abstracts completely from time and the institutional framework), that the entrepreneur needs to know his cash position, and financial position becomes the amount of cash which the assets of the business would produce on the day of the balance sheet if liquidated in an orderly fashion.

Although the image of the firm as cash box permeates the accounting literature and underlies many contributions to accounting theory it is clearly inadequate to serve a positive theory of accounting and cannot be recommended for the construction of a normative theory because it obviously concerns a subsystem of the firm and omits many important aspects of the total system which accrual accounting embraces.

OTHER DYNAMIC CONCEPTS OF FINANCIAL POSITION

We have drawn attention to the proposition that the balance sheet may be viewed as a statement of sources and uses of funds. Paton admitted this view in *Accounting Theory,* as an explanation for the equality of assets and equities: "The balance sheet presents a statement of all the property items at a given moment, and shows the concurrent distribution of ownership in the same" (p. 20). This has been referred to as the *static funds statement view*[6] and does not require Paton's additional assumption, that capital and liabilities are equities in the assets of the business. Goldberg, rejecting the proprietary and entity theories, proposed a new "commander" theory in which the balance sheet becomes a statement of the resources available to the managers of the business and of the sources from which they have been derived.[7] The idea is seductive and appears at first sight to possess the potential of explaining the balance sheet in its modern form, with various deferrals and accruals which can hardly be called properties or obligations in any meaningful sense of the words.

The problem remains, however, that only the first balance sheet of the entity—what we call the *opening* balance sheet—depicts sources and uses of funds; even for this proposition we must assume that the meaning of "funds" is clear, which is not the case. Thereafter the flow of funds through the business is divided into two streams—a revenue stream which is represented by the income statement, and a capital stream, which is represented by the balance sheet. In order to depict sources and uses of funds we require a quite separate model, now called a statement of changes in financial position, which is clearly the image of something quite different from whatever reality the balance sheet depicts.

Another dynamic view of financial position is that which sees the balance sheet as "a step between two income statements" in Hendriksen's picturesque phrase, or as the "sheet of balances," a list of leftovers. This was the view taken in *Accounting Terminology Bulletin No. 1.* We start with a quantity of data which register movements of values during a given period. From these data is extracted the part which is used for constructing the income statement, and what is left is utilized for constructing the balance sheet. Because of the double-entry accounting system, these leftovers are in the form of debit and credit balances; the debit balances are assets and the credit, equities.

Obviously, this explanation falls to the ground if we accept the proposition with which we started, namely, that the balance sheet is the alpha, or point of departure, of the accounting process.

The view of the balance sheet as a sheet of balances has been ascribed to the introduction of the matching principle, which will be discussed in chapter 14. If the primary purpose of accounting is the determination of net income (a proposition which has almost universal acceptance among accounting theorists) and net income is determined by matching against revenues the costs incurred to achieve those revenues, some relationships represented in a system of accounts will be excluded from the income determination process: receivables and payables, capital provided by stockholders, and revenues and costs of future periods, "in suspense" at the date of the balance sheet.

This is known as *period matching* and involves the definition of costs (equals expenses) as the value of resources consumed during a given period, and of revenues as the value of resources produced and exteriorized during a given period. We now start with the same concept of a quantity of data which registers the movement of values during a given period, and divide these data into two categories: values which have disappeared during the period through consumption (use) or loss, and values which have survived and will therefore affect future periods. It is a commonplace of accounting instruction to explain that revenues and expenses are period concepts; assets and liabilities are not. This explanation is not invalidated by the concept of the balance sheet as the point of departure for accounting, since a point has no time dimension.

This concept of the balance sheet is operational but does not help us to identify what goes into the balance sheet, only what goes out of it. If we could do the former we would be able to verify the claim that the residual type of balance sheet provides for the accountability of dollars invested, summarizes the structure of the entity, and prevents distortions from arising through the use of subjective valuations.

Finally, we may refer to the cash concept of financial position as the narrow meaning of the phrase. This is the view to which Canning first gave expression, that "accountants would like to mean by 'financial position' a position declared by direct positive measures of funds to be provided by enterprise operations."[8] This may be called *economic capital* and relates to what we have described as *economic income;* it has been an equally fertile source of ideas for accounting writers, even though it has had no noticeable effect on accounting practice. It belongs to the normative part of accounting theory.

One recent example of such influence, which may indicate the direction in which accounting practice will move, is seen in the Trueblood Report's seventh objective, to provide "a statement of financial position useful for predicting, comparing and evaluating enterprise earning power." From the preceding objectives we learned that earning power is essentially cash generation. Chapter 5 of the Trueblood report went on to assert that "this statement should provide information [about] uncompleted earnings cycles" and again, "Assets and liabilities should be grouped or segregated by the relative uncertainty of the amount and timing of prospective realization or liquidation."

Not only does this formulation restrict accounting to the liquidity cycle (Marx's *Geld—Ware—Geld*), but it suggests further the possibility of introducing into the balance sheet subjective goodwill as an item of great uncertainty as to amount and timing. The SEC's attempt to utilize economic accounting concepts in the form of Reserve Recognition Accounting was abandoned in 1981 (insofar as its use for primary financial statements was concerned) after experience of its application to oil and gas producing assets showed its limitations. However, the SEC remains committed to the view that "value-based" disclosures of oil and gas reserves is important supplementary information.

WHAT ARE ASSETS?

We can no longer postpone the task which we set ourselves early on in this book: a definition of assets is required, or at the very least, a definitive description. Assets are not only economic resources, or property, or "things of value owned by the firm," nor are they simply debit balances left over after closing the books, or expected future cash receipts. The FASB has addressed this issue in its *Statement of Financial Accounting Concepts No. 3,* which will be analyzed later in this chapter.

It is analytically useful for some purposes to regard assets as quantities multiplied by prices, to view assets as bundles of service potential. For our present purposes, however, this will not do; accounting is concerned, in the first instance, with *values,* defined as representations in money of objects described in words. As Paton stated, "Once it is recognized which assets have been increased and which have decreased, the entries follow almost as a matter of course."

We shall start with Paton's proposition that "any element, material or otherwise, for which the owners freely invest their funds, gives rise, at the outset, to an asset value."[9] For element we substitute object; the word "freely" is redundant, and we must interpret the words "invest" and "funds." We define investment as the allocation of scarce resources to a production objective; thus financial investment, a subclass, is the allocation of money for the production of a money return. Economics deals with saving and financial investment, which is why this theory proves inadequate as an explanation of accounting, although accounting may include financial investment and to that extent admit economic reasoning into its theory.

To define scarce resources brings us face to face with the central problem of economic theory, and one which has historically been obscured by the "veil of money." In practice, economics as a science of resource allocation is restricted to those resources which can be represented by prices; hence the technical apparatus of economics is a theory of relative prices. We share the problem, which is now empirical and not theoretical. To understand the nature of those scarce resources which are included by business entities under the term "assets," we may begin by noting the different ways in which assets may be recognized.

1. By purchase—perhaps the most common case, if we include barter.
2. By gift—not so common but, in these days of government largesse, not all that uncommon.
3. By discovery—if an employee of a store should find an envelope containing $100.00 after the last customer has left, we would expect the manager to require the registration of this occurrence, albeit with an identical liability to some unknown creditor. Accounting for the discovery of natural resources is not unknown.
4. By agreement—for example, when two partners admit a third and all three agree that goodwill should be recorded.
5. By production or the combination of factors of production—a process known as *transformation,* conversion, or adding value.

6. By sale—a credit sale causes the recognition of the new asset, "account receivable," as well as the extinction of the old one, "inventory." A cash sale triggers the recognition of the asset cash.
7. By barter, loan, bailment, consignment, or any other of the thousands of commercial transactions recognized by law or custom.

What can we say about the characteristics of objects capable of recognition in so many different ways within the context of the definition of investment provided above? Canning saw "any future service in money or any future service convertible into money (except those services arising from contracts the two sides of which are proportionately unperformed) the beneficial interest in which is legally or equitably secured to some person or set of persons."[10] Bearing in mind that an asset is a representation of such services and not the services themselves, we may ask the question, By what means are such services, not in present or future money, capable of representation in money? The answer, or an acceptable answer, is because someone will pay for them, which means that an asset (not being present or future money) can be identified as something potentially chargeable to another person or entity.

This asset concept undoubtedly underlies the view of the balance sheet as a basis for prediction, and the "uncompleted earnings cycle" idea which the Trueblood Report attempted to explain in connection with the proposition that the balance sheet should demonstrate the relative uncertainty of an asset's conversion into cash. In this model, assets are cash equivalents and could be grouped in respect of their expected values; for example, components of inventory might be found in several places in the balance sheet rather than in one item, depending upon the probability that a particular good would produce a specified amount. We have discussed this view at length in earlier chapters and concluded that it is too restrictive to base accounting theory on cash flow models. In the present context, it is not necessary to postulate cash receipts in order to assert that a value is chargeable to another entity.

It may be observed that this definition of asset does not render the term inappropriate for use in the balance sheets of nonbusiness entities, such as households, governments, charities, and, indeed, the accounts of the nation. Failure to understand the concept underlies many of the controversies in the area of accounting for not-for-profit organizations, including the debates about what shall be capitalized and whether depreciation should be charged as an expense. The latter problem is clarified by the observation that, if a taxpayer has paid for an item, the government unit acquiring it should not be encouraged to charge him again. Only when governments and other not-for-profit entities adopt business methods of financing (which is not an outlandish suggestion, and indeed, is being advocated by a number of respected public finance theorists) will government balance sheets appropriately contain assets in the business sense. For this type of situation it is sufficient to define assets as properties and view the primary purpose of the balance sheet as one of memorandum, serving the stewardship function.

The French and other more ancient cultures have solved this problem neatly by using the neutral terms *actif* (German: *Aktiva*) and *passif* (German: *Passiva*) for the two sides of the balance sheet. We might consider moving to similarly neutral terms, such as positive and negative, or do as the British have done and speak about "employment of funds" and "funds employed."

THE MEANING OF LIABILITIES

The ordinary meaning of liability as a debt or obligation is clearly inapplicable to the use of this word in accounting. Kohler included owners' equity in his definition,[11] and the old AICPA definition, although otherwise of a rare obscurity, nevertheless is clear on this point.

> Something represented by a credit balance that is or would be properly carried forward upon a closing... provided such credit balance is not in effect a negative balance applicable to an asset. Thus the word is used broadly to comprise not only items which constitute liabilities in the popular sense of debts or obligations....[12]

Not only is there a problem in deciding whether net worth is included in the concept "liabilities," but a further problem arises in determining the meaning of liability when only items other than net worth are considered. Perhaps the clearest example of this is found in the category known as *deferred credits,* including such items as deferred taxation and differences arising on consolidation. The definition offered by Sprouse and Moonitz ("*Liabilities* are obligations to convey assets or perform services, obligations resulting from past or current transactions and requiring settlement in the future.") referring only to "obligations," gives no indication of either problem.[13] And Ijiri's view, following Hatfield, that liabilities are negative assets, is of little help.[14]

Under the proprietary theory, liabilities were believed to represent debts owed by the owner or owners of a business; under the entity theory, the owner or owners are outside the firm, like its creditors; thus the transition from a proprietary theory of accounting to an entity theory is often invoked as an explanation for the contemporary inclusion of net worth under this heading. As a consequence, the American Accounting Association Committee on Accounting and Reporting Standards for Corporate Financial Statements recommended the substitution of the word "equities" in its 1957 Statement.[15]

If the credit balances appearing in a balance sheet represented sources of funds, then the word "liabilities" could be interpreted as a contemporary accounting synonym for *capital*. This would correspond with a view of the balance sheet as a statement of sources and applications of funds, which we have already examined and found wanting. In the fund theory, equities are defined as restrictions on the assets of the fund, which is the concept of capital used by some economic theorists, as a set of restrictions on production and distribution. Although this may explain the concept of liabilities used in government accounting and other applications of fund accounting, where the restrictions may be specified by law or the terms of a deed or gift, it does not lead to enlightenment in the more unstructured field of business; hence Vatter concluded that "[restrictions] may arise from legal, equitable, economic or even managerial considerations."[16]

FASB STATEMENT OF FINANCIAL ACCOUNTING CONCEPTS NO. 3, "ELEMENTS OF FINANCIAL STATEMENTS OF BUSINESS ENTERPRISES"

An FASB Concepts Statement dated December 1980 attempted to move closer to solving the problem by directing attention away from the position statement itself and focusing on the three "elements": assets, liabilities, and equity (= proprietor interest). In a note, the FASB pointed out that these elements could be called "financial position," but need not imply a particular financial statement. Only after establishing definitions, recognition criteria (attributes), and rules for display (presentation) could we describe adequately a statement of financial position, or balance sheet. Thus, the FASB definitions were a first screen on the way toward the financial statements.

Assets were defined as "probable future economic benefits obtained or controlled by a particular entity as a result of past transactions or events." This definition embraced three characteristics: (1) probable future benefit, (2) an entity which has a right to the benefit, and the power to exclude others from all or part thereof, and (3) a transaction or event [or circumstance?] which has already occurred. Other characteristics, such as cost, tangibility, exchangeability, and legal enforceability were not essential to the definition. Future economic benefit was synonymous with "service potential," which eventually results in net cash inflows to the enterprise. Once acquired, these benefits continue until collected, transferred to another entity, used, or lost through some other event or circumstance.

This definition poses certain problems.

1. Asset is a name given to the representation of an object. The FASB Exposure Draft (ED) *Objectives of Financial Reporting and Elements of Financial Statements of Business Enterprises* (December 29, 1977) attempted to distinguish between the

representation and the object by giving them different names. Criticism of this practice by respondents to the ED caused the FASB to revert to the customary English-language usage of the same name for both (for example, *inventory*), although this may be one source of confusion in this area.

2. Given the above characteristics, it is more accurate to define an asset as a *right* to a future economic benefit, rather than the benefit itself, and the element of an account rather than of a financial statement.
3. Destroying the property nexus leads to problems, similar to those which present themselves more strongly under the heading of liabilities, of determining what kind of rights to include under this heading, and what kind to leave out.
4. Even with a legal title to the benefit, the concept remains unclear. Consider the case of a legal proprietary interest in a mineral concession located in a foreign country. Such a concession may well be held at the pleasure of the host government, with the consequence that the owner cannot exclude others from the benefit.
5. "Benefit" is an unfortunate choice, given the difficulty of quantifying the term. The FASB has definitely not restricted it to the present value of future cash inflows; that would admit only cash, receivables, and possibly merchandise inventories. Nor has the FASB obviously eliminated those items currently accounted for as assets, in respect of which the benefits are quantifiable only as cost savings or cash received upon an unlikely liquidation. Paras. 101-102 of the Statement makes this point quite clear; most of the assets and liabilities we are accustomed to see in balance sheets will continue to qualify.
6. Another difficulty is encountered in paras. 19 and 26 of the Concepts Statement. In para. 19 an asset is a benefit "obtained or controlled" by the entity, and in para. 26 it ceases to be an asset when "collected." But if a benefit has been collected, surely it has been obtained?
7. Para. 27 of the Concepts Statement asserts that valuation accounts, such as the allowance for uncollectible receivables and a premium on a bond receivable, are part of the related asset. Although not explicitly stated, this category must include the valuation allowance on marketable equity securities and also accumulated depreciation. Does it also include a foreign currency translation difference which has been deferred instead of flowing through to the income statement? And is this a problem of measurement and not of definition?

Liabilities were defined as "probable future sacrifices of economic benefits arising from present obligations of a particular entity to transfer assets or provide services to other entities in the future as a result of past transactions or events." This definition embraced three characteristics: (1) a present duty or responsibility to one or more other entities requiring transfer or use of assets at a specified or determinable date, on occurrence of a specified event, or on demand; (2) an obligation, leaving little or no discretion to avoid the transfer or use; and (3) a transaction or other event which has already occurred. Payment in cash and legal liability are not essential to this definition, nor need the identity of the claimant be known.

Obligations originated in different ways: under contract or other agreement; by imposition by government; by voluntary acceptance or administrative action. Some obligations were purely moral or ethical. Once incurred, a liability continued as such until settled, otherwise discharged, or the entity's responsibility removed. Valuation accounts, such as bond premium or discount, were a part of the related liability.

Admitting such a wide spectrum of claims into the category "liability" has always proved troublesome. Earlier we pointed out the possibility of including stockholders' equity under this heading. Many ethical or moral obligations are systematically excluded from liabilities in corporate balance sheets, for example, customary severance pay (as distinct from a contractual obligation) and unfunded obligations of pension schemes.[17] The problem of uncertainty compounds these difficulties, as *FASB Statement No. 5,* "Accounting for Contingencies," indicates.[18]

In that Statement, the FASB made recognition of a liability affected by a contingency dependent on two criteria: it must arise out of a transaction or event which has already occurred, and the amount of the obligation must be determinable. It suffices, therefore, in order to avoid accounting for such loss contingencies by debiting the income statement and crediting a liability account, for the manager of the entity to assert that the amount cannot be reasonably determined.

The Concepts Statement contains a lengthy digression on uncertainty, which acknowledges the difficulties inherent in applying the definition, because it requires assessments of probabilities, when degrees of probability belong to the subject of recognition and measurement, and not of definition.

More difficult to understand is para. 42 of the Concepts Statement. It appears that this paragraph deals with the case of an asset or liability which conforms with the definition, but is not recorded and reported as such because of a recognition (measurement, attribute) difficulty. If the asset or liability in question has not been recognized, and yet a loss of future economic benefits, arising out of something which has already happened, is highly probable, some other accounting principle may require the loss to be recognized in determining income. In this case, the paragraph asserts, a valuation allowance should be established. By defining a valuation allowance as a part of the related asset or liability, however, the FASB necessarily assumes that an asset or liability has been recognized in this situation. However, a contractual agreement by a corporation to sell its unissued shares at a price below market, contingent upon an event which is virtually inevitable, would not be recorded or reported as an asset or a liability, nor would the loss be recognized in any way.

These problems aside, the FASB definition of liabilities does not raise new issues in the way the definition of assets does, especially if paraphrased to read as follows:

> A liability is any acknowledged obligation to transfer assets, perform services, or incur other liabilities in the future, which is established as existing at a particular point in time.

Equity was defined as a unitary construct, even though the Concepts Statement noted that different kinds of rights were embraced by the word. Equity was "the residual interest in the assets of an entity that remains after deducting its liabilities. In a business enterprise the equity is the ownership interest." Equity was the same as net assets, or assets minus liabilities, and was "enhanced or burdened" by increases and decreases in net assets from sources other than investments by owners and distributions to owners.

Whereas the definitions of assets and liabilities were merely problematical, the definition of equity is clearly incorrect. Only in the case of a sole proprietorship or partnership can the ownership interest in the enterprise be said to be an ownership interest in the assets of the enterprise. Stockholders of a corporation are part-owners of the corporation, not its assets. To assert otherwise is to lose sight of the fact that a corporation owns 100% of its assets, a fact which is the single most important aspect of corporate finance.

Moreover, to describe equity in terms of the arithmetical consequences of double-entry accounting is not to define it. In a closed system consisting of a balanced set of three elements, any change in one of the elements unaccompanied by an equal change in a second will necessarily affect the third. This tells us nothing about that third element, or the reasons for the change, yet it is referred to as the *distinguishing characteristic* of equity.

This observation leads to the basic weakness of the FASB's approach to explaining financial statements. It has been noted that a transaction, event, or circumstance may be an asset, under this approach, yet not appear in a financial statement because of recognition or display considerations. But the point of departure, as the title of the Concepts Statement made clear, was to explain assets, liabilities, and equity *which are balance sheet items*. How something could be a balance sheet item and yet not appear in a balance sheet is beyond comprehension.

It is clear that the FASB has proved unwilling or unable to advance beyond the point reached by the APB in its *Statement No. 4*. It will be recalled that that Statement adopted a proprietary equation, represented by: economic resources minus economic obligations equals residual interest. Substitution of the words asset, liability, and equity does nothing to enlighten us about what lies behind the concepts used by *APB Statement No. 4.* Again, it is surprising to see the proprietary theory of the balance sheet surviving long after the conditions which might have justified it have disappeared. Is this further evidence of the difficulty experienced by those trained in economics, in distinguishing between capital and assets? This distinction depends upon explicit recognition of the institutional framework of our society, a recognition which can also lead to acceptance of the proposition that a not-for-profit entity can have a capital, and even an equity element in its balance sheet.

INVESTMENTS BY AND DISTRIBUTIONS TO OWNERS

The Concepts Statement attempted to distinguish between two classes of transactions, events, and circumstances, depending upon whether or not equity was affected. (See Figure 8-1.) Changes in equity were then further divided into three classes: comprehensive income, changes in equity from transfers between the enterprise and its owners, and changes within equity. Comprehensive income (see chapter 13) was defined as the change in equity from nonowner sources, and could presumably also include changes within equity if they result in an increase of net assets, for example, gain on sale of Treasury stock. Hence the need to define the change in equity from nonowner sources.

Investments by owners (or capital contributions) were defined as increases of net assets resulting from transfers to an enterprise from other entities of something valuable, to obtain or increase ownership interests (or equity) in it. *Distributions to owners* (or capital distributions or dividends) were defined as decreases in net assets of a particular enterprise resulting from transferring assets, rendering services, or incurring liabilities by the enterprise to owners. Distributions by an enterprise to its owners decrease its net assets and decrease or terminate ownership interests of those that receive them. Reacquisition by an entity of its own equity securities by transferring assets or incurring liabilities to owners is a distribution to owners as that concept is defined in the Statement. It follows, that the purchase of treasury stock is a distribution to owners (dividend), and the sale of treasury stock is an investment by owners (contribution). A difference between the purchase and selling price of treasury stock, therefore, cannot be a gain and cannot enter into the determination of comprehensive income. Yet we speak of a "gain (or loss) on sale of treasury stock."

The difficulties posed by the definitions of *Statement of Financial Accounting Concepts No. 3* suggest that they should be regarded as tentative and not definitive. We are therefore encouraged to continue our search for these elusive concepts. One of the sources of the difficulties encountered is the frequent use of the phrase "net assets," a phrase which itself requires definition if it is to be meaningful.

THE SOCIAL CONSOLIDATION MODEL

It may be helpful, in attempting to construct an accounting theory which will explain the balance sheet and its elements, to refer to the idea of a social consolidation of accounts.

The accounts of the nation, comprising principally the national income, flow of funds, and balance of payments accounts prepared regularly by governments, are the products of economic statistics and not of accounting. That is to say, although these data are called "national income accounting" their production is based on statistical method and only the form is that of the account. However, it would be possible to approach this task, of representing the macroeconomic aggregates required by government officials, using accounting methodology; several writers have explained how this might be done.[19]

Basically, these writers propose the application to the problem of the techniques and methods of consolidations, sometimes called "accounting for business combinations." The accounts of individual enterprises (and other entities) would be combined to produce a consolidated account for the business sector, and consolidated accounts for the household and government sectors would be similarly prepared. The final consolidation would combine these sectorial consolidations into one super-consolidation for the nation as a whole. Those who have a taste for the grandiose may care to speculate on the extension of this process to provide a global consolidation for the entire world.

This potential social consolidation of accounts, while it does not exist, can provide a mental construct or framework within which we can comprehend the meaning of assets and liabilities, as well as proprietors' equity. Transactions between social entities result in the recognition of social values, called assets if they are capable of representation in money (recognition). Because of relationships between entities, these assets do not exist in any objective sense; they are subjective evaluations of reality made objective by interpersonal agreement. Liabilities are the assets of other entities than the one subject to these obligations, that is, liabilities can be regarded as appearing in the accounts of another entity as money, future money, or something else chargeable to the entity for which we are attempting to account. To determine liabilities, then, it is necessary to examine the environment for evidence of this type of claim; the gradual extension of liabilities to embrace long-term liabilities for taxes, amounts committed under certain kinds of leases, and pension obligations of a nonlegally binding nature illustrate this process.

The usefulness of the potential social consolidation model does not stop here. It also suggests the existence of obligations not represented by assets of another entity (and which would therefore be eliminated on consolidation), which may be viewed as obligations of society in general and which would appear in a comprehensive national balance sheet. Many of the accruals which are found among the liabilities of contemporary business firms are obligations of this kind. They include various kinds of provision for repairs, redecoration, warranties, and even the contingencies which failed to impress the FASB for self-insurance and other forms of equitable obligation arising out of prudent business conduct.

CHARACTERISTICS OF LIABILITIES

In the contemporary use of the term, liabilities include the following:

1. Debts and obligations, not restricted to legal obligations.
2. Estimates of future debts and obligations arising out of past transactions and events.
3. Adjustments to the amounts of debts and obligations required to apportion interest expense over the periods during which they will be outstanding.
4. Adjustments to the estimated future liability for taxes required to apportion taxation expense over the periods for which taxes are due.
5. Whether the gain represented by a credit difference arising on consolidation is contributed (like a donation) or earned (to be passed through the income statement) is an interesting question.

A *contingent* liability is not a part of this group of constructs; an *estimated* liability is. A contingent liability is a debt or obligation which may arise out of a past transaction or event, depending upon the occurrence of some future event which is either (1) improbable, or (2) accompanied by a corresponding new asset, such as a claim against a third party. An example of the former is a pending lawsuit claiming damages against the firm, which is being contested and the firm's lawyers confidently predict victory. An example of the latter is the existence of an investment in partly paid shares of stock in another company; if the unpaid capital is called, the liability will be equal to an addition to total assets.

FASB Statement No. 5, "Accounting for Contingencies," provided a test of our understanding of these concepts. The Statement restricts accrual of a liability (by recognizing an expense) to contingencies displaying two characteristics: (1) it is probable that, on the date of the financial statements, an asset has been impaired or a liability incurred, and (2) the amount of the loss can be reasonably estimated. However, the first of these is obscure, and the second, contentious.

Obviously, an impairment of an asset can be determined without necessarily recognizing a liability, but how can a loss accrual in the form of a liability be distinct from the liability itself? The accrual of warranty obligations which the Statement admitted is, in fact, a poor example of a contingency; the uncertainty lies in respect of the claimant, not the claim. A better example of the difficulty is provided by the so-called loss reserves of casualty insurers.

At any date a casualty insurance company may establish the probability of three classes of claims.

1. Damage has occurred and the insured has notified the company of a claim.
2. Damage has occurred and the insured has not yet notified the company of a claim, but can be expected to do so in the future.
3. Damage has not yet occurred, but there is a virtual 100% probability that it will, and that the company will be liable for damage caused because of the terms of its contract with the assured. An example would be hurricane insurance in Florida; it is virtually certain that a hurricane will occur, and cause severe damage, but it is not predictable.

The FASB Statement admitted the first two categories as loss contingencies which could be accrued as liabilities, but rejected the third on the grounds that a transaction or other event had not occurred at the date of the financial statements. Casualty insurers had, prior to the promulgation of this Statement, taken the view that acceptance of a liability should relate to the entire period of insurance coverage and not just to the year in which the casualty occurred. Thus, the practice in the industry was to accrue a liability by pro rata charges against income, so that hopefully the liability account would be big enough to cover most of the damage claims when they were finally received. The "transaction or other event" recognized by the insurers was acceptance of a contractual obligation vis-a-vis the insured property; the "transaction or other event" recognized by the FASB was the casualty loss.

The contentious nature of the Statement arises out of the fact that a liability is only recognized if the amount thereof can be reasonably estimated. In *FASB Interpretation No. 14,* "Reasonable Estimation of the Amount of a Loss," this proposition was examined more closely. If a single amount of loss cannot be estimated, but a range of likely amounts is known, two situations are distinguished. If one of the amounts in the range is more probable than any of the others, that amount should be accrued. If no amount is more probable than any other, the lowest estimate should be accrued. Besides contravening the rule of conservatism which is so often invoked in other contexts, this result can only lead to disputes between managers and accountants and to the omission of liabilities due to failure to agree on an amount.

CONTRACTUAL RIGHTS AND OBLIGATIONS

In a Research Report entitled *Recognition of Contractual Rights and Obligations*, published by the FASB in December 1980, Yuji Ijiri examined the problem of recognizing rights and obligations as assets and liabilities arising out of legally enforceable contracts. The following recognition points were identified:

1. The date the contract was signed.
2. The date the object of the contract was procured.
3. The date the object was ready for use.
4. The date the object was segregated for use of the other party.
5. The date the object was delivered.
6. The date of any advance payment, if one was made.
7. A construction progress point } In the case of long-term
8. A start of construction point } construction contracts

The criteria proposed for determination of the issue were—

- Conformity with the FASB definitions of asset and liability;
- Firmness of the commitment, that is, likelihood that its performance cannot be avoided;
- Decision usefulness, within the constraint of cost.

Nevertheless, some of the possible recognition points are ambiguous; for example, what if a contract is signed on one date, but purports to take effect on a different one? Further, the law of contract is particularly complex, and in some parts indeterminate; it would be impossible for an accountant to resolve asset and liability questions on the basis of the law. Thus, recognition of assets and liabilities remains a matter of managerial judgment or customs accepted by the entity. One of these customs could be an FASB statement requiring recognition at a particular point.

BALANCE SHEET STRUCTURE: DISPLAY CONSIDERATIONS

We have defined assets as investments and liabilities in terms which can include owners' equity, thus facilitating the explanation of accounting in terms of the basic equation of finance—

$$\text{Investment} = \text{Finance}$$

It follows that the balance sheet should provide information useful for financing decisions, that is, for determining the amount and form of finance required by investment. This is not the same question as that posed in comparative statics: given a quantity of resources, how shall it be optimally allocated?[20] Several viewpoints may be identified: proprietors, short- and long-term financiers, supply creditors, managers, financial analysts. The question arises whether there is one view of financial structure which can satisfy all their requirements?

As it happens, there appear to be a number of possibilities:

1. The unclassified balance sheet.
   a. Assets in order of decreasing liquidity, liabilities in the order in which they will be liquidated.
   b. The reverse order.
2. The classified balance sheet.
   a. Dual classification:
      fixed assets + current assets = long-term capital + current liabilities
   b. Triple classification:
      fixed assets + working capital = long-term capital
   c. A variety of other classification schemes is encountered in practice.

In each of these three forms the balance sheet may present the classes of assets and liabilities in a variety of sequences.

The choice between these alternatives seems to be a result of historical necessity rather than logic. In the United States, for example, the banks were the principal users of financial statements during the formative period and the emphasis of the balance sheet is still on liquidity; the first item in the balance sheet of General Motors is cash, which is more trivial than any other figure. However, utilities use the reverse order. In the United Kingdom, on the other hand, where the Companies Acts have been most influential, the emphasis is on stockholders' equity; in the traditional double-sided presentation this is the first item in the balance sheet, and the contemporary tabular form generally highlights stockholders' funds.

Since a variety of classifications could also be used to demonstrate financial structure—solvency, liquidity, relative uncertainty, method of valuation—the question necessarily arises whether one of these can be preferred for general purpose financial statements.

To answer this question we may refer to the model illustrated in Table 2-2 in Chapter 2.

WORKING CAPITAL	LONG-TERM DEBT
FIXED ASSETS	OWNERS' EQUITY

FIGURE 12-1

We can explain this construction in terms of investment and finance. To perform its economic function of producing goods and services, the enterprise must create a certain capacity and also provide funds for its activity in utilizing this capacity. At any point in time, capacity is a constant, and funds for activity, or current assets, will vary depending upon the immediate past and expected future level of activity. Finance must be provided from long-term sources for both long-term investment (in capacity) and for short-term investment (in activity) to the extent that the latter cannot be acquired with variable sources of finance. This amount constitutes the working capital requirement, defined in accounting as the excess of current assets over current liabilities.

The financial function is to provide the funds to make these investments, that is, capital, minimizing the cost of capital. This involves stratifying the assets in terms of risk as well as maturity, so that another model of the balance sheet might look like the one in Figure 12-2.

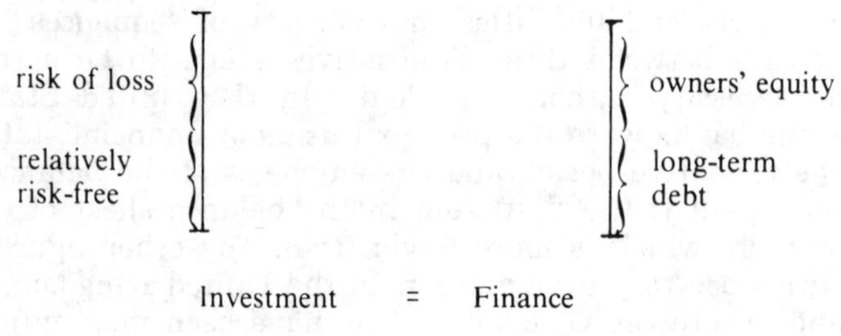

FIGURE 12-2

Measures of risk are not given in financial statements, and financial analysts are forced to use surrogates. One of these is a measure of the variability of the price of a company's stock relative to the variability of stock market prices in general (the *beta factor*). This can only be related to balance sheet investment risk on the assumption that the market has perfect knowledge, an assumption which is made by supporters of the *efficient market* hypothesis.

Another surrogate is the use of ratios—relationships between balance sheet items in terms of quantity; among the structure ratios most used by financial analysts are—

- Liquid ratio (liquid assets/current liabilities).
- Current ratio (current assets/current liabilities).
- Debt ratio (total debt/total assets).
- Debt/equity ratio (long-term debt/stockholders, equity).
- Fixed asset ratio (net fixed assets/total assets).

Having calculated these ratios, can analysts use them for the measurement of risk? Recent research indicates that they can. Several studies have affirmed the usefulness of ratio analysis as a predictor of business failure,[21] the pioneer work on this having been done by James O. Horrigan.[22] Other studies examining the proposition that financial reports contain "new information" have used financial ratios with some success.[23]

On the other hand, the classification of balance sheets into monetary and nonmonetary items, defining monetary in terms of probability of becoming or utilizing cash, has not been demonstrated to be useful. This is, of course, a different concept of monetary than the one used in constant dollar level accounting.

The calculation of financial ratios is affected by the existence of *off-balance sheet financing,* that is, sources of funds which are not recognized as liabilities. To the extent that an enterprise is able to make investments without incurring balance sheet liabilities, its debt situation is unclear. Many of these situations involve executory contracts, that is, agreements involving performance in the future. Until recently it was understood that executory contracts were not accounted for until at least one party had performed its obligation under the agreement, in part if not in whole.

FASB Statement No. 13, "Accounting for Leases," required a liability (and a corresponding asset) to be recorded and reported for a class of leases called *capital leases.* A lease is a good example of an executory contract; the lessor promises possession and use of the leased property for a future period, and the lessee promises to pay rent in the future. If a lease agreement is in substance a purchase, however, then *FASB Statement No. 13* requires both parties to reflect this fact in their financial statements. For such situations, what was off-balance sheet financing is put on the balance sheet, and the liability enters into the computation of the debt ratio and other ratios.

A number of other types of agreement which result in off-balance sheet financing have not yet been dealt with by the FASB; they include various types of guarantees, project financing arrangements, and conditional sales of assets. It can be anticipated with some confidence that the category "liabilities" will expand in the years to come as rules for recognizing this type of obligation as liabilities are agreed.

CONCLUSION

With all its faults, the modern balance sheet corresponds to the image of the firm presented in Table 2-3 in Chapter 2. Since we are dealing with concepts and not percepts, the only way in which we can validate this image is by interpersonal testing: that is, by finding out whether it is recognized and accepted by a majority of those to whom it is presented. Obviously, the subjects must be familiar with the real thing; it will not help to test the image with philosophers, artists, or economists unless they are also businessmen, managers of enterprises, or investors.

Recent research has established that three categories of user of financial statements—individual investors, institutional investors, and financial analysts—rate this kind of information as their most important source in arriving at buy and hold/sell decisions with regard to investments in common stocks. Of the financial statements, the income statement was rated most important, but the balance sheet was rated almost equally important by the majority of respondents to the survey. The individual investor group was found to be very heterogeneous, but a subgroup which resembled the institutional investors and financial analysts in terms of occupation and education also resembled them in the importance which they placed upon financial statements generally, and the balance sheet in particular.[24] These findings suggest a high degree of consumer satisfaction with the practical responses to the definition of asset, liability, and owners' equity which accountants have produced.

ENDNOTES

1. Paton, W.A., *Accounting Theory* (1922), Lawrence, Kansas: Scholars Book Co., 1973, p. 37.
2. Of the 600 companies surveyed in *Accounting Trends and Techniques,* (New York: AICPA annual publication) a total of 577 used the title "Balance Sheet" in 1946, which declined to 470 in 1965; however the number rose to 537 in 1975, and continues to increase.
3. Paton, William A., and Robert L. Dixon, *Essentials of Accounting,* New York: McMillan & Company, 1958, p. 35.
4. In *Accounting Theory* Paton wrote, "Cost gives true value for purposes of initial statement" but that subsequent evidence of value changes should be recognized. This kind of value change appears to have been used sparingly, contradicting the conventional wisdom, which holds that it was a real abuse during the 1920s. See Dillon, J., Gadis "Corporate Asset Revaluations: 1925-34," *The Accounting Historian's Journal*, Spring 1979, pp. 1-15.
5. Chambers, Raymond J., *Accounting, Evaluation and Economic Behavior,* Englewood Cliffs, N.J.: Prentice-Hall Inc., 1966, Ch. 1.
6. Sprouse, Robert T., "The Balance Sheet—Embodiment of the Most Fundamental Elements of Accounting Theory," in *Foundations of Accounting Theory,* University of Florida Press, 1971, pp. 90-104.
7. Goldberg, Louis, *An Inquiry into the Nature of Accounting,* Monograph No. 7, American Accounting Association, 1965.
8. Canning, John B., *The Economics of Accountancy,* New York: The Ronald Press Co., 1929, p. 191.
9. Paton, op. cit. p. 123.
10. Canning, op. cit. p. 22.
11. *A Dictionary for Accountants,* p. 263.
12. *Accounting Terminology Bulletin No. 1.*
13. Sprouse, Robert T., and Maurice Moonitz, "A Tentative Set of Broad Accounting Principles for Business Enterprise," *Accounting Research Study No. 3,* New York: AICPA 1962, p. 37.
14. Ijiri, Yuji, *The Foundations of Accounting Measurement,* Englewood Cliffs, New Jersey: Prentice-Hall, Inc., 1967.
15. AAA Committee on Accounting Concepts and Standards, *Accounting and Reporting Standards for Corporate Financial Statements and Supplements,* Columbus, Ohio, 1967, p. 7.
16. Vatter, William J., *The Fund Theory of Accounting and Its Implications for Financial Reports,* Chicago, 1947, p. 95.
17. *APBO No. 8,* "Accounting for the Cost of Pension Plans" (1966) prescribes that the maximum amount of the liability for unfunded pension commitments to be disclosed in the balance sheet is the amount to which the company is legally obligated.

18. Financial Accounting Standards Board, *Statement of Financial Accounting Standards No. 5,* "Accounting for Contingencies," Stamford, Conn., March, 1975.
19. Yu, S.C., "Micro-accounting and Macro-accounting," *The Accounting Review*, January, 1966, p. 8-20 and Most, Kenneth S., "The Accountant and Social Accounting," London: *Accountancy,* October, 1967, pp. 661-662.
20. It may be pointed out that finance theorists have adopted the economic problem of resource allocation as their central issue, with a consequent tendency to throw out the baby together with the bathwater.
21. For the methodology, see Beaver, W.H., J. Kennelly and W. Voss, "Predictive Ability as a Criterion for the Evaluation of Accounting Data," *The Accounting Review*, October 1968, pp. 675-683. See also Beaver, William H., "Market Prices, Financial Ratios and the Prediction of Failure," *Journal of Accounting Research*, Autumn 1968, pp. 179-192, Beaver, William H., "Financial Ratios as Predictors of Failure," *Empirical Research in Accounting: Selected Studies, 1966, Journal of Accounting Research, Supplement V, 1967*, pp. 71-111, Blum, Marc, "Failing Company Discriminant Analysis," *Journal of Accounting Research*, Spring 1974, pp. 1-25.
22. "The Determination of Long-term Credit Standing with Financial Ratios," *Empirical Research in Accounting: Selected Studies, 1966, Journal of Accounting Research, Supplement V, 1967,* pp. 44-62.
23. Gonedes, Nicholas J., "Capital Market Equilibrium and Annual Accounting Numbers: Empirical Evidence," *Journal of Accounting Research,* Spring, 1974, pp. 24-62.
24. Chang, Lucia, S. and Kenneth S. Most, *Financial Statements and Investment Decisions*, Vol. I, Florida International University, 1979; Vol. II, Florida International University, 1980.

SELECTED ADDITIONAL READINGS

Beaver, William H., "Market Prices, Financial Ratios and the Prediction of Failure," *Journal of Accounting Research,* Autumn 1968, pp. 179-192.

Chambers, Raymond J., *Accounting, Evaluation and Economic Behavior,* Englewood Cliffs, N.J.: Prentice-Hall, Inc., 1966, Ch. 5.

Cramer, Joe L. Jr. and Charles A. Neyhart, "A Comprehensive Accounting Framework for Evaluating Executory Contracts," *Journal of Accounting, Auditing and Finance*, Winter 1979, pp. 135-50.

Bird, Francis A., Lewis F. Davidson and Charles H. Smith, "Perceptions of External Accounting Transfers Under Entity and Proprietary Theory," *The Accounting Review,* April 1974, pp. 233-244.

Deakin, Edward B., "Distribution of Financial Accounting Ratios: Some Empirical Evidence," *The Accounting Review,* January 1976, pp. 90-96.

Financial Accounting Standards Board, Discussion Memorandum, *Accounting for Future Losses,* Stamford, Conn.: FASB, March 13, 1974.

———, Discussion Memorandum, "An Analysis of Issues Related to Conceptual Framework for Financial Accounting and Reporting: Elements of Financial Statements and Their Measurement," Stamford, Conn.: FASB, December 2, 1976, part I, chs. 3 and 4, and Appendix B.

———, *Statement of Financial Accounting Concepts No. 3,* "Elements of Financial Statements of Business Enterprises," Stamford, Conn.: FASB, December 1980, paras. 1-55, 74-82, 96-146.

Foster, George, *Financial Statement Analysis,* Englewood Cliffs, N.J.: Prentice-Hall, Inc., 1978, part II.

Glickman, Richard, and Richard Stahl, "The Case of the Misleading Balance Sheet," *Journal of Accountancy,* December 1968, pp. 66-68, 70-72 (and Letters to the Editor, May 1969, pp. 30, 32, 34).

Goldberg, Louis, *An Inquiry into the Nature of Accounting,* Monograph No. 7, American Accounting Association, 1965.

Hilton, Delmer P. "What *Is* the Balance Sheet," *New York Certified Public Accountant,* June 1970, pp. 485-491.

Holmes, Geoffrey, "Development of the Modern Form of Balance Sheet," *Accountancy,* April 1971, pp. 196-200.

Ijiri, Yuji, *Recognition of Contractual Rights and Obligations,* Research Report, Stamford, Conn: FASB, December 1980.

Ma, Ronald and Malcolm C. Miller, "Conceptualizing the Liability," *Accounting and Business Research,* Autumn 1978, pp. 258-65.

Meyer, Philip E., "The Accounting Entity," *Abacus,* December 1973, pp. 116-126.

Myers, John H., "A Set of New Financial Statements," *Journal of Accountancy,* February 1971, pp. 50-57 (and Letters to the Editor, July 1971, p. 31).

National Association of Accountants, "Fixed Asset Accounting: The Allocation of Costs," *Statement on Management Accounting Practices No. 7,* New York: NAA, March 1974.

Rappaport, Alfred, "Discussion of 'The Balance Sheet-Embodiment of the Most Fundamental Elements of Accounting Theory,'" in *Financial Accounting Theory I: Issues and Controversies,* ed. Zeff and Keller, New York: McGraw-Hill Book Company, 1973, pp. 174-183.

Sterling, Robert R., "Conservatism: The Fundamental Principle of Valuation in Traditional Accounting," *Abacus,* December 1967, pp. 109-132.

Sprouse, Robert F., "The Balance Sheet-Embodiment of the Most Fundamental Elements of Accounting Theory," in *Financial Accounting Theory I: Issues and Controversies,* ed. Zeff and Keller, New York: McGraw-Hill Book Company, 1973, pp. 164-174.

Walker, R.G., "Asset Classification and Asset Valuation," *Accounting and Business Research,* Autumn 1974, pp. 286-296.

Woolcott, Victor F., "The Case for a Comprehensive Financial Statement," *Financial Executive,* January 1972, pp. 18-25.

Case 12-1 Redeemable Preferred Stock

In 1979 the SEC approved the adoption of rules which would modify the financial statements prepared by corporations that had issued preferred stock with mandatory redemption requirements, or redeemable at the holder's option.

Preferred stock is often referred to as a "hybrid security" because it has characteristics of debt (fixed income) and equity (ownership rights). Traditionally, the equity aspect has prevailed in that preferred stock has been included in the balance sheet as a part of stockholders' equity. In recent years, some corporations have issued preferred stock which has an additional characteristic of debt: a fixed maturity, or redemption at the holder's option.

The SEC's rules required registrants to disclose mandatorily redeemable (or redeemable at the holder's option) preferred stock as a separate balance sheet item. Where this class of preferred stock existed, a general heading "shareholders' equity" would not be used, and a combined total for equity securities including redeemable preferred stock would be prohibited.

1. Discuss the implications of this decision for generalizations concerning the accounting basic equation, and the form and structure of the balance sheet.
2. Explain the relationship of the SEC's requirement and the FASB's definitions of liabilities, investments by and distributions to owners, and changes in equity from nonowner sources.

END OF CHAPTER QUESTIONS

1. Why should an examination of the basic financial statements begin with the balance sheet?
2. What are the implications of calling a balance sheet a "statement of financial position?"
3. What four concepts of the balance sheet can be identified in the accounting literature?
4. Discuss the relevance of the proprietary theory of accounting to the form and content of the balance sheet.
5. What do you understand by the phrase "uncompleted earnings cycle?" What is the significance of this phrase for understanding the balance sheet?
6. List the different ways in which an asset may come into existence. What are the common characteristics of these different kinds of asset?
7. How have "liabilities" been defined by (a) *Accounting Terminology Bulletin No. 1,* (b) *APB Statement No. 4,* (c) *FASB Statement of Financial Accounting Concepts No. 3*? Are these definitions the same, or do they display a tendency to broaden or narrow the concept?
8. What is the FASB definition of *assets*? What three characteristics does it embrace? How do you understand the phrase "possible future economic benefit?"
9. Introductory accounting texts often define assets as "things of value, owned by an entity." Does this definition correspond with the FASB's definition?
10. What is a "valuation account"? If a valuation account has a credit balance, is it a liability?

11. The accrual of a loss contingency is sometimes alleged to depend upon three basic financial reporting concepts: the time period (periodicity), measurement, and objectivity.
    a. Explain the chain of reasoning which links these three concepts with the accrual rule laid down in *FASB Statement No. 5*.
    b. What other basic concepts of accrual accounting underlie accounting for loss contingencies?
12. What is the FASB definition of *equity*? How does this definition relate to the one in *APB Statement No. 4*? What is the distinguishing characteristic of equity?
13. What are "investments by and distributions to owners?" What is the significance of these concepts for the measurement of comprehensive income?
14. Explain where a donation of land to a corporation by a local authority fits into the FASB's three types of changes in equity.
15. Discuss accounting for treasury stock in terms of the FASB's definitions of investments by and distributions to owners.
16. Explain what is meant by the "social consolidation model." How can it assist accountants to identify assets, liabilities, and equity?
17. What kind of liabilities did *FASB Statement No. 5* apply to? What is a "contingent liability?" How should it be reported?
18. What are "display considerations" in relation to the balance sheet? What practices can be identified in the United States? in the United Kingdom? How can these differences be reconciled?
19. What use of the balance sheet requires the solution of the display problem? What is the evidence that this use is justified by its results?
20. What is "off-balance sheet financing"? Give examples. Why should this kind of financing be included in balance sheet liabilities?

13

ASSETS, LIABILITIES, AND EQUITY

In the previous chapter we attempted to define the elements which enter into the construction of the balance sheet, and to explain its structure. In this chapter we will examine individual classes and items of assets and liabilities, and the components of stockholders' equity.

CLASSIFICATION OF ASSETS AND LIABILITIES[1]

In accounting terminology, a classified balance sheet is one which identifies subclasses of current assets and current liabilities. The problem of balance sheet classification goes beyond this, of course, and we have pointed to an alternative primary classification, corresponding with the theory of corporate finance, into

$$\text{Long-term (fixed) assets} + \text{Working capital} = \text{Long-term liabilities} + \text{Equity}$$

The right-hand side of this equation is often called *total capital employed*, and one use of the balance sheet, the calculation of profitability, relates pre- or after-tax earnings to total capital employed, as a ratio.

Apart from the terminology, there has been little discussion in the accounting literature of problems of balance sheet classification. The conventional assumption, that assets are listed (in the U.S.A.) in order of decreasing liquidity, and liabilities in the order in which they will be met, is often disproved in practice; real estate holdings may be liquidated on short notice, whereas some types of work in process may take months to complete and sell. Some bank loans which appear as current liabilities could not be repaid without destroying the entity as a business enterprise, whereas redeemable preferred stock is shown as such in the balance sheet even immediately prior to redemption. Utility companies use the reverse listing order.

Suggestions that assets and liabilities should be classified as monetary or nonmonetary have not been taken up, possibly because experience reveals the difficulty of making this distinction on rational, as distinct from definitional, grounds. The Trueblood Report proposed a distinction between assets in respect of their place in the liquidity cycle; Edwards and Bell's profit constructs pointed to a similar classification into realized and unrealized items; again, neither theorists nor practitioners have found these suggestions fruitful.

Classification of the components of stockholders' equity is invariably subject to legal considerations, such as the particular type of stock which is outstanding. However, we may note a move toward a unitary construct, with one item appearing in the balance sheet and its components listed in a note to the financial statements rather than in a Statement of Stockholders' Equity.

In this chapter we will utilize the conventional subclasses of items found in balance sheets published in the United States. It may be noted that many large corporations survey their shareholders and other financial statement users regularly, in order to find out what improvements they can make to their annual reports. The type of balance sheet with which we are familiar, therefore, appears to provide a high degree of consumer satisfaction.

CURRENT ASSETS AND CURRENT LIABILITIES

The distinction between current and noncurrent assets and liabilities depends upon the concept of working capital. Some critics of the working capital concept have taken the position that attention should be directed to cash instead, a position which will be examined in some detail in chapter 15.

Working capital is a measure of the long-term investment required by activity. To understand this concept we can start from the entrepreneur of economic theory, who stands ready with his cash box to pay for variable factors of production as he requires them and whose cash box is immediately replenished from the proceeds of sale. In this situation, working capital requirements are nil.[2]

Modifying this model to accommodate time and uncertainty, we note that the firm must acquire variable factors of production in advance of receiving the proceeds of sale of products or services. An estimate must be made of the minimum level of activity which will characterize the future, and long-term capital must be raised to cover this minimum requirement. This we call *working capital*.

We now introduce the problems of *supply* and *credit*. For a variety of reasons firms must acquire variable factors of production in advance of their use. These reasons include length of the supply chain, risk of interruption of supply, and need to minimize average per unit cost of each factor acquired. The supply problem serves to increase the minimum requirement found above. To the extent that credit is available, the investment in supply can be avoided so that this situation does not affect working capital; the asset and the liability cancel out in the equation:

Working capital = current assets − current liabilities

Finally, the need to extend credit to customers of the firm establishes investment in customer credit (accounts receivable), which also adds to the minimum requirement for working capital.

This presentation explains the classes "current assets" and "current liabilities" in the balance sheet in terms of financial and investment structure, rather than in the usual terms of solvency and liquidity. The relationship with solvency is this: a reduction of working capital is a reduction of funds for activity and, therefore, an indicator of declining production, sales, and profits. The relationship with liquidity is more apparent than real, because cash becomes available for payment of liabilities from a variety of sources. The liquid or "acid-test" ratio is only meaningful if a firm's liquidity position has become static and in any case is readily doctored before the year-end.

Early definitions of current assets characterized them as cash and near-cash; inventory was a current asset because it was expected to be turned into cash shortly after the balance sheet date. This view of inventory as a monetary asset was evident in the approach to foreign currency translation at that time. Current liabilities were short-term cash debts.

The inadequacy of a cash model of the firm led to a change in viewpoint. This was at first manifested by the adoption of a one-year time horizon; if the asset was expected to become cash within one year, or if the liability was payable within one year, it was current. Again, the one-year time period proved an unnecessary constraint, and current assets and liabilities were redefined in *Accounting Research Bulletin No. 43*, chapter 3A, to correspond more closely with the concept of working capital depicted above:

> **Current assets** Cash and other assets or resources commonly identified as those which are reasonably expected to be realized in cash or sold or consumed during the normal operating cycle of the business.
>
> **Current liabilities** Obligations whose liquidation is reasonably expected to require the use of existing resources properly classifiable as current assets or the creation of other current liabilities. They include obligations for items which have entered the operating cycle.

The link with a cash model was retained by defining the operating cycle as "the average time intervening between the acquisition of materials or services... and the final cash realization." This is a liquidity cycle and becomes an operating cycle only under the restrictive assumptions of the cash model of the firm. *APB Statement No. 4* did not add to our enlightenment; on the contrary, it tended to increase uncertainty by specifying only what current assets and liabilities *include*.[3]

The definition of current assets as investment in activity eliminates a number of theoretical problems; it explains prepaid expenses and deferrals generally and suggests the time period covered by the operating cycle. The "one year or less" rule clearly applies to the accounting cycle, and current assets could include investments for longer or shorter periods, depending on the length of the production process. The definition also indicates why next year's depreciation should not be classified as a current asset; it is investment in capacity, not activity. Only when the depreciation has been computed and accounted for as a cost can it enter into the current asset category, as a part of work in process or inventory cost.

The confusion apparent in *FASB Statement No. 6*, "Classification of Short-Term Obligations Expected to be Refinanced" and the subsequent *Interpretation No. 8*, could also have been avoided had the concept of current liabilities as a variable source of current assets been understood. It is not necessary to include the current portion of long-term debt in current liabilities to disclose the fact that it is due within one year, nor should temporary finance raised to cover construction costs be included in this category. Current liabilities, of course, can include obligations which will be settled other than by cash payment.

According to *ARB 43*, current assets include cash available for current operations, but many companies include all cash in this category, even if it is earmarked for payment for equipment, or for the acquisition of another company. The category also includes trade accounts, notes and acceptances receivable, and the prevailing (but not invariable) practice is to classify those receivables which mature more than one year after the balance sheet date as noncurrent. Other receivables are included only if collectible in the ordinary course of business within one year. Inventories of merchandise, raw materials, goods in process, finished goods, operating supplies, and maintenance materials and parts are current assets; they are *deferrals*: expenditure now, expense later. Thus, they are no different in kind from prepaid expenses and other deferred expenditures, and it was not necessary for the ARB to explain that the reason for including them in current assets was because, if not paid in advance, they would require the use of current assets during the operating cycle.

Current liabilities could include the following:

- Accounts payable
- Accrued expenses, including interest
- Notes payable—short term
- Dividends payable
- Current portion of long-term debt
- Taxes payable, including amounts withheld

- Advances and deposits
- Deferred revenue
- Credit balances on customer accounts receivable.

Of these, some may not be legal liabilities at the date of the balance sheet (accrued interest on notes payable); some are not obligations to pay cash in the amounts recorded (advances against orders; deferred revenue); and some are capable of being changed by future events (income tax payable).

The question whether current liabilities should be reported as liabilities and thus included in total capitalization, as compared with being deducted from current assets to show working capital, depends upon one's view of the balance sheet. A statement of what is owned and what is owed would highlight all liabilities and their total. A balance sheet which is simply a list of balances would also cause current liabilities to appear with other credit balances. If the purpose of the balance sheet is to depict financial *structure* (as compared with financial *position*) the display of working capital is more useful and informative. The very traditional French accountants have resolved this problem in the 1979 revised standardized financial statements under the *Plan Comptable Général* by showing current liabilities as liabilities in the balance sheet, and providing a separate schedule showing working capital and its components.

The interpretation of the function of the current asset classification has important implications for the valuation of these items. If we were concerned primarily with liquidity, we would wish to state these items at their current cash equivalents, that is, the amount which could be obtained from an orderly liquidation. Raw materials would have a lower value than their purchase price indicates, because the enterprise does not usually trade in such materials. Work in process inventories may be wholly unsalable as such, and, therefore, have a liquidation value of zero, or a small scrap value. Finished goods inventories, on the other hand, would have a value higher than their purchase or manufacturing cost.

Obviously this is not the current approach to valuation of current assets, and, therefore, liquidity is not the dominant characteristic. In this case, the lower of cost or market rule as such, when applied to inventories, appears indefensible; it results in inventories being reported at amounts which do not reflect the investment which has been made to bring them to their state and place of use in either historical or replacement cost. Note that it is not necessary to report inventories at the lower of cost or market in order to provide for a probable loss on sale; it may be provided for in the manner prescribed by *FASB Statement No. 5*, "Accounting for Contingencies." Note also that the lower of cost or market rule for current asset marketable equity securities can also be criticized in this context; if the investments are temporary uses of cash, they should be valued at proceeds (net realizable) value whether this is above or below cost.

NONCURRENT ASSETS

Logically, the creation of capacity precedes activity, which is why the traditional European form of balance sheet starts with noncurrent assets. These noncurrent assets include fixed assets, of which property, plant, and equipment, is the most common category, and also long-term investments and intangibles, which will be discussed separately.

Investment in equipment is called *fixed*, meaning that a change will increase or decrease capacity. This usage can be related to the economist's concepts of the short run, in which some factor of production is fixed, and the long run, in which all factors of production are variable. It is also called *noncurrent*, to distinguish it from working capital which is investment in activity; this usage can be ascribed to the United States practice of highlighting current assets in the balance sheet, by presenting them in first place. It is also called *property, plant, and equipment*, which restricts the classification to tangible fixed assets, in which case intangible fixed assets are classified separately. Finally, many commentators restrict themselves to *depreciable tangible assets* because they view the calculation of depreciation as the central issue.

By emphasizing the meaning of "fixed" we draw attention to the fact that the life of a fixed asset extends beyond any period of a length less than the capacity cycle. A baker's oven, for example, represents capacity to bake bread over a period of, say, twenty-five years, and any accounting for a shorter period, such as one year, necessitates an allocation procedure. As we have pointed out, all allocation is subjective and the ambivalence of depreciation results from this observation. Nevertheless, there is another problem involved in considering fixed assets which takes precedence over the depreciation issue. It is the recognition problem, the application of the investment theory of our asset definition to this class of resources. The valuation problem is intimately connected with the depreciation problem.

The view of an asset as the residual in a process of matching costs (= expenditures) with revenues produces the following thought process, expressed here in the phraseology of risk measurement.[4]

Measurement risk	Measurement procedure
1. Difficult to identify revenues arising from a given cost	1. Expense in current period
2. Estimated time duration of expected benefit or revenue flow subject to significant measurement error	2. Expense in current period
3. Estimated time duration of expected benefits subject to relatively small margins of error, but magnitude and timing of benefit or revenue flows subject to significant measurement error	3. (Capitalize) Choice of a systematic write-off basis over the expected time duration of expected benefits

A procedure which substitutes statistical for accounting method has been proposed by a committee of the American Accounting Association; based on the selection of a normative valuation model, it attempts to break out of the restrictions imposed by the double-entry model requiring balance sheet-income statement articulation.[5] This vision of a balance sheet which does not balance has been a perennial proposition of accounting theorists and is particularly relevant to the problem of asset recognition. For example, in the oil and gas industry it is generally agreed that the most useful information which the balance sheet could provide is the quantity and value of reserves of oil and gas. Although companies were required by *FASB Statement No. 19*. "Financial Accounting and Reporting by Oil and Gas Producing Companies" to report these reserves in quantities, the SEC was not satisfied with this disclosure and issued its own rules for a method called Reserve Recognition Accounting. These rules required oil and gas reserves to be valued and provided model statements to show results of operations during a period as the net effect of changes in the values of oil and gas reserves. This method of accounting was originally intended to be used in the primary statements of oil and gas companies, after an initial period of experimentation.

The rules provoked considerable controversy; a minority of accountants in the industry saw some merit in the approach, but the majority opposed it. Of greatest concern was the difficulty of determining oil and gas quantities in the ground and the rate at which they would be produced and sold; thus, it was believed, revisions of previous expectations would soon become the most important figures in the RRA statements. As a result of the first two years of experience with these statements, the SEC decided early in 1981 not to proceed with its intention to incorporate RRA in the basic financial statements, which would have caused the present value of oil and gas reserves to appear therein as assets. However, the requirement to publish supplementary RRA statements was continued, implementing an earlier proposition from the accounting profession itself, albeit in somewhat different form.[6]

Much of the literature on capital maintenance refers to the physical aspect of equipment and equates the asset to physical production capacity. It must be emphasized that accounts can contain only values, not physical objects, and the capacity to which we refer in the case of equipment is capacity to produce revenues. Otherwise we could not justify aggregating twenty acres on Manhattan Island with one million acres in West Texas and calling the result "land," far less the addition of land to plant and machinery.

THE VALUATION OF FIXED ASSETS

The valuation of fixed assets is much more difficult than the recognition problem. The use of historical cost as "the basis for" fixed asset valuation raises important questions of what to capitalize on installation and after installation, but equipment does not appear in balance sheets at historical cost but at cost less depreciation, which term includes amortization.

The reasoning which would justify the use of historical cost for valuing fixed assets on acquisition is illustrated by the following argument:

1. Decision models call for information on timing and amount of cash flow to the decision maker.
2. Future cash flows must be reduced by a discount factor to present values because of the time value of money.
3. Based on the assumptions of the capital asset pricing model, the net realizable value of a fixed asset is a usable estimate of the present value of future cash flows from that asset.
4. Replacement cost is a usable estimate of net realizable value in this case.
5. Historical cost is a usable surrogate for replacement cost.[7]

Disregarding for the moment the reference to a cash flow model, the argument can be seen to break down at any time after the date of acquisition of the fixed asset because the "historical cost" in question is cost to the firm, which includes location-specific costs, less accumulated depreciation expense, which is a function of the subjective evaluation of management. Even if it were possible to use the present value algorithm to calculate depreciation for all firms, we would still be faced with the choice of an infinite number of values for cost less depreciation in any particular case.

In this connection, we should not be misled by the form of the valuation. Accumulated depreciation is normally shown separately in financial statements instead of being deducted from cost in order to calculate written-down value directly. The purpose of this may be to disclose data for calculating such ratios as: accumulated depreciation/gross cost of fixed assets and net income/total investment at cost, which are useful for evaluating financial structure and analyzing profitability. The result, however, is to divorce balance sheet value from historical cost just as effectively as if depreciation were credited to the fixed asset account. This has been recognized by the FASB, which has defined an asset to include any valuation account related thereto.

Fixed asset accounting has been seen as an allocation process, where the cost or other basic value of the fixed asset is identified with periods in relation to an assumed pattern of consumption of asset services. The value of a fixed asset, in this view, is the sum of the expected future services and, under the conditions of perfect competition which underlie the capital asset pricing model, price may well equal their present value. This model has been examined by Wright, who defines "value in use" as *opportunity value*, the cost, loss, or sacrifice which would have to be incurred if the firm did not have those services.[8] Replacement cost under static conditions is found by solving for R in the equation:

$$C = \sum_{n=1}^{r} [RQ(n) - E(n)](1+i)^{-n} + S(T)(1+i)^{-T}$$

where C is the capital cost of the substitute machine.
$Q(n)$ is the number of units of service produced by the machine during the nth period of its life.
$E(n)$ is the operating expense incurred during that period.
i is the rate of interest, expressed as a fraction per period.
$S(n)$ is the salvage value of the machine at the end of the nth period, and
T is the economic life of the machine; that is, that life which leads to the minimum value of the average unit cost R. Hence, the existing machine at the end of the tth period of its life is given by:

$$V(t) = \sum_{n=t+1}^{T} [RQ(n) - E(n)](1+i)^{t-n} + S(T)(1+i)^{t-T}$$

and depreciation during the tth period by

$$\begin{aligned} D(t) &= V(t-1) - V(t) \\ &= RQ(t) - E(t) - iV(t-1) \end{aligned}$$

Wright attempted to show that the same approach could be used to calculate depreciation and, therefore, fixed asset value, if all the assumptions necessary to support opportunity value were relaxed. However, his theory of depreciation is only one of a number of attempts to arrive at replacement cost as the sum of the values of future services of an asset. Other authors have sought to examine the implications of the proposition that the value of a fixed asset is the present value of expected future net cash flows produced by that asset, and Edwards has shown the variety of depreciation methods and, thus, of fixed asset values, which this proposition can support.[9]

The fixed asset category includes nondepreciable fixed assets, of which land is the obvious example. A 1980 *Statement of Position* published by the AICPA added to this subcategory the "title plant" (inventory of documents relating to the investigation of titles insured) of title insurance companies.[10] By far the most important part of fixed assets is represented by depreciable assets.

DEPRECIATION IN THEORY AND PRACTICE

Attempts at defining depreciation have not always proved helpful; perhaps the most satisfactory is the simplest, "a reduction in the value of a fixed asset because of wear and tear from use or disuse, obsolescence, accident or inadequacy."[11] The AIA Committee on Terminology permitted itself a definition of *depreciation accounting* as "a system of accounting which aims to distribute the cost or other basic value of tangible capital assets, less salvage (if any), over the estimated life of the unit (which may be a group of assets) in a systematic and rational manner. It is a process of allocation, not valuation...."[12] *APB Statement No. 4* maintained depreciation at arm's length and talked about "some costs" being expensed on the basis of an attempt to allocate costs in a systematic and rational manner among the periods in which benefits are provided.

Paton described depreciation accounting without defining depreciation other than to draw attention to its "uncertain, provisional character."[13] It appears as if he saw depreciation as an expiry of property value, quite separate and distinct from any loss through abandonment, or the cost of replacement. Sterling thought so little of the subject that he failed to consider it an element in the determination of enterprise income.[14] Hicks has stated that "not all the economic theory of depreciation is well agreed among economists,"[15] and it was pointed out many years ago that unless wear and tear as a physical phenomenon is meant, depreciation does not belong in the economist's tool box.

Worse is to come: Keynes attributed to accountants' calculations of depreciation some, at least, of the blame for recessions and depressions, intensifying established up-and-down swings in the economy, and at least one accounting theorist supports this view.[16] Among the concepts which can be identified in the literature on economics, we find depreciation to be—

1. Exhaustion of utility of fixed capital;
2. Payment for fixed capital;
3. Replacement of fixed capital used up;
4. A "sunk" cost (i.e. an unrecoverable payment);
5. The opportunity cost of fixed capital;
6. A deduction from receipts of marginal net revenues.

Engineering economists and some accountants, however, have treated the subject as one deserving careful analysis. Hotelling presented a mathematical definition of depreciation as an element of unit cost,[17] and Brief has drawn attention to Ladelle's early contribution to the DCF method, sometimes referred to as the annuity method.[18] This type of approach is neatly encapsulated by a quotation from Lutz and Lutz:

> For the past hundred years accountants have been searching for the "true" depreciation method which would allocate the cost of the machine over its lifetime in accordance with the rate at which it is actually being "used up."[19]

THE CALCULATION OF DEPRECIATION

The problem can be readily demonstrated. We define depreciation as the expiry of a fixed asset through time, regardless of cause, and express this mathematically as:

$$D_l = C - S \qquad 1)$$

where D_l is depreciation over useful life
C is cost, and
S is salvage, if any

It will be seen that we have one equation with at least two unknowns (depreciation and life) and probably a third (salvage).

Now consider depreciation expense, that is, the allocation of depreciation to any period of time shorter than total useful life. This is defined mathematically as:

$$D_e = \frac{D_l}{L'} \qquad 2)$$

where D_e is the expense chargeable to any period and, by extension, to any product produced within that period, and L' is a measure of time in which—

1. All periods have equal weight, or,
2. The weighting of periods increases over time, or,
3. The weighting of periods decreases over time, or,
4. The weighting of periods fluctuates over time.

The determination of these questions at the time depreciation expense is calculated is an impossibility. It follows, therefore, that any explanation of depreciation in terms of something which has happened is false, no matter how desirable such a measurement might be.

In fact, we may define depreciation as a measure of the planned (or expected) sacrifice of value of a fixed (capacity) asset necessarily resulting from a planned (expected) sequence of production operations. Depreciation expense, then, is the analysis of depreciation by periods of time, and depreciation cost, the analysis of depreciation by process or product. It follows that depreciation expense cannot be a retrospective calculation of the effect of something which has occurred, and this observation may help to resolve the controversy. In particular, the possibility of identifying the effects of changes in expectations by splitting depreciation expense into an expected part and an acquisition gain disappears.

What is the meaning, then, of "cost less accumulated depreciation" for depreciable fixed assets (which includes intangible fixed assets subject to amortization)? As Wells points out, "this accounting model does not attempt to provide a valuation of the firm or a current measure of its financial position."[20] It can, however, be explained by the concept of an asset as a representation (or measure) of what is chargeable to present or future customers. In this case, the fact that the measurement is made at the time the asset was acquired, and remains in use throughout the life of the asset, distinguishes it only in degree from other similar measurements made on a day-to-day basis. In some cases, of course, firms do change their estimates of useful life, salvage value, and other predictions entering into the calculation of depreciation, as well as the algorithms by which this unusual mathematical problem is solved. The effects of these changes are accounted for as the effects of a change in accounting estimate.

APB Opinion No. 20, "Accounting Changes," requires the effect of an accounting change to be reported in the current and future periods affected. In the case of a change in the estimates on which depreciation has been calculated, this means that the error is spread over a number of years, rather than being recognized immediately. For example, assume that an asset with a five year life cost $1,000 and was assumed to have a salvage value of $500; straight-line depreciation is used. At the end of the third year it is discovered that salvage will be nil. The book value of $700 is written off under *APBO 21* by charges of $350 in each of the remaining two years. It is obvious, however, that the loss of salvage is attributable to something which has happened during the first three years, not the last two. Consider the case that the machine was damaged in use; it still serves its function, but is unsalable to another firm. Is it not strange to report that it has become more costly to operate (more valuable?) as a result of this accident?

APBO 20 also allows obsolescence to be ignored. Consider an asset which has a book value of $1,000 but a replacement cost of $500; assuming the same function is performed by the new asset, there is an economic loss of $500 to be recognized when it occurs. Since the difference would be spread over the remaining years of useful life in any case, it may be ignored for financial reporting purposes, except in current cost statements under *FASB Statement No. 33*.

The uncertainty attaching to the calculation of depreciation results in some variation in accounting practice. Fixed assets taken out of service and held for resale should be both revalued (at net realizable value) and transferred to current assets at that time; neither practice is believed to correspond with GAAP. In many cases, on the sale of a fixed asset, the difference between historical cost and sales proceeds is debited (even credited, in some cases) to the account for accumulated depreciation: this disposes of the difference, but does nothing to correct the effect of the past accounting for the fixed asset in question. Finally, a number of questions are resolved by applying income tax rules; this may mean adoption of the same depreciation method in the financial reports as is used for determining taxable income, or even capitalizing and charging to expense according as the Internal Revenue Service requires this treatment for tax purposes.

An additional twist was given to this subject by *FASB Interpretation No. 30*, "Accounting for Involuntary Conversion of Nonmonetary Assets to Monetary Assets." This Interpretation prohibits accounting for a difference between book value and insurance proceeds, when an asset is destroyed or damaged by an event against which the firm was insured, as an adjustment to the cost basis of property acquired as a replacement. A gain or loss must be recognized even where replacement is obligatory. From this it appears that some firms were increasing the book value of the replacement asset acquired by the loss on disappearance or damage of the old asset, with the consequence that the loss was carried forward to be written off, in the form of depreciation expense, in future years. This new GAAP, which follows the SEC's *Staff Accounting Bulletin (SAB) 21*, does not apply to LIFO conversions in certain circumstances.

THE MEANING OF COST

To state that fixed assets should be valued initially at cost and thereafter at their current value does not adequately explain accounting for fixed assets because we must identify the meaning of cost.

We define cost here as the sum of the representations in money of the sacrifices necessarily incurred to bring the fixed asset to its place and state of use. In public utility regulation the equivalent concept is *prudent cost*, the costs which would normally be paid by a reasonably prudent management. In some other businesses competition serves the same function as regulation, and the customer will not pay for more than his share of cost. However, it must be admitted that many firms enjoy unregulated monopoly powers and to that extent can include elements of waste and inefficiency in fixed asset values.

The constituents of cost can be considered in two types of situation: installation of purchased fixed assets and fixed assets constructed by the firm for itself. In the purchase situation, it is evident that to the price must be added freight, customs duties and other taxes, handling and storage charges, and such installation costs as wiring and concreting. The question whether to use invoice price net of trade discounts or net cash price after deducting cash discount is usually resolved in favor of the latter, on the grounds that the cash discount is a penalty for late payment. However, it must be admitted that more time is devoted by accountants to arguing whether a particular item of cost should be capitalized than to any other activity, so that the abandonment of the cost basis of accounting for fixed assets would reduce accounting costs dramatically.

In addition to the problems involved in deciding which expenditures to capitalize, there is the further difficulty, when a building is acquired together with its site, of separating the cost of the land from the cost of the building. A clearer example of the subjectivity of valuation in accounting could not be chosen. If the contract signed by the parties to the sale specifies the amounts agreed upon as values of land and building separately, this allocation is likely to be used in the accounts of the purchaser; yet it is well known that price and value are not equal. There are, in fact, an infinite number of possible solutions to this problem if "substance over form" is a principle of modern accounting.

Some of the problems of capitalization can be avoided by recording all the parts of an asset acquired in the same account. The difficulty of accounting for major replacements or radical rebuilding can often be minimized by separating the part replaced on original acquisition; for example, by accounting separately for the machine and the tool, or the housing and its contents.

Another complication encountered in practice is the basket purchase, where allocation is also necessary. There are an infinite number of solutions to this problem, some more reasonable than others. The simplest practice would appear to be to use the figures on which the executives concerned based the decision to acquire, since values contained in the agreement or bill of sale will often represent nothing more than negotiating positions.

Exchange of one nonmonetary asset for another, with or without an accompanying payment of cash, presents yet another problem. Because a large proportion of business transactions are of this kind, this subject is of great importance in accounting. *APB Opinion No. 29* attempted to provide for these exchanges to be accounted for at *fair value*, but failure to maintain this position, together with obscurities in the Opinion itself, have prevented the desired result from being achieved. In the first place, accounting for nonmonetary exchanges was made dependent upon determining whether the earning process has been completed, so that gain or loss could be recognized. Besides reflecting the difficulty of the FASB's definition of revenue (see chapter 14), this constraint eliminated two specified classes of exchange from fair value accounting (exchange of similar products, properties, and productive assets; exchange of one asset for another which is to be sold to a third party), and opened the door for other transactions to be accounted for at book value of the asset given up. In the second place, fair value was not defined with sufficient clarity; it could mean any of a variety of different "values," and it could be found either by reference to the asset given up or the asset received. Finally, it sufficed, in order to avoid fair value accounting, to assert that fair value was not determinable within reasonable limits. Although no research has been done in order to ascertain the effect of this Opinion, it is likely that it had less effect on accounting practice than it has had on accounting textbooks. "Cost" of fixed assets remains an uninterpretable construct, regardless of the method of depreciation used to reduce cost to carrying amount.

INTEREST ON CAPITAL AS A COST

Whether interest on capital employed should be included in the cost of fixed assets that require a time period to be brought to their state and place of use is a question which has been debated by accountants for many years.[21] An appreciation of the *time value of money*, which underlies all capital budgeting and investment analysis techniques, leads to the conclusion that it should, regardless of whether the investment was financed by equity capital or borrowed money. If two machines are acquired by the expenditure of $1,000 each, and the first is ready for use immediately, but the second requires six months to be brought to a usable state, then clearly the second machine cost more, and the additional cost can be represented by interest for the waiting period. This proposition has long been accepted in public utility rate regulation, and regulatory agencies permit utilities to charge an "allowance for interest during the construction period" to the cost of utility plant, with a credit to the income statement. For such utilities the amounts involved are often considerable, and investors would receive no return during the construction period if this practice were not permitted. The interest capitalized is charged to expense, and brought into the rate base, through the depreciation expense of future years, which is calculated on total cost, including the capitalized interest.

Some corporations which undertake large-scale investments over several years have adopted a policy of capitalizing interest on capital employed during the construction period, but only to the extent of interest expense, thus avoiding the issue of crediting the income statement with the difference between interest capitalized and interest expense actually incurred. In 1974 the SEC noted an increase in the number of companies following this practice and issued *ASR 163* in November of that year, imposing a moratorium. Corporations which had a policy of capitalizing interest prior to 1974 could continue to do so; others were prohibited from adopting the practice. Exceptions were made for public utilities and some real estate and savings and loan companies.

To resolve this issue the FASB issued *Statement No. 34*, "Capitalization of Interest Cost," in 1979. This Statement—

- Defines assets qualifying for the capitalization of interest, which is required if the effect is material;
- Provides rules for computing and recording such capitalization of interest;
- Prescribes certain disclosures of interest expense and amount capitalized.

Following this the SEC rescinded its 1974 *ASR 163*, but *FASB Statement No. 34* permitted retroactive restatement only in cases where financial statements had not previously been issued.

This Statement has been severely criticized, partly because its broad provisions permit the exercise of judgment, in contrast to *FASB Statement No. 13*, which contains quite specific bookkeeping instructions.[22] Familiarity with the history of *FASB Statement No. 13* does not necessarily find it a model of accounting standard-setting, however; the problem with *Statement No. 34* lies in what it says, rather than what it does not say.

In the first edition of this book I wrote, "The argument that only actual interest paid should be capitalized is based on a confusion between payment and cost which should need no further comment at this point."

Apparently this distinction has not been understood by the FASB. It is, however, a clear principle of accrual accounting, and its implications were well understood by the Accounting Principles Board, as can be seen from *APB Opinion No. 21*, "Interest on Receivables and Payables." That Opinion requires interest to be charged or credited to the income statement in certain cases, regardless of whether interest as such is actually received or paid. Indeed, calculated interest originating from the application of this Opinion can be capitalized as part of the cost of an asset under *Statement 34*, which restricts capitalization to the interest expenses of the period, whether paid or not. Interest imputed under *FASB Statement No. 13*, "Accounting for Leases," would also be included in interest expense.

The implementation problems which have preoccupied critics of *FASB Statement No. 34* can all be traced to the fundamental error of attempting to capitalize interest on loans instead of interest on asset costs. The latter would have presented only one major problem—determining the rate of interest to be used—and that has not given much difficulty in the analogous parts of *FASB Statement No. 13*. However, it is necessary to recognize that with *Statement No. 34* the FASB has at least begun to deal with this controversial and important issue, even though a number of nonaccounting factors can be seen to underlie the initiative, such as—

- The strains created by the time value of money concepts used in corporation finance being applied to accounting methods;
- The SEC's drive to constrain the freedom of corporations to capitalize expenditures;
- A possible move toward including interest on equity capital as a cost, which would reduce reported profits and might even lead to a tax deduction.

Although the FASB specifically excluded the capitalization of interest for a required holding period (as distinct from the construction period) and on assets such as routinely manufactured inventories, the same argument which supports permitted capitalization applies to these situations. It may be expected that the FASB will return to this subject to clarify and remove ambiguities and inconsistencies in the Statement, and conflicts with AICPA Statements of Position on accounting for real estate, and to extend the scope of interest capitalization.

COST OF OWN CONSTRUCTION

When a firm constructs fixed assets for its own use, the principles of cost ascertainment should apply. However, the area of controversy is magnified out of all proportion so that we appear to be considering a different problem.

The problem can be illustrated by an example. Suppose that a manufacturer of mattresses decides to construct a new factory and showroom instead of having a builder contract for the work. During a period of one year the employees do building construction instead of mattress manufacturing. No particular difficulty is presented by the bricks and other materials purchased for this purpose, although we may hazard a guess that the inefficiency of the labor force will result in more than the technically necessary amounts being used and more than the economically unavoidable prices being paid. There is also little argument about capitalizing the labor used (although similar questions can be raised concerning labor times and rates of pay) or such direct expenses as machine hire and related power or fuel costs.

Suppose, however, that the overhead costs of the mattress firm are considerable and must be met even in the shut-down state. (There is no normal production.) For income tax purposes there may be an advantage in charging these expenses to the period for the purpose of developing an agreed tax loss, and this is undoubtedly a factor in actual practice. From the viewpoint of replacement value theory, the overheads are costs of creating capacity and chargeable to future customers on the same basis as any other such costs. They should, therefore, be included in cost of construction.[23]

The next question is, if overhead, why not profit? Why not capitalize the price that would have been paid to a building contractor (obviously, higher than the expected cost of own construction, but not necessarily higher than actual cost) and show a profit or loss on the undertaking? Abstracting from tax considerations which would make such a solution awkward for many firms, the question reveals a failure to understand that profit is a residue which remains after transacting with the environment. It originates in the belief that profit is income and that the firm should have income for the period in question. The decision to build rather than to produce mattresses is a decision to have no income during the construction period.

The more usual situation is that of the firm which constructs its own fixed assets concurrently with production for external markets. The capitalization of direct materials, direct labor, and incremental overhead is not usually questioned, but the capitalization of normal overhead is. In this situation, the principles of costing applicable in the firm in question should be applied to the situation if the capacity used is part of normal capacity. If special capacity is created it should be regarded as causing incremental costs. These observations add weight to the proposition that current value cannot be found by multiplying historical costs by price indices; problems of cost allocation must be solved along the way.

INTANGIBLES

Tangible (from the Latin root *tango*, to touch) means, literally, "perceptible to the touch" and figuratively, "capable of being possessed or realized; real." Since accounts contain only values and not physical objects, reference to some as intangible assets does not imply literal tangibility but figurative. These are assets, the reality of which is in doubt because they cannot be possessed or realized. Hence Kohler's definition:

> *A capital asset* having no physical existence, its value being limited by the rights and anticipative benefits that possession confers upon the owner.[24]

The principal items which are classified as intangibles are goodwill, patents, trademarks, long-term investments, and long-term deferred charges. Research and development expenditures were an important example of long-term deferrals; since the issuance of *FASB Statement No. 2*, "Accounting for Research and Development Costs," providing generally that research and development costs are to be expensed as incurred, this class can be expected to disappear from published financial statements, although possibly continuing to be deferred in cost and managerial accounts and in some other situations. Leaseholds and leasehold improvements may sometimes be classified as intangibles but are more often shown under "Property, plant, and equipment," the current synonym for fixed assets. The AICPA annual survey *Accounting Trends and Techniques* makes no mention of leases under intangible assets.

We have noted that this class of assets meets with resistance from some financial statement users; economists who suspect the presence of monopoly; auditors who cannot verify intangibles because of the absence of physical substance; financial analysts who view them as evanescent; and bankers who find them difficult to liquidate. That this attitude is justified was demonstrated in 1980 with the promulgation of *FASB Statement No. 44*, "Accounting for Intangible Assets of Motor Carriers." The Motor Carrier Act of 1980 changed the rules regulating carriage of goods by road, causing permanent and substantial impairment of the value of some operating rights of interstate carriers. These operating rights were carried at cost, often without amortization, in the balance sheets of motor carriers. The Statement required affected motor carriers to identify these operating rights, however they had been accounted for at acquisition, and charge them to income in the year of impairment. They were required to be shown as an extraordinary item in that year, but subsequent write-offs of other intangible assets, such as goodwill, should not be reported as extraordinary.

Intangibles exclude current assets which are intangible (such as accounts receivable) suggesting that they should properly be included with noncurrent assets in one category. This is the prevailing practice in Europe. In the United States, however, intangibles are usually shown in the balance sheet as a separate class, or in a class entitled "Other assets" that includes long-term receivables and deferrals.

Questions which arise in respect of intangibles, and which may have implications for their recognition as assets, include—

1. Were they acquired in an arm's length transaction? It is relatively easy, for example, for the promoter of a company to assign a patent or trademark to the company and receive shares in the company as payment. The temptation to overvalue the asset must always be strong.
2. Can their expected future benefits be identified? The FASB answered this question in the negative in respect of R & D costs, but the problem exists with reference to other intangibles, such as goodwill and patents.
3. Can they be separated from the cost of other assets acquired? For example, a corporation may acquire the assets of another firm which has done extensive experimentation in order to arrive at the type of plant and machinery it has constructed for its own use. Naturally, the price paid for these assets includes the know-how that went into their construction, but is it separable? In the case of *FASB Statement No. 2* on "Accounting for Research and Development Costs" this question was posed in terms of alternative future uses.

In this section we will attempt to define the assets which are classified as intangibles and to review their common characteristics. We shall also consider the implications of these matters for balance sheet valuation, particularly in the light of the discernible trend for the so-called intangibles to assume greater importance in economic affairs.

ORGANIZATION COSTS

Legal and other costs are frequently incurred to establish a corporation or other form of organization; characteristically, these are expenditures which precede the entity's existence, and for this reason it appears illogical to charge them as expenses to any income statement during the entity's lifetime. It may be argued, however, that the value represented by organization costs is chargeable to its customers over the entity's lifetime and should be expensed in proportion to its sales. This would suggest the need for a method of amortization, and accountants sometimes follow the Internal Revenue Code (S. 248) which permits the organization expenditures of a corporation to be amortized over a sixty month period. This section does not apply to expenses of issuing stock or of corporate reorganization, which are treated as capital expenditure (more correctly, diminution of capital receipts).

Although capitalization of organization costs is apparently an accepted accounting principle, the definition of an asset in terms of probable future economic benefit throws doubt upon the inclusion of this item in the category, at least insofar as measurement of benefits is concerned.

GOODWILL

Nothing in accounting, with the possible exception of depreciation, has caused so much confusion as goodwill. At the present time, however, we can distinguish three generally accepted meanings of the word as used in accounting.

1. A theoretical construct: the present value of expected future profits, or net income in excess of a normal return on investment.[25]
2. An empirical observation: the excess of the price paid for a business over the fair market value of its net assets excluding goodwill.
3. An accounting technicality: on consolidating the accounts of a group, the excess of the amount paid by the parent for its holding over the parent's share of the net assets of the subsidiary.

Goodwill 1 and 2 originate in subjective valuation: the person who calculates expected future super-profits does so on the basis of his own vision of the future; the person who pays more for a business than the fair market value of its net assets has some private image of its future profitability. Attempts have been made to render this valuation objective, by predicting future profits as a function of past profits, and by identifying a normal return as the average return experienced by the industry as a whole in some recent period. In the last analysis, however, these devices appear simply as rationalizations. As Hendriksen states: "The assumption that the tangible assets can earn only a 'normal' rate while other factors are responsible for the excess is fiction."[26] There is usually no factual basis for assuming that the business will earn any return at all.

Canning and other writers, using concepts borrowed from the Fisherian theory of capital and income, view goodwill as a "master valuation account," the equivalent of the economist's "subjective goodwill." In this view, the value of the firm is the present value of an expected future stream of net cash flows, and in equilibrium this value V_0 will be equal to the amount invested in the firm, I. If expectations change, then $V_1 \ldots V_n$ will be greater or less than I; since I cannot change, the difference should be accounted for as goodwill. In this formulation, goodwill may be negative, and an accounting system based on Fisherian theories would undoubtedly have to find a place for this item.[27]

Goodwill 3 will be discussed in chapter 16 dealing with accounting for business combinations. In the United Kingdom, accountants have tended to use the phrase "cost of control" in place of "goodwill arising on consolidation," on the grounds that the excess of investment over net assets is effectively the price paid by the parent for control over the subsidiary. This appears to be an attempt to replace goodwill 1 with a new concept and one which is even more difficult to render objective.

The prevailing practice is to record goodwill 2 and 3 and thereafter to treat them identically. Expenditures designed to create super-profits are charged to expense in the period incurred, but expenditures for the purchase of goodwill may be capitalized, and usually are. For both types, there is a minority of firms which deduct goodwill from retained earnings where such exists and is greater than goodwill, or use retained earnings to reduce the amount capitalized as goodwill.

One of the situations discussed in *ARS No. 10*, "Accounting for Goodwill," lends particularly strong support to the argument that purchased goodwill should be a reduction of stockholders' equity, because it is in fact a payment for assets in excess of their determinable value. When a company purchases its own shares in the market (an increasingly common practice) at a price in excess of the price at issue plus a proportionate share of retained earnings since that date, it has paid for a part of its own goodwill. On retiring this treasury stock, the original price of the shares is debited to contributed capital and the balance of the purchase cost to retained earnings. The argument for capitalization of purchased goodwill would lead to the capitalization of the amount charged to retained earnings in excess of the proportionate part attributable to these shares, but this practice is neither recognized nor recommended. On the other hand, forcing companies acquiring their own shares in this way, usually in order to increase earnings per share by reducing the number of shares at issue, to recognize the fact that they had purchased goodwill and must amortize it over not more than forty years, might not be a bad idea.

PATENTS, COPYRIGHTS, TRADEMARKS, AND FRANCHISES

A patent is a government grant to an inventor, giving exclusive rights to produce and sell an invention. The first grant runs for seventeen years and the cost is very small; renewal for a further period, however, is more costly. The total cost of a patent, on the other hand, includes the research and development expenditure which preceded and led to the patentable discovery. Thus, the intangible asset "patents" will be discussed in conjunction with research and development expenditure.

However, costs of patent applications are often expensed when incurred, or a nominal amount is capitalized for memorandum purposes. In the latter case, amortization should extinguish the asset value over its useful life, which may be the period of the initial grant.

A copyright is an exclusive right, under the federal copyright laws, to reproduce and sell an original creation, such as a book, musical composition, or work of art, for the life of the author plus 50 years. Like patents, considerable expenditure may precede the granting of a copyright, for which the cost is insignificant. Because the direct cost of a copyright is small, the amount is usually expensed, except where a nominal value is capitalized for memorandum purposes. Purchased copyrights, on the other hand, may represent substantial investments.

A trademark is a distinctive identification of a manufactured product or service, registered under the appropriate federal law, for twenty-eight years, with renewal allowed. The remarks on copyright apply to trademarks.

Franchises are rights conferred by a manufacturer or holder of a patent or copyright upon a dealer or other third party, permitting him to make and sell, or just to sell, the invention or creation covered by the patent or copyright in a specific location or geographical area. The practice of franchising has grown considerably in recent years, and in many cases the franchisee makes a substantial payment to the franchisor for the rights acquired. Such is the case, for example, with the franchising of hotels or fast-food outlets, in which the initial franchise fee may take one of two forms:

1. The complex case where the amount paid clearly represents, in whole or in part, compensation for specific services to be provided by the franchisor, such as providing operating manuals and training managers, in site selection and design of facility, and staff assistance on opening.
2. The simple case where the payment does not clearly refer to such services. This is the more common case.[28]

Franchise payments are also made by public utility companies to governmental institutions for use of public property, in perpetuity or for a limited period of time. These payments together with associated legal fees and other expenditures are capitalized and amortized in accordance with *APBO No. 17*. Initial franchise fees of the simple case should receive the same treatment, except that the write-off period will be short; the complex case presents the possibility of charging parts of the initial franchise fee to expenses as the services specified are delivered. *FASB Statement No. 45*, "Accounting for Franchise Fee Revenue" (March 1981), established official accounting and reporting standards for revenue recognition of franchise fees and deferral of related costs in virtually the same terms as an AICPA Audit Guide issued in 1973.

RESEARCH AND DEVELOPMENT EXPENDITURE (R & D)

Prior to 1975, there was considerable variation in financial reporting practices where research and development expenditures were concerned. There were, and still are, four separate categories in which such expenditures fall to be considered for financial reporting purposes, and in which accounting practices may differ.

1. Research and development in the extractive industries.
2. Research and development by "development stage companies."[29]
3. Research and development by other companies.
4. Computer software research and development expenditures.

Within each of these situations, companies engaged in research and development might have followed one of the following policies, or some combination thereof:

1. Charge all R & D to expense as incurred, including property, plant, and equipment acquired for this purpose, keeping only memorandum records; for example, fixed assets for a nominal value of $1 each.
2. Capitalize R & D property, plant, and equipment, charge all other expenditure to expense as incurred.
3. Capitalize the direct costs of successful efforts; for example, those leading to marketable discoveries, and also property, plant, and equipment.
4. Capitalize all R & D costs, including the operating costs of research divisions, and amortize over future periods in proportion to sales or production of products invented or resources discovered.

FASB Statement No. 2, "Accounting for Research and Development Costs" October 1974, prescribed that, with certain exceptions, all R & D costs, whether materials, labor, equipment, facilities, contract services, or allocated overheads, must be charged to expense when incurred. The exceptions are the following:

1. R & D costs incurred for others under contract; that is, where reimbursement is expected.

2. R & D costs of the extractive industries.
3. A special case affecting regulated industries (see *APBO No. 2*, "Accounting for the 'Investment Credit'," *addendum*).
4. R & D materials, equipment, or purchased intangibles with alternative future uses.

This Statement raised many specific questions, and in February 1975, three interpretations were issued by the FASB. *Interpretation No. 4*, "Applicability of FASB Statement No. 2 to Business Combinations Accounted by the Purchase Method," required cost of an acquisition allocated to identifiable research and development assets *having no alternative future use* (emphasis supplied) to be charged to expense on consolidation of the acquiror's and acquiree's accounts prepared after the acquisition. Since *APBO No. 16* on Business Combinations required purchase accounting to allocate the cost of acquisition to each identifiable asset and the difference between the sum of the identifiable net assets and the acquisition price to goodwill, it would appear that this Interpretation must have the effect of transforming purchased R & D into goodwill, or placing acquiring companies in the farcical position of recognizing R & D as an asset and immediately thereafter recognizing the same amount as an expense.

Interpretation No. 6, "Applicability of FASB Statement No. 2 to Computer Software," attempted to clarify the distinction made by *Statement No. 2* between computer software activities which are and are not R & D. A broad interpretation of paragraph 31 of *SFAS 2* can conclude that virtually all computer software costs are R & D; the Interpretation specified that such costs which have a "sales orientation"—will be used in a computer or computer system sales operation "or administrative activities"—are not R & D costs. Regrettably, the Interpretation failed to resolve the problem, and the possible capitalization of some computer software costs which do not fall under the definition of R & D costs remains at issue.

It was in the "Basis for Conclusions" section of this Statement that the FASB first defined economic resources as "those *scarce* resources for which there is an *expectation of future benefits to the enterprise* either through use or sale." R & D benefits were too uncertain to qualify as assets.

Statement No. 2 has been criticized for failing to permit capitalization of some R & D costs, but has not received the sustained opposition that *Statement No. 8* received, for example. This may be because firms have discovered a variety of innovative arrangements which permit R & D costs to be funded in a manner obviating their write-off. Forming a limited partnership is probably the most common form of these arrangements; some companies have recorded the R & D as having been performed under a contract for a customer, the partnership. Others have used such partnerships to raise funds for R & D, accounted for as loans, or equity investments, or sale of future revenues.

FASB Statement No. 2 was regarded as too extreme a position to take in accounting for R & D expenditures by most foreign accounting associations, and the International Accounting Standards Committee's IAS 9, "Accounting for Research and Development Activities" (July 1978), permits companies to capitalize, and amortize against future revenues, R & D expenditures having determinable future benefits. United States accountants do not follow international accounting standards.

INTANGIBLE ASSETS—GENERAL CONCLUSIONS

There are, of course, many other examples of intangibles, such as the player contracts which appear on the balance sheets of football league clubs and are amortized over playing lives. The question of why are certain values separately disclosed in financial statements under the title "intangible assets" (sometimes, "other assets") is not easy to answer. The obvious answer—because they cannot be touched—has already been dismissed. Nevertheless, much of the obscurity surrounding the items included in this category is due to a continued preoccupation with nonexistent criteria of touch, taste, sight, sound, and smell.[30]

It is important, however, to recognize that intangibles are assets in exactly the same way that tangibles are. In the FASB's terminology, intangibles can be probable future economic benefits; whoever invented nylon can testify to that. In the framework provided in chapter 12, expenditure on developing or acquiring intangible assets is undertaken because it is believed that these intangibles can be charged to other entities or persons, and only when this belief is seen to be mistaken are they written off as losses. Nor is it necessary for an intangible asset to be separable, or for its expected future benefits to have a higher degree of certainty attached to them than those of tangible assets.

Examples found from balance sheets of corporations, in addition to long-term receivables and equity investments which are often reported under this heading, include—

- Startup costs, including preoperating losses (no longer capitalizable after *FASB Statement No. 7*, "Accounting for Development Stage Companies");
- Advertising and promotion costs;
- Relocation costs;
- Cost of converting manual files to computer files;
- Prepaid lease expenses;
- Repair part inventories;
- Ship expenses for a layup period;
- Publishers' bookplates;
- Interest on advance sales of oil and gas;
- Purchased credit files.

It is probable that the U.S. practice of showing separately a category "other assets," representing in the main, intangible assets, is another illustration of the influence of income taxation, since expensing or amortization of these assets invariably calls for special treatment under the Internal Revenue Code.

The subject of accounting for intangible assets was believed to have been settled by *APB Opinion No. 17*, "Intangible Assets" (1970). This Opinion restricts accounting for intangibles to their acquisition costs, and requires that they be written off by systematic charges to earnings (expense) over estimated life, not to exceed forty years. Changes in the estimate of useful life should be accounted for under *APB Opinion No. 20*. Promulgation of *FASB Statement No. 44*, "Accounting for Intangible Assets of Motor Carriers," in December 1980 suggests that either *APBO 17* and *20* were not understood, or were not being followed by a sizeable number of affected companies.

LONG-TERM LIABILITIES

The long-term financing of a business can be effected in a number of ways: by borrowing, by raising equity capital, by government subsidy of one kind or another, and even by customers, through various forms of advance payment. In this section we consider borrowing, a case where the recognition problem is acute.

An article in the *Financial Executive* recently stated that "existing accounting concepts of liability are so ill-defined that they are inadequate to deal with the increasingly sophisticated financing methods being practiced today."[31] The authors drew attention to some of the ways in which companies have obtained "off-balance sheet financing" by incurring obligations which need not be recognized as liabilities, including—

- Nonconsolidation of finance subsidiaries;
- Sales of receivables with recourse;
- Product financing arrangements;
- Operating leases drawn up in such a way as to qualify as such under *FASB Statement No. 13*, although technically capital in nature.

The FASB addressed this question in *Statement No. 47*, "Disclosure of Long-Term Obligations" (March 1981). Unconditional purchase obligations must be disclosed if not reported in the balance sheet. Such obligations include project financing arrangements, take-or-pay contracts, throughput contracts; and other commitments which are both unconditional and entered into for financing considerations. Appendix A to this Statement attempted to use the objectives of financial reporting in *Concepts Statement No. 1* to support this position, and went on to say that

> The Board's accounting recognition criteria project will consider criteria for balance sheet recognition of all contractual rights and obligations, whether or not unconditional and whether or not associated with financing arrangements.

Significantly, no attempt was made to use the definitions of elements contained in Concepts Statement No. 3 for the resolution of this problem.

FASB Statement No. 49, "Accounting for Product Financing Arrangements" (June 1981), requires a sale of inventory accompanied by an agreement to repurchase at the same price to be accounted for as a borrowing.

Of course, omission of some of these liabilities is compensated to a certain extent by the effects of inflation. Relating current borrowings to plant and other assets purchased in prior years and reported at historical costs makes the liabilities appear more burdensome than they are; historical cost debt ratios are often overstated. The measurement of reported liabilities is also a problem.

In market operations the value of a long-term liability is the sum of the expected future payments of interest and principal discounted at an appropriate rate. In theory, this rate is the marginal rate of substitution of future satisfactions for present ones, known in economics as the rate of interest. In practice, it is a function of the supply of and demand for loanable funds.

If a bond or debenture is issued to produce a rate of return to the investor equal to the current cost of this type of capital to this company, the book value and the market value of the debt are the same. Assume that a company issues a $1,000 bond bearing interest at 10 percent per annum and repayable at the end of ten years in the amount of $1,000. If the current rate of interest is 10 percent per annum, it is clear that the market value of the bond is $1,000. This is also the amount at which the bond will be recorded in the accounts. In all cases where interest payable differs from the product of the principal amount received and the relevant cost of capital, or where the principal amount repayable differs from the amount received, complications arise. These complications affect the determination of interest expense, but we are here considering their implications for the liability. They result in bond premiums and discounts.

Under this approach, a change in interest rates results in a change in the value of the liability, and, therefore, a change in premium or discount. Neither accounting theory nor practice require such an accounting treatment generally, although it is recognized in accounting for business combinations using the purchase method, at the date of acquisition. Thus, balance sheets which include amounts borrowed years ago at low interest rates overstate the liability in periods of high interest rates.

It is interesting to note that accountants experience no difficulty in accepting the proposition that the objective of financial reporting is to assist users to assess cash flows, and at the same time support a method of accounting for liabilities which results in bond premiums and discounts as "theoretically correct." This method results in the reported amount of the debt being different from the amount which will be repaid, and the reported amount of the interest expense being different from the periodical cash outflow for interest.

Changes in present value arising out of changes in interest rates during the life of the debt are not recorded or reported, nor are decreases of market value arising out of perceived financial difficulties of the borrower. Thus, the observation that the "theoretically correct" method of accounting for long-term debt is to record it at its present value on incurrence, and to amortize the difference between present and maturity value to interest expense over the life of the debt by using the interest method, must be looked at with a degree of skepticism.

Further, in the 1977 *FASB Statement No. 15*, "Accounting by Debtors and Creditors for Troubled Debt Restructuring," additional modifications were made to the theoretical basis of accounting for long-term debt. As a result of depressed economic conditions during the years 1975-77 many debtors were obliged to renegotiate loans with banks and other lenders. These renegotiations often involved reduction of the amount of the indebtedness, or of the rate of interest, or extensions of the time to maturity. In such cases the Statement lays down that the total future cash payments are to be regarded as the debtor's liability (and the creditor's receivable). If the sum of the future cash payments exceeds the carrying amount of the obligation, the effective interest rate is to be computed using the discounted cash flow method, and the excess amortized to expense as interest in accordance with this calculation regardless of the amounts designated as interest in the renegotiated agreement. If the sum of the future cash payments is less than the carrying amount of the obligation, the difference is recorded and reported as a gain in the borrower's income statement for the period in which the restructuring takes place. In this case, the future payments are debited against the written down liability, without reference to interest or principal. So much for present value in accounting, which is also disregarded on accounting for convertible debt.

CONVERTIBLE DEBT

A convertible security is an issue of preferred stock, bonds, or debentures which may be exchanged for common stock, at the owner's discretion, on terms specified at the time of issue.

There are many reasons for issuing convertible debt, a sound one and several unsound ones. When a company raises capital to finance a long-term construction project, as is the case with harbor works, pipelines, refineries, and chemical process plants, it is clear that no profits will be earned until operations start, and, therefore, a purchaser of common stock can expect no dividend during this period. As a corollary, interest paid on capital during the construction period is properly capitalized as part of the cost of the asset and will not, in this case, result in losses being shown during the construction period, thus postponing the dividend even further. In this situation, it is appropriate to finance construction with debt which can be converted into equity when operations start, thus providing an equity base for subsequent debt incurred to provide working capital or expand capacity.

Unsound reasons are (1) to avoid taxes by paying what would otherwise be nondeductible dividends in the form of interest, or (2) to induce hesitant investors to buy securities by adding the sweetener of the conversion right to the basic return. Tax avoidance is a legitimate collateral objective of business decision making, not a prime objective, and to confuse investors by placing them in an ambiguous position, not knowing whether they are creditors or proprietors, is an unfortunate way to establish a close business relationship with them. Likewise, to issue convertible debt to institutional investors which are precluded by law from purchasing common stocks is a form of deception which, though legal, has nothing else to commend it. Since a great deal of convertible debt has been issued for unsound reasons, it is hardly surprising that accountants have found it difficult to account for.

It is important to note that when convertible debt is issued to attract the speculator, the issuer can often sell the bonds initially at a price above the price of comparable straight debt. In such cases, the initial conversion price is greater than the market price of the common stock at the time of issue and does not decrease over time except for a provision to protect the holder from the effects of stock splits and dividends. As an example, suppose a company could issue debt at par, bearing interest at the rate of 10 percent per annum; it might instead issue convertible debt at a premium of 10 percent, bearing interest at the rate of 6 percent per annum and convertible into common stock at $33⅓ per share, at a time when the company's stock was selling at $20 per share.

The accounting problems which this situation presents are as follows:

1. What amount should be recorded as the debt liability?
2. What amount, if any, should be attributed to the conversion privilege and shown as paid-in capital?

With regard to the first of these questions, the APB in *Opinion No. 10* first recommended the separation of the debt liability from the value of the conversion privilege; *Opinion No. 12* suspended this ruling for further study of the problem, and *Opinion No. 14* eventually recommended that no portion of the proceeds be allocated to the conversion privilege, the entire amount being recorded as debt. The same *Opinion No. 14*, however, laid down a different basis for bonds issued with detachable warrants. In this situation, a bond issued is accompanied by a warrant, or option to purchase common stock in the future at a fixed price. *Opinion No. 14* held that, because the warrant is a separate security and can be traded apart from the bond, it can be accounted for by crediting the value of the warrant to stockholders' equity and the balance of the proceeds to the bond. *Opinion No. 14* provided that, if convertible debt is issued at a substantial premium, there is a presumption that the premium represents the value of the conversion feature and should be allocated to stockholders' equity. The question—what constitutes a substantial premium?—has never been satisfactorily answered. The viewpoint presented here is that a debt should appear in the balance sheet as such until it is converted. A warrant is a type of equity security and can, therefore, be accounted for as such.

Accounting for the conversion of convertible debt is another unsolved problem of accounting theory. If this is a nonmonetary exchange, the securities into which the debt is converted should be recorded at fair value; whether the fair value of the debt or the other security is more clearly apparent is a debatable question, particularly if both are quoted on markets. If this is not a nonmonetary exchange, or if it is considered an exchange of similar securities, the question of whether to record the transaction at fair value or carrying amount is usually resolved in favor of the latter, but to what extent should the par value of the security into which the debt is converted influence the amount at which the conversion is recorded? It will be appreciated that there are a number of alternatives here, some of which can provide the issuer of the convertible debt with a larger gain (or smaller loss) than others.

How can *FASB Statement of Financial Accounting Concepts No. 3*, "Elements of Financial Statements of Business Enterprises," help us to solve this problem? Not in respect of its definition of equity, which is a residual and affected only by enterprise operations, investments by owners and distributions to owners. The Statement confirms that a liability exists until something happens to remove the enterprise's responsibility to settle it, but it is silent on what constitutes settlement. Nor does the Statement's definitions of gains and losses (see chapter 14) help, as it is necessary first to ascertain whether there has been an increase or decrease in equity, which is precisely the question we are trying to answer.

DEFERRED CREDITS

Most deferred credits are actually estimated liabilities and bear the same relationship to long-term debt that accrued expenses bear to accounts payable. It would be appropriate, therefore, to group them with long-term debt under the heading "long-term obligations." Those arising on consolidation will be discussed in chapter 16.

This category of balance sheet liability is not much loved by accounting textbook writers, who restrict their attention to the two types of deferred taxes which will be considered further in the next sections of this chapter. Published balance sheets are replete with deferred credits, however, even though one category, the deferred premiums of casualty insurers relating to probable future liability for catastrophe losses, has been eliminated by *FASB Statement No. 5*. The category, besides deferred taxes and deferred investment tax credit, includes the following:

Advance payments received by oil and gas companies. These are very large sums which gas companies and other customers often pay to oil and gas producers to finance exploration and production, the understanding being that the advances will not be returned but, if commercially recoverable reserves are found, the advance payments will ensure that they are supplied to the financier and be taken into account in arriving at the price of the oil or gas. These advance payments can be likened to long-term deferred revenues.

Unfunded pension liabilities of enterprises operating such schemes. A firm which assures its employees of pensions but does not pay cash (or other property) to a trustee on their behalf will debit pension expense in accordance with *APB Opinion No. 8* with a credit to this account; pensions paid will be debited here. In some cases, firms with funded pension schemes will accrue part or all of the liability not yet funded in this category.

Deferred compensation Suppose that a movie actor who worries about his old age accepts payment for a film role in the form of "5% of the gross for each of the next 20 years." The film producer must estimate the liability in order to ascertain the cost of the film, the corresponding credit being a deferred credit.

In this discussion, it should be remembered that, in the context of accrual accounting, deferral is the technical term given to the practice of recognizing that a completed movement of values between one entity and another has an incomplete aspect from the viewpoint of one or both. Using the examples provided by Kohler, a receipt or accrual of revenue before it is earned is a transaction in suspense to both parties, whereas a payment or accrual of an expenditure before the object acquired is consumed by use or distribution is a transaction in suspense only to the entity incurring the expense.[32] In the potential social consolidation model, the former would be eliminated, whereas the latter would not, representing as it does either an increase in inventories or an increase in fixed assets.

DEFERRED TAXES

Tax deferral results from tax allocation, which is a consequence of differences between accounting net income and taxable income.

We have attempted to demonstrate the conceptual basis for accounting profit, or net income; taxable income is a term which can be understood only in the context of income tax legislation, which attempts to provide a means for financing public expenditures, equalizing personal incomes, and promoting certain economic objectives. There is no *prima facie* reason why these values should be identical, and there is no particular significance to the difference between them. Thus, the observation that the ratio of income tax expense to net income was .13 for Company *A* and .42 for Company *B*, at a time when the tax rate on *taxable income* was .48, is an observation which has no normative significance, although the analysis of the reasons for such differences may be relevant for making predictions.

So long as income tax was regarded as an appropriation of net income, rather than expense, the difference between accounting net income and taxable income did not lead to any additional disclosure, probably because it was widely understood that appropriations, being at the discretion of someone inside or outside the firm, had no normative significance. The amount reported as income tax was the estimated liability to pay income tax on the taxable income of the accounting period; as legislation put corporations on a pay-as-you-go basis, this estimate would not change simply because payments were substituted for liability to pay.

The introduction of the *matching principle* to explain why certain expenditures did not become expenses immediately, but were deferred as inventories and charged to expense only in the period when the goods were sold, drew the attention of some accounting theorists to the nature of income tax expense. The following assumptions were made:

1. The firm is a going concern; it will continue to make profits and pay income taxes on them.
2. Income tax is an expense and not a distribution of profit.
3. The amount of the expense is found by applying the income tax rate to the pretax accounting profit, and not by computing the income tax liability for the year.
4. The difference between income tax expense and income tax liability, insofar as it could be expected to result in higher or lower income tax payments in future years, should be deferred as either a credit or a debit balance in the balance sheet.

These assumptions were turned into accounting principles by *APB Opinion No. 11*, "Accounting for Income Taxes." This Opinion laid down that interperiod tax allocation was an integral part of the determination of income tax expense, and that the deferral method should be used to disclose its effects. Differences between accounting net income and taxable income are classified into *permanent differences*, which will not be reversed in a subsequent period, and *timing differences*, which will cause the income tax expense of a subsequent period to be greater or less because the income tax expense of an earlier period was less or more. A permanent difference would normally arise where the corporate income tax was being used to provide business with a disguised subsidy such as the mineral depletion allowances, whereas a timing difference would normally arise out of an attempt to lighten the burden of the corporate income tax on business liquidity in time of inflation, by permitting partial postponement of payment. This is the effect of the so-called accelerated depreciation methods used in income tax computations, whether or not they are used to arrive at accounting net income. Interperiod tax allocation applies to timing differences and not to permanent ones.

A related concept is that of intraperiod tax allocation. Differences between accounting net income and taxable income, arising out of the tax effects of extraordinary gains and losses, give rise to the need for tax allocation within a period. Shortly stated, if an extraordinary gain or loss is taxable or deductible and is shown separately in the income statement, the gain or loss should be disclosed on an "after tax effect" basis, with appropriate adjustment to the income tax expense account. Although there are suggestions that this is necessary if the financial statements are to be used by investors for prediction, it would be equally necessary simply to represent the impact of the extraordinary item on the company. Prior years' items similarly call for this type of tax allocation, as also does disclosure of the effects of disposing of a segment of the business.

In this situation, however, the question of which rate of tax to use will arise. The gain, for example, could be reduced by tax at (1) the actual rate, (2) the marginal rate, or (3) the average rate; in each case, where tax rates change, two or more rates of tax may fall to be considered. It would appear that this question can be answered only in the light of the facts of the particular case; if a gain gives rise to an identifiable tax liability, this amount should be used for the intraperiod allocation; where it simply increases taxable income, the highest or marginal rate should be used. The number and complexity of situations calling for intraperiod tax allocation suggest that no rule will prove workable for all cases.

It is difficult to justify the choice of the deferred method, rather than the liability method, of tax allocation. The unnecessary assumptions of the matching principle, to be discussed in chapter 14, may have been to blame. The reason for tax deferral itself is not hard to find; a flow-through treatment implies a government subsidy equal to the amount of tax saved, or a prepayment of tax on the timing difference. However, the tax is not saved in the former (more general) case, and the benefit is, at best, interest on the postponed payment for the postponement period. This would be clearer if the estimated liability to future income taxation were shown in the balance sheet, rather than a deferred credit.

Income taxation in the United States has become so complex that it is widely believed to be beyond human understanding at the present time. The tax implications of business operations are now dealt with by taxation specialists, and accountants do not presume to know how to determine income tax expense, or to handle the tax deferral aspect of tax accounting. These decisions, when an annual report is being prepared, are dealt with by a tax specialist, who is often a lawyer rather than a CPA. It may be that this aspect of accounting is no longer explicable by reference to accounting theory, in which subject accounting for income taxes must be treated as a given, a percept rather than a concept.

INTERPERIOD TAX ALLOCATION

Suppose a company has charged straight-line depreciation of $1,000 against revenue in arriving at accounting net income and accelerated depreciation of $2,000 in arriving at taxable income. *Ceteris paribus*, as the economists say, the tax saving of $1,000 times the current tax rate will lead to a subsequent increase in taxes of $1,000 times the future tax rate, because the company will have less depreciation to charge against revenue in arriving at future taxable income. To disclose this estimated future event arising out of something which has happened during the accounting period, the saving in tax should be deferred and amortized over the periods during which the income tax liability will be greater. In this way, something which affects only liquidity will not also affect the calculation of after-tax profitability.

We recognize the following four cases where interperiod tax allocation may be necessary:

1. Tax deduction now, expense later
2. Revenue now, taxable income later
3. Taxable income now, revenue later
4. Expense now, tax deduction later

Examples are (1) accelerated depreciation used only for tax purposes; (2) installment sales reported by the installment method for tax purposes only; (3) rent received in advance, taxable in the year of receipt; (4) provisions for estimated expenses which may be deducted only on an actual basis. The first two cases lead to a *deferred credit* for deferred taxation; the latter two to a deferred charge for deferred taxation, similar to a prepaid expense. *APBO No. 11* established a restriction on deferred tax charges by providing that the tax effects of operating loss carry forwards should not be recognized until the periods of realization. The reason for this, presumably, is that the tax effect is contingent on earning taxable income in the future; since the same applies to all aspects of tax deferral, we can identify in this restriction an obsolete view of assets as "things owned." In all cases where interperiod tax allocation is done, the rate to be used, according to *APBO No. 11*, is the rate applicable to the period when tax was deferred; apart from the question of materiality, there does not appear to be a good reason for failing to reflect in the financial statements the effect of significant changes in tax rates (or tax laws, for that matter).

There are three recognized methods of tax allocation.

1. The *net of tax* method, which is not much used in practice, and where the tax effect is netted against the applicable revenue, expense, asset, or liability.
2. The *deferred* method, which is the one recommended in *APBO No. 11*. It uses and maintains the tax rates in effect when the timing difference originates and does not accommodate subsequent changes in tax rates.
3. The *liability* method, which is often used outside the United States. This method uses tax rates in effect when income taxes are expected to be paid or recovered, and, when tax rates change subsequent to allocation, the deferral must be adjusted.

After experimenting with the deferred method, the United Kingdom accounting profession decided that it was too complex and misleading to be continued, and in 1977 a Statement of Accounting Practice recommended a partial allocation method. Under this method, only the portion of a timing difference expected to reverse in the foreseeable future is deferred. A corporation which can foresee heavy future investment in fixed assets sufficient to postpone the reversal of the timing difference caused by accelerated depreciation would not defer the tax effect from this source. Partial allocation resembles the liability method.

Approval of the deferred method by the APB is said to be "income oriented" because it does not involve adjustments of the current period's tax expense arising out of changes in tax rates affecting prior allocations. However, the current preoccupation of the SEC and the FASB with flowing as many changes as possible through the current income statement renders suspect this explanation.

Another explanation is that the deferred taxation account is not perceived as a liability.[33] This was the opinion of Professor Sidney Davidson who served on the APB at the time of *Opinion No. 11* and whose views may have prevailed.[34]

A related problem is the choice between comprehensive and special allocation. The latter is the approach which assumes a usefulness to investors' decision models, whereas comprehensive allocation makes no such assumption. For example, the allocation of the tax effects of deducting intangible drilling costs in the oil industry, while capitalizing them in the accounts, would be necessary under the special allocation approach, but could be omitted under comprehensive allocation because of the assumed offsetting effects of future depletion allowances. When depletion allowances were withdrawn, tax allocation for intangible drilling costs became mandatory, albeit in a restricted form.

There is an obvious conflict between comprehensive allocation under the deferred method and the objective of predicting future cash flows. It is possible to discern in the literature on tax allocation several other atavistic features: (1) the operating income view of the income statement, which makes corporate earnings a reflection of managerial performance; (2) a static funds statement view of the balance sheet; (3) the desire to remove factors causing business net income to fluctuate. In respect of this last, alternatives to tax deferral include the flow-through method, where income tax expense equals income tax accrual, and the partial allocation method.

Deferred investment tax credits are explicable only with reference to the fact that they presented the accounting profession with a new type of problem, which it proved unable to handle. The investment tax credit was clearly intended as a subsidy, a kind of business handout to stimulate investment and, thus, to raise the gross national product. If it had been an operating subsidy, it should have been credited to the income statement, a treatment preferred by the U.S. Treasury and eventually countenanced as one of the approved methods under *APB Opinion No. 4* (the flow-through method). As a capital subsidy it should have been credited to stockholders' equity, like any other donated capital. The other alternative admitted by *APB Opinion No. 4*—defer and amortize to income over the life of the asset—corresponds with no known meaning of liability; the only argument in favor of this treatment is that it is preferable to reducing the cost of the asset by the amount of the credit, which virtually guarantees that the benefit of the credit will go to customers and not to stockholders, through its effect on product costs. Over 500 of the 600 companies analyzed in *Accounting Trends and Techniques* use the flow-through method.

PROPRIETORSHIP OR STOCKHOLDERS' EQUITY

The prevailing view of the balance sheet, the *proprietary theory*, sees proprietorship as a residue: assets minus liabilities equals owners' equity. In this view, the balance sheet is a simple identity, an equality which derives from the fact that the two quantities are the same observations under different names. Economists see the balance sheet in this light because they do not distinguish between capital and assets. A balance sheet which was a simple identity would not be very useful, and we shall see that the magnitudes classified as ownership equities are derived independently of assets and liabilities in business accounting.

At the time assets are introduced into the firm's economy, the amounts of capital are determined in relation to those assets' values, whether we look at proprietorship or debt. At that time, however, the relationship is broken, so a liability can continue to exist long after the asset which it once represented has been used, lost, or sold. Similarly, the legal rights attaching to stockholders' equity, which the monetary amounts in the balance sheet represent, exist until extinguished by process of law.

The increases and decreases of stockholders' equity which are registered in the form of profits, losses, and distributions are likewise found outside the balance sheet. The income statement starts with sales and deducts from this representation of a relationship between the firm and its environment, the expenses for the same period. To some extent these expenses are a function of balance sheet values, but to a much larger extent they represent transactions with the firm's environment. The net income or loss for a period is therefore independently obtained, and cannot be regarded solely as a double-entry "plug."

In previous chapters we have discussed the entity, fund, and commander theories; it must be admitted that they do not shed light upon this controversy. The enterprise theory is an extension of the entity theory, in which the interests of social groups other than equity investors and lenders are given due weight. It is submitted that the enterprise theory, which supports "a value added" form of income statement, also supports the view of proprietorship as an independent variable. There is also Paton's residual equity theory, which recognizes the peculiar position of the proprietor, or common stockholder, as the bearer of residual risk and the owner of residual reward. In this view, the equation becomes—

$$\text{Assets} - \text{specific equities} = \text{residual equity}$$

The specific equities include, in addition to obligations of the nature of debt, preferred stock and other priority ownership interests. It has been suggested that this view sees capital contributed by common stockholders and retained earnings as the equity of the corporation *in itself*.[35] Such a viewpoint effectively closes the firm's system and separates it from the rest of the economic system; it is, therefore, inconsistent with the potential social consolidation model.

It must be confessed that the concept of proprietorship, more than any other in accounting, is explicable only by reference to the legal and institutional framework within which firms function, and for this reason has no counterpart in government, not-for-profit institution, or household accounting. For the same reason, subclassification of this item in the balance sheet always follows legal rules, even though from the viewpoint of the entity itself and its creditors there is no distinction between different types of residual equity—contributed capital at par, in excess of par, donated capital, retained earnings.

Recent years have seen a trend away from the presentation of the details of stockholders' equity in the balance sheet and towards the presentation of this item as one amount, or divided simply into contributed capital and retained earnings. Movements on the various accounts representing the components of equity have been disclosed in a separate Statement of Changes in Stockholders' Equity, or in a note to the financial statements. Since *FASB Statement No. 12*, "Accounting for Certain Marketable Securities," and *FASB Statement No. 52* on foreign currency translation, the components of stockholders' equity have acquired a new significance. Both of these call for changes in net assets to be debited directly to stockholders' equity instead of passing through the income statement. Gains and losses on transactions with treasury stock also affect stockholders' equity directly, as do donations, a form of capital subsidy. Are we seeing the process of a new form of financial statement developing, to account for transactions which affect stockholders' equity but do not enter into the determination of income?

Scott has drawn attention to the possibility of departing from the assumption that stockholders' equity can be accounted for only in accordance with legal constructs.[36] He suggests an economic classification of equities into "transitory" and "standing" sources of capital; distributable retained earnings would presumably belong under the former, and contributed capital under the latter. The proposed new Uniform Companies Act for the United States would provide for only two components of stockholders' equity: contributed capital and retained earnings. The SEC, in its Release 33-6097 on "Presentation of Redeemable Preferred Stock," effectively removed one component of legal stockholders' equity from the balance sheet equity class. Mandatorily redeemable preferred stock is in substance debt in many cases; the form is selected for tax reasons. The SEC required registrants with outstanding preferred stock subject to mandatory redemption, or where redemption was outside the issuer's control, to present separately—

1. preferred stocks of this nature,
2. nonredeemable preferred (or redeemable only at the issuer's option), and,
3. common stocks

together with appropriate footnote information. The SEC abandoned its earlier proposal to prohibit companies from disclosing a "stockholders' equity" section in the balance sheet if it included mandatorily redeemable preferred stock.

The problem of accounting for treasury stock also remains unsolved. Whether to use the par or the cost method is a fairly trivial issue compared with the question whether treasury stock should be carried as an asset or a contra-equity valuation adjustment.

Prior to World War I treasury stock was often accounted for as an asset, but over the past seventy years the view has prevailed that the purchase of treasury stock decreases both assets and stockholders' equity, because a corporation cannot own part of itself. As a legal proposition this is incorrect; a corporation is a person and has all the legal rights of a person, including that of owning shares. Further, one of the ways in which treasury stock originates is by donation, or for nonpayment of a subscription, in which situations the objective is to either sell the shares or use them as security for a loan. Finally, some corporations do account for treasury stock as an asset; General Motors Inc., for example, purchases its own stock on the market in order to have shares available to discharge its obligations under employee stock option schemes, and reports these shares as an asset in its published balance sheet.

Of great significance to this question is the related one: is the unissued share capital of a corporation an asset? The prevailing practice is to report in stockholders' equity only the amounts subscribed for shares issued, and not the par or market value of unissued shares. Yet unissued shares, particularly those of a corporation with publicly traded stock or of a corporation actively acquiring other companies by issuing stock in exchange for their assets, satisfy the FASB's definition of an asset.

It may be recalled that current practice recognizes additional paid-in capital from a variety of sources besides premiums received on the issue of shares. These sources include—

- Reacquisition of stock for less than the price at which it was sold to the public;
- Expiration of stock warrants and options unexercised;
- Reduction of stated capital on reorganization;
- Sale of treasury stock above cost;
- Donations of property to the company;
- Amounts subscribed on shares forfeited.

With reference to retained earnings, the practice of reporting appropriations of retained earnings has ceased, in spite of its survival in accounting textbooks. Retained earnings in the typical corporation is the sum of net income (loss) and prior period adjustments to date, less dividends distributed. However, some companies still debit share or bond issuance costs here.

CONCLUSION

It is difficult to examine a discipline which is changing rapidly, and in some ways radically, in order to relate theory and practice. Practices which do not fit the new conceptual framework can be viewed as obsolete as well as inconsistent; those which do fit can be hailed as illustrations of the framework's usefulness.

The task of the designers of the conceptual framework was to maintain a level of generality, leaving specific accounting decisions to those drafting statements and interpretations. It appears from our review of the present state of accounting for assets and liabilities, however, that strains in fitting specific accounting decisions into the conceptual framework have appeared with some frequency.

In the author's view, the principal cause of these strains is the sometimes explicit, sometimes concealed, cash flow model underlying the conceptual framework statements. Cash flow is a subsystem of a firm's operating system; assessing future cash flows cannot provide a satisfactory perspective for asset and liability recognition or measurement. It will be necessary for the FASB to return to the models used for internal corporate accountability if the problems of external financial reporting are to be solved within a consistent framework.

ENDNOTES

1. See chapter 2 for a discussion of classification in accounting.
2. This is the case in respect of the model presented by Sterling in his *Theory of the Measurement of Enterprise Income*, Kansas, 1971. We understand why his wheat trader should hold wheat, but why, if capital is freely available at the rate of interest, must he hold cash? See pp. 21-3.
3. See chapter 7, para. 25, *APB Statement No. 4*.
4. Rappaport, Alfred, "Discussion of 'The Balance Sheet—Embodiment of the Most Fundamental Elements of Accounting Theory'," reprinted in *Financial Accounting Theory I: Issues and Controversies*, ed. Zeff and Keller, New York: McGraw-Hill Book Company, 1973, p. 178.
5. Report of the 1966-68 Committee on External Reporting, "An Evaluation of External Reporting Practices," *The Accounting Review*, Supplement to Vol. XLIV, 1969, pp. 79-123.
6. Connor, Joseph E., "Discovery Value—the Oil Industry's Untried Method," *Journal of Accountancy*, May 1975, pp. 54-63. On RRA see the SEC's *Accounting Series Release No. 269*, also Releases 33-6126 and 6128 and *Staff Accounting Bulletin No. 35*. On discovery value, Paton and Littleton wrote, "It is hardly necessary to say that the acquisition of property through donation or discovery does not create an earned surplus."
7. Kenley, W.J. and G.J. Staubus, "Objectives and Concepts of Financial Statements," *Accounting Research Study No. 3*, Melbourne, Australia: Accountancy Research Foundation, 1972, p. 105.
8. Wright, F.K., "Towards a General Theory of Depreciation," *Journal of Accounting Research*, Vol. II, 1964, pp. 80-90.
9. Edwards, Edgar O., "Depreciation and the Maintenance of Real Capital," in *Depreciation and Replacement Policy*, ed. J.L. Meij, Chicago: Quadrangle Books, 1961.
10. SOP 80-1.
11. *Encyclopedic Dictionary of Business Finance*, Englewood Cliffs: Prentice-Hall, Inc., 1967, Vol. I, p. 201.
12. *Accounting Terminology Bulletin No. 1*, New York: AICPA, 1953, p. 25.
13. Paton, W.A., *Accounting Theory*, Lawrence, Kansas: Scholars Book Co., 1973, pp. 191-6.
14. in *The Theory and Measurement of Enterprise Income*, op cit.
15. Hicks, J.R. (with A.G. Hart), *The Social Framework*, New York: Oxford University Press, 1945, Note C, p. 244.
16. Keynes, J.M., *The General Theory of Employment, Interest and Money*, New York: Harcourt, Brace & World, Inc., 1965, p. 100, and Baxter, W.T., "The Accountant's Contribution to the Trade Cycle," *Economica*, Vol. XXII, 1955, pp. 164-72.
17. Hotelling, H., "A General Mathematical Theory of Depreciation," *Journal of the American Statistical Association*, Vol. XX, 1925, pp. 340-53.

18. Brief, Richard P., "A Late Nineteenth Century Contribution to the Theory of Depreciation," *Journal of Accounting Research*, Spring 1967, pp. 27-38.
19. Lutz, F. and V., *The Theory of Investment of the Firm*, Princeton, 1951, p. 7.
20. Wells, M.C., "A Note on the Amortization of Fixed Assets," *The Accounting Review*, April 1968, pp. 373-76.
21. See Anthony, Robert N., *Accounting for the Cost of Interest*, Lexington, Mass: Lexington Books, 1975.
22. Arcady, Alex T. and Charles E. Baker, "How to Implement the Controversial FASB Statement No. 34," *Journal of Accountancy*, March 1981, pp. 62-70.
23. The only recent discussion of this problem is found in *CASB Standard 404*, "Capitalization of Tangible Assets," Washington, D.C.: Cost Accounting Standards Board, 1973. It is consistent with the viewpoint presented in this chapter.
24. Kohler, Eric L., *A Dictionary for Accountants*, 4th ed., Englewood Cliffs, N.J., Prentice Hall, Inc., 1970, p. 235.
25. See Gynther, Reg. S., "Some 'Conceptualizing' on Goodwill," *The Accounting Review*, April 1969, pp. 247-55.
26. Hendriksen, Eldon S., *Accounting Theory*, Homewood, Ill.; Richard D. Irwin, Inc., rev. ed., 1970, p. 434.
27. See Canning, John B., *The Economics of Accountancy*, New York: The Ronald Press Co., 1929, p. 42.
28. Calhoun, Charles H., III, Accounting for Initial Franchise Fees," *Journal of Accountancy*, February 1975, pp. 60-67. The Industry Accounting Guide "Accounting for Franchise Revenue" published by the AICPA in 1973 deals mainly with the franchisor's revenue and not the franchisee's asset.
29. A company is considered to be in the development stage if (a) it is solely concerned with establishing a new business and has not started operating it, or (b) it has started operating but not yet derived significant revenues. Financial Accounting Standards Board, *Statement No. 7*, June 1975, *Accounting and Reporting by Development Stage Companies* ..., p. 2
30. See, for an illustration of this preoccupation, the exchange between G.O. May and counsel in *In the Matter of the Estate of E.P. Hatch, Deceased* (1912) in *Financial Accounting Theory I: Issues and Controversies*, ed. Zeff, S.A. and T.F. Keller, New York: McGraw-Hill Book Company 1973, p. 388.
31. Dieter, Richard and Arthur R. Wyatt, "Get It off the Balance Sheet," *Financial Executive*, January 1980, pp. 42-48.
32. Kohler, Eric L., *A Dictionary for Accountants*, Englewood Cliffs, N.J.: Prentice-Hall Inc., 4th ed. 1970, pp. 142-5.
33. Johnson, Arnold W., "The Interpretation of Financial Statements," *Financial Analysts Journal*, November-December 1968, pp. 75-83.
34. Davidson, Sidney, "Accelerated Depreciation and the Allocation of Income Taxes," *The Accounting Review*, April 1958, pp. 173-80.
35. Li, David H., "The Nature of Corporate Residual Equity under the Entity Concept," *The Accounting Review*, April 1960, pp. 285-63.
36. Scott, Richard A., "Owners' Equity, the Anachronistic Element," *The Accounting Review*, October 1979, pp. 750-63.

SELECTED ADDITIONAL READINGS

Accounting Trends and Techniques, New York: AICPA (Annual).

Anthony, Robert N., *Accounting for the Cost of Interest*, Lexington, Mass.: Lexington Books, 1975.

Baxter, W.T., *Depreciation*, London: Sweet & Maxwell, 1971.

Bierman, Harold Jr. and Roland E. Dukes, "Accounting for Research and Development Costs," *Journal of Accountancy*, April 1975, pp. 48-55.

Birkett, W.P. and R.G. Walker, "Accounting: A Source of Market Imperfection," *Journal of Business Finance and Accounting*, Summer 1974, pp. 171-193.

Burton, John C., Russell E. Palmer and Robert S. Kay, *Handbook of Accounting and Auditing*, Boston: Warren, Gorham & Lamont, 1981, especially chs. 17 and 19 through 26.

Clancy, Donald K., "What is a Convertible Debenture? A Review of the Literature in the U.S.A.," *Abacus*, December 1978, pp. 171-9.

Coughlan, Joseph D. and William K. Strand, *Depreciation: Accounting, Taxes, and Business Decisions*, New York: The Ronald Press Company, 1969.

Dieter, Richard, "Is Lessee Accounting Working?" *The CPA Journal*, August 1979, pp. 13-19.

Fess, Philip, "The Working Capital Concept," *The Accounting Review*, April 1966, pp. 266-270.

Financial Accounting Standards Board, Discussion Memorandum, *An Analysis of Issues Related to Accounting for Research and Development and Similar Costs*, Stamford, Conn: FASB, December 28, 1973.

Financial Accounting Standards Board Discussion Memorandum, *An Analysis of Issues Related to Accounting for Business Combinations and Purchased Intangibles*, Stamford, Conn.: FASB, August 19, 1976, Part Two.

Financial Accounting Standards Board, *Discussion Memorandum*, "An Analysis of Issues Related to Conceptual Framework for Financial Accounting and Reporting: Elements of Financial Statements and Their Measurement," FASB, December 2, 1976, ch. 3.

Financial Accounting Standards Board, *Statement of Financial Accounting Concepts No. 3*, "Elements of Financial Statements of Business Enterprises," FASB, December 1980, Appendix B.

Gynther, Reg S., "Some Conceptualizing on Goodwill," *The Accounting Review*, April 1969, pp. 247-255.

Hirschman, Robert W., "A Look at 'Current' Classifications," *Journal of Accountancy*, November 1967, pp. 54-58.

Huizingh, William, *Working Capital Classification*, Ann Arbor, Mich.: Bureau of Business Research, Graduate School of Business Administration, University of Michigan, 1967.

Lamden, Charles W., Dale L. Gerboth and Thomas W. McRae, *Accounting for Depreciable Assets*, New York: AICPA, 1975.

Livingstone, John Leslie, "Accelerated Depreciation, Cyclical Asset Expenditures and Deferred Taxes," *Journal of Accounting Research*, Autumn 1968, pp. 77-94.

Lowe, Howard D., "The Classification of Corporate Stock Equities," *The Accounting Review*, July 1961, pp. 425-433.

Melcher, Beatrice, *Stockholders' Equity*, New York: AICPA, 1973.

Moonitz, Maurice, "The Changing Concept of Liabilities," *Financial Accounting Theory I: Issues and Controversies*, ed. Zeff and Keller, New York: McGraw-Hill Book Company 1973, pp. 426-434.

Morland, D.P., "Accounting for Goodwill," *The Accountant*, March 13, 1975, pp. 340-344.

National Association of Accountants, "Fixed Asset Accounting: The Capitalization of Costs," *Statement on Management Accounting Practices No. 4*, New York: NAA, October 20, 1972.

Nurnberg, Hugo, *Cash Movements Analysis of the Accounting for Corporate Income Taxes*, East Lansing, Mich.: Graduate School of Business Administration, Michigan State University, 1971, chs. II and III.

Romano, Michael B., "Goodwill—A Dilemma," *Management Accounting*, July 1975, pp. 39-44.

Sprouse, Robert T., "Accounting for What-You-May-Call-Its," *Financial Accounting Theory II: Issues and Controversies*, ed. Keller & Zeff, New York: McGraw-Hill Book Company 1969, pp. 367-380.

Sprouse, Robert J. and Maurice Moonitz, "A Tentative Set of Broad Accounting Principles for Business Enterprises," *Accounting Research Study No. 3*, 1962, pp. 19-41.

Staubus, George J., "Statistical Evidence of the Value of Depreciation Accounting," *Abacus*, August 1967, pp. 3-22.

Stephens, Matthew J., "Inseparability and the Valuation of Convertible Bonds," *Journal of Accountancy*, August 1971, pp. 54-62.

Tearney, Michael G., "Accounting for Goodwill: A Realistic Approach," *Journal of Accountancy*, July 1973, pp. 41-45.

Van Seventer, A., "An Unsettled Problem in the Theory of Replacing Durable Assets: The Wemelsfelder-Traas Controversy," *The International Journal of Accounting Education and Research*, Spring 1974, pp. 45-81.

Wright, F.K., "Towards a General Theory of Depreciation," *Journal of Accounting Research*, Spring 1964, pp. 80-90.

Wright, F.K., "The Valuation of Tax-Depreciable Assets," *The International Journal of Accounting Education and Research*, Spring 1973, pp. 45-57.

Case 13-1 Barter Oil Inc.

Barter Oil Inc. acquired an oil lease in 1978 at a cost of $1,000. Between 1978 and 1982 the company spent $1 million on geological and geophysical costs and other activities designed to ascertain whether the leased property contained oil and/or gas reserves in commercially recoverable quantities. By June 30, 1982 these expenditures, totalling $1,001,000 had been capitalized, and the amount was carried as an asset under the category, "unproved properties."

On July 1, 1982 Barter Oil Inc. entered into an agreement with Splendid Gas Inc. which, on the basis of a study of the test data obtained from Barter, believed that gas would ultimately be produced from this property. Under the terms of the agreement, Splendid paid Barter $2 million in cash and undertook to spend a further

$5 million during the period 1982-85 on drilling wells and installing equipment for the purpose of producing any gas (or oil) which might be recoverable from this lease. In addition, Splendid transferred to Barter another oil lease in the same county, which was as yet untested.

In return, Barter transferred to Splendid a 50 percent interest in both leases.

1. Explain how *APB Opinion No. 29* could assist Barter Oil Inc. to decide how to account for this transaction.
2. Assuming that fair value is not determinable for either property, what different accounting solutions are there to this problem?

Case 13-2 Contingent Liabilities are Also Assets

Some European banks include in their balance sheets the total liability at the balance sheet date for acceptances and endorsements and, as an asset, the equal amount recoverable from third parties should they be called upon to make good these claims.

1. Does such an obligation conform to the FASB definition of a liability?
2. Does the amount recoverable conform to the FASB definition of an asset?
3. Should United States banks be required to account for liabilities under acceptances and endorsements in this way?

END OF CHAPTER QUESTIONS

1. Define *working capital*. Explain the significance of this concept (a) for the management of a business, (b) for the preparation of financial statements.
2. What are current assets? current liabilities?
3. How does a long-term liability become a current liability, and in what circumstances can this condition be ignored?
4. Do current liabilities consist only of legal obligations which must be met by the use of current assets?
5. Explain why the lower of cost or market rule is inappropriate for such current assets as inventories and marketable securities.
6. What is the difference between the following terms: fixed assets; noncurrent assets; property, plant and equipment; depreciable assets?
7. What argument justifies the use of historical cost based values for financial reporting, and what observation refutes it?
8. Explain Wright's concept of *opportunity value*, and the relationship between this concept and replacement cost depreciation. How is the value of a fixed asset determined under this approach?

9. Long-term construction contracts may be accounted for under the percentage-of-completion method.
   A. Discuss the theoretical and practical aspects of using the percentage-of-completion method (ignore taxation considerations).
   B. What conditions should be laid down to restrict the use of the percentage-of-completion method to situations in which it would fairly present the results of operations?
10. Property, plant and equipment (plant assets), generally represents a material portion of the total assets of most companies. Accounting for the acquisition and usage of such assets is therefore an important part of the financial reporting process.
    A. Distinguish between revenue and capital expenditures and explain why this distinction is important.
    B. Briefly define depreciation as used in accounting.
    C. Identify the factors that are relevant in determining the annual depreciation and explain whether these factors are determined objectively or whether they are based on judgement. (AICPA, May 1976)
11. A. Discuss the problems involved in accounting for nonmonetary exchanges, with particular reference to the exchange of unlike assets, with a relatively small cash payment ("boot") from one party to the transaction to the other.
    B. Explain the accounting problems arising in the following situations:
       (i) An automobile manufacturer in the United States ships trucks to a customer in South Africa, receiving in exchange a quantity of South African wine. The wine is shipped to a customer in England in exchange for a quantity of clothing textiles, which are sold for cash to a corporation in Canada.
       (ii) An oil company owns mineral rights over an area of 100,000 acres, of which 5,000 have been explored. A gas well has been discovered which will produce enough gas to pay for the cost of the entire 100,000 acres. The company trades the mineral rights to 10,000 unexplored acres for a 50 percent share in an oil well which has been drilled and completed, and which may or may not contain oil in economically recoverable quantities.
12. "Depreciation is a measure of the planned sacrifice of value for a planned sequence of productive operations." Discuss.
13. What criticism is levelled at *APB Opinion No. 20* insofar as it covers changes in accounting estimates used for depreciation calculations?
14. What is an "involuntary conversion"? How should insurance or other recoveries from such conversions be accounted for under *FASB Interpretation No. 30*?
15. What problems are associated with the measurement of an asset's cost? Why should interest be an element of an asset's

cost? Is the distinction between interest on capital and interest on assets clear? Wherein does it reside?

16. Some research and development expenditure is incurred in order to improve existing products, or to better serve existing customers. Some research and development expenditure is incurred in order to create new products which will be sold to a new market. Managers have been known to argue that the latter type of research and development expenditure should be deferred and charged to expense, under the matching principle, when sales of the new products are made.
    A. Explain why *FASB Statement No. 2* laid down that such expenditures (apart from the exceptions listed in the Statement) should be charged to expense in the period incurred.
    B. Discuss the methods whereby a manager could succeed in deferring such expenditures on the grounds that they are no different in kind from an investment in a new enterprise.
17. What is included in the accounting category "intangibles?" Does this class of items conform to the principles of classification?
18. What three accounting problems does "goodwill" present? What is the main difficulty in valuing expected future excess profits?
19. Explain the problems which arise in accounting for franchise revenues and costs by a franchisor, and how they are resolved by *FASB Statement No. 45*?
20. Trace the impact of the Internal Revenue Code on accounting for intangible assets.
21. What is off-balance sheet financing? Give examples, distinguishing between those which are still off-balance sheet, and those which are now included in balance sheet liabilities.
22. Discuss the relationship between the "theoretically correct" method of accounting for long-term debt, using premium and discount accounts, and (a) the theory of bond valuation, (b) the FASB definition of liability in *Concepts Statement No. 3*, (c) the objective of helping financial statement users to assess future cash flows to or from the enterprise.
23. What is the central problem of accounting for convertible debt? What accounting problem presents itself at the time of conversion?
24. Discuss the category "deferred credits." What are the common characteristics of items included under this heading?
25. Income tax allocation is required under generally accepted accounting principles.
    A. Explain the difference between interperiod and intraperiod tax allocation.
    B. Explain the reasons for each of these two forms of tax allocation.
    C. Discuss the alternative methods of interperiod tax allocation, and state which method corresponds with the reasons given under B.

26. Explain the basis for the analysis of stockholders' equity in corporate financial statements and discuss what alternative method of reporting this item might be more informative.
27. A. Compare the cost method with the par value method of accounting for treasury stock and state which portions of accounting theory are relevant to the explanation for each of these methods.
    B. In what circumstances would it be more informative to report treasury stock as an asset rather than as a reduction of stockholders' equity?

14

THE INCOME STATEMENT OR PROFIT AND LOSS ACCOUNT

Given conflicting views on what constitutes income, to which attention was drawn in chapter 8, it is only to be expected that we encounter difficulties when considering the form and content of the income statement. Even the name of this statement is an issue; although the majority of firms publish income statements, accountants still refer to it as the "P & L," short for profit and loss account.

An indication of the acute nature of the problem of income statement preparation was provided by the FASB in 1979. The Discussion Memorandum, "an analysis of issues related to Reporting Earnings" dated July 31, 1979, clearly showed an intention to adopt the word "earnings" in place of "net income," by defining it as

> ...the increase in net assets or owners' equity from all transactions and other events and circumstances affecting the enterprise during the period, excluding the effects of certain transactions with owners...(para II).

The Exposure Draft of a Statement of Financial Accounting Concepts on Elements of Financial Statements published on December 28 of the same year renamed this concept "comprehensive income." The new name was adopted by Concepts Statement No. 3, and both the ED and the Concepts Statement contained this note:

> *Comprehensive income* is the name used in this Statement for the concept that was called *earnings* in the FASB Exposure Draft, *Objectives of Financial Reporting and Elements of Financial Statements of Business Enterprises*...FASB Concepts Statement No. 1 ...and other conceptual framework documents previously issued....*Earnings* is not defined in this Statement. The Board has decided to reserve the term for possible use to designate a component part, as yet undetermined, of comprehensive income. (n. 1.)

In this chapter we will examine the historical development of the modern income statement and look at some of the unresolved issues of income statement presentation. The definition of the elements of the income statement will be seen to present particular problems at the present time.

HISTORY OF THE INCOME STATEMENT

Early double-entry accounting records suggest a process of comparison of opening and closing balance sheets to calculate profit for the period between them. Since profit was the result of a consumption and production process, what are now referred to as investments by and distributions to proprietors had to be eliminated. This has come to be known as the *capital maintenance approach to income determination*, but the description is anachronistic. Such calculations were not made regularly, and certainly not annually, and their purpose seems to have been to calculate increase or decrease in personal wealth.

During this period we find the origins of the profit and loss account as an analysis of the factors underlying this change in wealth. For example, a merchant would close off the account for a particular line of merchandise, to which he had debited purchases and credited sales, by transferring the balance to the account for profits and losses. Inventories presented a problem then as now, as is apparent from the writings of a German scholar of the Middle Ages named Grammateus (Schreiber). By the nature of its origins, however, the profit and loss account was only a partial analysis of the change in wealth.

Lee has identified the following six components of a double-entry accounting system:

1. The concept of an accounting entity.
2. The concept of algebraic opposition.
3. The concept of a single monetary unit of account.
4. The concept of proprietors' equity.
5. The concept of profit or loss as the increase or decrease of proprietors' equity.
6. The concept of an accounting period, over which to measure profit or loss.[1]

By the fifteenth century this link between the balance sheets at two dates had become explicit and comprehensive, so that the articulation of the profit and loss account with the balance sheet was possible. We look upon this as a critical aspect of double-entry accounting in that the income statement became a chain of evidence leading inexorably from one balance sheet to the next. The analysis of changes in wealth over time was the primary purpose of the profit and loss account.

This primary purpose led to the contemporary uses of the income statement: to provide data for evaluating management's effectiveness; to analyze profitability into its component parts; to aid the prediction of future profits; to support pricing decisions, particularly the price controls of trade associations, cartels, and government regulatory agencies; to determine the part of the increase in wealth which can safely be distributed as a dividend; to determine the ability of a firm to service its debt. The uses of the income statement now extend to the production of the social accounts, since in some countries business income statements are a primary source of national income statistics. Finally, the fact that the income statement analyzes a change of wealth makes it an object of great interest to the taxing authority, providing a point of departure for income and other types of business taxation.

The transition from a proprietary to an entity viewpoint, however, rendered inappropriate the concept of change in wealth. From the viewpoint of the stockholders of a corporation, wealth is measured by the market prices of their shares. If the stockholder wants to calculate the change in his wealth during a period, he compares the market value of his holdings at the beginning and end, adjusting for purchases, sales, and dividends.

It has been suggested that these viewpoints can be integrated by valuing the corporation's securities at market prices and including them in the balance sheet at the values thus found. The resulting difference between assets and liabilities would be something like the economist's "subjective goodwill," the present value of expected future income. The theory has many defects, one of them being the fallacy of composition, the belief that a price quoted for a marginal amount of a particular security is relevant for the entire stock. Principally, however, the difficulty is analytical. If we wish to analyze changes in investors' wealth, we must distinguish between those which are a function of the firm's operations and those which are due to other causes, such as economic changes unrelated to business operations.

This objective probably underlies the multistep income statement. A single-step income statement groups all revenues and all expenses into two classes; net income is found by deducting the latter from the former. The simplicity of this approach is not capable of achievement in practice because various APB Opinions require extraordinary items, gain or loss on discontinued operations, and effect of a change in accounting principle, to be disclosed separately on an after tax basis, after income from continuing operations and before net income. To this extent the theoretical case for a single-step income statement may be said to have been lost; at the very least, income from continuing operations is distinguished from net income.

Of the 600 companies surveyed in *Accounting Trends and Techniques*, however, approximately 60 percent use the single-step form, or show only income tax expense as a separate item before net income.[2] The other 40 percent use a variety of multistep forms, some showing gross margin and others, operating income, in the process of arriving at net income.

CURRENT OPERATING OR ALL-INCLUSIVE?

The difference between these two forms of income statement concerns presentation; a more fundamental problem, resting ultimately on the definition of income, concerns content. In other words, should the income statement embrace all changes in wealth, ending with a single figure which increases or decreases stockholders' equity? Or should the income statement display only the results of operations, in which case articulation requires another statement to reconcile net income with the change in stockholders' equity for the period?

The latter position implies an ability to manipulate income by deciding which elements of profit or loss should bypass the income statement. Attention was drawn to this problem by an early cause of conflict between the SEC and the American Institute's Committee on Accounting Procedure. This was the practice of writing off intangible assets directly to retained earnings, prohibited by the SEC in *ASR No. 50*, but not at that time a contravention of GAAP.

The proximate cause of action by the accounting profession was a situation which arose when two major oil companies were ordered by the Department of Justice to divest themselves of their controlling holdings in a third. One credited the profit on sale to the income statement, the other to retained earnings. Shortly after, *APBO No. 9*[3] appeared, which committed the profession to the all-inclusive approach. In recent years, however, analytical strain has begun to show, and there is some indication of a reversal of this decision.

APBO No. 9 distinguished between the *current operating performance* approach to the income statement, with emphasis on "ordinary, normal, recurring" operations during the period, and the *all-inclusive* approach, using the income statement to account for all periodic changes in proprietorship other than those resulting from nonreciprocal transfers. The principal elements of difference were seen to be *extraordinary items* (clearly, not "ordinary") and *prior period adjustments* (clearly, not "during the period"). With typical adroitness, the APB ruled that extraordinary items should be included in the income statement and shown separately, but that prior period items should be adjustments of opening retained earnings, with restatement of the prior periods affected. The effect of this Opinion was to maintain the distinction between capital and revenue implicit in the balance sheet/income statement dichotomy, and to move the income statement firmly away from an operating statement useful for charting trends and forming a view of "maintainable earnings." The Opinion did not express a preference between the single-step or multi-step forms, but clearly influenced a move away from the latter.

The principal argument supporting the all-inclusive income statement is based on the proposition that, over the total life of the business, lifetime net income should equal the sum of reported period net incomes. In this argument, the justification for excluding prior period adjustments from the income statement of the period is the restatement of the net income figures for the prior periods affected. However, the concept of lifetime net income (attributed to Canning) is meaningless in the context of the Hicksian consumption concept of income; at the end of the firm's life it is not in a position to consume anything. The concept of total lifetime net receipts (receipts from performing the entity's social function, excluding nonreciprocal transfers), on the other hand, is quite clear and unequivocally the sum of the periodic net receipts, but the income statement is not a statement of cash receipts and disbursements.

The SEC was a major influence in moving the accounting profession toward the all-inclusive income statement, but when Form 8–K was revised in January 1977 the SEC reaffirmed the importance of information about unusual and infrequently recurring items. It provided that current reporting of events of significance to investors should include reference to such items in the summary of earnings or operations and in management's discussion of quarterly income.

EXTRAORDINARY ITEMS AND PRIOR PERIOD ADJUSTMENTS

In *APB Opinion No. 9* extraordinary items were defined as the effects of transactions of a character significantly different from the typical or customary business activities of the entity. Examples given were material gains and losses from the sale of a plant, the sale of a segment of the business, the sale of an investment, the write-off of goodwill for unusual reasons, the condemnation or expropriation of properties, and the devaluation of a foreign currency. Extraordinary items did not include inventory or receivables write-downs, losses from discontinuance of a product line, or adjustments of contract prices. Nor did they include prior period adjustments.

The problems involved in identifying extraordinary items proved to be substantial and the APB returned to them in *APBO No. 30*.[4] Argument for classifying all income statement items into two categories—revenue (including gains) and expenses (including losses)—was also a factor leading to this opinion. Again the APB presented a masterly compromise, retaining the category of extraordinary items but defining it out of existence. The new criteria for extraordinary items required that they be *both* unusual ("possess a high degree of abnormality") and infrequent of occurrence ("not reasonably be expected to recur in the foreseeable future"). Not surprisingly, accountants found such items rare, and following the publication of *APBO No. 30* in 1973 extraordinary items virtually disappeared from published income statements, with a consequent decrease in their usefulness for the analysis of profitability.

There appears to be a move back to the identification of extraordinary items as such. *FASB Statement No. 4* required a gain or loss on the extinguishment of debt to be shown separately as an extraordinary item even in cases where the item did not meet the criteria of *APB Opinion No. 30*.[5] *FASB Statement No. 15* required gain on restructuring debt to be reported as an extraordinary item by the debtor.[6] *FASB Statement No. 44* requires the initial write-off of unamortized costs of interstate operating rights impaired by the Motor Carrier Act of 1980 to be reported as an extraordinary item.[7]

Besides these specific requirements there are a number of other situations which resemble treatment as an extraordinary item. We have referred to gains and losses on discontinued operations and effect of change in accounting principle. Also, *FASB Statement No. 2* requires the amount of research and development expenditure to be separately reported; *FASB Statement No. 5* has a similar requirement for loss contingencies accrued in some circumstances, and *FASB Statement No. 13* specifies disclosure of contingent rentals and other income statement items arising under lease agreements.[8]

One of the reasons for separate reporting of extraordinary items is the belief that they are indicative of the quality of earnings, of the extent to which net income is a result of normal business decisions as compared with casual results. Other indirect evidence relating to the quality of earnings includes—

- Disclosure of nonconservative accounting policies, such as failing to consolidate loss-making subsidiaries;
- Changes to accounting policies tending to increase current earnings, such as switching from accelerated to straight-line depreciation early in the asset's life;
- Reduction of research and development expenditures;
- Reduction of capital expenditures;
- Termination of auditors.

Prior years' adjustments are records of movements of values which took place in an accounting period other than the one in which they were recorded. By definition, in an efficient accounting system they should be rare. Examples given by *APBO No. 9* are adjustments or settlements of (prior periods') income taxes; contract renegotiation settlements; results of litigation. The criteria laid down in *APBO No. 9* were intended to be restrictive; such items—

1. Can be specifically identified with and directly related to the business activities of particular prior periods;
2. Are not attributable to economic events occurring subsequent to the date of the financial statements for the prior period;
3. Depend primarily on determination by persons other than management;
4. Were not susceptible of reasonable estimation prior to such determination.

As an example of the restrictive nature of these criteria, we may cite the SEC requirement that a company restate 1975 earnings to include a $2.7 million charge that previously had been reported as a prior period adjustment.[9] The expense arose out of settlement of claims against the company in respect of damages suffered through using one of its products during years 1970-1974. The SEC's requirement was the consequence of its chief accountant's decision that all items settled at the discretion of a company's management should be treated as current period items, in accordance with *APBO No. 9*.

Although prior period adjustments are useful information, permitting as they do the correction of prior year income statements, the SEC has always looked on them as potential devices for keeping losses out of the income statement. *FASB Statement No. 16*, "Prior Period Adjustments," permits only two types of prior period adjustment: correction of error (and what accountant will admit a mistake?) and realization of the tax benefits of preacquisition loss carryforwards of purchased subsidiaries.)[10] The tax benefits of other loss carryforwards recognized subsequent to the period of loss (because of uncertainty of realization prior to that time) are reported as extraordinary items under *APB Opinion No. 11*, "Income Taxes," para. 44.

However, while reducing the probability that prior period adjustments will be correctly reported, the APB and the FASB have concurrently increased the number of prior period adjustments of another kind. *APBO No. 20* divided accounting changes into three categories: in accounting principles, in accounting estimates, and in the reporting entity. Changes in accounting estimates—for example, of uncollectible receivables or fixed asset depreciation—should be allocated to the current, or the current and future, accounting periods. Changes in accounting principles should be recognized by including the cumulative effect in the earnings of the period of the change, except for a few specified changes (from LIFO to another inventory method; in method of accounting for long-term construction contracts; to or from the "full-cost" method used in the oil and gas industry). These few items require treatment as prior period adjustments. Changes in the reporting entity (the composition of a group) were required to be dealt with by restating the financial statements of all prior periods presented and thus show the effect on retained earnings at the beginning of the current period.

The requirement to report the effects of changes in accounting principles as current period items met with increasing resistance, and both the APB and the FASB have shown a marked tendency not to follow this rule, *FASB Statement No. 2*, "Accounting for Research and Development Costs" (October 1974), required retroactive effect to be given to the effects of changing to the method laid down by prior period adjustment. *FASB Statement No. 4*, "Reporting Gains and Losses From Extinguishment Debt" (March 1975), encouraged, but did not require restatement of prior periods. *FASB Statement No. 5*, "Accounting for Contingencies" (March 1975), at first prescribed the method of accounting dictated by *APBO No. 20*, but an amendment was soon published calling for the effect of any change to be treated as a retroactive restatement. The changes in accounting resulting from *FASB Statements No. 7*, *8*, and *12* are also to be accounted for wholly or partly by prior period adjustment.

Neither of these important issues was addressed in FASB Concepts Statement No. 3.

VALUE-ADDED FORM OF INCOME STATEMENT

Another alternative to these forms of income statement is the value-added form. The concept of value added is defined in economics as the total of factor costs, or payments made by the firm for its factors of production: labor (wages and salaries), land (rents), capital (interest and profits). "All the production actually carried on within the company, all the value it has added to the economy, has been compensated by the payments the company has made to land, labor and capital."[11] Materials and supplies are not factor costs, but payments to other firms for their factor costs. Taxes and depreciation are not readily accommodated in this formulation, but can be forced into the payments pattern. Income taxes are parts of profits; indirect taxes are payments of a different kind, and depreciation is a surrogate for replacement of fixed assets used up.

The value added by the firm, therefore, can be expressed as sales revenue minus purchases from other firms. In national income accounting, the income and product accounts of the nation are simple identities, in which factor payments are analyzed as inputs and summed as outputs. This is very different from the income statement of the firm, which does not equate revenues with receipts or expenses with payments. However, it is possible to construct an income statement in the value-added form, and this is the form required by the German Companies Acts. It is also in use in the United States; for example, by General Electric Inc., a corporation which is responsible for 1 percent of the country's GNP. The German form is shown on Figure 14-1, and the value-added statement of the United Kingdom subsidiary of a United States corporation on Figure 14-2.

It is noteworthy that the German form of value-added income statement (still called a profit and loss account) does not include dividends as factor payments, a practice which corresponds with the economist's view that profits are payments for risk.

The value-added form of income statement is of obvious usefulness to national income economists since it fits neatly into their model of the economy. In this connection, the words of the inventor of national income accounting are revealing:

> In attempting to give quantitative expression to empirical constructs, such as the national income, it is now generally recognized that a theoretical basis is necessary and that this basis should

Value-Added Income Statement
(German Form)

Sales		XXXX
Add: Net increase in inventories	XX	
Value of production of own equipment	XX	XXX
Total output		XXXX
Less: Purchases of materials and supplies		XXX
Operating income		XXXX
Add: Other income (interest, dividends, profit on sale of assets etc.)		XX
Total income		XXXX
Less: Wages and salaries	XXX	
Social security expenses	XX	
Depreciation	XXX	
Amortization	XX	
Interest	XX	
Taxes	XX	
Other expenses (e.g., losses)	XX	XXXX
Net income		XX

Figure 14-1

be the conscious concern of economists and not left in its practical aspects exclusively to businessmen, accountants and the Commissioners of Inland Revenue.[12]

One is reminded of Rowland Hill asking why the devil should have all the best tunes!

The usefulness of the value-added form of income statement to the business firm is primarily restricted to the observation of changes in the proportions of different factors of production through time. Since these changes are likely to be immaterial from one period to the next (substitution of machinery for labor, and vice versa), this is essentially a long-term kind of study. A secondary usefulness is the ability to compute turnover ratios more precisely, since the classification of assets and liabilities in the balance sheet is directly comparable with the classification of revenue and expenses in the income statement. A major drawback is the inability to use this form of income statement to analyze the cost structure of sales revenues and thus to undertake the analysis of profitability of sales. This is particularly important where the income statement is to be extended to cover segment, or line of business, reporting; or where costs are to be analyzed for the purpose of cost/volume/profit analyses.

The SEC requires cost of goods sold to be disclosed, and companies using a value-added form of income statement provide this information in the notes to the financial statements.

Value-Added Statement
(U.K. Form)
ESSO PETROLEUM COMPANY LTD.–U.K.

Value added statement 1979 Millions of pounds			
Gross revenue from sales of goods and services		3 112.5	
Excise duties and VAT		(708.8)	
Payments to suppliers for goods and services		(1 506.0)	
Value added		**897.7**	
Allocated as follows:			
Employees and annuitants			
Salaries, wages, pensions and benefits		116.3	13.0%
Providers of capital			
Interest on loans	127.0		
Foreign exchange gain on long-term loans	(1.0)		
Dividend	200.1	326.1	36.3%
Central and local government			
Provision for taxation on profits			
(used temporarily in the business)	231.9		
Rates, royalties and other taxes	50.0	281.9	31.4%
Retention in the business			
Depreciation and field restoration	99.3		
Increase in retained profit	74.1	173.4	19.3%
		897.7	**100.0%**

Figure 14-2

DEFINITION OF INCOME STATEMENT ELEMENTS—REVENUES

The income statement equation, in the all-inclusive form, is:

$$\text{Net income} = \text{Revenues} - \text{Expenses}$$

FASB Statement of Financial Accounting Concepts No. 3 does not mention net income, but defines *comprehensive income* as the change in equity (net assets) of an entity during a period from transactions and other events and circumstances from nonowner sources. It includes all changes in equity during a period except those resulting from investments by owners and distributions to owners.[13]

This definition presents alternatives: either the capital maintenance approach (comparison of balance sheets) or the income statement approach. If the latter approach is taken, it is necessary to define revenues and expenses.

Note that the FASB did not preclude the use of current cost or other measurement methods in arriving at comprehensive income. It did state that "the financial capital concept is the traditional view" in present primary financial statements, and indicated that "earnings," when eventually defined, might refer to return on physical capital as distinct from financial capital (para. 56). On the other hand, it also stated that "comprehensive income results from (a) exchange transactions...(b) the enterprise's productive efforts, and (c) price changes, casualties, and other effects of interactions between the enterprise and the...environment of which it is part." Although, no doubt, the percentage of completion method of accounting for long-term contracts could be included under (b), and the lower of cost or market rule for inventories under (c), it is unlikely that these categories were used to designate such anomalous accounting practices. They would easily fit the phrase "transactions and other events and circumstances." Note 29 confirms this observation.

Revenues were defined as

> inflows or other enhancements of assets of an entity or settlements of its liabilities (or a combination of both) during a period from delivering or producing goods, rendering services, or other activities that constitute the entity's ongoing major or central operations. (para. 63)

Prior to this publication the literature on accounting displayed three approaches to the definition of revenue.

1. As an inflow of assets or a decrease of liabilities resulting from activities which can change owners' equity. This definition, which was adopted by *APB Statement No. 4*, is logically defective if owners' equity is seen as a residual. Further, it confuses the two parts of a reciprocal exchange, the supply of a product or rendering of a service, and the consideration received therefor.

2. As an output of goods and services, which Paton and Littleton called "the product of the enterprise."[14] But this definition confuses the income statement with the production account, or account for "work in process." Some writers have attempted to counter the objection by introducing the criterion of exteriorization. In this approach, revenue is production transferred to customers during a given period. The concept is still too narrow, as it excludes not only completed production which the firm keeps for its own use (which some argue is not revenue) but also rent, interest, and dividend income, which are widely believed to constitute revenues.

3. As a surrogate for cash inflows from operations. Not only does this require identifying operations so as to exclude, for example, a bank loan to finance inventory purchases, but it also derives from an essentially pre-industrial model of the firm. Only in a small number of retail-type businesses could this concept be applied.

The FASB definition improved on the APB definition by omitting reference to owners' equity, but maintained the idea of an inflow of assets. The inadequacy of this concept is patent.

- A transaction which qualifies as a credit sale creates an asset, the account receivable, which follows the rendering of an invoice and never precedes it. How can revenue be recognized by an inflow of an asset in this case?
- An advance payment on a sale is obviously an inflow of an asset from an activity which constitutes a major operation of the entity, but is not a revenue.
- Property donated to a firm is an inflow of asset, but is not now reported as a revenue, and may in fact be a contribution of capital.

Why did the FASB maintain this position, in contrast to the much clearer view of *Accounting Terminology Bulletin No. 2* that "revenue results from the sale of goods or the rendering of services..." or the excellent definition of a Committee of the American Accounting Association?

> ...the monetary expression of the aggregate of products or services transferred by an enterprise to its customers during a period of time.[15]

One possible explanation is the survival of the so-called cash basis income statement and the involvement of auditors with its preparation and certification. True, both Concepts Statements Nos. 1 and 3 come out in favor of accrual accounting, but they see this as a more complete form of cash accounting, not different in kind.

> Accrual accounting attempts to record the financial effects on an enterprise of transactions and other events and circumstances that have cash consequences for the enterprise in the periods in which those transactions, events and circumstances occur rather than only in the periods in which cash is received or paid by the enterprise. (*Concepts Statement No. 3*, para 79)

Thus, if an entity sells goods on credit amounting to $10,000 during a period, and receives $5,000 from those sales on account, this $5,000 could be reported as "cash basis revenues" under the FASB definition. This appears to be another example of the subtle influence of income tax laws on accounting theory.

DEFINITION OF INCOME STATEMENT ELEMENTS—EXPENSES

The APB in *Statement No. 4* defined expenses as

> ...gross decreases in assets or gross increases in liabilities recognized and measured in conformity with generally accepted ac-

counting principles that result from those types of profit-directed activities of an enterprise that can change owners' equity.

Objections to this definition include—

- The word "gross"; what does it mean?
- Any kind of decrease in assets or increase in liabilities *can* change owners' equity, even repayment of a loan (gain or loss on retirement of debt);
- As with revenues, definition of expenses in terms of changes in equity is less than helpful if equity is itself a residual.

The FASB's Concept Statement No. 3 definition differs somewhat (para. 65). Expenses are outflows or other using up of assets or incurrences of liabilities (or a combination of both) during a period from delivering or producing goods, rendering services, or carrying out other activities that constitute the entity's ongoing major or central operations.

Whether the absence of a reference to generally accepted principles improves the definition is debatable; obviously, we are trying to create a framework for such principles, yet the principles themselves dictate the contents of the framework. The idea that expenses are outflows of assets or incurrences of liabilities makes expense determination a function of asset and liability determination; in addition, it is defective—

- Because incurring an expense causes a liability or a decrease in cash, not the other way around;
- Because some outflows of assets and incurrences of liabilities which take place during the enterprise's major operations are not expenses; payment of insurance premiums in advance and exchange of asset for liability are obvious examples.

However, the definition contains the germ of a usable concept, which could be expressed as follows:

> Expenses are resources used during a period of time which are capable of expression in money, regardless whether they originate from current, past, or future expenditures.

The desire to include "cash basis expenses" in the definition, as well as "cash basis revenues," may underlie the FASB's phraseology. Further evidence is provided by the first sentence of para. 66, "Expenses represent actual or expected cash flows (or the equivalent)."

An illustration of the nature of the problem facing the FASB in the preparation of the concepts statements was provided by n. 33 to para. 66, which stated, "Taxes and other expenses resulting from nonreciprocal transfers, as several comment letters noted, commonly do result directly from incurring liabilities." In the first place, firms pay taxes for benefits received from the taxing authority, which is the reason we account for income tax as an expense and not an appropriation. In the second place, another accounting principle which has become clear since *APB Opinion No. 11* is that income tax expense is found independently from income tax liability; hence tax allocation.

GAINS AND LOSSES

Prior to the FASB's Concept Statement No. 3, gains and losses were regarded as subclasses of revenues and expenses respectively. Principle R–9C of *APB Statement No. 4* confirmed this position.

> Revenue and expenses from other than sales of products, merchandise or services may be separated from other revenue and expenses and the net effects disclosed as gains or losses.

Even losses representing expired costs that produce no revenue were comprehended by this definition.

The FASB decided not to include gains and losses in revenues and expenses, but to define them as separate elements of financial statements. By this device the way has been opened to account for these items outside the income statement; note that the definitions refer to change in equity, in sharp contrast to the definitions of revenues and expenses.

> Gains are increases in equity (net assets) from peripheral or incidental transactions of an entity and from all other events and circumstances affecting the entity during a period except those that result from revenues or investments by owners. (para. 67)
> Losses are decreases in equity (net assets) from peripheral or incidental transactions of an entity and from all other transactions or other events and circumstances affecting the entity during a period except those that result from expenses or distributions to owners. (para. 68)

Thus donations of property to the entity, which we have seen as capable of inclusion under revenues, are also capable of inclusion under gains.

What constitutes "peripheral or incidental transactions"? If a corner gas station rents a few square yards of its land to a car salesman, is the rent a gain or a revenue? Suppose the garage owner takes advantage of a favorable price to buy a large quantity of lubricating oil and sells it to another station owner instead of using it in the service bay: Is this a revenue or a gain? If the station owner puts down money for an option on an adjoining lot, with an eye to expansion, and fails to exercise the option, is this an expense or a loss?

We are not helped by the further information provided by the FASB in paras. 70, 71, and 149. Some gains and losses are "net results"; this refers to profit on sale of marketable securities or other assets, or retirement of debt, but we cannot say that all profits are gains.[16] Other losses result from nonreciprocal transfers between an entity and a nonowner—is an advertising giveaway a loss? Yet other gains or losses result from holding assets and liabilities while their values change—why are these restricted to lower of cost or market write-downs and foreign exchange translation losses? And still other gains or losses result from catastrophes, but only "major casualty losses."

Consider the problem dealt with by the FASB in its *Interpretation No. 30*.[17] If nonmonetary assets, such as buildings or equipment are involuntarily lost (e.g., destroyed by fire or condemned by local government), the difference between their carrying amount and the proceeds of insurance or condemnation awards was accounted for by some firms as an adjustment to the cost basis of property acquired as replacement. In this interpretation of *APB Opinion No. 29*, "Accounting for Nonmonetary Transactions," the FASB required firms to recognize gain or loss, even in cases where replacement was obligatory. This rule does not apply to involuntary conversions of LIFO inventories at interim dates, or even at the end of the year in some cases, where the proceeds of the involuntary conversion are not reinvested by the relevant date.

It is clear that the FASB's primary object was to require firms adjusting the carrying value of property acquired to cease this practice, which has as its consequence failure to recognize a change in equity from nonowner sources. Whether this is accounted for as a revenue or gain, or an expense or loss, is a minor issue. For example, suppose that a dealer in land is the object of a condemnation proceeding, and the dealer is awarded fair market value for the land. Should this be accounted for as a gain (show only the difference between cost and market value in the income statement) or as a revenue, with the cost of the land charged to cost of sales? *FASB Interpretation No. 30* automatically converts all such transactions into "gains" or "losses" regardless of whether they arise out of "major or central operations" or "peripheral or incidental transactions."

It is suggested here that the distinction between revenues and gains, and expenses and losses, depends upon the informational content of the disclosure and can be resolved otherwise than by reference to subjective factors, such as intent. A major factor in the information approach is the concept of the *gross margin*. Calculation of gross margin is important in financial analysis; income from operations (the *net margin*) is a function of gross margin and selling and administrative expenses. Gross margin is found by deducting cost of goods sold from sales; the need to calculate this figure underlies the SEC's requirement that cost of goods sold must be disclosed if it is not apparent from the income statement. Because of a firm's pricing policy there tends to be a normative significance to the gross margin, which is why comparison from period to period is informative.

The question which the accountant asks in determining whether an item is to be included in revenues and expenses or reported as a gain or loss is bound up with the effect on gross margin. For example—

1. If a factory operates a cafeteria at a loss to facilitate production operations, the loss is a part of manufacturing expense and not a separate nonmanufacturing loss, even though it is the result of offsetting cafeteria expenses against cafeteria revenues.
2. If an oil company buys oil on the world market to supply its refineries, and consistently finds itself with an oversupply which is sold, sometimes at a profit and sometimes at a loss, sale of the excess supply is not a part of the company's revenues. The periodic profit or loss on trading is part of the cost of materials inventory.
3. If a manufacturer sells surplus equipment, the sale and the carrying amount of the equipment are not revenue or expense, because neither enters into the calculation of gross margin. Profit or loss on the sale will, therefore, be reported as a gain or a loss.

REALIZATION AND REVENUE RECOGNITION

The realization rule simply states that, when sales take place, they should be recorded as such on the invoice date. The definition of a sale as an invoiced delivery follows the legal rule and accords with common sense; delivery exteriorizes the transaction and the invoice shows that it is not a gift. Trade customs govern the rights of the customer to contest the invoice and experience reveals the probability that this will occur, which can be provided for. In the potential social consolidation model, sales being someone else's purchases, the transaction will be recorded in the same period by both parties.

Realization as a general criterion of revenue recognition seems to be of relatively recent origin, although most authorities include it in their lists of principles. The most complex of these propositions is that of Mattessich:

> 12. *Realization*. There exists a set of hypotheses, specifying which of the following three mutually exclusive effects are exercised by a *change* (in quantity, value, legal status, etc.) *of an entity's economic object(s)*. Such a change either: 1) affects the value assigned to the current income of the entity; or 2) does not affect the owner's equity of this entity (within the specified period); or 3) affects the owners' equity without affecting the current income of the entity.[18]

In this approach, economic events that increase income are called *revenues*, those that decrease it, *expenses*. In effect,

Mattessich extended the concept of realization to mean revenue and expense recognition. A number of contemporary writers would do the same, arguing that realization *can* mean that a value change has become sufficiently objective to be revenue or expense. The distinction between revenue recognition and realization was confused by Paton and Littleton,[19] and the resulting problem has been exposed at length by Windal.[20]

APB Statement No. 4 included realization as a pervasive measurement principle:

> P-2 *Realization*: Revenue is generally recognized when both of the following conditions are met: (1) the earning process is complete or virtually complete, and (2) an exchange has taken place.

This is typical circular reasoning: earnings are a function of revenue and revenue is recognized by earnings. The second restriction on revenue, that an exchange has taken place, is untenable, as the subsequent paragraphs of *Statement No. 4* clearly indicate.

The view that realization is a necessary condition for *net income* is attributable to Littleton, who argued that this followed from the proposition that revenue must be realized. There is some evidence that the view has been rejected; a 1973-1974 Committee of the American Accounting Association preferred the statement that income should be reported as soon as the level of uncertainty has been reduced to a tolerable level. This committee stated that "realization is not a determinant in the concept of income; it only serves as a guide in deciding when events otherwise resolved as being within the concept of income, can be entered in the accounting records in objective terms; that is, when the uncertainty has been reduced to an acceptable level."[21]

The FASB's view of realization, expressed in para. 83 of Concepts Statement No. 3 accords with the author's position. "Realization in the most precise sense means the process of converting noncash resources and rights into money and is most precisely used in accounting and financial reporting to refer to sales of assets for cash and claims to cash."

The reference to "cash and claims to cash" is unnecessary; a sale is realized in an arm's length transaction on rendering the invoice, regardless of the method of payment involved. Some would like accountants to abandon the term; it is suggested here that, if sales are included in the concept "revenue," realization should be restricted to the recognition of sales. The recognition of other revenues is *sui generis*. Revenue which accrues on a time basis is recognized in relation to the lapse of time and revenue which arises on the occurrence of a critical event—putting a process plant into operation under a turn-key contract—when that event occurs. This would also cover the accrual of dividends, commissions and "windfall" receipts.

In some cases, of course, the sale is one of form rather than substance, and this situation became scandalous in the land development and franchising industries in the 1960s and early 1970s. This led to the publication by the AICPA of an industry audit guide for real estate transactions which required special treatment for land sales with minimal down payments and long installment periods.[22] Similarly, transactions between related parties may purport to be sales but should be looked at critically,[23] and sales under product financing arrangements are loans and not sales, as *FASB Statement No. 49*, "Accounting for Product Financing Arrangements" (June 1981), confirmed.

On the other hand, genuine installment sales are sales, even though the collectibility may be low, as in the case of mail order sales of shavers to soldiers fighting overseas. In such cases, expenses should include a provision for estimated losses through bad debts.[24]

In principle, recognition ceases to be a problem once the proposition that revenues are outflows of goods and services, and not inflows of assets, is accepted. Obviously there are cases where the outflow of goods or services cannot be measured in money with sufficient certainty to be recorded; one such case might be the exchange of similar assets. When the seller agrees unconditionally to accept return of the property sold this does not necessarily negate the sale.

Directing attention to income determination rather than revenue recognition has led some accountants to argue that increase of value over time should be included in the concept of revenue.[25] In particular, this would rationalize accretion as an element of the Hicksian income concept. *Accretion* is the increase in value of growing crops or timber, or of mineral leases through the discovery of minerals in place. Some extractive industries do in fact include accretion in profit measurement, for example, by valuing ending inventories at selling prices. The percentage of completion method of accounting for long-term construction contracts, and the proportional performance method of accounting for service contracts, correspond with the notion that income is earned as work is done, rather than being the result of transactions with the environment. This is known as the *critical function theory*, the belief that income is earned at the moment of making the most critical decision, or performing the most critical act, in the operating cycle. Reserve recognition accounting (RRA) is an application of the critical function theory, as it assumes that income is earned on the discovery of oil and gas reserves, and thereafter each time that the market price of oil or gas changes.

The SEC's reversal of its plan to make RRA mandatory for the primary financial statements of oil and gas producers was announced as due to the uncertainty associated with the measurement of oil and gas reserves. This feature was well known at the time

RRA was adopted; it is a perennial subject of oil and gas accounting and taxation conferences. Other weaknesses were responsible for the failure of RRA; they have been alluded to in chapter 8. In general it can be said that an accounting system based on the critical function theory would go far beyond the modifications required in order to change the basis of recognizing revenue and expense.

The revenues of firms in the extractive industries are anomalous; the accounting treatment of inventories in agriculture and mining may be a survival from a preindustrial view of profit as the amount which will be distributed as a dividend to equity stockholders. The official position in the United States is that revenue recognition at the completion of production is recommended for precious metals having a fixed monetary value with no substantial costs of marketing and for agricultural and other mineral products only if the firm is unable to determine appropriate approximate costs. It is doubtful whether any of these criteria is applicable at the present time, except where production is sold forward.

Accounting for long-term construction contracts is still governed in the United States by *ARB 45* dated October 1955. This Bulletin allowed both the completed contract method and the percentage of completion method, but recommended the latter when estimates of costs to complete and extent of progress toward completion are reasonably dependable. The *AICPA SOP 81-1*, "Accounting for Performance of Construction-Type and Certain Production-Type Contracts," confirmed that the completed contract and percentage of completion methods are not interchangeable. Outside the United States there is considerable support for the proposition that long-term construction contracts should be carried at cost, less provisions for losses where applicable, because of the well-known fact that the risks associated with such contracts tend to peak around the completion date. A Standard published in the United Kingdom called for profit to be accrued on long-term contracts where "the outcome can be assessed with reasonable certainty" (paragraph 8), "it is reasonable to foresee profits in advance" (paragraph 10), and they are "estimated to arise over the duration of the contract" (paragraph 23).[26] The discretion which these criteria gives to optimistic directors caused much anxiety to United Kingdom accountants in such industries.

The desire to show a smooth trend of earnings, which the completed contract method precludes, is a consequence of the financial analyst's use of variability of earnings as a measure of risk. A company which has small losses in some years and large profits in others will find it more difficult to control the price at which its stock trades, and may face a higher cost of capital, than a company showing a relatively steady trend of earnings. However, the fact remains that long-term construction is a particularly hazardous, although potentially highly profitable, form of business undertaking, and the income statement should reveal this.

THE MEANING OF REVENUE AND EXPENSE

Revenue and expense are period concepts. One way to emphasize this point is to refer to them as *flow* concepts, but this may be deceptive since the subject matter of stocks and flows is the same. A flow is always a period phenomenon. Revenue relates to a specified period of time. All accounting represents movements of values, a *value* being any observation which can be represented quantitatively in terms of money. Which movements of values are covered by the term "revenue"? We may refer to the potential social consolidation model for an answer to this question. Revenue is a measure of *social output*, not of production. Social output is the product of the firm which increases the wealth of society and may be recognized either by other entities or by the firm itself; rent, interest, and dividend income are similar in that firm-to-firm transactions would be cancelled out in a social consolidation, but firm-to-consumer transactions would form part of the social product. That part of the production of the firm which is used for its own inputs, such as the oil company's gas production returned to the well to provide additional "drive," or the manure which a farmer uses as fertilizer, is revenue and at the same time, expense. The firm which produces its own equipment adds the value of such production to the social product, but uses as input only the depreciation of the equipment applicable to the period in question.

The potential social consolidation model directs attention to the relationship between the accounting entity and its environment. The business firm is viewed as a social organization having the function of producing and distributing goods and services which are chargeable to other accounting entities—other firms, households, and governments, at home and abroad. Government produces services which are, for the most part, distributed without consideration. Households are primarily consumer entities, whose basic social purpose is reproduction of the species. To the extent that they are producers of goods and services they can be regarded as business firms because their products are chargeable to other entities.

In this framework, the firm receives scarce resources from the rest of the economy (scarce relative to needs), which are either subjected to a transformation process (production), or transferred in substantially the same form to another supplying entity or to a consumer. Production, therefore, has an input phase and also an output phase, in which the object of the transformation process is exteriorized as a good or service chargeable to another entity.

It is this substitution of outputs for inputs which the income statement represents in terms of money. In this form it is called an *operating statement*. The income statement, according to the audit certificate of a CPA, purports to present the results of operations for a particular period. The modern income statement, however, does more than present the results of operations; it probably tries to do too much and would do a better job if it were divided into several statements.

The concept of social inputs and outputs is not the same as that of cash flows, and it is a mistake to view the income statement as a device for predicting net cash flows to the firm. Under certain conditions the funds statement, or statement of changes in financial position, can be useful for this purpose. However, it is well to acknowledge that cash flows are the most unpredictable aspects of business operations because they are dependent upon so many factors; profit, or net income, is only one.

The social consolidation model could have prevented the FASB from defining revenues and expenses in terms of inflows and outflows of assets. If, as the FASB has it, a revenue is an inflow of assets from a delivery and an expense is an outflow of assets from a delivery, then revenue to firm A must be expense to firm B. Obviously, not all revenues are expenses of others; a sale of land, a nondepreciable asset, never becomes expense to its purchaser.

The FASB's definition of revenue was called in question by *FASB Statement No. 48*, "Revenue Recognition when Right of Return Exists" (June 1981). This statement specified that a sale which confers upon the buyer a right to return should be recognized as revenue at the time of sale only if *all* the following conditions are met.

1. The seller's price to the buyer is substantially fixed or determinable at the date of sale.
2. The buyer has paid the seller, or the buyer is obligated to pay the seller and the obligation is not contingent on resale of the product.
3. The buyer's obligation to the seller would not be changed in the event of theft or physical destruction or damage of the product.
4. The buyer acquiring the product for resale has economic substance apart from that provided by the seller.
5. The seller does not have significant obligations for future performance to directly bring about resale of the product by the buyer.
6. The amount of future returns can be reasonably estimated.

If these conditions are not met, revenue may not be recognized; if they are, then sales revenue and cost of sales should be reduced to reflect estimated returns, and expected costs or losses should be accrued.

It is obvious that the FASB's definition of revenue was of no assistance in this problem area; it was not even mentioned in the statement. Further, the method presented by this statement conflicts with the method of hospital accounting for contractual adjustments under Medicare and Medicaid; the AICPA Hospital Audit Guide requires these to be accounted for in a similar manner to uncollectible receivables, as an expense.

The four accounting terms—expenditure, payment, expense, and cost—must be carefully distinguished. An *expenditure* is an outflow of assets, any resource, not just cash. A *payment* is an outflow of cash. An *expense* is a using up of a resource during a period. A *cost* is a sacrifice (including a using up) of a resource for a given purpose or object. These four concepts may coincide; if I pay $x for food today in order to throw a party for my friends tonight, $x measures expenditure, payment, expense, and cost. However, if part of the purchase consists of a food which spoils before it can be eaten, that part is not a cost of the party. It is, in fact, an expense which is not a cost, or the cost of nothing—a loss.

Questions sometimes arise about expenses connected with sales, which might conceivably be deducted therefrom in arriving at revenue. The proceeds of sales, for example, are reduced by selling expenses, and revenue could be shown net of these expenses. The extent to which expenses are deducted from revenues in the presentation of the income statement is bound up with the use of the income statement, principally its analysis through ratios. As a result, there may be a good reason for showing net income for some operations instead of revenue and expense; the case of discontinued operations is an example. However, this does not transform net income into revenue or change the concept of expense. The inclusion of a provision for bad debt losses as an expense is explicable within the framework of the potential social consolidation model; a bad debt is a transfer payment, not a reduction of revenue.

MATCHING AND THE MEASUREMENT OF EXPENSE

Expense measurement is typically more difficult than revenue recognition, because the biggest element of revenue is sales of goods and services, which are dated. However, in the case of governmental and other not-for-profit organizations, the problem of revenue recognition is equally acute; it is a mistake to regard tax receipts or charitable contributions as revenues of such organizations. One of the principal problems in accounting for not-for-profit organizations is the measurement of their contributions to the social product; even the FASB is in agreement on this point.[27]

Until quite recently the problem of expense measurement appeared to be soluble by reference to the *matching principle*.

The 1964 Committee of the American Accounting Association on the Matching Concept defined it as the process of reporting expenses on the basis of a cause and effect relationship with reported revenues.[28] The committee viewed the matching principle as purporting to relate efforts expended with results achieved to arrive at a difference representing profit or loss from operations during a specified period of time.

In 1969 Arthur Thomas confirmed the 1964 Committee's approach.[29] He pointed out, however, that to be justifiable any allocation method must meet three criteria:

1. Be additive, that is, the sum of the parts must equal the whole;
2. Be unambiguous, that is, result in only one set of parts;
3. Be defensible, that is, be superior to all other allocations.

It is this last criterion which the matching principle fails to meet; in Thomas' terminology, such an allocation is *incorrigible*. In spite of this incorrigibility, *APB Opinion No. 11* referred to the matching process as "one of the basic processes of income determination," and *APB Opinion No. 2* had also seen matching in this light.

The importance of reliance on the matching principle for expense determination is evident from a survey of contemporary accounting textbooks. The matching principle is cited as the justification for the currently acceptable accounting treatment of inventories, depreciable assets, pensions, leases, and intangible assets generally. In these and other instances, alternatives are supported if they expressly purport to match expenses with revenues.

Prior to 1940 there was no mention of matching, and expenses and revenues were to be determined by reference to periods of time. In a 1935 textbook, McKinsey and Noble stated that "just as the accounts should show, at the end of the fiscal period, all the income earned during the period, they should also show all the expenses incurred in earning that income."[30]

Transaction-based accounting theories came under strain in the particular area of accounting for cost of goods sold. The practice of charging expenses to the income statement in the period in which they were incurred, which appeared rational to the retailer or wholesaler, came under question in the case of the manufacturer. The practice of capitalizing what would otherwise be expenses (in inventory) and then charging them against revenues in the period of sale was not easily defended in the absence of a new concept. Accountants still display great anxiety in capitalizing labor; for example, in computer software costs.

The period which followed 1940 saw the investigation of several difficult accounting problems affecting income determination, such as accounting for leases, pension costs, income taxation, and research and development; in each case, the matching principle appeared to offer guidelines to a solution.

Serving to underpin the matching principle is the assumption that the income statement is a surrogate for cash flow. This view has been expressed by several writers, more recently by John C. Burton: "Income is measured by an averaging approach (called matching) which is designed to show the longrun average net cash inflow at the current level of activity."[31] The relationship between income flows and cash flows is complex, affected as it is by credit relationships and investment/disinvestment decisions which bypass the income statement because they do not affect the measurement of net income, quite apart from the obvious problem that activity level is a continuous variable. Net income plus depreciation, plus or minus other amortizations and deferrals, is probably a better measure of longrun average net cash flow from operations.

DECLINE OF THE MATCHING PRINCIPLE

The first sign that official thinking on accounting principles found the matching principle less than useful appeared in the Accounting Principles Board's *Statement No. 4* (1970),[32] in Note 6 to the section on "Income Determination":

> The term *matching* is often used in the accounting literature to describe the entire process of income determination. The term is also often applied in accounting, however, in a more limited sense to the process of expense recognition or in an even more limited sense to the recognition of expenses by associating costs with revenue on a cause and effect basis.... Because of the variety of its meanings, the term *matching* is not used in this statement.

The principal academic critic of matching is Robert T. Sprouse. In 1971, he wrote about "the notion that... an accounting theory... can be constructed on the basis of the pre-eminence of the income statement and the application of the 'matching' concept. Which of these two... is the chicken and which is the egg is difficult to determine... both are sterile."[33]

FASB Statement No. 2 ("Accounting for Research and Development Costs") and *No. 5* ("Accounting for Contingencies") both referred to the matching principle in the sections headed "Basis for Conclusions." They used the same words to point out that *APB Statement No. 4*:

> explicitly avoids using the term "matching" because it has a variety of meanings in the accounting literature. In its broadest sense, matching refers to the entire process of income determination—described in paragraph 147 of *APB Statement No. 4* as "identifying, measuring and relating revenue and expenses of an enterprise for an accounting period." Matching may also be used in a more limited sense to refer only to the process of expense recognition or in an even more limited sense to refer only to the:
>
> (*FASB Statement No. 2*) recognition of expenses by associating costs with revenue on a cause and effect basis. In the following discussion, matching is used in its most limited sense to refer to the process of recognizing costs as expenses on a cause and effect basis.
>
> (*FASB Statement No. 5*) process of expense recognition or in an even more limited sense to refer to the recognition of expenses by associating costs with revenue on a cause and effect basis.

Statement No. 2 concluded that this notion of matching cannot be applied to research and development costs. *Statement No. 5* concluded that this matching "is a consideration in relation to accrual for such matters as uncollectible receivables and warranty obligations" and by implication, that it is not a consideration in relation to self-insurance, threat of expropriation, and the catastrophe losses of property and casualty insurance companies.

Bierman and Dukes wrote, in their analysis of *FASB Statement No. 2*, "If the Board had chosen to argue that matching was not an important criterion (it wisely did not do so), then its conclusion might be understandable. But to argue that expensing of R & D is consistent with matching is a conclusion that is difficult to comprehend."[34] It seems, however, from a close reading of the FASB's comments under the heading "Basis for Conclusions" that while the Board had not formally abandoned the matching principle, it had very serious reservations about its usefulness.

FASB Statement of Financial Concepts No. 3, however, reverted to the pre-*APB Statement No. 4* position:

> Thus, recognition of revenues, expenses, gains, and losses and the related increments or decrements in assets and liabilities—including matching of costs and revenues . . . is the essence of using accrual accounting to measure performance of business enterprises. (para. 85) Matching of costs and revenues is combined or simultaneous recognition of the revenues and expenses that result directly and jointly from the same transactions or other events. (para. 86).

The problem is that matching produces the same difficulties as are encountered in its absence. Contemporary income statement preparation concentrates on consumption and output, and since we have divorced income determination from transactions, the fundamental problem is bound up with the interaction of inputs in the revenue-producing process. Only an imputation system can serve the purposes of financial accounting, as indeed of economic theory.

For example, in the case of depreciation, the principle that expense must be matched with revenue does not help us to proceed with the allocation of total depreciation to periods of time. All methods are equally arbitrary, whether based on years of useful life, units of output, hours of production, or estimated net revenues. It cannot even be demonstrated that value flows of cost to expense accompany sales on the basis of physical flows of goods or services, even though such a result may be viewed as common sense or desirable. The measurement of value flows is a subjective operation because value is a subjective phenomenon.

Thus, when the matching principle is invoked to resolve expense determination questions, the result is to increase controversy. A recent example is the previously mentioned FASB standard on accounting for research and development. A continuing example is the debate on accounting for preproduction costs in the petroleum industry, where all participants are for matching but will agree on nothing else.

The most basic objection to the matching principle, however, is that it makes expense determination a function of revenues, whereas it should be quite clear that expenses are to be determined independently of revenues and even in the absence of revenues. Indeed, to assert that revenues and expenses are simultaneously determined is to assert that the income statement is a simple identity and thus useless for business analysis and prediction. This position was clearly enunciated in the FASB discussion memorandum on research and development costs: "Even if conceptually desirable, matching is not usually possible; in practice, most costs are independently identified with a period of time in much the same way that revenues are identified with a period of time."[35]

THE ALLOCATION PROBLEM

In economic theory, costs are found by imputing revenues (receipts) to factors of production, using the techniques of marginal analysis. The fact that time is an important variable in accounting presents insuperable obstacles to a similar approach, and Thomas has demonstrated conclusively that an empirically verifiable, as distinct from an operational, method of allocating expenses as a function of revenue is not known.[36]

By separating expense measurement from revenue recognition, however, we are identifying a different problem. Income statement preparation is a process of matching the expenses of a specified period with the revenue of the same period, a process known as *period matching*. If the two flows of the income statement are measured independently of each other, the balance (net income) can be interpreted and analyzed; the income statement can then be viewed as a behavioral equation and not a simple identity.

In the context of this book, expenses are found by testing for chargeability to customers or recipients of services. All expenditure is viewed logically as asset creating, since it is absurd to assume that the firm's managers will acquire goods and services for purposes other than investment. Expense measurement is the identification of assets which have expired, in the conventional idiom, or values which have been consumed, in the terminology used here. The continuous method of expense measurement postulates a causal relationship between the asset and time, or between the asset and a given activity. Thus, some expenses can be "metered" into the income statement as if they were being issued from inventory; the perpetual inventory approach to finding cost of goods sold is the clearest example of this process. The periodic inventory method finds the asset value at the end of the period, defined as the amount which is (subjectively) estimated to be chargeable to future customers and calculates expense as the residue, using the equation:

Opening inventory (assets at the beginning of the period) plus expenditure during the period minus closing inventory (asset at the end of the period) equals consumption

In neither case can the result be more than a usable approximation of some perceived reality.

A loss is an expense which did not produce an output. The net loss which results from an excess of expenses over revenue can be explained in the same terms. An expense which could not have contributed to output may be identifiable, such as a casualty loss or a value adjustment resulting from a change in expectations, or plans. Other losses are not identifiable and may be merged with expenses. In management accounting an attempt is made to separate expenses into costs and losses, and the analysis obtained is frequently reported in income statements presented to management. It would be useful, although possibly embarrassing to managers, if such a differentiation were made in published financial statements. One of the consequences of a current value approach to financial statement preparation should be the reporting of losses (and gains) separately from expenses.

AN IDEA FOR INCOME STATEMENT CLASSIFICATION

We have rejected the primary classification of income statement items by *nature* (or type) as less informative than classification by *object* (or function). In this connection, we should be aware of the prevalence of bastard classifications in published income statements, where, for example, "cost of goods sold" is followed by "depreciation and amortization."

It is also common to find revenue analyzed by type, without a corresponding analysis of expenses. In the case of interest and dividend revenue, it may be assumed that expenses are negligible but this need not be the case. The difficulty of allocating expenses to revenue is no different in kind from the problem of allocating expenses to periods.

Gains and losses could usefully be classified in relation to the part of the operating cycle in which they originate. In this way, responsibility for these items could be attributed to the managers of the functions which experience these results in the same way that expenses can be associated with the revenues resulting from them.

Referring again to Table 2-3, it is possible, although not always easy, to analyze the total results of an enterprise into the following categories:

1. Results of capital management; for example, profits (losses) derived from trading in own stock or obligations; credits from unclaimed dividends.
2. Results of equipment management; for example, profits (losses) derived from disposing of equipment.

3. Results of managing working capital—financial (cash discounts, interest on temporary financial investments), credit (bad debt expense), supply (profits or losses on sale of surplus inventories, depreciation of raw materials).
4. Results of input management—expenses not used for production.
5. Results of production management—cost variances; profits (losses) on sale of scrap.
6. Results of marketing management, the difference between sales revenues and cost of sales.

The extension of this type of analysis to line of business, or segment, reporting can be viewed as the ultimate form of income statement classification. The FASB in *Statement No. 14* required annual financial statements to provide segmental information about revenue, operating profit or loss and identifiable assets for each line of business and geographical area, as well as certain information about major customers. The original exposure draft would have required this information in interim statements, and the fact that *FASB Statement No. 14* omitted this provision, and that *FASB Statement No. 21* withdrew nonpublic enterprises from its scope, are to be regretted, since this was one of the most important improvements to financial reporting in recent years.[37]

The analysis of profitability from the information presented in the income statement typically proceeds via ratios; setting net sales equal to 100, the other items are calculated as percentages of sales. With the diversification characteristic of modern businesses these ratios are difficult to evaluate because they represent averages of widely dispersed measures. For example, cost of goods sold representing 70 percent of net sales may conceal the following details:

	Total Firm	**Segment A**	**Segment B**
Sales	100	50	50
Cost of goods sold	70	25	45

In the case of disposal of a segment of the business, the effect of discontinued operations on future maintainable profits cannot be evaluated unless this type of detail is known. There is considerable investor interest in disclosure of the assets, liabilities, revenues, and expenses of all "lines of business," as they are called, but *APBO No. 30* addressed only the effect of disposal on net income. The APB required the results of continuing operations to be disclosed separately from discontinued operations and any gain or loss on disposal of a segment to be reported in conjunction with the related results of discontinued operations. Intraperiod tax allocation was required and so was restatement of prior periods.

During this period there was considerable pressure on several U.S. government agencies to require the publication of line-of-business data. Some economists regarded one result of the post-World War II wave of mergers and acquisitions to be the suppression of market information. These economists started with the assumption that profits spurred competition; when a firm was acquired by another firm, usually because it was profitable, details of this profitability were merged in the consolidated statements of the acquirer. These pressures came to rest in the U.S. Department of Justice, which issued its own rules on the subject as a part of its antitrust administration. Others, including financial analysts, saw the problem in the rise of the conglomerate, whose financial statements combine figures from a variety of different kinds of business and are therefore difficult to analyze. Their pressures affected the SEC.

After the promulgation of *FASB Statement No. 14*, the SEC adopted Regulation S–K, which had been recommended by the Advisory Committee on Corporate Disclosure, to require additional information:

1. The name of a major customer or customers under common control.
2. Financial information about geographical areas not currently significant if they had been in the past and were expected to be so again.
3. Revised information by class of similar product or service, where material, within an industry segment.[38]

This last requirement drew attention to one of the weaknesses of the approach taken by the FASB, which had made the identification of segments depend upon the internal organization of the firm (profit centers), rather than external markets. In the case of an electrical manufacturer, for example, refrigerators might be reported under "Electrical products," "Consumer durables," or "Small appliances"; or if supplied to food processors, they might be divided between "Consumer products" and "Industrial products." If a segment "Foreign sales" was reported, some refrigerators might find themselves in that category. The numerical rules laid down by the FASB could permit firms to combine categories which had once been reported separately, and produce other odd results. For example, a product line which constituted less than 10 percent of a firm's sales need not be reported, no matter how important a part of the total market that 10 percent might represent. Thus, General Motors reported that it was in one industry, the automobile industry, even though its defense equipment sales represent a major portion of that market, and may be responsible for a disproportionate share of GM's profit or loss in any year.

We should look upon *FASB Statement No. 14* as a start in the process of making useful line-of-business information available to financial statement users, rather than a definitive answer to the problem.

EARNINGS PER SHARE

A general discussion of the problems of income statement preparation cannot conclude without reference to earnings per share. This essentially statistical calculation was made an accounting technique by *APB Opinion No. 15*, although *FASB Statement No. 21* withdrew nonpublic enterprises from its scope.[39] The calculation of earnings per share is particularly meaningless in the case of private corporations formed with a capital of 100 shares and which become prosperous; consider the per share earnings of such a company with a net income of $500,000. The comparison of earnings per share between public companies is difficult, and the principal analytical use of the earnings per share figure is to validate or extrapolate a share price, using a hypothetical price/earnings ratio. If it is assumed that two firms should have the same price/earnings ratio, then their earnings per share become directly comparable in terms of market prices.

The FASB and the APB have required a number of income statement and other items to be presented together with their effects on earnings per share: extraordinary items, effect of change in accounting principle, loss or gain on discontinuance of a line of business, prior period adjustments. However, although earnings per share must be reported on the face of the income statement, these other effects may be reported either in the income statement or in the notes to the financial statements.

The calculation of earnings per share is complicated, and its presentation may involve six or more separate numbers depending upon the complexity of the corporation's capital structure and the nonoperating items in the income statement. It is suggested here that accountants would serve users better if this time and effort were devoted to calculating, reporting, and analyzing return on investment, a ratio which is not required and seldom disclosed, and to the factors underlying changes in this ratio. Such an approach would help resolve some of the problems of income statement preparation.

CONCLUSION

The determination of revenues, expenses, gains, and losses is a continuing preoccupation of accounting practitioners and theorists. Its importance lies in the fact that the result of combining this element is the determination of net income (or "comprehensive income"). A diversity of practices, both customary and required by promulgated GAAP, suggests that the conceptual problems involved have not yet been resolved.

Many of the difficulties are referred to such practical considerations as whether an asset resulting from a sale is collectible, or realizable; whether a transaction effectively transfers the risk of ownership; whether a future benefit or cost (receipt or payment) is measurable; whether the earning process is complete. It is clear that conditions affecting the management of a particular enterprise often override conceptual approaches to definition, recognition, and measurement in this area.

ENDNOTES

1. Lee, Geoffrey Alan, "The Coming of Age of Double-entry: the Giovanni Farolfi Ledger of 1299-1300," *The Accounting Historian's Journal*, Fall 1977, pp. 79-96.
2. AICPA, 1980.
3. "Reporting the Results of Operations," *Opinions of the Accounting Principles Board No. 9*, New York: AICPA, December 1966.
4. "Reporting the Results of Operations—Reporting the Effects of Disposal of a Segment of a Business, and Extraordinary, Unusual and Infrequently Occurring Events and Transactions," *Opinions of the Accounting Principles Board No. 30*, New York: AICPA, June 1973.
5. "Reporting Gains and Losses from Extinguishment of Debt," Stamford, Conn.: Financial Accounting Standards Board, March 1975.
6. "Accounting by Debtors and Creditors for Troubled Debt Restructurings," Stamford, Conn., Financial Accounting Standards Board, June 1977.
7. "Accounting for Intangible Assets of Motor Carriers," Stamford, Conn., Financial Accounting Standards Board, December 1980.
8. *FASB Statement No. 2*, "Accounting for Research and Development Costs," October 1974; *FASB Statement No. 5*, "Accounting for Contingencies," March 1975; *FASB Statement No. 13*, "Accounting for Leases," November 1976.
9. A.H. Robins, Inc.
10. Financial Accounting Standards Board, June 1977.
11. Heilbronner, Robert L., *Understanding Macro-economics*, Englewood Cliffs, N.J., Prentice-Hall, Inc., 3rd edition, 1970, p. 28.
12. Stone, Richard, *The Role of Measurement in Economics*, Cambridge, England, 1951, p. 3.
13. *Statement of Financial Accounting Concepts No. 3*, "Elements of Financial Statements of Business Enterprises," Financial Accounting Standards Board, December 1980, para. 56.
14. Paton, W.A. and A.C. Littleton, *An Introduction to Corporate Accounting Standards*, American Accounting Association Monograph No. 3, 1940, p. 46.
15. American Accounting Association Committee on Concepts and Standards for Accounting and Reporting, "Accounting and Reporting Standards for Corporate Financial Statements—1957 Revision," *Accounting Review*, October 1957, pp. 536-546.
16. Is the equity pickup of an investor, being its share of the investee's profits, revenue or gain?
17. "Accounting for Involuntary Conversions of Nonmonetary Assets to Monetary Assets," Financial Accounting Standards Board, September 1979.
18. Mattessich, Richard, *Accounting and Analytical Methods*, Homewood, Ill.: Richard D. Irwin, Inc. 1964, p. 43.
19. Paton and Littleton, op. cit. pp. 48-49.
20. Windal, Floyd, *The Accounting Concept of Realization*, Occasional Paper No. 5, East Lansing: Bureau of Business Research, Michigan State University, 1961 and "The Accounting Concept of Realization," *The Accounting Review*, April, 1961, pp. 249-258.
21. AAA Committee on Concepts and Standards—External Reporting, "Report of the 1973-74 Committee on Concepts and Standards—External Reporting," *The Accounting Review*, Supplement to Vol. XLIX, 1974, p. 209.
22. "Accounting for Retail Land Sales" and "Accounting for Profit Recognition on Sales of Real Estate," *AICPA Industry Accounting Guides*, New York: AICPA, 1973.

23. Auditing Standards Executive Committee, "Related Party Transactions," *Statement on Auditing Standards 6*, New York: AICPA, July, 1975.
24. The old realization rule of *ARB 32* seems rather optimistic: "Profit is realized when a sale is effected in the ordinary course of business, unless collection of the sale price is not reasonably assured."
25. For example, in the AAA Committee's 1957 Revision, cited above: "The essential meaning of realization is that a change in an asset or liability has become sufficiently definite and objective to warrant recognition in the accounts."
26. Accounting Standards Steering Committee, SSAP 9, "Stocks and Work in Progress," *The Accountant*, June 12, 1975, pp. 751-755.
27. See *FASB Statement of Financial Accounting Concepts No. 4*, "Objectives of Financial Reporting by Nonbusiness Organizations," December 1980, for an extensive discussion of this problem.
28. American Accounting Association, 1964 Concepts and Standards Research Study Committee—The Matching Concept, "The Matching Concept," *The Accounting Review*, April, 1965, p. 369.
29. Thomas, Arthur L., *AAA Studies in Accounting Research No. 3*, "The Allocation Problem in Financial Accounting," Evanston, Ill.: American Accounting Association, 1969.
30. McKinsey, James O. and Howard S. Noble, *Accounting Principles*, Cincinnati: South-Western Publishing Company, 1935, p. 253.
31. Burton, John C., Emmanuel Saxe Distinguished Accounting Lecture, "In our opinion, these financial statements present fairly," City University of New York, February 18, 1975.
32. *APB Statement No. 4*, "Basic Concepts and Accounting Principles Underlying Financial Statements of Business Enterprises," New York: AICPA, October, 1970.
33. Sprouse, Robert T., "The Balance Sheet—Embodiment of the Most Fundamental Elements of Accounting Theory," in *Foundations of Accounting Theory*, University of Florida Press, 1971, pp. 90-104.
34. Bierman, Harold Jr. and Roland E. Dukes, "Accounting for Research and Development Costs," *Journal of Accountancy*, April 1975, pp. 48-55.
35. *Discussion Memorandum on Accounting for Research and Development and Similar Costs*, Financial Accounting Standards Board, p. 26.
36. Thomas, Arthur L., op. cit., and American Accounting Association, *Studies in Accounting Research No. 9*, "The Allocation Problem in Financial Accounting Theory—Part II," 1974.
37. *FASB Statement No. 14*, "Financial Reporting for Segments of Business Enterprise," December 1976; *FASB Statement No. 21*, "Suspension of the Reporting of Earnings Per Share and Segment Information by Nonpublic Enterprises," April 1978; Stamford, Conn.: Financial Accounting Standards Board.
38. See *Accounting Series Release 236*, December 23, 1977.
39. *APB Opinion No. 15*, "Earnings per Share," 1969; see also the lengthy APB publication "Computing Earnings per Share: Accounting Interpretations of Section 2011, Earnings per Share," July, 1970.

SELECTED ADDITIONAL READINGS

Accounting Principles Board, *Statement No. 4*, "Concepts and Accounting Principles Underlying Financial Statements," New York: AICPA, October 1970, paras. 61-72; 134-135; 148-164; 180-187.

American Accounting Association Committee on Concepts and Standards Underlying Corporate Financial Statements, "Accounting and Reporting Standards for Corporate Financial Statements, 1957 Revision," *The Accounting Review*, October 1957, pp. 536-546.

American Accounting Association Committee on Concepts and Standards—Inventory Measurement, "A Discussion of Various Approaches to Inventory Measurement," Supplementary Statement No. 2, *The Accounting Review*, July 1964, pp. 700-714.

American Accounting Association 1964 Concepts and Standards Research Study Committee—The Matching Concept, "The Matching Concept," *The Accounting Review*, April 1965, pp. 368-372.

American Institute of Accountants, *Accounting Terminology Bulletin No. 1*, *Review and Resume*, New York: American Institute of Accountants, August 1953; *Accounting Terminology Bulletin No. 2, Proceeds, Revenue, Income, Profit and Earnings*, March 1955, *Accounting Terminology Bulletin No. 3*, *Cost, Expense and Loss,* July 1957.

Backer, Morton, "Financial Reporting and Security Investment Decisions," *Financial Analysts Journal*, March/April 1971, pp. 67-72, 79.

Barden, Horace G., *Accounting Research Study No. 13*, "The Accounting Basis for Inventories," New York: AICPA, 1973.

Beams, Floyd A., "Income Reporting: Continuity with Change," *Management Accounting*, August 1972, pp. 23-27.

Bedford, Norton M., *Income Determination Theory: An Accounting Framework*, Reading, Mass.: Addison-Wesley, 1965.

Benke, Ralph L. Jr., and James Don Edwards, *Transfer Pricing: Techniques and Uses*, National Association of Accountants, 1980.

Bernstein, Leopold A., "Extraordinary Gains and Losses—Their Significance to the Financial Analyst," *Financial Analysts Journal*, November/December 1972, pp. 49-52, 88-90.

Carroll, Thomas J., "The Accountants' Extraordinary Dilemma," *World*, Peat, Marwick, Mitchell & Co., Summer 1974.

Cirtin, Arnold, "Interest Expense—Is It Really a 'Non-Operating' Expense?," *CPA Journal*, October 1973, pp. 877-880.

"Dollar Values in the Social Income Statement," *World*, Peat, Marwick, Mitchell & Co., Spring 1973.

FASB *Discussion Memorandum*, "an analysis of issues related to Conceptual Framework for Financial Accounting and Reporting: Elements of Financial Statements and Their Measurement," Stamford, Conn.: Financial Accounting Standards Board, December 2, 1976, Part I, chs. 5/6 and Appendix A.

FASB *Discussion Memorandum*, "an analysis of issues related to Reporting Earnings," Stamford, Conn.: FASB, July 31, 1979.

FASB *Statement of Financial Accounting Concepts No. 3*, "Elements of Financial Statements of Business Enterprises," Stamford, Conn.: FASB, December 1980, paras. 56-89, 147-178.

Jaenicke, Henry R., Research Report, *Survey of Present Practices in Recognizing Revenues, Expenses, Gains and Losses*, Stamford, Conn.: Financial Accounting Standards Board, January 1981.

Kreiser, Larry, "Toward a More Social Income Statement," *Financial Executive*, June 1980, pp. 24-26.

Most, Kenneth S., "A Proposal for the Abolition of 'Extraordinary Events and Transactions,'" *The Singapore Accountant*, Vol. 9, 1974, pp. 23-29.

Most, Kenneth S., "The Value of Inventories," *Journal of Accounting Research*, Spring, 1967, pp. 39-50.

Rueschhoff, Norlin G., "The 'Funds-Flow' Income Statement: An Advance in Presentation," *CPA Journal*, September 1973, pp. 809-811.

Snaveley, H. Jim, "Financial Statement Restatement," *Journal of Accountancy*, October 1976, pp. 91-100.

Snaveley, Howard J., and Allan H. Savage, "Clean Surplus vs. Current Operating Performance—Gaps in APB Opinion No. 9," *New York Certified Public Accountant*, February 1970, pp. 124-129.

Thomas, Arthur L., *Revenue Recognition*, Michigan Business Reports No. 49, Ann Arbor, Mich.: Bureau of Business Research, University of Michigan, 1966.

Wheeler, James E. and Willard H. Galliart, *An Appraisal of Interperiod Income Tax Allocation*, New York: Financial Executives Research Foundation, 1974.

Windal, Floyd, "The Accounting Concept of Realization," *The Accounting Review*, April 1961, pp. 249-258.

Case 14-1 Extinguishment of Debt

One of the recognized types of "gain" or "loss" is the difference between the carrying value of a debt obligation and the amount at which it is acquired in order to be retired. The following chronology is relevant to accounting for this difference.

1966— *APB Opinion No. 9* severely curtailed the number of items which could be directly charged or credited to Retained Earnings, and distinguished between extraordinary and prior years' items.

1972— *APB Opinion No. 26* stated that all early extinguishments of debt were alike, and required gains and losses to be classified as ordinary or extraordinary in accordance with—

1973— *APB Opinion No. 30*, which defined extraordinary items so narrowly that gains or losses from early extinguishment of debt would not qualify.

1975— *FASB Statement No. 4* called for gains and losses on early extinguishment of debt to be reported as extraordinary, if material. However, this Statement made an exception for cash purchases of debt made to satisfy current or future sinking fund requirements.

1. Are all extinguishments of debt before scheduled maturities fundamentally alike? (*APBO 26*, para. 19)
2. What concept of materiality might be relevant in the application of *FASB 4*?
3. To what extent was *FASB 4* a measured response to a problem which had become apparent in the application of

APBO 26, and to what extent was it a sudden response to a few scandalous situations reported to the SEC?

Case 14-2 Northway Airlines, Inc.

In 19X3 Northway Airlines, Inc. sued Phillips Aircraft, Inc. for $30 million, claiming that this was the amount of loss it suffered through delays in obtaining delivery of aircraft ordered by Northway from Phillips. The court awarded Northway $25 million in 19X5; Phillips appealed and the appeal court reversed the decision. In 19X7 Northway sued again; late in 19X7 attorneys for both sides concluded a settlement in which Phillips agreed to pay Northway $10 million in consideration for dropping the claim.

Under the terms of the settlement, Northway agreed to lease ten aircraft from Phillips for two years from January 1, 19X8. The quarterly rental, payable in advance, was $2,500,000 per plane. The $10 million due to Northway would be allowed to them as a rebate of 10 percent on each of the four quarterly rental payments due in 19X8.

1. How, and in which fiscal year(s), should Northway account for this $10 million?
2. How, and in which fiscal year(s), should Phillips account for the claim against the company?

Case 14-3 Capital or Revenue Expenditure?

In 1981 the U.S. Federal Communications Commission approved a change in accounting rules designed to ensure the financial welfare of the nation's telephone companies. Under the rules which govern the operation of these monopolies, they are permitted to recover their costs in their prices, but must raise their capital from investors and lenders. These rules are applied in somewhat different ways by various state commissions, called public utility (or service) commissions.

The Commission's decision involved accounting procedures covering the cost of installing a new phone or moving an existing one, a cost incurred almost entirely in the form of labor (wages of installers). Until the new rule this cost was capitalized together with expenditures on equipment, and charged to expense through amortization. Thus, the telephone companies were required to borrow in expensive money markets to finance such expenditures. The old rule had the effect of spreading installation costs over all customers, since a typical installation costing $100 was charged to a residential customer as a smaller fee of, say, $40. Under the new rule the consumer may be charged the full cost of an installation, or else a smaller fee may result in part of the cost being spread over all customers during the period when the installation occurred.

1. Could this problem ever arise in a nonregulated enterprise, such as an oil company or a meat-packing plant?
2. In the absence of regulation, what would be the reasons for wanting an accounting standard to cover this type of situation?
3. How does the FASB's definitions of asset and expense help to resolve this accounting problem?

Case 14-4 The Accounting Piscatorial Society

The following annual financial report was submitted to the members of the Accounting Piscatorial Society.

Accounting Piscatorial Society
Statement of Revenues and Expenditures
Year to December 31, 1980

	Budget	Actual
Revenues		
Membership dues	$ 6,800	$ 5,410
Sales of rods, lures, and flies	1,000	723
Sales of books on fishing	1,000	355
Total revenues	$ 8,800	$ 6,488
Expenditures		
Printing fishing books	$ 5,300	$ 2,310
Printing membership roster	1,500	—
Postage, telephone and other expenses	2,000	455
Total expenditures	$ 8,800	$ 2,765
Revenues less expenditures	$ —	$ 3,723
Beginning Balance	3,678	3,678
Ending Balance	$ 3,678	$ 7,401

Prepared on the cash basis.

(signed) William Wordsworth, CPA
Treasurer

1. Do the items called "revenues" correspond with the FASB definition of revenues?
2. What is the meaning of "expenditures" in this statement?
3. List the possible sources of difference between the revenues and expenditures listed in the statement and conventional accrual-basis revenues and expenses. Do you agree that the same name should be used for both?
4. What is the statement presented for the Accounting Piscatorial Society? What is the "ending balance"?

Case 14-5 The Used Truck Allowance

In 1980 a large corporation in the business of leasing automobiles and trucks agreed to a settlement of the SEC's charges that it had violated the reporting provisions of the 1934 Act. The company filed amendments to pending S–7 registration statements and to its 1979 10–K report.

The issue concerned a so-called Used Truck Allowance (UTA) which the company received from its main truck supplier. The UTA was a payment received from the supplier in connection with the purchase of a new truck which was paid for in full. Originally, this payment was received only if a used truck was traded in to the supplier in part exchange for the new one. For many years prior to 1979, however, the UTA was paid by the supplier solely on the purchase of a new truck. The company booked the UTA as income immediately, regardless of whether it traded in any used trucks to the supplier, or sold them elsewhere. A further aspect of the company's accounting was that the UTA was received when billed, and not necessarily when the new truck was purchased. No UTA was receivable when a truck was purchased to expand the company's fleet, however.

The SEC contended that the UTA should have been accounted for as a reduction of the purchase price of the new truck, and not as additional proceeds on sale of the old one. It had also been suggested that the UTA should be deferred and amortized to income over the life of the new truck. The company and its auditors argued that (a) to treat the receipt as a discount would affect the amount of the investment tax credit, (b) acknowledgment of a discount of this kind might also be contrary to the antitrust laws, and (c) it was believed to be industry practice to credit a UTA to income on receipt or on disposal of the used truck, based upon the fact that the UTA required the sale of an old truck as well as the purchase of a new one.

The consequence of the settlement with the SEC was that the company restated its financial statements back to 1975; the effect was slight for years 1975-77, but the last two years' earnings were reduced by 11.9 percent and 5.2 percent respectively.

1. Did the UTA correspond with the FASB's definition of revenue, or with the FASB's definition of asset (an allowance can be a part of an asset in that definition)?
2. What other parts of the conceptual framework are relevant to the solution of this accounting problem? To what conclusion do they lead?
3. The SEC asserted that "the company should have accounted for the allowance as a reduction of the purchase price for new equipment and amortized the acquisition price of the new vehicles, less estimated residual value, over the life of the underlying equipment. When these vehicles were sold, the

company would have then reflected gain or loss on the disposition of the vehicles measured as the difference between the carrying value of the assets and the consideration received." Is there any difference between the method of accounting required by the SEC and that laid down as appropriate by any *Intermediate Accounting* textbook published during the period 1977-79?

END OF CHAPTER QUESTIONS

1. What are the two approaches to the measurement of income? Why is one more informative than the other?
2. List the essential ingredients of a double-entry accounting system. Which would be absent in a nonarticulated system?
3. Explain the social uses of the income statement, and identify the factor underlying the change from a proprietary to an entity viewpoint.
4. Distinguish between: multistep and single step, current operating and all-inclusive—as classifiers of income statements.
5. What is the reason for excluding from the measurement of operating income the categories: extraordinary items, gains and losses on discontinued operations, and effect of change of accounting principle?
6. How has the APB's definition of an extraordinary item been modified by the FASB?
7. How has the APB's prescribed method of accounting for a change in accounting principle been modified by the FASB?
8. Argue the case for prior period adjustments to be abolished as components of the change in equity.
9. What is meant by the phrase "quality of earnings"? What factors are indicative of this quality?
10. How does a value-added income statement differ from the conventional form of income statement? How are changes in inventories reported in such a statement? What information is highlighted in a value-added statement?
11. Define *revenues* as perceived by the FASB. Critically examine this definition.
12. Explain what is meant by *cash basis income* and its relation to income determination theory.
13. Define *expenses* as perceived by the FASB. Critically examine this definition.
14. How did the FASB distinguish gains from revenues and losses from expenses? What is the informational significance of such a distinction?
15. Explain why revenue is recognized when a sale takes place. How can a sale take place without revenue being recognized?
16. How is revenue recognized other than that arising from sales?
17. Define *realization* in accounting.
18. What is the social output concept of revenue?

19. Distinguish carefully between: expenditure, expense, payment, cost. Where in this group of concepts does "cost of goods sold" belong?
20. What is the *matching principle?* Why was it adopted? What useful purpose does it serve? Is there one matching principle, or are there two?
21. Discuss the rules governing accounting for pension cost in relation to the general principles of expense determination. Refer specifically to the accrual method and the matching principle.
22. What is the allocation problem? Discuss its significance to the process of income measurement.
23. What alternative approaches to income statement classification are there, other than the conventional forms and the value-added form?
24. Explain the role of segment reporting in aiding the objectives of income statement reporting.
25. The most often-quoted piece of corporate annual report data is earnings per share.
    A. Explain why earnings per share is so important to financial statement users.
    B. Discuss the characteristics of earnings per share which make this ratio less useful to financial statement users than your explanation in A indicates that users believe it to be.
    C. What other ratio could be of interest to financial statement users as a substitute for earnings per share, and how would you suggest that it should be calculated?

15

THE STATEMENT OF CHANGES IN FINANCIAL POSITION

The third basic financial statement, the statement of changes in financial position, received this name in 1971 when its importance was recognized by *APB Opinion No. 19.*[1] Prior to that date it was often called a statement of source and application of funds, or a funds statement. The last is shorter and equally familiar to accountants, and will be used throughout this chapter.

HISTORY OF THE FUNDS STATEMENT

The funds statement is a relatively recent addition to the set of financial statements, and it is, perhaps for this reason, comparatively misunderstood.[2] Corporations have published funds statements in much the same form as today since 1862 in England and 1863 in the United States, which was noted by Cole in a textbook published in 1908.[3] H. A. Finney was instrumental in familiarizing the accounting profession with the construction of funds statements, through his textbooks and by means of a series of articles published in the *Journal of Accountancy* during the 1920s. By the end of World War II, the funds statement was commonly presented in annual reports either as a separate statement or in a footnote. In 1963 its presentation was recommended, but not required, by *APB Opinion No. 3,*[4] and in 1970 the SEC made it an obligatory part of a financial statement filing.[5] *APB Opinion No. 19* laid down that, when financial statements purporting to be in accordance with generally accepted accounting principles are presented, a statement of changes in financial position should be provided; this has been interpreted to mean that this statement is required whenever such financial statements are published to external users. A funds statement is usually presented by multinational and larger domestic corporations domiciled in other countries, but international accounting standards have not yet mandated publication. Research has established that users regard this statement as important as, and in some cases more important than, the balance sheet.

The word *funds* used here is derived from the more specialized term "fund" to denote a property subject to a set of restrictions. In finance, a fund is a sum of money or other property set aside for a specific purpose, such as a revolving fund for certain types of expenditures, a petty cash fund, a pension fund, or a sinking fund with which to liquidate debt. Since the entity can be viewed as a set of properties subject to the restrictions placed upon their use by proprietors, other financiers, and state regulators, it can be represented as a group of funds. Vatter has suggested that fund accounting be applied to business entities, as it is already used for not-for-profit undertakings.[6] Anyone familiar with fund accounting will agree that if accountants had been commissioned to create a system of accounting to induce the maximum of obscurity into the affairs of men, they would have invented fund accounting. A survey by Anton reported, however, that companies thought such fund accounting would be desirable, although they found it impossible to construct it on a departmental basis.[7] There is no evidence that fund accounting, as distinct from funds statements, is used for business operations.

From the beginning, four concepts of funds were identifiable in the statements presented. These were cash and cash equivalents; current assets; working capital; and all financial resources (assets, liabilities, and stockholders' equity). Cole favored the all financial resources approach, but Finney's advocacy resulted in the acceptance of the working capital approach by academics and eventually by a majority of corporations presenting this type of statement. In a research study prepared some years before the publication of *APBO No. 19,* Perry Mason identified additional funds concepts, such as short-term monetary assets, net monetary assets, and all significant financial events.[8] *APBO No. 3,* published in 1963 (which was superseded by *APBO No. 19*), recommended the use of the "all significant financial events" concept to include interfirm transactions of a type which do not change working capital or cash, and did not favor the use of a cash flow approach. *APBO No. 19* recommended "a broad concept embracing all changes in financial position" which can be equated with the "all significant financial events" approach. This Opinion also called for changes in working capital or cash resulting from operations and the effects of extraordinary items to be prominently disclosed, and for the statement to begin with income (or loss) before extraordinary items, adjusted for items which do not use or provide working capital. It is clear that the authors of the Opinion were not quite ready to discard the working capital concept as a fundamental element of the statement.

Yu has suggested that the most useful concept of funds is that of *all economic resources* and that the statement should take a form similar to the one used by national income accountants to present the flow of funds in the national accounts.[9] He argues that the cycle of business operations involves a continuous movement of resources into and out of the firm, so that data restricted to stocks and income flows are incomplete. His statement would start with revenue flows rather than net income, and distinguish between financial and nonfinancial flows. *APBO No. 19* stated that the total revenue flow approach was an acceptable alternative to starting with net income before extraordinary items.

Because of a lack of standardization in the form and content of the funds statement, there have been several attempts in recent years to rethink its nature and objectives. A major research study was sponsored by the AICPA in 1978, and the FASB's conceptual framework project includes a discussion memorandum dated December 15, 1980; both of these will be examined later in this chapter, after an attempt to clarify the existing situation has been made.

WHAT IS THE FUNDS STATEMENT?

The contemporary funds statement depicts the movements of values into, through, and out of an entity during a specified period of time. These values may be assets, liabilities, contributions and withdrawals of capital, revenues, and expenses. Referring to the flow chart in Table 2-3, such movements are represented as a third dimension, including internal movements of values through the entity. They can be represented by the equation:

$$\triangle \text{ assets equals } \triangle \text{ liabilities plus } \triangle \text{ owner's equity.}$$

Since we have defined assets as investment, and liabilities and owner's equity as capital or sources of finance, the funds statement can be seen as a period statement of the investing activities of the enterprise and the financing of these investments. This viewpoint comes out clearly in *APB Opinion No. 19* which gives as the first objective of the statement

> to summarize the financing and investing activities of the entity, including the extent to which the enterprise has generated funds from operations during the period.

This last concept is sometimes referred to as *self-financing.*

The second objective is "to complete the disclosure of changes in financial position during the period." One change in financial position, namely, the change in retained earnings, is typically shown either in the income statement itself or else in a separate statement of changes in owners' equity. The second objective, therefore, calls for the statement to explain all other changes in financial position, as a means of demonstrating financing and investing activities.

The meaning of funds in this context can be equated to "means of payment," which is a set of observations ranging from the narrowest to the widest. The narrowest observation is cash in the form of coin and banknotes. Next we have bank checks and other forms of bank transfer. Following this we have various other forms of negotiable instrument, such as bills of exchange and promissory notes, tobacco receipts, dock warrants to bearer, bills of lading with documents attached, and the like. We also have certain specialized forms of bank credit, such as the letter of credit which is widely used in international trade. We may also include in this category near-cash items, such as securities freely traded on a recognized exchange and which are available for the settlement of obligations.

Beyond this, however, is a wider set of observations of values which can be used for transactions: receivables, which can be assigned as well as hypothecated; inventories which can be bartered or returned to suppliers; equipment, which can be used in non-monetary exchanges. In fact, all of the resources which can be the subject of investment can be included in the category "means of payment." This is the explanation of the definition of funds as "all economic resources" and of the broad concept of the APB, embracing all changes in financial position. Indeed, very few of the transactions, events, and circumstances which provide the raw material of accounting are excluded from the funds statement; one, on which there is general agreement, is a stock dividend. Other accounting events which appear in the funds statement but are not funds flows include depreciation, amortization, the equity pickup in respect of investee profits and losses, and movements on the deferred income tax accounts; these appear only because they must be added back or deducted from net income to arrive at funds provided by operations.

This view permits us to see all concepts of funds as parts of this broad concept. A funds statement which depicts the net change in working capital simply highlights changes in the relatively narrow concept of funds as current assets minus current liabilities. In operational terms, we eliminate from the period's changes in assets and liabilities the changes in working capital items, so that the net change of funds is equal and opposite to the net change in working capital. A funds statement that depicts all significant financial events incorporates all changes in assets, liabilities, and owners' equity arising from transacting with the environment; under the conditions of the double-entry system, these will cancel out (the total inflows and outflows will equal each other). There can be no difference, however, in the amounts for items included in each type of funds statement; moreover, where an analysis of net change in working capital accompanies a funds statement which is prepared under the working capital concept of funds, the individual changes in current assets and liabilities will be the same as if they had been included in an events type of funds statement. Some textbooks have begun to demonstrate the preparation of period cash flow statements which they call "Statement of Changes in Financial Position—Cash Basis." Whatever the usefulness of such statements, they are not the cash basis funds statements referred to in several places in *APB Opinion No. 19.*

It may be surmised that the different forms of funds statement arose from specific user needs. For example, the financiers of a company which has executed an indenture in connection with its bonded debt, requiring working capital to be maintained at a certain level, will be interested to see the net change in working capital at the end of each accounting period. The directors of a company which has a chronic shortage (or surplus) of cash will be interested in a funds statement which highlights the net change in cash.

CASH FUNDS FLOWS

It follows from the above that cash flows are a part of funds flows and not a surrogate therefor, or vice versa. In terms of the movement of values, cash is one of a great number of values moving between the firm and its environment. Ultimately, the cycle of the entity's economy is a liquidity cycle, from and to cash, but cash is not an independent variable in the production and distribution of goods and services. A profitable firm will obtain cash (given time and a knowledgeable financial manager), and an unprofitable firm will lose cash; the possession of cash does not of itself ensure profits or even survival.

Nor is it correct to regard cash held by the firm as undifferentiated (or generalized) purchasing power. The cash held by a business entity is earmarked for payments of wages, rents, interest, and for goods and services supplied, of a highly specific kind. Therefore, if we were to calculate the effects of inflation on a firm's cash position, we should need a specific index of those things on which the firm spends its money, and not a general purchasing power index. Similarly, the definition of funds as cash does not imply free availability for dividends.

It is, of course, necessary to recognize the critical role played by cash (and similar means of payment) in the operation of any economic entity. If the entity cannot pay its bills, it will fail in its mission; a human being who cannot pay for food may die of starvation. Every firm must have an efficient subsystem to account for and to aid in planning and controlling cash flows. It is a fundamental error of observation, however, to confuse cash flows with income (or profit) flows. The complex nature of the relationship between cash flows and income flows is depicted in Table 15-1. It will be evident that only a firm which has few credit transactions, which has a relatively small inventory (or does not expect any change in inventory from one period to another), and which is relatively labor—rather than capital—intensive can equate cash flows to income flows. Some cash flow statements illustrated in intermediate accounting textbooks attempt to simplify this complex picture by showing financing and investing activities not involving cash as notes to the funds statement, and not part of the funds statement itself.

TABLE 15-1 Origins of Differences Between Receipts/Payments, Revenue/Expense

1. Payments in advance
   A. Acquisitions which will become expenses
      (a) depreciable fixed asset purchases
      (b) prepayments
      (c) construction of own equipment
      (d) inventory items
      (e) advance payments to suppliers
   B. Payments which will be cancelled by receipts
      (a) nondepreciable fixed asset purchases
      (b) loans advanced
      (c) investment securities purchased
2. Payments cancelling previous receipts—loan repayments
3. Revenues not producing receipts—unpaid credit sales
4. Expenses not corresponding with payments
   (a) purchases on credit
   (b) accrued expenses
   (c) accrued tax liabilities
   (d) imputed costs
   (e) accrued loss contingencies
5. Receipts which will be cancelled by future payments—loans received
6. Deferred revenues
7. Noncash transactions
   (a) capital contributions in kind
   (b) barter transactions
   (c) subsidies in kind
8. Income tax allocations
9. Investor's share in profits/losses of investees, adjusted where appropriate for additional depreciation and goodwill amortization

If it were desired to present a statement of cash flows as a basic financial statement, in order to assist users to predict future cash flows, the statement would need to distinguish between—

- Cash flow from operations;
- Other recurring in- and outflows, such as open market bond purchases and dividends receivable and payable;
- Investments in plant and equipment needed to maintain capacity;
- Investments to increase capacity, including cash raised and repaid from and to shareholders and bondholders;
- Extraordinary receipts and payments; cash in- or outflows from discontinued operations, and prior period items.

Given the great variety of different types of cash receipts and payments, this classification could present as many problems as does accrual accounting. How should a seasonal bank loan received to finance merchandise purchases be classified? It certainly results from operations, but if the borrowing is an annual event, it could be classified as a recurring loan. Should it be divided into two parts if this year's loan finances more purchases than last year's loan did?

Many commentators have pointed out that cash receipts and disbursements behave in an unpredictable manner over short periods of time, and are completely unpredictable in the long run. The transition from cash to accrual accounting has always been regarded as an improvement, and the FASB's conceptual framework accepts the proposition that financial reports prepared on the accrual basis are more useful in assessing future cash flows. A statement of cash flow would obviously be informative if the entity had liquidity problems; in the extreme situation of insolvency, accrual accounting must be supplemented by liquidation accounts.

A method of integrating the cash-basis funds statement with the two other basic financial statements has been demonstrated by the author, without attracting much interest.[10]

STRUCTURE OF THE FUNDS STATEMENT

Since the funds statement presents the flow of all funds through the firm, to understand its structure we require a model of the firm. The *see-through* model of economic theory is of no use, lacking as it does the dimensions of time and space. The *plumbing* model shown as Figure 15-1 is of some help.

This model recognizes the flow of funds implicit in Table 2-3. We must be on guard against the error of believing that it represents some physical flow, assimilable to the flow of a liquid, for example. With this caution, we observe that funds are received from three primary sources: owners, creditors, and customers. To these we may add government, if subsidy is recognized. A secondary source is the liquidation of assets or disinvestment (not shown). Funds are disbursed to factors of production, which are combined in the form of inventories; to customers, in the form of supplier credit; for equipment (fixed assets); and for dividends and taxes. The separate identification of interest in Figure 15-1 can be explained by the fact that the model was devised for the study of finance.

One problem which the model highlights is the treatment of depreciation. Conventional funds statements for the most part incorporate the net income figure from the income statement, which is not a fund flow. It is, therefore, necessary to accommodate the nonfund items in the income statement, of which depreciation is usually the major item of significance, either by adding it back to net income or by deducting it from investment in fixed assets to show net investment. The model proposed by Yu eliminates this difficulty by showing expenses net of depreciation.

However, a funds statement which starts with revenues can be criticized from another viewpoint. Objectively, the most comprehensive form of Yu's funds statement is the pre-closing trial balance.

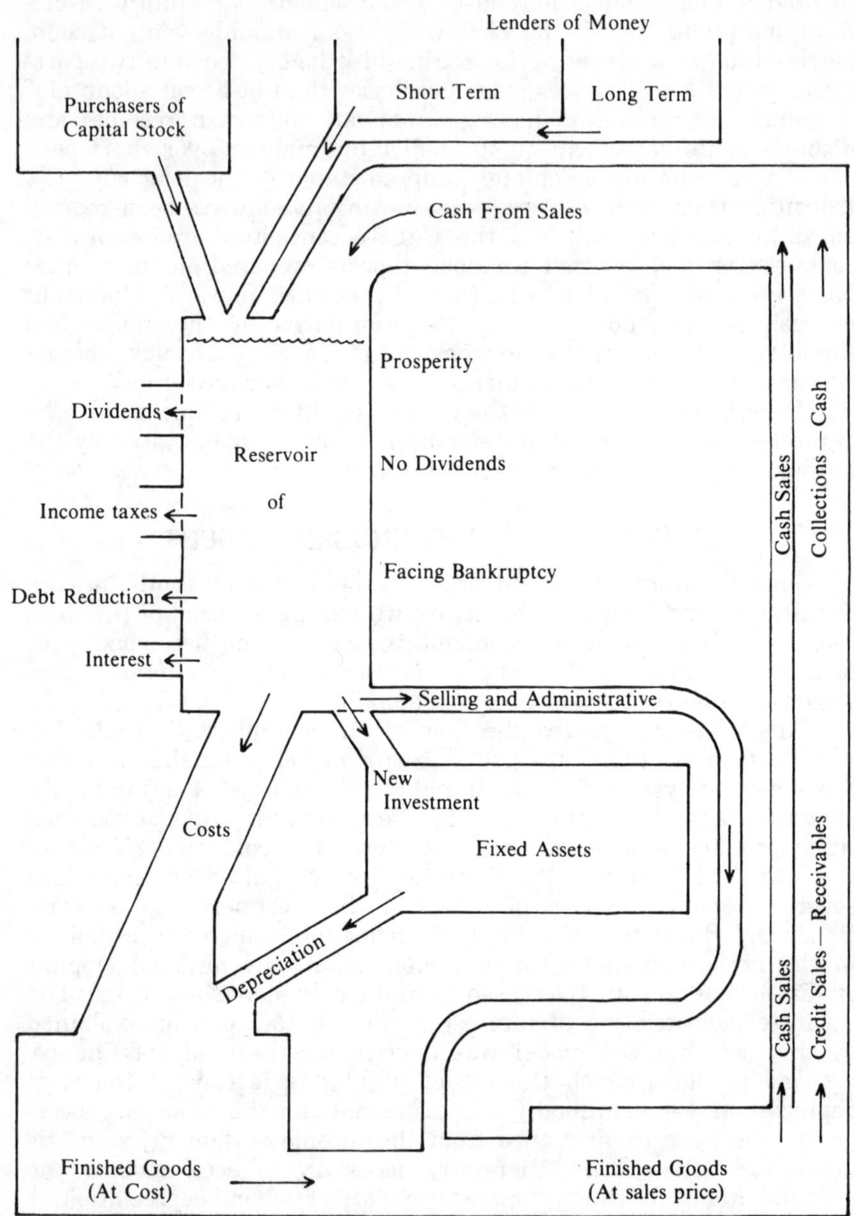

FIGURE 15-1 CASH FLOW THROUGH A BUSINESS

Source: John A. Griswold, *Cash Flow Through A Business,* Dartmouth: The Amos Tuck School of Business Administration, 1955, p. 2.

This is because, if we equate the objects accounted for with economic resources and obligations, the pre-closing trial balance includes them all. It is obvious that the trial balance requires further interpretation before it can be made useful, which is why we analyze it into an income statement and a balance sheet. The same data can be analyzed for presentation as a funds statement by eliminating nonfund accounting entries. This leads to a funds statement in the form of Figure 15-1, rather than that proposed by Yu.

The prevailing practice is to classify sources into funds provided from operations and a gallimaufry of other inflows, and to classify uses by balance sheet items. The problem of determining what is provided by operations has been mentioned; there is also the problem of defining operations. The effect of *APBO No. 30,* "Reporting the Results of Operations, etc.," has been to include any transaction in operations if it is not of an unusual nature and of infrequent occurrence. Sale of equipment, for most firms, does not meet these criteria. Prior to *APBO No. 30,* it was clear that the gain or loss on such a transaction should be deducted from or added back to net income in arriving at funds provided by operations, and the actual sale proceeds shown among other sources. If such sales are now regarded as part of ordinary operations, this treatment is no longer justified, and the textbook method of reporting them is obsolete. However, it was pointed out in chapter 14 that the unitary income statement is proving unmanageable, and the effect of *APBO No. 30* on the funds statement is only one of the factors which call for this Opinion to be revised.

USES OF THE FUNDS STATEMENT

The literature on funds statements provides the following list of perceived uses of funds flow information:

- Assessing future fund flows
- Assessing the "quality of earnings" by identifying the relationship between income and change in working capital, or cash
- Reporting the reasons for changes in working capital or cash.
- Improving interperiod and interfirm comparisons by eliminating deferrals and accruals
- Providing answers to a number of "where got—where gone" questions, such as why the firm has not increased the dividend when profits have risen, or what happened to the proceeds of a stock issue

Research has established the importance of the funds statement to external users. Clarkson found that institutional investors placed importance on growth in working capital and growth in cash flows per share.[11] Hawkins and Campbell found that funds flows analysis was used to examine how a company financed capital expenditures and dividends.[12] Backer and Gosman found funds statements used in credit analysis.[13] A survey of attitudes of financial statement users identified cash flow information as highly important, and Beaver's research suggests strongly that changes in elements of working capital are regarded by analysts as indicators of business failure.[14]

Anton reported that in 1951 nearly all companies preparing funds statements used them internally in decision making, and it is unlikely that the situation has changed in the last thirty years.[15] Small businesses relied heavily on funds statement presentation to bankers, but would probably be better served by cash forecasts. The growth of cash budgeting over the past twenty-five years suggests that the short-term uses of the funds statement, emphasized in the Anton study, may have been replaced by long-term uses, such as evaluating and planning changes in capital and asset structures.

Like most of the subjects examined in this book, the uses of the funds statement have not been researched scientifically. Nor has there been much imagination shown in identifying additional uses for this statement. Since it is not complicated by accruals and deferrals required for the calculation of revenues and expenses, it is particularly suited for reporting operations in cases where income determination is not important. This is the case of the development stage enterprise, and a requirement to report a funds statement together with a balance sheet for such entities would be sufficient. *FASB Statement No. 7,* however, required them to report an income statement in addition.[16]

In this connection, it is interesting to note that the role of accounting for changing prices in relation to the funds statement has not yet been explored. *FASB Statement No. 33* and other official pronouncements calling for replacement or current cost disclosures have simply ignored this possibility. Those companies which have reported price-level adjusted financial statements, such as Indiana Telephone Corporation, have simply thrown the resulting asset and liability changes, including purchasing power gains and losses, into the funds statement. The view of the funds statement presented in this chapter raises questions about this practice. Indeed, it is arguable that funds statements in historical terms are equally valid in times of changing price-levels and in periods of constant prices. One firm of financial analysts which prepares replacement cost adjusted financial statements as a part of the information supplied to clients has developed the statement shown in Table 15-2, which is based on a concept of cash flow as net income plus depreciation and deferred taxes.[17]

Another situation in which the funds statement would be useful is in reports by public figures, such as politicians, on changes in their wealth. It is often difficult to determine whether money, goods, and services made available to such individuals are constituents of their personal incomes or contributions to their political expenses, but the question is usually irrelevant; what the public wants

TABLE 15-2 INFLATION EFFECTS ON CASH FLOW ($000s)

Reported net income	$ 71,700	
+ depreciation, depletion, and amortization	34,000	
+ deferred income taxes	4,300	
Reported cash flow from operations	$110,000	$110,000
Capital maintenance requirements due to inflation		
Receivables net of current liabilities	(35,800)	
One-year weighted price change in cost of goods sold = 6.8% $35,800 × 6.8%	= (2,400)	
Cost of goods sold—replacement cost increment	8,100	
Fixed asset increase in replacement cost	52,800	58,500
Sustainable operating cash flow		51,500
Less: Dividends and growth investments		
Dividends paid	23,300	
Increase in inventory above capital maintenance requirement	15,400	
Increase in monetary working capital above capital maintenance requirement	(1,400)	
Capital expenditure exceeding capital maintenance requirement	3,800	41,100
Net cash flow before financing requirement		$ 10,400

Note: Positive net cash flow implies no financing requirement.

to know is the source of their funds and the uses to which they are put.

For long-term uses it is possible that cumulative sources and uses of funds are more informative than period sources and uses. The latter can provide clues to short-term future financing and investment decisions. A decline in working capital may presage business failure but may also suggest a future stock or bond issue. An increase in fixed asset investment unaccompanied by an increase in working capital also indicates a probable future issue of stock or bonds. This type of prediction can sometimes be made by examining the structure of the period funds statement, to see the relationships between short-term financing and investment and long-term financing and investment. Evaluation of the capital and asset structure of a business for the purpose of long-term predictions, however, involves studying the flow of funds over the investment cycle of the firm, which may be as long as twenty-five years and longer in the case of public utilities. Brief *et al.* have demonstrated a graphical method of displaying cumulative income and cumulative cash flows to suppliers of capital.[18]

DISSATISFACTION WITH THE FUNDS STATEMENT

A 1976 study by an independent investment research firm asserted that the funds statement is an important analytical tool for investors, but criticized most current presentations as miscellaneous collections of plus and minus changes in balance sheet items.[19] This study contained the surprising assertion that the predominant emphasis on working capital serves little purpose "since working capital is not an important analytical figure." It appeared that the principal use of the funds statement by analysts was as a source of information about capital expenditures and other matters affecting assets and liabilities, which could be more easily obtained from a statistical tabulation. The study expressed a preference for a form of funds statement balanced to cash and incorporated in the management discussion section of the annual report. Otherwise the authors had no clear idea about what to do with the funds statement, even though they considered it an important part of the financial statements.

Another recent critical study likewise points out that whereas the income statement has achieved a definitive form, the same cannot be said of the funds statement.[20] The author believed that the statement should disclose financing and investing activities in a form corresponding to the structure of these activities:

Financing equals equity plus debt
Investing equals short-term assets plus long-term assets

Short-term assets differs from working capital in that borrowings at interest, including the current portion of debt, would be excluded.

The author also drew attention to what he termed "loose practices" in the preparation of the funds statement, and this appears to be the area in greatest need of improvement. The problems include the following.

- *Presentation* Although the report, or tabular, form is almost universal, and perhaps 90 percent of funds statements balance to the change in working capital, a great variety of presentations is encountered. Some firms use a balanced format, some show a difference between sources and uses as a balancing figure. Some balance to working capital, others to cash plus marketable securities, or liquid assets minus bank overdrafts, or even, in the case of some utilities, net change in property, plant and equipment. Having selected a balancing figure, some statements end with the net change, while others provide a reconciliation such as

Net decrease in working capital, 19X0	$ 700
Working capital on January 1, 19X0	800
Working capital at December 31, 19X0.	$ 100

- *What to include* Although *APB Opinion No. 19* seems clear enough in requiring all changes in financial position to be presented, some still see the funds statement as basically a cash flow analysis and, therefore, seek to exclude non-monetary exchanges, such as settlement of liabilities by issuing stock to the creditors. Whether financing should be shown gross or net is another issue; if a firm repays a $100,000 loan and then borrows another $100,000, some would omit these transactions from the statement.
- *Structure* The category "funds provided by operations" is fairly well understood in practice, but thereafter the sequencing of items appears random, not even ordered by size. There would seem to be a basis for classifying both sources and uses in a more or less standard manner.
- *Change of sign* What to do with a category which provided an inflow last period and an outflow this is a real problem, particularly if comparative statements are presented. The difficulty is most acute if one year shows funds provided from operations and the next, because of a loss which is greater than depreciation expense, a use of funds under this heading. Using the report form means that one literally does not know where to start.
- *Related events* We have referred to the possibility of netting some transactions, and to the case of sales of equipment, where the proceeds may be divided into a gain or loss and a reduction of the asset and its accumulated depreciation.
- *Materiality* All discussions of materiality proceed from the viewpoint of effect on net income, but in preparing the funds statement we should consider the relationship between an item and total fund flows.
- *Working capital constituents* Since most funds statements feature the change in working capital, and *APB Opinion No. 19* states that the net change in working capital items should always be shown, the question of what to include in working capital is of the greatest importance. Inclusion of short-term investments which are earmarked for capital expenditures, or the current portion of a long-term debt which is about to be refinanced, are obvious problems here.
- *Capital maintenance* Should this concept be formally recognized, by dividing investments into those required to maintain capital, and those which are expansionary?
- *Consolidation* Should the investor's share of the investee's fund flows be included in the case of equity accounting? Consolidated statements incorporate 100 percent of the fund flows of subsidiaries, but equity accounting conventionally excludes the funds flows of the investee.

HEATH'S PROPOSALS FOR IMPROVING THE FUNDS STATEMENT

In a 1978 research monograph sponsored and published by the AICPA, Loyd Heath criticized existing funds statements as the product of unclear, misleading, and unattainable objectives.[21] In his view, *APB Opinion No. 19* addressed itself to three kinds of changes: in cash or near-cash resources (debt-paying ability); in capital structure; and in long-term assets. He, therefore, proposed that several different statements are required to communicate this information, now crammed into a single statement. These would be—

- Statement of cash receipts and payments;
- Statement of financing activities, showing movements on loan and equity financing accounts;
- Statement of investing activities, showing movements on equipment and other long-term investment accounts.

An article presenting these views in the *Journal of Accountancy* was severely criticized by several accounting scholars on the grounds—

- That after calling the objectives of *APB Opinion No. 19* unattainable, Heath eventually adopted them.
- That the preparation of three separate schedules to do what the statement of changes in financial position does in one is not an improvement.
- That a statement of cash receipts and disbursements has limited informational content and suggests a reversion to a more primitive age of cash basis accounting.
- That the working capital basis of preparing a funds statement is preferable to the cash basis, because it eliminates timing fluctuations arising out of the sequence: accounts receivable to cash to accounts payable.[22]

The desire to substitute a cash flow statement for the widely used working capital change statement clearly represented a major factor in Heath's reasoning, and a subsequent *Journal of Accountancy* article demonstrated this clearly.[23] In it the author condemned working capital as a useless concept. He argued that the basis of classification of assets and liabilities as current or noncurrent is uncertain; that changes in working capital were not good predictors of business failure; and that working capital does not help users of statements to evaluate financial flexibility, the ability to finance survival in a period of adversity. An unclassified balance sheet accompanied by a schedule of receivables and "financing liabilities" classified by maturities was proposed as "a modest proposal" to improve the form of the balance sheet.

THE FASB DISCUSSION MEMORANDUM

In December 1980 the FASB issued a lengthly Discussion Memorandum on funds flows, extending the subject to cover liquidity and financial flexibility.[24] At the outset, the DM declared its interest only in the past; no attempt would be made to consider forecast information. In the light of what is known of investors' information needs, and of the FASB's own acknowledged objective of assisting users to assess future cash flows, this restriction appeared surprising.

The DM took as its point of departure a static concept of funds as "an asset, a group of assets, or a group of assets and liabilities." It defined liquidity as a measure of time between the reporting date and the date on which cash flows are expected to arise, mitigating this unusual view by providing an alternative definition as "a quality of an asset or a liability." Financial flexibility referred to the ability of an enterprise to alter the amount and timing of future cash flows in order to respond to unexpected needs and opportunities. Emphasis on cash flows was marked, suggesting that respondents to the DM were not encouraged to raise questions about working capital.

This emphasis was based on the following proposition:

> ...if future cash flows are assessed directly from information about past cash flows, users will need information about actual cash receipts and payments.

The wider perspective of *APB Opinion No. 19,* which took the "all financial resources" definition of funds as its point of departure, was thus abandoned. Specific questions posed by analysts were cited as reasons for a historical cash flow statement, and it was asserted that these questions required explanation of the differences between income flows and cash flows.

Horngren has drawn attention to such uses of the funds statement by financial analysts as—

1. The prediction of future earnings and dividends;
2. The prediction of the impact of capital expenditures on financial position;
3. The determination of operating policies;
4. The determination of financial policies.

Some of these uses go beyond the possibilities of cash flow analysis, which is clearly inadequate to demonstrate the enterprise's financing and investing activities.

The narrowed perspective was also evident from the DM's statement of transactions generally referred to as funds flows transactions.

- Cash collections from customers and cash payments to employees, suppliers, and governments
- Acquisition and disposition [*sic*] of long-term assets, such as fixed assets and investments in affiliated enterprises
- Increases and decreases in borrowings and equity capital

The DM provided several illustrations of different forms of statement of cash transactions, and one form of report of working capital provided (starting with sales). It also demonstrated an original combined income/cash statement which simply started with cash receipts and payments and then showed the accruals necessary to convert from the cash to the accruals basis.

In addition to examining various alternatives to conventional funds statements, the DM devoted considerable space to a discussion of the related problems of disclosing liquidity and financial flexibility. Liquidity means "nearness to cash" for both assets and liabilities, and may be assessed by incorporating in financial statements information about the expected timing of cash inflows and outflows; alternatively, it may be expressed by disclosing liquidation values, rather than historical costs. The basic issue addressed by the DM was the classification of the balance sheet and the possibility of basing a classification scheme on "nearness to cash."

Financial flexibility was believed to be an important characteristic about which financial statement users would wish to be informed; the DM did not have any specific idea how, but suggested certain types of information which were relevant, such as the existence of unused lines of credit.

Evidence of the extent of the FASB's dissatisfaction with the funds statement is the observation that, throughout the DM, no mention was made of existing forms and practices, or of any research undertaken to ascertain their strengths and weaknesses.

The FASB's effort to direct attention away from the working capital concept of funds, and toward the cash concept, is a direct consequence of adopting the financial reporting objective of helping users to assess future cash flows. It may or may not be true that information about past cash flows is useful in predicting future cash flows; what little evidence is available on this point tends not to support this proposition.

For example, it has been suggested that information about past investing activities should be classified for this purpose into—

- Spending to maintain existing capacity;
- Expanding existing lines of business;
- Entering new lines of business;
- Complying with regulatory requirements.[25]

Obviously, expenditures for these purposes can be expected to fluctuate widely from year to year.

Thus, acceptance of the "assessing future cash flows" objective does not lead of necessity to a cash flow form of funds statement. The point which must be emphasized is that cash flow is a subsystem of the firm, and, therefore, a cash flow statement is a subsidiary part of the financial statements, not a basic statement.

THE IMPORTANCE OF THE CURRENT/NONCURRENT DISTINCTION

It is instructive to reflect on this aspect of capital maintenance. The fundamental problem of business finance is to raise capital. Capital is invested in two distinct forms—fixed assets and working capital. The distinction between these is of great significance.

Consider the baker, for example. A baker's oven has a life of, say, twenty-five years. Customers cannot be expected to pay for the oven every time they buy a loaf of bread. The loaf includes an infinitesimal contribution for the use of the oven which over many years and millions of loaves pays for the equipment. But the customer who buys a loaf of bread does expect to pay for the flour and other ingredients it contains and for the labor and other conversion costs incurred in order to bake it. That part of capital which is invested in materials and operating costs is called *working capital.*

Contrary to Heath's assertion, then, the prime objective of classifying assets and liabilities as current and noncurrent is to determine working capital. It is not, as many commentators have stated, primarily to measure liquidity and short-term financial health that we are interested in working capital. This secondary objective is derived from the primary one, as we shall see.

It is also a mistake to direct attention to current assets and away from working capital. This error is widespread and can be observed in the common practice of referring to working capital as "net working capital."

An illustration will indicate why this is so. On December 31 a corporation has equipment which cost $1,000 and current assets totalling $500. The corporation owes suppliers $250, because December 31 is a Wednesday and bills are paid on a Friday. How much capital (fixed plus working) does the corporation need? If the finance director makes the mistake of raising $1,500 instead of $1,250 the corporation is overcapitalized and risks the consequences of being unable to service the superfluous capital.

It is not due to lack of understanding, then, that many bond indentures require the indebted corporation to maintain working capital at a specified level, or that the form of funds statement which shows the change in working capital is so common a part of corporate financial statements.

Another illustration will indicate why. Suppose that our baker realizes a contribution margin of ten cents per loaf. Suppose further that overheads and the baker's living expenses amount to $1,000 weekly. Obviously, the baker must sell 10,000 loaves weekly to survive. Now, suppose that to buy flour and other ingredients and to pay wages, the baker needs working capital of $2,000 for a volume of 10,000 loaves weekly. Clearly, if working capital falls to, say, $1,500, the baker cannot maintain the required volume and will soon be out of business. Equally clearly, if the baker can accumulate more than $2,000 of working capital and, thus, produce and sell more than 10,000 loaves weekly, the business can expand further and has a safety margin against a decline in demand.

CASH PROVIDED BY OPERATIONS

APB Opinion No. 19, "Reporting Changes in Financial Position," provides for a number of choices in the preparation of the Statement of Changes in Financial Position (SCFP). One is the choice of the cash basis, in the following words.

> The Statement should prominently disclose working capital or cash provided from or used in operations for the period.... In either case the resulting amount of working capital or cash should be appropriately described, e.g., "Working capital provided from (used in) operations for the period, exclusive of extraordinary items." (para. 10).
>
> a. If the format shows the flow of cash, changes in other elements of working capital (e.g., in receivables, inventories, and payables) constitute sources and uses of cash and should accordingly be disclosed in appropriate detail in the body of the statement. (para. 12)

None of the SCFP—Cash Basis formats illustrated in textbooks, or in the FASB Discussion Memorandum of December 15, 1980, conforms to these specifications. Cash receipts from sales or other operating sources are not cash from operations *for the period;* they include cash receipts from operations for the preceding year. Cash payments to suppliers and others are not related solely to operations *for the period;* they include payments of purchases and expenses for the prior year. Thus, the result of deducting one from the other, or of adding back and deducting increases and decreases, is to produce a figure which can best be described as "net excess of cash received from customers over cash payments to suppliers of goods and services."

What this format achieves is simply a conversion of accrual accounting to cash accounting. Combined with other cash receipts and payments, it results in a statement of net cash flows. A part of such a statement could be designated as, "Cash provided by operations for the period," but it would exclude collection of the prior year's receivables and payments of the prior year's payables.

THE SITUATION IN PRACTICE

About 10 percent of United States corporations publishing financial statements present an SCFP—Cash Basis; others mainly balance to the net change in working capital. Some utilities balance to the additions to property, plant and equipment, and a few corporations present their SCFP in the form, sources = uses.

Of the corporations presenting an SCFP—Cash Basis, none arrives at a different figure of "funds (cash) provided from operations" than would have been identified under this heading in an SCFP—Working Capital Basis. None uses the textbook/FASB format. Is everyone out of step?

Assume that the only nonfund item in the income statement is depreciation. By adding back depreciation we show the amount of funds which would have been provided from operations—

1. If no credit had been given or received, and
2. If there had been no necessity to carry inventories.

In this sense, it is the SCFP and not the income statement which shows the "long-run average net cash inflow at the current level of activity."

The question now arises: if the SCFP is prepared on a working capital basis, does the meaning of this figure for "funds provided from operations" differ? The answer is, obviously not.

CONCLUSION

The statement of changes in financial position provides a good example of our lack of knowledge of the factors underlying accounting practices. True, the funds statement is only one hundred years old, and human behavior changes very slowly. Nevertheless, it should be possible to state the objectives of presenting the funds statement more clearly, and to determine more closely the form and content which best reflects these objectives.

Tracking changes in liquidity has become of major importance since inflation and the accompanying high interest rates have placed a premium on holding cash. Many firms which would in former times have attempted to remain liquid are now finding the opportunity cost too high; it is still possible to substitute financial flexibility for liquidity by negotiating lines of credit for use in emergencies. According to the SEC, financial flexibility is also affected by the existence of debt with interest tied to the prime rate, a matter which requires disclosure, including the effects of future changes in prime on the firm's liquidity. Such information is probably more appropriately disclosed in the notes to the statements than in the statements themselves, whereas changes in liquidity are readily apparent from conventional financial statements.

On the other hand, firms for which liquidity and financial flexibility are not an issue should not be burdened with additional reporting. The repeated emphasis on cash flow accounting is beginning to complicate annual report preparation. In its 1980 annual report, Sun Company, Inc. presented three years' consolidated statements of changes in financial position—working capital basis as part of the financial statements, and an additional statement entitled "Statements of Cash Flow of Sun Company Businesses" for 1979 and 1980. These statements, which were analyzed by industry segments, were conventional statements of changes in financial position—cash basis, and resembled not at all statements of receipts and payments. In 1980, Sun had an increase in funds provided from operations, but a decrease in working capital, as compared with 1979; cash and near-cash items also declined.

The SEC's *Accounting Series Release No. 142* prohibited the disclosure of cash flow per share on the grounds that there was no accepted definition of the concept. The critical problem, of course, is the definition of cash flow, since the number of shares to be used in the calculation can be found in the same manner as for earnings per share.

Although there is considerable support from the accounting profession for defining funds as cash plus cash equivalents (readily marketable assets held in place of cash), working capital is a more comprehensive concept of funds. However, consideration should be given to expanding fund flow information by providing statements to show the effects of inflation accounting and of segment fund flows. Financial flexibility should be dealt with in the notes to the financial statements, and in management's discussion and analysis of those statements.

ENDNOTES

1. "Reporting Changes in Financial Position," New York: AICPA, 1971.
2. See Rosen, L.S. and Don T. DeCoster, "'Funds' Statements: A Historical Perspective," *The Accounting Review,* January 1969, pp. 124-136.
3. Cole, William Morse, *Accounts: Their Construction and Interpretation etc.,* New York: Houghton Mifflin Co., 1908, pp. 99-101.
4. Superseded by *APB Opinion No. 19.*
5. *Accounting Series Release No. 117,* Washington, D.C.: October 14, 1970.
6. Vatter, W.J., *The Fund Theory of Accounting,* Chicago, 1947.
7. Anton, Hector R., *Accounting for the Flow of Funds,* Boston, Mass: The Houghton Mifflin Co., 1962, p. 26.
8. Mason, Perry, "Cash Flow Analysis and the Funds Statement," *Accounting Research Study No. 2,* New York: AICPA, 1961.
9. Yu, S.C., "A Flow-of-Resources Statement for Business Enterprises," *The Accounting Review,* July 1969, pp. 571-582.
10. Most, Kenneth, S., "Two Forms of Experimental Accounts," *The Accounting Review,* January 1969, pp. 145-52. See also Vatter, W.J., "Operating Confusion in Accounting—Two Reports in One," *The Journal of Business,* July 1963, pp. 290-301, and the FASB Discussion Memorandum "Reporting Funds Flows, Liquidity and Financial Flexibility," December 15, 1980, p. 52.
11. Clarkson, Geoffrey P.E., *Portfolio Selection: A Simulation of Trust Investment,* Englewood Cliffs, N.J.: Prentice-Hall, Inc., 1962.

12. Hawkins, David F. and Walter J. Campbell, *Equity Valuation: Models, Analysis and Implications,* New York: Financial Executives Research Foundation, 1978.
13. Backer, Morton and Martin L. Gosman, *Financial Reporting and Business Liquidity,* New York: National Association of Accountants, 1978.
14. Beaver, William H., "Alternative Accounting Measures as Predictors of Failure," *The Accounting Review,* January 1968, pp. 113-22.
15. Anton, op cit Ch. 7.
16. "Accounting and Reporting by Development Stage Enterprises," Stamford, Conn: Financial Accounting Standards Board, June 1975.
17. Duff and Phelps, Inc., Chicago.
18. Brief, Richard P., Barbara Merino, and Ira Weiss, "Cumulative Financial Statements," *The Accounting Review,* July 1980, pp. 480-90.
19. *A Management Guide to Better Financial Reporting,* Arthur Andersen & Co., 1976, pp. 81-82.
20. Lewis, Sherman L., "Needed: A More Definitive Funds Statement," *Journal of Accountancy,* September 1976, pp. 48-50.
21. Heath, Loyd, *Financial Reporting and the Evaluation of Solvency,* Accounting Research Monograph No. 3, New York: AICPA, 1978.
22. Heath, Loyd, "Let's Scrap the 'Funds' Statement," *Journal of Accountancy,* October 1978, pp. 94-103; and replies by Largay, James A. III; Swanson, Edward P.; and Vangermeersch, Richard, *Journal of Accountancy*, December 1979, pp. 88-96.
23. Heath, Loyd, "Is Working Capital Really Working?" *Journal of Accountancy,* August 1980, pp. 55-62.
24. See n. 10.
25. Postek, Thomas S., *Cash Flow: Is More Information Needed?* Financial Accounting Standards Board, 1981.

SELECTED ADDITIONAL READINGS

Anton, Hector R., *Accounting for the Flow of Funds,* Boston, Mass.: The Houghton Mifflin Co., 1962.

Arnett, Harold E., *Proposed Funds Statement for Managers and Investors,* New York: National Association of Accountants, 1979.

Beams, Floyd A. and Robert H. Strawser, "Preferences for Alternative Presentations of the Statement of Changes in Financial Position," *Massachusetts CPA Review,* November/December 1973, pp. 14-18.

Buzby, Stephen L., and Haim Falk, "A New Approach to the Funds Statement," *Journal of Accountancy,* January 1974, pp. 55-61.

European Federation of Financial Analysts' Societies, *Fourth Report of the Corporate Information Committee,* Paris, France: May 1976.

FASB Discussion Memorandum, *An Analysis of Issues Related to Reporting Funds Flows, Liquidity, and Financial Flexibility,* Stamford, Conn.: Financial Accounting Standards Board, December 15, 1980.

Giese, J.W. and T.P. Klammer, "Achieving the Objectives of APB Opinion No. 19," *Journal of Accountancy,* March 1974, pp. 54-61.

Goldberg, L., "The Funds Statement Reconsidered," *The Accounting Review,* October 1951, pp. 485-491.

Heath, Loyd C., *Financial Reporting and the Evaluation of Solvency,* Accounting Research Monograph No. 3, New York: AICPA, 1978.

Henry, Evan J., "A New Funds Statement Format for Greater Disclosure," *Journal of Accountancy,* April 1975, pp. 56-62.

Horngren, Charles T., "The Funds Statement and Its Use by Analysts," *Journal of Accountancy,* January 1956, pp. 55-59.

Käfer, Karl and V.K. Zimmerman, "Notes on the Evolution of the Statement of Source and Application of Funds," *International Journal of Accounting Education and Research,* Spring 1967, pp. 89-121.

Mason, Perry, "Cash Flow Analysis and the Funds Statement," *Accounting Research Study No. 2,* New York: AICPA 1961.

Rosen, L.S. and Don T. DeCoster, "'Funds' Statements: A Historical Perspective," *The Accounting Review,* January 1969, pp. 124-136.

Rosen, L.S., "'Funds' Statements: Prime Disclosure Vehicle of the 1980's?" *CA Magazine,* July 1974, pp. 48-53.

Spiller, Earl A. and Robert L. Virgil, "Effectiveness of APB Opinion No. 19 in Improving Funds Reporting," *Journal of Accounting Research,* Spring 1974, pp. 112-142.

Vatter, W.J., "Operating Confusion in Accounting—Two Reports in One," *The Journal of Business,* July 1963, pp. 290-301.

Yu, S.C., "A Flow of Resources Statement for Business Enterprises," *The Accounting Review,* July 1969, pp. 571-582.

Case 15-1 Bali Furniture Inc.

Bali Furniture was a retailer of imported furniture in a large U.S. city. It was operated by Joe and Stan Blair, who inherited the business from their father. Each owned 25 percent of the equity; the other 50 percent was owned by their widowed mother and unmarried sister.

The income statement for the year 1981 showed a small loss of $4,000 after charging depreciation amounting to $300. Comparative balance sheets at the beginning and end of 1981 are shown below.

Bali Furniture Inc. Balance Sheets	December 31 1981	1980
Current assets		
Cash	$ 750	$ 1,100
Accounts receivable	19,800	25,700
Receivable from officers and employees	39,700	14,700
Inventory	148,000	152,000
Total current assets	208,250	193,500
Equipment at cost	100,000	100,000
less: Accumulated depreciation	(82,000)	(81,700)
Equipment—net	18,000	18,300
Total assets	$226,250	$211,800

Liabilities		
Current	$120,000	$101,550
Stockholders' equity		
Capital stock	40,000	40,000
Retained earnings	66,250	70,250
Total liabilities and stockholders' equity	$226,250	$211,800

1. Prepare a Statement of Changes in Financial Position for the year 1981, in a suitable form.
2. How did you decide which form to use?

END OF CHAPTER QUESTIONS

1. Explain the historical development of the statement of changes in financial position as part of the basic financial statements.
2. Distinguish between fund accounting and funds statements.
3. How does the funds statement articulate with the balance sheet and income statement?
4. What are the objectives of the funds statement according to *APBO 19?*
5. Discuss the meaning of *funds* in the context of contemporary practice.
6. What is the meaning of "all significant financial events"?
7. What does a statement of cash flows present? What would be the most useful form of such a statement?
8. List the differences between the concepts of "receipts and payments" and of "revenues and expenses."
9. What problems are encountered when considering the structure of the funds statement? How can they be resolved?
10. List the uses of the funds statement and discuss which of them are most important to users.
11. How can the funds statement be adapted to show the effects of changing prices?
12. What are the reasons for the current dissatisfaction with the statement of changes in financial position? Which "loose practices" are frequently encountered?
13. Discuss Heath's recommendations for reform of the funds statement.
14. What three sets of information were discussed in the FASB's Discussion Memorandum dated December 1980? How was each defined?
15. What is meant by the "narrowed perspective" of the Heath and FASB approaches?
16. Discuss the importance of the current/noncurrent classification in the light of contemporary criticism of the working capital concept.

17. What do you understand by the phrase "cash provided by operations," and how does it differ, if at all, from "funds provided by operations"?
18. A. Explain what is meant by the "all financial resources" concept of funds.
    B. Provide two examples of transactions which would neither increase nor decrease working capital or any of its components, but would be reported in a statement of funds flows because of the "all financial resources" concept.
    C. Explain why these transactions should be reported in a statement of funds flow.
    D. Suggest alternative methods of disclosing these transactions, and discuss their relative usefulness to the financial statement user.

16

ACCOUNTING FOR BUSINESS COMBINATIONS

A business combination occurs when a corporation and one or more incorporated or unincorporated businesses are brought together as one accounting entity.[1] Some of the same accounting problems are experienced in connection with partnerships, particularly when a new partner is admitted who makes payments to the old partners or into the firm. With the decline in use of the partnership which has accompanied the growth of the corporate form, these problems have tended to fall into neglect. Even though there is currently a revival of partnerships between corporations, the subject of partnership accounting generally will not be discussed here. Partnership between corporations will be considered together with the equity method of accounting.

Some of the most complicated technical problems in accounting occur in accounting for business combinations, called *consolidation*. The subject is only about one hundred years old, as the first published consolidation in the United States appeared in 1862. In recent years a considerable controversy has arisen; an FASB project to reconsider accounting standards in this area was taken off its agenda in 1981.[2]

In this chapter we will examine some of these difficult accounting issues, which have produced very little accounting literature for all their complexity. We will look at the principal controversy—purchase or pooling?—the accounting entity problem, and accounting for goodwill arising on consolidation. We will also look at the equity method of accounting, closely related to consolidation, and foreign currency translation insofar as it affects the financial statements of a parent with foreign subsidiaries.

OBJECTIVE OF CONSOLIDATION

The rationale behind consolidations was given by *APB Statement No. 4.* as R6 of Chapter 7,II.22:

> Consolidated financial statements are presumed to be more meaningful than the separate statements of the component legal entities... usually necessary for fair presentation in conformity with generally accepted accounting principles if one of the enterprises in a group directly or indirectly owns over 50% of the outstanding voting stock in the other enterprises... essentially as if the group were a single enterprise composed of branches or divisions.

This objective was also that of *ARB 40* and *ARB 51,* parts of which still apply to consolidations.

In the case of a group of companies under common ownership, consolidation permits the managers of the group to exercise their functions of planning, coordinating, controlling, and so forth, in relation to the group as a whole. In this respect, the accounts conform to the same rules as the accounts for an individual company. The basic rules of consolidation, that the capital of the holding company is the capital of the group and that majority control results in 100 percent consolidation, are derived from the objective of representing to the directors of a holding company the assets and liabilities under their control and the revenues and expenses for which they are responsible.

The objective of consolidation for mergers and acquisitions serves this purpose and also restricts the ability of the directors of a group to manipulate group results so as to conceal from investors and other interested parties unfavorable results of individual companies. The first step in this direction is the move from accounting for investments under the cost method to the equity method. By carrying investments in subsidiaries at cost and crediting dividends receivable to income, a holding company can conceal current operating losses by continuing to declare upstream dividends from the companies concerned, if necessary postponing the payments or returning them to those companies in the form of loans. By accruing its share in the net incomes of the group companies, the holding company reports subsidiaries' profits and losses for the periods in which they are registered by the subsidiaries. Consolidation extends these observations to return on investment, since it permits the net income of the group to be related to its net assets (or total assets, if preferred).

The *APB Statement No. 4* objective is defective in two main respects. The word "usually" provided holding companies with an option, which many took, to exclude from the consolidation holdings which might make the financial statements look in some way worse. Its unnecessary assumption has given rise to application problems, which will be discussed later. The assumption is, that to give effect to substance over form, the reality of the situation should be overlooked, and a nonexistent head office/branch relationship substituted.

These application problems can be placed in the following useful consolidation framework.

Step 1. Revalue the assets and liabilities of the acquired or merged company (Revaluation).
Step 2. Combine the financial statements of the constituent companies (Combination).
Step 3. Eliminate intercompany transactions and unrealized intercompany profits (Elimination).
Step 4. Substitute the net assets of the subsidiaries for the investment of the parent (Substitution).
Step 5. Separate the minority interests in the subsidiaries (Separation).

THE "PURCHASE OR POOLING" CONTROVERSY

Dominating all other issues is the question of whether the pooling method of consolidation should be preferred to the purchase method, or even permitted. Although this was long believed to be an issue confined to the United States, recent research suggests that pooling accounting is widely used elsewhere.[3] Pooling modifies the above framework in these respects:

Step 1. Revaluation does not take place.
Step 2. Combination is effected as if the pooled company had always been a member of the group.
Step 3. It is restricted to current asset and liability adjustments, and recurring noncurrent asset and liability adjustments, under para. 56 of *APB Opinion No. 16*.
Step 4. Goodwill would only arise under quite exceptional conditions in a pooling.

The purchase or pool[4] alternatives emerged during the 1950s as responses to the problem posed by a business combination effected by an exchange of stock.[5] If Company *A* acquires all or the majority of the net assets of Company *B* for cash, no question of value at date of acquisition arises for the transaction as a whole, although the values of individual assets and liabilities may well present difficulties. If the combination is effected by an exchange of *A*'s stock for *B*'s stock (or net assets), a valuation problem arises in respect of the entire transaction, although not, to the theorist, a particularly unusual one.

The purchase method used the fair value (either of the stock issued by *A* or of the net assets acquired) as the cost to *A* of its acquisition. The pooling method simply recorded *B*'s assets and liabilities at book value and, the ownership interest in *B* being transferred, *B*'s retained earnings were brought forward intact into the combined accounts.

In the latter part of 1950, the Committee on Accounting Procedure of the then AIA issued *ARB No. 40,* "Business Combinations."[6] This bulletin stated as the criterion for a pooling of interests that all or substantially all of the equity interests in predecessor corporations continue as such in a surviving corporation. Size and continuity of management were "other factors to be taken into consideration." *ARB No. 40* required the accountants to look beyond the legal form of the acquisition to "the attendant circumstances" and, thus, left the choice of purchase or pooling relatively free. However, the size characteristic appears to have been respected, since research showed that during this period combinations of large companies were treated as poolings.[7] The effect of *ARB*s *Nos. 40, 43,* and *48* was to legitimize carrying forward the retained earnings of the constituent corporations on a merger or acquisition, which would otherwise have been proscribed by paragraph 3 of Chapter 1 (*a*) of *ARB No. 43* (earned surplus of a subsidiary corporation created prior to acquisition does not form part of consolidated earned surplus). Again, some companies using pooling did not carry forward the acquired company's retained earnings, but capitalized the amount as they would have done in purchase accounting, although the effect of the ARBs was to discourage this practice.

It may be noted that the practice of amortizing goodwill arising on consolidation to expense became widespread during this period, and Wyatt believes this to have been significant in causing many companies to choose pooling accounting.

The differences between purchase and pooling accounting are summarized in Table 16-1.

TABLE 16-1
Differences Between

Purchase	**and**	**Pooling**
1. All assets and liabilities which comprise the bargained cost of an acquired company (or the constituent parts of a merged company) are consolidated with the assets and liabilities of the parent; whether recorded by the subsidiary or not.		1. The recorded assets and liabilities of the acquired (or merged) company are combined with the recorded assets and liabilities of the parent.
2. The assets and liabilities of the acquired (merged) company are revalued to correspond with the substance of the transaction.		2. Only those changes in asset and liability valuation are made as are necessary to put all companies on the same basis of accounting.
3. Equity of the parent issued as consideration for the acquisition (or merger) is recorded by the parent at "fair value."		3. Equity issued by one company in exchange for equity in another may be recorded at par, or book value of the net assets acquired.
4. Retained earnings of the acquired (merged) company prior to the acquisition (merger) date are capitalized.		4. Retained earnings of the combined companies are (in most cases) carried forward unchanged.

5. Any excess of the cost of a subsidiary over the parent's share of net assets acquired is capitalized as "goodwill arising on consolidation" and amortized to expense over not more than 40 years. In some countries, this excess may be deducted from stockholders' equity. Any excess of the parent's share of the net assets of a subsidiary over their cost is used to reduce tangible fixed assets proportionately, and after their extinguishment, shown as a deferred credit and amortized to income over not more than 40 years. In most countries this amount is not used to reduce asset values, and there is no amortization requirement.
6. The consolidated income statement shows revenues and expenses of the acquired (merged) corporation from the date of acquisition (merger) to the balance sheet date.
7. The consolidated net income is affected by amortization of positive or negative goodwill and also by changes in depreciation and even cost of goods sold consequent upon asset revaluation.

5. The consequence of pooling is that the amount of any excess of cost over share of net assets will be relatively small, and is deducted first from other contributed capital and then from combined retained earnings; the reverse situation is shown as other contributed capital (*ARB No. 40*).
6. The income statements of the corporations (after eliminations) are combined for the entire fiscal period.
7. Apart from eliminations there is no difference between combined pretax income and the sum of the pretax net incomes of the combined corporations. There may be a tax effect arising out of the merger or acquisition, particularly if effected by an exchange of shares.

A number of attempts have been made to rationalize the purchase versus pooling issue on the basis of distinguishing between them in respect of circumstantial characteristics. Perhaps the least convincing argument asserts that pooling accounting conforms to the entity theory, and purchase accounting to the proprietary theory. We have pointed out elsewhere that valuation at acquisition price is more consistent with an entity viewpoint, and at current value with a proprietary viewpoint, but these valuations coincide when a business combination takes place. Indeed, the confusion of the APB on this point is indicated by the observation that *APBO No. 16* explicitly adopted the entity theory (para. 29) whereas the contemporaneous *Statement No. 4* explicitly adopted the proprietary theory (paras. 21, 23).

A second argument concerns the medium of exchange; it is asserted that a business combination effected by the issuance of stock is different in kind from a purchase involving cash or other assets, because the latter involves no change in the total assets of the entity. Those who have travelled this far will have no difficulty in identifying this argument as specious, even though it played a major part in the APB's decision to require combinations effected by an exchange of common stock to be accounted for as poolings.

A third argument concerns the size of the combining companies, in that the acquisition of a very small by a very large company is clearly a purchase; whereas the merger of two very large companies appears to be a mere union of ownership interests. Quite apart from the problems involved in arriving at size criteria in terms of assets, revenues, or number and value of shares exchanged, it is obvious that very large companies do not merge simply because the directors of the one enjoy the conversation of the directors of the other. Economic forces are at play just as much in this case as in any other.

More pertinent is the argument that it is illogical to recognize the economic facts in the case of the subsidiary, by revaluing its assets and liabilities, while continuing to ignore them in the case of the parent, by failing to revalue. We have earlier endorsed current value as the basic model for valuing nonmonetary assets and, therefore, regard current practice as defective in both purchase and pooling accounting.

Other criteria put forward as arguments supporting pooling are: that the firms combined were previously independent entities without significant intercorporate investments; that there is a continuity of ownership interests (or at least, intention to continue as a stockholder) and/or management; and that the business activities are carried on virtually unchanged. It is submitted that, in these rare cases, some form of pooling can be justified on the legal grounds that if retained earnings are capitalized the stockholders may suffer damage through having their rights to future dividends restricted by the merger. However, this is not an argument in favor of consolidating assets and liabilities recorded at acquisition prices (historical cost).

APB Opinion No. 16 provided that if certain conditions were met, primarily that two previously independent companies effected a business combination by an exchange of stock in circumstances which did not suggest a plan to avoid purchase accounting, pooling was mandatory. In all other cases, purchase accounting must be used.

Both *Accounting Research Study No. 5,* on accounting for business combinations, and *No. 10,* on accounting for goodwill, concluded that virtually all group accounts are best consolidated under the purchase method; a similar conclusion was reached in a recent study by a major committee of the AAA.[8] This by no means demonstrates conclusively that pooling is wrong, but such unusual unanimity of opinion indicates a consensus that the arguments for pooling are weak. The rule laid down by *APBO No. 16,* that a business combination which meets all of the therein specified conditions should be accounted for as a pooling of interests, can therefore be viewed as perverse, especially in the light of the fact that management's freedom to choose the accounting method which has the better economic effect has not been noticeably restricted. This was made very clear by General Electric's 1976 acquisition of Utah International. This acquisition was structured so that it could be accounted for as a pooling, but it was a purchase in every other sense of the word.[9]

WHY IS PURCHASE ACCOUNTING PREFERRED?

The GE/Utah International case illustrates clearly why purchase accounting is preferred. By using pooling accounting, approximately $1.5 billion of assets acquired through the merger, mainly in the form of valuable mineral leases, were omitted from GE's consolidated balance sheet. A large but unknown amount of goodwill was also omitted. The excess of these asset values over Utah's historical cost will flow to the credit of GE's income statements over about fifteen years, the average life of a mineral lease, without any corresponding depreciation, depletion, or amortization, and without any write-off of goodwill arising on consolidation. Thus, the form of accounting selected permitted GE to influence its profits and its profitability for years to come.

But is pooling ever justified on economic, as distinct from legal, grounds? We shall assume the existence of two or more accounting entities (not necessarily legal entities) which have been operating independently for periods of time coterminous with t_n, and which have each distributed less than the sum of their earnings in the form of dividends or as withdrawals. The income statements of each entity constitute a time series of revenues, expenses, and net income; their balance sheets constitute time series of assets, liabilities, and stockholders' equity, and the last, through the statements of retained earnings, present a time series of the effects of financing and investment decisions.

It is apparent that the effect of merger or acquisition at t_n causes a break in these time series. If the group were simply a continuation of the individual companies, the only change being the combination of ownership interests, the trends shown by a succession of financial statements unaffected by the special features of purchase accounting would be very informative, more informative than the broken series produced by purchase accounting. Herein lies the attraction of pooling.

To examine this proposition, we may list the main reasons for business combinations.

1. To secure a source of supply
2. To secure a channel of distribution
3. To acquire production facilities
4. To acquire marketing facilities

5. To obtain assets cheaply, by purchasing majority control rather than the assets themselves, or by bargain purchase of a going concern
6. To obtain tax deductions or otherwise reduce future taxation
7. To reduce variability of earnings; for example, by combining sales of hot dogs with sales of ice cream
8. To acquire management skills or to provide them in place of existing management
9. To acquire location advantages
10. To expand a product line
11. To acquire new technology
12. To achieve lower unit costs through economies of scale

In relatively few cases, therefore, will the future profits of the consolidated entity be directly comparable with the sum of the previous profits of the entities participating in the business combination. The argument that purchase accounting distorts financial results by charging to expense a fictitious goodwill amortization and, therefore, produces misleading information, depends upon an untenable assumption—that nothing has changed except the ownership interests in the companies concerned.[10]

It is perhaps not surprising that *APBO 16* resulted in 39 Accounting Interpretations between 1970 and 1973 (when the APB was replaced by the FASB) and gave rise to considerable SEC criticism. An example of the latter was *ASR 146,* which stated that firms purchasing their own shares in the open market for use in acquiring the assets or stock of the companies they wished to take over were circumventing the purchase accounting requirements of *APBO 16.*

THE ACCOUNTING ENTITY

The basic criterion governing choice of accounting entity is control over assets. However, control is difficult to define, and, particularly in the United States, there appears to be a strong belief that not all controlled assets should be combined.

The *modified entity* concept of accounting for business combination is believed to regard the majority and minority interests in the equities of subsidiaries as different kinds of capital. Under this concept, the price paid by the parent company for its interest in the subsidiary should be extrapolated to the total net assets of the subsidiary, and the minority interest valued accordingly. However, a survey of accounting textbooks and recent CPA examination questions revealed that a modified revaluation procedure is believed to be used, the asset in question being revalued only by the investor's share of the difference between book value and fair market value. No research on this point could be found.

The *parent company* viewpoint may explain contemporary accounting for business combinations, or at least the textbook view of such accounting, better than does the modified entity viewpoint. Under the former the subsidiaries are treated like branches and the minority interests shown as liabilities to outside parties. This view does not necessarily lead to eliminating only the parent's share in unrealized intercompany profits, as has been argued[11] and is consistent with the observation that minority interests tend to be acquired if the subsidiary is retained.[12]

In the United States, the usual condition for control is ownership of a majority voting interest; that is, over 50 percent of the outstanding voting equity. If, however, preferred stock has received a majority of votes because the preferred dividend is in arrears, this does not constitute control in the sense of a business combination. *ARB*s *43* and *51* listed as exceptions to the rule (1) where control is likely to be temporary; (2) where it does not rest with the majority owners, as in reorganization or in bankruptcy; (3) where the minority interest is very large in relation to the equity of the shareholders of the parent in the consolidation (but this would not invalidate the selection of the entity under the potential social consolidation model); (4) where it would be more informative to stockholders and creditors to provide them with separate statements for one or more subsidiaries; (5) in some cases where the subsidiaries are in a foreign country and their assets and net income are subject to controls and exchange restrictions. Kohler gives more specific reasons: where a subsidiary is about to be disposed of, or where a subsidiary's operations are unrelated to those of its parent. He also produces two other exceptions: a subsidiary, the financial statements of which bear a date differing from that of the controlling company's statements, and a subsidiary, control of which has been acquired at a figure substantially and unaccountably in excess of or less than the corresponding fraction of its net assets at the date of consolidation.[13] Current attitudes favor reducing the list of exceptions.

ARB 43 proposes these alternatives to normal consolidation for foreign subsidiaries

1. To furnish (a) statements in which only domestic subsidiaries are consolidated and (b) suitable summaries of foreign subsidiaries' assets, liabilities, net income, and the parent company's equity therein. Intercompany profits would still be eliminated.
2. To consolidate and also furnish (b).
3. To consolidate and furnish a separate consolidation for domestic companies only.
4. To consolidate and furnish parent company statements showing investment in and income from foreign subsidiaries separately from domestic subisidaries.

There is wide variation in practice in the United States. Conglomerates consolidate all controlled corporations, including finance companies, but General Motors does not consolidate General Motors Acceptance Corporation nor does General Electric consolidate its finance companies. Some companies with overseas subsidiaries consolidate all; others consolidate some; a few consolidate none. Further, because the relative positions of parent and subsidiary bondholders and other creditors and the assets against which their claims rank are not apparent from consolidated financial statements, loan agreements frequently provide for the submission of additional statements (called *consolidating* financial statements) showing this information.

In spite of these limitations, in the United States the consolidated financial statements are considered the primary statements of the group, and Regulation S-X, Rule 4-02 of the SEC requires consolidated statements to be filed for a group of corporations controlled by one of them.

A 1981 SEC proposal would require the disclosure of restrictions on the ability of subsidiaries to advance or loan funds to the parent company. Disclosure would be required when the proportionate share of net assets of subsidiaries (after eliminations) under such restriction exceeds 25 percent of consolidated net assets at the end of the most recent year. The proposal applies equally to equity-method accounted companies.

The notes to the financial statements would disclose the following:

- Restrictions on both consolidated and unconsolidated subsidiaries, to remit cash dividends or repay loans and advances.
- The amounts of undistributed earnings of consolidated and unconsolidated subsidiaries and 50 percent or less owned equity-accounted affiliates, and the amounts restricted as to dividends. Undistributed earnings would be reconciled to consolidated earnings.
- The significance of the aggregate amount of restricted net assets to consolidated net assets as at year-end.
- Condensed financial information for the parent company in lieu of full financial statements.

In addition, new rules reducing the requirements to file separate financial statements for subsidiaries are being considered, together with a requirement to provide summarized financial information on 10 percent or more holdings, besides the condensed financial statements required for 20 percent or more holdings accounted for under the equity method.

In the United Kingdom the Companies Act, 1948, requires the filing of consolidated accounts with the Registrar of Companies for all groups, except where one of six reasons apply: (1) impracticality; (2) insignificance; (3) disproportionate expense or delay; (4) misleading effect; (5) harmful effect; (6) divergent nature of the businesses concerned. In cases (5) and (6) the approval of the Department of Trade and Industry must be obtained. The prevailing view in the United Kingdom is that control is not only a question of majority vote but can exist where, for example, the directors of Company *A* have power to appoint the majority of the directors of Company *B*. In addition, the practice of obtaining control of a company through acquiring its shares in the names of different companies under common control is recognized in the United Kingdom. However, it must be admitted that fractionated voting power results in control of large corporations being acquired with relatively small percentage holdings; most of the *Fortune* 500 companies are controlled by holders of under 10 percent of the voting equity.

The annual report of a U.K. company will provide the separate financial statements of the parent as well as the consolidation. The annual report of a European company may not provide a consolidation, but whether it does or not, summaries of the financial statements of the principal subsidiaries are often given.

The proposed Seventh Directive of the European Economic Community (EEC) concerning group accounts introduced several features which will accentuate the differences between United States and European practices.

1. Consolidation was made dependent upon *de facto,* rather than *de jure,* control. Although criticized as subjective, this is no more so than United States companies' decisions whether to consolidate or not.
2. A so-called horizontal, or Community, consolidation of subsidiaries operating in or controlled from EEC countries was required. This introduces a new accounting entity, consisting of a part of a group, and would necessitate recognition of a regional management structure and creation of a regional accounting system.
3. A so-called vertical consolidation, whereby each subsidiary (called a dependent undertaking) registered in an EEC country would be required to prepare a group consolidation to include its own subsidiaries.

The last two provisions would place new responsibilities on accountants and call for new and different accounting standards covering business combinations.

Change in the accounting entity severely affects the analysis and interpretation of group financial statements over time. Step-by-step acquisitions, reciprocal holdings, and change of accounting period present particularly ferocious problems. If a subsidiary's fiscal year is not coterminous with that of the parent, it is customary to follow the SEC rule that different fiscal years may be combined if they end not more than ninety days apart. These difficulties are not helped by a conflict between *APB Opinion No. 16* and *No. 20.*

APB Opinion No. 16 provided—

- That a pooling should be reported by showing the results of operations as if the companies had been combined as of the beginning of the period, and restating financial statements presented for prior periods;

- That a purchase should be reported by showing the results of operations of the combined entity as from the date of the combination, but pro forma information concerning results of operations of the current and prior periods as though the companies had combined at the beginning of the earliest period presented must be given in the footnotes.

APB Opinion No. 20 provided that "accounting changes which result in financial statements that are in effect the statements of a different reporting entity should be reported by restating the financial statements of all prior periods presented in order to show financial information for the new reporting entity for all periods."

GOODWILL ARISING ON CONSOLIDATION

In Chapter 13, we established the proposition that firms may pay in advance for the prospect of future super-profits. Purchase accounting ensures that, if such a payment is made when a subsidiary is acquired, or on a merger, it will be kept in evidence and not hidden from view. In this section we consider the disposition of this goodwill arising on consolidation.

The possibility of a bargain purchase also exists. The reasons why the owners of a corporation may be willing to dispose of their interest for less than the value of the net assets need not concern us here, but they sometimes do. Having accepted the importance of recognizing changes in current and realizable values as a regular feature of accounting, we cannot deny the effects of a favorable purchase. The disposition of the resulting credit should follow the same logic as does accounting for goodwill arising on consolidation. It is sometimes called *negative goodwill.*

There are essentially three possible methods of disposing of goodwill.

1. Carry forward at the same amount from the date it arises until the subsidiary is sold or discontinued, either as an asset or as an identifiable deduction from stockholders' equity.
2. Deduct from stockholders' equity (specifically, retained earnings) immediately, as it arises, or immediate write-off to the income statement.
3. Capitalize as a depreciable asset and amortize to expense in the same way that any depreciable asset is amortized.

APBO No. 17 adopted number 3. and placed a maximum limit of forty years on useful life. The Opinion appears to call for a straight-line method of amortization, but it has been established that accelerated amortization is appropriate when savings and loan association mergers create short-lived customer goodwill subject to progressive deterioration. It is regrettable that *APBO No. 17* has been interpreted as if it recommends a forty-year useful life in all circumstances. Otherwise, the treatment of goodwill arising on consolidation as a depreciable fixed asset corresponds with the perception of goodwill as a payment and with the definition of an asset as an estimate of what is chargeable to future customers.

The observation that the goodwill which a firm generates for itself is not capitalized as a depreciable fixed asset is sometimes voiced as an objection to the practice recognized by *APBO No. 17.* In fact, the expectation of future profits in this situation is not divided into "normal" and "exceptional" components, and it has been suggested earlier in this book that such a separation is sometimes irrational. Irrational or not, where a payment is made it must be dealt with. Amortization represents an expense, a consumption of value during a specified period, and not necessarily a cost associated with any particular revenue.

The method of accounting for negative goodwill laid down by *APBO No. 17* is not consistent with the view of goodwill as a depreciable fixed asset. To reduce recorded fixed asset values proportionately (except for marketable securities held as investments) is explicable only as a device for eliminating the observation. However, this Opinion did accept that the residue of negative goodwill should be deferred and amortized systematically through credit to the income statements of not more than forty years.

The practice of carrying forward the amount established for goodwill without amortization is supported by the argument that goodwill is an intangible asset with an unlimited life. It is refuted by the observation that the factors underlying goodwill arising at the date of acquisition or merger have limited effects and are unrelated to other subsequent factors creating goodwill.

The practice of charging goodwill against retained earnings enjoyed a certain popularity in the United States during the period prior to 1952, and recent attempts to revive it are associated with the firm of Arthur Andersen & Co. The authors of *ARS No. 10,* "Accounting for Goodwill," both partners in this accounting firm, recommended this treatment, and the rationale has been explained by Chambers.

> ...the goodwill of a going concern runs to the constituents, not to the firm....That cash has been paid may be recognized in the record; but its effect is in no way to increase the adaptability of the firm, and the indicated treatment of it is to reduce the amount of the residual equity from the price paid to the current cash equivalent of the new firm's component assets and liabilities.[14]

The view that purchased goodwill has no measurable separate existence is a question of fact in each case and may be relevant to the ascertainment of any asset value.

ACCOUNTING FOR AN EXCHANGE OF SHARES

We have mentioned the fact that accounting for business combinations is more difficult when shares of one corporation are exchanged for the shares or net assets of another. We have also drawn attention to the permissive nature of generally accepted accounting principles in the United States where accounting for nonmonetary exchanges is concerned.

In this context, *APBO 16* requires that assets acquired by the exchange of stock are measured by the value of the stock given in exchange, unless the value of the assets acquired can be more objectively measured. The possibility of the latter is more apparent than real; a written agreement placing values on the individual assets or liabilities of the acquired (or merged) corporation will contain only negotiating figures from the buyer's viewpoint, as he would be unlikely to reveal his true estimates. For example, a buyer may agree to give $100,000 for the shares in a corporation which has two assets, *X* which the vendor values at $75,000 and *Y* which the vendor values at $25,000. In this case, the buyer may value *X* at $150,000 and regard *Y* as worthless; yet a slavish adherence to the letter of *APBO No. 16* would result in the agreed amounts being recorded in the consolidation. Few accounting authorities recommend that the seller's estimates of value should be recorded.

Use of the value of the stock given in exchange for shares or net assets is clearly the most informative practice, yet the least objective. Conventional valuation models simply multiply the number of shares exchanged by their market price on the date the transaction was agreed. What if the acquiring corporation holds the shares as treasury stock having bought them at a lower (or higher) price? A profit or loss on treasury stock being unknown to accountants, the difference will be adjusted on the account for capital in excess of par or stated value. One of the advantages of the FASB's desire to distinguish gains and losses from revenues and expenses is the possibility of recognizing such realized differences without calling them part of income.

However, the significance of market price for shares which are not actually traded is questionable. The market price of shares on a given date represents the marginal rate of substitution of shares for cash of a relatively small number of shareholders; those who do not choose to sell at that price believe it undervalues the shares, and they are a majority. Further, market price is affected by many factors other than the exchange value of the shares, such as the seller's liquidity problems or the buyer's gullibility. Burton has examined this question in some detail and pointed out an additional complication.[15] Exchange of stock for stock is usually based on some relationship between their prices per share and earnings per share. The recommended method of valuing the acquisition, however, uses only the price of the acquiring company's stock. If that stock sells at a high *P/E* ratio, the acquiring company will be willing to pay a premium over net asset values to achieve the result of consolidating the acquired company's earnings. This means goodwill arising on consolidation which is a function of the market price of the acquiror's shares.

For example, assume a case in which Company *A*'s stock sells at $60 and Company *B*'s stock at $20; a 3:1 exchange ratio is agreed. Shortly after the merger, the market prices of the two stocks decline to $45 and $15 respectively, which approximates book value per share. It is clear that acquisitions and mergers effected during boom stock market conditions often result in the capitalization of substantial amounts of goodwill arising on consolidation unless accounted for as poolings of interests.

This is not an argument in favor of pooling accounting, or a criticism of the use of the value of shares given in exchange as the estimate of the value of the shares or net assets acquired. On the contrary, it confirms the reason previously given for the use of purchase accounting in all cases, and the essentially subjective nature of all accounting allocations. The presumption that market values provide the evidence for valuation may be overcome in this case, as in the case of accounting for interest on receivables and payables.

EQUITY METHOD OF ACCOUNTING FOR COMMON STOCK INVESTMENTS

The traditional method of accounting for investment in common stocks was to record the investment at cost and to accrue as revenue dividends declared on such investments. Typically, the cost of these investments was not written up or down in accordance with changes in the market prices or underlying net asset values, except that good practice called for amortization in the case of permanent diminution of value, and write-off where the investment became valueless. In the case of marketable securities carried as current assets whose market value is less than cost, they were to be shown at market value under *ARB 43,* but market value could be merely annotated if the decline was believed temporary. If the investments in question are truly current assets, that is, temporary uses of working capital substituting for cash, it is difficult to see how the holder can argue that a decline in market value is "temporary."

Following the AICPA's industry audit guide of 1973, investment companies must now account for changes in the market values of their portfolios, and this is a common practice of nonbusiness entities such as estates, trusts, and individual investors. The use of market values for long-term investments was, until recently, virtually unknown outside of these situations, although one U.K. company (Burmah Oil Ltd.), which started life as an investment company, continued to account on this basis after becoming a producing and trading group. Changes in the carrying amount of investments are credited or debited to a revaluation reserve and not to the income statement. *FASB Statement No. 12,* "Accounting for Certain Marketable Securities," provides that marketable equity securities shall be carried at the lower of cost or market, unless accounted for under the equity method; this statement, which will be discussed in chapter 17, has been criticized for not requiring such securities to be carried at market value.

The equity method of accounting was developed to reflect the results of operations for unconsolidated subsidiaries. Under this method, the investor's share of the profits or losses of the investee are accrued by the former; the practice is known as "picking up" the share of investee earnings. The investment account grows by the algebraic sum of the profits or losses accrued minus the dividends received from the investee. Impairment of the investment, indicated by a succession of operating losses, should be recognized by amortization or write-off; given the optimism of most managers, it is doubtful whether this situation is common.

One problem which is typically insoluble within the framework of historical cost accounting is the situation which arises when the investment account is reduced below zero. This may arise through the investor's share of the investee's losses exceeding the carrying amount of the investment, but also through dividends received exceeding cost of investment plus accumulated earnings. A practice admitted by *APB Opinion No. 18* is to discontinue applying the equity method and not provide for additional losses unless the investee's obligations have been guaranteed by the investor. If the investee's profitability recovers, the investor resumes applying the equity method only after its share of net income exceeds the share of net losses not recognized during the period equity accounting was suspended.[16]

It is possible, however, for the situation to arise as a result of a partial distribution by the investee, in which funds not required for asset replacement are paid to shareholders instead of being accumulated by the investee. An example would be a shipping company which is going out of business; for a number of years, and up to the amount standing to the credit of the retained earnings account, the shipping company may declare and pay dividends in excess of earnings. An investor could still have a sizeable amount to come after recovering cost plus share of post-acquisition earnings, and this amount would not be reflected as an asset if *APB Opinion No. 18* were followed.

The equity method was extended to less than majority situations by *APBO 18;* it must be used when investment in voting stock gives the investor *significant influence* over the investee, and ownership (direct or indirect) of 20 percent or more of the voting stock of the investee is presumed to satisfy that condition, in the absence of evidence to the contrary. The Opinion draws attention to two investment situations:

1. Holdings of 50 percent or less of the voting stock of corporations which give the investor ability to exercise signifi-

cant influence over the operating and financial policies of the investee.
2. Corporate joint ventures, where the investor takes essentially a partnership position and is responsible for his share of profits and losses, besides being liable to contribute additional amounts of capital, if required.

In respect of the latter, although ability to exercise influence can be indicated by representation on the board of directors, participation in policy decisions and other evidence, investment (direct or indirect) in 20 percent or more of the voting stock of an investee is presumed to give the investor "significant influence." The 20 percent limit can be traced to a similar provision in U. K. professional standards, and to the French legal concept of *participations* (more than 20 percent holdings) which must be classified separately in the corporation's balance sheet. Application has given considerable trouble in connection with the following:

- Income tax allocation *(ABP Opinions Nos. 23* and *24).*
- Marketable equity securities (*FASB Statement No. 12* and *Interpretation No. 13*).
- Leases (*FASB Statement No. 13, Interpretation No. 21,* and para. 15 of *APBO 18* itself).

Even the basic concept presented a problem, which was dealt with in *FASB Interpretation No. 35,* "Criteria for Applying the Equity Method of Accounting for Investments in Common Stock." This Interpretation requires an evaluation of all the facts and circumstances relating to the investment to see if the 20 percent presumption is valid. Evidence, such as a lawsuit or complaint to a government agency, by the investee against the investor, or concentration of other shares in the hands of a majority group, or failure to obtain information or obtain representation on the investee's board, may indicate inability to exercise effective control.

APBO 18 goes well toward consolidation on a pro rata basis, but it stops short of reporting the full effects of pro rata consolidation.[17] Only the equity pickup of profit or loss and the carrying amount of the investor's investment need be reported, causing the method to be referred to as "one line consolidation." The investment account can be very different from the investor's share in the net assets of the investee, depending on the price which was paid for the investment and the number of years since purchase. *APBO 18* states that the difference between this equity method and consolidation lies in the details reported and that the investor's net income and stockholders' equity will be the same whether an investment in a subsidiary is consolidated or accounted for under the equity method. This may be true for subsidiaries if their assets and liabilities are revalued, but not for corporate joint ventures and 20 to 50 percent investments, where revaluation is unlikely to be practicable. Thus, goodwill arising on consolidation and goodwill arising on the application of the equity method are not the same.

In this connection, some writers have suggested that unrealized profit eliminations are reasonable only where the equity method is viewed as a "one-line consolidation," and not for a nonsubsidiary investment, unless the investor and investee do not transact on an arm's length basis.[18] The same critics have pointed out the potential inconsistency between the treatment of unrealized profits arising out of *upstream* (subsidiary to parent) and *downstream* (parent to subsidiary) sales in equity accounting and in consolidated accounting generally. However, in this as in other accounting problem areas, empirical evidence on the difficulty in question is lacking.

FASB Statement No. 12 created another opportunity for the equity method to be different from a one-line consolidation. Whereas a subsidiary's marketable equity securities are aggregated with the parent's for the purpose of calculating the valuation allowance (cost or lower carrying amount less market value), each portfolio is treated separately if the equity method is applied. Consider a case where the parent has a portfolio which cost $1,500 and has a market value of $1,850; whereas the subsidiary has a portfolio which cost $2,500 and has a market value of $1,650. In the limiting case of a 100 percent subsidiary, the valuation allowance charged to income in the consolidation would be $500 ($4,000 – $3,500), but the net effect on the equity method would be an $850 reduction in the equity pickup.

It is apparent from contemporary published financial statements that *APBO No. 18* is not followed by all the corporations affected. Accounting for 20 to 50 percent interests is done in a variety of ways, the most common being as follows:

1. Cost plus equity in post-acquisition earnings.
2. "The equity method"; presumably a partial consolidation of the investee's net income and net assets, subject to additional (or reduced) depreciation on revaluation of investee assets, and amortization of goodwill. Use of the equity method presupposes knowledge by the investor of the fair market value of the investee's assets, but it is still not clear whether absence of such knowledge in itself precludes application of the equity method.
3. Pro rata, or proportional, consolidation seems to be particularly applicable to joint ventures and other forms of partnership between corporations, involving as it does combination of the investor's percentage of the investee's revenues, expenses, assets, and liabilities. Active participation by the investor in the activities of the investee, and the fact that the investor will pay a pro rata share of the investee's debts if called upon to do so, are the underlying reasons for proportional consolidation.

APBO No. 18 also mentions the market value method in terms which suggest that it conforms to generally accepted accounting principles in certain special circumstances.

In *APBO No. 23* it was held that a timing difference may result from including undistributed earnings of a subsidiary in the pretax accounting income of a parent, but that tax allocation need not be made if evidence shows that remittance of earnings will be postponed indefinitely, or be taxfree.[19] *APBO No. 24* took the opposite view in respect of an investee's earnings accrued under the equity method, because significant influence over an investee differs from control over a subsidiary.[20] This distinction, if valid, seriously undermines the argument in support of the equity method of accounting for all investments where significant influence does not mean control.

FOREIGN CURRENCY TRANSLATION

By definition, the multinational enterprise is a cluster of corporations of different nationalities such that the combined operations of entities not reporting in the reference currency are material in amount. Historically, currency translation techniques were developed for domestic corporations having relatively minor foreign operations, often in the form of branches. Prior to World War II, textbook writers did not treat this as a question of great importance. *The Accountants' Handbook,* 3rd edition (1943) devoted less than two pages (out of 1,450) to accounting for foreign branches. The 5th edition (1970) allocated slightly more space to this problem area, devoting to it a total of 7½ pages out of nearly 2,000. Some *Advanced Accounting* texts include foreign branch accounts in the subject matter covered.

One assumption of these writers was that the foreign branch or subsidiary existed solely to provide cash, whether in the form of dividends or other, to the domestic corporation. The viewpoint is clearly marked in Kester whose work was often quoted as authoritative in this connection.[21] The disturbed monetary conditions following World War II rendered this assumption difficult to work with, and the strain is already noticeable in the 4th edition of Finney and Miller, *Principles of Accounting—Advanced* (1952), chapter 29.

This assumption is no longer tenable where multinational enterprises are concerned, for a number of reasons.

1. Consolidated financial statements do not purport to present cash availability generally, except as an incidental piece of information which is normally presented in a funds statement. The emphasis of contemporary financial statements is on period residual net income and its origins, on resources

and obligations at a given point in time, and on the flow of resources through the entity for a given period.

2. The all-inclusive form of income statement has been interpreted as implying that gains and losses arising out of currency translation should not be restricted to fluctuations in the value of monetary or current assets and liabilities or to differences arising out of remittances.
3. The flow of remittances and dividends cannot be assumed one-way; that is, from subsidiary to parent. Multinational enterprises conduct extensive banking operations involving transfers between all parts of the system.
4. The time-scale involved in global investment is such that remittances from the parent to the subsidiary may continue for a number of years before any prospect of a reverse flow can be entertained.
5. Many countries restrict remittances and dividends by reference to factors other than cash availability to the remitting corporation. There is no presupposition in such cases that net current or net monetary assets are transferable, and the cash transfer assumption would lead logically to the nonconsolidation of subsidiaries subject to these restrictions. This contradicts the basic purpose of consolidation, which is to provide an image of an economic entity, regardless of monetary instability or nonconvertibility.
6. Multiple exchange rates for a particular currency, even in the case of subsidiaries which are permitted to make remittances, imply that the cash transfer assumption cannot lead to a generally acceptable translation result in all cases. Purely artificial rates, a function of political factors as well as inefficiency of money markets, are similarly suspect. Thus, even where a specific exchange rate is available, its significance may be debatable.

It appears, therefore, that an alternative theoretical basis must be found for the currency translation problem, to develop new accounting principles for the financial statements of multinational enterprises. This proposition concerns published financial reports and internal management reports equally, since there is no real reason why the former should differ from the latter, except with respect to the degree of disaggregation involved.

The currency translation approaches proposed in the publications of professional associations and individual scholars include the following:

1. Net current assets (working capital) at the closing rate, net fixed assets minus noncurrent liabilities at the transaction date rate. Revenues and expenses at the average rate for the period, except for depreciation, where the rate used for the fixed assets applies (*ARB 43* method).

2. Net monetary assets at the closing rate, net nonmonetary assets at the transaction rate. Revenues and expenses at the average rate, except for depreciation (NAA method). This method differs from the previous one mainly in respect of the rates used for inventories and long-term liabilities.
3. The modified AICPA method, in which long-term receivables and payables may be translated at closing rates "in many circumstances," as remodified after the devaluation of the U.S. dollar. A 1971 APB proposal would have permitted U.S. corporations with noncurrent foreign currency obligations to defer the difference between the amount at the transaction rate and the amount at the closing rate and charge it to expense over the unexpired period of the loan.
4. Translate all items in the accounts at the current or closing rate and remittances at the actual rate and take only realized gains/losses to the income statement (the new European approach).
5. Adjust accounts stated in a currency other than the reference currency for inflation in the country concerned, except net worth and external debt, then translate all items at the current or closing rate (the Zenoff and Zwick net assets method).[22] The reverse procedure was proposed by the APB, which would result in the adjustment of foreign currency financial statements in terms of the purchasing power of the reference currency, and was adopted by the FASB in *Statement No. 8*.
6. The *temporal* method, described by Lorensen[23] and adopted by *FASB Statement No. 8*. The temporal method resembles the NAA monetary/nonmonetary method, except for certain complications affecting mainly the translation of inventory values.
7. The functional currency method of *FASB Statement No. 52* (December 1981).

FASB STATEMENT NO. 8

FASB Statement No. 8, "Accounting for the Translation of Foreign Currency Transactions and Foreign Currency Financial Statements," illustrates most of the difficulties of accounting standard-setting: a short-run response to a situation perceived as urgent; selecting an unusable accounting theory on which to base GAAP; adopting a new and untested accounting method without consideration of its economic consequences; inflexibility in the light of varying situations; the politicization of the standard-setting process.

The devaluation of the U.S. dollar in 1973 drew attention to the possibility that U.S. corporations might have suffered losses which were not being disclosed because of the method of foreign currency translation used. *FASB Statement No. 1* (December 1973) merely called for certain disclosures to be made in financial statements that included amounts denominated in a foreign currency and then translated into U.S. dollars. Corporations were required to identify which assets and liabilities were translated at the current rate and which at historical rates; which rates were used for which income statement accounts; the method of accounting for exchange adjustments and, if any part was deferred, of disposing of the deferral. They were also required to disclose the aggregate exchange adjustments included in the income statement and the aggregate deferral and a few other items of interest. The Statement did not require any corporation to change its accounting methods.

Soon after this Statement appeared, in a Discussion Memorandum dated February 21, 1974, the FASB's objective of producing a new accounting method which would conform with its view of accounting theory became known. In an Exposure Draft dated December 31, 1974, the FASB argued that businesses should present their financial statements in conformity with the generally accepted accounting principles that would apply had all assets, liabilities, revenues, and expenses been measured and recorded in the reporting currency. This was the basic proposition of *Accounting Research Study No. 12,* "Reporting Foreign Operations of U.S. Companies in U.S. Dollars," which can now be seen to have provided an unsound basis for developing a method of accounting for foreign operations.

The temporal method which was proposed in *ARS No. 12* had a further defect; it required all exchange adjustments (debit and credit differences arising on translation) to flow through the income statement for the period in which they were ascertained. The effect on companies having foreign operations was to increase the number and size of the income statement effects of foreign transactions and operations for any accounting period, even an interim period, regardless of their origin or ultimate disposition.

The temporal method was made mandatory by *FASB Statement No. 8*. Published research found that 403 out of 511 companies surveyed were affected to the extent that they had to adapt their foreign currency translation practices to correspond with the new standard. This research was also concerned with economic effects, and found—

- That current and potential cash costs were being incurred to minimize noncash exchange adjustments;
- That a majority of firms changed the mix between local currency and U.S. dollar debt to reduce exchange adjustments;
- That one-third of the respondents believed that cash borrowing costs were significantly higher because of such changes; extra interest expense was not as visible or immediate a reduction of income as translation adjustments would be.[24]

In addition to these effects, many of the companies incurred additional cash costs to hedge accounting exposure, rather than economic exposure, to the effects of exchange rate changes and to obtain expert banking advice to that end. This was confirmed by one of the FASB's research projects.[25] Effects on net income were highly visible in interim and annual financial statements published after this GAAP became effective.

The economic and accounting problems presented by application of *FASB Statement No. 8* were brought to the attention of the Board on frequent occasions, and it eventually agreed to reconsider the Statement. An exposure draft of a new statement was issued in 1980, and a revised exposure draft and new Statement in 1981.

THE FASB'S NEW APPROACH TO FOREIGN CURRENCY TRANSLATION

The new FASB Statement introduced major changes in accounting for foreign operations, and some minor changes in accounting for foreign currency transactions by U.S. corporations. *FASB Statement No. 8* adopted the "two transaction approach" to accounting for transactions denominated in a currency other than the currency of account, and this was retained intact. Under the two transaction approach, the value of a transaction in U.S. dollars is determined by the exchange rate on the date it takes place; the effects of subsequent exchange rate changes are reported as foreign exchange gains or losses and do not affect the value of the transaction. Exceptions were made for transactions intended and effective as hedges of a net investment in a foreign entity, or other identifiable foreign currency commitment, which were to be deferred.

The FASB's new approach to foreign currency translation was made dependant upon a concept entitled the "functional currency." A functional currency is generally the currency of the country in which an entity is located, but not necessarily so. If a foreign entity generates and expends cash primarily in another currency such as the U.S. dollar, then that other currency is its functional currency. In this case, the provisions of *FASB Statement No. 8* apply; the foreign currency transactions of the foreign entity are translated into its functional currency using the temporal method. There are two minor modifications; deferred income taxes and unamortized policy acquisition costs of a stock life insurance company are to be translated at the current or closing rate, and not at historical rates, as under *Statement No. 8*.

If the functional currency of the foreign entity is not the U.S. dollar, then (a) all assets, liabilities, and, therefore, the total stockholders' equity are translated at the current (closing) rate, and (b) the weighted average rate of exchange is used to translate all revenues, expenses, gains, and losses for a period. The resulting exchange adjustment, which after the initial restatement is composed of the effect of restatement of opening net assets plus the difference between the weighted average and current exchange rates multiplied by foreign currency net income, is credited to a separate component of stockholders' equity. Thus, translated stockholders' equity consists of three elements: contributed capital at historical cost, retained earnings at amount brought forward on restatement plus net income and minus dividends subsequent thereto, and translation adjustment. This last is to be called "Equity Adjustment from Foreign Currency Translation" and is to be transferred to the income statement only on sale or substantially complete liquidation of the foreign entity.

Another innovation was a prescription for incorporating the effect of inflation on the currency of a country operating in a highly inflationary environment. Financial statements in such a currency were to be restated for the effects of changing prices prior to translation, using an appropriate index of inflation in the foreign country.

Finally, the *FASB Statement No. 8* requirement to disclose the effects of foreign currency translation on the income statement was abandoned. Disclosure was restricted to (a) the aggregate transaction gain or loss included in determining net income, and (b) a reconciliation of the opening and closing balances of the account for equity adjustment from foreign currency translation.

EVALUATION OF THE NEW FASB APPROACH

The change of posture demonstrated by the FASB in this matter is remarkable primarily because of the implicit acceptance of a situational response to an accounting problem. Prior to the 1980 exposure draft, the FASB had been firmly against the idea that the situation of a corporation might justify adoption of an alternative accounting principle; accounting for leases was an obvious case where a situational approach might have been more useful than the legalistic approach ultimately adopted. At the time when *FASB Statement No. 8* was proposed, several sources pointed out that the effect of an exchange rate change on a foreign entity differed according as its finance was obtained from U. S. or foreign markets, without persuading the FASB to accommodate this proposition in its pronouncement.

There are other noteworthy features of the new Statement.

1. The FASB adopted entirely different objectives for foreign currency translation. The new objectives were (a) to preserve the financial results and relationships that are expressed in the foreign currency financial statements, and (b) to provide information which is generally compatible with the expected economic effects of exchange rate changes. This contrasts with the former objective, to account for the operations of the foreign entity as though they had been effected in the reporting currency.
2. The FASB in effect retained the superseded GAAP while at the same time promulgating new GAAP. Whether this was

due to an inability to write off the intellectual capital invested in the temporal method, or a genuine need to provide for a new situation in a traditional way, the fact is that accountants must now learn and apply two entirely different methods of accounting for foreign operations.
3. The concept of a functional currency, while no doubt clear enough in the majority of cases, is confusing in a significant minority, in spite of the provision of detailed guidelines for determining the functional currency in a given situation. Consider, for example, the case of a Norwegian subsidiary of a U. S. oil company, which obtains its loan capital and sells its production in sterling, pays substantial income and other taxes in Norwegian crowns, and pays out the bulk of its costs in U. S. dollars.
4. A new concept of realization has been created, namely, sale or substantially complete liquidation of a subsidiary. The old concept of realization would have required, for example, that the part of the equity adjustment from foreign currency translation which related to translation of a long-term loan be recognized as a gain or loss at the latest on the date of repayment of the loan.
5. A degree of discretion has been awarded to corporations in the timing of gain or loss recognition. To the extent that sale or liquidation of a foreign subsidiary can be accelerated or delayed, they are able to advance or postpone income statement items.
6. One of the reasons for changing *FASB Statement No. 8* was to reduce the volatility of reported earnings of corporations with foreign operations. Consider, however, that the effects of exchange rate changes which under *FASB Statement No. 8* flowed into the income statement gradually, quarter by quarter, will now arrive there suddenly, in one large amount, during a quarter or year when a foreign subsidiary is sold or substantially liquidated.

It is not surprising that the FASB should have so much difficulty with this intractable subject. It combines the problems of foreign currency translation with those of accounting for business combinations in a mixture of exceptional complexity. Accountants in other countries have not been noticeably more successful in accounting for gains and losses on foreign currency translation, and indeed, what constitutes the profit, or net income, of a corporation which has ongoing foreign operations is a question which appears almost impossible to answer.

Some see the requirement to report translation adjustments, which may include both realized and unrealized gains and losses, as a component of stockholders' equity, to be a retrograde step. When taken together with the similar treatment of unrealized losses on noncurrent portfolios of marketable equity securities, under *FASB Statement No. 12,* this provision could lead to an unforeseen return to a situation which *APB Opinion No. 30* was believed to have done away with, the so-called dirty surplus.

CONCLUSION

Accounting for business combinations presents us with a vivid illustration of accounting practice divorced from accounting theory. The use of accounts to represent increasingly complex human systems is a key characteristic of the development of accounting. As Sombart wrote in *Der Moderne Kapitalismus:* "Accounting grew by means of constructions using accounts; by putting them into accounts, the writer of an unanalyzed and personalized collection of notes... built them into a firm sequence of thoughts, on which all subsequent accounting could be based." (Author's trans.) The process continues; since consolidated accounts came into general use, we have seen the creation of other forms of combination of accounts, particularly the social system of national income, product and wealth accounts, and the combined accounts of complex governmental organizations.

It is clear that neither ownership nor control is a necessary condition for the usefulness of consolidations, and that diversity of operations does not render them meaningless. Valuation is not a different problem but the same: the critical aspect is the agreement of those who will use the financial statements. As far as disclosure is in question, the answer lies in determining whether structure or performance is revealed with greater clarity.

The study of accounting for business combinations is illuminated by the study of social accounting, and the accountants for the nation are capable of learning much from the practice of consolidation. It is to be hoped that these areas of accounting can be brought together so that principles may be agreed which can support even more complex and extensive accounting representations of the human condition. Even the idea of a world consolidation is not outside the bounds of possibility, providing that difficult problems of translating foreign currencies with different underlying inflation rates can be overcome. Among the proposals which have been made for this purpose are the use of purchasing power parities, or exchange rates weighted for differences in purchasing power, and artificial currencies such as the Eurodollar, which are baskets of different currencies weighted to produce a money index.

ENDNOTES

1. "Accounting for Business Combinations," *APB Opinion No. 16,* New York: AICPA 1970, para. .01.
2. "an analysis of issues related to Business Combinations and Purchased Intangibles," Stamford, Conn.: Financial Accounting Standards Board, August 19, 1976.

3. Lee, T.A., "Accounting for and Disclosure of Business Combinations," *Journal of Business Finance and Accounting,* Spring 1974, pp. 1-21.
4. The term "pooling" seems to have arisen in U.S. cases involving determining the rate bases of regulated utilities, which would explain the fact that the name is unknown outside the U.S.A.
5. Wyatt, Arthur R., *Accounting Research Study No. 5,* "A Critical Study of Accounting for Business Combinations," New York, AICPA, 1963, p. 14.
6. Restated in *ARB No. 43* and again in *ARB No. 48.*
7. *ARS No. 5,* p. 27. Even so, *ARB No. 48* effectively eliminated the size criterion.
8. Committee to Prepare a Statement of Basic Accounting Theory, *A Statement of Basic Accounting Theory,* American Accounting Association, 1966, p. 19.
9. See the annual reports of General Electric, Inc. for the years 1975 and 1976.
10. Snaveley, H.J., "Pooling Should be Mandatory," *The CPA Journal,* December 1975, pp. 23-26.
11. Smolinski, Edward J., "The Adjunct Method in Consolidations," *Journal of Accounting Research,* Autumn 1963, pp. 149-78.
12. For further discussion of this point see *Consolidated Financial Statements,* Accountants International Study Group, 1973, pp. 24-25.
13. Kohler, Eric, *A Dictionary for Accountants,* Englewood Cliffs, N.J.: Prentice-Hall, Inc., 1975, 5th ed., pp. 114-5.
14. Chambers, R.J., *Accounting, Evaluation and Economic Behavior,* Englewood Cliffs, N.J.: Prentice-Hall, Inc., 1966, p. 211.
15. Burton, John C., *Accounting for Business Combinations,* New York: Financial Executives Research Foundation, 1970, pp. 23-25.
16. "The Equity Method of Accounting for Investments in Common Stock," *APB Opinion No. 18,* New York: AICPA, 1971, para. 19 i.
17. Reklau, David L., "Accounting for Investments in Joint Ventures—A Reexamination," *Journal of Accountancy,* September 1977, pp. 96-103.
18. King, Thomas E. and Valdean C. Lembke, "Reporting Income Under the Equity Method," *Journal of Accountancy,* September 1976, pp. 65-71.
19. "Accounting for Income Taxes—Special Areas," *APB Opinion No. 23,* New York: AICPA 1972.
20. "Accounting for Income Taxes—Investments in Common Stock Accounted for by the Equity Method (other than Subsidiaries and Corporate Joint Ventures)", New York: AICPA, 1972.
21. Kester, Roy B., *Advanced Accounting*, New York: The Ronald Press Co., 1946, 4th ed.
22. Zenoff, David B. and Jack Zwick, *International Financial Management,* Englewood Cliffs, N.J.: Prentice-Hall Inc., 1969, chs. 3, 12 and 13.
23. Lorensen, Leonard, *Accounting Research Study No. 12,* "Reporting Foreign Operations of U.S. Companies in U.S. Dollars," New York: AICPA, 1972.
24. Shank, J.K., J.F. Dillard, and R.J. Murdoch, *Assessing the Economic Impact of FASB No. 8,* Financial Executives Institute, 1979.
25. Folks, W.R., T.G. Evans, and M. Jilling, *The Impact of Statement of Financial Accounting Standards No. 8 on the Foreign Exchange Risk Management Practices of American Multinationals: An Economic Impact Study,* Financial Accounting Standards Board, 1978.

SELECTED ADDITIONAL READINGS

Business Combinations

Accounting Principles Board Opinion No. 16, "Business Combinations," New York: AICPA 1970.

———, *No. 17,* Intangible Assets," New York: AICPA 1970.

Accountants International Study Group, *Consolidated Financial Statements,* New York, 1973.

——, *Accounting for Goodwill,* New York, 1975.

Andrews, Wesley T. Jr., "The Evolution of APB Opinion No. 17, *Accounting for Intangible Assets;* a Study of the U.S. Position on Accounting for Goodwill," *The Accounting Historians Journal,* Spring 1981, pp. 37-49.

Arthur Andersen & Co., "Comments to the Securities and Exchange Commission in Response to Requests for Comments on Proposed Accounting Series Release No. 146: Containing Recommendations on Fundamental Changes Needed in Accounting for Business Combination and Goodwill," Chicago: Arthur Andersen & Company, November 12, 1973.

Baxter, George C., and James C. Spinney, "A Closer Look at Consolidated Financial Statement Theory," *CA Magazine,* January, 1975, pp. 31-36 and "Closer Look, Part II," *CA Magazine,* February 1975, pp. 31-35.

Burton, John C., *Accounting for Business Combinations,* New York: Financial Executives Research Foundation, 1970.

Catlett, George R. and Norman O. Olson, *Accounting Research Study No. 10,* "Accounting for Goodwill," New York: AICPA 1968.

Copeland, Ronald M. and Joseph F. Wojdak, "Income Manipulation and Purchase-Pooling Choice," *Journal of Accounting Research,* Autumn 1969, pp. 188-195.

Financial Accounting Standards Board, *an analysis of issues related to Business Combinations and Purchased Intangibles,* Stamford, Conn.: Financial Accounting Standards Board, April 19, 1976.

Lee, T.A., "Accounting for and Disclosure of Business Combinations," *Journal of Business Finance and Accounting,* Spring 1974, pp. 1-21.

Miller, Malcolm, "Goodwill—An Aggregation Issue," *The Accounting Review,* April 1973, pp. 280-291.

Moonitz, Maurice, *The Entity Theory of Consolidated Statements,* Brooklyn, N.Y.: The Foundation Press, 1951.

Nelson, Kenneth and Robert H. Strawser, "A Note on APB Opinion No. 16," *Journal of Accounting Research,* Autumn 1970, pp. 284-289.

Rayburn, Frank R., "Another Look at the Impact of Accounting Principles Board Opinion No. 16—An Empirical Study," *Merger and Acquisitions,* Spring 1975, pp. 7-9.

Smolinski, Edward J., "The Adjunct Method in Consolidations," *Journal of Accounting Research,* Autumn 1963, pp. 149-178.

Snaveley, H.J., "Pooling Should Be Mandatory," *The CPA Journal,* December 1975, pp. 23-26.

Tearney, Michael G., "Accounting for Goodwill: A Realistic Approach," *Journal of Accountancy,* July 1973, pp. 41-45.

Wyatt, Arthur R., *Accounting Research Study No. 5,* "A Critical Study of Accounting for Business Combinations," New York: AICPA 1963.

The Equity Method Of Accounting

Accounting Principles Board, *Opinion No. 18,* "The Equity Method of Accounting for Investments in Common Stock," New York: AICPA 1971.

Barrett, Edgar M., "Accounting for Intercorporate Investments: A Behavioral Field Experiment," *Journal of Accounting Research,* Empirical Research in Accounting, 1971, pp. 50-65.

———, *APB Opinion No. 18:* "A Move Toward Preferences of Users," *Financial Analysts Journal,* July/August 1972, pp. 47-50, 52-55.

Financial Accounting Standards Board, *Interpretation No. 35,* "Criteria for Applying the Equity Method of Accounting for Investments in Common Stock," May 1981.

King, Thomas E., and Valdean C. Lembke, "Reporting Investor Income Under the Equity Method," *Journal of Accountancy,* September 1976, pp. 65-71.

Lynch, Thomas Edward, "Accounting for Investments in Equity Securities by the Equity and Market Value Methods," *Financial Analysts Journal,* January/February 1975, pp. 62-69.

O'Connor, Melvin C., and James C. Hamre, "Alternative Methods of Accounting for Long-term Nonsubsidiary Intercorporate Investments in Common Stock," *The Accounting Review,* April 1972, pp. 308-319.

Reklau, David L., "Accounting for Investments in Joint Ventures—A Re-examination," *Journal of Accountancy,* September 1977, pp. 96-103.

Other Forms of Consolidation

"An Annual Report for the Federal Government," *Fortune,* May 1973, pp. 193-199, 322, 324.

Most, Kenneth S., "An Accountant Looks at Social Accounting," *Accounting and Business Research,* Autumn 1972, pp. 264-274.

Yu, S.C., "An Appraisal of Macroaccounting," in *Aspects of Contemporary Accounting,* Gainesville, Fl.: University of Florida, 1966, pp. 25-43.

Foreign Currency Translation

Aliber, Robert Z. and Clyde P. Stickney, "Accounting Measures of Foreign Exchange Exposure," *The Accounting Review,* January 1975, pp. 44-57.

Bursk, Edward C., John Dearden, David F. Hawkins, and Victor M. Longstreet, *Financial Control of Multinational Operations,* New York: Financial Executives Research Foundation, 1971, chs II, IV and Appendix B.

Dietermann, Gerard J., "Evaluating Multinational Performance under FAS No. 8," *Management Accounting,* May 1980, pp. 49-55.

Financial Accounting Standards Board, *Statement of Financial Accounting Standards No. 8,* "Accounting for the Translation of Foreign Currency Transactions and Foreign Currency Financial Statements," Stamford, Conn.: Financial Accounting Standards Board, October 1975.

———, *Statement of Financial Accounting Standards No. 52*, "Foreign Currency Translation," Stamford, Conn: Financial Accounting Standards Board, December 1981.

Folks, W.R., T.G. Evans, and M. Jilling, *The Impact of Financial Accounting Standard No. 8 on the Foreign Exchange Risk Management Practices of American Multinationals: An Economic Impact Study,* Stamford, Conn.: Financial Accounting Standards Board, 1978.

Case 16-1 Curtiss-Wright Corporation

Early in 1980, Curtiss-Wright announced that it had changed to the equity method of accounting for its 14.3 percent interest in Kennecott Copper, a corporation approximately six times bigger than its stockholder. Curtiss-Wright asserted that it had enough influence over Kennecott to justify the adoption of the equity method.

The change in accounting principle added $7.5 million (91 cents per share) to Curtiss-Wright's earnings for the first nine months of 1979, and 10 cents per share to 1978 income, restated. It was known that Curtiss-Wright used the equity method for two other investments of less than 20 percent, but both companies were very small and virtually controlled by Curtiss-Wright appointees on their boards. In announcing the Kennecott change, Curtiss-Wright stated that the adoption of the equity method was appropriate "in view of our ownership of a substantial block of Kennecott's voting stock and the participation of our representatives on Kennecott's board." Curtiss-Wright had an agreement with Kennecott not to seek more than 21 percent of its voting stock, but three of its directors served on Kennecott's board of eighteen. Curtiss-Wright's auditors concurred with the change, noting that four of the remaining Kennecott directors served by mutual consent.

1. Did Curtiss-Wright's change of accounting principle comply with *APB Opinion No. 18?*
2. List the reasons for and against the use of the equity method in minority (less than 50 percent but at least 20 percent) holdings.
3. Would it have made any difference if Curtiss-Wright had claimed significant influence with a holding of 9.9 percent of Kennecott Copper?
4. Did anything happen after 1979 to suggest that Curtiss-Wright should not have adopted the equity method in this case?

Case 16-2 Sperry Corporation

Sperry Corporation fiscal year ends March 31. The interim report for the first quarter of the 1981/82 fiscal year showed a 75 percent earnings decline, which was particularly disappointing to the chairman who was facing mandatory retirement at age 65 shortly after the year's end.

Two factors contributed to the decline: higher interest rates and foreign currency translation. With regard to the latter, 44 percent of Sperry's business was overseas, and the foreign currency translation losses were due in large part to the translation of $500 million in computer financing leases. With currencies moving up and down in relation to the U.S. dollar, the value of these receivables could fluctuate by as much as $5 million a day. Without these factors, operating results would have exceeded those of the previous year, and this fact led the board to raise Sperry's quarterly dividend from 44 cents to 48 cents in spite of the reduced net income. Continued high interest rates and a strong dollar meant that second quarter results would also probably be down.

Obviously disappointed by what he regards as "the somewhat frivolous FASB effect" in the first quarter, reported *The Wall Street Journal* for July 10, 1981, the chairman said that Sperry may be a "classic example" of the strong effect the Financial Accounting Standards Board *Statement No. 8* can have on companies with a large portion of overseas business.

Under consideration was a proposal to end the practice of finance leasing and to sell or rent instead.

1. Explain why finance leasing overseas results in foreign exchange translation gains and losses under *FASB Statement No. 8*.
2. Can such exchange gains and losses be reported even in cases where the corporation has no economic exposure to exchange gains or losses because receivables under lease agreements are equal to payables in foreign currencies?
3. Discuss the social and economic implications of an accounting standard promulgated by a private sector organization such as the FASB which causes business firms to change their operating policies.

END OF CHAPTER QUESTIONS

1. When a business combination is effected by an exchange of common stock, the transaction is accounted for as a purchase or as a pooling of interests, depending on the circumstances. The methods are not optional and each yields significantly different results as to financial position and results of operations.
   Required:
   Discuss the *supportive* arguments for each of the following:
   A. Purchasing method.
   B. Pooling of interests method (AICPA, November 1979).
2. The concept of the accounting entity often is considered to be the most fundamental of accounting concepts, one that pervades all of accounting.
   Required:
   A. What is an accounting entity? Explain.
   B. Explain why the accounting entity concept is so fundamental that it pervades all of accounting.
   C. Provide examples of three different applications of the accounting entity concept. (AICPA adapted, May 1975)
3. What is the objective of accounting consolidation?
4. What are the constituent parts of the consolidation framework? Explain each part carefully.

5. What parts of the consolidation framework differ if pooling is used instead of purchase accounting?
6. What are the reasons for business combinations, and how does the reason affect the choice of method, purchase or pooling?
7. What two different viewpoints may be adopted in consolidating the accounts of a subsidiary which is not wholly owned with those of its parent? How do they affect the consolidation?
8. Discuss the grounds on which a subsidiary may be excluded from a consolidation, and critically evaluate each of them. What method of accounting is required for a subsidiary which is not consolidated? What alternative disclosures are available to corporations which do not consolidate foreign subsidiaries?
9. Why is it important to disclose restrictions on the ability of a consolidated subsidiary to advance or loan funds to the parent?
10. Discuss the new accounting problems posed by the proposed Seventh Directive of the European Economic Community.
11. Explain the conflict between *APB Opinions 16* and *20* in respect of a change in the accounting entity.
12. Discuss the concept of "goodwill arising on consolidation," and explain the various methods whereby such a difference could be accounted for. How does *APB Opinion No. 17* require positive and negative goodwill be accounted for?
13. What problems arise in accounting for an acquisition effected by exchange of shares?
14. Discuss the difficulties which may be encountered in applying *APB Opinion No. 18.*
15. What is "pro rata" or proportional consolidation, and how does it differ from the equity method? For what type of investment would it be particularly appropriate?
16. Discuss the particular provisions of GAAP for income tax allocation and accounting for marketable equity securities in the application of equity accounting.
17. A new terminology has been invented by the FASB for foreign currency translation.
    A. Define the terms *measure* and *denominate* as used in this context, and give brief examples which distinguish between amounts measured in, and amounts denominated in, a particular currency.
    B. Explain the temporal method prescribed by *FASB Statement No. 8,* and state what changes were made to this method by *FASB Statement No. 52*.
    C. State the circumstances in which the temporal method will be applied although *FASB Statement No. 8* has been superseded by a new Statement.
18. Discuss the economic consequences of *FASB Statement No. 8,* and explain the reasons for its replacement.
19. State the rules applicable to accounting for foreign currency transactions, distinguishing between a hedge of an identifiable commitment or net investment, and a speculative hedge.

20. Evaluate the new method prescribed by the FASB for accounting for foreign currency operations and financial position in the light of—
    A. The FASB's objective of reducing the fluctuations caused by *FASB Statement No. 8,* and,
    B. The widely held belief that management should not influence the amount of reported net income by using accounting methods devoid of economic substance.

17

CURRENT PROBLEMS OF ACCOUNTING THEORY AND PRACTICE

Accounting standard-setting bodies have been extremely kind to financial statement preparers in the past. They have failed to restrict alternatives, in any meaningful way, in the three areas which lend themselves best to manipulation of net income—inventory valuation, depreciation accounting, and consolidations. Cynical accountants could point out that auditors will adopt a rigid position on imputing interest on receivables and payables under *APBO 21*, possibly affecting income by several thousand dollars, while permitting choice of a depreciation method which affects the income statement in millions of dollars.

We have drawn attention to the problems of accounting consolidations in chapter 16, and discussed depreciation accounting in chapter 14. In this chapter we will first look at the problem of inventory valuation and at accounting for marketable equity securities, which was influenced by inventory accounting. We will then examine several emerging accounting issues, look at some other aspects of accounting theory which appear to have been ignored by the FASB, and end this book by drawing certain conclusions.

INVENTORIES

Inventories are, for most business firms and for many other entities, a major factor in the determination of period expense. By definition, expense is a measure of consumption during a given period: consumption by use or by distribution. Transformation is not consumption, and inventories are expenditures in process of transformation.

Economics is of little assistance in dealing with the accounting problems presented by inventories. Economic theory abstracts from time, and inventories represent factors of production in suspense (between markets) because of the production time period; economists would just as soon they did not exist. Only in national income accounting are economists obliged to confront the existence of inventories. In this context they are assimilated to sales and reported as output at selling prices. There exists a restricted set of cases where accountants adopt the same viewpoint, principally in the extractive industries, and it is possible that the view of finished product inventories as exteriorized in substance but not in form applies to a wider range of observations.

One of the accounting problems in this area is the recognition of inventories which arise through accretion. *Accretion* is the term used for natural growth through reproduction or age, and is applied also to increased value resulting from aging wood, liquor, or tobacco. It would be a foolish farmer who did not record livestock births and deaths, or transfers to and from the number of milk-bearing heifers. Similarly, the addition to a stock resulting from natural growth should be recognized by accountants as an increase in inventory, with a corresponding credit to revenue. Taxation complications probably underlie the fact that this practice is not more common. From the potential social consolidation viewpoint, we are discussing an increase in social wealth, not simply a transformation process.

Accretion due to aging is a more difficult concept because the increased value is not realizable until the aging process is complete. Growing timber is an acute form of this problem, because timber may be cut before or after its optimal growth. Replacement value of growing and aging inventories is normally a function of cost and interest rates; in periods of glut or shortage, and in times of inflation, these other factors should be reflected in the accounts only where the inventories are held for sale and need not be replaced in the ordinary course of business.

It will be obvious by now that inventories always represent social revenues either of other firms or individuals or of the entity of account. The prevailing practice of showing these expenditures as assets and not as expenses is consistent with the idea of social consolidation and the avoidance of double counting. Again, the separation of inventories of salable goods (including work in process) from inventories of supplies to be consumed in such operations as maintenance or in auxiliary production, such as power generation, can be seen as a distinction without a difference.

The particular problem raised by inventories is that there are an infinite number of possible methods of arriving at their value. In a few cases, where exteriorization is a mere technicality, differential net revenue is relatively objective. If this type of direct valuation is not available, we are attempting to solve a problem of subjective valuation similar to the one whereby depreciation is calculated. This problem is a function of inventory quantities and the related prices.[1]

The determination of inventory quantities is frequently a matter of great difficulty because of physical features making a count either impossible or uneconomic. The basic choice between perpetual and periodic inventory methods is supplemented by statistical methods which recognize the fact that error is unavoidable.

The pricing operation is equally imprecise because of our inability to validate this type of valuation, which Thomas calls *incorrigible*. The areas of choice include the following:

1. Market prices (FIFO, LIFO, average, weighted average, standard, specific replacement, selling price less normal markup; lower of cost or market)
2. Transfer prices (unit cost, process cost, differential cost; these may be actual or standard)
3. Cost centers, or points at which costs are collected

There has been very little accounting rule making on these questions; 1. and 2. are covered by *ARB 43*, chapter 4; 3. has been tackled, without great success, by the Cost Accounting Standards Board which does not provide GAAP for financial reporting. *ARB 43* defined inventory and excluded from the category a depreciable asset which has been retired from use and is held for sale. This kind of asset has the economic characteristics of an inventory, but its inclusion in this category would distort the inventory turnover ratio. On the other hand, the inventory turnover ratio is easily distorted, for example, if the ending inventory is particularly high because of expected future sales; the correct way to deal with such statistical problems is by annotating the data, not by redefining it.

Para. 5 of the appropriate chapter of *ARB 43* provides that inventories should be valued at cost, which is almost impeccably stated as "the sum of the applicable expenditures and charges directly or indirectly incurred in bringing an article to its existing condition and location." A more contemporary view would substitute for the last phrase, "to its state and place of use" and specify that "applicable" means "necessary." Para. 6 permits a choice of that valuation method which "most clearly reflects periodic income"; since we do not know what income is, this constraint is ineffective. Finally, *ARB 43* provides that a departure from the cost basis is required when the utility of the goods is no longer as great as its cost, and utility is defined as market value. Statement 6 of *ARB 43* provides generally for replacement cost to be used if it is lower than historical cost, and it lays down specific lower of cost or market (LCM) rules which appear to be particularly relevant to retail businesses. These rules established a "ceiling" in the form of net realizable value, and a "floor" in the form of net realizable value reduced by a normal profit margin. No guidance on what constitutes a normal profit margin was provided.

The LCM rule is obviously an application of balance sheet conservatism; its income statement effect is believed to be similar, but may lead to overstatement in subsequent periods. It has been criticized for a number of reasons.

- It is asymmetrical; losses are recognized but not gains.
- It leads to multiple valuations; some items are included in inventories at historical cost, others at replacement cost, yet others at net realizable value, or net realizable value less a hypothetical profit margin.
- It does nothing to restrict the ability of a firm's management to manipulate earnings by the choice of a particular valuation method (sometimes called "cost flow assumption").[2]

THE LIFO PROBLEM

LIFO presents an interesting example of the attempt to solve accounting problems within accounting and nonaccounting frameworks. The last-in, first-out method of inventory valuation (LIFO) was first proposed by the American Petroleum Institute in 1936 to reflect the fact that low-cost oil and gas reserves were being replaced by high-cost discoveries. Since inventories did not at that time represent a substantial proportion of oil companies' balance sheet assets, the effect on their balance sheets was not an overriding consideration. LIFO was permitted by the Internal Revenue Service in 1938 for fungible goods only, but the restriction was gradually relaxed; the dollar value method was admitted generally in 1949 after having been introduced for retail department stores several years earlier.

A distinction is often made between "natural" LIFO, where cost flows demonstrably reflect physical flows, and "artificial" LIFO, where cost flows demonstrably contradict physical flows. There is no necessary connection between physical flows and cost accounting, and the relation of one to the other is simply a convenient assumption which may be refuted by the facts of a particular case. Thus, to discuss LIFO generally with reference to this special case is unsound, and we will proceed to examine LIFO in the general case without reference to the physical flow of goods. The LIFO physical flow raises other valuation problems, such as the determination of the condition of the undisturbed first-in material, which belong to the subject of inventory valuation generally.

It is also common to find LIFO discussed as a variant of the base stock method of inventory valuation. In fact, these are conceptually two different approaches, since the base stock method involves determining a normal inventory quantity and LIFO does not, although they appear to have similar consequences. Base stock is a fixed asset for all practical purposes and, therefore, does not conform with the current asset criteria which apply to inventory valuation. Historically, attempts to persuade the Internal Revenue Service to allow the base stock method for tax purposes preceded the adoption of LIFO, and the failure of this approach led to advocacy of the LIFO method.

Because the rise of the use of LIFO took place during a period of inflation and because one of the consequences of its adoption is to shield holding gains from income taxation, a number of commentators have attempted to explain LIFO as a method of partially adjusting financial statements for the effects of inflation. It has been claimed that LIFO matches current costs (inventory quantities used X recent prices paid) with current revenues, and the resulting gross margin, therefore, represents current value gross profit. As a result, a considerable literature arguing the pros and cons of LIFO emerged during the period 1945-1970.

A sudden increase in world commodity prices during 1974 produced a flurry of articles in 1975 to explain the large number of corporate adoptions of LIFO for 1974 or 1975. It is clear, however, that LIFO is purely a tax avoidance method of inventory valuation and can only be justified within a tax law framework; the fact that firms adopting LIFO must conform their financial reporting is an isolated instance of this situation in the United States, and no generalizations of an accounting theory nature can be made from this observation. It may be noted, however, that in some countries conformity of financial reporting is a condition of expense deductibility or revenue deferral over a wide range, and in those jurisdictions accounting theorists must accommodate the fact in their generalizations. To save taxes, any company should adopt LIFO when it has inventories that are a significant part of total assets, faces increases in input prices, can reasonably expect to maintain or increase inventory levels, and does not expect an increase in tax rates. A formula which can be used to predict tax savings is—

Marginal tax rate X Inflation Rate X Beginning inventory at FIFO = Current year's tax savings.

For example, if the tax rate is 50 percent, the inflation rate is 15 percent yearly, and the beginning LIFO inventory is $10 million, tax of $750,000 could be saved in the year LIFO is adopted.

LIFO may be examined within the frameworks of income taxation, financial and managerial accounting, securities analysis, or organization theory; it also has macroeconomic implications.

TAX ASPECTS OF LIFO

LIFO is likely to be adopted at a time when input prices, more particularly those of raw materials, have risen sharply. By valuing inventory at beginning-of-period prices and by calculating cost of sales at the prices of the period, the firm creates hidden reserves which are shielded from income and property taxation. As long as prices and inventory levels do not decline, this shield remains, and in this case the tax saving is permanent. If input prices decline to their former level or inventory is liquidated, the hidden reserves disappear and, if profits are earned, the tax saved becomes payable. In this case, the permanent saving is restricted to interest on the tax postponed for the postponement period. Should tax rates increase in the meantime, the higher tax paid may eliminate this saving.

LIFO aims at stabilizing taxable income from period to period in time of rising prices, but prices which rise also fluctuate, so the effect of adopting LIFO on profits of periods subsequent to the one of adoption is unknown. The immediate liquidity problem, however, may be so acute that the risks are acceptable; this was certainly the case in 1974/75 when one company claimed to have saved $100 million in federal income tax payments by adopting LIFO.

LIFO is available to virtually all taxpayers; when adopted it must be used consistently for financial reporting generally as well as for tax accounting, although the position with regard to interim reporting so far has permitted other inventory valuation methods. A breach of this consistency requirement may cause the Internal Revenue Service to prescribe a method of its choice for the year of breach and subsequently. Taxpayer election is irrevocable, and a change to another inventory valuation method requires the permission of the Commissioner of Internal Revenue. In both cases, the consequences may be a sharply higher tax liability, but IRS regulations permit this liability to be spread over a number of years, thus mitigating somewhat the rigor of the conditions surrounding LIFO.[3]

Adoption of LIFO involves disclosure of the accounting change in published financial statements, but the IRS has fought to restrict publication of the effect on earnings, while the SEC has favored inclusion of a note on this effect in the company's annual reports and SEC filings. A controversy between these two agencies early in 1975 resulted in a compromise; the effect on net income must be stated in the year of change; in subsequent years, the notes to financial statements published must state the difference between opening and closing inventories under LIFO and the method previously used. Further IRS regulations in 1979 and 1980 relaxed the effect of the conformity rule to the point where it has become possible to report inventories at FIFO in the balance sheet while using LIFO in the income statement, and at the time of writing moves were under foot to abolish the conformity rule entirely.

ACCOUNTING ASPECTS OF LIFO

Since adoption for tax purposes implies adoption for all other financial reporting purposes, the accounting aspects of LIFO may be discussed without reference to the tax effects. However, it should be remarked that, because LIFO is an acceptable method of inventory valuation generally and the Internal Revenue Code only restricts those adopting LIFO for tax purposes, it may be adopted for financial reporting purposes exclusively. If a firm used LIFO for financial reporting and, say, FIFO for tax accounting, it would reduce reported earnings in times of rising prices; the more likely scenario is that this change would be made by a positive profit difference firm to report lower profits to the IRS without reducing its reported earnings or earnings per share. The switch from another method of inventory valuation to LIFO would be made by a negative profit difference firm, that is, one which would report lower profits using LIFO.

Accounting aspects of LIFO are frequently presented under the "advantages-disadvantages" dichotomy, summarized as follows.

Advantages of LIFO	Disadvantages of LIFO
1. Eliminates the effects of specific price-level changes from the calculation of period net income, thus producing a form of "operating net income." Eliminates the so-called paper profits from the income statement and provides a better matching of current costs with current revenues.	1. *(a)* The current preference for an all-inclusive statement of net income would call for a statement of holding gains or losses, which LIFO does not provide. *(b)* Full price-level adjustment would be preferable to partial. *(c)* The effects of general price-level changes are not eliminated, and specific price changes may not be fully eliminated. *(d)* Changes in inventory levels can move the user far from the "operating net income" concept. *(e)* Fails to reveal the current value of inventories in the balance sheet.
2. Improves the "quality of earnings" in times of rising prices, by smoothing and by maintaining net income at a lower level than with other inventory valuation methods.	2. *(a)* The lower reported earnings may translate into lower stock prices (although the empirical evidence is equivocal on this point). *(b)* Smoothing is undesirable; firms whose profitability fluctuates should demonstrate this fact. *(c)* LIFO can cause fluctuations!
3. The LIFO cost flow assumption is no more unrealistic than any other cost flow assumption, and LIFO permits the firm to adapt to its circumstances where conservation of cash flow is a primary consideration.	3. Other profit manipulations can accompany LIFO; by timing purchases a company's management can cause higher or lower costs to flow into the income statement, thus increasing or decreasing reported net earnings at will.

4. It is a "cheap" form of tax avoidance from the accounting viewpoint, requiring many inventory calculations but only one annual accounting entry, the "LIFO adjustment."

4. *(a)* It is expensive in its use of the time of senior accountants, who must monitor the effects of price changes and inventory levels on profits to advise management of appropriate actions to be taken.

   (b) LIFO cannot be used with a perpetual inventory system since, even if inventories drop to zero during the year, the beginning LIFO valuation can be used if they are replenished at any time before the year's end. Management accounts and other internal financial statements must use FIFO or average cost methods of inventory valuation, so that management decisions based on the situation shown by these financial statements will not be informed on the effect of those decisions on taxable income or reported profits. This feature undermines the credibility of the accounting function and is probably a more serious disadvantage of LIFO than is the more frequently discussed undervaluation of inventory problem. Since the 1980 LIFO rules changes permitted the use of another inventory method for internal management reporting, however, this has ceased to be a problem.

SECURITIES ANALYSIS AND LIFO

Financial analysts use ratios to render financial statements of different companies comparable, in order to evaluate them in relation to each other. LIFO affects the figures for cost of sales, net income before and after taxes, taxation expense, inventories, current assets, total assets, and stockholders' equity. It is obvious that measures of profitability, security, liquidity, activity, and operating efficiency are therefore influenced. It is clear that because companies adopt LIFO at different dates, the financial statements of otherwise comparable companies yield analytical results which are difficult to evaluate, even if all use the LIFO method for inventory valuation. If some companies use LIFO and others FIFO or average cost, the analyst may be aware of this possible cause of variation but can adjust the statements only with difficulty—for example, by restating LIFO inventories and the related retained earnings at FIFO or average cost.

In cruder terms, the LIFO company reports lower earnings in times of rising prices than the FIFO company, and superficial comparison will favor the latter over the former. Although the prices of the securities of companies switching to LIFO will drop after their results are published, longer-run studies suggest that this impact is not significant.[4] The fact that many companies adopted LIFO in 1975, at a time when the stock exchanges were at their lowest price level for many years, may suggest a belief that the market will be sophisticated enough to remember the change when profits and stock exchange prices subsequently increase.

OTHER ASPECTS OF LIFO

The effects of the adoption of LIFO on managerial behavior have not been researched; it is clear that the change must be decided at a high level of management, that it occupies substantial amounts of executive and administrative time, and that these effects are significant. We have referred to several behavioral aspects of LIFO—its effects on the credibility of accounts, the opportunity for manipulation of earnings which it presents, and the impact of the change on managers, financial analysts, and the investing public.

In the hands of a fraudulent manager LIFO could lead to one of the simplest and most common corporate swindles; the company reports lower earnings, causing its share price to drop; the management buys shares at depressed prices; the company subsequently reports substantial increases in earnings and its share prices rise, permitting the management to sell at a profit. The low per-share book value of common stock which accompanies statement of inventories at LIFO cost reinforces this effect.

From the macroeconomic viewpoint, LIFO inventory valuation has two predominant defects. It tends to increase corporate liquidity in times of inflation, making it more difficult for government to use income taxation for counter-cyclical purposes. However, this objection has little practical significance; since government tends to spend more than its tax receipts during periods of inflation, it is difficult to say whether the combined effect on inflation is good or bad. Secondly, the incorporation of inventory changes in the calculation of gross national product is seriously affected by the fact that inventories are valued on different bases. Again, the error inherent in national income accounting is so great that the effect of LIFO is unlikely to be more serious than the effect of the other assumptions and approximations of national income economists.

MARKETABLE SECURITIES

An accounting entity which acquires an equity or debt interest in another entity accounts for such interests as investments. They are actually disinvestments, capital transferred from the accounting entity to another entity, and should, therefore, be shown separately from other assets in the balance sheet, unless the investment is simply a temporary form of holding cash. Such long-term investments may be a permanent revenue producing part of the entity's assets, or a strategic support for enterprise activities falling short of control, or significant influence, over the investee.

Investments held for specific purposes are often called *funds*. A firm may establish a pension fund without transferring assets to trustees, and purchase investments to assure discharge of its obligations; such funds are also often established to provide a source of cash for construction of new facilities. Investments may be marketable or nonmarketable, a distinction which relates to liquidity, not value. A given marketable security may be readily liquidated at a price, yet a nonmarketable security may take more time to sell, but fetch a higher price.

Thus, accounting for investments is affected by whether they are equity or debt, current or noncurrent, marketable or nonmarketable, and even the type of enterprise which holds them. Holdings of 20 percent or more in the voting equity of an investee calls for the equity method of accounting; more than 50 percent, for consolidation, unless a good reason can be found to avoid the latter.

Not surprisingly, a variety of practices exist in accounting for investments. Debt securities and nonmarketable securities may be carried at cost, interest and dividends being credited to income, unless evidence shows permanent impairment of value, in which case they should be written down, or off. Some companies create valuation allowances for such value declines on a regular basis; others avoid the issue until forced by their auditors or others to take action. It is generally believed that current asset debt securities may be treated in the same fashion, but it is difficult to argue that investments which are held as a temporary outlet for working capital are going to be held until their value recovers.[5] All declines in value should be accounted for, and in view of the fact that current assets are used to finance operations, increases also. Before *FASB Statement No. 12*, it was customary to annotate the current market value of securities reported as current assets, where different from their cost.[6]

Prior to *FASB Statement No. 12*, market value was used for equity securities only (a) by some companies for current portfolios where market was below cost, and (b) by investment companies affected by the AICPA Industry Audit Guide "Audits of Investment Companies" (1973) and SOP 77-1, "Financial Accounting and Reporting by Investment Companies."

FASB Statement No. 12 purported to extend the use of market value for marketable securities. For firms other than investment companies and in situations where the equity method was not applicable, marketable securities had to be carried at the lower of cost or market. The difference between cost and market, when the latter was lower, constituted a valuation allowance. A distinction was made between current asset securities and fixed asset securities in the treatment of the valuation allowance. Changes in the valuation allowance applicable to current asset securities should be debited or credited to the income statement; changes in the valuation allowance applicable to fixed asset (noncurrent) securities should be debited or credited to stockholders' equity. Realized gains and losses should be included in the income statement in both cases.

This statement has a number of defects, some of which were alluded to by Norgaard and Grinnell.[7] They deplored the extension of the "lower-of-cost-or-market" rule; the absence of a standard for some entities maintaining large portfolios, such as insurance companies; the "total portfolio" approach, which permits some unrealized gains to be realized through deferring the write-off of losses on other securities; and the opportunities for manipulation presented by the differential treatment of current and noncurrent portfolios.

Quite apart from these criticisms, the Statement bears other marks of being a hastily concocted stopgap designed to force investors to recognize the severe decline in stock market prices during 1973-1974, but capable of producing anomalous results more confusing than those resulting from the preceding conditions. *FASB Interpretation No. 12* dealt with the case of a firm which had previously provided for a decline in the market value of its marketable securities by amortization. An "allowance" account, or provision for amortization, was to be written back by credit to the income statement. Since such an allowance would previously have been debited to the income statement of a prior period, in the case of a current portfolio the only damage done was to cause the decline in value to be recognized in a period in which it did not occur. However, in the case of a noncurrent portfolio, the valuation allowance established on first applying *Statement No. 12* would be debited to stockholders' equity, thus providing the reporting company with an unusual form of windfall gain.

Again, the definition of realized gains and losses in terms of the difference between cost price and selling price, disregarding the valuation allowance, raises the prospect of the same portfolio producing, in the same period, *both* a gain and a loss because the selling price was above cost, and the sale also caused an increase in the valuation allowance.

Most important, perhaps, is the fact that in this instance the FASB has introduced the idea that a change in value may be neither a gain nor a loss, but simply a restatement of capital.

From the viewpoint presented in this book, the solution to the problem of accounting for investments generally should be consistent with the definitions in chapter 12. Investments representing a substitute for money would be valued at present value for debt securities and net realizable value for equity securities, and accounting for them by full or partial consolidation would not be an alternative. The equity method of accounting, often called "one line consolidation," can only be regarded as an interim solution to investment accounting. Investments representing a permanent feature of the firm's asset structure should be accounted for at replacement value, which would be the current value of the investee's capacity if in fact the purpose of the investment was to acquire a share in that capacity. Full or partial consolidation would be used for all investments in which control over assets, liabilities, revenue, and expenses was acquired.

Investments carried forward as current assets can be assimilated to a simultaneous purchase and sale at the end of one accounting period and the beginning of the next, so that increase or decrease in value is a gain or loss forming part of profit. In the case of long-term investments, however, changes in value do not represent gains or losses, unless capable of being interpreted as production or consumption of value. In all other cases they are restatements of capital and should not be credited or debited to the income statement.

ACCOUNTING FOR LEASES

The problem of accounting for leases embraces most of the conceptual issues discussed in this book: extension of the traditional accounting model, valuation of assets and liabilities, the measurement of revenue and expense. It has proved difficult for the APB, which dealt with the subject in several opinions,[8] and for the FASB. The latter issued two exposure drafts of a proposed statement before the lengthy and complex *FASB Statement No. 13* appeared.[9] In spite of so much preparation and detailed prescription, this Statement proved insufficient, and seven further statements (Nos. 17, 22, 23, 26, 27, 28, and 29) and six interpretations (Nos. 19, 21, 23, 24, 26, and 27) were found necessary between 1976 and 1979. These publications were combined in *Accounting for Leases*, dated May 1980.[10] It is common knowledge that substantial managerial, accounting, and legal talent is engaged on devising leases which will not be subject to the capitalization provisions of *Statement No. 13* as amended and interpreted. The absence of any amendments or interpretations after 1979 suggests that the FASB has recognized the impossibility of policing this area, which at one time appeared to account for nearly half the FASB's work load.

A lease is an executory contract; both use of the leased property and payment of rent (or hire) are normally contingent for all parts of the period covered by the lease which lie in the future. In some cases, rent is paid in advance for the entire period of the lease; in others, an existing lease is acquired by a third party, with payments additional to those specified by the lease (called premiums) being made to the lessee or the lessor. Until recently, the usual practice was to account for leases as follows:

1. Rent was charged to expense by the lessee, or credited to revenue by the lessor, on a strict time apportionment basis. Rent paid or received in advance was accounted for as a prepayment or deferred income.
2. Premiums were capitalized and charged to expense by amortization on a time basis, usually straight-line depreciation over the remainder of the term.
3. Expenses incurred in using the leased property, such as repairs for which the lessee was responsible, were accounted for as such and not related to the rent expense.
4. Commitments under leases were footnoted as contingent liabilities only where unusual features were present, such as penalties payable on cancellation or hypothecation of the lease contract.

Several developments led to a reconsideration of traditional accounting for leases. The volume of leasing expanded greatly after World War II as the growth of savings fueled the creation of financial intermediaries specializing in such transactions. It became much easier for businesses, which previously were obliged to purchase buildings or equipment, to lease them instead. Tax benefits for lessors were also a factor in this situation; an unprofitable corporation obtains no tax shield from depreciation and may be able to execute an advantageous lease with a profitable corporation which can use the deductions.

In addition, a new practice of raising capital by sale-and-leaseback developed. In such a transaction, the owner of a building or equipment sells it to a financial institution and executes a simultaneous lease on terms which effectively reimburse the purchaser with interest over the term. Such a lease would be a *net lease*, under which all outgoings for the building or equipment leased are paid by the lessee. In many cases, this transaction was in substance a loan from the financial institution, and the lease a matter of form, which should not affect accounting for the asset in question.

Further, installment sales of equipment have increasingly taken the form of a lease with a bargain purchase option at the expiry of the term. Sale-and-leaseback financing and equipment sales in the form of leasing involve leases having sale or financing characteristics, and are called *capital leases*.

Finally, some financial analysts regarded the exclusion of leased properties from assets, and of obligations under leases from liabilities, as rendering the financial statements of leasing entities noncomparable with those of owning entities. This viewpoint was marked in *ARS No. 4* by John Myers.

Many critics of *Statement No. 13* support the general proposition that contracts which are in form leases but in substance purchases should be accounted for as purchases, and the lease obligation treated as an accounting liability. Mechanical rules to be applied in making such a determination, however, appear to be inconsistent with the application of professional judgment and to lead inevitably to avoidance measures on the part of both lessors and lessees. Thus, general criticisms of *Statement No. 13* include the following:

- The complexity of the statements and interpretations suggest that the authors did not possess a clear view of the field of leasing transactions. For example, it would have been useful to exempt from the scope of the standards any lease which has less than one year to run and is not part of a series of leases of the same property for a longer period of time.
- It is not clear what constitutes the asset and the liability under a lease; it is a right to use a property which is conveyed, and not the property itself.
- Converting rental expense into depreciation plus interest does not render expense determination less subjective.
- The detailed rules are obviously aimed at preventing avoidance of the application of the leasing standards; this in itself suggests that compliance will be largely voluntary.
- The "cookbook" rules provide management with many opportunities to allow the form of a transaction to affect net income in a desired direction.
- The disclosure provisions, while they are extremely complex, do not get to the root of the matter, which is whether future cash flows will cover future lease obligations.

The technical objections to the standards and interpretations are too numerous to be considered here. We may point to one of the problem areas, that of accounting for the lease of a building or a part of a building. Provisions of *Statement No. 13* in this area even conflict with other accounting standards; for example, a profit could be reported on leasing a building in a case where no profit could be reported on sale due to the down payment being too low.

The rules governing leveraged leases, which are also extremely complex, have increased the difficulty of administering such transactions. A leveraged lease involves three parties: a lessee, a long-term creditor, and a lessor. The creditor provides financing on a nonrecourse basis in an amount sufficient to provide the lessor with substantial financial leverage; the lessor obtains the tax benefits of ownership of the leased asset. The Statement provides the additional rule that the lease would be a direct financing lease disregarding the 90 percent of fair value criterion.

The lessor's net investment under a leveraged lease declines during the early years, increases as a consequence of reversal of the tax benefits, and is liquidated when the leased asset is sold at the termination of the lease. The Statement requires the lessor to recognize income throughout the period of the lease in a manner which produces a constant rate of return during the period in which net investment is positive and no return when it is negative. In effect, an internal rate of return is found for positive net cash flows; negative net cash flows are ignored. A computer program must be used to calculate rate of return and develop schedules for recording interest, income, and amortization.[11]

Obviously, in real life negative net cash flows cannot be ignored. Thus, a leveraged lease transaction must now be evaluated three ways:

1. Economic effect, which uses net present value techniques
2. Tax effect, which uses the provisions of the tax code
3. Accounting effect, which uses *Statement No. 13* as amended and interpreted

This is another example of accounting standard-setting having unforeseen economic consequences, and ignoring the complexities of the real world in which leasing is a viable alternative to purchasing in those cases where it is not simply a purchase in disguise. The boot and shoe industry, for example, has leased machinery from the United Shoe Machinery Company for over one hundred years because it is more economic and practical to lease than to buy. The fact that the machine was an asset of the USM Co. and, therefore, did not appear in the balance sheet of the shoe manufacturer did not seem confusing to analysts or financiers of that industry.

ACCOUNTING FOR PENSION COSTS AND BENEFITS AND FOR PENSION FUNDS

Variability in accounting for the cost of pension schemes led the Accounting Principles Board to issue *APB Opinion No. 8* in 1966, ostensibly to clarify a preference stated in *ARB 47* for accrual accounting.[12] *APBO 8* was based, in part, on the conclusions of *ARS 8*, "Accounting for the Cost of Pension Plans," published in 1965. Briefly, *APBO 8* required the use of actuarial cost methods in determining pension cost (expense) but permitted a measure lying between a minimum and a maximum and which fell short of true accrual accounting. In particular, *APBO 8* countenanced a forty-year period for amortization of unfunded vested benefits, and did not allow full recognition of the effects of increases or decreases in prior service cost arising out of changes in the terms of a pension plan. It also allowed deferral of recognition of actuarial losses (and gains) over a period which could extend to twenty years.

During the following decade, there was a substantial increase in the number and size of pension schemes in both the private and public sectors. Pension benefits were often granted employees as a substitute for immediate pay increases, one which would affect the income statement only gradually as a limited pension cost accrual took place under *APBO 8*. In addition, the Employment Retirement

Income Security Act of 1974 attempted to stop some of the more flagrant ways in which firms frustrated their employees' expectations, through bankruptcy, merger, voluntary termination of plans, and even fraud. ERISA (as it is known) and similar legislation in other countries had a minor effect on accounting for pension plans, which *FASB Interpretation No. 3* recognized without modifying *APBO 8* in any way.

There are five actuarial cost methods in current use for defined benefit plans, which fall into two categories: cost methods and benefit methods. Cost methods assume that the pension cost of each year of employee service is a proportional part of the present value of estimated future pension benefits. Benefit methods relate the cost of future pension benefits to current employment conditions. These methods can differ materially on such calculations as: timing of employer's contribution to the pension fund; recognition of pension expense; and accumulation of fund balances and liability for unfunded benefits.

FASB Statement No. 36, "Disclosure of Pension Information," amended *APBO 8* as an interim measure designed to introduce more comparability between firms in respect of pension scheme disclosures. It required the following:

- A statement that pension plans exist, and identification of employee groups covered
- A statement of accounting and funding policies
- The provision for pension cost (pension expense) for each period income statement presented
- Nature and effect of significant accounting matters, such as change in accounting method or circumstances affecting the plan
- For defined benefit plans covered by *FASB Statement No. 35* (see later), information about the actuarial values of vested and nonvested benefits, plan assets available to meet benefits, assumed rates of return used in making actuarial determinations, and the date at which this information was prepared. If these data are not available, the reasons for nondisclosure should be revealed.[13]

A Discussion Memorandum entitled "Employer's Accounting for Pensions and Other Postemployment Benefits" was published by the FASB in February 1981. Major issues, besides those which imply lack of comparability through use of different accounting and measurement methods, include the following:

- Disclosing the effect of inflation on a pension plan
- Accounting for unaccrued costs of providing pensions for employees of discontinued operations. Some companies have failed to accelerate accrual of such expenses following a shutdown, on the grounds that the obligation is of a long-term nature[14]

- Accounting for termination benefits, often substantial and rarely accrued. Many firms simply charge these payments to expense when the employee is terminated

Besides the accounting problems of the employer there are also serious accounting issues to be confronted by pension plans themselves, which frequently command very large asset positions. In addition, a desirable separation of enterprise management from plan management is sometimes not achieved, leading to the real danger that the enterprise will transfer its business failures (or even worse, those of the principal stockholders) to the plan in discharge of the funding obligation. These issues were addressed by *FASB Statement No. 35*, "Accounting and Reporting by Defined Benefit Pension Plans," which established standards of financial accounting and reporting for the annual financial statements of such plans, whether covered by ERISA or not.[15] This Statement did not *require* the preparation and publication of financial statements covering a plan; it merely specified what information must be disclosed *if* such statements are published. Such information should be useful in assessing a plan's present and future ability to pay benefits when due.

The annual financial statements of a plan shall include—

- A statement of net assets available for benefits as of the end of the plan year;
- A statement of changes during the year in net assets available;
- Information on the actuarial present value of accumulated plan benefits, which may be at the beginning or end of the plan year (in the former case, net assets at that date and change in net assets for the preceding year must be given);
- Information about the effects of factors affecting the year-to-year change in actuarial present value.

The Statement also laid down certain accounting principles on the accrual basis, requiring investments to be presented at fair value (current selling price) but operating assets at cost less accumulated depreciation. Changes in actuarial assumptions were to be viewed as changes in estimates, which permitted them to be deferred and amortized over long periods of time.

It is not possible in this space to give adequate coverage to this long and complex Statement, although it deserves special study as a first attempt to apply the accounting standard-setting process to what is in effect a trust fund. One observation may be permitted: the Statement assumes that current value of investments and actuarial present value of future benefits are the principal information requirements of plan beneficiaries and other interested parties. The essence of a pension plan, however, is the provision of a dated stream of future cash flows to beneficiaries, about which current or present value tells nothing. For example, a plan may have an expectation of cash flows starting in the year 2,000, the present value of which exceeds the present value of pension obligations starting in 1990. As in the case of lease obligations, a statement of year-by-year expected cash in- and outflows would be inestimably more valuable to the user than current or present values, however calculated.

Hopefully, *FASB Statement No. 35* is a first attempt to come to grips with the problem of accountability for pension funds, and to aid in the elimination of the abuses which often accompany such funds.

OIL AND GAS ACCOUNTING

The accounting problems of the petroleum industry have become the object of FASB and SEC attention since the energy crisis which started in 1974. For nearly fifty years there has been a real difference of opinion within the industry on a number of technical accounting questions; one of these is how to account for preproduction costs. These are expenditures incurred in order to find, acquire rights to, and develop the ability to produce from, underground reserves of oil and gas.

Practices within the industry are very diverse and constitute a spectrum rather than a dichotomy. At one extreme there are companies which expense all such expenditures with the exception of real property acquisition costs, which they capitalize in accordance with conventional rules concerning such costs. At the other extreme, there are companies which capitalize all but a few such expenditures on the grounds that these expenditures are equivalent to manufacturing costs and, therefore, should be aggregated to arrive at the cost of goods (oil or gas) available for sale.

Perhaps a majority of the largest oil companies, prior to 1974, utilized a method known as "successful efforts" which capitalized most of these preproduction expenditures and carried them forward until a determination could be made whether the object of the expenditures—a leased property or well—contained exploitable reserves of oil or gas. If it was determined that it did not, the object was called a "dry hole" and the accumulated expenditures written off to expense at that time. If it did, then the accumulated expenditures were transferred to a "producing properties" account, to be charged to expense over the period in which the oil or gas was produced by means of (in the United States at least) a unit of production depletion calculation.

A minority of the largest companies and perhaps as many as one-half of the smaller so-called independents utilized a method known as "full cost" which did not write off dry holes as discovered. Instead, all preproduction expenditures were accumulated either on a country-by-country basis, or by fields, which are regional deposits of fossil fuels. An upper limit of net realizable value was set for these "cost centers" and was found by calculating the present value of the reserves they represented and deducting therefrom the present value of future lifting costs, expenditures necessary to achieve production. The total capitalized costs in each cost center were then charged to expense in the period in which the oil and gas was produced by means of a unit of production depletion calculation.

It was widely believed that the effect of the coexistence of these dissimilar accounting methods was to render the financial statements of petroleum companies noncomparable. During the 1960s and 1970s, the debate was confined to the industry, and the American Petroleum Industry collected and published details of the accounting methods in use in the industry.[16] These publications revealed that differences were much wider than is suggested by the successful efforts/full cost dichotomy. By the beginning of the 1970s, the issue had been laid before the Accounting Principles Board, which found them so intractable that it could not issue an opinion.

The energy crisis focused public attention on the profits of oil and gas companies and on the difficulty of ascertaining the cost of a barrel of oil or an mcf of gas. As a result, the U.S. Congress mandated the SEC to determine a uniform method of making such cost calculations, and the SEC indicated to the FASB that it would issue accounting rules if the FASB did not act by the end of 1977.[17] (The FASB had previously issued *Statement No. 9* which required all oil and gas producers to use income tax allocation in respect of timing differences arising out of intangible drilling costs, without ruling on how to account for such costs.)[18] *FASB Statement No. 19* required a form of successful efforts accounting, slightly different from the method used by any of the companies using successful efforts but substantially different from the full cost method.[19]

The opponents of the successful efforts method brought pressure to bear on the United States government, and in 1978 the SEC published a docket, which included *Accounting Series Release No. 253*. This ASR prescribed that companies using the successful efforts method must follow *FASB Statement No. 19*, but the full cost method was an acceptable alternative. If the latter were used, it must follow prescribed methods, subsequently published in *ASR 257* and *258*. *ASR 253* also asserted that neither accounting method was capable of providing sufficient information on oil and gas reserves and their cost, and announced that the SEC would prescribe a new method, Reserve Recognition Accounting (RRA), to be published as a supplementary statement but, after a period of experimentation, to become the primary method for accounting for oil and gas production and sale. As was noted in chapter 8, RRA was recognized by the SEC in 1981 as unsuitable for financial statements, although the presentation of supplementary RRA information continued to be required.

Following the 1978 actions of the SEC, the FASB issued *Statement No. 25* suspending the application of *Statement No. 19* insofar as it prescribed successful efforts accounting.[20] *Statement No. 25* also rescinded the *Statement No. 19* definitions of reserves and physical quantities) required by *FASB Statement No. 19* to be published as supplementary information, not as an integral part of the financial statements. The method of accounting for oil and gas preproduction and production costs must be disclosed, together with certain other details of capitalized and expensed costs. Following the abandonment of RRA in 1981, the FASB announced that it would develop a comprehensive package of required reporting by oil and gas companies, but without considering the relative merits of successful efforts or full cost accounting.

This sequence of events is very instructive, as it reveals the following:

- The political element in the formulation of accounting standards.
- The dependence of the FASB upon the SEC, and the power of the latter in the accounting standard-setting arena.
- The selection of a false problem for resolution. Except in the first and last years of the life of an oil and gas company, use of the successful efforts or full cost method would not render financial statements less comparable than would any number of other accounting and reporting alternatives which might be used by the companies concerned.
- Lack of research—the debate would not have reached the point of confrontation had the parties involved informed themselves about the difficult issues which arise in the process of accounting for natural resources.
- Partial analysis of an accounting problem. None of the protagonists ever considered whether the unit of production depletion method was appropriate for foreign reserves subject to great political risks, or other accounting issues peculiar to the industry, such as how to account for oil and gas acquired by payment of income tax to a host government, rather than by direct purchase.
- Absence of a conceptual framework within which questions of capitalization and expensing can be resolved.
- Absence of an appreciation of the economic consequences of an accounting decision, or of any method whereby assertions of economic consequences could be determined. For example, many critics of *FASB Statement No. 19* argued that it would have the effect of reducing the amount of capital available to drill for oil and gas.
- The difference between financial statements and financial reporting, exemplified by requirements to provide certain information in the financial statements themselves, and other information outside those statements.

WHAT THE FUTURE HOLDS FOR ACCOUNTANTS

In the first edition of this book attention was directed to the weakness of the FASB's position and the poor quality of its output during the first years of its life. These factors were recognized by the FASB's trustees, and a 1978 study led to certain changes in the structure and methods of operation of the Board.

Unfortunately, these changes have not improved the situation. The FASB has been demonstrably weak in dealing with the SEC and in its failure to police its own standards, and the standards themselves have not improved in quality or significance. Nor is the FASB an inexpensive operation; it employs 100 persons, whereas the APB never employed more than ten.

If the FASB is in fact mainly responsible for technical improvements in accounting practices, under the direction of the SEC, then it would appear that its most significant defect has been a failure to study the economic consequences of its standards. To evaluate the economic impact of accounting standards would require—

- Identification of existing practices in a scientific manner;
- Assessment of the extent to which each is used, and by which kinds of firms;
- Assessment of the significance of these practices to the financial statements of the firms concerned;
- Evaluation of the effect of a new ruling on management's behavior and particularly its resource allocation decisions;
- Determination of the extent of opposition to change, and of political support of resistance to change.

In an article on the future of financial reporting, Dr. Robert Sprouse, a member of the FASB and a respected scholar, discussed four responses to the current system of financial reporting.[21] First come the reactionists (reactionaries) who represent arch-conservatism and are usually found in the ranks of the accountancy profession itself. They support the status quo and particularly the traditional emphasis on conservatism in valuation. They would, if possible, eliminate changing accounting methods if it were not possible to eliminate accounting alternatives, and they wish to see accounting standard-setting remain in the hands of the profession.

Next come the pragmatists, who occupy a middle ground by recognizing that some change is inevitable. They would be satisfied if the range of accounting alternatives were narrowed, and if similar businesses adopted the same accounting methods and reporting dates. A third group, the disciplinists, restrict the task of reducing available alternative accounting methods by placing it within a conceptual framework. They believe that such a framework would lead to consistent standards and also resolve accounting problems in the absence of promulgated standards.

Finally, the revolutionaries stand ready to take over should the others falter. They argue that the entire current system is faulty and should be scrapped. They are impatient with the progress which the FASB is making toward a conceptual framework, and often have their own, different frame of reference, such as economic theory. They want income statements which will directly improve investment decisions and lead to better capital allocation within the economy. Some hold the view that numerous financial statements should be presented, embracing historical cost, replacement cost, current market value, and present value of future net cash flows so that the user can pick and choose the data which will assist in the evaluation of performance. In recent years this group has become less vocal, disillusioned with their own lack of effectiveness as "shock troops" and with the lengthy time it takes to force professional associations to make even minor changes, such as modifying the audit certificate.

This analysis is significant because it failed to identify any constituency for corporate social accountability disclosures, or socio-economic accounting as it is sometimes called. The debates in which U.S. accountants engage have changed their focus only slightly over the years; Table 17-1 provides an interesting comparison of issues as perceived in 1950 and 1981.

TABLE 17-1 Comparison of Issues Affecting Accountants as Seen in 1950 and 1981

Thomas Henry Sanders	John C. Burton
1. What can best be expressed in accounts, and what outside, in statistical or narrative form	1. Declining importance of financial statements
2. Role of American Accounting Association in development of GAAP	2. Future-oriented reporting
3. Full disclosure of departures from GAAP	3. Liquidity disclosures
4. Tax and accounting depreciation in times of rising prices	4. Inflation accounting
5. Extension of matters covered by Accounting Research Bulletins and Accounting Releases; harmony between the two sources	5. Foreign currency translation
6. Pension costs	6. Pension costs
7. Development of GAAP	7. Municipal accounting
8. The underlying assumptions of accounting	

Sources: Sanders, Thomas Henry, "An Analysis of the Forces which Are Shaping the Future of Accountancy," *Journal of Accountancy*, October 1950, pp. 282-9. Burton, John C., "Emerging Trends in Financial Reporting," *Journal of Accountancy*, July 1981, pp. 54-66.

CORPORATE SOCIAL ACCOUNTABILITY

In the United States, corporate social reporting has not affected the financial statements themselves. Public relations personnel have often taken the lead in preparing such material for the annual report. Questions have been raised about the objectivity of this information, its relation to the financial statements themselves, and its potential auditability. It has remained largely voluntary; the SEC requires disclosure of material matters which could affect capital needs, operating costs, and litigation. The SEC's preoccupation with environmental issues indicates one source of the pressures forcing it to act.

In Europe the situation is different. In 1976 the OECD issued extensive guidelines covering corporate morality and social disclosure. The EEC has addressed these issues in its Directives on corporate reporting. France has adopted legislation specifying the content of social reports, and German companies have voluntarily taken the lead in providing such information. In marked contrast to the U.S. experience, European companies place great importance on labor-related information about employment, salaries, social costs, and benefits to consumers; and many link this information with performance reporting as reflected in the income statement.

It is widely believed that progress in the United States will not be achieved until research has been conducted in such areas as (a) measurement of social costs and benefits; (b) behavioral factors such as capital allocation decisions and employee and consumer satisfaction; and (c) macroeconomic effects of preferred policies. However, involvement of private and public accountants in areas outside of the traditional fields of financial and managerial accounting was indicated by the responses of partners in the eight largest CPA firms to the question: "To the best of your knowledge, in which of the following areas has your firm been involved in social program engagements?"[22]

RESPONSES

Area	No.	Percent
Education	28	88
Welfare programs (including programs to aid disadvantaged groups)	26	81
Health	24	75
Transportation	23	72
Urban, rural, and/or regional planning and economic development	21	66
Housing	21	66
Crime prevention and law enforcement	19	59
Recreation	16	50
Pollution abatement and control	10	31

These data do not begin to reflect the extent to which accountants are engaged in public interest accounting or socially desirable activities outside the field of accounting itself. Many accountants believe, however, that the potential contributions which accountants can make to the solution of social problems is very great and hardly yet begun.

An increasing awareness of their social responsibilities on the part of business firms has led to the use of annual and interim reports for disclosures of the efforts being made by firms in this area, with which accountants have become increasingly involved. This involvement is reflected by the publication of the AICPA's *Statement on Auditing Standards 8*, "Other Information in Documents Containing Audited Financial Statements," in December 1975. This statement requires the auditor to familiarize himself with such disclosures and to disassociate himself from the financial statements if he concludes the other information to be false or misleading.

The most extensive disclosures in the United States concern environmental matters such as conservation and pollution control, equal opportunity employment practices and other personnel matters, product safety, education, and involvement in community projects. Comparable developments in other countries include the *Social Report* which German companies now provide in their annual reports. The social report describes the contributions which the company has made to the economy in the form of payments to suppliers, employees, and governments, and quantifies the benefits which employees have derived from the company during the period covered. Emphasis on employees is consistent with the modern view of the importance of the worker to society, both as producer and consumer.

For 1975, the German subsidiary of Royal Dutch/Shell, Deutsche Shell A.G., entitled its annual report *Geschäftsbericht/Sozialbericht* (Annual Report/Social Report). This report attempted to integrate the two concepts by identifying the company's business and social goals and by quantifying expenditures for the latter. The extensive changes which this policy introduced make the German Shell 1975 annual report required reading for those interested in such developments. The German subsidiary of Mobil Oil Corporation, Mobil Oil A.G., also reported in great detail on social aspects of its operations and provided the interesting statement summarized in Figure 17-1.

Much of the interest in socioeconomic accounting stems from the ideas of David Linowes, who defined it as "the application of accounting in the field of the social sciences."[23] Linowes' views were formed, in part, by his experiences as adviser to governments of developing countries, and it appears that the generalization of accounting methods is an even more urgent problem in developing countries. Enthoven has categorized this problem as a three-way extension: *horizontal*, referring to the sectorization of the economy; *vertical*, referring to the interrelationships of costs and benefits; and

FIGURE 17-1
Business Output and Value Added in DM Millions

	1975	1974	Change in %
Sales	4168.5	3937.6	+ 5.9
Other revenues	171.5	280.4	-38.8
Total output	4340.0	4218.0	+ 2.9
Purchases from suppliers	3180.4	2977.7	+ 6.8
Expenditures for the environment, research and development of energy, including investing for the year	214.5	110.4	+94.3
Total purchases	3394.9	3088.1	+ 9.9
Value added	945.1	1129.9	-16.4
Distribution of value added			
To the State (taxes)	710.9	749.0	- 5.1
To the financiers (interest)	38.5	43.7	-11.9
To stockholders (dividends)	38.0	180.0	-78.9
To the corporation (retained)	2.0	9.5	-78.9
To employees	155.7	147.7	+ 5.4
Total	945.1	1129.9	
Payments to employees			
Wages and salaries	113.4	100.2	+13.2
Compulsory social charges	11.9	9.7	+22.7
Pensions	22.9	31.9	-28.2
Voluntary social charges of which	7.5	5.9	+27.1
Meals	2.1	1.6	+31.3
Savings scheme	1.5	1.3	+15.4
Training	1.1	0.9	+22.2
Medical and Sports	0.3	0.3	—
Other	2.5	1.7	+47.1

Source: Mobil Oil A. G. Annual Report (translation by author).

time, referring to the need for a prospective as well as a retrospective mode.[24]

The critical step which must be taken before the input-output model known as an account can be used for the solution of social problems is the measurement of the output function. There is no equivalent outside of business of the measurement we call "revenue" in business operations. *Cost/benefit* analysis is a contemporary term for what was originally thought of as *cost/performance* analysis, and the translation of performance as benefit has not helped to clarify the nature of the measurement intended. This problem has been discussed extensively by public finance theorists in recent years, and the absence of a measure of social outputs constitutes the principal obstacle in the way of developing a theory of distribution of goods and services produced by the public sector.

As an indication of interest in English-speaking countries, the Directors' Review section of the 1979 annual report of The Burmah Oil Company Ltd. (U.K.) contained the following statement.

Statement of added value (£m.)

Added value	**1979**	**1978**
Sales net of duties	1,087	985
Less: cost of materials and services purchased	814	783
Value added by trading	273	202
Investment income	5	5
Total added value	278	207
Shared as follows		
Reinvested in the business – depreciation, depletion amortization and retentions	64	27
Employees		
wages, salaries, pension fund contributions, and other benefits	160	152
Government		
taxation on profits	23	9
External providers of funds		
interest on borrowing (net)	20	17
minorities' share of profits	1	1
	21	18
Stockholders		
dividends	10	1
	278	207

A wider concept of socioeconomic accounting results from the view that a new conceptual framework is required for replacing the accounting methods characteristic of a capitalistic society. It is pointed out by those who hold this view that contemporary accounting practices are dominated by the information needs of shareholders and creditors and of the managers who serve the former. In a society dedicated to improvement of the welfare of all its members, to the goals of worker satisfaction and consumer justice, these dominant needs are anachronistic. An information system must satisfy the information needs of workers and external consumer groups as well as those of capitalists, and managers should serve all interested parties and not one group to the exclusion of all others. Accounting must be adapted to provide measures of success in achieving more goals than just profitability.

It is not clear how these goals can be quantified under a common denominator such as money. They include the humanization of labor, occupational safety, job protection, elimination of discrimination, increasing employee benefits, worker participation in decision making, environmental protection, product safety, price regulation, and the production of public, as well as private, goods. However, some steps which must be taken to implement these radical changes are already visible. They are accounting for social costs and benefits and accounting for human resources.

Economists distinguish between two kinds of cost: internal and external. Internal costs are social sacrifices for which the firm can be made to pay, either because it can acquire the resources in question only by operations in markets, or because the government can levy a tax on the firm for use of the public good in question. External costs are all other social sacrifices, which fall on other firms or on society in general. If a firm emits noxious fumes which cause suffering to the residents of a nearby neighborhood, or if it produces a raw material which is dangerous to the user, the sacrifices in question are external costs from the viewpoint of the firm, although internal to the society of which all these entities form part.

There are, of course, many benefits or firm outputs for which the firm cannot demand payment. Typically, an employer of labor will provide workers with transferable skills, improve the tax base for the entire community, attract communications which would not otherwise be made available, and create a host of external benefits which probably exceed in value the sum of external costs. Although the socioeconomic viewpoint is consumer oriented, the measurement of social benefits has not been extensively discussed, leading to the inference that the motives of those who espouse this viewpoint may sometimes be political rather than social.

Having said this, however, it must be observed that the development of accounting has always been toward embracing wider sets of observations, and accounting for social costs is already a fact in some firms and does not present any particular problems. Accounting for social benefits is in a different category because of the necessity to identify a single group having a homogeneous value system as a prerequisite for all such valuations. It may be that this singular application of the doctrine of conservatism will always be a feature of accounting. The development of indicators outside the accounting system is essentially a statistical problem, comparable with the measurement of earnings per share, with which many accountants will be prepared to grapple. This does not, however, transform it into an accounting problem.

Whether or not socioeconomic accounting benefits business firms directly, by reducing their cost of capital, is an interesting question; one research project using efficient market methodology claimed that the market values social disclosure positively, and asserted that a portfolio of securities of disclosing firms outperformed portfolios of firms that did not make such disclosures.[25]

HUMAN RESOURCE ACCOUNTING

The 1960s saw the birth of a new idea in accounting, that human resources should be accounted for as assets.[26] It should be pointed out that this does not state that human resources should be accounted for in the same way as other resources; the idea that human beings involve accounting entities in obligations has not yet been considered by human resource accounting theorists.

The initiative for this development came from a management scientist named Rensis Likert, Director of the Institute for Social Research of The University of Michigan. Likert observed that many management decisions resulting in short-run labor cost savings were associated with subsequent losses, either through the deteriorating morale of the remaining workers or through subsequent expenses to rebuild the labor force. This led him to hypothesize that if human resources were accounted for as assets, managers would not be so ready to dispose of them to improve liquidity.

Initially, cost-based allocation methods were proposed, as in the R.G. Barry Corporation. Barry was a manufacturing firm in Ohio, and three researchers from the University of Michigan worked on preparing financial statements for the corporation which included human resource accounting.[27] The assets were recorded at acquisition cost, including recruiting, hiring, training, and development expenditures. Cost was amortized to periods in a manner similar to depreciation calculations, and skills made obsolete or lost through termination were written off when the fact was established. The R.G. Barry Corporation published supplementary statements incorporating human resource accounting for several years, but the recession of the 1970s saw the suspension of this practice, although the statements would have shown the effects of layoffs, terminations, and other management actions designed to protect liquidity.

The accounting firm of Touche Ross & Co. in Canada has attempted to construct a different form of human resource accounting, based on opportunity cost concepts. In this case, opportunity cost was defined as estimated billings lost when the employee was not producing chargeable time. It will not surprise the reader to learn that this model drew attention to the high value of a CPA firm's partners.[28]

Other suggested forms of human resource accounting include a replacement cost model (Flamholtz)[29] and income value models based upon capitalizing future net receipts or employee earnings (Hermanson; Lev and Schwartz).[30] Economic value models have been tested experimentally at several offices of public accounting firms in the United States. The most significant development is the reported attempt in recent years by corporations of the size of American Telephone & Telegraph, Texas Instruments, and General Telephone and Electric (GTE) to implement accounting subsystems through which managers are held responsible for the company's investments in human resources.

The theoretical underpinnings of human resource accounting are, to say the least, shaky. Accountants have never distinguished between human and other resources; slaves were carried as business assets when slavery was legal, and sporting corporations such as football franchises capitalize amounts paid for player contracts. Advances to employees and liabilities for wages and expenses are included as a matter of course. The cost of labor services is as much a problem as the cost of, say, leased premises, and only in rare cases does the amount charged to the income statement correspond with the amount paid as wages for the same period.

Why, then, should human resources be accounted for in a special manner? It is possible that we are again in the presence of the labor theory of value, that most perverse and resilient of paradoxes. In Marxist terms, the value of a commodity is determined by the labor time required to produce it. The Marxist explanation of profit is that it occurs solely through exploitation of the labor power of the workers. The future net receipts or excess earnings referred to in the economic value models are Marx's surplus labor value and the sole source of profit. Hence, the effect of human resource accounting is to allocate subjective goodwill to the workers from whom it originates.

The failure of the labor theory of value in economics is only one of the arguments against human resource accounting. The principal weakness is the assumption that, in the allocation of the joint product of labor and capital, labor will get less than its full share. It is at least arguable that, during the last hundred years, labor has obtained not only its share but also most of the share which should have accrued to capital; hence the contemporary phenomenon of "profitless prosperity." This observation is consistent with modern wage theory and, if true, means that the value of human resources is an asset to the labor force and not to the firms which employ labor. While being chargeable to the firm's customers, the value of human resources is chargeable in the first instance to the firm itself. Insofar as the firm has contractual rights to the worker's services, we are dealing with an executory contract which, if accounted for, produces *both an asset and a liability*.

Using the simpler present value method of human resource valuation, the error lies in expressing value to the firm as:

$$V=\sum_{t=r}^{T}\frac{I(t)}{(1-r)^{t-r}}$$

Where $I(t)$ = annual earnings to retirement and T = retirement age

This is value *to the employee*; if there is any value *to the firm* it would be expressed as:

$$V=\sum_{t=r}^{T}\frac{[E(t)-I(t)]}{(1-r)^{t-r}}$$

Where $E(t)$ = the annual contribution to the firm made by the employee and

$I(t)$ = the employee's earnings as in the previous equation.

Given the strength of contemporary unionism and the likelihood that any such value to the firm would quickly become known to the workers involved in its generation, it is obvious that an asset of this kind, once found, would not survive beyond the next balance sheet date.

APPEARANCE AND REALITY

At the beginning of this book we drew attention to the necessity to distinguish between percepts and concepts. At the end, we feel obliged to restate this necessity in terms of the conflict between the appearance of things and their reality, which is a constant feature of the human condition.

Accounting theory attempts to bring order into a complex and confused set of observations by placing them in the context of a framework or system within which they may be explained. What it cannot do is to eliminate the complexity and confusion of the observations themselves. Thus, although there should not be any conflict between theory and practice, between the logical and the empirical, the truth of this statement escapes demonstration. It must be accepted on faith alone.

How does the real world conform to the image which the accounting theorist has of it? The answer must be: not very well. Participants in the process of producing goods and services are not always rational in the sense that their actions are aimed at maximizing output for a given input, or minimizing inputs for a specified output. Many—perhaps most—investment decisions are not influenced to any considerable degree by return on investment considerations. Government intervention, family relationships, individual human weaknesses, all affect business behavior to a marked extent, often in ways inconsistent with the accountant's view of how it should behave.

Nor is the accountant himself free from this discrepancy between appearance and reality. We may cite the practice of expensing individually minor items of equipment which, over a period of time, may add up to a material amount. Or of consolidating, or equity-accounting, corporate accounts covering different periods of time, ending on different dates. Or of combining productive assets having different economic lives for the purpose of calculating group depreciation. To examine the composition of the aggregates reported in financial statements as assets, liabilities, revenues, and expenses is a sobering experience for anyone dedicated to uniform accounting principles.

The predilection of standard-setting institutions in the United States for specifying accounting method in some detail can be seen to be defective when these differences between appearance and reality are taken into account. It may also serve to undermine the public accountant's authority and, thus, professional responsibility, by placing him in the position of insisting on a standardized response to an accounting problem of little significance, while remaining flexible on issues involving material amounts. Materiality, in this context, is dependent upon the statistical concept of the significant digit: net income of $10,732,484 means "more or less $10 million" and may mean something quite different if arrived at after charging depreciation of $50 million.

Three philosophical observations underlie the viewpoint of the author of this book: all valuation is subjective; all accounting allocations are incorrigible; individuals must make decisions in the face of an unknown tomorrow. Accounting has developed as a sophisticated and consistent response to the problems presented by these three observations; it has served society well, and the many efforts to extend its applicability indicate that this service is acknowledged widely. Accounting standard-setters should take great care not to weaken this powerful instrument of social equity, particularly by the pronouncement of ambiguous, or even contradictory, standards. After all, it is preferable to have to function with contradictory practices than to pay homage to contradictory principles.

ENDNOTES

1. Most, Kenneth S., "The Value of Inventories," *Journal of Accounting Research*, Spring 1967, pp. 39-50.
2. See also Dasburg, John H. and C. Richard Morehead, "Can GAAP Still Support Inventory Valuation After Thor?" *Journal of Accountancy*, October 1979, pp. 68-76.
3. The complicated tax rules governing the use of LIFO in the United States are found in the Internal Revenue Code, Section 472 and the regulations which have been issued thereunder. These regulations have been substantially modified during the period 1979-81.
4. Sunder, Shyam, "Stock Price and Risk Related to Accounting Changes in Inventory Valuation," *The Accounting Review*, April 1975, pp. 305-15. This example of efficient market research should be read with the observations in chapter 3 in mind.
5. See *ARB 43*, Ch. 3A, as amended, para. .09.
6. *FASB Statement No. 12*, "Accounting for Certain Marketable Securities," Financial Accounting Standards Board, 1975.
7. Notgaard, Corinne T. and D. Jacque Grinnell, "New Accounting and Reporting Requirements for Marketable Equity Securities," *Michigan CPA*, September-October 1976, pp. 33-38.
8. *APBO 5*, "Reporting of Leases in Financial Statements of Lessee," (1964); *APBO 7*, "Accounting for Leases in Financial Statements of Lessors," (1966); *APBO 27*, "Accounting for Lease Transactions by Manufacturer or Dealer Lessors," (1972); *APBO 31*, "Disclosure of Lease Commitments by Lessees," (1973).
9. *FASB Statement No. 13*, "Accounting for Leases," Financial Accounting Standards Board, 1976.
10. *Accounting for Leases, FASB Statement No. 13 as amended and interpreted through May 1980*, Financial Accounting Standards Board, May 1980.

11. Grant, Edward B. and Raymond C. Witt, "A Look at Leveraged Leases under FAS. No. 13," *Management Accounting*, February 1979, pp. 49-52.
12. *APBO 8*, "Accounting for the Cost of Pension Plans," (1966).
13. *FASB Statement No. 36*, "Disclosure of Pension Information," Financial Accounting Standards Board, May 1980.
14. Best, Lawrence C. and Paul A. Gerwirtz, "Plant Closings: The Pension Cost Controversy," *Financial Executive*, November 1980, pp. 12-19.
15. *FASB Statement No. 35*, "Accounting and Reporting by Defined Benefit Plans," Financial Accounting Standards Board, March 1980.
16. American Petroleum Institute, *Report on Certain Petroleum Industry Practices—1974*, Washington, D.C.: American Petroleum Institute. It is remarkable that two of the largest companies using the full cost method, Texaco and Occidental, were excluded from this survey.
17. The Energy Policy and Conservation Act of 1975, Public Law 94-163, Title V, Section 503 grants power to the SEC to prescribe rules for accounting by oil and gas producers and also permits the SEC to rely on accounting practices developed by the Financial Accounting Standards Board.
18. *FASB Statement No. 9*, "Accounting for Income Taxes—Oil and Gas Producing Companies (An Amendment of APB Opinions Nos. 11 and 23," Financial Accounting Standards Board, 1975.
19. *FASB Statement No. 19*, "Financial Accounting and Reporting by Oil and Gas Producing Companies," Financial Accounting Standards Board, 1977.
20. *FASB Statement No. 25*, "Suspension of Certain Accounting Requirements for Oil and Gas Producing Companies (Amendment of FASB Statement No. 19)," Financial Accounting Standards Board, 1979.
21. Sprouse, Robert T., "Prospects for Progress in Financial Reporting," *Financial Analysts Journal*, September 1979, pp. 79-85.
22. American Accounting Association Committee on Measures of Effectiveness for Social Programs, "Report of the Committee on Measures of Effectiveness for Social Programs," *The Accounting Review, Supplement to Vol. XLVII, 1972, pp. 337-96.*
23. Linowes, David F., *"Socio-Economic Accounting," Journal of Accountancy*, November 1968, pp. 37-42.
24. Enthoven, Adolf J.H., *Accountancy and Economic Development Policy*, New York: American Elsevier Publishing Co. Inc., 1973.
25. Anderson, John C. and Alan W. Frankle, "Voluntary Social Reporting: An Iso-Beta Portfolio Analysis," *The Accounting Review*, July 1980, pp. 467-79.
26. The pioneer publication was Roger H. Hermanson's *Accounting for Human Assets*, Occasional Paper No. 14, Michigan State University, 1964.
27. Brummet, R. Lee, Eric G. Flamholtz and William C. Pyle, *Human Resource Accounting: Development and Implementation in Industry*, Ann Arbor, Mich.: Foundation for Research on Human Behavior, 1969.
28. Alexander, Michael O., "Investments in People," *Canadian Chartered Accountant*, July 1971, pp. 38-45.
29. Flamholtz, Eric G., "A Model for Human Resource Valuation: A Stochastic Process with Service Rewards," *The Accounting Review*, April 1971, pp. 253-67; "Toward a Theory of Human Resource Value in Formal Organizations," *The Accounting Review*, October 1972, pp. 666-78.
30. Hermanson, op. cit.; Lev, Baruch and Aba Schwartz, "On the Use of the Economic Concept of Human Capital in Financial Statements," *The Accounting Review*, January 1971, pp. 103-18.

SELECTED ADDITIONAL READINGS

General

Benston, George J., "Accounting Standards in the United States and the United Kingdom: Their Nature, Causes and Consequences," *Vanderbilt Law Review*, January 1975, pp. 235-268.

Briloff, Abraham J., *Unaccountable Accounting*, New York: Harper & Row, 1972. *More Debits than Credits: The Burnt Investor's Guide to Financial Statements*, New York: Harper & Row, 1976.

Buckley, John W., "The FASB and Impact Analysis," *Management Accounting*, April 1976, pp. 13-17.

Garber, Dean and Bill Jarnagin, "The FASB, Eliminator of Managed Earnings," *Financial Analysts Journal*, March 1979, pp. 64-72.

Kirk, Donald J., "The FASB: Serving its Constituency," *Management Accounting*, June 1976, pp. 11-14, 25.

May, Robert G. and Gary L. Sundem, "Research for Accounting Policy: An Overview," *The Accounting Review*, October 1976, pp. 747-763.

Sprouse, Robert T., "Prospects for Progress in Financial Reporting," *Financial Analysts Journal*, September 1979, pp. 79-85.

Williams, Thomas H. and Charles H. Griffin, "On the Nature of Empirical Verification in Accounting," *Abacus*, December 1969, pp. 157-178.

LIFO

Keister, Orville, "LIFO and Inflation," *Management Accounting*, May 1975, pp. 27-31.

Moonitz, Maurice, "The Case Against LIFO as an Inventory Pricing Formula," *Journal of Accountancy*, June 1953, pp. 682-690.

Slocum, Elliott L. and Kathryn C. Buckner, "LIFO—A Problem Child," *Atlanta Economic Review*, July/August 1976, pp. 17-22.

Marketable Securities

Blum, James D. and Herbert L. Jensen, "Accounting for Marketable Securities in Accordance with FASB Statement No. 12," *Management Accounting*, September 1978, pp. 33-41.

Financial Accounting Standards Board, *Statement No. 12*, "Accounting for Certain Marketable Securities," Financial Accounting Standards Board, 1975.

Norgaard, Corinne T. and D. Jacque Grinnell, "New Accounting and Reporting Requirements for Marketable Equity Securities," *Michigan CPA*, September-October 1976, pp. 33-38.

Leases

Financial Accounting Standards Board, *Accounting for Leases, FASB Statement No. 13 as amended and interpreted through May 1980*, Financial Accounting Standards Board, May 1980.

Financial Accounting Standards Board, *Research Report*, "The Economic Effects on Lessees of FASB Statement No. 13, Accounting for Leases," Financial Accounting Standards Board, 1981.

Grant, Edward B. and Raymond C. Witt, "A Look at Leveraged Leases under FASB 13," *Management Accounting*, February 1979, pp. 49-52.

Accounting for Pension Funds and Costs

Accounting Principles Board, *APB Opinion No. 8*, AICPA, 1968.

Financial Accounting Standards Board, *Statement No. 35*, "Accounting and Reporting by Defined Benefit Plans," Financial Accounting Standards Board, 1980.

Financial Accounting Standards Board, *Statement No. 36*, "Disclosure of Pension Information," Financial Accounting Standards Board, 1980.

Financial Accounting Standards Board, *Accounting for Pensions by Employers*, Financial Accounting Standards Board, 1980.

Oil and Gas Accounting

Adkerson, Richard C., "Can reserve recognition accounting work?"*Journal of Accountancy*, September 1979, pp. 72-81.

Connor, Joseph E., "Reserve recognition accounting: Fact or Fiction?" *Journal of Accountancy*, September 1979, pp. 92-99.

Cooper, Kerry, Steven M. Flory, Steven D. Grossman, and John C. Groth, "Reserve recognition accounting: A proposed disclosure framework," *Journal of Accountancy*, September 1979, pp. 82-91.

Financial Accounting Standards Board, *Statement No. 19*, "Financial Accounting and Reporting by Oil and Gas Producing Companies," Financial Accounting Standards Board, 1977, and *Statement No. 25*, "Suspension of Certain Accounting Requirements for Oil and Gas Producing Companies," Financial Accounting Standards Board, 1979.

Ijiri, Yuji, "Oil and gas accounting: Turbulence in financial reporting," *Financial Executive*, August 1979, pp. 18-27.

Socioeconomic Accounting

Cook, James S. Jr., Lewis F. Davidson and Charles H. Smith, "Social Costs and Private Accounting," *Abacus*, December 1976, pp. 87-99.

Enthoven, Adolf J.H., *Accountancy and Economic Development Policy*, New York: American Elsevier Publishing Co. Inc., 1973.

Estes, Ralph, *Accounting and Society*, Los Angeles, Calif., Melville Publishing Company, 1973.

Ramanathan, Kavasseri V., "Theory of Corporate Social Accounting," *The Accounting Review*, July 1976, pp. 516-528.

Schreuder, Hein, "Employees and the Corporate Social Report: The Dutch Case," *The Accounting Review*, April, 1981, pp. 294-308.

Human Resource Accounting

Brummet, R. Lee, Eric G. Flamholtz, and William C. Pyle, "Human Resource Measurement—A Challenge for Accountants," *The Accounting Review*, April 1968, pp. 217-224.

Flamholtz, Eric G., "A Model for Human Resource Valuation: A Stochastic Process with Service Rewards," *The Accounting Review*, April 1971. "Toward a Theory of Human Resource Value in Formal Organizations," *The Accounting Review*, October 1972, pp. 666-678.

Lev, Baruch and Aba Schwartz, "On the Use of the Economic Concept of Human Capital in Financial Statements," *The Accounting Review*, January 1971, pp. 103-118.

The Future

Brown, Victor H., "The economic impact of financial accounting standards," *Financial Executive*, September 1979, pp. 32-39.

Carmichael, Douglas Roy, "What does the independent auditor's opinion really mean?" *Journal of Accountancy*, November 1974, pp. 83-7.

Linowes, David F., "Communications Satellites: Their Impact on the CPA," *Journal of Accountancy*, September 1981, pp. 58-66.

Case 17-1 Crude Oil and Product Exchanges

Oil companies frequently exchange inventory with other oil companies to facilitate refining and marketing operations. For example, a company which is short of crude for a refinery in Europe may exchange a cargo of oil with a company which needs crude for a refinery in the United States. This may simply involve rerouting two tanker ships. Alternatively, a company which is short of regular gasoline in New York, but has a surplus of unleaded in Iowa, may exchange that unleaded for regular with another company which has the opposite problem.

The companies involved in such an exchange adjust inventory quantities, taking the difference in standard cost to a "loss or gain" account; sometimes one company will require a payment from the other because the values of the two quantities are different. The Internal Revenue Service, however, refuses to allow this treatment. The IRS contends that one of the cornerstones of the existence of inventory is the element of title; since in the usual case one of the parties (or both) has not yet obtained delivery, the oil or product is a receivable, not inventory.

1. Why is this issue important to the IRS? To the oil companies' auditors responsible for reporting on the companies' financial statements?
2. Is there any part of GAAP relevant to the solution of this problem?
3. How can the FASB's conceptual framework support the position of the oil companies on this question?

Case 17-2 Social Responsibility and Social Demands

The following quotation appeared in a newspaper article in 1981:

> During the lean years of the 1970s, many financially strapped states and depressed older cities were hard put to find money either for maintenance or for new construction. With teachers, welfare recipients, garbage collectors and senior citizens all expecting higher salaries or more services, government priorities tipped toward meeting social demands.

1. What is the meaning of the word *social* as used in this context?
2. Explain the problem to which this quotation draws attention, and discuss how the meaning of *social* contributes to the underlying factors.
3. What can accountants do to help?

Case 17-3 Seven Major Oil Companies

The fact that oil companies use different accounting principles and methods to account for apparently similar operations has been extensively discussed in recent years. This was one of the factors responsible for Accounting Research Study No. 11 (The Field Report), which was intended, at the time, to lay the groundwork for a pronouncement of the Accounting Principles Board on this subject.[1] The committee on Extractive Industries of the Accounting Principles Board published a report in 1973, entitled *Accounting and Reporting Practices in the Oil and Gas Industry*, which gave the history of APB involvement in this problem and drew attention to one particular aspect of it, the "full-cost" versus "successful efforts" controversy. The report stated that "all attempts by the Committee to find the one theoretically best method of accounting in the oil and gas industry met with vehement resistance from either one or both of the factions supporting the alternative methods of accounting. The results of the aborted attempts to find one method of accounting also makes it clear that the major issue is whether or not the two basic methods of accounting for the oil and gas industry should be allowed as equally acceptable alternatives."

The intention of the APB was to narrow the range of alternative accounting practices within the industry, presumably to improve the suitability of oil companies' financial statements for financial analysis. This point has also been the subject of several comments in the financial press.[2] A leading authority on petroleum accounting, Stanley Porter, has put the problem in a wider perspective and drawn a conflicting conclusion:

> Variations in the accounting treatment accorded apparently similar transactions are common to all phases of the accounting for petroleum exploration, development and production operations. Differences resulting from these variations may each have a significant and material effect for a small and/or non-integrated producer, but in the matter of comparison between major companies most of these differences will not materially affect the financial statements.[3]

[1]*Financial Reporting in the Extractive Industries*, An Accounting Research Study by Robert E. Field, American Institute of Certified Public Accountants, 1969.

[2]See for example, "The Numbers Game," *Forbes*, December 1, 1973, pp. 49-50.

[3]Porter, Stanley P., *Petroleum Accounting Practices*, New York: McGraw-Hill Book Company, 1965, p. 322.

One of the classical techniques of financial analysis, designed to render the financial statements of different size companies comparable, is to convert the statements to common size. This involves expressing each item as a percentage of sales (income statement); total assets (balance sheet); sources of funds (statement of changes in financial position).

In order to test the hypothesis, that the existence of very different methods of accounting for oil and gas preproduction costs leads to financial statements which are noncomparable, you have been provided with the common size income statements, balance sheets, and statements of changes in financial position of seven major U.S. oil companies (exhibits I-III on pages 544-546). These financial statements are for the year 1972, before the energy crisis directed attention to these differences and before the SEC and the FASB sought to eliminate them.

The exhibits do not reveal the names of the seven oil companies, which are identified by the letters A through G. Appendix A lists the (abbreviated, but recognizable) names of the seven companies, and describes their 1972 accounting practices in respect of exploration, development, and related expenditures.

1. Identify each of the seven companies designated by letters A through G, using the differences in accounting practices as a guide.
2. Do the common size financial statements indicate the use of different accounting methods other than in relation to oil and gas preproduction costs? Are they more or less significant than the full-cost/successful efforts differences?

APPENDIX A

EXTRACTS FROM 1972 ANNUAL REPORTS' NOTES ON ACCOUNTING POLICY REGARDING EXPLORATION, DEVELOPMENT, AND RELATED EXPENSES

The annual reports of major oil companies are available to the public by simply writing to the headquarters office of the company. The following extracts from the notes to the financial statements in the 1972 annual reports cover the treatment of exploration, development, and related expenses.

TEXACO

"Depreciation,* depletion, and amortization of properties, plant, and equipment related to exploration and producing activities are determined on the unit-of-production basis by applying the ratio of produced oil and gas to estimated recoverable oil and gas reserves.

With respect to exploration activities, the company capitalizes lease acquisition costs and costs related to the exploration for and development of oil and gas reserves, with the principal exceptions of expenditures in the U.S. for lease rentals and for intangible drilling costs applicable to dry holes. As a result, finding and development costs are allocated to the periods in which revenue is recognized as the oil and gas reserves are produced and sold."

*[For operations other than exploration and producing, depreciation is provided generally on the group plan with the depreciation rates based on estimated useful life applied to the cost of each class of property.]

EXXON

"Costs of productive wells, both tangible and intangible, as well as productive acreage are capitalized and amortized on the unit of production method. Costs of that portion of undeveloped acreage likely to be unproductive, based largely on historical experience, are amortized over the period of exploration. Minimum work commitments are capitalized to the extent such expenditures relate to the acquisition of acreage expected to be productive; otherwise they are treated as nonproductive acreage costs. Other exploratory expenditures, including Geophysical costs, Dry hole costs and annual lease rentals, are charged to income as incurred."

GULF

Exploration & Production Expenditures

"In the petroleum industry the most significant accounting policy relates to the method of accounting for the exploration, drilling, and equipping of producing oil and gas wells. In this regard, the company's capitalization policy follows the 'successful effort' concept except that successful G & G costs are not capitalized. All exploratory costs, including G & G costs, annual delay rentals on undeveloped leases and all dry hole costs are charged to income as incurred.

Depreciation, Depletion, Amortization, & Retirements

"Provisions for depreciation and depletion of base and well equipment, intangible drilling costs applicable to productive wells, and undeveloped and developed leasehold costs represent charges per unit of production based on the estimated proved and developed oil and gas reserves."

ATLANTIC RICHFIELD

Exploratory & Development Costs

"Costs of drilling exploratory wells are expensed as incurred, under the probabilities indicated by experience, but capitalized and credited to expense if the well proves to be productive. Costs of drilling development wells, under the expectation of productivity, are initially capitalized but charged to expense if the well is determined to be unproductive. In general other exploratory costs, including geological and geophysical costs and lease rentals, are charged to expense as incurred.

Intangible Development Costs

"Intangible development costs applicable to productive wells are capitalized and amortized on the unit-of-production method."

PHILLIPS

Exploratory Costs

"Undeveloped oil and gas leaseholds are capitalized and that portion of the costs applicable to properties which it is estimated will be surrendered is amortized over the estimated holding period. Dry holes and undeveloped lease rentals are expensed. Geological and Geophysical costs resulting in the acquisition or retention of leases are capitalized with the remainder being expensed."

GETTY

Leasehold Costs

"Undeveloped leasehold costs are capitalized and amortized at rates which should provide full amortization on abandonment of unproductive leases. Costs of abandoned leases are charged to the accumulated amortization reserve accounts and costs of productive leases are transferred to the developed property accounts.

Development Costs

"Costs of drilling and developing producing wells, including both tangible and intangible expenditures, are capitalized and amortized by the unit-of-production method within each production operating district.

Exploratory Costs

"Substantially all exploration costs and all dry-hole losses are charged to operating income, except that portions of geophysical costs applicable to domestic leases acquired are capitalized and amortized based on experience or, where leases are productive, on a unit-of-production basis."

EXHIBIT I
Seven Major Oil Companies Common Size Financial Statements
— 1972 Income Statements — % of Sales

	A	B	C	D	E	F	G
Sales and other operating revenues	100.0	100.0	100.0	100.0	100.0	100.0	100.0
Dividends, interest, and royalties	1.9	3.2	1.4	1.8	1.9	1.1	1.4
	101.9	103.2	101.4	101.8	101.9	101.1	101.4
Purchases and operating expenses	42.2	69.2	42.1	60.7	60.9	57.0	62.7
Selling, general, and administrative expenses	9.6	8.2	12.0	8.5	10.6	10.4	7.9
Depreciation, depletion, and amortization	4.8	4.9	7.7	6.3	7.9	8.2	7.8
Interest expense	1.2	1.2	1.9	1.6	2.1	1.7	0.5
Taxes — income and general	28.8	6.4	18.0	6.3	4.5	5.4	7.9
— excise	8.0	2.9	13.8	13.3	10.6	13.5	8.8
Total Expenses	94.6	92.8	95.5	96.7	96.6	96.2	95.6
Net income after taxes, before minority interest	7.3	10.4	5.9	5.0	5.3	5.0	5.8
Minority interest	0.3	0.2					0.8
Net income attributable to stockholders	6.9	10.2	5.9	5.0	5.3	5.0	5.0
Extraordinary items — net			(3.3)				0.3
Net income after extraordinary items	6.9	10.2	2.6	5.0	5.3	5.0	5.3
Dividends	3.8	5.2	4.1	3.4	3.5	2.8	1.6
Additions to/reduction of retained earnings	3.1	5.0	(1.5)	1.6	1.8	2.2	3.7
Net income after taxes/total assets	7.5%	7.5%	4.8%	4.2%	4.6%	4.6%	4.1%
Net income attributable/stockholders equity	12.5	12.4	8.3	6.5	7.8	7.6	5.2
Depreciation, depletion, and amortization/gross fixed assets	4.7	3.6	5.3	4.2	5.7	5.4	3.9

EXHIBIT II
Seven Major Oil Companies Common Size Financial Statements — 1972 Balance Sheets — % of Total Assets

Assets	A	B	C	D	E	F	G
Fixed assets — gross	103.6	98.4	116.5	123.8	119.7	137.2	145.2
— accumulated depreciation and depletion	45.0	33.0	58.3	58.0	62.9	72.2	77.2
— net	58.6	65.4	58.2	65.8	56.8	65.0	68.0
Current assets	32.9	25.9	31.4	24.2	30.7	27.0	26.0
Other assets	8.5	8.7	10.4	10.0	12.5	8.0	6.0
Total Assets	100.0	100.0	100.0	100.0	100.0	100.0	100.0
Capital and Liabilities							
Stockholders' equity — capital stock	12.2	18.6	15.9	21.6	18.6	18.0	4.0
— retained earnings	44.6	41.1	42.1	42.5	39.1	41.0	63.0
— total	56.8	59.7	58.0	64.1	57.7	59.0	67.0
Minority interests	2.5	0.7	2.6		0.1	1.0	9.0
Long-term debt	12.0	11.4	20.8	17.5	24.2	21.0	5.0
Current liabilities	22.0	18.0	16.0	14.1	14.8	14.0	15.0
Deferrals and other reserves — tax	3.5	9.7	1.6	1.2	1.9	2.0	0.5
— other	3.2	0.5	1.0	3.1	1.3	3.0	3.5
Total Capital and Liabilities	100.0	100.0	100.0	100.0	100.0	100.0	100.0
Accumulated depreciation and depletion/ gross fixed assets	43.4%	33.0%	50.0%	46.9%	52.5%	52.6%	53.2%
Current ratio	1.5	1.4	2.0	1.7	2.1	1.9	1.8

EXHIBIT III
Seven Major Oil Companies
Common Size Financial Statements — 1972
Statements of Changes in Financial Position — % of Total Sources/Uses

Sources	A	B	C	D	E	F	G
Net income attributable to stockholders	42.2	51.9	28.7	25.5	29.8	23.6	21.4
Minority interest in net income	2.2	0.9	1.4				3.6
Depreciation, depletion, and amortization	29.2	24.9	37.0	32.2	44.9	38.3	34.5
Other adjustments	5.0	−0.7	2.9	5.8	−0.7	16.2	17.4
Funds Provided by Operations	78.6	77.0	70.0	63.5	74.0	78.1	76.9
Other sources:	4.4	3.5	13.3	28.5	11.1	8.4	13.8
Sales of properties and investments			7.4	7.0			4.6
Other reductions in investments	15.1	7.2	8.3		10.0	13.5	4.7
Increase in long-term debt				1.0	4.0		
Increase of capital stock	1.9	12.3	1.0		0.9		
Decreases in working capital							
Total Sources	100.0	100.0	100.0	100.0	100.0	100.0	100.0
Uses							
Investment in fixed assets	54.7	65.0	43.6	48.3	53.4	60.5	76.9
Other investments	3.2	1.5	3.1		2.2	2.1	
Reduction in long-term debt	16.6	3.2	21.3	6.1	11.7	7.3	2.5
Reduction in capital stock		0.5					3.9
Cash dividends — stockholders	23.5	26.4	20.0	17.5	19.7	13.2	6.8
— minority interest	1.1	0.2	0.7				1.1
Increases in working capital			11.3	22.3	12.5	15.0	7.9
Other uses	0.9	3.2		5.8	0.5	1.9	0.9
	100.0	100.0	100.0	100.0	100.0	100.0	100.0

UNION

Amortization of Non-Productive Acreage Costs

"Leasehold costs of exploratory acreage are capitalized. Full amortization of the non-productive portion of such costs is provided over the lease holding period. Costs of successful leases are transferred to productive properties and depleted.

"Geophysical costs are capitalized and the portion applicable to acreage acquired is amortized in the same manner as the leasehold cost. The portion not related to acreage acquired is fully amortized currently.

"Leasehold rentals and geological costs are charged to income as incurred.

Provision for Dry Hole Losses

"The costs of drilling and equipping exploratory and development wells are capitalized. Dry holes are fully provided for currently."

END OF CHAPTER QUESTIONS

1. Explain the "cost flow" assumptions underlying the FIFO, LIFO, and average cost methods of valuing inventories.
2. Discuss the reasons why firms adopt LIFO in times of inflation.
3. What is the current state of the LIFO conformity rule?
4. Explain the implications for financial reporting of the failure of accounting standard-setting bodies to lay down rules on inventory valuation other than the "lower of cost or market" rule. Why do you think this failure has occurred?
4. Under *FASB Statement No. 12*, a corporation which holds marketable equity securities and classifies its balance sheet is required to designate separate current and noncurrent portfolios.
   A. Why do corporations invest in such securities?
   B. How does a corporation distinguish between current and noncurrent portfolios?
   C. Does the accounting treatment of these two classes of portfolio laid down in *FASB Statement No. 12* relate to the factors mentioned in your answers to A and B?
5. Under what conditions is a lease classified as a capital lease (a) by a lessor (b) by a lessee?
6. Explain the distinction between a direct financing and a sales-type lease from the viewpoint of a lessor. Does this distinction affect the lessee?
7. Discuss the different methods of accounting for initial direct costs required by *FASB Statement No. 13* for three types of

leases, and explain how accounting theory can be invoked to justify each.

8. Under what conditions will the amount of lessor's revenue (lessee's expense) under an operating lease differ from the amount of net rent receivable (payable) under the lease for a given period? Under what conditions does this difference represent different economic circumstances (or, to what extent is it simply a bookkeeping difference)?
9. What is the basic reason for capitalizing some leases? What subsidiary reasons have been proposed? What is the most important piece of information concerning a lease?
10. Discuss the rules applicable to accounting for pension cost under *APB Opinion No. 8* in the light of general principles of expense determination under the accrual method.
11. Why is accounting for pension plans an important social issue? What has the FASB done to reflect society's interest in this question? What more needs to be done to discharge a duty of accountability here?
12. Why is accounting for preproduction expenditures in the petroleum industry a difficult problem? What are the reasons for the major split in the industry between supporters of two different accounting methods?
13. Discuss Reserve Recognition Accounting from the viewpoint of (a) resolving the differences in accounting for preproduction costs by petroleum companies, and (b) implementing the objectives of financial reporting.
14. What does the petroleum industry accounting problem tell us about the relationship between the FASB and the SEC?
15. How do you perceive the future of an independent profession of public accountant in the United States? What issues will preoccupy accountants in the year 2000?
16. Explain the concept of corporate social accountability. What impact on financial reporting does this concept have?
17. Discuss the concept of socioeconomic accounting from the viewpoint of the firm and of society as a whole.
18. What is human resource accounting? What forms can it take? Why has it not been adopted throughout industry? Is there any reason to suppose that it would be more readily embraced by United States firms than by, say, Japanese firms?
19. Discuss the somewhat pessimistic paragraphs which conclude this book in the light of the factors which underlie the author's viewpoint. Rewrite these paragraphs in an optimistic tone, giving reasons to support your divergent viewpoint.

AUTHOR INDEX

SUBJECT INDEX